# HIDDEN® Hawaii

"A bible."
—*Honolulu Advertiser*

"The perfect choice for the visitor who wants an active
vacation in the islands."
—*Travel & Leisure*

"Paints a vivid picture of each island's history, natural wonders
and unique qualities."
—*Travel Holiday*

"Explores even deeper for the hidden places at the heart of island life."
—*American Bookseller*

"A view no travel agent can offer. Riegert's adventures are crammed with
fascinating insider's advice."
—*Los Angeles Times*

"Unlike many guides that claim to offer inside information,
this one actually delivers."
—*Vancouver Sun*

"Offers the best of all worlds to the Hawaii visitor."
—*Dallas Morning News*

# HIDDEN®

# Hawaii

## Including Oahu, Maui, Kauai, Lanai, Molokai, and the Big Island

### Ray Riegert

**THIRTEENTH EDITION**

Ulysses Press®

**BERKELEY, CALIFORNIA**

Published by:  ULYSSES PRESS
                P.O. Box 3440
                Berkeley, CA 94703
                www.ulyssespress.com

ISSN 1097-3222
ISBN 1-56975-424-1

Printed in Canada by Transcontinental Printing

40 39 38 37 36 35 34 33 32

EDITORIAL DIRECTOR: Leslie Henriques
MANAGING EDITOR: Claire Chun
PROJECT DIRECTOR: Lily Chou
EDITORIAL ASSOCIATES: Lynette Ubois, Laura Brancella,
   Leona Benten
TYPESETTERS: Lisa Kester, James Meetze
CARTOGRAPHY: Pease Press
HIDDEN BOOKS DESIGN: Sarah Levin
INDEXER: Sayre Van Young
FRONT COVER PHOTOGRAPHY: Douglas Peebles
COLOR INSERT: Robert Holmes Photography
ILLUSTRATOR: Jen-Ann Kirchmeier
CONTRIBUTING WRITER: Leslie Henriques

Distributed in the United States by Publishers Group West
and in Canada by Raincoast Books

HIDDEN is a federally registered trademark
of BookPack, Inc.

Ulysses Press 悉 is a federally registered
trademark of BookPack, Inc.

*To Jim Chanin,*
*for years of friendship*

Throughout this 25th Anniversary
Edition, places that were in
the original book are marked with a

# Acknowledgments

Since this book is now entering its thirteenth edition, there are several generations of people to thank. The person to whom I owe the deepest gratitude has been working on the project since the very beginning. I met my wife Leslie when I first arrived in the islands to write *Hidden Hawaii*. Since then she has contributed to the book as an editor, writer, researcher and innovator. Her energy and spirit have been an inspiration throughout.

The current edition results from the efforts of several people. Claire Chun skillfully shepherded the book through many stages. Lily Chou worked her magic as the project director. My wife Leslie and Sarah Levin devoted their talents to the cover design (while I'm at it, Leslie deserves an extra thanks for all her help with the researching and writing of this edition); Douglas Peebles submitted a terrific cover photo; and Robert Holmes provided outstanding interior photos. Lynette Ubois, Lisa Kester, James Meetze, Laura Brancella and Leona Benten aided and abetted with research and other matters large and small. My son Keith and daughter Alice also merit a warm note of thanks for their encouraging smiles and infectious energy.

Special thanks are also due to those friends from long ago who worked on the very first *Hidden Hawaii*—Sebastian Orfali, Sayre Van Young, Peter Beren, Suellen Ethnebuske, John Orfali, Phil Gardner and Carlene Schnabel, Jen-Ann Kirchmeier and Marlyn Amann. To all of them, I want to extend a *mahalo nui loa*—thank you a thousand times for your *kokua*.

# What's Hidden?

At different points throughout this book, you'll find special listings marked with a hidden symbol:

**◄ HIDDEN**

This means that you have come upon a place off the beaten tourist track, a spot that will carry you a step closer to the local people and natural environment of Hawaii.

The goal of this guide is to lead you beyond the realm of everyday tourist facilities. While we include traditional sightseeing listings and popular attractions, we also offer alternative sights and adventure activities. Instead of filling this guide with reviews of standard hotels and chain restaurants, we concentrate on one-of-a-kind places and locally owned establishments.

Our authors seek out locales that are popular with residents but usually overlooked by visitors. Some are more hidden than others (and are marked accordingly), but all the listings in this book are intended to help you discover the true nature of Hawaii and put you on the path of adventure.

\*

# Write to us!

If in your travels you discover a spot that captures the spirit of Hawaii, or if you live in the region and have a favorite place to share, or if you just feel like expressing your views, write to us and we'll pass your note along to the author.

We can't guarantee that the author will add your personal find to the next edition, but if the writer does use the suggestion, we'll acknowledge you in the credits and send you a free copy of the new edition.

ULYSSES PRESS
P.O. Box 3440
Berkeley, CA 94703
E-mail: readermail@ulyssespress.com

# Contents

# Maps

## OUTDOOR ADVENTURE SYMBOLS

The following symbols accompany national, state and regional park listings, as well as beach descriptions throughout the text.

| Symbol | Activity | Symbol | Activity |
|---|---|---|---|
| | Camping | | Waterskiing |
| | Hiking | | Windsurfing |
| | Biking | | Kayaking/Canoeing |
| | Swimming | | Boating |
| | Snorkeling or Scuba Diving | | Boat ramps |
| | Surfing | | Fishing |

# Preface

Hawaii. What images does the word bring to mind? Crystal blue waters against a white sand beach. Palm trees swaying in a soft ocean breeze. Volcanic mountains rising in the hazy distance. Bronzed beach boys and luscious Polynesian women. Serenity. Luxury. Paradise.

To many it conjures still another dream—the perfect vacation. There is no more beautiful hideaway than this spectacular chain of tropical islands. For over a century Hawaii has been the meeting place of East and West, a select spot among savvy travelers. These adventurers are attracted not by Hawaii's famed tourist resorts—which are usually crowded and expensive—but by the opportunity to travel naturally and at low cost to an exotic locale.

As you'll find in the following pages, it is possible to tour economically through Hawaii's major sightseeing centers. It's even easier to explore the archipelago's more secluded realms. Few people realize that most of Hawaii's land is either rural or wilderness, and there's no price tag on the countryside. You can flee the multitudes and skip the expense by heading into the islands' endless backcountry. And if you venture far enough, you'll learn the secret that lies at the heart of this book: The less money you spend, the more likely you are to discover paradise.

Quite simply, that's the double-barreled purpose of *Hidden Hawaii*—to save you dollars while leading you to paradise. Whatever you're after, you should be able to find it right here. When you want to relax amid the comforts of civilization, this book will show you good restaurants, comfortable hotels, quaint shops and intriguing nightspots.

When you're ready to depart the beaten track, *Hidden Hawaii* will guide you to untouched beaches, remote campsites, underwater grottoes and legendary fishing holes. It will take you to the Pacific's greatest surfing beaches, on hiking trails across live volcanoes, into flower-choked jungles, through desert canyons and up to the top of the world's most massive mountain.

*Hidden Hawaii* is a handbook for living both in town and in the wild. The first chapter covers the nuts and bolts—how to get to the islands, what to bring and what to expect when you arrive. Chapter Two prepares you for outdoor life—swimming, hiking, camping, skindiving and living off the land. The third chapter, covering Hawaii's history and language, will familiarize you with the rich tropical culture.

The last six chapters describe individual islands. Each island is divided geographically. Here you'll find specific information on sightseeing, hotels, restaurants, shops, nightspots and beaches.

This book is not intended for those tourists in plastic leis who plop down on a Waikiki beach, toast for two weeks, then claim they've seen Hawaii when all they've really seen is some bizarre kind of Pacific Disneyland. No, *Hidden Hawaii* is for adventurers: people who view a vacation not as an escape from everyday routine, but rather as an extension of the most exciting aspects of their daily lives. People who travel to faraway places to learn more about their own homes. Folks like you and me who want to sit back and relax, but also seek to experience and explore.

Ray Riegert
Honolulu, 1979

# Preface to the 25th Anniversary Edition

Every author sets out to change the world, at least with the first book he writes. Having a knack for doing things backwards, my first book changed me. The rest of the world remained exactly the same, but by the time I finished writing *Hidden Hawaii* 25 years ago, I had met my wife, discovered a new career and found a second home.

It took years for all the changes to reveal themselves. Finding romance in paradise led to two children, the book evolved into a series of over 30 guidebooks and the series grew a publishing company we have been running ever since.

Strange that a writing project I ventured into as an excuse to travel would become a personal watershed. At the time I was a journalist with an idea for an adventure travel book on the 50th state. After convincing a credulous publisher I was an expert on Hawaii (I had spent a week on one of the islands the year before), I set off for the airport with a royalty advance in one hand and a knapsack in the other.

I started on Kauai since that was the only island I knew even vaguely. Supplementing meager payments from my publisher with unemployment checks and staying in places that didn't qualify even for the budget guide I was researching, I learned on the fly how to write a book.

By the time I returned home to California, I was hooked on travel for life. The book hit a cultural vein. It was the late '70s. Lonely Planet, Moon and John Muir had recently begun showing Frommer and Fodor that the counterculture knew how to travel, too, and that we could do it with a lot more imagination and fewer footprints. *Hidden Hawaii* was swept up in the wave they helped create and before we had time to book our next trip my wife and I were ourselves signing meager checks for a motley group of writers venturing off to hidden Mexico, Florida and other points around the compass. Ulysses Press was born.

John Lennon said that "life is what happens while you're making other plans." I never even reached the planning stage. That first book rocked my world.

It opened a new path and I just followed it out to the highway. We were soon doing books on every destination that still promised undiscovered locales. And every two years my wife and I, then my wife and son and I, and ultimately my wife, son and daughter and I, ventured back out to the islands to do a new edition of *Hidden Hawaii*.

Which brings us to the hefty tome you are holding in your hands. It's the 13th edition: the biggest and, I hope, the best one yet. Since it marks 25 years since that scrawny original hit the bookshelves, we've put a turtle icon in the margin to honor the places, some of them mom-and-pop operations that looked even then like they'd be swept away by the trade wind, that have been in the book since the first edition. Like *Hidden Hawaii*, they are there for travelers and local people who are looking for something a bit out of the ordinary, something adventurous or odd, a spot that evokes the natural beauty and mesmerizing spirit of the islands, or maybe just something cheap and easy where they can kick back and breathe in the perfumed air of the islands.

The air, redolent of earth and ocean and frangipani, is the first thing I sense and the last I remember each time I visit the islands. That rich, fecund atmosphere, moisture-laden and pregnant, is the medium in which Hawaii works its magic. I went there originally to create something but soon found I was more clay than creator. What I thought a quarter century ago was merely a cluster of islands deep in the Pacific opened for me an entire world.

Ray Riegert
Berkeley, California
December 2004

# Introduction

Reading *Hidden Hawaii* brought back memories of my long and frustratingly unconsummated love affair with the islands. Throughout my childhood I listened spellbound as my father and uncles swapped tales of sun-washed beaches far across the Pacific. Like millions of other sailors and GIs, they had toured distant lands courtesy of that great travel agent, Uncle Sam. Between battles they recuperated under swaying coco palms, swilling warm beer and bartering with the natives. Stale Lucky Strikes were traded for hand-forged bolo knives and intricately carved hardwood spears. And though their travels took them far beyond "Pearl," to me the atolls, jungles and magical reefs of which they spoke all spelled Hawaii.

"Hawaii Granted Statehood," the headline ran. I folded the damp newspaper, hurled it toward my customer's front porch and pedaled angrily along my paper route. *They* had done it, by a simple stroke of an administrative pen. My dream of retiring to the islands at age fifteen gave a violent lurch. Hawaii suddenly shifted from the distant edge of the unknown Orient to just another state. The Iowa of the Pacific. Offshore California. No more need for a passport or an interpreter. No gorging on exotic mahimahi and poi—the fabled Sandwich Islands would now feed me on McBurgers and cola.

I survived the disillusionment of statehood and though, two years later, I squandered my meager savings (earmarked for passage to the islands) on a battered motorbike, the dream did not fade entirely. Friends-of-friends returned from two-week Hawaiian idylls, faces and arms tanned to an improbable richness. Wilted leis would be casually draped over lampshades and mantlepieces, a not-so-subtle reminder of their brief fling in the sun. I could only wait.

Later, the islands subverted my college career. In the storm clouds gathering above the campus, I saw the foam of a turquoise wave curling around a slender surfer. Rain-washed ivy dissolved into frangipani and bougainvillea. The neo-Gothic monstrosity of the campus library became a battered volcanic grotto, rumbling with echoes of ocean rollers. My instructors, unable to see beyond the tips of their umbrellas, rewarded my visions of paradise with neat lines of zeroes.

Flunking out of college, however, almost brought me my dream. I found myself low man on the totem pole on a disabled fishing boat, drifting helplessly across the gulf of Alaska. There seemed little promise of sunburns and coco palms in those cold, relentless waves. And then the captain took a close look at the charts.

"Well, boys, if this keeps up, we'll just head for Hawaii," he muttered. It had already been two endless weeks. Given the force of wind and current, we would hail the islands' sparkling shores within a month.

But it was just another lost chance, thwarted by an annoyingly efficient Norwegian chief engineer who dreamed of cod and boiled salmon heads rather than pineapple and passion fruit. The ancient engine coughed to life and took us north, back into the Big Grey.

Like many early explorers before me, I now took the only reasonable alternative left in my unsuccessful quest for the islands: I gave up. I went south instead, to a land where coconuts and tequila create a dream of their own. I traded my vision of a Polynesian outrigger for a ticket on the Greyhound, drawn to the irresistible warmth of a Mexican sun. Hawaii receded over the horizon.

A few years later, returning north through California, land of surprises, the dream suddenly reappeared. My partner Lorena and I were invited to a birthday luau honoring King Kamehameha, father of the islands. In the shade of a redwood forest we feasted on rich, greasy barbecued pork, delicate raw fish, tropical fruits, palm hearts and that exotic beverage, Budweiser-on-tap. Frustrated Hawaiians weaving another year's dream from Maui smoke, we lay back on soft aromatic pine needles, lulled into fantasies of graceful sea canoes, the melancholy summons of conch shell trumpets, the rhythmic sweep of the paddles . . . carrying us off to the islands.

We could resist no longer; we determined to make the big break with the mainland. Having already written a travel book on Mexico, I now had the ultimate justification. We would go to Hawaii and return with knowledge and advice to pass on to others—while also earning a royalty that would guarantee a long rest on a hidden beach. Lorena was enthusiastic; between the native herbs and tropical sunsets, she could pass many many days. The final lure was thrown to us by our publisher: the promise of an advance to finance the journey. "But only when you've finished your camping book on Mexico," he warned.

$$\bullet \ \bullet \ \bullet$$

"Hey, Carl, remember the book you were going to do on Hawaii?" I held the phone in a white-knuckled grip. Publishers are notorious for their twisted humor. Surely "remember" and "were going to do" were just sad attempts to cheer me toward my deadline.

"Yeah," I answered, "I have my Hawaiian shirt on right now. The one you bought me at Goodwill. *Remember?*"

There was a short, cynical laugh.

"Well, Ray Riegert just wrote it for you. Looks like it's time to play spin-the-globe again."

I slammed the phone down. Moments later I was trudging through the dusty Mexican streets, snarling at burros and stray dogs. At least my new recipe for mai tais wouldn't be wasted!

• • •

Good travel writers must constantly walk a tightrope between telling too much and not telling enough. The lazy tourist demands to be led by the nose to a comfortable yet inexpensive hotel and from there to a tasteful, quaint café. Nothing can be left to the demons of surprise and chance. Restless natives laboring over tom-toms in the middle of the night must be courtesy of the local tourist bureau, a civic contribution to amuse the traveler, rather than an inconvenient rebellion.

And with the distance between the islands and the continental U.S. reduced to nothing more than a quick lunch and a few drinks on a passenger jet, the pressures of tourism have become enormous. Hawaii's very lure is in danger of becoming its downfall.

This has created a situation in which a responsible and imaginative writer can perform a service both to adventurers and to the places they travel to see. A sensitive and aware guidebook like *Hidden Hawaii* helps educate and, in so doing, creates sensitive and aware travelers. The vast majority of guidebooks are not actually guides but consumer directories: where to spend your money with a minimum of distraction. That type of book actually steers us away from the heart of a place and an understanding of its peoples, on to nothing more than a superficial tour of the "sights." Ray Riegert shows us a Hawaii blessed with an incredible richness of cultures, history, topography and climates.

*Hidden Hawaii* not only points out attractive and inexpensive alternatives in meals, lodging, entertainment and shopping, but also takes us beyond Hawaii's often overdeveloped facade: where to watch whales; how to find the best parks, trails and campsites; how to live on the beach, foraging, fishing and diving; where to go shell collecting, volcano gazing . . . a variety of information as broad as the interests of travelers who want a lot out of a trip without going bankrupt. *Hidden Hawaii* demonstrates a very encouraging trend: I like guidebooks that are starting points for my own explorations, not addictive crutches. A little help can, and should, go a long way. Travel is a creative activity, one that should enhance the traveler as well as the places and people visited.

This is a book with an underlying attitude of respect and an awareness that it is more often one's attitude, rather than physical presence, that can be destructive. The hiker's motto, "Walk softly on the earth," is just as valid to the traveler strolling the streets of Lahaina as it is to the explorer on the trails of Kauai or the hidden beaches of Molokai.

It's up to *us* to keep hidden Hawaii unspoiled and enjoyable for everyone.

Carl Franz
San Miguel de Allende, 1979

No alien land in all the world has any deep, strong charm for me but that one, no other land could so longingly and so beseechingly haunt me, sleeping and waking, through half a lifetime, as that one has done. Other things leave me, but it abides; other things change, but it remains the same. . . . In my nostrils still lives the breath of flowers that perished twenty years ago.

—*Mark Twain, 1889*

# ONE

# The Aloha State

Hawaii is an archipelago that stretches more than 1500 miles 11/9across the North Pacific Ocean. Composed of 132 islands, it has eight major islands, clustered at the southeastern end of the chain. Together these larger islands are about the size of Connecticut and Rhode Island combined.

Each island, in a sense, is a small continent. Volcanic mountains rise in the interior, while the coastline is fringed with coral reefs and white-sand beaches. In the parlance of the Pacific, they are "high islands," very different from the low-lying atolls found elsewhere in Polynesia.

The northeastern face of each island, buffeted by trade winds, is the wet side. The contrast between this side and an island's southwestern sector is sometimes startling. Dense rainforests in the northeast are teeming with exotic tropical plants, while across the island you're liable to see cactus growing in a barren landscape!

Deciding to take a vacation in Hawaii is easy; the hard part comes when you have to choose which islands to visit. All six are remarkably beautiful places, each with unique features to offer the traveler. Eventually, you should try to tour them all, but on a single trip you'll probably choose only one, two or three. Traveling to more in the course of a typical vacation is counterproductive.

To help you decide which to see, I'll briefly describe the key features of each. For more detailed information, you can turn to the introductory notes in each of the island chapters.

My personal favorites are the Big Island and Kauai, the easternmost and westernmost islands in the chain, and I often recommend to friends unfamiliar with Hawaii that they visit these two islands. That way they manage to travel to both ends of the chain, experiencing the youngest and most rugged, and the oldest and most lush, of all the islands. The two offer a startling contrast, one that quickly shatters any illusion that all the islands are alike.

**Oahu**, Hawaii's most populous island, is dominated by the capital city of Honolulu. Featuring the Waikiki tourist center, this is the most heavily touristed island. It's too crowded for many visitors. But Oahu is a prime place to mix city living with country exploring. It's also rich in history, culture and beautiful beaches.

The island of **Hawaii**, or the Big Island, is true to its nickname. Located at the southeastern end of the Hawaiian chain, and dominated by two 13,000-foot volcanoes, this giant measures more than twice the size of all the other islands combined. It's a great place to mountain climb and explore live volcanoes, to snorkel along the sun-splashed Kona Coast, or to tour orchid farms in the verdant city of Hilo.

**Maui**, the second largest island, is one of Hawaii's favorite destinations for first-time visitors. Haleakala alone, the extraordinary crater that dominates the island, makes the "Valley Isle" worth touring. The island also sports many of Hawaii's nicest beaches and provides an offshore breeding ground for rare humpback whales.

Directly to the west, lying in Maui's wind shadow, sits the third smallest and most secluded island. **Lanai** is an explorer's paradise, with a network of jeep trails leading to hidden beaches and scenic mountain ridges. There are only 2800 people and about 20 miles of paved road here. If you are seeking an idyllic retreat, this is the place.

**Molokai**, slightly larger but nearly as remote, provides another extraordinary hideaway. With white-sand beaches, a mountainous interior and a large population of Hawaiians, the "Friendly Isle" retains a unique sense of old Hawaii. Here you can visit a former leper colony on the windswept Kalaupapa Peninsula, a pilgrimage that could prove to be the most inspiring of all your experiences in Hawaii.

The oldest island in the chain, **Kauai** is also the archipelago's prettiest, most luxuriant island. Located at the northwestern end of the chain, it is filled with jewel-like beaches and uninhabited valleys. Along the north shore are misty cliffs that fall precipitously to the sea; from the island's center rises a mountain that receives more rainfall than any place on earth; and along Kauai's southern flank there's a startling desert region reminiscent of the Southwest.

Only seven of the major islands are inhabited: the eighth, Kahoolawe, although sacred to Hawaiians, was used for decades as a bombing range for the U.S. Navy, then was finally turned over to the state of Hawaii in 1994. The seventh island, Niihau, is inhabited but is privately owned and off-limits to the public.

The islands are located 2500 miles southwest of Los Angeles, on the same 20th latitude as Hong Kong and Mexico City. It's two hours earlier in Hawaii than in Los Angeles, four hours be-

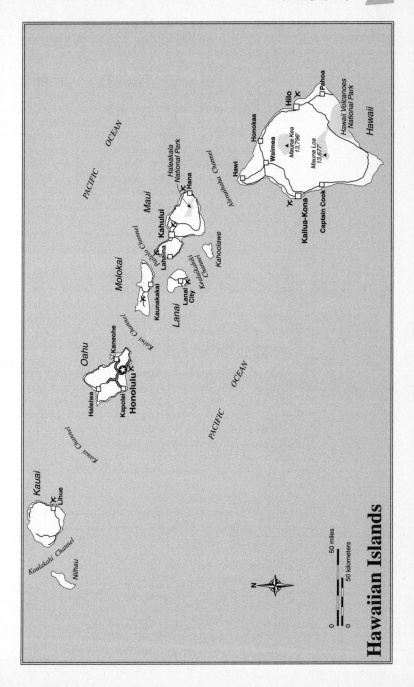

Hawaiian Islands

fore Chicago and five hours earlier than New York. Since Hawaii does not practice daylight-saving, their time difference becomes one hour greater during the summer months.

## When to Go

**SEASONS**

There are two types of seasons in Hawaii, one keyed to tourists and the other to the climate. The peak tourist seasons run from mid-December until Easter, then again from mid-June through Labor Day. Particularly around the Christmas holidays and in August, the visitors centers are crowded. Prices increase, hotel rooms and rental cars become harder to reserve, and everything moves a bit more rapidly. Shop around, however; package deals that include discounts on published rates are available.

If you plan to explore Hawaii during these seasons, make reservations several months in advance; actually, it's a good idea to make advance reservations whenever you visit. Without doubt, the off-season is the best time to hit the islands. Not only are hotels more readily available, but campsites and hiking trails are also less crowded.

Climatologically, the ancient Hawaiians distinguished between two seasons—*kau*, or summer, and *hooilo*, or winter. Summer extends from May to October, when the sun is overhead and the temperatures are slightly higher. Winter brings more variable winds and cooler weather.

The important rule to remember about Hawaii's beautiful weather is that it changes very little from season to season but varies dramatically from place to place. The average yearly temperature is about 78°, and during the coldest weather in January and the warmest in August, the thermometer rarely moves more than 5° or 6° in either direction. Similarly, sea water temperatures range comfortably between 74° and 80° year-round.

Seeking a cooler climate? Head up to the mountains; for every thousand feet in elevation, the temperature drops about 3°F. If you climb high enough on Maui or the Big Island, you might even encounter snow!

Crucial to this luxurious semitropical environment is the trade wind that blows with welcome regularity from the north-

## ISLAND COLORS

Each of the main islands has designated a specific bloom as its island flower. Oahu has the *ilima*, a small golden blossom, and the Big Island has the red *lehua*, a furry flower with needle petals resembling a bottlebrush plant. Maui spotlights the *lokelani*, or pink cottage rose while Kauai's pick is the *mokihana*, which is actually a light green berry. Molokai's flower of choice is the small, white *kukui* blossom and Lanai's is the vibrant orange *kaunaoa*.

east, providing a natural form of air-conditioning. When the trades stop blowing, they are sometimes replaced by *kona* winds carrying rain and humid weather from the southwest. These are most frequent in the winter, when the Hawaiian islands receive their heaviest rainfall.

While summer showers are less frequent and shorter in duration, winter storms are sometimes quite nasty. I've seen it pour for five consecutive days, until hiking trails disappeared and city streets were awash. If you visit in winter, particularly from December to March, you're risking the chance of rain.

A wonderful factor to remember through this wet weather is that if it's raining where you are, you can often simply go someplace else. And I don't mean another part of the world, or even a different island. Since the rains generally batter the northeastern sections of each island, you can usually head over to the south or west coast for warm, sunny weather.

Sometimes nasty weather engulfs the entire chain, but there's usually a sunny refuge somewhere. I once spent a strenuous period along the Kona Coast working on a suntan. Across the island near Hilo, flood warnings were up. Twenty-five inches of rain dropped in 24 hours; five feet of water fell in seven days. Toward the end of the week, when my major problem was whether the tan would peel, officials in Hilo declared a state of emergency.

## CALENDAR OF EVENTS

Something else to consider in planning a visit to Hawaii is the amazing lineup of annual cultural events. For a thumbnail idea of what's happening when, check the calendar below. You might just find that special occasion to climax an already dynamic vacation. For a comprehensive listing with current updates, check the Hawaii Visitors & Convention Bureau website at www.gohawaii.com.

**Early January**    At Maui's **Annual Festival of Hula** local hula *halaus* compete for Halau of the Year.

**JANUARY**

**During January**    On Maui, the Four Seasons Resort Wailea sponsors the **Whales Alive Celebration**, an international gathering with discussions, whale watching, entertainment and an art exhibit.

**Mid-January or February**    The month-long **Narcissus Festival** begins with the Chinese New Year. During the weeks of festivities, there are open houses, street parties and parades in Honolulu's Chinatown.

**Early February**    Usher in **Chinese New Year** with Lahaina locals: a colorful lion dance, food booths, Chinese calligraphy and the traditional fireworks are among the festivities.

**FEBRUARY**

**February through March**    The Japanese community celebrates its **Cherry Blossom Festival** in Honolulu with tea ceremonies, kabuki theater presentations, martial arts demonstrations and crafts exhibits.

**Late February**   The world's greatest female bodyboarders compete in the **Extreme Bodyboard Series** at the birthplace of the sport, The Pipeline in Oahu. The annual **Whale Day Celebration** on Maui includes food by Maui's top chefs, a Hawaiian craft fair and a carnival for the kids. On Kauai, rodeo events, lei making and ukulele contests, entertainment, food booths and a canoe race are all part of the **Waimea Town Celebration**.

## MARCH

**During March**   On Maui, you can volunteer to help the Pacific Whale Foundation count humpbacks during **The Great Whale Count** in late February/early March. Athletes compete in Kauai's **Prince Kuhio Ironman/Ironwoman Canoe Race**. **Art Maui** is a month-long juried art show featuring new work by local artists.

**Mid-March**   Celebrate the "Mother of Hawaii" with exhibits, entertainment and storytelling at Maui's **Queen Kaahumanu Festival**.

**March 26**   Major festivities on Kauai mark the **Prince Kuhio Festival**, commemorating the birthdate of Prince Jonah Kuhio Kalanianaole, Hawaii's first delegate to the U.S. Congress.

**Late March/Early April**   The **East Maui Taro Festival** in Hana celebrates taro, the staple of the Hawaiian diet, with exhibits, lectures, music, hula, and, of course, food.

## APRIL

**Early April**   The **International Pro Board Windsurfing Competition** is a popular ten-day tournament that's held at Hookipa Beach Park on Maui. The week-long **Merrie Monarch Festival** on the Big Island pays tribute to David Kalakaua, Hawaii's last king. Festivities include musical performances, pageants and a parade. Buddhist temples on all the islands mark **Buddha Day**, the luminary's birthday, with special services. Included among the events are pageants, dances and flower festivals. Maui's annual birthday party for **Lahaina's Banyan** honors the famous tree with cake and exhibits. For the eco- and creative-minded, the Kaahumanu Center in Kahului, Maui, sponsors the **Trash Art Show**, a glimpse into the wonders of—what else—trash art.

## MAY

**During May**   **Molokai Ka Hula Piko** marks the birth of hula on Molokai. Hula dancers, local musicians and Hawaiian craftspeople display their many talents. Held for four weekends in May (and sometimes in June), the **50th State Fair** in Oahu features agricultural exhibits, food stalls, dances, music and displays of island arts and crafts.

**May 1**   **Lei Day** is celebrated in the islands by people wearing flower leis and colorful Hawaiian garb. In Oahu's Kapiolani Park, there are pageants and concerts.

**Mid-May**    Maui's **Mother's Day Orchid Show** presents award-winning orchids. The **Maui Music Festival** fills two days and nights with jazz at the Kaanapali resort.

**Late May**    The Molokai **Ka Hula Piko Festival** honors Maunaloa's art form with hula performances.

**During June**    In Honolulu, the music, dance and customs of more than 40 Pacific Rim areas are showcased at the annual **International Festival of the Pacific**. This two-week event features performers from American Samoa, New Zealand, Guam and Hawaii. Also on Oahu, the **Aloha State Games**, featuring Olympic-style events, take place statewide. *Halaus* from around the world participate in Oahu's **Annual King Kamehameha Hula Competition**. On Maui, the **Maui Symphony Fest & Chamber Music Festival** features chamber music by internationally acclaimed artists. Staged at the Eddie Tam Complex in Makawao, the **Upcountry Fair** is where the 4-H crowd swings into action. Enjoy the live entertainment and local delicacies and, if you're an aspiring performer, don't miss the Star Search. On Kauai, a barbecue and jam session get things rolling at the **Kauai Cowboy Round-up** in Waimea; this week-long celebration of cowboy culture culminates with the Paniolo Challenge and Mule Races.

**June 10–11**    **King Kamehameha Day**, honoring Hawaii's first king, is celebrated on all six islands with parades, chants, hula dances and exhibits.

**Mid-June**    In Lahaina, the annual **Shapers Phoai Na Keiki Nalu** showcases surfers under 12.

**June through August**    On Oahu and the other islands, Buddhists perform colorful **Bon Dances** every weekend to honor the dead.

**JUNE**

**During July**    On the Big Island, the **Hilo Orchid Society Flower Show** is a showy demonstration of tropical colors. On Maui, more than 100 different wines from California, Oregon and Washington, as well as Australia, are sampled at the **Kapalua Wine & Food Symposium**. The **Pineapple Festival**, held in Lanai City, features contemporary Hawaiian music, pineapple cooking contests and arts and crafts.

**Early July**    "Cowboy Town" Makawao, in Maui's ranchland, promotes its **Parade & Rodeo** as a Maui-style Fourth of July.

**Late July**    **Ocean Concepts Bayfest**, one of Oahu's biggest water carnivals, presents three days of rides, games and watersports. On Kauai, Poipu celebrates its sugar heritage with **Koloa Plantation Days**, a week-long event featuring a sunset block party, ethnic cooking demonstrations, a rodeo, nature walks, a Polynesian revue and a parade through old Koloa Town.

**JULY**

**During August**    On Oahu, you can see the dramatic **Haleiwa Cup**, a one-mile ocean swim from Haleiwa Beach Park to Puena

**AUGUST**

Point and back, which draws more than 350 swimmers. In Honolulu, dancers six to twelve years old gather to compete in the **Queen Liliuokalani Keiki Hula Festival**. In addition to a raw onion–eating contest, **The Maui Onion Festival** features food booths, live music, a farmers market and an onion recipe contest.

**August 21**   Local residents celebrate **Admission Day**, the date in 1959 when Hawaii became the 50th state.

**Late August**   Visitors to Molokai won't want to miss the **Molokai Ranch Professional Rodeo**, a full two-day rodeo with barbecues and live bands.

**SEPTEMBER**   **During September**   The six-person **Hana Relay**, a 54-mile Maui swim from Kahului to Hana, is one of autumn's more challenging events. The **Haleakala Run to the Sun** is a 38-mile run from the ocean to the 10,023-foot peak of Haleakala. Molokai's **Bankoh Na Wahine** draws canoers from around the world for a grueling race from Molokai to Oahu.

**Early September**   The **Queen Liliuokalani Canoe Regatta** is staged on Oahu. Everyone keeps their eyes on Maui's **Wilson Kapalua Open Tennis Tournament**; it has Hawaii's largest tennis purse. A six-person relay across the nine-mile channel from Lanai to Kaanapali draws 50 international teams to the **Maui Channel Relay Swim**.

**Late September**   The **Hawaii County Fair** in Hilo on the Big Isle features an orchid show, steer show, lei contest, agricultural displays, plus exhibits of Hawaiian arts and crafts. The **Maui Marathon** is run from the Kaahumanu Shopping Center in Kahului to Kaanapali. Participants vie in hula, song-writing and slack-key guitar competitions during the week-long **Kauai Mokihana Festival**.

**Late September and during October**   The highlight of Hawaii's cultural season is the **Aloha Week** festival, a series of week-long celebrations featuring parades, street parties and pageants. Each week, a different island stages the festival and the entire sequence ends with a **Molokai-to-Oahu Canoe Race**. The **Maui County Fair** features agricultural exhibits and arts-and-crafts displays at the Wailuku War Memorial Complex.

**OCTOBER**   **During October**   The **Honolulu Orchid Show** in Honolulu presents thousands of orchids and other tropical plants. The EMC **Kaanapali Classic** tournament on Maui draws top stars from the PGA Tour.

**Mid-October**   The **Ironman Triathlon World Championship** on the Big Island tests the stamina of the world's best-conditioned athletes. **The Emalani Festival** commemorates Queen Emma's historic trek up Kauai's Waimea Canyon and into the Alakai Swamp with a royal procession, authentic hula, traditional Hawaiian music and exhibits at Kokee State Park.

**Late October** **Halloween in Lahaina** is a memorable street party with a parade, food fair, music and dancing on Front Street.

**Early November** The Big Island's **Kona Coffee Cultural Festival** celebrates the coffee harvest with a parade, international food bazaar and musical entertainment.

**Mid-November** Sail out to snorkel with over 200 Hawaiian spinner dolphins during Oahu's **Dolphin Rendezvous**.

**During November** **Hula O Na Keiki**, a children's hula performance on Maui, gives prizes for top performers in traditional and modern forms of the dance. Surfers and landlubbers alike gather for the **Hawaiian Pro Surfing Championships** on Oahu. The **Aloha Classic Windsurfing** at Hookipa Beach on Maui is a key event during the Pro Boardsailing Association World Tour.

**November through December** The world's greatest surfers compete on Oahu's north shore in a series of contests including the **Pipeline Masters**, **World Cup of Surfing** and the **Hawaiian Pro Surfing Classic**. With 20-foot waves and prize money topping $50,000, these are spectacular events. Hawaiian and other crafts are showcased at the **Lokahi Pacific Christmas Craft Fair**, held at the War Memorial Sports Complex in Wailuku, Maui.

**During December** **Honolulu City Lights** at Honolulu's City Hall marks the Christmas season. Maui celebrates with arts and crafts, music and dance at the **Na Mele O Maui Festival**. On Molokai, local communities take turns hosting **Christmas crafts fairs**. Oahu puts on the two-day **Festival of Art & Fine Crafts** at Thomas Square Park featuring over 110 arts and crafts vendors.

**Early December** Buddha's enlightenment is commemorated on all the islands with **Bodhi Day** ceremonies and religious services.

**Mid-December** Runners by the thousands turn out for the **Honolulu Marathon**.

**Before You Go**

**VISITORS CENTERS**

The **Hawaii Visitors & Convention Bureau**, a state-run agency, is a valuable resource from which to obtain free information on the islands. With branches on each of the four largest islands, the Bureau can help plan your trip and then offer advice once you reach Hawaii. ~ 2270 Kalakaua Avenue, Suite 801, Honolulu; 808-923-1811, 800-464-2924; www.gohawaii.com

*Oahu* ~ 733 Bishop Street, Suite 1520, Honolulu; 808-524-0722, 877-525-6248; www.visit-oahu.com

*Big Island* ~ 250 Keawe Street, Hilo, 808-961-5797; and 250 Waikoloa Beach Drive, Suite B-15, Waikoloa, 808-886-1655

*Maui* ~ 1727 Wili Pa Loop, Wailuku; 808-244-3530; www.visitmaui.com

*Kauai* ~ 4334 Rice Street, Suite 101, Lihue; 808-245-3971; www.kauaivisitorsbureau.com

**PACKING**   When I get ready to pack for a trip, I sit down and make a list of everything I'll need. It's a very slow, exact procedure: I look in closets, drawers and shelves, and run through in my mind the activities in which I'll participate, determining which items are required for each. After all the planning is complete and when I have the entire inventory collected in one long list, I sit for a minute or two, basking in my wisdom and forethought.

Then I tear the hell out of the list, cut out the ridiculous items I'll never use, halve the number of spares among the necessary items, and reduce the entire contents of my suitcase to the bare essentials.

Before I developed this packing technique, I once traveled overland from London to New Delhi carrying two suitcases and a knapsack. I lugged those damned bundles onto trains, buses, jitneys, taxis and rickshaws. When I reached Turkey, I started shipping things home, but by then I was buying so many market goods that it was all I could do to keep even.

I ended up carrying so much crap that one day, when I was sardined in a crowd pushing its way onto an Indian train, someone managed to pick my pocket. When I felt the wallet slipping out, not only was I unable to chase the culprit—I was so weighted down with baggage that I couldn't even turn around to see who was robbing me!

I'll never travel that way again, and neither should you. Particularly when visiting Hawaii, where the weather is mild, you should pack very light. The airlines permit two suitcases and a carry-on bag; try to take one suitcase and maybe an accessory bag that can double as a beach bag. Dress styles are very informal in the islands, and laundromats are ubiquitous, so you don't need a broad range of clothing items.

Remember, you're packing for a semitropical climate. Take along a sweater or light jacket for the mountains, and a poncho to protect against rain. But otherwise, all that travelers in Hawaii require are shorts, bathing suits, lightweight slacks, short-sleeved shirts and blouses, and summer dresses or muumuus. Rarely do visitors require sport jackets or formal dresses. Wash-and-wear fabrics are the most convenient.

For footwear, I suggest soft, comfortable shoes. Low-cut hiking boots or tennis shoes are preferable for hiking; for beachgoing, there's nothing as good as sandals.

There are several other items to squeeze in the corners of your suitcase—sunscreen, sunglasses, a towel and, of course, your copy of *Hidden Hawaii*. You might also consider packing a mask, fins and snorkel, and possibly a camera.

Accommodations in Hawaii range from funky cottages to B&B inns to highrise condos. You will find inexpensive family-run hotels, middle-class tourist facilities and world-class resorts. Generally, the farther a hotel is from the beach, the less it costs.

    Whichever you choose, there are a few guidelines to help save money. Try to visit during the off-season, avoiding the high-rate periods during the summer and from Christmas to Easter. (If you do come during high season, book well in advance.) Rooms with mountain views are less expensive than ocean view accommodations. Another way to economize is by reserving a room with a kitchen. In any case, try to reserve far in advance.

    To help you decide on a place to stay, I've described the accommodations not only by area but also according to price (prices listed are for double occupancy during the high season; prices may decrease in low season). *Budget* hotels are generally less than $60 per night for two people; the rooms are clean and comfortable, but lack luxury. The *moderately* priced hotels run $60 to $120, and provide larger rooms, plusher furniture and more attractive surroundings. At *deluxe*-priced accommodations you can expect to spend between $120 and $180 for a double in a hotel or resort. You'll check into a spacious, well-appointed room with all modern facilities; downstairs the lobby will be a fashionable affair, and you'll usually see a restaurant, lounge and a cluster of shops. If you want to spend your time (and money) in the island's very finest hotels, try an *ultra-deluxe* facility, which will include all the amenities and price well above $180.

**Bed-and-Breakfast Inns**    The bed-and-breakfast business in Hawaii becomes more diverse and sophisticated every year. Today there are several referral services that can find you lodging on any of the islands. Claiming to be the biggest clearinghouse in the state, **Bed and Breakfast Honolulu (Statewide)** represents over 400 properties. ~ 3242 Kaohinani Drive, Honolulu, HI 96817; 808-595-7533, 800-288-4666, fax 808-595-2030; www. hawaiibnb.com.

**LODGING**

◆◆◆◆◆◆◆◆◆◆◆◆◆◆◆◆◆◆◆◆◆◆◆◆◆◆◆◆◆◆◆◆◆◆◆◆◆◆◆◆◆◆◆◆◆◆◆◆◆◆◆◆

### UNDER THE STARS

If you plan on camping, you'll need most of the equipment required for mainland overnighting. In Hawaii, you can get along quite comfortably with a lightweight tent and sleeping bag. You'll also need a knapsack, canteen, camp stove and fuel, mess kit, first-aid kit (with insect repellent, water purification tablets and Chapstick), toilet kit, a pocket knife, hat, waterproof matches, flashlight and ground cloth.

The original association, **Bed and Breakfast Hawaii**, claims more than 200 locations. This Kauai-based service was founded in 1979 and is well known throughout Hawaii. ~ P.O. Box 449, Kapaa, HI 96746; 808-822-7771, 800-733-1632, fax 808-822-2723; www.bandb-hawaii.com. For other possibilities, contact **Hawaiian Islands Bed & Breakfast**. ~ 808-261-7895, 800-258-7895, fax 808-262-2181; www.lanikaibeachrentals.com.

You can also try the Maui-based **Affordable Accommodations**, which offers help finding all types of lodging. ~ 2825 Kauhale Street, Kihei, HI 96753; 808-879-7865, 888-333-9747, fax 808-874-0831; www.affordablemaui.com. Or call **All Islands Bed & Breakfast**, an Oahu-based reservation service that represents over 700 bed and breakfasts. ~ 463 Iliwahi Loop, Kailua, HI 96734; 808-263-2342, 800-542-0344, fax 808-263-0308; www.all-islands.com.

While the properties represented by these agencies range widely in price, **Hawaii's Best Bed & Breakfasts** specializes in small, upscale accommodations on all the islands. With about 100 establishments to choose from, it places guests in a variety of privately owned facilities; most are deluxe priced. ~ P.O. Box 563, Kamuela, HI 96743; 808-885-4550, 800-262-9912, fax 808-885-0559; www.bestbnb.com.

**CONDOS**   Many people visiting Hawaii, especially those traveling with families, find that condominiums are often cheaper than hotels. While some hotel rooms come with kitchenettes, few provide all the amenities of condominiums. A condo, in essence, is an apartment away from home. Designed as studio, one-, two- or three-bedroom apartments, they come equipped with full kitchen facilities and complete kitchenware collections. Many also feature washer/dryers, dishwashers, air-conditioning, color televisions, telephones, lanais and community swimming pools.

Utilizing the kitchen will save considerably on your food bill; by sharing the accommodations among several people, you'll also cut your lodging bill. While the best way to see hidden Hawaii is obviously by hiking and camping, when you're ready to come in from the wilds, consider reserving a place that provides more than a bed and a night table.

**DINING**   A few guidelines will help you chart a course through Hawaii's countless dining places. Within a particular chapter, the restaurants are categorized geographically, with each restaurant entry describing the establishment as budget, moderate, deluxe or ultra-deluxe in price.

To establish a pattern for Hawaii's parade of dining places, I've described not only the cuisine but also the ambience of each establishment. Restaurants listed offer lunch and dinner unless otherwise noted.

Dinner entrées at *budget* restaurants usually cost $8 or less. The ambience is informal café style and the crowd is often a local one. *Moderately* priced restaurants range between $8 and $16 at dinner and offer pleasant surroundings, a more varied menu and a slower pace. *Deluxe* establishments tab their entrées above $16, featuring sophisticated cuisines, plush decor and more personalized service. *Ultra-deluxe* restaurants generally price above $24.

Breakfast and lunch menus vary less in price from restaurant to restaurant. Even deluxe-priced kitchens usually offer light breakfasts and lunch sandwiches, which place them within a few dollars of their budget-minded competitors. These early meals can be a good time to test expensive restaurants.

**TRAVELING WITH CHILDREN**

Hawaii is an ideal vacation spot for family holidays. The pace is slow, the atmosphere casual. A few guidelines will help ensure that your trip to the islands brings out the joys rather than the strains of parenting, allowing everyone to get into the *aloha* spirit.

Use a travel agent to help with arrangements; they can reserve spacious bulkhead seats on airlines and determine which flights are least crowded. They can also seek out the best deals on inexpensive condominiums, saving you money on both room and board.

Planning the trip with your kids stimulates their imagination. Books about travel, airplane rides, beaches, whales, volcanoes and Hawaiiana help prepare even a two-year-old for an adventure. This preparation makes the "getting there" part of the trip more exciting for children of all ages.

And "getting there" means a long-distance flight. Plan to bring everything you need on board the plane—diapers, food, books, toys, and extra clothing for kids and parents alike. I found it

**SOMETHING BORROWED**

The **Hawaii State Public Library System** provides facilities for residents and non-residents alike, with 50 branches scattered throughout the islands. Visitors can check out books by simply applying for a library card with a valid identification card. The following cities and towns are among many where you can borrow light beach-reading material as well as books on Hawaii: Honolulu, Kailua and Waimanalo on Oahu; Hilo, Kailua-Kona and Pahala on the Big Island; Kahului, Wailuku and Hana on Maui; Lanai City on Lanai; Kaunakakai on Molokai; and Waimea, Lihue and Princeville on Kauai. For a complete list of libraries, check the state library system's website. ~ www.hcc.hawaii.edu/hspls.

helpful to carry a few new toys and books as treats to distract my son and daughter when they got bored. When they were young children, I also packed extra snacks.

Allow extra time to get places. Book reservations in advance and make sure that the hotel or condominium has the extra crib, cot or bed you require. It's smart to ask for a room at the end of the hall to cut down on noise. And when reserving a rental car, inquire to see if they provide car seats and if there is an added charge. Hawaii has a strictly enforced car seat law.

Besides the car seat you may have to bring along, also pack shorts and T-shirts, a sweater, sun hat, sundresses and water-proof sandals. A stroller with sunshade for little ones helps on sightseeing sojourns; a shovel and pail are essential for sandcastle building. Most importantly, remember to bring a good sunblock. The quickest way to ruin a family vacation is with a bad sunburn. Also plan to bring indoor activities such as books and games for evenings and rainy days.

Most towns have stores that carry diapers, food and other essentials. However, prices are much higher in Hawaii. To economize, some people take along an extra suitcase filled with diapers and wipes, baby food, peanut butter and jelly, etc. If you're staying in Honolulu, ABC stores carry a limited selection of disposables and baby food. ~ 2432 Koa Avenue, Honolulu; 808-921-2799. Shopping outside Waikiki in local supermarkets will save you a considerable sum: Star Market is open from 5 a.m. to 2 a.m. ~ 2470 South King Street, Honolulu; 808-973-1666.

A first-aid kit is always a good idea. Also check with your pediatrician for special medicines and dosages for colds and diarrhea. If your child does become sick or injured in the Honolulu area, contact Kapiolani Medical Center (808-983-6000). On the Windward Coast of Oahu, call Castle Medical Center (808-263-5500); on the North Shore, Kahuku Hospital (808-293-9221); and on the leeward side, Wahiawa General Hospital (808-621-8411). On the Big Island's east side, there's Hilo Medical Center

## TIME OUT

If you find yourself in need of a parenting break, check out the summer and holiday programs offered at many of the islands' resorts and large hotels. Hula lessons, lei making, storytelling, sandcastle building and various sports activities keep *keikis* (kids) over six happy while also giving Mom and Dad a break. As an added bonus, these resorts offer family plans, providing discounts for extra rooms or permitting children to share a room with their parents at no extra charge. Check with your travel agent or directly with the facility.

(808-974-4700); in Kona, **Kona Community Hospital** (808-322-9311); Maui, **Maui Memorial Hospital** (808-242-2343); Lanai, **Lanai Community Hospital** (808-565-6411); Molokai, **Molokai General Hospital** (808-553-5331); and Kauai, **Wilcox Memorial Hospital and Health Center** (808-245-1100). There's also a **Hawaii Poison Center** in Honolulu. ~ 808-941-4411.

Hotels often provide access to babysitters. On Oahu, **Aloha Babysitting Service** is a bonded babysitting agency. ~ 808-732-2029, fax 808-735-1958.

When choosing which island to visit, consider how many diversions it will take to keep your children happy. Oahu offers numerous options, from the Honolulu Zoo to theme parks to museums, while the outer islands have fewer attractions. It might be helpful to read the introductory passages to each of the island chapters before planning your vacation.

## WOMEN TRAVELING ALONE

Traveling solo grants an independence and freedom different from that of traveling with a partner, but single travelers are more vulnerable to crime and should take additional precautions. An option for those who are alone but prefer not to be is to join a tour group. A multitude abound that are tailored to your specific interests; see "The New Travel" section in Chapter Two for ideas.

It's unwise to hitchhike and probably best to avoid inexpensive accommodations on the outskirts of town; the money saved does not outweigh the risk. Bed and breakfasts, youth hostels and YWCAs are generally your safest bet for lodging, and they also foster an environment ideal for bonding with fellow travelers.

Keep all valuables well-hidden and hold on to cameras and purses. Avoid late-night treks or strolls along beaches or through undesirable parts of town, but if you find yourself in this situation, continue walking with a confident air until you reach a safe haven. A fierce scowl never hurts.

These hints should by no means deter you from seeking out adventure. Wherever you go, stay alert, use your common sense and trust your instincts.

Throughout the islands there are many organizations that can help you in case of emergency. On Oahu, contact the **Sex Abuse Treatment Center**. ~ 808-524-7273. **Women Helping Women**, a domestic violence shelter on Maui, can provide referrals. ~ 808-579-9581; www.whwmaui.net.

For more helpful hints, get a copy of *Safety and Security for Women Who Travel* (Traveler's Tales).

## GAY & LESBIAN TRAVELERS

**The Gay & Lesbian Community Center**, specializing in support groups and community outreach, supplies Oahu visitors with gay-relevant information. Stop by during office hours to pick up lesbian and gay newspapers and brochures. It's located in the YWCA; call for office hours. ~ 2424 Beretania Street, Honolulu; 808-951-7000, fax 808-951-7001; www.glcc-hawaii.org.

For monthly updates on the gay and lesbian scene in Hawaii, pick up a copy of *Da Kine* at bars and clubs in Waikiki, the main library and the Academy of Arts Theater. Along with coverage of news and entertainment, it provides a calendar of events and a listing of services. ~ 2410 Cleghorn Street #2302, Honolulu, HI 96815; 808-923-7378, fax 808-922-6124; e-mail ha@gte.net.

The *Pocket Guide to Hawaii*, published by **Pacific Ocean Holidays**, is also helpful for gay travelers. It comes out three times a year and lists the best and hottest establishments and beaches that Hawaii has to offer. Send $5 per copy (via mail only) if ordering from the mainland; otherwise, it's distributed free by local gay businesses. This outfit can also help book vacation packages. ~ P.O. Box 88245, Honolulu, HI 96830; 808-923-2400, 800-735-6600 reservations only; www.gayhawaii.com.

A photography hint: Buy your film in the islands and have it developed before you leave to avoid X-ray damage. Never carry undeveloped film in your checked luggage.

**Hawaiinet Tour & Travel Services Network, Inc.** offers special tour packages to both gays and straights. They can help decide on hotels, condos and restaurants. This gay-owned company also delivers Hawaiian paper order baskets to the mainland. ~ P.O. Box 15671, Honolulu, HI 96830; 808-545-1119, fax 808-524-9572; www.hawaiinet.com.

Spanning the entire Hawaiian chain, the Big Island–based **Black Bamboo Hawaii** unearths the best cottages and houses for gay and straight travelers. This service also arranges car rentals, hiking tours, birdwatching trips and other sporting activities for its guests. ~ P.O. Box 211, Kealakekua, HI 96750; 808-328-9607, 800-527-7789; www.blackbamboohawaii.com. For information on the gay and lesbian scene on Maui, contact **Both Sides Now, Inc.** They can provide details on lodging, upcoming events and social gatherings. ~ P.O. Box 5042, Kahului, HI 96733; 808-244-4566; www.mauigayinfo.com. Lesbians can also call **Contact Dykes.** ~ 808-879-2971.

Women can call the **Women's Events Information Line** for goings-on around Maui. ~ 808-573-3077.

For further information, be sure to look under "gay-friendly travel" in the index at the end of the book.

**SENIOR TRAVELERS**   Hawaii is a hospitable place for senior citizens to visit. Countless museums, historic sights and even restaurants and hotels offer senior discounts that can cut a substantial chunk off vacation costs. The national park system's Golden Age Passport, which must be applied for in person, allows free admission for anyone 62 and older to the two national parks in the islands.

The **American Association of Retired Persons** (AARP) offers membership to anyone over 50. AARP's benefits include travel discounts with a number of firms. ~ 601 E Street NW, Washington, DC 20049; 800-424-3410; www.aarp.org.

**Elderhostel** offers reasonably priced, all-inclusive educational programs in a variety of locations throughout the year. ~ 11 Avenue de Lafayette, Boston, MA 02111; 877-426-8056, fax 617-426-0701; www.elderhostel.org.

Be extra careful about health matters. Consider carrying a medical record with you—including your medical history and current medical status as well as your doctor's name, phone number and address. Make sure your insurance covers you while you are away from home.

**DISABLED TRAVELERS**

The **Commission on Persons with Disabilities** publishes a survey of the city, county, state and federal parks in Hawaii that are accessible to travelers with disabilities. They also provide "Aloha Guides to Accessibility," which cover Oahu, Maui, Kauai and the Big Island, and give information on various hotels, shopping centers, and restaurants that are accessible. ~ 919 Ala Moana Boulevard, Room 101, Honolulu, HI 96814; 808-586-8121, fax 808-586-8129; e-mail accesshi@aloha.net.

The **Society for Accessible Travel & Hospitality** offers information for travelers with disabilities. ~ 347 5th Avenue, Suite 610, New York, NY 10016; 212-447-7284, fax 212-725-8253; www.sath.org. **Travelin' Talk**, a network of people and organizations, also provides assistance. ~ P.O. Box 1796, Wheatridge, CO 80034; 303-232-2979; www.travelintalk.net. **Access-Able Travel Source** has worldwide information online. ~ 303-232-2979; www.access-able.com.

Be sure to check in advance when making room reservations. Some hotels feature facilities for those in wheelchairs.

**FOREIGN TRAVELERS**

**Passports and Visas**    Most foreign visitors are required to obtain a passport and tourist visa to enter the United States. Contact your nearest United States Embassy or Consulate well in advance to obtain a visa and to check on any other entry requirements.

**Customs Requirements**    Foreign travelers are allowed to carry in the following: 200 cigarettes (1 carton), 50 cigars or 2 kilograms (4.4 pounds) of smoking tobacco; one liter of alcohol for personal use only (you must be 21 years of age to bring in alcohol); and US$100 worth of duty-free gifts that include an additional quantity of 100 cigars. You may bring in any amount of currency, but must fill out a form if you bring in over US $10,000. Carry any prescription drugs in clearly marked containers. (You may have to produce a written prescription or doctor's statement for the customs officer.) Meat or meat products, seeds, plants, fruits and narcotics are not allowed to be brought into the United States. Contact the **United States Customs Service** for further information. ~ 1300 Pennsylvania Avenue NW, Washington, DC 20229; 202-927-6724; www.customs.ustreas.gov.

**Driving**   If you plan to rent a car, an international driver's license should be obtained prior to arrival. Some rental car companies require both a foreign license and an international driver's license. Many car rental agencies require that the lessee be at least 25 years of age; all require a major credit card. Seat belts are mandatory for the driver and all passengers. Children under the age of 6 or weighing less than 60 pounds should be in the back seat in approved child safety restraints.

> Don't let the sun ruin your vacation. Those beet-red tourists you see wincing along forgot their sunblock. Avoid the sun between 11 a.m. and 2 p.m. or you'll be wincing, too.

**Currency**   United States money is based on the dollar. Bills come in six denominations: $1, $5, $10, $20, $50 and $100. Every dollar is divided into 100 cents. Coins are the penny (1 cent), nickel (5 cents), dime (10 cents), quarter (25 cents) and dollar (100 cents).

You may not use foreign currency to purchase goods and services in the United States. Consider buying traveler's checks in dollar amounts. You may also use credit cards affiliated with an American company such as Interbank, Barclay Card, VISA, MasterCard and American Express.

**Electricity and Electronics**   Electric outlets use currents of 110 volts, 60 cycles. For appliances made for other electrical systems, you need a transformer or adapter. Travelers who use laptop computers for telecommunication should be aware that modem configurations for U.S. telephone systems may be different from their European counterparts. Similarly, the U.S. format for video-tapes is different from that in Europe; U.S. Park Service visitors centers and other stores that sell souvenir videos often have them available in European format.

**Weights and Measurements**   The United States uses the English system of weights and measures. American units and their metric equivalents are as follows: 1 inch = 2.5 centimeters; 1 foot (12 inches) = 0.3 meter; 1 yard (3 feet) = 0.9 meter; 1 mile (5280 feet) = 1.6 kilometers; 1 ounce = 28 grams; 1 pound (16 ounces) = 0.45 kilogram; 1 quart (liquid) = 0.9 liter.

## MAIL

If you're staying in a particular establishment during your visit, you can usually have personal mail sent there. Otherwise, for cardholders, **American Express** will hold letters for no charge at its Honolulu office for 30 days, and will provide forwarding services. If you decide to use their facilities, have mail addressed to American Express, Client Mail, 2424 Kalakaua Avenue, Honolulu, HI 96815. ~ 808-922-4718. If you don't use this service, your only other recourse is to have mail sent to a particular post office in care of general delivery.

During the 19th century, sleek clipper ships sailed from the West Coast to Hawaii in about 11 days. Today, you'll be traveling by a less romantic but far swifter conveyance—the jet plane. Rather than days at sea, it will be about five hours in the air from the West Coast, nine hours from Chicago, or around 11 hours if you're coming from the East Coast.

**Transportation**

**GETTING TO THE ISLANDS**

Aloha, American, Continental, Delta, Hawaiian, Northwest and United fly regular schedules to Honolulu. American, Delta and United also offer flights to Maui, American and United to the Big Island, and United serves Kauai. This nonstop service is particularly convenient for travelers who are interested in visiting the outer islands while bypassing Honolulu.

Foreign carriers include Air Canada, Air New Zealand, All Nippon Airways, China Airlines, Japan Airlines, Korean Airlines, Philippine Airlines and Qantas Airlines.

Whichever carrier you choose, ask for the economy or excursion fare, and try to fly during the week; weekend flights are generally higher in price. To qualify for the lower price fares, it is sometimes necessary to book your flight two weeks in advance and to stay in the islands at least one week. Generally, however, the restrictions are minimal. Children under two years of age can fly for free, but they will not have a seat of their own. Each passenger is permitted two large pieces of luggage plus a carry-on bag. Shipping a bike or surfboard will cost extra.

In planning a Hawaiian sojourn, one potential moneysaver is the package tour, which combines air transportation with a hotel room and other amenities. Generally, it is a style of travel that I avoid. However, if you can find a package that provides air transportation, a hotel or condominium accommodation and a rental car, all at one low price—it is worth considering. Two experienced Hawaii packagers are **Suntrips** (800-786-8747; www.suntrips.com) and **Pleasant Hawaiian Holidays** (866-867-4567; www.hawaii-hawaii.com). Prices are often low, but be forewarned: Some packages will preplan your entire visit, dragging you around on air-conditioned tour buses. Look for the package that provides only the bare necessities while allowing you the greatest freedom.

**BY AIR** Most inter-island transportation is by plane. **Aloha Airlines** and **Hawaiian Airlines**, the state's major carriers, provide frequent inter-island jet service. If you're looking for smooth, rapid, comfortable service, this is certainly it. You'll be buckled into your seat, offered a low-cost cocktail and whisked to your destination within 20 to 40 minutes.

**GETTING BETWEEN ISLANDS**

Now that you know how to fly quickly and comfortably, let me tell you about the most exciting way to get between islands. Several carriers, including **Island Air**, **Molokai Air Shuttle**, **Pacific Wings** and **Paragon Air**, fly twin-engine propeller planes. These small airplanes travel at low altitudes and moderate speeds over the islands. Next to chartering a helicopter, they are one of the best ways to see Hawaii from the air.

**BY FERRY**   The only inter-island ferry services run between Lahaina, Maui, and the islands of Molokai and Lanai. **Expeditions Inc.** makes the trip from Lahaina, Maui, to Manele Harbor, Lanai, five times a day. ~ 808-661-3756, 877-464-6284. **Molokai Ferry** runs between Lahaina, Maui, and Kaunakakai, Molokai, once a day. ~ 658 Front Street, Suite 10, Lahaina; 808-667-6165, 800-275-6969; www.molokaiferry.com.

**CAR RENTALS**   Renting a car is as easy in Hawaii as anywhere. Every island supports several rental agencies, which compete fiercely with one another in price and quality of service. So before renting, shop around: check the listings in this book, and also look for special temporary offers that many rental companies sometimes feature.

There are several facts to remember when renting a car. First of all, a major credit card is essential. Also, many agencies don't rent at all to people under 25. Regardless of your age, many companies charge several dollars a day extra for insurance. The insurance is optional and expensive, and in many cases, unnecessary. (Many credit cards provide the same coverage when a rental is charged to the card. Find out if you credit card company offers this coverage.) Your personal insurance policy may also provide for rental cars and, if necessary, have a clause added that will include rental car protection. Check on this before you leave home. But remember, whether you have insurance or not, you are liable for the first several thousand dollars in accident damage.

A vigorous agricultural inspection keeps unwanted pests out of Hawaii. If you forgot that apple tucked into your backpack, a sniffing dog inspector may tag you.

Rates fluctuate with the season; slack tourist seasons are great times for good deals. Also, three-day, weekly and monthly rates are almost always cheaper than daily rentals.

Other than on the island of Lanai, I don't recommend renting a jeep. They're more expensive and less comfortable than automobiles, and won't get you to very many more interesting spots. In addition, the rental car collision insurance provided by most credit cards does not cover jeeps. Except in extremely wet weather when roads are muddy, all the places mentioned in this book, including the hidden locales, can be reached by car.

**TWO**

# The Land
# and Outdoor Adventures

**GEOLOGY** More than 25 million years ago a fissure opened along the Pacific floor. Beneath tons of sea water molten lava poured from the rift. This liquid basalt, oozing from a hot spot in the earth's center, created a crater along the ocean bottom. As the tectonic plate that comprises the ocean floor drifted over the earth's hot spot, numerous other craters appeared. Slowly, in the seemingly endless procession of geologic time, a chain of volcanic islands, now stretching almost 2000 miles, has emerged from the sea.

On the continents it was also a period of terrible upheaval. The Himalayas, Alps and Andes were rising, but these great chains would reach their peaks long before the Pacific mountains even touched sea level. Not until about 25 million years ago did the first of these underwater volcanoes, today's Kure and Midway atolls, break the surface and become islands. It was not until about five million years ago that the first of the main islands of the archipelago, Niihau and Kauai, broke the surface to become high islands.

For a couple of million more years, the mountains continued to grow. The forces of erosion cut into them, creating knife-edged cliffs and deep valleys. Then plants began germinating: mosses and ferns, springing from windblown spores, were probably first, followed by seed plants carried by migrating birds and on ocean currents. The steep-walled valleys provided natural greenhouses in which unique species evolved, while transoceanic winds swept insects and other life from the continents.

Some islands never survived this birth process: the ocean simply washed them away. The first islands that did endure, at the northwestern end of the Hawaiian chain, proved to be the smallest. Today these islands, with the exception of Midway, are barren uninhabited atolls. The volcanoes that rose last, far to the southeast, became the mountainous archipelago generally known as the Hawaiian Islands.

With several distinct biological regions, there's much more to the islands than lush tropics. Rainforests give way to dry forests, and to coastal habitats where the vegetation is specially suited to withstand wind and salt. Higher in altitude are the bogs, pools of standing water containing rare life forms that have been forced to adapt to a difficult environment. Highest in altitude is the alpine zone, consisting of bare volcanic surfaces scattered with clumps of low-growing herbs and shrubs. Subzero temperatures, frost and even snow help keep this region desolate.

Hawaii's luxurious parks, mountain retreats and deserted beaches make it a paradise for campers and backpackers. Because of the varied terrain and the islands' microenvironments, it's possible to experience all kinds of outdoor adventures. One day you can hike through a steaming rainforest filled with tropical flowers; the next night you can camp atop a volcanic crater in a stark, windblown area that resembles the moon's surface; then you'll descend to a curving white-sand beach populated only by shorebirds and tropical fish.

Paradise means more than physical beauty, however. It also involves an easy life and a bountiful food supply. The easy living is up to you; just slow down from the frantic pace of mainland life and you'll discover that island existence can be relaxing.

As for wild food—you'll find it hanging from trees, swimming in the ocean and clinging to coral reefs. Just be sure to use the proper techniques in taking from the environment and always keep Hawaii's delicate ecosystem in mind.

In this chapter I'll pass along a few facts I've learned while exploring Hawaii. I don't advise that you plan to live off the land. Hawaii's environment is too fragile to support you. Anyway, living that way is a hell of a lot of work! I'll just give a few hints on how to supplement your provisions with a newly caught fish or a fresh fruit salad. That way you'll get a full taste of the islands.

Obviously, none of these techniques were developed by me personally. In fact, most of them date back centuries to the early days, when Polynesian explorers applied the survival skills they had learned in Tahiti and the Marquesas to the newly discovered islands of Hawaii. So as you set out to fish along a coral reef, hunt for shellfish in tidepools or gather seaweed at low tide, give a prayerful thanks to the generations of savvy islanders who have come before you.

▼▼▼▼▼▼▼▼▼▼▼▼
## Flora and Fauna

### FLORA

Many of the plants you'll see in Hawaii are not indigenous. In fact, much of the lush vegetation of this tropical island found its way here from locations all over the world. Sea winds, birds and seafaring settlers brought many of the seeds, plants, flowers and trees from the islands of the South Pacific, as well as from other, more distant regions. Over time, some plants adapted to Hawaii's unique ecosystem and climate, creating strange new lineages and evolving into a completely new ecosystem. This process has long interested scientists, who call the Hawaiian Islands one of the best natural labs for studies of plant evolution.

Sugar cane arrived in Hawaii with the first Polynesian settlers, who appreciated its sweet juices. By the late 1800s, it was well established as a lucrative crop. The pineapple was first planted during the same century. A member of the bromeliad family, this spiky plant is actually a collection of beautiful pink, blue and purple flowers, each of which develops into a fruitlet. The pineapple is a collection of these fruitlets, grown together into a single fruit that takes 14 to 17 months to mature. Sugar cane and pineapple are still the main crops in Hawaii, although competition from other countries and environmental problems caused by pesticides have taken their toll.

Visitors to Hawaii will find the islands a perpetual flower show. Sweetly scented plumeria, deep red, shiny anthurium, exotic ginger, showy birds of paradise, small lavender crown flowers, highly fragrant gardenias and the brightly hued hibiscus run riot on the islands and add color and fragrance to the surrounding area. Scarlet and purple bougainvillea vines, and the aromatic lantana, with its dense clusters of flowers, are also found in abundance.

The beautiful, delicate orchid thrives in Hawaii's tropical heat and humidity. Cultivated primarily on the Big Island, the most popular orchids are the *dendrobium*, which can come in white, purple, lavender, or yellow; the *vanda* (bamboo orchid), which is lavender with white lavender and often used for making leis; and the popcorn, which has small, yellow flowers. The wild *vanda*, with its white and lavender petals, can be spotted along the side of the road year-round.

Unfortunately, some new arrivals to the islands, such as mongoose and palm-grass, have become pests and invasive weeds, upsetting the balance of Hawaii's ecosystem.

Hawaii's most unusual plant is the silversword. Delicate looking, this silvery green plant is actually very hardy. It thrives on the moonscape of Haleakala, 6000 to 10,000 feet above sea level on Maui. Very adaptable, it can survive in extreme hot and cold temperatures with little moisture. Its silvery hairs reflect the sun and its leaves curl inward, protecting the stalk and creating a sort of bowl where rain is collected and stored. The plant lives from five to thirty years, waiting until the right moment before sprouting a three- to nine-foot stalk composed of hundreds of small, reddish flowers—and then it dies. In the same family as the sunflower, this particular type of silversword lives only on Haleakala and has been close to extinction for many years. Now protected, it is currently making a comeback.

Another curious specimen found on the leeward slopes of Haleakala and on the Big Island is the protea. With 1500 varieties, this remarkable plant comes in a myriad of shapes, sizes and colors. Some look like pin cushions, others resemble corn cobs. Originally from South Africa and Australia, the Hawaiian plant is a hybrid.

Although many people equate the tropics with the swaying palm tree, Hawaii is home to a variety of exotic trees. The famed banyan tree, known for pillarlike aerial roots that grow vertically downward from the branches, spreads to form a natural canopy. When the roots touch the ground, they thicken, providing support for the tree's branches to continue expanding. The candlenut, or *kukui*, tree, originally brought to Hawaii from the South Pacific islands, is big, bushy and prized for its nuts, which can be polished and strung together to make leis. The state tree, it provided early Hawaiians with oil, light and natural remedies. Covered with tiny pink blossoms, the canopied monkeypod tree has fernlike leaves that close up at night. With its cascades of bright yellow or pink flowers, the cassia tree earns its moniker—the shower tree.

Found in a variety of shapes and sizes, the ubiquitous palm does indeed sway to the breezes on white-sand beaches, but it also comes in a short, stubby form, the Samoan coconut, featuring more frond than trunk. The fruit, or nuts, of these trees are prized for their oil, which can be utilized for making everything from margarine to soap. The wood (rattan for example) is often used for making furniture.

**FRUITS AND VEGETABLES**   There's a lot more to Hawaii's tropical wonderland than gorgeous flowers and overgrown rainforests. The islands are also teeming with edible plants. Roots, fruits, vegetables, herbs and spices grow like weeds from the shoreline to the mountains. Following is a list of some of the more commonly found edibles.

*Avocado:* Covered with either a tough green or purple skin, this pear-shaped fruit sometimes weighs as much as three pounds. It grows on ten- to forty-foot-high trees, and ripens from June through November.

*Bamboo:* The bamboo plant is actually a grass with a sweet root that is edible and a long stem frequently used for making furniture. Often exceeding eight feet in height, the most common bamboo is green until picked, when it turns a golden brown.

*Banana:* Polynesians use banana trees not only for food but also for clothing, medicines, dyes and even alcohol; culturally, it represents man. The fruit, which grows upside down on broad-leaved trees, can be harvested as soon as the first banana in the bunch turns yellow.

*Breadfruit:* This large round fruit grows on trees that reach up to 60 feet in height. Breadfruit must be boiled, baked or fried.

*Coconut:* The coconut tree is probably the most important plant in the entire Pacific. Every part of the towering palm is used. Most people are concerned only with the hard brown nut, which yields delicious water as well as a tasty meat. If the coconut is still green, the meat is a succulent jellylike substance. Otherwise, it's a hard but delicious white rind.

*Guava:* A roundish yellow fruit that grows on a small shrub or tree, guavas are extremely abundant in the wild. They ripen between June and October.

*Lychee:* Found hanging in bunches from the lychee tree, this popular summer fruit is encased in red, prickly skin that peels off to reveal the sweet-tasting, translucent flesh.

*Mango:* Known as the king of fruits, the mango grows on tall shade trees. The oblong fruit ripens in the spring and summer.

*Maui onion:* Resembling an ordinary yellow onion in size and color, these bulbs are uncommonly mild. They are grown on the south side of Haleakala in rich volcanic soil, and enjoy enough sun and altitude to make them very sweet. A member of the lily family, the Maui onion is best eaten raw.

*Mountain apple:* This sweet fruit grows in damp, shaded valleys at an elevation of about 1800 feet. The flowers resemble fluffy crimson balls; the fruit, which ripens from July to December, is also a rich red color.

*Papaya:* This delicious fruit, which is picked as it begins to turn yellow, grows on unbranched trees. The sweet flesh can be bright orange or coral pink in color. Summer is the peak harvesting season.

*Passion fruit:* Known as *lilikoi* on the islands, this tasty yellow fruit is oval in shape and grows to a length of about two or three inches. It's produced on a vine and ripens in summer or fall.

*Taro:* The tuberous root of this Hawaiian staple is pounded into a grayish purple paste known as *poi*. One of the most nutritious foods, it has a rather bland taste. The plant has wide, shiny, thick leaves with reddish stems; the root is white with purple veins. Taro is also served in other forms, such as chips and popsicles.

**FAUNA**

In Hawaii, it seems there is more wildlife in the water and air than on land. A scuba diver's paradise, the ocean is also a promised land for many other creatures. Coral, colorful fish and migrating whales are only part of this underwater community. Sadly, many of Hawaii's coral reefs have been dying mysteriously in the last several years. No one is sure why, but many believe this is partially due to runoff from pesticides used in agriculture.

### STEP LIGHTLY

Hawaii's wilderness is home to pigs, goats, tropical birds, deer and mongooses, as well as a spectacular array of exotic and indigenous plants. All exist in one of the world's most delicate ecological balances. There are more endangered species in Hawaii than in all the rest of the United States. So keep in mind the maxim that the Hawaiians try to follow. *Ua mau ke ea o ka aina i ka pono:* The life of the land is preserved in righteousness.

For adventure lovers, Maui, and to a lesser extent the Big Island, offer excellent opportunities for whale watching. Every year, humpback whales converge in the warm waters off the islands to give birth to their calves. Beginning their migration in Alaska, they can be spotted in Hawaiian waters from November through May. The humpback, named for its practice of showing its dorsal fin when diving, is quite easy to spy. They feed in shallow waters, usually diving for periods of no longer than 15 minutes. They often sleep on the surface and breathe fairly frequently. Unlike other whales, humpbacks have the ability to sing. Loud and powerful, their songs carry above and below the water for miles. The songs change every year, yet, incredibly, all the whales always seem to know the current one. Quite playful, they can be seen leaping, splashing and flapping their 15-foot tails over their backs. The best time for whale watching is from January to April.

Spinner dolphins are also favorites among visitors. Named for their "spinning" habit, they can revolve as many as six times during one leap. They resemble the spotted dolphin, another frequenter of Hawaiian waters, but are more likely to venture closer to the shore. Dolphins have clocked in with speeds ranging from 9 to 25 mph, a feat they often achieve by propelling themselves out of the water (or even riding the bow wave of a ship). Their thick, glandless skin also contributes to this agility. The skin is kept smooth by constant renewal and sloughing (bottlenoses replace their epidermis every two hours). Playful and intelligent, dolphins are a joy to watch. Many research centers are investigating the mammals' ability to imitate, learn and communicate; some believe that dolphin intelligence may be comparable to that of humans.

One of the few mammals to live in the Hawaiian islands before the Polynesians' arrival, the Hawaiian monk seal has been hunted nearly to the point of extinction. Now protected as an endangered species, this tropical seal is found mostly on the outer

## AQUACULTURE THE ANCIENT WAY

Ancient Hawaiians would have fared well on the television series *Survivor*; they had fishtrapping down pat. Using enclosed brackish water off the coast, fish were bred and maintained in fishponds through ingenious use of *makaha*, sluice gates that controlled the in- and outflow of water. Designed to allow young fish in and keep the ready-to-eat fish from escaping, the gates also helped control the growth of algae, the lowest but most vital rung on the pond food ladder. This ancient technique is still practiced in Oahu's Kaneohe Bay, where the **Kualoa Ranch** maintains an operational pond and sells its produce. ~ Kualoa Ranch, Kaneohe; 800-231-7321; www.kualoa.com.

islands, although it is occasionally spotted on Kauai, and more rarely, on Oahu. Closely related to the elephant seal, the monk seal is not as agile or as fond of land as other seals.

Green sea turtles are common on all of the Hawaiian islands, although this was not always the case. Due to the popularity of their shells and meat, they spent many years on the endangered species list, but are now making a comeback. Measuring three to four feet in diameter, these large reptiles frolic in saltwater only, and are often visible from the shore.

Hawaii is also home to many rare and endangered birds. Like the flora, the birds on the islands are highly specialized. The state bird, the nene, or Hawaiian goose, is a cousin to the Canadian goose and mates for life. Extinct on Maui for many years, several nenes were reintroduced here in the late 1960s. There's still some doubt as to whether they will produce a self-sustaining wild population. They currently live in the wild in the West Maui Mountains, on the Big Island and on Kauai. Once thought to be native to high-elevation habitats, biologists now believe that these rare birds may be more suited to a sea-level environment. The slopes of Haleakala are also home to two other endangered birds: the crested honeycreeper and the parrotbill.

On the endangered species list for many years, the Hawaiian hawk, or *io*, has had its status changed to "threatened." Existing exclusively on the Big Island, the regal *io* is found in a variety of habitats from forest to grassland, but is most often sighted on the slopes of Mauna Kea and Mauna Loa.

There *are* a few birds native to Hawaii that have thus far avoided the endangered species list. Two of the most common birds are the yellow-green *amakihi* and the red *iiwi*.

Known in Hawaiian mythology for its protective powers, the *pueo*, or Hawaiian owl, a brown-and-white-feathered bird, resides on Kauai, the Big Island and in Haleakala crater. On Oahu the Hawaiian owl is considered an endangered species.

The *koae kea*, or "tropic bird," lives on Haleakala, as well as in Kilauea Crater and Kauai's Waimea Canyon. Resembling a seagull in size, it has a long, thin white tail and a striking striping pattern on the back of the wings.

One common seabird is the *iwa*, or frigate, a very large creature measuring three to four feet in length, with a wing span averaging seven feet. The males are solid black, while the females have a large white patch on their chest and tail. A predatory bird, they're easy to spot raiding the nesting colonies of other birds along the offshore rocks. If you see one, you may want to seek cover; legend says they portend a storm. Other native birds that make the islands their home are the Hawaiian stilt and the Hawaiian coot—both water birds—along with the black noddy, American plover and wedge-tailed shearwater.

Not many wild four-footed creatures roam the islands. Deer, feral goats and pigs were brought here early on and have found a home in the forests. Some good news for people fearful of snakes: There is nary a serpent (or a sea serpent) in Hawaii, although lizards such as skinks and geckos abound.

One can only hope that with the renewed interest in Hawaiian culture, and growing environmental awareness, Hawaii's plants and animals will continue to exist as they have for centuries.

▼ ▼ ▼ ▼ ▼ ▼ ▼ ▼ ▼ ▼ ▼ ▼ ▼ ▼
## Outdoor Adventures

Opportunities for adventuring abound in the islands. In this section you'll find information on popular ocean-based activities, including advice on creative ways to scare up your own supper.

Some, like torchfishing, are part of time-honored Hawaiian traditions. You'll also find some general tips on hiking and camping in the islands (for more specific information, see individual island chapters). For information about other outdoor adventures such as diving, kayaking, surfing, snuba and more, please see individual island chapters.

**OCEAN SAFETY**  Many water lovers never realize how awesome the sea can be. Particularly in Hawaii, where waves can reach 30-foot heights and currents flow unobstructed for thousands of miles, the ocean is sometimes as treacherous as it is spectacular. Dozens of people drown every year in Hawaii, many others are dragged from the crushing surf with broken backs, and countless numbers sustain minor cuts and bruises.

These accidents can be entirely avoided if you approach the ocean with a respect for its power as well as an appreciation of its beauty. All you have to do is heed a few simple guidelines. First, never turn your back on the sea. Waves come in sets: one group may be small and quite harmless, but the next set could be large enough to sweep you out to sea. Never swim alone.

Don't try to surf, or even bodysurf, until you're familiar with the sports' techniques and precautionary measures. Be extremely careful when the surf is high.

If you get caught in a rip current, don't swim *against* it: swim *across* it, parallel to the shore. These currents, running from the shore out to sea, can often be spotted by their ragged-looking surface water and foamy edges.

Around coral reefs, wear something to protect your feet against coral cuts. Particularly good are the inexpensive Japanese *tabis*, or reef slippers. If you do sustain a coral cut, clean it with hydrogen peroxide, then apply an antiseptic or antibiotic substance. This is also a good procedure for octopus bites.

When stung by a Portuguese man-of-war or a jellyfish, rinse the affected area with sea water to remove any tentacles. For jellyfish stings only, you might also try vinegar or isopropyl alcohol.

The old Hawaiian remedies, which are reputedly quite effective, involve applying urine or green papaya.

If you step on the sharp, painful spines of a sea urchin, soak the affected area in very hot water for 15 to 90 minutes. Another remedy calls for applying urine or undiluted vinegar. If the pain persists for more than a day, or you notice swelling or other signs of infection, consult a doctor.

Oh, one last thing. The chances of encountering a shark are about as likely as sighting a UFO. But should you meet one of these ominous creatures, stay calm. He'll be no happier to see you than you are to confront him. Simply swim quietly to shore. By the time you make it back to terra firma, you'll have a hell of a story to tell.

## FISHING

While you're exploring the islands, the sea will be your prime food source. Fishing in Hawaii is good year-round, and the off-shore waters are crowded with many varieties of edible fish. For deep-sea fishing you'll have to charter a boat, and freshwater angling requires a license; so I'll concentrate on surf-casting. It costs nothing to fish this way.

In the individual island chapters, you'll find information on the best spots to fish for different species; in the "Addresses" section of those chapters, you'll usually see a fishing supply store listed. For information on seasons, licenses and official regulations, check with the Aquatic Resources Division of the State Department of Land and Natural Resources. This agency has offices on most of the major islands.

The easiest, most economical way to fish is with a hand-held line. Just get a 50- to 100-foot line, and attach a hook and a ten-ounce sinker. Wind the line loosely around a smooth block of wood, then remove the wood from the center. If your coil is free from snags, you'll be able to throw-cast it easily. You can either hold the line in your hand, feeling for a strike, or tie it to the frail end of a bamboo pole.

### SERVICE IN THE SUN

If you're looking for a fun and fulfilling way to spend ten days, contact **Sierra Club Outings**. Their guided service trips lead you into the islands' most desolate wilderness areas, through lush tropical forests and to coastal waters, restoring natural settings by removing manmade structures and fencing and conducting research on marine wildlife. Adventurers are able to snorkel, hike and enjoy beautiful views while helping to preserve Hawaii's paradise. ~ 85 2nd Street, 2nd Floor, San Francisco, CA 94105; 415-977-5522, fax 415-977-5795; www.sierraclub.org/outings/national.

Beaches and rocky points are generally good places to surf-cast; the best times are during the incoming and outgoing tides. Popular baits include octopus, eel, lobster, crab, frozen shrimp and sea worms.

**TORCHFISHING & SPEARFISHING**   The old Hawaiians also fished at night by torchlight. They fashioned torches by inserting nuts from the *kukui* tree into the hollow end of a bamboo pole, then lighting the flammable nuts. When fish swam like moths to the flame, the Hawaiians speared, clubbed or netted them.

Today, it's easier to use a lantern and spear. (In fact, it's all *too* easy and tempting to take advantage of this willing prey: Take only edible fish and only what you will eat, and follow state rules on size and season limits for some species.) It's also handy to bring a facemask or a glass-bottomed box to aid in seeing underwater. The best time for torchfishing is a dark night when the sea is calm and the tide low.

During daylight hours, the best place to spearfish is along coral reefs and in areas where the bottom is a mixture of sand and rock. Equipped with speargun, mask, fins and snorkel, you can explore underwater grottoes and spectacular coral formations while seeking your evening meal. Spearguns can be purchased inexpensively throughout the islands.

**CRABBING**   For the hungry adventurer, there are several crab species in Hawaii. The most sought after are the Kona and Samoan varieties. Kona crabs are found in relatively deep water, and can usually be caught only from a boat. Samoan crabs inhabit sandy and muddy areas in bays and near river mouths. All you need to catch them are a boat and a net fastened to a round wire hoop secured by a string. The net is lowered to the bottom; then, after a crab has gone for the bait, the entire contraption is raised to the surface.

**SQUIDDING**   Between June and December, squidding is another popular sport. Actually, the term is a misnomer: squid inhabit deep water and are not usually hunted. What you'll really be after are octopuses. There are two varieties in Hawaii, both of which are commonly found in water three or four feet deep: the *hee*, a greyish-brown animal that changes color like a chameleon, and the *puloa*, a red-colored mollusk with white stripes on its head.

Both are nocturnal and live in holes along coral reefs. At night by torchlight you can spot them sitting exposed on the bottom. During the day, they crawl inside the holes, covering the entrances with shells and loose coral.

The Hawaiians used to pick the octopus up, letting it cling to their chest and shoulders. When they were ready to bag their prize,

# The New Travel

Travel has become a personal art form. A destination no longer serves as just a place to relax: It's also a point of encounter. To many, this new wave in travel customs is labeled "adventure travel" and involves trekking glaciers or dusting the cliffs in a hang glider; to others, it connotes nothing more daring than a restful spell in a secluded resort. Actually, it's a state of mind, a willingness not only to accept but seek out the uncommon and unique.

Few places in the world are more conducive to this imaginative travel than Hawaii. Several organizations in the islands cater specifically to people who want to add local customs and unusual adventures to their vacation itineraries.

The **Nature Conservancy of Hawaii** conducts natural history day hikes of Oahu, Maui and Molokai. Led by expert guides, small groups explore untrammeled beaches, rainforest and an ancient bog. The tours provide a singular insight into the plant and animal life of the Islands. Reservations should be made at least one month in advance. ~ P.O. Box 1716, Makawao, HI 96768, 537-4508 on Oahu; 808-572-7849 on Maui; and P.O. Box 220, Kualapuu, HI 96757, 808-553-5236 on Molokai; www.nature.org.

**Hawaiian Adventure Tours** features a ten-day tour of Kauai, Maui and the Big Island, including hiking and snorkeling. ~ P.O. Box 1269, Kapaau, HI 96755; 808-889-0227, 800-659-3544; www.hawaiianadventuretours.com.

**Paradise Safaris** offers a sunset stargazing trip. Small groups enjoy a sunset view at the summit of Mauna Kea, and learn about the mountaintop observatory's telescope. ~ P.O. Box 9027, Kailua-Kona, HI 96745; 808-322-2366, 888-322-2366; www.maunakea.com.

**EarthVoice Hawaii** is an environmentally and culturally active nonprofit that aims to generate respect and responsibility for the natural world and interest in Hawaiian culture and customs. Activities run the gamut from nature walks to volcano watches to stepping through waterfalls. ~ P.O. Box 1433, Honokaa, HI 96727; 888-464-1080; www.earthmediahawaii.com.

When you're ready to take up the challenge of this style of freewheeling travel, check with these outfits. Or plan your own trip. To traditional tourists, Hawaii means souvenir shops and fast-food restaurants. But for those with spirit and imagination, it's a land of untracked beaches and ancient volcanoes waiting to be explored.

they'd dispatch the creature by biting it between the eyes. You'll probably feel more comfortable spearing the beast.

**SHELLFISH GATHERING**

Other excellent food sources are the shellfish that inhabit coastal waters. The ancient Hawaiians used pearl shells to attract the fish, and hooks, some made from human bones, to snare them. Your friends will probably be quite content to see you angling with store-bought artificial lures. Oysters and clams, which use their muscular feet to burrow into sand and soft mud, can be collected along the bottom of Hawaii's bays. Spiny lobsters, rarely found in Hawaii waters, are illegal to spear, but can be taken in season with short poles to which cable leaders and baited hooks are attached. You can also just grab them with a gloved hand but be careful—spiny lobsters live up to their name! You can also gather limpets, though I don't recommend it. These tiny black shellfish, locally known as *opihi*, cling tenaciously to rocks in the tidal zone. In areas of very rough surf, the Hawaiians gather them by leaping into the water after one set of waves breaks, then jumping out before the next set arrives. Being a coward myself, I simply order them in Hawaiian restaurants.

**SEAWEED GATHERING**

There are still some people who don't think of seaweed as food, but it's very popular among Japanese, and it once served as an integral part of the Hawaiian diet. It's extremely nutritious, easy to gather and very plentiful.

Rocky shores are the best places to find the edible species of seaweed. Some of them float in to shore and can be picked up; other species cling stubbornly to rocks and must be freed with a knife; still others grow in sand or mud. Low tide is the best time to collect seaweed: more plants are exposed, and some can be taken without even getting wet.

## A FRUIT FOR ALL SEASONS

Coconuts are one of those blessings from heaven, providing food, fuel, water, shade and building materials. The fronds were used with *pili* grass to thatch roofs, the hollowed trunks are made into *pahu*, or drums, and the fiber can be dried for fuel. It was also fashioned into ropey sandals that allowed Hawaiians to walk across razor-sharp lava. Nutritionally, the water inside is sterile and full of healthful enzymes, and the meat can be eaten or pressed into cream and oil. Most importantly, coconuts grow well close to the ocean, offering welcome shade from the harsh tropical sun.

Camping in Hawaii usually means pitching a tent or reserving a cabin. Throughout the islands there are secluded spots and hidden beaches, plus numerous county, state and federal parks. All of these campsites, together with hiking trails, are described in the individual island chapters; it's a good idea to consult those detailed listings when planning your trip. The camping equipment you'll require is listed in the "Packing" section of the preceding chapter. You might also want to obtain some hiking maps; they are available from **Hawaii Geographic Maps & Books**. ~ 49 South Hotel Street #215, Honolulu; 808-538-3952, 800-538-3950.

Before you set out on your camping trip, there are a few very important matters that I want to explain more fully. First, bring a campstove: firewood is scarce in most areas and soaking wet in others. It's advisable to wear long pants when hiking in order to protect your legs from rock outcroppings, spiny plants and insects. Also, if you are going to explore the Mauna Kea, Mauna Loa or Haleakala volcanoes, be sure to bring cold-weather gear; temperatures are often significantly lower than at sea level and these peaks occasionally receive snow.

Most trails you'll be hiking are composed of volcanic rock. Since this is a very crumbly substance, be extremely cautious when climbing any rock faces. In fact, you should avoid steep climbs if possible. Stay on the trails: Hawaii's dense undergrowth makes it very easy to get lost. If you get lost at night, stay where you are. Because of the low latitude, night descends rapidly here; there's practically no twilight. Once darkness falls, it can be very dangerous to move around. You should also be careful to purify all of your drinking water. And be extremely cautious near streambeds as flash-flooding sometimes occurs, particularly on the windward coasts. This is particularly true during the winter months, when heavy storms from the northeast lash the islands.

Another problem that you're actually more likely to encounter are those nasty varmints that buzz your ear just as you're falling asleep—mosquitoes. Hawaii contains neither snakes nor poison ivy, but it has plenty of these dive-bombing pests. Like me, you probably consider that it's always open season on the little bastards. With most of the archipelago's other species, however, you'll have to be a careful conservationist.

# THREE

# History and Culture

**POLYNESIAN ARRIVAL**   The island of Hawaii, the Big Island, was the last land mass created in the ongoing dramatic geologic upheaval that formed the Hawaiian islands. But it was most likely the first island to be inhabited by humans. Perhaps as early as the third century, Polynesians sailing from the Marquesas Islands, and then later from Tahiti, landed on Hawaii's southern tip. The boats were formidable structures, catamaran-like vessels with a cabin built on the platform between the wooden hulls. The sails were woven from *hala* (pandanus) leaves. Some of the vessels were a hundred feet long and could do 20 knots, making the trip to Hawaii in a month. Entire families crossed the 2500 miles of untracked ocean with all the provisions they needed for their new home.

The Polynesians had originally come from the coast of Asia about 3000 years before. They had migrated through Indonesia, then pressed inexorably eastward, leapfrogging across archipelagoes until they finally reached the last chain, the most remote—Hawaii.

These Pacific migrants were undoubtedly the greatest sailors of their day, and stand among the finest in history. When close to land they could smell it, taste it in the seawater, see it in a lagoon's turquoise reflection on the clouds above an island. They knew 150 stars. From the color of the water they determined ocean depths and current directions. They had no charts, no compasses, no sextants; sailing directions were simply recorded in legends and chants. Yet Polynesians discovered the Pacific, from Indonesia to Easter Island, from New Zealand to Hawaii. They made the Vikings and Phoenicians look like landlubbers.

**CAPTAIN COOK**   They were high islands, rising in the northeast as the sun broke across the Pacific. First one, then a second and, finally, as the tall-masted ships drifted west, a third island loomed before them. Landfall! The British crew was ecstatic. It meant fresh water, tropical fruits, solid ground on which to set their boots and a chance to carouse with the native women. For their captain, James Cook, it was another in an amazing career of discoveries. The man whom many call history's greatest explorer was about to land in one of the last spots on earth to be discovered by the West.

He would name the place for his patron, the British earl who became famous by pressing a meal between two crusts of bread. The Sandwich Islands. Later they would be called Owhyhee, and eventually, as the Western tongue glided around the uncharted edges of a foreign language, Hawaii.

It was January 1778, a time when the British Empire was still basking in a sun that never set. The Pacific had been opened to Western powers over two centuries before, when a Portuguese sailor named Magellan crossed it. Since that time, the British, French, Dutch and Spanish had tracked through in search of future colonies.

They happened upon Samoa, Fiji, Tahiti and the other islands that spread across this third of the globe, but somehow they had never sighted Hawaii. Even when Cook finally spied it, he little realized how important a find he had made. Hawaii, quite literally, was a jewel in the ocean, rich in fragrant sandalwood, ripe for agricultural exploitation and crowded with sea life. But it was the archipelago's isolation that would prove to be its greatest resource. Strategically situated between Asia and North America, it was the only place for thousands of miles to which whalers, merchants and bluejackets could repair for provisions and rest.

Cook was 49 years old when he shattered Hawaii's quiescence. The Englishman hadn't expected to find islands north of Tahiti. Quite frankly, he wasn't even trying. It was his third Pacific voyage and Cook was hunting bigger game, the fabled Northwest Passage that would link this ocean with the Atlantic. On January 18, 1778, Captain Cook's HMS *Resolution*, along with the HMS *Discovery*, spotted Oahu.

But these mountainous islands were still an interesting find. He could see by the canoes venturing out to meet his ships that the lands were inhabited; when he finally put ashore on Kauai, on January 20, Cook discovered a Polynesian society. He saw irrigated fields, domestic animals and high-towered temples. The women were bare-breasted, the men wore loincloths. As his crew bartered for pigs, fowls and bananas, he learned that the natives knew about metal and coveted iron like gold.

If iron was gold to these "Indians," then Cook was a god. He soon realized that his arrival had somehow been miraculously timed, coinciding with the Makahiki festival, a months-long celebration highlighted by sporting competitions, feasting, hula and exaltation of the ruling chiefs. Even war ceased during this gala affair. Makahiki honored the roving deity Lono, whose return to Hawaii on "trees that would move over seas" was foretold in ancient legend. Cook was a strange white man sailing tall-masted ships—obviously he was Lono. The Hawaiians gave him gifts, fell in his path and rose only at his insistence.

But even among religious crowds, fame is often fickle. After leaving Hawaii, Cook sailed north to the Arctic Sea, where he failed to discover the Northwest Passage. He returned the next year to Kealakekua Bay on the Big Island, arriving at the tail end of another exhausting Makahiki festival. By then the Hawaiians had tired of his constant demands for provisions and were suffering from a new disease that was obviously carried by Lono's archangelic crew—syphilis. This Lono was proving something of a freeloader.

Tensions ran high. The Hawaiians stole a boat. Cook retaliated with gunfire. A scuffle broke out on the beach and in a sudden violent outburst, which surprised the islanders as much as the interlopers, the Hawaiians discovered that their god could bleed. The world's finest mariner lay face down in foot-deep water, stabbed and bludgeoned to death.

Cook's end marked the beginning of an era. He had put the Pacific on the map, his map, probing its expanses and defining its fringes. In Hawaii he ended a thousand years of solitude. The archipelago's geographic isolation, which has always played a crucial role in Hawaii's development, had finally failed to protect it, and a second theme had come into play—the islands' vulnerability. Together with the region's "backwardness," these conditions would now mold Hawaii's history. All in turn would be shaped by another factor, one which James Cook had added to Hawaii's historic equation: the West.

**KAMEHAMEHA AND KAAHUMANU**  The next man whose star would rise above Hawaii was present at Cook's death. Some say he struck the Englishman, others that he took a lock of the great leader's hair and used its residual power, its *mana*, to become king of all Hawaii.

Kamehameha was a tall, muscular, unattractive man with a furrowed face, a lesser chief on the powerful island of Hawaii. When he began his career of conquest a few years after Cook's death, he was a mere upstart, an ambitious, arrogant young chief. But he fought with a general's skill and a warrior's cunning, often plunging into the midst of a melee. He had an astute sense of technology, an intuition that these new Western metals and firearms could make him a king.

In Kamehameha's early years, the Hawaiian islands were composed of many fiefdoms. Several kings or great chiefs, continually warring among themselves, ruled individual islands. At times, a few kings would carve up one island or a lone king might seize several. Never had one monarch controlled all the islands.

But fresh players had entered the field: Westerners with ample firepower and awesome ships. During the decade following Cook, only a handful had arrived, mostly Englishmen and Americans, and they had not yet won the influence they soon would wield. However, even a few foreigners were enough to upset the balance of power. They sold weapons and hardware to the great chiefs, making several of them more powerful than any of the others had ever been. War was imminent.

When Captain Cook came ashore in 1778, there were approximately 300,000 Hawaiian residing there.

Kamehameha stood in the center of the hurricane. Like any leader suddenly caught up in the terrible momentum of history, he never quite realized where he was going or how fast he was moving. And he cared little that he was being carried in part by Westerners who would eventually want something for the ride. Kamehameha was no fool. If political expedience meant Western intrusion, then so be it. He had enemies among chiefs on the other islands; he needed the guns.

When two white men came into his camp in 1790, he had the military advisers to complement a fast expanding arsenal. Within months he cannonaded Maui. In 1792, Kamehameha seized the Big Island by inviting his main rival to a peaceful parley, then slaying the hapless chief. By 1795, he had consolidated his control of Maui, grasped Molokai and Lanai, and begun reaching greedily toward Oahu. He struck rapidly, landing near Waikiki and sweeping inland, forcing his enemies to their deaths over the precipitous cliffs of the Nuuanu Pali.

The warrior had become a conqueror, controlling all the islands except Kauai, which he finally gained in 1810 by peaceful negotiation. Kamehameha proved to be as able a bureaucrat as he had been a general. He became a benevolent despot who, with the aid of an ever-increasing number of Western advisers, expanded Hawaii's commerce, brought peace to the islands and moved his people inexorably toward the modern age.

He came to be called Kamehameha the Great, and history first cast him as the George Washington of Hawaii, a wise and resolute leader who gathered a wartorn archipelago into a kingdom. Kamehameha I. But with the revisionist history of the 1960s and 1970s, as Third World people questioned both the Western version of events and the virtues of progress, Kamehameha began to resemble Benedict Arnold. He was seen as an opportunist, a megalomaniac who permitted the Western powers their initial foothold in Hawaii. He used their technology and then, in the manner of great men who depend on stronger allies, was eventually used by them.

As long a shadow as Kamehameha cast across the islands, the event that most dramatically transformed Hawaiian society occurred after his death in 1819. The kingdom had passed to Kamehameha's son Liholiho, but Kamehameha's favorite wife, Kaahumanu, usurped the power. Liholiho was a prodigal son, dissolute, lacking self-certainty, a drunk. Kaahumanu was a woman for all seasons, a canny politician who combined brilliance with boldness, the feminist of her day. She had infuriated Kamehameha by eating forbidden foods and sleeping with other chiefs, even when he placed a taboo on her body and executed her lovers. She drank liquor, ran away, proved completely uncontrollable and won Kamehameha's love.

It was during Kamehameha's rule that the first permanent building was erected in the islands—the "Brick Palace" in Lahaina.

It was only natural that when he died, she would take his *mana*, or so she reckoned. Kaahumanu gravitated toward power with the drive of someone whom fate has unwisely denied. She carved her own destiny, announcing that Kamehameha's wish had been to give her a governmental voice. There would be a new post and she would fill it, becoming in a sense Hawaii's first prime minister.

And if the power, then the motion. Kaahumanu immediately marched against Hawaii's belief system, trying to topple the old idols. For years she had bristled under a polytheistic religion regulated by taboos, or *kapus*, which severely restricted women's rights. Now Kaahumanu urged the new king, Liholiho, to break a very strict *kapu* by sharing a meal with women.

Since the act might help consolidate Liholiho's position, it had a certain appeal to the king. Anyway, the *kapus* were weakening: these white men, coming now in ever greater numbers, defied them with impunity. Liholiho vacillated, went on a two-day drunk before gaining courage, then finally sat down to eat. It was a last supper, shattering an ancient creed and opening the way for a radically new divinity. As Kaahumanu had willed, the old order collapsed, taking away a vital part of island life and leaving the Hawaiians more exposed than ever to foreign influence.

Already Western practices were gaining hold. Commerce from Honolulu, Lahaina and other ports was booming. There was a fortune to be made dealing sandalwood to China-bound merchants, and the chiefs were forcing the common people to strip Hawaii's forests. The grueling labor might make the chiefs rich, but it gained the commoners little more than a barren landscape. Western diseases struck virulently. The Polynesians in Hawaii, who numbered 300,000 in Cook's time, were extremely susceptible. By 1866, their population had dwindled to less than 60,000. It was a difficult time for the Hawaiian people.

**MISSIONARIES AND MERCHANTS**    Hawaii was not long without religion. The same year that Kaahumanu shattered tradition, a group of New England missionaries boarded the brig *Thaddeus* for a voyage around Cape Horn. It was a young company—many were in their twenties or thirties—and included a doctor, a printer and several teachers. They were all strict Calvinists, fearful that the second coming was at hand and possessed of a mission. They were bound for a strange land called Hawaii, 18,000 miles away.

Hawaii, of course, was a lost paradise, a hellhole of sin and savagery where men slept with several wives and women neglected to wear dresses. To the missionaries, it mattered little that the Hawaiians had lived this way for centuries. The churchmen would save these heathens from hell's everlasting fire whether they liked it or not.

The delegation arrived in Kailua on the Big Island in 1820 and then spread out, establishing important missions in Honolulu and Lahaina. Soon they were building schools and churches, conducting services in Hawaiian and converting the natives to Christianity.

The missionaries rapidly became an integral part of Hawaii, despite the fact that they were a walking contradiction to everything Hawaiian. They were a contentious, self-righteous, fanatical people whose arrogance toward the Hawaiians blinded them to the beauty and wisdom of island lifestyles. Where the natives lived in thatch homes open to the soothing trade winds, the missionaries built airless clapboard houses with New England–style fireplaces. While the Polynesians swam and surfed frequently, the new arrivals, living near the world's finest beaches, stank from not bathing. In a region where the thermometer rarely drops much below 70 degrees, they wore long-sleeved woolens, ankle-length dresses and claw-hammer coats.

And yet the missionaries were a brave people, selfless and God-fearing. Their dangerous voyage from the Atlantic had brought them into a very alien land. Many would die from disease and overwork; most would never see their homeland again. Bigoted though they were, the Calvinists committed their lives to the Hawaiian people. They developed the Hawaiian alphabet, rendered Hawaiian into a written language and, of course, translated the Bible. Theirs was the first printing press west of the Rockies. They introduced Western medicine throughout the islands and created such an effective school system that, by the mid-19th century, 80 percent of the Hawaiian population was literate. Unlike almost all the other white people who came to Hawaii, they not only took from the islanders, they also gave.

But to these missionaries, *giving* meant ripping away everything repugnant to God and substituting it with Christianity. They would have to destroy Hawaiian culture in order to save it. Though instructed by their church elders not to meddle in island politics, the missionaries soon realized that heavenly wars had to be fought on earthly battlefields. Politics it would be. After all, wasn't government just another expression of God's bounty?

They allied with Kaahumanu and found it increasingly difficult to separate church from state. Kaahumanu converted to Christianity, while the missionaries became government advisers and helped pass laws protecting the sanctity of the Sabbath. Disgusting practices such as hula dancing were prohibited.

Politics can be a dangerous world for a man of the cloth. The missionaries were soon pitted against other foreigners who were quite willing to let the clerics sing hymns, but were damned opposed to permitting them a voice in government. Hawaii in the 1820s had become a favorite way station for the whaling fleet. As the sandalwood forests were decimated, the island merchants began looking for other industries. By the 1840s, when over 500 ships a year anchored in Hawaiian ports, whaling had become the islands' economic lifeblood.

Like the missionaries, the whalers were Yankees, shipping out from bustling New England ports. But they were a hell of a different cut of Yankee. These were rough, crude, boisterous men who loved rum and music, and thought a lot more of fornicating with island women than saving them. After the churchmen forced the passage of laws prohibiting prostitution, the sailors rioted along the waterfront and fired cannons at the mission homes. When the smoke cleared, the whalers still had their women.

Religion simply could not compete with commerce, and other Westerners were continuously stimulating more business in the islands. By the 1840s, as Hawaii adopted a parliamentary form of government, American and British fortune hunters were replacing missionaries as government advisers. It was a time when anyone, regardless of ability or morality, could travel to the islands and become a political powerhouse literally overnight. A consumptive American, fleeing the mainland for reasons of health, became chief justice of the Hawaiian Supreme Court while still in his twenties. Another lawyer, shadowed from the East Coast by a checkered past, became attorney general two weeks after arriving.

The situation was no different internationally. Hawaii was subject to the whims and terrors of gunboat diplomacy. The archipelago was solitary and exposed, and Western powers were beginning to eye it covetously. In 1843, a maverick British naval officer actually annexed Hawaii to the Crown, but the London government later countermanded his actions. Then, in the early 1850s, the threat of American annexation arose. Restless Californians, fresh from the gold fields and hungry for revolution, plotted unsuccessfully in Honolulu. Even the French periodically sent gunboats in to protect their small Catholic minority.

Finally, the three powers officially stated that they wanted to maintain Hawaii's national integrity. But independence seemed increasingly unlikely. European countries had already begun claiming other Pacific islands, and with the influx of Yankee missionaries and whalers, Hawaii was being steadily drawn into the American orbit.

**THE SUGAR PLANTERS**    There is an old Hawaiian saying that describes the 19th century: The missionaries came to do good, and they did very well. Actually the early evangelists, few of whom profited from their work, lived out only half the maxim. Their sons would give the saying its full meaning.

This second generation, quite willing to sacrifice glory for gain, fit neatly into the commercial society that had rendered their fathers irrelevant. They were shrewd, farsighted young Christians who had grown up in Hawaii and knew both the islands' pitfalls and potentials. They realized that the missionaries had never quite found Hawaii's pulse, and they watched uneasily as whaling became the lifeblood of the islands. Certainly it brought wealth, but whaling was too tenuous—there was always a threat that it might dry up entirely. A one-industry economy would never do; the mission boys wanted more. Agriculture was the obvious answer, and eventually they determined to bind their providence to a plant that grew wild in the islands—sugar cane.

> The missionaries kept many of their old eating habits. They preferred salt pork to fresh beef, dried meat to fresh fish. They considered coconuts an abomination and were loath to eat bananas.

The first sugar plantation was started on Kauai in 1835, but not until the 1870s did the new industry blossom. By then, the Civil War had wreaked havoc with the whaling fleet, and a devastating winter in the Arctic whaling grounds practically destroyed it. The mission boys, who had prophesied the storm, weathered it quite comfortably. They had already begun fomenting an agricultural revolution.

**THE GREAT MAHELE**    Agriculture, of course, means land, and until the 19th century all Hawaii's acreage was held by chiefs. So in 1848, the mission sons, together with other white entrepreneurs, pushed through the Great Mahele, one of the slickest real estate laws in history. Rationalizing that it would grant chiefs the liberty to sell land to Hawaiian commoners and white men, the mission sons established a western system of private property.

The Hawaiians, who had shared their chiefs' lands communally for centuries, had absolutely no concept of deeds and leases. What resulted was the old $24-worth-of-beads story. The benevolent Westerners wound up with the land, while the lucky Hawaiians got practically nothing. Large tracts were purchased for cases of whiskey; others went for the cost of a hollow promise. The entire island of Niihau, which is still owned by the same family, sold for $10,000. It was a bloodless coup, staged more than 40 years before the revolution that would topple Hawaii's monarchy. In a sense it made the 1893 uprising anticlimactic. By then Hawaii's future would already be determined: white interlopers would own four times as much land as Hawaiian commoners.

Following the Great Mahele, the mission boys, along with other businessmen, were ready to become sugar planters. The *mana* once again was passing into new hands. Obviously, there was money to be made in cane, a lot of it, and now that they had land, all they needed was labor. The Hawaiians would never do. Cook might have recognized them as industrious, hardworking people, but the sugar planters considered them shiftless. Disease was killing them off anyway, and the Hawaiians who survived seemed to lose the will to live. Many made appointments with death, stating that in a week they would die; seven days later they were dead.

Foreign labor was the only answer. In 1850, the Masters and Servants Act was passed, establishing an immigration board to import plantation workers. Cheap Asian labor would be brought over. It was a crucial decision, one that would ramify forever through Hawaiian history and change the very substance of island society. Eventually these Asian workers transformed Hawaii from a chain of Polynesian islands into one of the world's most varied and dynamic locales, a meeting place of East and West.

The Chinese were the first to come, arriving in 1852 and soon outnumbering the white population. Initially, with their long pigtails and uncommon habits, the Chinese were a joke around the islands. They were poor people from southern China whose lives were directed by clan loyalty. They built schools and worked hard so that one day they could return to their native villages in glory. They were ambitious, industrious and—ultimately—successful.

*Too* successful, according to the sugar planters, who found it almost impossible to keep the coolies down on the farm. The Chinese came to Hawaii under labor contracts, which forced them to work for five years. After their indentureship, rather than re-enlisting as the sugar bosses had planned, the Chinese moved to the city and became merchants. Worse yet, they married Hawaiian women and were assimilated into the society.

These coolies, the planters decided, were too uppity, too ready to fill social roles that were really the business of white men. So in the 1880s, they began importing Portuguese, over 20,000 of them. But the Portuguese thought they already *were* white men, while any self-respecting American or Englishman of the time knew they weren't.

The Portuguese spelled trouble, and in 1886 the sugar planters turned to Japan, with its restricted land mass and burgeoning population. The new immigrants were peasants from Japan's southern islands, raised in an authoritarian, hierarchical culture in which the father was a family dictator and the family was strictly defined by its social status. Like the Chinese, they built schools to protect their heritage and dreamed of returning home someday; but unlike their Asian neighbors, they only married other Japanese. They sent home for "picture brides," worshipped their ancestors and Emperor and paid ultimate loyalty to Japan, not Hawaii.

The Japanese, it soon became evident, were too proud to work long hours for low pay. Plantation conditions were atrocious; workers were housed in hovels and frequently beaten. The Japanese simply did not adapt. Worst of all, they not only bitched, they organized, striking in 1909.

So in 1910, the sugar planters turned to the Philippines for labor. For two decades the Filipinos arrived, seeking their fortunes and leaving their wives behind. They worked not only with sugar cane but also with pineapples, which were becoming a big business in the 20th century. They were a boisterous, fun-loving people, hated by the immigrants who preceded them and used by the whites who hired them. The Filipinos were given the most menial jobs, the worst working conditions and the shoddiest housing. In time, another side of their character began to show—a despondency, a hopeless sense of their own plight, their inability to raise passage money back home. They became the untouchables of Hawaii.

During the heyday of the whaling industry, more American ships visited Hawaii than any other port in the world.

**REVOLUTIONARIES AND ROYALISTS** Sugar, by the late 19th century, was king. It had become the center of island economy, the principal fact of life for most islanders. Like the earlier whaling industry, it was drawing Hawaii ever closer to the American sphere. The sugar planters were selling the bulk of their crops in California; having already signed several tariff treaties to protect their American market, they were eager to further strengthen mainland ties. Besides, many sugar planters were second-, third- and fourth-generation descendants of the New England missionaries; they had a natural affinity for the United States.

There was, however, one group that shared neither their love for sugar nor their ties to America. To the Hawaiian people, David Kalakaua was king, and America was the nemesis that had long threatened their independence. The whites might own the land, but the Hawaiians, through their monarch, still held substantial political power. During Kalakaua's rule in the 1870s and 1880s, anticolonialism was rampant.

The sugar planters were growing impatient. Kalakaua was proving very antagonistic; his nationalist drumbeating was becoming louder in their ears. How could the sugar merchants convince the United States to annex Hawaii when all these silly Hawaiian royalists were running around pretending to be the

Pacific's answer to the British Isles? They had tolerated this long enough. The Hawaiians were obviously unfit to rule, and the planters soon joined with other businessmen to form a secret revolutionary organization. Backed by a force of well-armed followers, they pushed through the "Bayonet Constitution" of 1887, a self-serving document that weakened the king and strengthened the white landowners. If Hawaii was to remain a monarchy, it would have a Magna Carta.

But Hawaii would not be a monarchy long. Once revolution is in the air, it's often difficult to clear the smoke. By 1891, Kalakaua was dead and his sister, Liliuokalani, had succeeded to the throne. She was an audacious leader, proud of her heritage, quick to defend it and prone to let immediate passions carry her onto dangerous ground. At a time when she should have hung fire, she charged, proclaiming publicly that she would abrogate the new constitution and reestablish a strong monarchy. The revolutionaries had the excuse they needed. They struck in January 1895, seized government buildings and, with four boatloads of American marines and the support of the American minister, secured Honolulu. Liliuokalani surrendered. Sanford Dole, a missionary's son whose name eventually became synonymous with pineapples, became Hawaii's first president.

It was a highly illegal coup; legitimate government had been stolen from the Hawaiian people. But given an island chain as isolated and vulnerable as Hawaii, the revolutionaries reasoned, how much did it really matter? It would be weeks before word reached Washington of what a few Americans had done without official sanction, then several more months before a new American president, Grover Cleveland, denounced the renegade action. By then the revolutionaries would already be forming a republic.

Not even revolution could rock Hawaii into the modern age. For years, an unstable monarchy had reigned; now an oligarchy composed of the revolution's leaders would rule. Officially, Hawaii was a democracy; in truth, the Chinese and Japanese were hindered from voting, and the Hawaiians were encouraged not to bother. Hawaii, reckoned its new leaders, was simply not ready for democracy. Even when the islands were finally annexed by the United States in 1898 and granted territorial status, they remained a colony.

More than ever before, the sugar planters, alias revolutionaries, held sway. By the early 20th century, they had linked their plantations into a cartel, the Big Five. It was a tidy monopoly composed of five companies that owned not only the sugar and pineapple industries, but the docks, shipping companies and many of the stores, as well. Most of these holdings, happily, were the property of a few interlocking, intermarrying mission families— the Doles, Thurstons, Alexanders, Baldwins, Castles, Cookes and others—who had found heaven right here on earth. They golfed together and dined together, sent their daughters to Wellesley and their sons to Yale. All were proud of their roots, and as blindly paternalistic as their forefathers. It was their destiny to control Hawaii, and they made very certain, by refusing to sell land or provide services, that mainland firms did not gain a foothold in their domain.

What was good for the Big Five was good for Hawaii. Competition was obviously not good for Hawaii. Although the Chinese and Japanese were establishing successful businesses in Honolulu and some Chinese were even growing rich, they posed no immediate threat to the Big Five. And the Hawaiians had never been good at capitalism. By the early 20th century, they had become one of the world's most urbanized groups. But rather than competing with white businessmen in Honolulu, unemployed Hawaiians were forced to live in hovels and packing crates, cooking their poi on stoves fashioned from empty oil cans.

Political competition was also unhealthy. Hawaii was ruled by the Big Five, so naturally it should be run by the Republican Party. After all, the mission families were Republicans. Back on the mainland, the Democrats had always been cool to the sugar planters, and it was a Republican president, William McKinley, who eventually annexed Hawaii. The Republicans, quite simply, were good for business.

The Big Five set out very deliberately to overwhelm any political opposition. When the Hawaiians created a home-rule party around the turn of the century, the Big Five shrewdly co-opted it by running a beloved descendant of Hawaii's royal family as the Republican candidate. On the plantations they pitted one ethnic group against another to prevent the Asian workers from organizing. Then, when labor unions finally formed, the Big Five attacked them savagely. In 1924, police killed 16 strikers on Kauai. Fourteen years later, in an incident known as the "Hilo massacre," the police wounded 50 picketers.

The Big Five crushed the Democratic Party by intimidation. Polling booths were rigged. It was dangerous to vote Democratic—

**THE LAST QUEEN**

Queen Lydia Paki Kamakaeha Liliuokalani, the last reigning monarch of the islands, took the throne in 1891 after her brother David Kalakaua, the Merry Monarch, died. Born in Honolulu, she learned to write music as a child. An accomplished musician, she played the piano, organ, ukulele and guitar. It was after her overthrow and confinement in Iolani Palace that she went on to write the islands' much beloved song "Aloha O'e."

workers could lose their jobs, and if they were plantation workers, that meant losing their houses as well. Conducting Democratic meetings on the plantations was about as easy as holding a
hula dance in an old missionary church. The Democrats went
underground.

Those were halcyon days for both the Big Five and the Republican Party. In 1900, only five percent of Hawaii's population was
white. The rest was composed of races
that rarely benefitted from Republican
policies. But for the next several decades,
even during the Depression, the Big Five kept
the Republicans in power.

Some Polynesians migrated to the
Hawaiian islands due to population pressures that caused
famine. The lack of food
sources led them to abandon
their smaller, less abundant
Pacific islands.

While the New Deal swept the mainland,
Hawaii clung to its colonial heritage. The islands were still a generation behind the rest of
the United States—the Big Five enjoyed it that
way. There was nothing like the status quo when
you were already in power. Other factors that had
long shaped Hawaii's history also played into the
hands of the Big Five. The islands' vulnerability, which had always favored the rule of a small elite, permitted the Big Five to
establish an awesome cartel. Hawaii's isolation, its distance from
the mainland, helped protect their monopoly.

**THE JAPANESE AND THE MODERN WORLD**    All that ended on
December 7, 1941. On what would afterwards be known as the
"Day of Infamy," a flotilla of six aircraft carriers carrying over
400 planes unleashed a devastating assault on Pearl Harbor.
Attacking the Pacific Fleet on a Sunday morning, when most of the
American ships were unwisely anchored side by side, the Japanese
sank or badly damaged six battleships, three destroyers and sev-
eral other vessels. Over 2400 Americans were killed.

The Japanese bombers that attacked Pearl Harbor sent shock
waves through Hawaii that are still rumbling today. World War II
changed all the rules of the game, upsetting the conditions that
had determined island history for centuries.

Ironically, no group in Hawaii would feel the shift more thoroughly than the Japanese. On the mainland, Japanese-Americans
were rounded up and herded into relocation camps. But in Hawaii
that was impossible; there were simply too many (160,000—fully
one-third of the island's population), and they comprised too large
a part of the labor force.

Many were second-generation Japanese, *nisei*, who had been
educated in American schools and assimilated into Western society. Unlike their immigrant parents, the *issei*, they felt few ties to
Japan. Their loyalties lay with America, and when war broke out
they determined to prove it. They joined the U.S. armed forces and
formed a regiment, the 442nd, which became the most frequently

decorated outfit of the war. The Japanese were heroes, and when the war ended many heroes came home to the United States and ran for political office. Men like Daniel Inouye and Spark Matsunaga began winning elections and would eventually become United States senators.

By the time the 442nd returned to the home front, Hawaii was changing dramatically. The Democrats were coming to power. Leftist labor unions won crucial strikes in 1941 and 1946. Jack Burns, an ex-cop who dressed in tattered clothes and drove around Honolulu in a beat-up car, was creating a new Democratic coalition.

Burns, who would eventually become governor, recognized the potential power of Hawaii's ethnic groups. Money was flowing into the islands—first military expenditures and then tourist dollars, and non-whites were rapidly becoming a new middle class. The Filipinos still constituted a large part of the plantation force, and the Hawaiians remained disenchanted, but the Japanese and Chinese were moving up fast. Together they formed a majority of Hawaii's voters.

Burns organized them, creating a multiracial movement and thrusting the Japanese forward as candidates. By 1954, the Democrats controlled the legislature, with the Japanese filling one out of every two seats in the capital. Then, when Hawaii attained statehood five years later, the voters elected the first Japanese ever to serve in Congress. Today one of the state's U.S. senators and a congressman are Japanese. On every level of government, from municipal to federal, the Japanese predominate. They have arrived. The *mana*, that legendary power coveted by the Hawaiian chiefs and then lost to the sugar barons, has passed once again—to a people who came as immigrant farm-workers and stayed to become the leaders of the 50th state.

The Japanese and the Democrats were on the move, but in the period from World War II until the present day, everything was in motion. Hawaii was in upheaval. Jet travel and a population boom shattered the islands' solitude. While in 1939 about 500 people flew to Hawaii, now about seven million visitors land every year. The military population escalated as Oahu became a key base not only during World War II but throughout the Cold War and the Vietnam War, as well. Hawaii's overall population exploded from about a half-million just after World War II to over one million at the present time.

No longer did the islands lag behind the mainland; they rapidly acquired the dubious quality of modernity. Hawaii became America's 50th state in 1959, Honolulu grew into a bustling highrise city, and hotels and condominiums mushroomed along the beaches of Maui, a neighboring island. Outside investors swallowed up two of the Big Five corporations, and several partners in the old monopoly began conducting most of their business outside Hawaii. Everything became too big and moved too fast for Hawaii to be entirely vulnerable to a small interest group. Now, like the rest of the world, it would be prey to multinational corporations.

By the 1980s, it would also be of significant interest to investors from Japan. In a few short years they succeeded in buying up a majority of the state's luxury resorts, including every major beachfront hotel in Waikiki, sending real estate prices into an upward spiral that did not level off until the early 1990s. During the rest of the decade, the economy was stagnant, with real estate prices dropping, agriculture declining and tourism leveling off at seven million visitors annually.

One element that has not plateaued during the last ten years is the Native Hawaiian movement. Nativist sentiments were spurred in January 1993 by the 100th anniversary of the American overthrow of the Hawaiian monarchy. Over 15,000 people turned out to mark the illegal coup. Later that year, President Clinton signed a statement issued by Congress formally apologizing to the Hawaiian people. In 1994, the United States Navy returned the island of Kahoolawe to the state of Hawaii. Long a rallying symbol for the Native Hawaiian movement, the unoccupied island had been used for decades as a naval bombing target. By 1996, efforts to clean away bomb debris and make the island habitable were well under way, although completion of the clean-up is still years off. Then in 1998, the issue of Hawaii's monarchy arose again when demonstrators marched around the entire island of Oahu and staged rallies to protest the 100th anniversary of the United States' annexation of Hawaii.

Today, numerous perspectives remain to be reconciled, with grassroots movements working to secure a degree of autonomy for Hawaii's native people. The most common goal seems to be a status similar to that accorded the American Indians by the federal government, although there are still those who seek a return to an independent Hawaii, either as a restored monarchy or along democratic lines. Also pending resolution is the distribution of land to Native Hawaiians with documented claims, as well as a financial settlement with the state government. It's a complex situation involving the setting right of injustices of a century past.

## Hawaiian Culture

Hawaii, according to Polynesian legend, was discovered by Hawaii-loa, an adventurous sailor who often disappeared on long fishing trips. On one voyage, urged along by his navigator, Hawaii-loa sailed toward the planet Jupiter. He crossed the "many-colored ocean," passed over the "deep-colored sea," and eventually came upon "flaming Hawaii," a mountainous island chain that spewed smoke and lava.

History is less romantic. The Polynesians who found Hawaii were probably driven from their home islands by war or some similar calamity. They traveled in groups, not as lone rangers, and shared their canoes with dogs, pigs and chickens, with which they planned to stock new lands. Agricultural plants such as coconuts, yams, taro, sugar cane, bananas and breadfruit were also stowed on board.

Most important, they transported their culture, an intricate system of beliefs and practices developed in the South Seas. After undergoing the stresses and demands of pioneer life, this traditional lifestyle was transformed into a new and uniquely Hawaiian culture.

It was based on a caste system that placed the *alii* or chiefs at the top and the slaves, *kauwas*, on the bottom. Between these two groups were the priests, *kahunas* and the common people or *makaainanas*. The chiefs, much like feudal lords, controlled all the land and collected taxes from the commoners who farmed it.

Life centered around the *kapu*, a complex group of regulations that dictated what was sacred or profane. For example, women were not permitted to eat pork or bananas; commoners had to prostrate themselves in the presence of a chief. These strictures were vital to Hawaiian religion; *kapu* breakers were directly violating the will of the gods and could be executed for their actions. And there were a lot of gods to watch out for, many quite vindictive. The four central gods were *Kane*, the creator; *Lono*, the god of agriculture; *Ku*, the war god; and *Kanaloa*, lord of the underworld. They had been born from the sky father and earth mother, and had in turn created many lesser gods and demigods who controlled various aspects of nature.

It was, in the uncompromising terminology of the West, a stone-age civilization. Though the Hawaiians lacked metal tools, the wheel and a writing system, they managed to include within their inventory of cultural goods everything necessary to sustain a large population on a chain of small islands. They fashioned fish nets from native *olona* fiber, made hooks out of bone, shell and ivory, and raised fish in rock-bound ponds. The men used irrigation in their farming. The women made clothing by pounding mul-

**A SLICE OF THE PIE**
In ancient Hawaii, each island was divided like a pie into wedge-shaped plots, *ahupuaas*, which extended from the ocean to the mountain peaks. In that way, every chief's domain contained fishing spots, village sites, arable land and everything else necessary for the survival of his subjects.

berry bark into a soft cloth called *tapa*, dyeing elaborate patterns into the fabric. They built peak-roofed thatch huts from native *pili* grass and *hala* leaves. The men fought wars with spears, slings, clubs and daggers. The women used mortars and pestles to pound the roots of the taro plant into poi, the islanders' staple food. Bread, fruit, yams and coconut were other menu standards.

The West labeled these early Hawaiians "noble savages." Actually, they often lacked nobility. The Hawaiians were cannibals who practiced human sacrifice during religious ceremonies and often used human bone to fashion fish hooks. They constantly warred among themselves and would mercilessly pursue a retreating army, murdering as many of the vanquished soldiers as possible.

But they weren't savages either. The Hawaiians developed a rich oral tradition of genealogical chants and created beautiful lilting songs to accompany their hula dancing. Their musicians mastered several instruments including the *ukeke* (a single-stringed device resembling a bow), an *ohe hano ihu* or nose flute, rattles and drums made from gourds, coconut shells or logs. Their craftsmen produced the world's finest featherwork, tying thousands of tiny feathers onto netting to produce golden cloaks and ceremonial helmets. They used fruit and a natural glue from local trees to capture live birds for their exquisite featherwork. After taking a few feathers from the bird, they would release it back into the environment.

The Hawaiians helped develop the sport of surfing. They also swam, boxed, bowled and devised an intriguing game called *konane*, a cross between checkers and the Japanese game of go. They built networks of trails across lava flows, and created an elemental art form in the images—petroglyphs—that they carved into lava rock along the trails.

They also achieved something far more outstanding than their varied arts and crafts, something that the West, with its awesome knowledge and advanced technology, has never duplicated. The Hawaiians created a balance with nature. They practiced conservation, establishing closed seasons on certain fish species and carefully guarding their plant and animal resources. They led a simple life, without the complexities the outside world would eventually thrust upon them. It was a good life: food was plentiful, people were healthy and the population increased. For a thousand years, the Hawaiians lived in delicate harmony with the elements. It wasn't until the West entered the realm, transforming everything, that the fragile balance was destroyed. But that is another story entirely.

**PEOPLE**    Because of its unique history and isolated geography, Hawaii is truly a cultural melting pot. It's one of the few states in the union in which caucasians are a minority group. Whites, or *haole* as they're called in the islands, comprise only about 22 percent of Hawaii's 1.2 million population. Japanese constitute 18 percent, Filipinos 13 percent, Hawaiians and part-Hawaiians account for 21 percent, Chinese about 3 percent and other racial groups 23 percent. It's a very vital society, with one fifth of the people born of racially mixed parents.

One trait characterizing many of these people is Hawaii's famous spirit of aloha, a genuine friendliness, an openness to strangers, a willingness to give freely. Undoubtedly, it is one of the finest qualities any people has ever demonstrated. Aloha originated with the Polynesians and played an important role in ancient Hawaiian civilization.

The aloha spirit is alive and well in the islands, although bad attitudes toward *haole*, the term used for whites, are not unknown. All parties, however, seem to understand the crucial role tourism has come to play in Hawaii's economy, which means you're not likely to experience unpleasantness from the locals you'll meet—unless you behave unpleasantly. A smile goes a long way.

**ECONOMY**

For years, sugar was king in Hawaii, the most lucrative part of the island economy. Today, tourism is number one. About four million Americans, and almost seven million travelers worldwide visit the Aloha State every year. It's now a $10 billion business that expanded exponentially during the 1970s and 1980s, leveled off in the 1990s.

With 44,542 personnel stationed in Hawaii, the U.S. military is another large industry. Concentrated on Oahu, where they control one-quarter of the land, the armed forces pour more than $3 billion into the local economy every year.

One reason for the decline of the sugar industry in the islands is because it takes one ton of water to produce a pound of sugar.

Sugar, like other agricultural crops in the islands, was threatened by urban development. Since the construction industry is a $4.8 billion business, new housing developments are competing more and more with agricultural land.

Pineapple is another island crop that's ailing. Stiff competition from the Philippines, where labor is relatively cheap, has reduced Hawaii's pineapple plantations to a few relatively small operations.

Hawaii is one of the only places in the United States that grows coffee. The islands also do a booming business in macadamia nuts, orchids, anthuriums, guava nectar and passion fruit juice. Together, these industries have created a stable economy in the 50th state. The per capita income is greater than the national average, and the standard of living is generally higher.

**CUISINE**

Nowhere is the influence of Hawaii's melting pot population stronger than in the kitchen. While in the islands, you'll probably eat not only with a fork, but with chopsticks and fingers as well. You'll sample a wonderfully varied cuisine. In addition to standard American fare, hundreds of restaurants serve Hawaiian, Japanese, Chinese, Korean, Portuguese and Filipino dishes. There are also fresh fruits aplenty—pineapples, papayas, mangoes, bananas and tangerines—plus local fish such as mahimahi, marlin and snapper.

The mainstay of the traditional Hawaiian diet is poi, a purplish paste pounded from baked or steamed taro tubers. It's pretty bland fare, but it does make a good side dish with imu-cooked pork or tripe stew. You should also try *laulau*, a combination of fish, pork and taro leaves wrapped in a *ti* leaf and steamed. And don't neglect to taste baked *ulu* (breadfruit) and *opihi* (limpets). Among the other Hawaiian culinary traditions are *kalua* pig, a shredded pork dish baked in an *imu* (underground oven); *lomi-lomi* salmon, which is salted and mixed with onions and tomatoes; and chicken *luau*, prepared in taro leaves and coconut milk.

A good way to try all these dishes at one sitting is to attend a luau. I've always found the tourist luaus too commercial, but you might watch the newspapers for one of the special luaus sponsored by civic organizations.

Japanese dishes include sushi, sukiyaki, teriyaki and tempura, plus an island favorite—*sashimi*, or raw fish. On most any menu, including McDonald's, you'll find *saimin*, a noodle soup filled with meat, vegetables and *kamaboko* (fishcake).

You can count on the Koreans for *kim chi*, a spicy salad of pickled cabbage and *kalbi*, barbecued beef short ribs prepared with soy and sesame oil. The Portuguese serve up some delicious sweets including *malasadas* (donuts minus the holes) and *pao doce*, or sweet bread. For Filipino fare, I recommend *adobo*, a pork or chicken dish spiced with garlic and vinegar, and *pochero*, a meat

## SOUNDS FISHY

What are all those strange-sounding fish dishes on the menu? A quick translation will help you when choosing a seafood platter from Hawaiian waters. Firm-textured with a light taste, the most popular fish is mahimahi, or dolphin fish (no, it's not one of those amazing creatures that do fancy tricks on the waves); its English equivalent is dorado. Ahi is yellowfin tuna and is especially delicious as sashimi (raw) or blackened. *Opakapaka* is pink snapper and is a staple of Pacific Rim cuisine. Other snappers include *uku* (gray snapper), *onaga* (ruby snapper) and *ehu* (red snapper). *Ono* (which means delicious in Hawaiian) is king mackerel or wahoo, a white fish that lives up to its name.

entrée cooked with bananas and several vegetables. In addition to a host of dinner dishes, the Chinese have contributed treats such as *manapua* (a steamed bun filled with barbecued pork) and oxtail soup. They also introduced crack seed to the islands. Made from dried and preserved fruit, it provides a treat as sweet as candy.

As the Hawaiians say, *"Hele mai ai."* Come and eat!

The language common to all Hawaii is English, but because of its diverse cultural heritage, the archipelago also supports several other tongues. Foremost among these are Hawaiian and pidgin. Hawaiian, closely related to other Polynesian languages, is one of the most fluid and melodious languages in the world. It's composed of only twelve letters: five vowels—*a, e, i, o, u* and seven consonants—*h, k, l, m, n, p, w.* The glottal stop ('), when used, counts as a thirteenth letter.

## LANGUAGE

At first glance, the language appears formidable: how the hell do you pronounce *humuhumunukunukuapuaa?* But actually it's quite simple. After you've mastered a few rules of pronunciation, you can take on any word in the language.

The first thing to remember is that every syllable ends with a vowel, and the next to last syllable usually receives the accent.

The next rule to keep in mind is that all the letters in Hawaiian are pronounced. Consonants are pronounced the same as in English (except for the *w,* which is pronounced as a *v* when it introduces the last syllable of a word—as in *ewa* or *awa.* Vowels are pronounced the same as in Spanish: *a* as in *among, e* as in *they, i* as in *machine, o* as in *no* and *u* as in *too.* Hawaiian has four vowel combinations or diphthongs: *au,* pronounced *ow; ae* and *ai,* which sound like *eye;* and *ei,* pronounced *ay.* As noted above, the glottal stop (') occasionally provides a thirteenth letter.

By now, you're probably wondering what I could possibly have meant when I said Hawaiian was simple. I think the glossary that follows will simplify everything while helping you pronounce common words and place names. Just go through the list, starting with words like aloha and luau that you already know. After you've practiced pronouncing familiar words, the rules will become second nature; you'll no longer be a *malihini.*

Just when you start to speak with a swagger, cocky about having learned a new language, some young Hawaiian will start talking at you in a tongue that breaks all the rules you've so carefully mastered. That's pidgin. It started in the 19th century as a lingua franca among Hawaii's many races. Pidgin speakers mix English and Hawaiian with several other tongues to produce a spicy creole. It's a fascinating language with its own vocabulary, a unique syntax and a rising inflection that's hard to mimic.

Pidgin is definitely the hip way to talk in Hawaii. A lot of young Hawaiians use it among themselves as a private language.

At times they may start talking pidgin to you, acting as though they don't speak English; then if they decide you're okay, they'll break into English. When that happens, you be one *da kine brah.*

So *brah*, I take *da kine* pidgin words, put 'em together with Hawaiian, make one big list. Savvy?

*aa* (ah-**ah**)—a type of rough lava

*ae* (eye)—yes

*aikane* (eye-**kah**-nay)—friend, close companion

*akamai* (ah-kah-**my**)—wise

*alii* (ah-**lee**-ee)—chief

*aloha* (ah-**lo**-ha)—hello; greetings; love

*aole* (ah-**oh**-lay)—no

*auwe* (ow-**way**)—ouch!; oh no!

*brah* (bra)—friend; brother; bro'

*bumby* (**bum**-bye)—after a while; by and by

*da kine* (da kyne)—whatdyacallit; thingamajig; the best

*dah makule guys* (da mah-**kuh**-lay guys)—senior citizens

*diamondhead*—in an easterly direction (Oahu only)

*duh uddah time* (duh **uh**-duh time)—once before

*ewa* (**eh**-vah)—in a westerly direction (Oahu only)

*e komo mai* (eh kohmoh mai)—welcome, come in

*hale* (**hah**-lay)—house

*haole* (**how**-lee)—Caucasian; white person

*hano hou* (hah nah hou)—encore

*hapa* (**hah**-pa)—half

*hapa-haole* (**hah**-pa **how**-lee)—half-Caucasian

*heiau* (hey-**yow**)—temple

*hele on* (**hey**-lay on)—go, move, outta here

*hoaloha* (ho-ah-**lo**-ha)—friend

*holo holo* (**ho**-low **ho**-low)—to visit

*howzit?* (hows-it)—how you doing? what's happening?

*huhu* (hoo-hoo)—angry

*hukilau* (**who**-key-lau)—community fishing party

*hula* (**who**-la)—Hawaiian dance

*imu* (**ee**-moo)—underground oven

*ipo* (**ee**-po)—sweetheart

*kahuna* (kah-**who**-nah)—priest; specialist or expert in any field

*kai* (kye)—ocean

*kaka-roach* (**kah**-kah roach)—ripoff; theft

*kamaaina* (kah-mah-**eye**-nah)—one born and raised in Hawaii; a longtime island resident

*kane* (**kah**-nay)—man

*kapu* (**kah**-poo)—taboo; forbidden

*kaukau* (cow-cow)—food

*keiki* (**kay**-key)—child

*kiawe* (key-**ah**-vay)—mesquite tree

*kokua* (ko-**coo**-ah)—help

*kona winds* (**ko**-nah winds)—winds that blow against the trades

*kuli kuli* (koo-lee koo-lee)—be quiet, be still

*lanai* (lah-**nye**)—porch; also island name

*lauhala* (lau-**hah**-lah) or *hala* (**hah**-lah)—a pandanus tree whose leaves are used in weaving

*lei* (lay)—flower garland

*lolo* (low-low)—stupid

*lomilomi* (**low**-me-**low**-me)—massage; salted raw salmon

*luau* (**loo**-ow)—Hawaiian meal

*mahalo* (mah-**hah**-low)—thank you

*mahalo nui loa* (mah-**ha**-low **new**-ee **low**-ah)—thank you very much

*mahu* (**mah**-who)—gay; homosexual

*makai* (mah-**kye**)—toward the sea

*malihini* (mah-lee-**hee**-nee)—newcomer; stranger

*mauka* (**mau**-kah)—toward the mountains

*nani* (**nah**-nee)—beautiful

*ohana* (oh-**hah**-nah)—family

*okole* (oh-**ko**-lay)—rear; ass

*okolemaluna* (oh-ko-lay-mah-**loo**-nah)—a toast: bottoms up!

*ono* (**oh**-no)—tastes good

*pahoehoe* (pah-**hoy**-hoy)—smooth or ropy lava

*pakalolo* (pah-kah-**low**-low)—marijuana

*popakiki* (poh-poh-**key**-key)—stubborn; hard head

*pali* (**pah**-lee)—cliff

*paniolo* (pah-nee-**oh**-low)—cowboy

*pau* (pow)—finished; done

*pilikia* (pee-lee-**key**-ah)—trouble

*puka* (**poo**-kah)—hole

*pupus* (**poo**-poos)—hors d'oeuvres

*shaka* (**shah**-kah)—hand greeting

*swell head*—"big head"; egotistical

*tapa* (**tah**-pah)—also *kapa*; fabric made from the beaten bark of mulberry trees

*wahine* (wah-**hee**-nay)—woman

*wikiwiki* (**wee**-key-**wee**-key)—quickly; in a hurry

*you get stink ear*—you don't listen well

Music has long been an integral part of Hawaiian life. Most families keep musical instruments in their homes, gathering to play at impromptu living room or backyard jam sessions. Hawaiian folk tunes are passed down from generation to generation. In the earliest days, it was the sound of rhythm instruments and chants that filled the air. Drums, including the *pahu hula*, were fashioned from hollowed-out gourds, coconut shells or hollowed sections of coconut palm trunks, then covered with sharkskin. Gourds and coconuts, *uliuli*, adorned with tapa cloth and feathers, were also filled with shells or pebbles to produce a rattling sound. Other instruments included the nose flute, or *ohe*, a piece of bamboo similar to a mouth flute, but played by exhaling through the nostril; the bamboo organ; and *puili*, sections of bamboo split into strips, which were struck rhythmically against the body. Stone castanets, *illili*, and *ke laau* sticks are also used as hula musical instruments.

Western musical scales and instruments were introduced by explorers and missionaries. As ancient Hawaiian music involved a radically different musical system, Hawaiians had to completely re-adapt. Actually, Western music caught on quickly, and the hymns brought by missionaries fostered a popular musical style—the *himeni,* or Hawaiian church music.

Hawaii has been the birthplace of several different musical instruments and styles. The ukulele, modeled on a Portuguese guitar, quickly became the most popular Hawaiian instrument. Its small size made it easy to carry, and with just four strings, it was simple to play. During the early 1900s, the steel guitar was exported to the mainland. Common in country-and-western music today, it was invented by a young man who experimented by sliding a steel bar across guitar strings.

The slack-key style of guitar playing also comes from Hawaii, where it's called *ki ho'alu*. When the guitar was first brought to Hawaii in the 1830s by Mexican and Spanish cowboys, the Hawaiians adapted the instrument to their own special breed of music. In tuning, the six (or twelve) strings are loosened so that they sound a chord when strummed and match the vocal range

## THE JUMPING FLEA

Legend has it that the ukulele was introduced to the islands in 1879 when the *Ravenscrag* arrived in Honolulu from the island of Madeira, bringing a boatload of Portuguese to work the sugar cane fields. Known as a *braguinha* by the Portuguese, the Hawaiians named it the ukulele, or "jumping flea," for the way one's fingers dance across the instrument. King David Kalakaua was purported to design and play his own instruments after he was taught by Augusto Dias, whose shop he visited frequently. Other notable Hawaiian royalty ukulele players included Queen Emma, Queen Liliuokalani, Prince Leleiohoku and Princess Likelike.

of the singer. Slack-key is played in a variety of ways, from pluck-ing or slapping the strings to sliding along them. A number of different tunings exist, and many have been passed down orally through families for generations. Some of the more renowned guitarists playing today include Keola Beamer, Raymond Kane and Cyril Pahinui.

During the late 19th century, "*hapa*-haole" songs became the rage. The ukulele was instrumental in contributing to this Ha-waiian fad. Written primarily in English with pseudo-Hawaiian themes, songs like "Tiny Bubbles" and "Lovely Hula Hands" were later introduced to the world via Hollywood.

The Hawaiian craze continued on the mainland with radio and television shows such as "Hawaii Calls" and "The Harry Owens Show." In the 1950s, little mainland girls donned plastic hula skirts and danced along with Hilo Hattie and Ray Kinney.

It was not until the 1970s that both the hula and music of old Hawaii made a comeback. Groups such as the Sons of Hawaii and the Makaha Sons of Niihau, along with Auntie Genoa Keawe and the late Gabby Pahinui, became popular. Before long, a new form of Hawaiian music was being heard, a combination of ancient chants and contemporary sounds, performed by such islanders as Henry Kapono, Kalapana, Olomana, the Beamer Brothers, Bla Pahinui, the Peter Moon Band and the Brothers Cazimero.

Today many of these groups, along with other notables such as Hapa, the Kaau Crater Boys, Brother Noland, Willie K., Del Beazley, Butch Helemano and Obrien Eselu, bring both innova-tion to the Hawaiian music scene and contribute to the preser-vation of an ancient tradition. The trend continues with hybrid infusions of reggae and rock, while performers like Kealii Reichel and groups like Kapena maintain the soft-edged sounds so well-suited to the islands.

An entire new category of music has become established in Hawaii: dubbed "Jawaiian," the sound incorporates Jamaican reggae and contemporary Hawaiian music, and is especially pop-ular amongst the state's younger population. Pro-sovereignty groups like Sudden Rush have taken this trend one step further, laying down their message-imbued rap lyrics on reggae tunes and Hawaiian classics to create a truly unique genre. In addition, now-deceased masters of Hawaiian song like Gabby Pahinui and Israel Kamakawiwoole have gained renewed popularity and re-spect for the links they created between old and contemporary Hawaiian music.

Tune in to KPOA-FM 93.5 and 102.7 for island sounds and Hawaiian music.

Along with palm trees, the hula—swaying hips, grass skirts, col-orful leis—is linked forever in people's minds with the Hawaiian

**HULA**

Islands. This western idea of hula is very different from what the dance has traditionally meant to native Hawaiians.

Hula is an old dance form, its origin shrouded in mystery. The ancient hula, *hula kahiko*, was more concerned with religion and spirituality than entertainment. Originally performed only by men, it was used in rituals to communicate with a deity—a connection to nature and the gods. Accompanied by drums and chants, *hula kahiko* expressed the islands' culture, mythology and history in hand and body movements. It later evolved from a strictly religious rite to a method of communicating stories and legends. Over the years, women were allowed to study the rituals and eventually became the primary dancers.

"Hula is the language of the heart, and therefore the heart beat of the Hawaiian people."
—KING KALAKAUA

When westerners arrived, the *hula kahiko* began another transformation. Explorers and sailors were more interested in its erotic element, ignoring the cultural significance. Missionaries simply found it scandalous and set out to destroy the tradition. They dressed Hawaiians in western garb and outlawed the *hula kahiko*.

The hula tradition was resurrected by King David Kalakaua. Known by the moniker "Merrie Monarch," Kalakaua loved music and dance. For his coronation in 1883, he called together the kingdom's best dancers to perform the chants and hulas once again. He was also instrumental in the development of the contemporary hula, the *hula auwana*, which added new steps and movements and was accompanied by ukuleles and guitars rather than drums.

By the 1920s, modern hula had been popularized by Hollywood, westernized and introduced as kitschy tropicana. Real grass skirts gave way to cellophane versions, plastic leis replaced fragrant island garlands, and exaggerated gyrations supplanted the hypnotic movements of the traditional dance.

Fortunately, with the resurgence of Hawaiian pride in recent decades, Polynesian culture has been reclaimed and *hula kahiko* and traditional chants have made a welcome comeback. Hula *halaus* (schools) are serious business throughout the islands (and even on the mainland). Competitions bring together *halau* throughout the islands.

## FOUR

# Oahu

Honolulu, Somerset Maugham once remarked, is the meeting place of East and West. Today, with its highrise cityscape and crowded commercial center, Hawaii's capital is more the place where Hong Kong meets Los Angeles. It's the hub of Hawaii—a city that dominates the political, cultural and economic life of the islands.

And it's the focus of Oahu as well. Honolulu has given Oahu more than its nickname, The Capital Island. The city has drawn three-fourths of Hawaii's population to this third-largest island, making Oahu both a military stronghold and a popular tourist spot.

With military installations at Pearl Harbor and outposts seemingly everywhere, the armed forces control about one-quarter of the island. Most bases are off-limits to civilians; and tourists congregate in Honolulu's famed resort area—Waikiki. Both defense and tourism are big business on Oahu, and it's an ironic fact of island life that the staid, uniformly dressed military peacefully coexist here with crowds of sun-loving, scantily clad visitors.

The tourists are attracted by one of the world's most famous beaches, an endless white-sand ribbon that has drawn sun worshippers and water lovers since the days of Hawaiian royalty. In ancient times Waikiki was a swamp; now it's a spectacular region of world-class resorts.

Indeed, Waikiki is at the center of Pacific tourism, just as Honolulu is the capital of the Pacific. Nowhere else in the world will you find a population more varied or an ambience more vital. There are times when Waikiki's Parisian-size boulevards seem ready to explode from the sheer force of the crowds. People in bikinis and wild-colored aloha shirts stroll the streets, while others flash past on mopeds.

During the 1980s this sun-splashed destination became a focal point for millions of wealthy tourists from Japan. As a result, Waikiki has moneychanging shops, restaurants displaying menus in Japanese only, stores where the clerks speak no English and an entire mall filled with duty-free shops.

Today the development that created modern-day Waikiki continues, albeit at a slower pace and on a less intense scale, at the Koolina Resort, along the south central Oahu coast near residential Ewa Beach, with the JW Marriott Ihilani Resort & Spa providing a flagship hotel for the resort. Nearby, work continues on the development of Kapolei as a "second city" for Oahu, planned for as many as 200,000 people and designed to reduce the population concentration on urban Honolulu.

So hurry. Visitors can still discover that just beyond Honolulu's bustling thoroughfares stretches a beautiful island, featuring countless beaches and two incredible mountain ranges. Since most of the tourists (and a vast majority of the island's 902,704 population) congregate in the southern regions around Honolulu, the north is rural. You can experience the color and velocity of the city, then head for the slow and enchanting country.

As you begin to explore for yourself, you'll find Oahu also has something else to offer: history. *Oahu* means "gathering place" in Hawaiian, and for centuries it has been an important commercial area and cultural center. First populated by Marquesans around A.D. 500, the island was later settled by seafaring immigrants from Tahiti. Waikiki, with its white-sand beaches and luxurious coconut groves, became a favored spot among early monarchs.

Warring chiefs long battled for control of the island. Kamehameha I seized power in 1795 after landing troops along the coast just east of Waikiki, proceeding inland and sweeping an opposing army over the cliffs of Nuuanu Pali north of Honolulu. Several years earlier the British had "discovered" Honolulu Harbor, a natural anchorage destined to be one of the Pacific's key seaports. Over the years the harbor proved ideal first for whalers and sandalwood traders and eventually for freighters and ocean liners.

By the 1840s, the city, originally a village called Kou, had grown into a shipping port and the commercial and political capital of the Hawaiian kingdom. Here in 1893 a band of white businessmen illegally overthrew the native monarchy. Almost a half-century later, in an ill-advised but brilliantly executed military maneuver, the Japanese drew the United States into World War II with a devastating air strike against the huge naval base at Pearl Harbor.

There are some fascinating historical monuments to tour throughout Honolulu, but I recommend you also venture outside the city to Oahu's less congested regions. Major highways lead from the capital along the east and west coasts of this 608-square-mile island, and several roads bisect the central plateau en route to the North Shore. Except for a five-mile strip in Oahu's northwest corner, you can drive completely around the island.

Closest to Honolulu is the east coast, where a spectacular seascape is paralleled by the Koolaus, a jagged and awesomely steep mountain range. This is Oahu's rain-swept Windward Coast. Here, traveling up the coast past the bedroom communities of Kailua and Kaneohe, you'll discover beautiful and relatively untouched white-sand beaches. On the North Shore are some of the world's most famous surfing spots—Waimea Bay, Sunset, the Banzai Pipeline—where winter waves as high as 20 to 30 feet roll in with crushing force.

The Waianae Range, rising to 4040 feet, shadows Oahu's western coast. The sands are as white here, the beaches as uncrowded, but I've always felt slightly uncomfortable on the Leeward Coast. Theft can be a problem here. Wherever you go on Oahu, never leave valuables unattended, but be particularly watchful around this area.

*Text continued on page 64.*

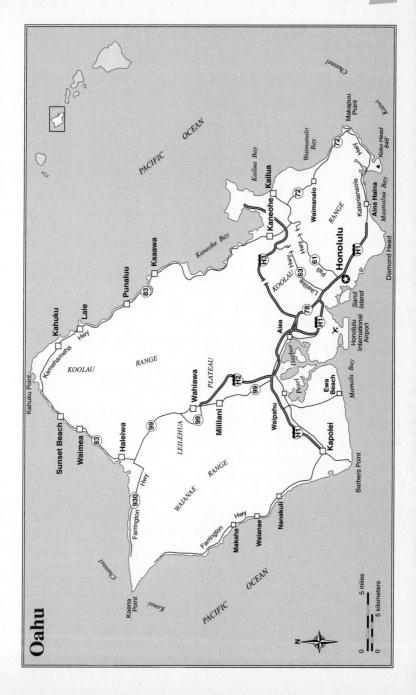

# Oahu

*Oahu Getaway*

## Three-day Itinerary

**Day 1**
- Check into a hotel or condo in Waikiki then make tour reservations for the next day for Iolani Palace and/or Pearl Harbor.

- Explore **Waikiki Beach**, take a stroll over to **Kapiolani Park** (page 68), or just kick back. In the evening, seek out a spot to listen to Hawaiian music. Dine in Waikiki.

**Day 2**
- Spend the morning sightseeing in Honolulu. If you are going to **Pearl Harbor** (page 104) try for an early-morning tour. (Allow 1.5 hours.)

- Head back downtown to visit the **Mission Houses Museum** (page 85) (allow .5 hour) and then continue along South King Street to **Iolani Palace** (page 86). (Allow 45 minutes for the tour of the palace, reservations needed.)

- If you opted not to go to Pearl Harbor earlier, drive up the Pali Highway to the **Nuuanu Pali Lookout** (page 104), stopping at **Queen Emma's Summer Palace** (page 104) on the way.

- Return to Downtown Honolulu and have lunch, then stroll through the nooks and crannies of **Chinatown** (page 91).

- In the afternoon either visit the **Hawaii Maritime Center** (page 90) and **Foster Botanical Garden** (page 92) or return to Waikiki for a canoe ride, a swim or a hike up **Diamond Head** (page 69).

- Hop on a bus and have dinner at an eatery in Ward Centre or Restaurant Row.

**Day 3**
- Drive around the island. Get up *early* in the morning (when the water is clear) and snorkel at **Hanauma Bay** (page 114). (Allow at least 1 hour.)

- Continue along the Kalanianaole Highway, Route 72, stopping at the **Halona Blowhole** (page 115) to see the ocean in its fury and **Makapuu** or **Sandy Beach** (page 120) to watch the body surfers.

- Continue on Route 72 to the bedroom community of **Kailua** (page 122), then take Route 83 (Kahekili Highway) to the **Byodo-In Temple** (page 124) for a short stroll through a peaceful oasis. (Allow .5 hour.)

- Continue along Route 83, stopping for a picnic lunch at **Kahana Bay** (page 126).

- Take a short hike through **Ahupuaa o Kahana State Park** (page 126), past small Hawaiian farms. (Allow 1.5 hours.)

- Continue along Route 83 to **Sunset Beach** (page 137) or **Waimea Bay** (page 137) for a dip in the ocean. (If it's winter and the surf's up, don't go swimming—just watch the surfers ride those magnificent waves.)

- Next, drive through **Haleiwa** (page 138), stopping at **Matsumoto's** (page 143) for a shave ice (with azuki beans) and a stroll around town.

- Take Route 99 to H2 to Honolulu, stopping in **Chinatown** (page 95) for dinner.

Between the Koolau and Waianae ranges, remnants of the two volcanoes that created Oahu, spreads the Leilehua Plateau. This fertile region is occupied by sugar and pineapple plantations as well as several large military bases.

Geologically, Oahu is the second-oldest island in the chain; two million years ago it was two individual islands, which eventually were joined by the Leilehua Plateau. Among its geographic features is the *pali*, an awesome wall of sheer cliffs along the windward coastline, and three famous tuff-cone volcanoes—Diamond Head, Punchbowl and Koko Head.

Hosting millions of tourists each year, Oahu has become a favorite location among travel agents. Many people can't even conceive of visiting Hawaii without going to "the gathering place," and some never venture out of Waikiki. But if, like me, you think of a vacation in terms of experiencing the crowds, and then leaving them behind—plan on venturing outside of Waikiki and Honolulu to unspoiled rural Oahu.

## Waikiki

To understand the geography of Waikiki you need only know about Waikiki Beach. And to understand Waikiki Beach, you must know two things. The first is that major hotels line the beach, practically from one end to the other, and are used as landmarks by visitors and local residents alike. The other fact to remember is that to visitors Waikiki Beach is a single sandy ribbon two miles long, but to local folks it represents many beaches in one. When you park your beach towel here, consider that every few strides will carry you into another realm of Waikiki's culture and history.

Waikiki is where Hawaiian tourism began, and its reputation as a retreat dates back centuries, though not a single hotel here was built before the 20th century. It is believed that the area was a favorite recreation site for the long-ago kings of Oahu and Maui, and a sacred place as well. The site of the Royal Hawaiian Hotel was previously a *heiau pookanaka*, or sacrificial temple, and strictly off limits to the common people.

This fabled peninsula extends two miles from the Ala Wai Yacht Harbor to Diamond Head and measures a half-mile in width from the Ala Wai Canal to the Pacific. Kalakaua Avenue, the main drag, is packed elbow to elbow with throngs of visitors. Paralleling the ocean, this broad boulevard is all at once noisy, annoying, exciting, cosmopolitan and fascinating. Today, visitors from Japan, Korea and Australia, arriving in ever-increasing numbers, add to the international atmosphere.

But the main appeal is still the district's white-sand corridor. Dotting the beach are picnic areas, restrooms, showers, concession stands and beach equipment rentals. Most of the beach is protected by coral reefs and sea walls, so the swimming is excellent, the snorkeling fair. This is also a prime area for surfing. Two- to four-foot waves, good for beginners and still challenging to experienced surfers, are common here.

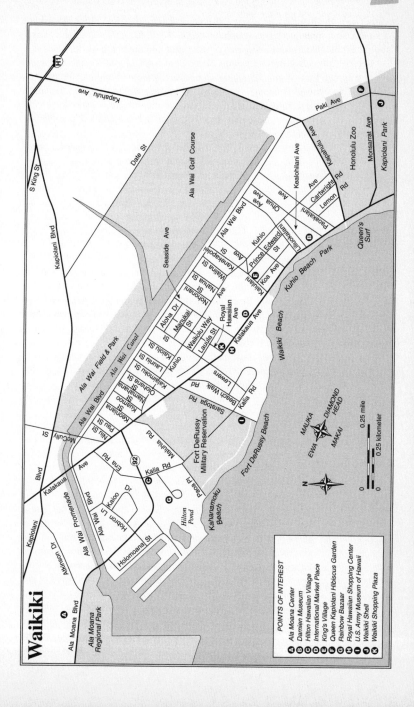

# Waikiki

POINTS OF INTEREST

- Ⓐ Ala Moana Center
- Ⓑ Damien Museum
- Ⓒ Hilton Hawaiian Village
- Ⓓ International Market Place
- Ⓔ King's Village
- Ⓕ Queen Kapiolani Hibiscus Garden
- Ⓖ Rainbow Bazaar
- Ⓗ Royal Hawaiian Shopping Center
- Ⓘ U.S. Army Museum of Hawaii
- Ⓙ Waikiki Shell
- Ⓚ Waikiki Shopping Plaza

**SIGHTS**     It's difficult to visit Waikiki and not spot the **Hilton Hawaiian Village**. The *Guinness Book of World Records* notes the massive resort for having two of the tallest mosaics in the world. The rainbow-patterned murals flank both sides of the Rainbow Tower. Even if you're staying somewhere else on the island, be sure to wander through the shops and gardens of the complex; the landscaped grounds include 22 acres of indigenous flora sprinkled with koi ponds, penguin and flamingo habitats, and a number of squawking cockatoos.

In the sweeping Kalia Tower, the resort has established a satellite branch of the **Bishop Museum** with material you won't find in the main headquarters. Visitors are met with *oli* (traditional chants) and move through the exhibits to the rhythms of Hawaii's musical heritage. There are vivid life-size scenes of life in Waikiki over the past two centuries, and an impressive collection of art and photographs. ~ Hilton Hawaiian Village, 2005 Kalia Road; 808-949-4321, fax 808-947-7898; www.hawaiianvillagehilton.com.

The western flank of Waikiki Beach sits near the Hilton Hawaiian Village. Here you will find a pretty lagoon fringed by palm trees. The curving strand nearby, fronting the resort, is called **Kahanamoku Beach**. Named for Hawaii's great surfer, Duke Kahanamoku, it features numerous facilities. Beach stands rent everything from towels, chairs and air mattresses to snorkel sets, surfboards and Hobie-cat sailboats.

**Fort DeRussy Beach**, owned by the military but open to the public, features the area's widest swath of white sand. It is also beautifully backdropped by a grove of palm trees. There are restrooms, picnic tables and barbecues, plus tennis, squash and volleyball courts on the property.

The nearby **U.S. Army Museum of Hawaii** has every weapon from Hawaiian shark teeth blades to Vietnam-era instruments of destruction. You can also trace the United States' unending series of military campaigns from the uniforms and equipment (ours and theirs) on exhibit here. Closed Monday. ~ Kalia Road, Fort DeRussy; 808-438-2821, fax 808-438-2819.

Past Fort DeRussy Beach stretches a palisade of highrise hotels. Lining the beachfront, they provide numerous facilities for thirsty sunbathers or adventuresome athletes. Continue on and you will pass the Sheraton strip, a lengthy stretch of Waikiki Beach fronted entirely by hotels. This section marks Waikiki's center of action. The first hotel is the **Outrigger Reef on the Beach**, followed by the **Halekulani**, a pricey property that many consider Waikiki's best hotel. Next is the **Sheraton Waikiki**. A highrise structure built with two curving wings, it resembles a giant bird roosting on the beach.

The hotels here are so famous that the nearby strand is named **Royal-Moana Beach**. Stretching between the Royal Hawaiian and

Moana hotels, it has been a sun-soaked gathering place for decades. That's because these two grand dames are Waikiki's oldest hotels.

The **Royal Hawaiian Hotel** is Hawaii's "Pink Palace," a Spanish Moorish–style caravansary painted shocking pink. Built in 1927, it is a labyrinth of gardens, colonnades and balconies; the old place is certainly Waikiki's most interesting edifice. ~ 2259 Kalakaua Avenue; 808-923-7311, fax 808-924-7098; www. royal-hawaiian.com.

The **Sheraton Moana Surfrider Resort**, built in 1901, was Waikiki's first resort. Its vaulted ceilings, tree-shaded courtyard and spacious accommodations reflect the days when Hawaii was a retreat for the rich. Further delving into the history of the place can be done in its Historical Room, containing interesting photographs and memorabilia dating from the hotel's conception. The **Moana Banyan tree**, planted on the grounds in 1904, stretches 150 feet across and 75 feet high. The Moana's beach is also the site of one of Waikiki's most renowned surfing spots, **Canoe's Surf**. ~ 2365 Kalakaua Avenue; 808-922-3111, 888-488-3535, fax 808-923-0308; www.starwood.com/hawaii.

Just beyond the Moana is **Kuhio Beach Park**, which runs along Kalakaua Avenue from Kaiulani to Kapahulu avenues. In addition to a broad sandy beach and a creative layout that includes a banyan tree, traditional healing stones and a cascading fountain, there are numerous facilities here—picnic areas, beach equipment rentals, showers and restrooms, as well as lifeguards. The shady pavilions in this public park also attract local folks who come to play cards and chess. Needless to say, this convenient beach is often quite crowded. Diners like it because of its proximity to many Waikiki budget restaurants; parents favor the beach for its protective sea wall, which provides a secure area where children can swim; and people-watchers find it an ideal place to check out the crowds of tourists and local residents. The park features broad walkways, grassy areas and artificial waterfalls and tidepools. ~ Kalakaua Avenue.

### ON THE TRAIL OF HISTORY

You can explore the hidden past of Hawaii's most popular tourist destination on the **Waikiki Historic Trail**. Just follow the surfboard-shaped markers that denote historic sights along the beach and streets. Or take the guided Queen's Tour, which covers a portion of the trail. The free and highly entertaining two-hour tour (offered at 9 a.m. Tuesday, Thursday and Saturday) is led by native Hawaiian storytellers and historians. ~ It begins and ends at the Royal Hawaiian Shopping Center's Fountain Courtyard, 2233 Kalakaua Avenue; 808-737-6442.

HIDDEN ▶

Tucked behind St. Augustine Catholic Church (808-923-1024), on a side street near the beach, sits the tiny **Damien Museum**, a tribute to Father Damien, the Belgian priest best known for his work in Kalaupapa, the leper colony on Molokai. Father Damien established churches throughout the islands, but his dedication to those suffering from Hansen's Disease (leprosy) is what made him a Hawaiian hero. The exhibits include his glasses, chalice and other unassuming belongings, as well as his prayer book and vestments. Photos depicting his final years on Molokai, where he, too, died of the disease, paint an evocative portrait of this selfless man. The museum is currently being renovated. ~ 130 Ohua Avenue.

HIDDEN ▶

The strand just beyond Kuhio Beach Park is called **Queen's Surf**. Here also are picnic areas, shady pavilions, restroom facilities and showers. Something of a Bohemian quarter, this pretty plot draws gays, local artists and a wide array of intriguing characters. On the weekends, conga drummers may be pounding out rhythms along the beach while others gather to soak in the scene.

**Kapiolani Park** next door extends across 140 acres on both sides of Kalakaua Avenue. Hawaii's oldest park, this tree-studded playland dates back to 1887. Perhaps more than anything else, it has come to serve as a jogger's paradise. From dawn 'til dark, runners of all ages, colors, sizes and shapes beat a path around its perimeter. But Kapiolani offers something to just about anyone. There are tennis courts, softball and soccer fields, an archery area, and much more. To fully explore the park, you must visit each of its features in turn.

HIDDEN ▶

Across from Kapiolani Park, the **Queen Kapiolani Hibiscus Garden**, with its colorful flowerbeds and shady pavilion, is a pretty place to stroll and picnic. ~ Monsarrat and Paki avenues.

**AUTHOR FAVORITE**

sights

The **Waikiki Aquarium** is the place where you can finally discover what a *humuhumunukunukuapuaa*, that impossibly named fish, really looks like. (Don't be surprised if the name proves to be longer than the fish.) Within the aquarium's glass walls, you'll see more than 420 different species of aquatic animals and plants originating from Hawaiian and South Pacific waters. Ranging from rainbow-hued tropical fish to staghorn coral, they constitute a broad range of underwater species. Then there are Hawaiian monk seals (an endangered species) and other intriguing wildlife. A biodiversity exhibit features a rotating display of creatures not native to Hawaii. Admission. ~ 2777 Kalakaua Avenue; 808-923-9741, fax 808-923-1771; www.waquarium.org.

The **Waikiki Shell**, located in Kapiolani Park, is a great place for an evening under the stars with Diamond Head as a backdrop. General admission means lawn seating, which is the perfect way to enjoy the Honolulu Symphony backing up headliners like Burt Bacharach, local favorites like Kalapana, or megastars like Bob Dylan. Check with the Blaisdell Center box office to see if anything is scheduled for the Shell while you're in town and plan to go. ~ 808-527-5400, 808-591-2211, fax 808-591-8072; www.blaisdell center.com.

The park's grandest feature is the **Honolulu Zoo**. Like city zoos everywhere, this tropical facility has a resident population of elephants, giraffes, ostriches, zebras, hippos, Sumatran tigers, lions, alligators and so on. But it also includes animals more common to the islands, creatures like the nene (a rare goose), Komodo dragons and Galápagos tortoises. Perhaps most interesting of all, there is an outstanding population of tropical birds. Admission. ~ 808-971-7171, fax 808-971-7173; www.honoluluzoo.org.

Kapiolani Park includes a stretch of beach called **Sans Souci**, a popular spot where residents and visitors share the sand and reef-sheltered waters. It's also an easy place to set out for a kayak paddle to the marine preserve off Diamond Head or to head toward Waikiki, which stands in highrise silhouette.

The beach is bordered to the west by the **Natatorium**, a saltwater pool and grandstand built in the 1920s as a monument to those Hawaiians who lost their lives in World War I. Closed in 1979 due to slipshod maintenance and deterioration, it is slated to be restored. However, legal challenges have put the start of restoration on hold pending environmental, health and best-use issues. The City continues to say it will pursue a full restoration that includes the saltwater pool as well as the landmark arch at the entrance. Opponents, however, don't believe the restoration is worth the millions of dollars it will take; they are also skeptical that the fully restored pool would be hygienic for the public.

Sans Souci is certainly not a hard place to find, since one of the world's most famous landmarks rises just behind it. More than any other place in the islands, **Diamond Head** is the trademark of Hawaii. A 760-foot crater, it is the work of a volcano that has been dead for about 100,000 years. To the Hawaiians it was known as *Leahi*. They saw in its sloping hillsides the face of an ahi, or yellowfin tuna. Then, in the 19th century, sailors mistook its volcanic glass rocks for rare gems and gave the promontory its present name. Formed 350,000 years ago, this natural landmark was a sacred place to the ancient Hawaiians. A *heiau* once graced its slopes and King Kamehameha is said to have worshiped here, offering a human sacrifice to the Polynesian war god.

It is possible to drive into the gaping maw of this old dragon. Just take Kalakaua Avenue until it meets Diamond Head Road, then follow the latter around to the inland site of the crater. From there a tunnel leads inside. Once within, there is a steep three-quarter-mile trail climbing to the rim of the crater. From here you can gaze along Oahu's southeast corner and back across the splendid little quarter called Waikiki.

**LODGING**   While it may no longer be the simple country retreat it was at the 20th century's turn, Waikiki does have one advantage: believe it or not, it's a great place to find low-rent hotels. A lot of the cozy old hostelries have been torn down and replaced with highrises, but a few have escaped the urban assault. Some of those skyscrapers, too, are cheaper than you might think. One thing to consider when staying in Waikiki is that it is not exactly quiet. Early-morning garbage trucks and late-night party-goers make considerable street noise. Streets on the outskirts (Saratoga Road) are less noisy than those in the heart of things (e.g., Lewers and Beach Walk). Ask for rooms off the street or high in the sky! Let's take a look at some of the better bargains Waikiki has to offer.

What better combination can you ask for than a place that is both a hotel *and* a hostel? At the **Island Hostel/Hotel,** located inside the Hawaiian Colony building, you can book a room with private bath or join fellow travelers in a coed dorm room. The dorm includes kitchen privileges. ~ 1946 Ala Moana Boulevard; phone/fax 808-942-8748. BUDGET.

**The Polynesian Hostel Beach Club** offers both private and dormitory accommodations (baths are shared in either case) in this apartment building. Private rooms have their own refrigerators and all have bathrooms and can sleep up to six people. Laundry facilities and a full kitchen are available for guests, as well as a barbecue and outdoor deck area. It is the closest hostel to the beach, which is one block away. ~ 2584 Lemon Road; 808-922-1340, 877-504-2924, fax 808-262-2817; www.hostelhawaii. com, e-mail polynesian@hostelhawaii.com. BUDGET.

**AUTHOR FAVORITE**

Waikiki was little more than a thatch-hut village when its first deluxe hotel went up in 1901. Today the **Sheraton Moana Surfrider Resort** retains the aura of those early days in its Colonial architecture and Victorian decor. Insist on a room in the main building with its traditional appointments and turn-of-the-20th-century ambience. Downstairs are restaurants, bars, a lobby filled with wicker furniture, and an ancient banyan tree beneath which Robert Louis Stevenson once wrote. A throwback to colonial times, tea is served every afternoon at the Banyan Veranda. ~ 2365 Kalakaua Avenue; 808-922-3111, 800-782-9488, fax 808-924-4799; www.sheraton-hawaii.com. ULTRA-DELUXE.

Budget travelers should also consider a stay at **Hostelling International—Waikiki**. This helpful facility features single-sex dormitory-style accommodations and private studio units available for couples. The latter are plain cinder block rooms with private baths. Open to both men and women, the hostel provides bedding and a common kitchen and creates a family-style atmosphere conducive to meeting other travelers. High-speed internet access is available for a fee. Seven-day maximum stay. ~ 2417 Prince Edward Street; 808-926-8313, fax 808-922-3798; www. hostelsaloha.com. BUDGET.

Some of the walls are still cinderblock, but the price is right at the **Waikiki Prince Hotel**. All 30 guest rooms have air conditioning and cable television; many of the units are equipped with kitchenettes (which are outfitted with mini-refrigerators, microwaves, stoves and utensils). ~ 2431 Prince Edward Street; 808-922-1544, fax 808-924-3712; www.waikikiprince.com, e-mail info@waikikiprince.com. BUDGET.

A lowrise hotel tucked away in the shadow of vaulting condominiums, **The Breakers** is truly a find. Dating to the 1950s, this Waikiki original consists of 64 rooms and 15 suites surrounding a pool and landscaped patio. Shoji doors add to the ambience while kitchenettes in every room and a location one block from the beach round out the features. ~ 250 Beach Walk; 808-923-3181, 800-426-0494, fax 808-923-7174; www.breakers-hawaii.com, e-mail breakers@aloha.net. MODERATE.

Rising higher from the ground, while still keeping costs low, is the **Royal Grove Hotel**, a six-story, 87-unit establishment. If  you can get past the garish pink exterior here, you'll find the rooms more tastefully designed. All accommodations are carpeted and comfortably furnished, and some are decorated in simple but appealing styles. There are TVs and phones in all of the rooms, plus an almond-shaped pool and spacious lobby. Rents vary according to which wing of this sprawling building your bags are parked in. Most rooms even have kitchenettes with microwaves, as well as air conditioning, so it's hard to go wrong here. ~ 151 Uluniu Avenue; 808-923-7691, fax 808-922-7508; www.royal grovehotel.com, e-mail rghawaii@gte.net. BUDGET.

**Kai Aloha Apartment Hotel** offers intimacy combined with  modern convenience; each guest room has air conditioning, an all-electric kitchen, radio, telephone with voice mail, cable television and carpeting. Studio apartments feature lovely rattan furniture and are attractively decorated with old drawings and paintings. The one-bedroom apartments will comfortably sleep four people. Daily maid service is provided. ~ 235 Saratoga Road; 808-923-6723, fax 808-922-7592; www.magickhawaii.com/kaialoha, e-mail kai.aloha@gte.net. MODERATE.

Dominating the mid-range hotel scene in Waikiki are the Outrigger's OHANA hotels. It seems like everywhere you turn in this tourist enclave another one looms above: There are over a dozen.

The OHANA Village is located on a busy street a block from the beach, but it offers rooms with or without kitchenettes at reasonable cost. You can expect street noise. The lobby contains about five different shops selling a variety of clothing and sundries. If you don't feel like walking to the beach there's a pool. ~ 240 Lewers Street; 808-923-3881, 800-462-6262, fax 808-922-2330; www.ohanahotels.com. DELUXE.

Located a stone's skip from the beach, the OHANA Waikiki Tower is a 438-unit colossus. Each room comes with carpeting, telephone, TV, cable movies, refrigerator and shared lanai; many rooms also have microwave ovens. The decor is bland but the furniture comfy. Downstairs is an open-air lobby with adjoining restaurant and pool. ~ 200 Lewers Street; 808-922-6424, 800-462-6262, fax 808-923-7437; www.ohanahotels.com. DELUXE.

The Ewa Hotel has 90 rooms. Tucked away on a back street one block from the beach, this pastel-and-rattan establishment has a 1980s aura about it. Close to Kapiolani Park and offering kitchenettes in many rooms, it is particularly convenient for families. ~ 2555 Cartwright Road; 808-922-1677, 800-359-8639, fax 808-923-8538; www.ewahotel.com, e-mail mail@ewahotel.com. MODERATE.

About the same size is the Waikiki Hana Hotel, a 73-room place that offers a restaurant and small lobby. Quiet (for Waikiki), friendly and comfortable, its rooms are brightly decorated and trimly appointed with air conditioning and color televisions. Some have kitchenettes and lanais. ~ 2424 Koa Avenue; 808-926-8841, fax 808-924-3770. MODERATE.

The Aston Honolulu Prince Hotel was once a college dormitory. Today it's a ten-story hotel with a comfortable lobby. The standard rooms are small and blandly decorated. Located about

## CINEMA ALFRESCO

Drive-in movies are a thing of the past, but that doesn't mean you can't watch a film in the great outdoors. Few settings are more idyllic than Queen's Surf Beach, across from the Honolulu Zoo in Waikiki, where hit films are shown on a 30-foot screen several weekends each month. The Sunset on the Beach festivities start at 4 p.m. with a craft fair featuring the work of local artisans. Pick up some snacks or a plate lunch at one of the food booths and find a comfy spot on the sand or pier. Live music begins at about 4:30 p.m., followed by the movie at sunset. Call 808-523-2489 or 808-923-1094 to find out what's playing and when.

three blocks from the beach, this hotel also has one- and two-bedroom apartments available with full kitchens. ~ 415 Nahua Street; 808-922-1616, 800-922-7866, fax 808-922-6223; www.aston-hotels.com, e-mail hop@aston-hotels.com. MODER-ATE TO DELUXE.

**Holiday Inn Waikiki**, another good bargain, is easy walking distance from both Ala Moana Center and the beach. For the price, accommodations at this 17-story caravansary are relatively plush. Each room has air conditioning, television, telephone, decorations, carpeting, a shower-tub combination, as well as a small refrigerator. The room I saw was quite spacious and contained a king-size bed. There's also a fitness center. ~ 1830 Ala Moana Boulevard; 808-955-1111, 888-992-4545, fax 808-947-1799; www.holiday-inn.com, e-mail holinnwk@pixi.com. MODERATE TO DELUXE.

The **Waikiki Grand Hotel** is right across the street from lush Kapiolani Park. The standard rooms in this ten-story building are comfortable, pleasant places to park your bags. Downstairs there's a windswept lobby. ~ 134 Kapahulu Avenue; 808-923-1511, 800-922-7866, fax 808-922-8785. MODERATE.

**Celebrity Resorts Honolulu** is a modern, attractive complex of three low-slung buildings surrounding a garden and swimming pool. The rooms are decorated in a tropical theme with rattan fur-niture and come with all-electric kitchenette, telephone, TV and air conditioning. ~ 431 Nohonani Street; 808-923-7336, 800-423-8604, fax 808-923-1622; www.celebrityresorts.com. MODERATE TO DELUXE.

The **Aston Coconut Plaza Hotel**, a ten-story highrise, has ac-commodations with kitchenettes; all guest rooms have refrigera-tors and microwaves; standard rooms have a wet bar. Decorated in Mexican tile and furnished with wicker, the rooms are attrac-tively appointed. The lobby adds elements of elegance in the form of an open-air lounge and a small pool. Continental breakfast in-cluded. ~ 450 Lewers Street; 808-923-8828, 800-922-7866, fax 808-923-3473; www.aston-hotels.com. MODERATE.

The **Queen Kapiolani Hotel** is a 314-room facility that rises 19 stories above nearby Kapiolani Park. There's a spacious lobby, three floors of public rooms, several shops and a swimming pool here. The guest rooms are plainly decorated and modest in size. Located one block from the beach. ~ 150 Kapahulu Avenue; 808-922-1941, 800-367-2317, fax 808-922-2694; www.queenkapiolani.com, e-mail reservations@queenkapiolani.com. MODERATE TO ULTRA-DELUXE.

The **Hawaiiana Hotel** is an intimate, lowrise facility that of-fers a garden courtyard arrangement with rooms surrounding ei-ther of the hotel's two pools. Some of the rooms have a private lanai; all have wicker armoires, kitchenettes and pastel decor. ~ 260 Beach Walk; 808-923-3811, 800-367-5122, fax 808-926-

5728; www.hawaiianahotelatwaikiki.com, e-mail hawaiiana@lava.net. MODERATE.

If you'd like to stay directly across the street from the beach, check into the **Aston Waikiki Circle Hotel**. This 14-story hotel-in-the-round has air-conditioned rooms, many with an ocean view, which is the main advantage here. ~ 2464 Kalakaua Avenue; 808-923-1571, 800-922-7866, fax 808-926-8024; www.aston-hotels.com. DELUXE TO ULTRA-DELUXE.

**The Cabana at Waikiki** is a lodging option for gay and lesbian visitors. The hotel has 15 nicely decorated one-bedroom suites, with queen beds in the bedroom and a queen sofa-bed in the living room. Rattan furnishings and Hawaiian prints convey a tropical feel. All suites have TV/VCR/stereos and microwave-equipped kitchenettes, complete with coffeemakers, toasters and blenders. There is an eight-person jacuzzi for guest use. Continental breakfast and cocktails are included. ~ 2551 Cartwright Road; 808-926-5555, 877-921-2121, fax 808-926-5566; www.cabana-waikiki.com, e-mail marlin800@aol.com. DELUXE.

There are three attractive facilities on the edge of Waikiki that are removed from the crowds. The **New Otani Kaimana Beach Hotel** rests beside beautiful Sans Souci Beach in the shadow of Diamond Head. Its two restaurants and oceanside bar lend the feel of a big hotel, but the friendly staff and standard rooms create a family atmosphere. ~ 2863 Kalakaua Avenue; 808-923-1555, 800-356-8264, fax 808-922-9404; www.kaimana.com, e-mail rooms@kaimana.com. DELUXE.

HIDDEN ▶ Another hotel is equally secluded from the bustle of Waikiki. Located even closer to the fabled crater, the **Diamond Head Beach Hotel** is an ultra-contemporary establishment. The rooms are done in a tasteful, Balinese-themed style, and many come with a kitchen. Located on the ocean, this 13-story facility is one of the most chic resting places around. ~ 2947 Kalakaua Avenue; 808-922-1928, fax 808-924-8980; www.marcresorts.com, e-mail dhb@lava.net. ULTRA-DELUXE.

Offering well over 2500 rooms, the **Hilton Hawaiian Village** is the largest resort in the islands and Waikiki's premier family hotel. The grounds provide a Disneyesque atmosphere that keeps children of all ages engaged—fireworks on Friday evening, shopping malls, restaurants and nightly entertainment, not to mention a penguin pool, flamingos, cockatoos and koi ponds. Seaside diversions include paddle boats and surfboards as well as numerous swimming pools to dip in, an acre of sand for sandcastle-making and an ocean of fun. Not to be overlooked, the rooms are attractively furnished and well-cared for and the service is friendly and welcoming. ~ 2005 Kalia Road; 808-949-4321, fax 808-946-8039; www.hiltonhawaiianvillage.com. ULTRA-DELUXE.

Exuding elegance and refinement, the **Halekulani,** whose name means "house befitting heaven," is where the elite come to get away from it all. If you want to splurge, you can, too. The guest rooms and facilities are luxurious and the personalized service radiates with Hawaiian hospitality. If you don't want to float in the oceanfront swimming pool (which boasts an orchid made of 1.25 million South African glass mosaic tiles that reflect the changing light), you can visit the spa, indulge in an in-room massage or dine in one of their award-winning dining rooms. ~ 2199 Kalia Road; 808-923-2311, 800-367-2343, fax 808-926-8004; www.halekulani.com. ULTRA-DELUXE.

The grand dame of Hawaiian hotels captures the sense of Old Hawaii. Built in 1927 and affectionately known as the "Pink Palace," the **Royal Hawaiian Hotel** is an elegant, Spanish Moorish–style building complete with colonnaded walkways and manicured grounds. This castle away from home is decorated in French provincial fashion and features a fabulous lobby bedecked with chandeliers. Adjacent to the original building is a 17-story tower that brings the room count to 528. Worth visiting even if you never check in. ~ 2259 Kalakaua Avenue; 808-923-7311, 800-782-9488, fax 808-931-7098; www.royal-hawaiian.com. ULTRA-DELUXE.

**CONDOS**

The **Royal Kuhio,** a good bet for families, is a 389-unit highrise two blocks from Waikiki Beach. One-bedroom units feature fully equipped kitchens and balconies with ocean or mountain views. Studios are $120; one-bedroom units are $140. A two-bedroom suite with a living room, dining area and two bathrooms is $250. ~ 2240 Kuhio Avenue; 808-923-0555, 800-927-0555, fax 808-923-0720; www.waikikicondos.com, e-mail info@waikikicondos.com.

At the **Aston Waikiki Beach Tower,** all 140 units feature contemporary furniture, wetbars, kitchens and beautiful lanais. The kids will enjoy the pool. One-bedroom units begin at $540. Two-bedroom suites for up to six guests start at $640. ~ 2470 Kalakaua Avenue; 808-926-6400, 800-922-7866, fax 808-926-7380; www.aston-hotels.com, e-mail res.awt@aston-hotels.com.

**ISLAND SOUL**

When visiting the islands, be sure to sample some of Hawaii's local talent. Oahu is the ideal island to seek out Hawaiian sounds. Many of these musicians—Keola Beamer, Kealii Reichel, Henry Kapono, Olomana and the Brothers Cazimero to name a few—may be playing at a local club. Consult the daily newspapers, or tune in to **KCCN** at 100 on the radio dial. This all-Hawaiian station is the home of island soul.

At **Winston's Waikiki Condos**, one-bedroom condos rent for $99 to $155 (lower monthly rates available) for one to four people. All suites are comfortably furnished with rattan furniture and feature lanais and full and complete kitchens. The units, just one block from the beach, are well-maintained and clean. Some units have washers and dryers. Patrick Winston offers special deals for *Hidden Hawaii* readers, so make sure you call ahead and mention this book. Seven-day minimum stay. ~ 417 Nohonani Street, Suite 409; phone/fax 808-924-3332, 800-545-1948; www.winstonswaikikicondos.com, e-mail winston@iav.com.

In 1795 near present-day Waikiki, Kamehameha began a decisive battle in his campaign to unite the Hawaiian Islands, defeating the forces of Kalanikupule.

The **Outrigger Waikiki Shore** offers 29 studios and one- and two-bedroom units. These condos feature complete kitchens, washer/dryers and great views. Studios are $200 while one-bedroom units are $350, with a two-night minimum. Two-bedroom units accommodating up to six start at $325. ~ 2161 Kalia Road; 808-923-3111, fax 808-924-4957; www.outrigger.com, e-mail wsr@outrigger.com.

At **Aston at the Waikiki Banyan** one-bedroom units are $215 to $260 for one to four people. These highrise ocean and mountain view units have full kitchens, rattan furniture and lanais. One block from the beach. ~ 201 Ohua Avenue; 808-922-0555, 800-922-7866, fax 808-922-0906; www.aston-hotels.com, e-mail res.ban@aston-hotels.com.

**DINING**

This tourist mecca is crowded with restaurants. Since the competition is so stiff, the cafés here are cheaper than anywhere else on the islands. There are numerous American restaurants serving moderately good food at modest prices, so diners looking for standard fare will have no problem. But as you're probably seeking something more exotic, I'll also list some interesting Asian, Hawaiian, health food and other offbeat restaurants.

If you decide to go to **Nick's Fishmarket**, plan on eating seafood. You have never seen such a list of fresh fish dishes. Not that much of it will seem familiar, but there is mahimahi, *opakapaka* and ahi. Or if you prefer to dine on something you recognize, how about shrimp scampi, abalone, lobster or scallops? The service is attentive. ~ 2070 Kalakaua Avenue; 808-955-6333; e-mail nick waikiki@aol.com. ULTRA-DELUXE.

For a just-before-midnight snack—they close at 11:00—or to satisfy cravings for a hot bowl of noodle soup, you're never too far from an **Ezogiku**. Rub shoulders with Japanese tourists at the counter in one of these hole-in-the-wall eateries serving ramen in a variety of styles, including curry, pork and wonton. There are three locations to choose from in Waikiki. ~ 2420 Koa Avenue, 808-922-2473, fax 808-926-2207; 2546 Lemon Road, 808-923-

2013; 2146 Kalakaua Avenue, 808-926-8616; www.ezogiku.com,
e-mail info@ezogiku.com. BUDGET.

To find an affordable meal on Kalakaua Avenue, the oceanfront strip, try the bottom floor of the **Waikiki Shopping Plaza**.
Here about a dozen ethnic and American restaurants offer takeout
food as well as full-course sitdown dinners. ~ 2250 Kalakaua
Avenue; 808-923-1191, fax 808-922-4579. BUDGET TO MODERATE.

The food is pretty standard fare at the Sheraton Waikiki's
**Ocean Terrace Restaurant** but the view deserves five stars. Set
poolside next to the beach in one of the state's largest hotels, this
open-air dining room provides a welcome means to dine on the
water. Popular for breakfast, lunch and dinner, the evening menu
centers around rotating theme buffets, such as prime rib and
shrimp and crab night or steak and seafood night. ~ 2255
Kalakaua Avenue; 808-922-4422 ext. 71777, fax 808-931-8530.
ULTRA-DELUXE.

For oceanfront dining, **The Beachside Cafe** is true to its name.
With indoor and patio dining and a big buffet bar, it's a standard-
fare American restaurant lacking in imagination but filled with
beautiful views. Open for breakfast, lunch and dinner, the café
serves steak, hamburgers and egg dishes, as well as offering a
prime rib and crab leg dinner buffet. Ask for a table outside. ~
Sheraton Moana Surfrider Resort, 2365 Kalakaua Avenue; 808-
922-3111, fax 808-924-4759; e-mail samuel.garnier@sheraton.
com. DELUXE TO ULTRA-DELUXE.

Italian *and* Chinese? Sounds like an odd pairing, but **Ciao
Mein**'s hybrid menu is nonetheless delicious on both sides. On the
Chinese side try spicy kung pao chicken, Szechuan eggplant or the
savory flavors of Mongolian sizzle. If you're craving Italian, start
with the carpaccio followed by pasta in a light tomato basil sauce.
Everything is served family style, which means shared dishes that
make this a great place to go with kids or in a group. Located on
the third floor of the Hyatt Regency Waikiki, the decor is Euro-
chic. ~ 2424 Kalakaua Avenue; 808-923-1234, fax 808-921-
6018. DELUXE.

Fans whir overhead and a bar sits in the back; sheet music covers and old Matson oceanliner menus stand framed along the
walls. Hard to believe someone would create this ambience for
their restaurant, then name the place **Cheeseburger in Paradise**.
But burgers it is, plus a selection of breakfast dishes for the morning. ~ 2500 Kalakaua Avenue; 808-923-3731, fax 808-923-
1070; www.cheeseburgerland.com, e-mail chzyburger@aol.com.
BUDGET TO MODERATE.

Apart from the bustle of Waikiki but still right on the beach
is the **Hau Tree Lanai**. Here beneath the interwoven branches of
twin hau trees you can enjoy patio dining with a view that extends across Waikiki to the distant mountains. I favor the place

for its breakfast (the French toast is delicious), but they also have a lunch and dinner menu that ranges from steamed vegetables to curried chicken to fresh island fish. In the evening the place is illuminated by torches, and soft breezes wisp off the water, adding to the enchantment. ~ New Otani Kaimana Beach Hotel, 2863 Kalakaua Avenue; 808-921-7066; www.kaimana.com, e-mail hautreelanai@kaimana.com. ULTRA-DELUXE.

Innovative, high-quality cuisine and excellent service make the **Diamond Head Grill** one of Hawaii's best restaurants. The oven-roasted *onaga* is one of those oh-so-good dishes that makes you want to order it each time you visit. The refined and artful presentation is complemented by the eatery's New Age decor with deco highlights. There's entertainment Wednesday through Saturday nights. No lunch. ~ W Honolulu hotel, 2885 Kalakaua Avenue; 808-922-3734, fax 808-791-5164; www.diamond headgrill.com. ULTRA-DELUXE.

For an informal and lively ambience, head over to **Davey Jones Ribs**. Pizza and pasta dishes as well as seafood and chicken are served at this friendly dining room. ~ 250 Lewers Street; 808-923-7427, fax 808-922-7001. MODERATE.

Favored by both tourists and locals for its low prices, **Seaside Bar & Grill** has a budget-priced early-bird special of steak or mahimahi nightly until 7 p.m. Choose any two items—lobster tail, crab legs, mahimahi, fried shrimp or New York steak—and they'll throw in a house salad as well. The fish is frozen and the place is actually two blocks from the "seaside," but for low-rent dining it's worth considering. ~ 2256 Kuhio Avenue; 808-922-8227, fax 808-922-8227. BUDGET.

An L-shaped counter with swivel chairs is the most decor you can expect at **Fatty's Chinese Kitchen**. The prices on plate lunches and dinners are a throwback, too. With dozens of choices, including many "noodle in soup" dishes, Fatty aims to suit every palate. ~ Kuhio Mall, 2345 Kuhio Avenue; 808-922-9600. BUDGET.

**AUTHOR FAVORITE**

One of the ethnic restaurants most popular with local folks is **Keo's in Waikiki**. Fulfilling to all the senses, this intimate place is decorated with fresh flowers and tropical plants. The cuisine includes such Southeast Asian dishes as the "evil jungle prince," a sliced beef, shrimp or chicken entrée with coconut milk, fresh basil and red chili. You can choose from dozens of fish, shellfish, fowl and meat dishes. The menu offers a lot of variety, and is highly recommended. ~ 2028 Kuhio Avenue; 808-951-9355; www.keosthaicuisine.com, e-mail keos@keosthaicuisine.com. MODERATE TO DELUXE.

The blue skies and green palms of the Caribbean never seem far away in Hawaii, and they feel even closer at **Cha Cha Cha Restaurant**. With its tropical color scheme and festive decor, this "Caribe/Mex" eatery serves up Mexican dishes such as burritos, tacos and quesadillas prepared Caribbean style with unusual spices and sauces. ~ 342 Seaside Avenue; 808-923-7797, fax 808-926-7007. BUDGET TO MODERATE.

A great place for breakfast, the **Waikiki Broiler** has inexpensive specials every morning. Dining is outdoors under thatched umbrellas or in a dining room with an outdoor feel. It's on a busy corner so the atmosphere is not exactly idyllic, but it's hard to match the prices—at dinner you can enjoy teriyaki steak and chicken entrées. ~ 200 Lewers Street; 808-923-8836, fax 808-924-3316. MODERATE.

**Perry's Smorgy**, with its two locations—at the OHANA Coral Seas Hotel and on Kuhio Avenue—has an inexpensive, prix-fixe buffet at dinner, lunch and breakfast. With an extensive salad bar, plus a host of meat and fish platters, this all-you-can-eat emporium is hard to beat. I'd suggest the OHANA branch; it's two blocks from the beach. ~ OHANA Coral Seas Hotel, 250 Lewers Street, 808-922-8814; and also at 2380 Kuhio Avenue, 808-926-0184, phone/fax 808-922-1907; www.perryshawaii.com, e-mail perrysrestaurants@hotmail.com. BUDGET TO MODERATE.

Italian specialties at affordable prices draw nightly crowds to **Arancino's**. The place has the feel of a New York–style bistro, with excellent, home-style standards like eggplant parmigiana that are worth the potential 20-minute wait. ~ 255 Beach Walk; 808-923-5557, fax 808-922-0105; www.arancino.net, e-mail info@arancino.net. MODERATE.

Dishes like macadamia nut–crusted *opakapaka* and marinated rack of lamb make **Bali by the Sea** a special favorite. Plush seating, nautical lamps, fresh flowers and soft ocean breezes add to the charm of this elegant restaurant. Dress code. Closed Sunday. ~ Hilton Hawaiian Village, 2005 Kalia Road; 808-949-4321, fax 808-947-7926. ULTRA-DELUXE.

The **Shore Bird Beach Broiler** is a beachfront dining room that's a great place to enjoy a reasonably priced dinner and an ocean view. This is a cook-your-own-food facility that offers hand-carved steaks, fresh fish, teriyaki chicken and barbecued ribs. One of the best bargains on Waikiki Beach, the Shore Bird is inevitably crowded, so try to dine early. ~ Reef Hotel, 2169 Kalia Road; 808-922-2887, fax 808-923-4056. MODERATE TO DELUXE.

It's not surprising that Waikiki's most fashionable hotel, the Halekulani, contains one of the district's finest restaurants. Situated on an open-air balcony overlooking the ocean, **La Mer** has a reputation for elegant dining in intimate surroundings. French-inspired dishes include crispy-skin *onaga* fillet, confit tomato with truffle juice and fried basil, and rack of lamb with a dijon mustard crust, provençal-style vegetables and creamy potatoes. Add the filigree woodwork and sumptuous surroundings and La Mer is one of the island's most attractive waterfront dining rooms. Formal attire required. Dinner only. ~ 2199 Kalia Road; 808-923-2311, fax 808-926-8004; www.halekulani.com. ULTRA-DELUXE.

Downstairs from La Mer is **Orchids**, serving a mix of Hawaiian and world cuisine like steamed *onaga* with sesame oil and shiitake mushrooms, lemon-rosemary roasted island chicken and roasted lamb chops. Orchids is open for breakfast, lunch, dinner and Sunday brunch. ~ 2199 Kalia Road; 808-923-2311, fax 808-926-8004; www.halekulani.com. ULTRA-DELUXE.

**GROCERIES** The best grocery store in Waikiki is also the biggest. Prices at **The Food Pantry** are inflated, but not as much as elsewhere in this tourist enclave. ~ 2370 Kuhio Avenue; 808-923-9831. There are also two smaller groceries: **Ala Wai Pantry** ~ 2211 Ala Wai Boulevard, 808-922-2818; and **Food Pantry** ~ 438 Hobron Lane, 808-947-3763.

**ABC Discount Stores**, a chain of sundry shops with branches all around Waikiki, are convenient, but have a very limited stock and even higher prices.

If you are willing and able to shop outside Waikiki, you'll generally fare much better price-wise. See "Groceries" in Greater Honolulu.

**SHOPPING** This tourist mecca is a great place to look but not to buy. Browsing the busy shops is like studying a catalog of Hawaiian handicrafts. It's all here. You'll find everything but bargains. With a few noteworthy exceptions, the prices include the unofficial tourist surcharges that merchants worldwide levy against visitors. Windowshop Waikiki, but plan on spending your shopping dollars elsewhere.

One Waikiki shopping area I do recommend is **Duke's Lane**. This alleyway, running from Kalakaua Avenue to Kuhio Avenue near the International Market Place, may be the best place in all Hawaii to buy jade jewelry. Either side of the lane is flanked by mobile stands selling rings, necklaces, earrings, stick pins, bracelets and more. It's a prime place to barter for tiger's eyes, opals and mother-of-pearl pieces.

The main shopping scene is in the malls. **Waikiki Shopping Plaza** has five floors of stores and restaurants. Here are jewelers, sundries and boutiques, plus specialty shops like **Borders Express**, with an excellent line of magazines as well as paperbacks and bestsellers. ~ 2250 Kalakaua Avenue; 808-922-4154.

The **Royal Hawaiian Shopping Center** is a four-story complex that runs for two blocks along Kalakaua Avenue, from Lewers

Street to the Outrigger Waikiki. On the *makai* side (facing the ocean), it fronts the grounds of the Royal Hawaiian and the Sheraton Waikiki. It is Waikiki's largest mall and features Euro-American designer boutiques, upscale shops, numerous restaurants and fast-food kiosks, as well as an indoor shooting gallery and showroom. A weekly schedule of Hawaiiana and other cultural performances provides an entertaining respite from the pressures of shopping. One of Waikiki's more unusual shops is in the center. Check out the **Little Hawaiian Crafts Shop** (808-926-2662) on the third floor, where you'll find an interesting selection of traditional and contemporary Hawaiian crafts including carved *koa* wood bowls, Niihau shell leis, Hawaiian quilts, ceramics and glassware. ~ 2233 Kalakaua Avenue.

Then there's **King's Village**, a mock Victorian town that suggests how Britain might have looked had the 19th-century English invented polyethylene. The motif may be trying to appear antiquated, but the prices are unfortunately quite contemporary. ~ 131 Kaiulani Avenue at Kalakaua Avenue.

The **Waikiki Trade Center** is a strikingly attractive mall. With an air of Milanese splendor about it, this glass-and-steel complex is a maze of mirrors. In addition to the stained-glass windows and twinkling lights, there are several worthwhile shops. ~ Kuhio and Seaside avenues.

The **International Market Place**, a Waikiki institution since 1957, is closing for a complete makeover. No doubt its old charm will disappear, but let's hope that its local soul will return in some fashion when it reopens in 2008.

Hilton Hawaiian Village contains the **Rainbow Bazaar**, an array of shops spread around the grounds of Hawaii's largest resort complex. This plaza contains a number of stores specializing in island fashions, plus gift shops and import emporia. The

**AUTHOR FAVORITE**

If you're in the market for a ukulele, stop by **The Ukulele House**, which carries everything from children's souvenir ukes for $10 to $25 to musically playable instruments ranging from $80 all the way to $2000-plus for vintage models. This world-famous supplier of vintage and unique ukuleles is also home of the world's largest ukulele. If you would like to try playing a ukulele on your visit to Hawaii, you can take free lessons here. Free lessons are also offered at the Orchid Court on the third floor of the Royal Hawaiian Shopping Center five days a week. ~ Royal Hawaiian Shopping Center, 2233 Kalakaua Avenue; 808-923-8587, fax 808-593-9796.

shopping center has been designed in Oriental style, with curving tile roofs and brilliantly painted roof beams. You can stroll along an Asian arcade, past lofty banyan trees and flowering gardens, to stores filled with rare art and Far Eastern antiquities. ~ 2005 Kalia Road.

Island-based **Local Motion** has opened an architecturally distinguished flagship shop for its line of logowear and sporting gear, including surfboards, body boards and backpacks. ~ 1958 Kalakaua Avenue; 808-979-7873; www.localmotionhawaii.com.

**Island Treasures Antique Mall** has Waikiki's best selection of Hawaiiana in a multilevel complex that's home to a number of individual vendors. Fun for browsing and a purchase if you find something priced right. The shops open in the early afternoon and stay open until 10 p.m., which makes it a good tie-in with an evening stroll. Call for hours. Closed Monday. ~ 2145 Kuhio Avenue; 808-922-8223.

Looking for a vintage silk shirt? Those famous Hawaiian styles, like the one Montgomery Clift sported in *From Here to Eternity*, are among the alluring items at **Bailey's Antiques and Aloha Shirts**. This place carries over 7000 Hawaiian shirts, and is the world's largest vintage shirt store. If an original silky is beyond your means, they also have reproductions as well as collectibles like Zippo lighters. ~ 517 Kapahulu Avenue; 808-734-7628; e-mail baileysantiques@webtv.net.

**Peggy's Picks** ranges from Hawaiiana to an eclectic array of collectibles at affordable prices. ~ 732 Kapahulu Avenue; 808-737-3297.

**NIGHTLIFE** Hawaii has a strong musical tradition, kept alive by excellent groups performing their own compositions as well as old Polynesian songs. I'm not talking about the "Blue Hawaii"–"Tiny Bubbles"–"Beyond the Reef" medleys that draw tourists in droves, but *real* Hawaiian music as performed by Henry Kapono, the Brothers Cazimero, Keola and Kapono Beamer, Marlene Sai, Melveen Leed and others.

**AUTHOR FAVORITE**
**Duke's Canoe Club** in the Outrigger Waikiki offers a beachfront setting, a distant view of Diamond Head, and plenty of atmosphere. Duke refers to Duke Kahanamoku, the Olympic swimming champion and surfer who helped restore surfing to a position of cultural prominence. The decor documents his career with archival photography and memorabilia. It draws overflowing crowds, particularly on Sunday afternoons when Henry Kapono performs. ~ Outrigger Waikiki, 2335 Kalakaua Avenue; 808-922-2268, fax 808-923-4204.

If you spend any time in Honolulu, don't neglect to check out such authentic sounds. One or more of these musicians will probably be playing at a local club. Consult the daily newspapers.

Over at **Nick's Fishmarket** there's live entertainment nightly. Expect to hear light rock, jazz, soul or blues while munching on half-price *pupus*. ~ 2070 Kalakaua Avenue; 808-955-6333, fax 808-946-0478; e-mail nickwaikiki@aol.com.

On Friday and Saturday nights, a contemporary Hawaiian group stars at the **Paradise Lounge**. Other forms of live entertainment are offered nightly. Choose between table or lounge seating in this carpeted club, which is decorated with Hawaiian landscapes painted by local artists. ~ Hilton Hawaiian Village, 2005 Kalia Road; 808-949-4321, fax 808-951-5458.

There's Hawaiian music nightly at the **Mai Tai Bar**. Grab an umbrella-topped table on the terrace for primo ocean views. ~ Royal Hawaiian Hotel, 2259 Kalakaua Avenue; 808-923-7311.

The **Esprit Nightclub** is a congenial spot situated right on Waikiki Beach. This cozy club features bands that play music from different eras Tuesday through Saturday, has special guests on Sunday and Monday and offers spectacular ocean views every night of the week. ~ Sheraton Waikiki Hotel, 2255 Kalakaua Avenue; 808-922-4422, fax 808-923-8785.

A group performs mellow Hawaiian music nightly at the **Shorebird** at the Outrigger Reef. ~ Outrigger Reef, 2169 Kalia Road; 808-922-2887.

Tired of the old nine-to-five grind? For a change of pace try **Scruples**, where the schedule is eight to four. 8 p.m. to 4 a.m. that is. Promising "dance and romance," this popular nightspot features dancing to Top-40 tunes. Cover and two-drink minimum. ~ 2310 Kuhio Avenue; 808-923-9530, fax 808-926-8804.

The **Cellar** specializes in dancing, with Top-40 hits spun by a deejay Tuesday through Sunday. It's a top spot for a hot night. Cover. ~ 205 Lewers Street; 808-923-9952.

Nearby, **Waikiki Broiler** has karaoke Tuesday through Sunday. ~ 200 Lewers Street at Kalia Road; 808-923-8836.

If you like sophisticated jazz to accompany dinner or drinks Wednesday and Thursday, the **Diamond Head Grill** is the place to go. The vocalists and musicians are first rate, and the decibel level is suitable for either concentrating on the music, conversation or food, which is some of the best in the Islands. Friday and Saturday nights offer deejay dancing. ~ W Honolulu hotel, 2885 Kalakaua Avenue; 808-922-3734, fax 808-791-5164; www.diamondhead grill.com.

Cruise into **Wave Waikiki** and catch a deejay spinning hip-hop, house and dance music nightly. Rock bands take the stage Wednesday and Saturday. Cover after 9 p.m. ~ 1877 Kalakaua Avenue; 808-941-0424; www.wavewaikiki.com.

With room for 300 of your closest friends, **Moose McGilly-cuddy's** is a prime place to dance to live bands Monday through Saturday. Deejays also spin Top-40 music. Known for its weird pictures, this establishment is easily spotted. Just look for the only building on Lewers Street sporting a stuffed moose head. Occasional cover. ~ 310 Lewers Street; 808-923-0751; www. moosewaikiki.com, e-mail honomoose@aol.com.

For an authentic *tourist* experience accompanied by a genuine aloha spirit, join the busloads of Waikiki visitors who are caravanned to Barbers Point for **Germaine's Luau**, the ultimate in Hawaiian kitsch. At Germaine's you'll get to witness the unearthing ceremony of a pig from its underground *imu* (oven), dine on Hawaiian-style food and watch Polynesian dancers (or join them on stage), all at a beachfront site as the sun sets on the Pacific. ~ 808-949-6626, 800-367-5655, fax 808-949-4218; www.germainesluau.com.

**GAY SCENE**   The gay scene is centered around several clubs on Waikiki's Kuhio Avenue and in Eaton Square, near the corner of Eaton and Hobron streets, not far away.

On a short street near Kuhio and Lewers is **In Between**, a great place to bend an elbow with island regulars. ~ 2155 Lauula Street; 808-926-7060; www.inbetweenonline.com.

Club goers hang in and out at **Angles Waikiki**, where a bar in the center of the room provides a place to socialize, as does the lanai outside. There are pool tables and videos, as well as a dancefloor. Every Wednesday, crowds compete for cash prizes in the Best Chest/Best Buns contest, and Sensually Certified, an all-male revue, entertains on Thursday and Sunday nights. ~ 2256 Kuhio Avenue; 808-926-9766; www.angleswaikiki.com, e-mail angles.waikiki@juno.com.

**Fusion Waikiki** is another gay club open until 4 a.m. This hot spot taking up the second and third floors of the Paradise Building features dancing to house and underground deejay music. There are male strip shows and female impersonation performances on Friday and Saturday. Cover. ~ 2260 Kuhio Avenue; 808-924-2422.

## CATCH A WAVE

All along Waikiki Beach, concessions offer rides on **outrigger canoes.** They are long, sleek fiberglass crafts resembling ancient Polynesian canoes. Each seats four to six passengers, plus a captain. For very cheap you can join the crew on a low-key wave-riding excursion that will have you paddling as hard and fast as you can to catch waves and ride them far into the shore.

Near Diamond Head, **Hula's Bar and Lei Stand,** with an ocean view and a disco complete with strobe-lit dancefloor and videos, rocks nightly until 2 a.m. ~ Waikiki Grand Hotel, 134 Kapahulu Avenue; 808-923-0669.

Tucked away in the back of Eaton Square, a little hideaway off Ala Moana Boulevard, **P-10A,** a private coffee bar that gives gay guys an alternative place to meet. It's an alcohol- and smoke-free relaxing retreat, serving coffee and tea. For entertainment there are video games, X-rated movies and, most importantly, conversation in this low-key, quiet hangout. Although it's a private club, it costs no more than a night at a bar. Open from 6 p.m. weekdays and 24 hours from Friday to Monday morning; there's live entertainment Friday and Saturday nights. Cover. ~ Eaton Square, Hobron and Eaton streets; 808-942-8536.

Next door, the exclusively gay **Michaelangelo** serves up $2 beer and well drinks to a mix of locals and tourists. There's pool, darts and video games to pass the time at this relaxed cruise bar. ~ Eaton Square, Hobron and Eaton streets; 808-951-0008.

Dance any night of the week 'til 4 a.m. to deejay-spun house, disco and hip-hop mixes at **Venus Nightclub.** They feature a male revue and female impersonators. Cover. ~ 1349 Kapiolani Boulevard; 808-951-8671.

**WAIKIKI BEACH** Famous all over the world, the strand in Waikiki is actually several beaches in one. Kahanamoku Beach, Fort DeRussy Beach, Royal-Moana Beach, Kuhio Beach Park and Queen's Surf form an unbroken string that runs from the Ala Wai Canal to Diamond Head Crater. Together they comprise Waikiki Beach. Since going to the beach in this busy enclave also means exploring Waikiki itself, I have placed the beach descriptions in the sightseeing section on the preceding pages.

**BEACHES & PARKS**

For a historical and cultural tour of Hawaii's state capital, simply head toward Downtown Honolulu. A financial center for the entire Pacific Rim, Honolulu's importance to both North America and Asia is manifest in the highrise cityscape. The historical significance of this port city is evident from the 19th-century buildings that lead to the financial district in the heart of the city.

**Downtown Honolulu**

A fitting place to begin your tour is among the oldest homes in the islands. The buildings at the **Mission Houses Museum** seem to be borrowed from a New England landscape, and in a sense they were. The Frame House, a trim white wooden structure, was cut on the East Coast and shipped around the Horn to Hawaii. That was back in 1821, when this Yankee-style building was used to house missionary families.

**SIGHTS**

Like the nearby Chamberlain House and Depository and other structures here, the Frame House represents one of the missionaries' earliest centers in Hawaii. It was in 1820 that Congregationalists arrived in the islands; they immediately set out to build and proselytize. In 1831, they constructed the Chamberlain House and Depository from coral and used it as the mission store. The neighborhood's Printing Office, built of the same durable material ten years later, was used by the first press ever to print in the Hawaiian language. The Mission Houses complex tells much about the missionaries, who converted Hawaiian into a written language, then proceeded to rewrite the entire history of the islands. The museum is run by the Hawaiian Mission Children's Society. Guided tours daily. Closed Monday. Admission. ~ 553 South King Street; 808-531-0481, fax 808-545-2280; e-mail mhm@lava.net.

In the mid-1840s, writer Herman Melville worked in Honolulu as a pin boy in a bowling alley.

Opposite, at South King and Punchbowl streets, is the **Kawaihao Church**. This imposing edifice required 14,000 coral blocks for its construction. Completed in 1842, it has been called the Westminster Abbey of Hawaii because coronations and funerals for Hawaiian kings and queens were once conducted here. Services are still performed in Hawaiian and English every Sunday at 10:30 a.m.; attending them is not only a way to view the church interior, but also provides a unique cultural perspective on contemporary Hawaiian life. Also note that the tomb of King Lunalilo rises in front of the church, and behind the church lies the cemetery where early missionaries and converted Hawaiians were buried.

Across South King Street, the brick structure with stately white pillars is the **Mission Memorial Building**, constructed in 1916 to honor those same early church leaders. The nearby Renaissance-style building with the tile roof is **Honolulu Hale**, the City Hall. You might want to venture into the central courtyard, an open-air plaza surrounded by stone columns.

As you continue walking along South King Street in a westerly direction toward the center of Honolulu, **Iolani Palace** will appear on your right. The palace (*iolani* means "bird of heaven" in Hawaiian) is the only royal residence on American soil. Built for King Kalakaua in 1882, this stunning Renaissance-style mansion served as a royal residence until Queen Liliuokalani was overthrown in 1893. Later the ill-starred monarch was imprisoned here; eventually, after Hawaii became a territory of the United States, the palace was used as the capitol building. Guided tours (running every half hour from 9 a.m. to 2 p.m.) lead you past the *koa* staircases, the magnificent chandeliers and the Corinthian columns that lend a touch of European grandeur to this splendid building.

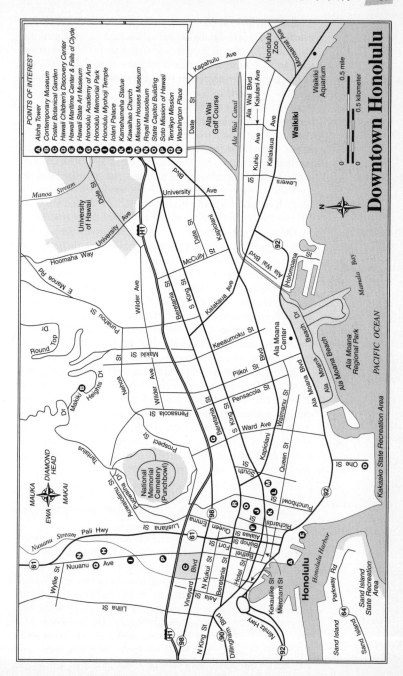

**Downtown Honolulu**

POINTS OF INTEREST

- Ⓐ Aloha Tower
- Ⓑ Contemporary Museum
- Ⓒ Foster Botanical Garden
- Ⓓ Hawaii Children's Discovery Center
- Ⓔ Hawaii Maritime Center & Falls of Clyde
- Ⓕ Hawaii State Art Museum
- Ⓖ Honolulu Academy of Arts
- Ⓗ Honolulu Memorial Park
- Ⓘ Honolulu Myohoji Temple
- Ⓙ Iolani Palace
- Ⓚ Kamehameha Statue
- Ⓛ Kawaiaho Church
- Ⓜ Mission Houses Museum
- Ⓝ Royal Mausoleum
- Ⓞ Soto Mission of Hawaii
- Ⓟ State Capitol Building
- Ⓠ Tenrikyo Mission
- Ⓡ Washington Place

The land around the Palace was significant to the Hawaiian people even before the royalty set up house. A Hawaiian temple stood here until it was probably destroyed in 1819. King Kamehameha III relocated his court from Lahaina to this location in 1845. After his residence was torn down, the current palace incarnation was constructed.

Also located on the palace grounds is **Iolani Barracks**, where the Royal Household Guards were stationed, and the **Coronation Pavilion**, upon which the King was crowned. You can tour the palace grounds for free, but there's an admission charge for the building. Reservations are strongly advised; children under five are allowed only in the video theater and basement galleries. Tours are given Tuesday through Saturday. Closed Sunday and Monday. ~ South King and Richards streets; 808-522-0832, fax 808-532-1051; www.iolanipalace.org, e-mail kanaina@iolanipalace.org.

Directly across the street rises the **Kamehameha Statue**, honoring Hawaii's first king. A huge gilt-and-bronze figure cast in Italy, it is covered with flower leis on special occasions. The spear-carrying warrior wears a feather cape and helmet. Behind him stands **Aliiolani Hale**, better known as the Judiciary Building, home to Hawaii's Supreme Court. Back in the days of the monarchy, it served as the House of Parliament. Docent-led tours of the Judiciary History Center are available Thursday and Friday, and by appointment. ~ 808-539-4999, fax 808-539-4996; www.jhchawaii.org, e-mail jhc@yahoo.com.

Behind Iolani Palace is the **State Capitol Building**. Unlike the surrounding structures, this is an ultramodern building, completed in 1969. Encircled by flared pillars that resemble palm trees, the capitol represents a variety of themes. Near the entrance there's a statue of Father Damien, who died of leprosy on Molokai Island, and Queen Liliuokalani, Hawaii's last reigning monarch. The House and Senate chambers are designed in a cone shape to resemble volcanoes, and the open-air courtyard is a commentary on the state's balmy weather. Tours of the capitol building and the legislature are given Monday, Wednesday and Friday. ~ Bounded by South Beretania, Richards and Punchbowl streets; 808-586-0178, fax 808-586-0019.

Since 1967 the State of Hawaii has set aside a percentage of revenues to fund the State Foundation on Culture and the Arts. The result is an art collection grown to more than 5000 pieces ranging from fabrics to paintings, glasswork to bronze sculpture. Art from the collection is exhibited in 285 buildings throughout the State. To provide a museum setting for a portion of the collection, the State purchased the historic Richard Street YMCA, a noteworthy 1920s architectural monument across the street from Iolani Palace, and created **Hawaii State Art Museum**, with three galleries on the second floor offering a total of 12,000 square feet

of exhibit space. Closed Sunday and Monday. ~ One Capitol
District Building; 808-586-0900; www.state.hi.us/sfca.

**Washington Place**, the governor's residence, is steeped in history. Captain John Dominis began construction in 1846, but never
got to live here because he died at sea be-
fore the house was completed four years
later. His famous daughter-in-law, however,
made the house a palace. Queen Liliuokalani
was living in Washington Place when she was
overthrown, marking the end of the Hawaiian
monarchy. When she was released from prison,
she returned to Washington Place despite several
other more comfortable living options. It has been
speculated that her residence here was an act of politics and bravery: the home was cramped—at least by
royal standards—but located near the new government's
center of power. She did not, it would appear, wish to be forgotten. Washington Place has continued to serve its government
over the years, providing living quarters for 12 governors and
their families. Tours are available Wednesday between 10 a.m.
and 2 p.m.; one-week advance reservations are required. ~ 320
South Beretania Street; 808-586-0248.

> The State's art collections, on dis-
> play in public places, are high-
> lighted in an excellent historic
> walking tour booklet of down-
> town Honolulu. It's available
> free from the State Founda-
> tion for Culture and the
> Arts. ~ 250 Hotel Street,
> 2nd floor; 808-586-0304.

**St. Andrews Cathedral**, thought to be the only example of
French-Gothic architecture in Hawaii, was erected in 1862 of
stone shipped from England. The cathedral's eight bells have the
names of eight Hawaiian monarchs and the dates of their reigns
engraved on them, and can perform 40,320 different melodic
changes. As if that wasn't enough of a claim to fame, the organ
is the second largest in Hawaii. Sunday mass, including the hymns,
is conducted in Hawaiian. ~ Beretania and Alakea streets; 808-
524-2822, fax 808-537-4177.

Let the kids burn off some steam at the 38,000-square-foot
**Hawaii Children's Discovery Center**. Four major galleries sponsor
interactive exhibits that are hands-on and educational (for example, "Fantastic You" will teach kids everything they need to know
about the human body), but don't worry, they'll never catch on.
You can picnic (or nap) at the park across the street. Be forewarned: the Center does not accommodate strollers (although it is
wheelchair accessible), so bring a carrier. Closed Monday. Admission. ~ 111 Ohe Street; 808-524-5437, fax 808-524-5400;
www.discoverycenterhawaii.org.

**WATERFRONT**  For a tour of Honolulu's waterfront, head down
Richards Street from the State Capitol Building toward Pier 7.
Next to the **Aloha Tower Marketplace**, a festive market bazaar
with shops, food and music, the imposing and historic **Falls of
Clyde** lies berthed. A completely restored century-old sailing ship,
the *Falls of Clyde* is reputedly the only fully rigged four-masted

ship in the world. In the old days it was used to carry sugar and oil across the Pacific. Honolulu was then a harbor filled with tall-masted ships, so crowded at the dock that they bumped one another's gunwales. Part of this proud fleet, the *Falls of Clyde* was built in Scotland and sailed halfway round the world. For a single admission charge you can tour this marvelous piece of floating history and, when in port, view the **Hokulea**, a double-hulled canoe that has sailed several times to Tahiti. A 60-foot replica of an ancient Polynesian craft, it follows the traditional designs of the boats used by the early Tahitians. Since 1975, this fragile craft has been sailed between Hawaii and French Polynesia by Hawaiian navigators, re-creating more than 100,000 miles of historic sea voyages. Using no modern instruments, navigating by stars and wave patterns, they traced the course of their ancestors.

The fascinating **Hawaii Maritime Center** (adjacent to the *Falls of Clyde*) traces the archipelago's maritime history from the era of Polynesian exploration to the days of the great ocean liners and beyond. Skeletal remains of a humpback whale and an 1800-pound blue marlin are draws. Other displays focus on the old whaling trade and seaplanes; there's also an interactive program for kids. Admission. ~ Pier 7, Honolulu Harbor; 808-536-6373, fax 808-536-1519; www.bishopmuseum.org.

From the Hawaii Maritime Center, follow the roadway along the water to **Aloha Tower** at Pier 9. You'll see it nearby, rising like a spire along the water's edge. In the early 20th century, when many visitors arrived in luxurious ocean liners, this slender structure was Hawaii's answer to the Statue of Liberty. It greeted guests when they arrived and bade them farewell upon departure. Now dwarfed by the skyscrapers of Downtown Honolulu, proud Aloha Tower still commands an unusual view of the harbor and ocean.

**sights**

**AUTHOR FAVORITE**

A jewel in Honolulu's art community is **Honolulu Academy of Arts**. Founder Anna Rice Cooke originally donated over 4000 works in 1927. Today the internationally recognized museum boasts over 34,000 pieces and is worth spending an afternoon perusing. Emphasizing Eastern and Western artworks, the museum may exhibit such items as author James Michener's collection of *ukiyo-e* prints from Japan or the Samuel H. Kress Foundation collection of Italian Renaissance paintings. In addition, traditional arts of Africa, the Pacific and the Americas are also displayed. Several elegantly landscaped courtyards add to the beauty. Closed Monday. Admission. ~ 900 South Beretania Street; 808-532-8700, fax 808-532-8787; www.honoluluacademy.org, e-mail academypr@honoluluacademy.org.

Any day between 9 a.m. and sunset you can ride an elevator to the tenth-floor observation deck for a crow's-nest view.

It's also fun to wander the nearby wharves, catching glimpses of the shops and pleasure boats that still tie up around Honolulu's historic port. You can take in the city's fishing fleet, as well as several tour boats, at **Kewalo Boat Basin**, also known as Fisherman's Wharf, midway between Waikiki and Downtown Honolulu. ~ Ala Moana Boulevard and Ward Avenue.

To see where all that delicious seafood you've been eating comes from, stop by the **Honolulu Fish Market**. Here auctioneers    ◄ HIDDEN
sell the day's catch. For the real experience, get there at 5:30 in the morning. Those not quite as industrious should note it's all over by noon. ~ Near the Honolulu Harbor (Pier 38).

It's not far to **Fort Street Mall**, a seven-block stretch of Downtown Honolulu that is an attractive pedestrian thoroughfare with a few restaurants. The mall is also a good place to spend a little time shopping. Located miles from the Waikiki tourist beat, the stores here cater to local people, so you'll be able to discover objects unobtainable in kitschier quarters.

Fort Street Mall leads to **Merchant Street**, center of the old downtown section of Honolulu. The 19th- and early-20th-century buildings in this neighborhood re-create the days before Hawaii became the 50th state, when the islands were almost totally controlled by "The Big Five," an interlocking group of powerful corporations. Today the brick-rococo district remains much the same on the outside. But the interiors of the buildings have changed markedly. They now house boutiques and gourmet restaurants downstairs and multinational corporations on the upper floors.

**CHINATOWN**    After proceeding away from the waterfront all the way to the end of Merchant Street, take a right on Nuuanu Avenue, then a left on Hotel Street. As you walk along this thoroughfare, which seems to change its identity every block or two, you will pass from Honolulu's conservative financial district into one of its most intriguing ethnic neighborhoods, **Chinatown**.    ◄ HIDDEN

The Chinese first arrived in Hawaii in 1852, imported as plantation workers. They quickly moved to urban areas after completing their plantation contracts, became merchants and proved very successful. Many settled right here in this weather-beaten district, which has long been a center of controversy and an integral part of Honolulu's history. When bubonic plague hit the Chinese community in 1900, the Caucasian-led government tried to contain the pestilence by burning down afflicted homes. The bumbling white fathers managed to raze most of Chinatown, destroying businesses as well as houses.

Despite the renovation of select buildings, Hotel Street, the spine of Chinatown, retains a seedy air with a sailor's port-of-call feel. Refurbished shops stand cheek-by-jowl with quaint, time-worn stores. You'll still encounter the other side of Chinatown, the late-night face of the neighborhood. Strung like a neon ganglion along the thoroughfare are porno movie places, flophouses, barrooms and pool halls. This was once a booming red-light district, the haunt of a motley collection of characters.

The ultimate emblem of Chinatown's revitalization is **Maunakea Marketplace**. This Amerasian shopping mall, with a statue of Confucius overlooking a brick courtyard, houses an Oriental antique shop and a Chinese art store. The most interesting feature is the produce market, a series of traditional hanging-ducks-and-live-fish stalls inside an air-conditioned building. ~ Hotel and Maunakea streets; 808-524-3409.

*HIDDEN* ►    The best way to visit this neighborhood is on one of the **Chinatown Walking Tours** sponsored by the Chinese Chamber of Commerce. Chinatown today is an eclectic community, containing not only Chinese, but Filipinos, Hawaiians and more recent arrivals from Vietnam and Laos. To fully understand Hawaii's melting-pot population, it's important to visit this vibrant district. The walking tour is given on Tuesday mornings, and will carry you past temples and other spots all around the neighborhood. Fee. ~ 42 North King Street; 808-533-3181, fax 808-533-6967.

Continuing north along Hotel Street across Nuuanu Stream, turn right on College Walk and follow it a short distance upstream. You'll pass the **Izumo Taishakyo Mission**, a Japanese Shinto shrine. Take a minute to stop in to see the bell and gate.

Proceed farther and you will arrive at **Foster Botanical Garden**. This 14-acre plot is planted with orchids, palms, coffee trees, poisonous plants and numerous other exotic specimens. There are about 4000 species in all, dotted around a garden that was first planted over 125 years ago. You can meditate under a bo tree or wander through a "prehistoric glen," a riot of ancient ferns and unusual palms. Or you can stroll through and marvel at the universe of color crowded into this urban garden. Visitors are advised

## HEART OF A NEIGHBORHOOD

Some of Chinatown's woodframe buildings still suggest the old days and traditions. Wander down side streets like Maunakea Street and you will encounter import stores, Chinese groceries and noodle factories. You might also pop into one of the medicinal herb shops, which feature unique potions and healing powders. There are chop suey joints, acupuncturists and outdoor markets galore, all lending a priceless flavor of the Orient.

to bring insect repellent. Admission. ~ 50 North Vineyard Boulevard; 808-522-7065, fax 808-522-7050; www.co.honolulu.hi.us/parks/hbg.

When you're done enjoying Foster Botanical Garden, stop by the adjacent **Kwan Yin Temple**, where the smell of incense fills the air and Buddhist tranquility pervades. For a brief moment you'll feel like you're in China rather than Honolulu. ~ 50 North Vineyard Boulevard.    ◀ HIDDEN

On the way back to Chinatown, walk along the other side of Nuuanu Stream and stop at the **Cultural Plaza**. This Asian-style shopping mall is bounded by Kukui, Maunakea and Beretania streets, and by the stream. You'll find porcelain, Chinese jewelry, housewares, gifts, medicinal herbs, Chinese cake shops and several restaurants. Don't miss the open-air market selling fresh vegetables, tropical fruits, fish, chicken feet, pigs' heads and other exotic items. The market entrance is in the back of the plaza.

On the outskirts of Chinatown is the **Hawaii Theatre**. After years of painstaking restoration, it is a study in neoclassical architecture. With gilded decor, Corinthian columns and striking mosaics, it has been elevated again to the grand status it enjoyed when the theater first opened in 1922. In 1929, it was the first movie theater in the islands to show movies with sound. Tours are available at this nationally registered historic place. Shows, concerts, festivals, ethnic programs and films are presented here. Closed Monday. Admission. ~ 1130 Bethel Street; 808-791-1306, 808-528-0506 (tickets), fax 808-528-1675; www.hawaiitheatre.com.

If you're in the mood for a movie fix, head to the **Signature Theater** complex at Dole Cannery Square. Hawaii's largest cineplex with 18 screens, it also features Hawaii's best cinematic selection, including foreign films you'll find nowhere else on the island. ~ 735-B Iwilei Road; 808-526-3456.

The **Town Inn**, on the outskirts of Chinatown, allows you to capture the local color of Honolulu's Chinese section, though the hotel itself is rather nondescript. The 26 rooms are clean, carpeted and sparsely furnished—some even have air conditioning—and all are practically devoid of decoration. First-come, first-served. ~ 250 North Beretania Street; 808-536-2377. BUDGET.    **LODGING**

The **Aston Executive Centre Hotel**, a highrise in the financial district, has about 90 comfortable guest rooms. Its location and perks aimed at business folks (computer ports, 24-hour fitness center, daily newspaper) make this an ideal spot for a business trip. Other amenities include laundry facilities and a spa. A complimentary breakfast is included. ~ 1088 Bishop Street; 808-539-3000, fax 808-523-1088; www.astonexecutivecentre.com, e-mail resexc@aston-hotels. ULTRA-DELUXE.

**DINING**    As you get away from Waikiki you'll be dining with a more local crowd and tasting foods more representative of island cuisine, so I would certainly advise checking out some of Honolulu's eating places.

Ward Centre, situated midway between Waikiki and Downtown Honolulu, is a focus for gourmet dining. A warren of wood-paneled restaurants, it features several outstanding eateries.

Consider **Compadres**, upstairs in the same complex. This attractive Mexican restaurant, with oak bar and patio dining, prepares dishes from south of the border as well as salads, steaks and seafood. It specializes in tropical ambience, good food and fish-bowl-size margaritas. ~ 1200 Ala Moana Boulevard; 808-591-8307, fax 808-593-2901. BUDGET TO DELUXE.

**Ryan's Grill** is one of Honolulu's hottest after-work hangouts for singles who want to become un-single, and the place is packed from 5 p.m. until after 1 a.m. Comfortable leather chairs and marble-topped tables create a cozy, modern atmosphere. Grilled and steamed fish and fowl, pizzas, salads and fettuccine are among the many culinary options for those who go to eat instead of drink. ~ 1200 Ala Moana Boulevard; 808-591-9132, fax 808-591-0034. MODERATE.

Honolulu has numerous seafood restaurants. Some of them, fittingly enough, are located right on the water. But for an authentic seafront feel, it's nice to be where the fishing boats actually come in. **Fisherman's Wharf** provides just such an atmosphere. This family restaurant serves seafood dishes as well as pasta and steaks. ~ 1009 Ala Moana Boulevard; 808-538-3808, fax 808-521-5210. DELUXE.

Located in the ultracontemporary Restaurant Row shopping mall, **Sunset Grill** is a minimalist's delight. Track lights, exposed pipes, raw wood and poured concrete establish a kind of early-21st-century motif. The only area devoted to excess is the kitchen, which serves up a lavish array of *kiawe*-grilled dishes, such as smoke-infused marinated salmon. It's hard to go wrong here. No lunch Saturday or Sunday. ~ 500 Ala Moana Boulevard, #1-A;

**AUTHOR FAVORITE**

**Wisteria Restaurant** has been pleasing local Japanese Hawaiians for years. This is where they come to celebrate birthdays, anniversaries and other milestones. The setting is padded booths—coffeeshop style. The food is Japanese home-style cooking, just like *obachan* (grandma) used to make. The sukiyaki and teriyaki are particularly tasty. No lunch Saturday and Sunday. ~ 1206 South King Street; 808-591-9276, fax 808-596-0976. MODERATE.

808-521-4409, fax 808-523-5190; www.sunsetgrill.biz, e-mail sschroeder@sunsetgrill.biz. MODERATE TO DELUXE.

Fresh *ono*, mahimahi, *opakapaka* and ahi highlight the vast seafood menu at **John Dominis**. A sprawling establishment midway between Waikiki and Downtown Honolulu, it features huge pools filled with live fish. The wood-paneled dining room overlooks the water and the chefs know as much about preparing seafood as the original Polynesians. For landlubbers, steak and veal are also on the menu. No lunch. ~ 43 Ahui Street; 808-523-0955, fax 808-526-3758; www.johndominis.com. ULTRA-DELUXE.

Near the city's financial center there's a modest restaurant that I particularly like. The food at **People's Café** is primarily Polynesian: this is a good spot to order poi, *lomi* salmon, *kalua* pig and other island favorites. *Ono, ono!* Closed Sunday. ~ 1310 Pali Highway; phone/fax 808-536-5789. BUDGET.

There is nothing else in Honolulu quite like **La Mariana Sailing Club**. Located on the shores of the Keehi Lagoon and reached through the industrial port area off Sand Island Access Road, La Mariana Sailing Club plays host to an assortment of old salts who dance the hula, sing, party and provide more local color than you'll find just about anywhere else in town. What's more, the food, with a focus on fresh fish, seafood, prime rib and steaks, is good and the service friendly. ~ 50 Sand Island Access Road; 808-848-2800, fax 808-841-2173. MODERATE TO DELUXE.  ◄ *HIDDEN*

For the true flavor of China, head over to Chinatown, just a few blocks from the financial district. Amid the tumbledown buildings and jumble of shops, you'll happen upon **Double Eight Restaurant**. Although the service is forgettable and the decor nonexistent, they do know how to cook up Hong Kong–style delicacies. One fortuitous sign of quality is that few of the employees speak any English. Good luck and *bon appetit!* ~ 1113 Maunakea Street; 808-526-3887. BUDGET.  ◄ *HIDDEN*

There's **Mylan Restaurant** right in the heart of Chinatown. Small it may be, but this café represents a triple threat to the competition—attractive decor, good prices and excellent food. The menu covers the spectrum of Vietnamese dishes, with a smattering of Italian and vegetarian fare, and the interior, lined with tropical paintings, is easy on the eyes. ~ 1160 Maunakea Street; 808-528-3663. BUDGET TO MODERATE.  ◄ *HIDDEN*

And there's a little bit of every other ethnic cuisine at the food stalls in **Maunakea Marketplace**. Here you'll find vendors dispensing steaming plates of Thai, Chinese, Japanese, Hawaiian, Filipino, Korean, Vietnamese and Italian food. Italian? Small tables are provided. ~ Hotel and Maunakea streets. BUDGET.

By way of Filipino food, **Mabuhay Cafe** comes recommended by several readers. It's a plainly adorned place on the edge of Chinatown that serves a largely local clientele. The menu is exten-  ◄ *HIDDEN* sive, covering all types of Filipino dishes. ~ 1049 River Street; 808-545-1956. BUDGET.

**Indigo** is one of Chinatown's treats. This Eurasian dining room casts an aura of the Orient with its dark wicker chairs, ornamental gong and intaglio-carved furnishings. You can expect more than a dozen dim sum dishes. The soups and salads include tomato-garlic crab soup and goat cheese wontons. Among the entrées, they offer miso-marinated seared salmon and Mongolian lamb chops with mint-tangerine sauce. What an adventure! No lunch Saturday. Closed Sunday and Monday. ~ 1121 Nuuanu Avenue; 808-521-2900, fax 808-537-4164; www.indigo-hawaii. com. MODERATE TO DELUXE.

For anyone who thinks a meal without meat isn't a meal, a visit to **Legend's Buddhist Vegetarian Restaurant** might make a health-food nut out of you. Yes, it's vegan (i.e., no animal products)—but the dim sum is darn good. Run by the same people as Legend Seafood Restaurant, this eatery is located in the same building. No dinner. Closed Wednesday. ~ 100 North Beretania Street; 808-532-8218. BUDGET.

A giant red neon sign announces that you've arrived at **Sam Choy's Breakfast, Lunch & Crab**, a noisy, bustling restaurant with marine decor accentuated by a dry-docked fishing boat. Chef Sam Choy, a local boy who has helped Hawaii Regional cuisine establish an international reputation, serves crab (Dungeness, Maryland Blue, Florida Gold, Alaskan King) fresh from the open kitchen. There's also lobster, shrimp, fish and, for those unclear on the concept, chicken and beef dishes. ~ 580 North Nimitz Highway; 808-545-7979, fax 808-521-3887; www.samchoy.com. MODERATE TO ULTRA-DELUXE.

**GROCERIES**   Midway between Waikiki and Downtown Honolulu there's a **Safeway** store. ~ 1121 South Beretania Street; 808-592-6499. There's another **Safeway** in Downtown Honolulu. ~ 1360 Pali Highway; 808-538-3953.

Also look for **The Carrot Patch**, with its health and diet products and sandwiches. ~ 700 Bishop Street; 808-531-4037.

## THE MERRY MONARCH

The king who commissioned the Iolani Palace, David Kalakaua, was a world traveler with a taste for the good life. Known as the Merry Monarch, he planned for his coronation the greatest party Hawaii had ever seen. He liked to spend money with abandon and managed to amass in his lifetime a remarkable collection of material goods, not the least of which was his palace.

**R. Field Wine Co.** specializes in fine wines and gourmet groceries. ~ 1460 South Beretania Street; 808-596-9463.

You might want to browse around the mom-and-pop grocery stores spotted throughout Chinatown. They're marvelous places to pick up Chinese foodstuffs and to capture the local color.

Don't miss the **Open Market** in Chinatown. It's a great place to shop for fresh foods. There are numerous stands selling fish, produce, poultry, meat, baked goods and island fruits, all at low-overhead prices. ~ Along North King Street between River and Kekaulike streets.

◀ HIDDEN

One of Honolulu's sleeker shopping malls is **Ward Centre** on Ala Moana Boulevard. Streamlined and stylized, it's an elite enclave filled with designer shops, spiffy restaurants, boutiques and children's shops. Adorned with blond-wood facades, brick walkways and brass-rail restaurants, the shopping complex provides a touch of Beverly Hills. ~ 1200 Ala Moana Boulevard.

**SHOPPING**

Anchoring Ward Centre at the far end is **Borders Books & Music** (808-591-8995), a superstore that is chockablock with everything for your reading and listening pleasure. They have two floors of paperbacks, hardbacks, audiotapes and CDs.

Just down the walkway in Ward Centre, you can home in on **Sedona**, the self-proclaimed "unique place to find yourself." It stocks aromatherapy oils, visionary music, inspirational gifts—and personal psychic readings. ~ 808-591-8010.

**Black Pearl Gallery** features lustrous Tahitian black pearls that highlight its jewelry collection. ~ 808-597-1477.

In the same complex, there's an excellent selection of women's clothing and accessories at **The Ultimate You**. This designer consignment store offers great bargains. ~ 808-591-8388.

Ala Moana Center may be the biggest, but the smaller **Ward Warehouse**, on Ala Moana Boulevard between Waikiki and Downtown Honolulu, is a shopping center worth visiting. It features stores such as **Native Books/Na Mea Hawaii** (808-596-8889), which stocks locally crafted items and an extensive collection of books on the islands. **Nohea Gallery** (808-596-0074) displays quilts, jewelry, pottery, glassware, lamps and wooden bureaus—all made in Hawaii by local artists. ~ 1020 Ala Moana Boulevard.

A California-style affair complete with white stucco walls and curved tile roof, **Aloha Tower Marketplace** is located on the waterfront overlooking Honolulu Harbor. With its flagstone walkways and open-air courtyards, it's worth stopping by even if buying something is the last thing on your mind. Among the over 70 shops are about 25 devoted to apparel, a handful of galleries and perhaps three dozen specialty shops. Among them are **Hapa Collections** (808-528-0395), which sells Hawaiian tourist poster prints of the 1920s and other art. Tucked between the Hawaii

Maritime Museum and Aloha Tower, it's set near one of the busiest parts of the harbor. ~ Pier 8; 808-528-5700.

If you're seeking Oriental items, then Chinatown is the place. Spotted throughout this neighborhood are small shops selling statuettes, pottery and other curios. It's also worthwhile wandering through the **Chinese Cultural Plaza**. This mall is filled with Asian jewelers, bookstores and knickknack shops. ~ Corner of Beretania and Maunakea streets; 808-521-4934.

At the edge of Chinatown along Nuuanu Avenue are several galleries and shops worthy of a visit. The **Pegge Hopper Gallery** is here, displaying acrylic paintings and the female portraits for which she is renowned. Open Tuesday through Saturday or by appointment. ~ 1164 Nuuanu Avenue; 808-524-1160; www. peggehopper.com.

**NIGHTLIFE** A harbor view and Hawaiian contemporary music played on Thursday, Friday and Saturday by acoustic guitarists and bands make **Kincaid's** a good choice for a relaxing evening. This lounge is part of a popular Honolulu restaurant in Ward Warehouse. ~ 1050 Ala Moana Boulevard; 808-591-2005.

Near downtown, the ultracontemporary Restaurant Row offers several nightspots including a restaurant called **The Ocean Club**. This upscale club features nightly deejay dance music. Dress code. Cover. ~ 500 Ala Moana Boulevard; 808-526-9888.

**Chai's Island Bistro** in the Aloha Tower Marketplace often hosts Hawaiian entertainers. It's a fairly intimate setting, especially if you get there early and have dinner. You can get up-close and personal. Call and check who will be there—you're apt to find Jerry Santos or the Brothers Cazimero. ~ Aloha Tower Marketplace, 1 Aloha Tower Drive; 808-585-0011, fax 808-585-0012; www.chaisislandbistro.com.

One of Honolulu's hot spots is **Kapono's**, in the Aloha Tower Marketplace. Presenting live local music from both up-and-coming musicians to old-time favorites, it's where you might be able to hear its owner perform. A not-to-miss Hawaiian musician, Henry Kapono was once part of the Hawaiian duo Cecilio & Kapono.

**AUTHOR FAVORITE**

There's nothing quite like a Friday or Saturday evening at **La Mariana Sailing Club**. A festive group of locals takes over the floor to entertain you with their song and dance. If you're lucky, it will be someone of note who dropped by to talk story or strum his or her uke. There's live piano music Wednesday through Saturday evenings. ~ 50 Sand Island Access Road; 808-848-2800, fax 808-841-2173.

Now he's on his own, and most Fridays you can find him at his restaurant and bar making people happy. ~ Aloha Tower Marketplace; 808-536-2161.

**Indigo**, an attractive Asian restaurant with a patio, has hip-hop dancing, acoustic jazz and contemporary music Tuesday through Saturday. On several nights the sound is live; other nights it's deejay driven. Closed Sunday and Monday. Cover. ~ 1121 Nuuanu Avenue; 808-521-2900.

For something more refined and classical, consider **Chamber Music Hawaii**, which presents a series of concerts annually at several different locations around the city. They also perform on the windward side of the island. ~ 650 Ewalei Road; 808-524-0815.

The **Hawaii Theatre** offers the best in Broadway performances, dance troupes, classical music and much more. The Hawaii International Film Festival is held here every November. ~ 1130 Bethel Street; 808-791-1305, 808-528-0506 (tickets).

The **Honolulu Symphony**, with a season that runs from September to May, provides a delightful schedule of programs. ~ 650 Ewalei Road; 808-524-0815, box office 808-524-0815.

At the **Hawaii Opera Theater**, you can see works like Saint-Saens' *Samson and Delilah*, Puccini's *Madame Butterfly* and *Die Fledermaus* by Strauss. This regional company features stars from the international opera scene. ~ 987 Waimanu Street; 808-596-7372, box office 808-596-7858.

A variety of youth- and family-oriented productions are performed by the **Honolulu Theater for Youth**, at a number of venues throughout Oahu. The company also tours the neighbor islands. Make reservations two weeks in advance. ~ 2846 Ualena Street; 808-839-9885.

**KAKAAKO WATERFRONT PARK** 🏃 Located near downtown Honolulu and popular with local picnickers, this rock-fringed park has a promenade with an uninterrupted view spanning from Diamond Head to the harbor. There are picnic tables, pavilions, showers, restrooms and large grassy plots. There's a surfing break offshore but no swimming. ~ End of Cooke Street off Ala Moana Boulevard.

**BEACHES & PARKS**

◀ *HIDDEN*

**SAND ISLAND STATE RECREATION AREA** 🏃 🛶 This 140-acre park wraps around the south and east shores of Sand Island, with sections fronting both Honolulu Harbor and the open sea. Despite the name, there's only a small sandy beach here, and jet traffic from nearby Honolulu International might disturb your snoozing. But there is a great view of Honolulu. While the swimming and snorkeling are poor here, there are good surf breaks in summer and fishing is usually rewarding. *Papio* and *moano* are the prime catches. Facilities include restrooms and a picnic area.

◀ *HIDDEN*

~ From Waikiki, take Ala Moana Boulevard and Nimitz Highway several miles west to Sand Island Access Road.

▲ State permit required for tent camping in the grassy area facing the ocean.

▼▼▼▼▼▼▼▼▼▼▼▼▼
**Greater Honolulu**

Framed by the Waianae Range in the west and the Koolau Range to the east, Honolulu is a nonstop drama presented within a natural amphitheater. Honolulu Harbor sets the stage to the south; at the center lie Waikiki and Downtown Honolulu. Wrapped around these tourist and business centers is a rainbow-shaped congeries of sights and places that, for lack of a better name, constitutes "Greater Honolulu."

Greater Honolulu is where most of the people of Honolulu live. It extends from navy-gray Pearl Harbor to the turquoise waters of the prestigious Kahala district and holds in its ambit some of the city's prettiest territory.

These points of interest are dotted all across the city and require a bit of planning to see. You'll need to ride buses or taxis or rent a car, but it is well worth the extra effort. You'll be away from the crowds of tourists and get a chance to meet the locals and get a singular perspective on island life and culture.

Many of the points of interest below are frequented more by local residents than tourists. Others contain an interesting mix of local folk and out-of-towners. In any case, be sure to take the time to explore some of these outlying spots.

**SIGHTS**

**KALIHI–NUUANU AVENUE AREA** The first district is actually within walking distance of Downtown Honolulu, but it's a relatively long walk, so transportation is generally advised. Nuuanu Avenue begins downtown and travels uphill in a northeasterly direction past several noteworthy points. First stop is **Soto Mission of Hawaii**, home of a meditative Zen sect. Modeled after a temple in India where the Buddha gave his first sermon, this building is marked by dramatic towers, and beautiful Japanese bonsai plants decorate the landscape. ~ 1708 Nuuanu Avenue.

Here and at nearby **Honolulu Myohoji Temple** the city seems like a distant memory. The latter building, placidly situated along a small stream, is capped by a peace tower. ~ 2003 Nuuanu Avenue.

Uphill from these shrines lies **Honolulu Memorial Park**. There is an ancestral monument here, bordered on three sides by a pond of flashing carp and a striking three-tiered pagoda. ~ 22 Craigside Place. This entire area is a center of simple yet beautiful Asian places of worship. For instance, **Tenrikyo Mission** is a wood-frame temple that was moved here all the way from Japan. One intriguing fact about this fragile structure is that large sections were built without nails. ~ 2236 Nuuanu Avenue.

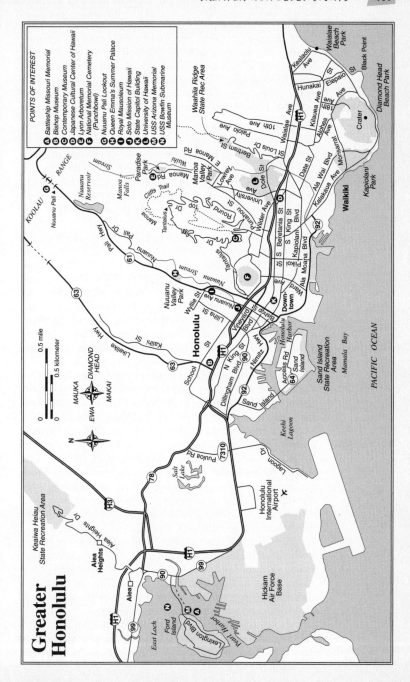

## Greater Honolulu

**POINTS OF INTEREST**

- **Ⓐ** Battleship Missouri Memorial
- **Ⓑ** Bishop Museum
- **Ⓒ** Contemporary Museum
- **Ⓓ** Japanese Cultural Center of Hawaii
- **Ⓔ** Lyon Arboretum
- **Ⓕ** National Memorial Cemetery (Punchbowl)
- **Ⓖ** Nuuanu Pali Lookout
- **Ⓗ** Queen Emma's Summer Palace
- **Ⓘ** Royal Mausoleum
- **Ⓙ** Soto Mission of Hawaii
- **Ⓚ** State Capitol Building
- **Ⓛ** University of Hawaii
- **Ⓜ** USS Arizona Memorial
- **Ⓝ** USS Bowfin Submarine Museum

KOOLAU RANGE

Nuuanu Pali

Nuuanu Reservoir

Manoa Stream

Wailhi Stream

Paradise Park

Manoa Falls

Manoa Cliffs Trail

Tantalus Dr

Round Top Dr

Manoa Rd

E Manoa Rd

Bertram St

Waahila Ridge State Rec Area

St Louis Dr

Palolo Ave

10th Ave

Waialae Ave

HI

Kealaolu Ave

Waialae Beach Park

Black Point

Diamond Head Beach Park

Crater

Diamond Head

Kapiolani Park

Waikiki

Kalakaua Ave Monsarrat

Ala Wai Blvd

Date St

Kilauea Ave

Aluhea Ave

Alohea Ave

Hunakai St

Elepaio St

18th Ave

Manoa Valley Park

University Ave

Lowrey Ave

Dole St

Wilder Ave

Punahou St

S Beretania St

S King St

Kapiolani Blvd

Ala Moana Blvd

92

Piikoi St

Ward Ave

Pensacola St

Downtown

Honolulu Harbor

Sand Island

Sand Island State Recreation Area

Mamala Bay

PACIFIC OCEAN

Nuuanu Valley Park

Wyllie St

Lilha St

Nuuanu Ave

Vineyard Blvd

Bishop St

Pali Hwy

61

63

Nuuanu Stream

Tantalus Dr

Honolulu

School St

Kalihi St

Likelike Hwy

N King St

Nimitz Hwy

Dillingham Blvd

90

HI

63

92

64

Access Rd

Sand Island

Keehi Lagoon

Puuloa Rd

7310

Lagoon Dr

Honolulu International Airport

78

H3

Salt Lake

Aiea Heights Dr

Aiea Heights

Keaiwa Heiau State Recreation Area

Aiea

H1

99

90

East Loch

Ford Island

Lexington Blvd

Pearl Harbor

Hickam Air Force Base

H1

99

N

MAUKA

MAKAI

EWA

DIAMOND HEAD

0    0.5 mile
0    0.5 kilometer

HIDDEN ►

The Hawaiian people also have an important center here. The **Royal Mausoleum** is situated across the street from the Tenrikyo Mission. This was the final resting place for two of Hawaii's royal families, the Kamehameha and Kalakaua clans. Together they ruled 19th-century Hawaii. Today the area is landscaped with palms, ginger, plumeria and other beautiful plants and flowers. ~ 2261 Nuuanu Avenue.

**PUNCHBOWL AND TANTALUS**   It is a few miles from Downtown Honolulu to **Punchbowl**, the circular center of an extinct volcano. You'll find it northeast of town, at the end of Ward Avenue and just off Prospect Drive, which circles the crater. A youngster in geologic terms, the volcano is a mere 150,000 years old. From the lip of the crater, there is a marvelous vista sweeping down to Diamond Head, across Honolulu and all the way out to the Waianae Range.

The most important feature here, however, is the **National Memorial Cemetery**, located in the extinct volcano known as *Puowaina*, Hawaiian for "hill of sacrifice." Over 42,000 war dead have been interred, including victims of both World Wars, as well as the Korean, Spanish-American and Vietnam wars. There is also an impressive monument to the "Courts of the Missing," which lists the names of soldiers missing in action. Ironically, of all the people buried here, the most famous was not a soldier but a journalist—Ernie Pyle, whose World War II stories about the average GI were eagerly followed by an entire nation. Near his grave you will also find the burial site of Hawaii's first astronaut, Ellison Onizuka, who died in the *Challenger* space shuttle disaster. Guided walking tours are offered by the American Legion. Fee. ~ 808-946-6383, fax 808-947-3957; e-mail aldepthi@hawaii.rr.com.

HIDDEN ►

You can explore the heights by following Tantalus Drive as it winds up the side of **Tantalus**, a 2013-foot mountain. Together with Round Top Drive, Tantalus Drive forms a loop that circles through the residential areas hidden within this rainforest. There are spectacular views all along the route, as well as hiking trails that lead from the road into verdant hilltop regions. Here you'll encounter guava, banana, eucalyptus and ginger trees as well as wildflowers and an occasional wild pig.

One of the best views of all is found at **Puu Ualakaa Park**, a lovely retreat located along the drive. The vista here extends from Diamond Head west to Pearl Harbor, encompassing in its course a giant swath of Honolulu and the Pacific. If you were a fan of *Blue Hawaii*, you might recall the view from here. It's where Elvis decides he wants to become a tour guide.

En route stop by the **Contemporary Museum**. In addition to changing exhibitions of contemporary art, the museum features the works of several well-known artists in its sculpture garden and galleries, including David Hockney, Robert Arneson, Charles Arnoldi and Tom Wesselman. Boasting five galleries, an inspired gift shop and a gourmet café, the museum is nevertheless up-staged by its magnificently landscaped grounds. Closed Monday. Admission. ~ 2411 Makiki Heights Drive; 808-526-1322, fax 808-536-5973; www.tcmhi.org, e-mail info@tcmhi.org.

**CROSS-ISLAND EXPRESS**    Along the outskirts of Honolulu, there are several more points of interest. The best way to tour them is while traveling along the two highways that cut across the Koolaus, connecting Honolulu directly with the island's Windward Coast.

The Likelike Highway, Route 63, can be reached from Route H-1, the superhighway that serves Honolulu. Before heading up into the mountains, you will encounter the **Bishop Museum** near the intersection of Routes 63 and H-1. Built around the turn of the 20th century, it houses a stellar collection of Hawaiian and Pacific artifacts.

Here you'll also find an outrigger canoe, thrones, primitive artworks and fascinating natural-history exhibits. There are drums made with shark skin, and helmets decorated with dog teeth and pearl shells. The 19th-century whaling trade is represented with menacing harpoons and yellowing photographs of the oil-laden ships. Of all the exhibits, the most spectacular are cloaks worn by Hawaiian kings and fashioned from tens of thousands of tiny feathers. There are displays capturing the Japanese, Chinese and Filipino heritage in Hawaii and a hall devoted to other cultures of the Pacific. The museum also houses a planetarium, various children's activities, and a gift shop. Admission. ~ 1525 Bernice Street; 808-847-3511, fax 808-847-8249; www.bishopmuseum. org, e-mail shop@bishopmuseum.org.

**AUTHOR FAVORITE**

**sights**    Founded in 1889 by Charles Reed Bishop in honor of his late wife, Princess Bernice Pauahi Bishop, the last descendant of the royal Kamehameha family, the **Bishop Museum** now includes a plethora of artifacts, documents and photographs about Hawaii as well as other Pacific island cultures. Built on the original site of the Kamehameha Schools for Boys, a school estab-lished to educate Hawaiian children, the museum was created to augment their education and instill a greater pride in their Hawaiian heritage. The one remaining building from the school, which was relocated in the '60s, is Bishop Hall. The museum is a must-see for anyone interested in Hawaiiana. See above for more information.

The other, more scenic road across the mountains is the Pali Highway, Route 61. As it ascends, it passes **Queen Emma's Summer Palace**. Constructed in 1848, the palace was originally used as a mountain home by King Kamehameha IV and his wife, Queen Emma. Today the gracious white-pillared house is a museum. Here you can view the Queen's personal artifacts, as well as various other period pieces. The Palace's gardens are especially beautiful; you can almost see the Queen entertaining her guests by the lily pond. The gift shop has a nice selection of local crafts and books. Admission. ~ 808-595-3167, fax 808-595-4395; www.daughtersofhawaii.org, e-mail doh1903@hawaii.rr.com.

HIDDEN ►

You can also walk the tree-shaded grounds of **Nuuanu Pali Drive** and follow until it rejoins the highway. This residential boulevard, with its natural canopy and park-like atmosphere, is one of Honolulu's many idyllic hideaways.

Farther along Pali Highway, there is a turnoff to **Nuuanu Pali Lookout**. It is a point that must not be missed, and is without doubt Oahu's finest view. Gaze down the sheer, rugged face of the Koolau cliffs as they drop 3000 feet to a softly rolling coastal shelf. Your view will extend from Makapuu Point to the distant reaches of Kaneohe Bay, and from the lip of the cliff far out to sea. It was from these heights, according to legend, that a vanquished army was forced to plunge when Kamehameha I captured Oahu in 1795.

**PEARL HARBOR**  Many people consider a trip to Pearl Harbor a pilgrimage. It was here on a sleepy Sunday morning, December 7, 1941, that the Japanese launched a sneak attack on the United States naval fleet anchored in the port, immediately plunging the nation into World War II. As Japanese planes bombed the harbor, over 2400 Americans lost their lives. Eighteen ships sank that day in the country's greatest military disaster.

The "leaping flea," better known as the ukulele, was introduced to Hawaii by the Portuguese in 1879. It's now a fundamental instrument used in Hawaiian music.

The battleship USS *Arizona* was hit so savagely by aerial bombs and torpedoes that it plunged to the bottom, entombing over 1100 sailors within its hulk; today they remain in that watery grave. A special **USS Arizona Memorial** was built to honor them; it's constructed directly above the ship, right in the middle of Pearl Harbor. The memorial includes a shrine with the name of each sailor who died aboard the ship carved in marble. Gazing at this too, too long list of names, and peering over the side at the shadowy hull of the ship, it's hard not to be overcome by the tragic history of the place. Daily from 8 a.m. to 3 p.m., there's a 75-minute program that includes free boat tours out to this fascinating memorial. Remember, no bathing suits or bare feet are permitted. Pearl Harbor, several miles northwest of Downtown Honolulu, can be reached by car or bus. ~ 808-422-2771, fax 808-483-8608; www.nps.gov/usar.

Anchored nearby the *Arizona* visitors center is the **USS Bowfin Submarine Museum**. This World War II–era submarine is a window into life beneath the waves. It provides an excellent opportunity to tour the claustrophobic quarters in which 80 men spent months at a time. The accompanying museum, filled with submarine-related artifacts, will help provide an even fuller perspective. Admission. ~ 808-423-1341, fax 808-422-5201; www.bowfin.org.

For another perspective on World War II, visit the **Battleship Missouri Memorial**. Launched in 1944, the *Missouri*, or Mighty Mo as it is usually called, was the last U.S. battleship ever built. It was aboard this 887-foot vessel on September 2, 1945, that General Douglas MacArthur accepted the surrender of the Japanese forces, thus ending World War II. The decommissioned battleship is now docked in Pearl Harbor, off Ford Island, within sight of the USS *Arizona* Memorial. Tours depart from the ticket office of the *Bowfin* submarine. Guided tours are available, or you can tour the Mighty Mo on your own, getting a first-hand glimpse of its massive armaments, the surrender deck and the commanding bridge. Plan to spend an hour on the self-guided tour. Reservations recommended. Admission. ~ 808-423-2263, 888-877-6477; www.ussmissouri.org, e-mail bigmo@ussmissouri.org.

**ALA MOANA–MOILIILI–KAPAHULU–KAIMUKI AREA**    Bordering the *ewa* direction of Waikiki, just Diamond Head–side of Downtown Honolulu, is Ala Moana (which means "pathway to the sea"). Its claim to fame is a very large family-oriented park that extends from the Ala Wai Yacht Harbor along the ocean to Kewalo Basin. **Ala Moana Beach Park** is where Honolulu residents flock to on the weekends to hold family reunions or company picnics, or to play volleyball, softball or tennis with their friends. The sandy beach that lines the park is a safe place for swimmers, especially near **Magic Island** (Ala Moana Regional Park), the peninsula on the east side of the park. Long-distance swimmers practice swimming the length of the park, while joggers run alongside the shore to get into shape. Watching the sun set from this spot is the sport of choice for many locals and tourists alike.

Across the street, **Ala Moana Center** is the shop-'til-you-drop capital of the islands (and almost anywhere else in the U.S.). In addition to over 200 shops, Ala Moana Center is the main transfer point for most island buses, so if you ride TheBus, you'll likely end up here at some point. ~ www.alamoana.com.

Just *mauka* (toward the mountains) of Ala Moana are several working-class communities—Moiliili, Kapahulu and Kaimuki. They skirt the University of Hawaii on one side and Waikiki on the other. What's best about these neighborhoods is the handful of restaurants that are far enough away from the madding crowd of Waikiki to make eating out a pleasure. Restaurants in every budget category can be found in these enclaves, and best of all, you'll more than likely be dining with a local crowd.

HIDDEN ► In Moiliili, the **Japanese Cultural Center of Hawaii** sponsors a permanent exhibit focusing on Hawaiian-Japanese culture. In addition to the gallery, there's a little gift shop. The Resource Center contains an extensive collection of books, pamphlets, periodicals and oral histories of the Japanese in Hawaii. It also hosts festivals marking traditional Japanese holidays; call ahead for details. Closed Sunday and Monday. Admission. ~ 2454 South Beretania Street; 808-945-7633, fax 808-944-1123; www.jcch. com, e-mail info@jcch.com.

**MANOA VALLEY**   Residents of a different sort are found in the city's beautiful Manoa Valley, a couple of miles northeast of Waikiki. Among the elegant homes decorating the region are some owned by the New England families that settled in Hawaii in the 19th century.

The **University of Hawaii** has its main campus here; almost 20,000 students and 2000 faculty members attend classes and teach on these grounds, which are set amid rolling lawns and backdropped by the Koolau Mountains. ~ 2444 Dole Street; 808-956-8111; www.hawaii.edu.

Don't miss the opportunity to visit the **University of Hawaii Art Gallery**. The gallery, employing modular and movable walls, constantly reinvents itself to the configurations of visiting exhibits. Closed Saturday; closed mid-May to late August. ~ Art Building, University of Hawaii at Manoa; 808-956-6888; www.hawaii. edu/artgallery, e-mail gallery@hawaii.edu.

HIDDEN ► Also on campus is the **East-West Center**, a private research facility. Designed by noted architect I. M. Pei, the center strives to promote the mutual understanding and cooperation among Pacific Rim cultures. The center also contains a number of priceless Asian artworks, well worth viewing. ~ John Burns Hall, 1601 East-West Road; 808-944-7111; www.eastwestcenter.org, e-mail ewcinfo@eastwestcenter.org.

From campus you can head deeper into Manoa Valley along Oahu Avenue and Manoa Road. You'll pass the **Waioli Tea Room**

**SWAP 'EM, *BRAH***

For a variety of secondhand items, try the **Kam Super Swap Meet**. It's a great place to barter for bargains, meet local folks and find items you'll never see in stores. It's open on Wednesday, Saturday and Sunday. ~ 98-850 Moanalua Road; 808-483-5535.

(808-988-5800), a cozy dining room tucked into a garden setting where you can enjoy breakfast or high tea, a bakery and a gift shop. Here also is the **Little Grass Shack** that was once occupied by novelist Robert Louis Stevenson (or so the story goes), and a small chapel replete with stained-glass windows. ~ 2950 Manoa Road.

Farther down Manoa Road is **Lyon Arboretum**, a magnificent 194-acre garden with over 8000 plant species, research greenhouses, hiking trails and perhaps the world's largest collection of palm trees. Closed Sunday. ~ 3860 Manoa Road; 808-988-0456; www.hawaii.edu/lyonarboretum.

**KAHALA AREA**   **Diamond Head Beach Park**, a twisting ribbon of white sand, nestles directly below the famous crater. Whenever the wind and waves are good, you'll see windsurfers and surfers galore sweeping in toward the shoreline. The coral reef here makes for good skindiving, too. It's a pretty beach, backdropped by the Kuilei cliffs and watched over by the **Diamond Head Lighthouse**.

From Diamond Head, continue east along Diamond Head Road and Kahala Avenue. These will lead through the Kahala District, home to the island's elite. Bordered by the ocean and the exclusive Waialae Country Club is a golden string of spectacular oceanfront homes with carefully manicured lawns.

Tobacco heiress Doris Duke, a socialite celebrity of the mid-20th century, built a fantasy home on a five-acre site on the lava rock headland called Black Point, just to the east of Diamond Head. Duke, who died in 1993, created a museum of the house, which she'd romantically named **Shangri La**, after the legendary Himalayan valley where peace and good health prevailed. Intrigued by Islamic art, Duke designed the home with Islamic architectural features, furnishings and artworks. The museum, in Kahala, is open to a limited number of visitors daily, with departures from the Honolulu Academy of Arts. Advance bookings are required for the docent-led tour. ~ For details and tour options contact the Honolulu Academy of Arts; 808-532-3685.

**LODGING**

An inexpensive place for both men and women across from Ala Moana Park is the YMCA **Central Branch**. It's handily situated across the street from Ala Moana Center and a block from the beach. And you're welcome to use the gym, pool, saunas, television room and coffee shop. You can also expect the usual Y ambience—long sterile hallways leading to an endless series of identical, cramped, uncarpeted rooms. You will pay several dollars more for a private bathroom, but low prices help make up for the lack of amenities. ~ 401 Atkinson Drive; 808-941-3344, fax 808-941-8821; e-mail hidomen@aol.com. BUDGET.

The **Nuuanu** YMCA has inexpensive accommodations for men. Complete athletic facilities are available. ~ 1441 Pali Highway; 808-536-3556, fax 808-521-1181. BUDGET.

The **Pagoda Hotel** is sufficiently removed from the crowds but still only a ten-minute drive from the beach. Spacious studio and one-bedroom units put the accent on rattan furniture. The carpeted rooms feature views of the hotel garden or distant mountains. Two-bedroom units in the adjoining Pagoda Terrace offer kitchens. Ask for a room in the new wing, which is substantially nicer than the old one. ~ 1525 Rycroft Street; 808-941-6611, 800-367-6060, fax 808-955-5067; www.pagodahotel.com, e-mail reservation@hthcorp.com. MODERATE.

In Manoa Valley, the **Fernhurst YWCA** is an appealing three-story lowrise that provides a residence for women. Rooms are single or double occupancy with shared baths. Among the facilities are microwaves, laundry, dining room and lounge. Rates include breakfast and dinner Monday through Friday. ~ 1566 Wilder Avenue; 808-941-2231, fax 808-945-9478. BUDGET.

**Hostelling International—Honolulu** is a dormitory-style crash pad with separate living quarters for men and women, although there is one studio available. Shared kitchen facilities, television lounge, garden patio and laundry are available. Visitors can book island tours through the hostel. ~ 2323-A Sea View Avenue; 808-946-0591, fax 808-946-5904; www.hiayh.org.com, e-mail hihostel@lava.net. BUDGET.

**DINING**

*HIDDEN* ►

In Kalihi, **Meg's Drive-In** is a small eatery serving breakfast, local-style plate lunches and daily specials such as fried noodles with teriyaki beef. You can take your meal to go or dine on the adjoining lanai. No dinner Saturday. Closed Sunday. ~ 743 Waiakamilo Road; 808-845-3943. BUDGET.

For prime rib, crab legs, shrimp and vegetable tempura, try the **Pagoda Floating Restaurant**. This restaurant-in-the-round sits above a pond populated with gaily colored tropical koi. Several cascades and a fountain feed the pond. The surrounding grounds have been carefully landscaped. This dining room offers lunch and dinner buffets with changing featured entrées such as oxtail stew, *misoyaki*, butterfish and *kalua* pork. ~ 1525 Rycroft Street; 808-941-6611, fax 808-946-6596; www.pagodahotel. com. DELUXE.

To go where the local gentry dine, head to **Alan Wong's Restaurant**. Appetizers in the form of quarter-sized burgers made from an ahi tuna combination hint at bigger and better things to come. You can select from a menu filled with locally caught fish, home-grown produce and a wealth of poultry and meat dishes like macadamia nut and coconut–crusted lamb chops. One of the *in* places to dine on Hawaiian Regional cuisine, so reservations are suggested. ~ 1857 South King Street; 808-949-2526, fax 808-951-9520; www.alanwongs.com, e-mail reservations@alan wongs.com. DELUXE.

A star in the Honolulu culinary scene is **Chef Mavro's**. Chef George Mavrothalassitis, formerly of the Four Seasons Resort in Wailea, presides over his own corner in Honolulu. The unassuming building on South King Street does not hint at what awaits inside—an elegant yet understated dining room adorned with local artwork. The French-inspired cuisine arrives at the table in an equally sublime presentation. The dishes are five-star and the service impeccable. One claim to fame of Chef Mavro is the perfect pairing of the wine with every item on the menu. A place for that special night. Dinner only. Closed Monday. ~ 1969 South King Street; 808-944-4714; www.chefmavro.com, e-mail mavro@gte.net. ULTRA-DELUXE.

**McCully Chop Suey**, one of Honolulu's best budget-priced Chinese restaurants, is rather bland but offers a menu that contains everything imaginable. There are over 160 items to choose from—two dozen poultry dishes, eight different sizzling platters, and a host of beef, noodle and seafood dishes. ~ 2005 South King Street; phone/fax 808-946-4069. BUDGET.

Right next to Waikiki, in Ala Moana Center, there are numerous ethnic takeout restaurants that share a large dining pavilion called **Makai Market**. Best of all is **Patti's Chinese Kitchen** (808-  946-5002, fax 808-943-4355), a crowded and noisy gathering place. At Patti's you can choose from over 20 entrées plus a side  order of fried rice or *chow fun*. The courses include dim sum, orange chicken, beef and broccoli, tofu, beef tomato, sweet-and-sour ribs, barbecued pork and shrimp with vegetables. There's also the **Poi Bowl** (808-949-8444), a takeout stand serving traditional  Hawaiian dishes. **Tsuruya Noodle Shop** (808-946-7214) features bowls of Japanese soba and udon noodles. ~ BUDGET.

Or you can ride the escalator to the upper level of Ala Moana Center. Here **Shirokiya**, a massive Asian department store, features an informal Japanese à la carte–style buffet. ~ 808-973-9111. MODERATE.

**AUTHOR FAVORITE**

Hawaii's foremost bed-and-breakfast inn rests in a magnificent old mansion near the University of Hawaii campus. Set in the lush Manoa Valley, the **Manoa Valley Inn** is a 1915 cream-colored Victorian featuring seven guest rooms and an adjacent cottage. Decorated with patterned wallpaper and old-style artworks, the rooms are furnished in plump antique armchairs. Guests enjoy a spacious veranda and lawn. For luxury and privacy, this historic jewel is one of the island's finest spots. ~ 2001 Vancouver Drive; 808-947-6019, fax 808-946-6168; www.manoavalleyinn.com, e-mail manoavalleyinn@aloha.net. MODERATE TO DELUXE.

Hawaiian regional cuisine accented by island fruits is featured at the **Prince Court**. The Hawaii Prince Hotel's harborside restaurant, this dining room is known for dishes like sea scallops and lobster. An extensive wine list is another plus at this Polynesian-style dining room appointed with floral bouquets. ~ 100 Holomoana Street; 808-956-1111. ULTRA-DELUXE.

Near the University of Hawaii campus, there are pizzas, sub sandwiches and chicken dinners at **Magoo's Pizza**. Open for lunch on weekends and dinner daily, it's a great place to snack or stop for a cold beer. ~ Puck's Alley, 1015 University Avenue; 808-949-5381. BUDGET TO MODERATE.

Fiery Szechuan-style cooking is done with competence and style at the tastefully elegant **King Tsin Restaurant**, a popular Chinese eatery. The locale is well away from Waikiki's hustle and bustle, although still easily reached. The extensive menu offers legendary potstickers, honey-glazed spareribs, garlic eggplant and other spicy treats. Most items are hot, but there are a few mild dishes for the more timid. No lunch on Tuesday. ~ 2140 Beretania Street; 808-946-3273. MODERATE.

Quantity and quality don't usually come together, particularly where gourmet restaurants are concerned. But at **Sam Choy** you can count on platter-size portions of macadamia-crusted *ono*, Oriental lamb chops or oven-roasted duck. Considered one of the top Hawaiian cuisine restaurants on the island, it sits with unassuming grace on the second floor of a strip mall. Eat heartily (and well)! Dinner and Sunday brunch. ~ 449 Kapahulu Avenue, Suite 201; 808-732-8645, fax 808-732-8683; www.samchoy.com. DE-LUXE TO ULTRA-DELUXE.

**Irifune** is a warm and friendly Japanese eatery frequented by a local crowd. In fact, around dinnertime, you will likely find yourself in line. The decor gives off a fun, casual air: fishing nets, Kabuki masks and other assorted wallhangings. On the menu are tasty curry, sushi, teriyaki and tempura dishes, plus several other Asian delectables. Closed Sunday and Monday. ~ 563 Kapahulu Avenue; 808-737-1141. MODERATE.

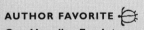

**AUTHOR FAVORITE**

**Ono Hawaiian Foods** is a must for all true Hawaii lovers. It's a hole-in-da-wall eatery on a busy street. But if you're lucky enough to get one of the few tables, you can feast on *laulau, kalua* pig, *pipikaula*, poi and *haupia*. The walls are papered with signed photographs of local notables and the place is packed with locals, notable and otherwise. Closed Sunday. ~ 726 Kapahulu Avenue; 808-737-2275. MODERATE.

For local-style plate lunches, cruise in to **Rainbow Drive-In**.    ◄ *HIDDEN*
Popular with *kamaainas* and tourists alike, the menu includes
hamburger steak, beef curry, breaded mahimahi, chili and fried
chicken served with two scoops of rice and various salads. ~
3308 Kanaina Avenue; 808-737-0177. BUDGET.

Waialae Avenue, a neighborhood strip a mile or so outside
Waikiki, has developed into a gourmet ghetto. **Azteca Mexican**    ◄ *HIDDEN*
**Restaurant** is a vinyl-booth-and-plastic-panel eatery that serves a
delicious array of Mexican food. ~ 3617 Waialae Avenue; 808-735-
2492. MODERATE.

Award-winning **3660 On the Rise** is a local favorite, blending
Asian influences with a definite touch of California cuisine. Try
their signature ahi katsu: deep-fried ahi wrapped in nori with a
wasabi-ginger sauce. Finish off the meal with Harlequin crème
brûlée, which is difficult to describe without salivating but basically involves vanilla-bean custard and chocolate mousse glazed
with caramel. Dinner only. Closed Monday. ~ 3660 Waialae Avenue; 808-737-1177, fax 808-735-6105; www.3660.com, e-mail
3660@flex.com. ULTRA-DELUXE.

For spicy and delicious Asian dishes, it is hard to find a more
appealing place than **Hale Vietnam**. A family restaurant that draws
a local crowd, it has traditional Vietnamese soup and a host of
excellent entrées. ~ 1140 12th Avenue; 808-735-7581. MODERATE.

**Foodland** supermarket in the Ala Moana Center just outside    **GROCERIES**
Waikiki is cheaper than Waikiki groceries, but still more expen-
sive than other Greater Honolulu stores. ~ 1450 Ala Moana
Boulevard; 808-949-5044.

Also in the Ala Moana Center, **Vim N Vigor** has a variety of
vitamins, supplements and health foods, as well as a juice bar and
lunch counter. ~ 1450 Ala Moana Boulevard; 808-955-3600;
www.vimnvigor.com.

In Moiliili near the University, **Star Market** is open 5 a.m. to 2
a.m. ~ 2470 South King Street; 808-973-1666. In Kahala, there's
a **Star Market** in the Kahala Mall that's open 6 a.m. to 12 a.m. ~
808-733-1366.

The best place in Honolulu to buy health foods is at **Down To**
**Earth Natural Foods**. ~ 2525 South King Street; 808-947-7678.
**Kokua Market** is another excellent choice. ~ 2643 South King
Street; 808-941-1922.

Scattered around town are several shops that I recommend you    **SHOPPING**
check out. At **Lanakila Crafts** most of the goods are made by the
disabled, and the craftsmanship is superb. There are shell necklaces, woven handbags, monkeypod bowls, Hawaiian pillows
and homemade dolls. You'll probably see these items in other
stores around the islands, with much higher price tags than here

at the "factory." ~ 1809 Bachelot Street; 808-531-0555; www.lanakilahawaii.org.

Out at the Bishop Museum be sure to stop by **Shop Pacifica**, which offers a fine selection of Hawaiiana. There are books on island history and geography, an assortment of instruments that include nose flutes and gourds, plus cards, souvenirs and wooden bowls. ~ 1525 Bernice Street, near the intersection of Routes 63 and H-1; 808-848-4158.

**Ala Moana Center**, on the outskirts of Waikiki, is the state's largest shopping center. This multitiered complex has practically everything. Ala Moana features three department stores: **Sears** (808-947-0252), **Macy's** (808-941-2345) and a Japanese emporium called **Shirokiya** (808-973-9111). The designer shops, appropriately, are on the upper levels. ~ 1450 Ala Moana Boulevard; 808-955-9517; www.alamoanacenter.com.

For crafts, sushi, fresh produce and even feng shui advice, visit the Honolulu Street Market. Open Saturday from 8 a.m. to 2 p.m. ~ 90 Pohukaina Street; 808-221-6042.

One of Honolulu's more upscale shopping centers is **Kahala Mall**, where you'll find designer shops galore. This attractive complex also hosts almost 100 moderately priced stores. **Barnes & Noble** (808-737-3323) has a superstore here. In addition to a comprehensive line of books, they sell tapes and CDs and have an onsite café. ~ 4211 Waialae Avenue; 808-732-7736.

**NIGHTLIFE**  Outside Honolulu there are usually a couple of spots to hear Hawaiian music. Pick up a copy of *Spotlight's Oahu Gold* or *This Week Oahu* magazine to see what's going on.

At **Rumours**, theme nights are the spice of life. Salsa, retro, hip-hop and Top 40 are all featured, along with "Big Chill" night on Friday featuring '60s music. Located in the Ala Moana Hotel, this club is decorated with artwork and neon fixtures. Cover. ~ 410 Atkinson Drive; 808-955-4811; www.alamoanahotel.com.

Over by the University of Hawaii's Manoa campus, there's **Anna Bannana's**. A popular hangout for years, this wildly decorated spot has all types of live music on Friday and Saturday nights. There's an open mic on Monday, and a deejay on Wednesday. Cover for live shows. ~ 2440 South Beretania Street; 808-946-5190.

The **Manoa Valley Theatre** stages a half dozen Broadway and off-Broadway productions with local actors. Recent offerings include *Cabaret*, *The Graduate* and *The Laramie Project*. ~ 2833 East Manoa Road; 808-988-6131; www.manoavalleytheatre.com.

**BEACHES & PARKS**

HIDDEN ▶

**KEAIWA HEIAU STATE RECREATION AREA** 🏃 Amazing as it sounds, this is a wooded retreat within easy driving distance of Honolulu. Situated in the Koolau foothills overlooking Pearl Harbor, it contains the remains of a *heiau*, a temple once used by Hawaiian healers. There's a forest extending to the far reaches of the mountains and a loop hiking trail. Facilities include picnic area, showers and restrooms. ~ Located in Aiea Heights. To get there from Honolulu, take Route 90 west to Aiea, then follow Aiea Heights Drive to the park.

▲ Tents only. State permit required.

**ALA MOANA REGIONAL PARK** 🏊 🎣 🏄 This 119-acre park is a favorite with Hawaii residents. On weekends every type of outdoor enthusiast imaginable turns out to swim, snorkel, fish (common catches are *papio*, bonefish, goatfish and *moano*), jog, sail model boats and so on. It's also a good place to surf; there are three separate breaks here: "Concessions," "Tennis Courts" and "Baby Haleiwa" all have summer waves. There's a curving length of beach, a grassy park area, a helluva lot of local color and facilities that include a picnic area, restrooms, showers, concession stands, tennis courts, a recreation building, a bowling green and lifeguards. Fun fact: in the opening credits of "Gilligan's Island," the ship set sail out of the harbor near here. ~ On Ala Moana Boulevard at the west end of Waikiki, across from Ala Moana Center.

◀ HIDDEN

**DIAMOND HEAD BEACH PARK** 🏊 🎣 🏄 ⛵ Heaven to windsurfers, this twisting ribbon of white sand sits directly below the crater. It's close enough to Waikiki for convenient access but far enough to shake most of the crowds. The Kuilei cliffs, covered with scrub growth, loom behind the beach. Snorkeling is good—a coral reef extends offshore through this area. There's also a good year-round surf break called "Lighthouse." And for the anglers, your chances are good to reel in *ulua*, *papio* or *mamao*. A shower is the sole facility. ~ Located just beyond Waikiki along Diamond Head Road at the foot of Diamond Head; watch for parked cars.

◀ HIDDEN

**KUILEI CLIFFS BEACH PARK AND KAALAWAI BEACH** 🏊 🎣 🏄 ⛵ Extending east from Diamond Head Beach Park, these sandy corridors are also flanked by sharp sea cliffs. Together they extend from Diamond Head Lighthouse to Black Point. The aquatic attractions are the same as at Diamond Head Beach Park and both beaches can be reached from it (or from cliff trails leading down from Diamond Head Road). A protecting reef makes for good swimming at Kaalawai Beach (which can also be reached via a public accessway off Kulumanu Place).

**WAIALAE BEACH PARK** 🏊 🎣 Smack in the middle of Honolulu's prestigious Kahala district, where a million dollars buys a modest house, sits this tidy beach. Its white sand neatly groomed, its spacious lawn shaded by palms, Waialae is a true find. It has good swimming and fishing. There are bathhouse facilities, beachside picnic tables and a footbridge arching across the stream that divides the property. To the west of the park lies **Kahala Beach**, a long, thin swath of sand that extends all the way to Black Point. There's good snorkeling near the Kahala Mandarin Oriental Hotel. ~ Located on the 4900 block of Kahala Avenue in Kahala.

## Southeast Oahu

Out past Honolulu, beyond the glitter of Waikiki and the gilded neighborhoods of Kahala, the pace slows down, the vistas open up and Oahu begins to look more like a tropical island. The road—Route 72, the Kalanianaole Highway—leads out of Honolulu and hugs the rugged coastline as it climbs up and down and back and forth along the edge of a series of volcanic ridges. The jagged, jade-colored peaks of the Koolau Mountains on one side and the sparkling blue sea on the other provide some of the most striking scenery the state has to offer.

**SIGHTS**

The highway streams through Hawaii Kai and other residential areas, then ascends the slopes of an extinct volcano, 642-foot **Koko Head**. Here Madame Pele is reputed to have dug a hole for the last time in search of fiery volcanic matter.

**Koko Crater**, the second hump on the horizon, rises to over 1200 feet. This fire-pit, according to Hawaiian legend, is the vagina of Pele's sister. It seems that Pele, goddess of volcanoes, was being pursued by a handsome demigod. Her sister, trying to distract the hot suitor from Pele, spread her legs across the landscape.

From the top of Koko Head, a well-marked road and sidewalk lead down to **Hanauma Bay**, one of the prettiest beaches in all Hawaii. The word *hanauma* means "the curved bay," and you will clearly see that Hanauma Bay was once a circular volcano, one wall of which was breached by the sea. This breathtaking place is a marine preserve filled with multicolored coral and teeming with underwater life. Little wonder that Hollywood chose this spot as the prime location for Elvis Presley's movie, *Blue Hawaii*. Elvis' grass shack was right here, and the strand was also a setting in the classic film *From Here to Eternity*.

The swimming and snorkeling are unmatched anywhere and the mazework of coral formations along the bottom adds to the snorkeling adventure. Or you can stroll along the rock ledges that fringe the bay and explore **Toilet Bowl**, a tidepool that "flushes" as the waves wash through it. The best time to come is early morning before other swimmers stir up the waters. Hanauma Bay is an extremely popular picnic spot among local folks, so it is also advisable to visit on a weekday rather than face bucking the crowds on Saturday and Sunday. Because of its popularity, the preserve cuts off entrance to the park when the parking lot is full (another good reason to arrive early). Closed Tuesday. ~ Located on Kalanianaole Highway about 12 miles east of Waikiki; 808-396-4229.

From Hanauma Bay the highway corkscrews along the coast. Among the remarkable scenes you'll enjoy en route are views of Lanai and Molokai, two of Oahu's sister islands. On a clear, clear day you can also see Maui, an island that requires no introduction.

At an overlook you will encounter **Halona Blowhole**, a lava tube through which geysers of seawater blast. During high tide and when the sea is turbulent, these gushers reach dramatic heights. *Halona* means "peering place," and that is exactly what everyone seems to do here. You can't miss the spot, since the roadside parking lot is inevitably crowded with tourists. Between December and April this vista is also a prime whale-watching spot.

Just beyond spreads **Sandy Beach**, one of Hawaii's most renowned bodysurfing spots. It's a long, wide beach piled with fluffy sand and complete with picnic areas and showers. Inexperienced

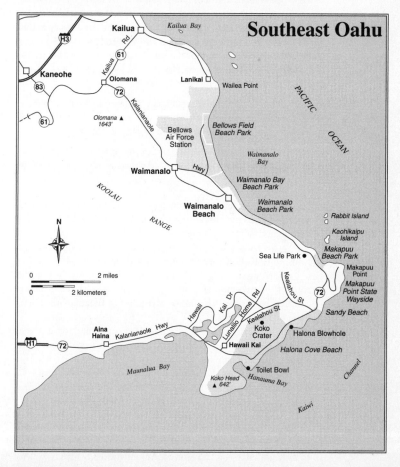

Southeast Oahu

SCENIC DRIVE

# A Hawaiian Cultural Tour

You're on the right island to get a true sense of what life was (and is) like for the Hawaiian people.

**BISHOP MUSEUM**      Our tour begins at the Bishop Museum (page 103), with its exceptional exhibits of Hawaiiana. Three floors of the grand hall give you a feel for Polynesian history over the centuries. Allow 1.5 hours.

**IOLANI PALACE**      Next, head downtown to Iolani Palace (page 86). Be sure to make reservations ahead of time if you want to see the phenomenal woodwork inside the palace. Stroll the grounds and imagine what it was like to be dressed in the long-sleeved outfits of the royal family in this heat! Most Friday afternoons the Royal Hawaiian Band plays at the Royal Bandstand. Allow 45 minutes for the tour. Stroll across the street to see the **statue** of King Kamehameha, Hawaii's first king. If you're lucky, it will be a holiday and he'll be draped in flower leis.

**ROYAL MAUSOLEUM**      It's about six blocks west (*ewa*) to Nuuanu Avenue. Head toward the mountains (*mauka*) and you'll arrive at the Royal Mausoleum (page 102), where Hawaii's royals are interred.

**QUEEN EMMA'S SUMMER PALACE**      After paying your respects, backtrack to Route H-1, head Diamond Head direction (east) and get off on

bodysurfers are better off enjoying the excellent sunbathing here, since the dramatic shorebreak that makes the beach so popular among bodysurfers is dangerous for beginners.

**HIDDEN ►**      Across from the beach, a sign points you to a side road that leads up to **Koko Crater Botanical Gardens**, a 60-acre collection of cacti, plumeria and other water-thrifty plants. A brochure at the start of the two-mile loop trail guides you through the drought-resistant landscape. ~ Kealahou Street, off of Kalanianaole Highway; 808-522-7060.

Route 72 rounds Oahu's southeastern corner and sets a course along the eastern shoreline. It also climbs to a scenic point from which you can take your first view of the Windward Coast. You will be standing on **Makapuu Point**. Above you rise sharp lava cliffs, while below are rolling sand dunes and open ocean. The slope-faced islet just offshore is Rabbit Island. The distant headland is Makapuu Peninsula, toward which you are bound.

From this perfect perch you can also spy a complex of buildings. That's **Sea Life Park**, a marineworld attraction comparable to those in California and Florida. Among the many features at this

the Pali Highway (Route 61) traveling *mauka* toward Kaneohe/Kailua. You'll soon come to Queen Emma's Summer Palace (page 104). A comfortable New England–style home rather than a grand building, it was built in 1843 for the wife of King Kamehameha IV. Allow half an hour to tour her residence and lovely grounds.

**NUUANU PALI LOOKOUT**    Continue up the highway to the Nuuanu Pali Lookout (page 104). This is where King Kamehameha I overwhelmed his enemies. The view is not to be missed.

**ULUPO HEIAU**    You'll want to see at least one *heiau* (ancient temple) on this tour. Your best bet is to continue your drive on Route 61. As you descend into Kailua, you'll encounter Ulupo Heiau (page 122), located behind the YMCA. According to legend, this temple was built by the leprechaun-like *Menehunes*.

**HEEIA STATE PARK**    Farther along Kaneohe Bay is Heeia State Park (page 131), where the ancient Hawaiians built one of the largest fishponds in the islands.

**UNWINDING**    Now that you've had a day of sightseeing, round things out with an invigorating canoe ride at **Waikiki Beach** (page 85) and then dine at **Ono Hawaiian Foods** (page 110) on poi and *lomi* salmon or kalua pig. Be sure to check out the Hawaiian music scene: the Brothers Cazimero or Olomana often perform at **Chai's Island Bistro** (page 98) in Aloha Tower Marketplace.

park is the "Hawaiian Reef Tank," a 300,000-gallon oceanarium inhabited by about 4000 sea creatures. To see it you wind through a spiral viewing area that descends three fathoms along the tank's glass perimeter. At times a scuba diver will be hand-feeding the fish. Swimming about this underwater world are sharks, stingrays, turtles and a variety of lesser-known species. As well as several interactive programs, the park also features a turtle lagoon, penguin habitat and the only known *wholphin* (half whale, half dolphin) living in captivity. Admission. ~ Makapuu Point; 808-259-2501, fax 808-259-7373; www.sealifeparkhawaii.com.

Across the road from Sea Life Park spreads **Makapuu Beach Park**, another fabled but daunting bodysurfing spot that is set in a particularly pretty location. Nearby black lava cliffs are topped by a white lighthouse and **Rabbit Island** is anchored just offshore. Rabbit Island, located off Makapuu Point, resembles a bunny's head, but was actually named for a former rabbit-raising farm there. Makapuu Beach itself is a short, wide rectangle of white sand. It's an ideal place to picnic, but when the surf is up, beware of the waves.

The road continues along the shoreline between soft sand beaches and rugged mountain peaks. For the next 30 miles your attention will be drawn back continually to those rocky crags. They are part of the **Koolau Range**, a wall of precipitous mountains that vault up from Oahu's placid interior. Their spires, minarets and fluted towers are softened here and there by lush, green valleys, but never enough to detract from the sheer beauty and magnitude of the heights. Light and shade play games along their moss-covered surfaces, while rainbows hang suspended between the peaks. If wind and weather permit, you will see hang gliders dusting the cliffs as they sail from the mountains down to the distant beach.

The road continues through **Waimanalo**, an old ranching area that today has been turned to fruit and flower cultivation. Outside town you will see **Olomana Peak**. Favored by rock climbers, it is a double-barreled peak that seems to belong in the Swiss Alps.

**LODGING**

If you want to follow the footsteps of James Michener and hang out at Waimanalo Beach, you might consider tucking yourself into **Trade Winds Inn**. Here you'll find six bedrooms (most with a queen-size bed and ceiling fan) and a full bath, plus barbecue facilities, a billiard room, and use of a kitchen. ~ Waimanalo; 808-259-7792, 866-625-6946, fax 808-259-0203; www.beach househawaii.com, e-mail beachhousehawaii@aol.com. MODER-ATE TO DELUXE.

**Nalo Winds Bed & Breakfast** offers "a home away from home." There are three accommodations, each with private bath, queen-size beds, fresh flowers and ceiling fans; one suite sleeps up to six people. Ideal for families. Boogieboards, snorkeling gear, beach chairs and a barbecue round out the amenities. Fresh papaya grow on the trees, and for a lazy afternoon in the sun, sink into the hammock with a good book. For those who can't get away from it all, there's even internet access. ~ Hihimanu Street, Waimanalo; 808-224-6213, 866-625-6946, fax 808-524-0999; www.beachhousehawaii.com, e-mail beachhousehawaii@ aol.com. MODERATE.

**DINING**

Spotted along Oahu's southeastern shore are a couple of moderately priced restaurants (and an expensive but worthy one) that may prove handy if you're beachcombing or camping. All are located on or near Route 72 (Kalanianaole Highway).

You're bound to feel Eurocentric at the **Swiss Haus**, where the menu includes wienerschnitzel, bratwurst and, for non-meat lovers, vegetarian pasta. On the dessert menu you'll find Swiss chocolate mousse, peach melba and fresh fruit tarts. The wood-paneled Old World look features pictures of villages that make you yearn for the Matterhorn. Closed Monday. ~ Niu Valley Shopping Center, 5730 Kalanianaole Highway; 808-377-5447, fax

808-377-1151; e-mail swisshausllc@juno.com. MODERATE TO DELUXE.

**Dave's Ice Cream** scoops up gourmet ice cream in flavors like azuki bean, cotton candy and *poha*, made from gooseberries grown on the Big Island. It also serves guava and passion fruit sherbet, among many other selections. ~ 41-1537 Kalanianaole Highway, Waimanalo; 808-259-0356. BUDGET.

**Keneke's** has breakfasts, plate lunches and sandwiches at greasy-spoon prices. No gourmet's delight, this tiny eatery is well placed for people enjoying Waimanalo's beaches. ~ 41-857 Kalanianaole Highway, Waimanalo; 808-259-5266. BUDGET.

◀ HIDDEN

A convenient place to shop in Oahu's southeast corner is at the Koko Marina Shopping Center's **Foodland**. ~ 7192 Kalanianaole Highway, Hawaii Kai; 808-395-3131. Proceeding north along the coast, there's **Mel's Market**, a small store in Waimanalo. Its crowded aisles contain a cornucopia of Hawaii's culinary ingredients, from *kim chi* and cream cheese to ahi tuna and tempura batter. ~ 41-1029 Kalanianaole Highway, Waimanalo; 808-259-7550.

**GROCERIES**

There aren't many places on Oahu more Hawaiian than Waimanalo, so **Naturally Hawaiian** fits the landscape nicely. Featuring fine art and homemade gifts, the shop sells *puka*-shell necklaces, *koa* wood pieces, prints and paintings, and Hawaiian commemorative stamps. ~ 41-1025 Kalanianaole Highway, Waimanalo; 808-259-5354; www.naturallyhawaiian.com.

**SHOPPING**

**HANAUMA BAY NATURE PRESERVE** One of Oahu's prettiest and most popular beaches, this curving swath of white sand extends for almost a half-mile. The bottom of the bay is a maze of coral reef, and the entire area has been designated a ma-

**BEACHES & PARKS**

**AUTHOR FAVORITE**

Tucked away in unassuming fashion in a business park is one of my favorite dining spots. You'll have to travel all the way to Hawaii Kai, several miles east of Waikiki, to find **Roy's Restaurant**. It is, to say the least, ultracontemporary, from the magazine clips framed on the walls to the cylindrical fish tank near the door. One of the most innovative of Hawaii's Pacific Rim cuisine dining rooms, it specializes in fresh local ingredients. Wildly popular, so reserve in advance. Dinner only. ~ 6600 Kalanianaole Highway, Hawaii Kai; 808-396-7697, fax 808-396-8706; www.roysrestaurant.com, e-mail honolulu@roysrestaurant.com. DELUXE TO ULTRA-DELUXE.

rine preserve; fishing is strictly prohibited. As a result, the skin-diving is unmatched and the fish are tame enough to eat from your hand. (Just beware of "Witch's Brew," a turbulent area on the bay's right side, and the "Molokai Express," a wicked current sweeping across the mouth of the bay.) You can also hike along rock ledges fringing the bay and explore some mind-boggling tidepools. Crowded though it is, this is one strand that should not be bypassed. Get here early—the beach closes at 7 p.m. (it opens at 6 a.m.), and once the parking lot fills up, entrance to the park is cut off. Facilities include a picnic area, restrooms, showers, a snack bar, snorkeling equipment rentals and lifeguards. Closed Tuesday. Parking fee, $1; nonresident day-use fee, $5 per person. ~ Located about nine miles east of Waikiki. Take Kalanianaole Highway (Route 72) to Koko Head, then turn onto the side road near the top of the promontory. This leads to a parking lot; leave your vehicle and walk the several hundred yards down the path to the beach. ~ 808-396-4229.

Ihiihilauakea Preserve is a 30-acre site above Hanauma Bay protected by the Nature Conservancy. A dry dusty crater in summer, the preserve is home to the rare *Marsilea villosa* fern, which lies dormant until the wet weather.

HIDDEN ►

**HALONA COVE BEACH** This is the closest you'll find to a hidden beach near Honolulu. It's a patch of white sand wedged between Halona Point and the Halona Blowhole lookout. Located directly below Kalanianaole Highway (Route 72), this is not exactly a wilderness area. But you can still escape the crowds massed on the nearby beaches. Swimming and snorkeling are good when the sea is gentle but extremely dangerous if it's rough. Prime catches are *ulua*, *papio* and *mamao*. There are no facilities. ~ Stop at the Halona Blowhole parking lot on Kalanianaole Highway (Route 72), about ten miles east of Waikiki. Follow the path from the right side of the lot down to the beach.

**SANDY BEACH** This long, wide beach is a favorite among Oahu's youth. The shorebreak makes it one of the finest, and most dangerous, bodysurfing beaches in the islands. Surfing is good and very popular but beware of rip currents. Lifeguards are on duty. It's a pleasant place to sunbathe, but if you go swimming, plan to negotiate a pounding shoreline. Anglers try for *ulua*, *papio* and *mamao*. There are picnic areas, restrooms and showers. Should you want to avoid the crowds, head over to **Wawamalu Beach Park** next door to the east. ~ Head out on Kalanianaole Highway (Route 72) about 12 miles east of Waikiki.

**MAKAPUU POINT STATE WAYSIDE** This state park encompasses Makapuu Beach, lookout and the lighthouse that overlooks the east Oahu coast. The mile-long asphalted trail leading to the lighthouse has become a popular family excursion; you can take the trail's uphill segments at a leisurely pace. The heat can be draining by midday, so a morning or afternoon hike is recommended, particularly on weekends when crowds abound. Panoramic views are the reward, with brisk tradewinds likely. The two islands offshore nearby are bird sanctuaries. The large one is known as Rabbit Island. The Hawaiians call it Manana Island, which means to stretch out or protrude. ~ Off Kalanianaole Highway between Sandy Beach and Makapuu Lookout.

**MAKAPUU BEACH PARK** Makapuu is set in a very pretty spot with lava cliffs in the background and Rabbit Island just offshore. This short, wide rectangle of white sand is Hawaii's most famous bodysurfing beach. With no protecting reef and a precipitous shoreline, Makapuu is inundated by awesome swells that send wave riders crashing onto shore. Necks and backs are broken with frightening regularity here, so if the waves are large and you're inexperienced—play the spectator. If you take the plunge, prepare for a battering! Snorkeling is usually poor and surfing is not permitted here. Common catches are *ulua*, *papio* and *mamao*. The only facilities are restrooms and a lifeguard. ~ Located on Kalanianaole Highway (Route 72) about 13 miles east of Waikiki.

**WAIMANALO BEACH PARK AND WAIMANALO BAY BEACH PARK** Located at the southeast end of Waimanalo's three-and-a-half-mile-long beach is a spacious 38-acre park. It's studded with ironwood trees and equipped with numerous recreation facilities including a playground, a basketball court and a baseball field. Waimanalo Beach Park and Waimanalo Bay Beach Park, a mile farther north, are both excellent spots for picnicking, swimming, snorkeling, bodysurfing and sunbathing. The latter is farther removed from the highway in a grove of ironwood trees known to local residents as "Sherwood Forest." Waimanalo is a good place to fish for *papio*, bonefish, milkfish and goatfish. There are picnic areas, restrooms and showers at both. ~ Waimanalo Beach Park is located at 41-741 Kalanianaole Highway (Route 72) about 15 miles east of Waikiki. Waimanalo Bay Beach Park is on Aloiloi Street a mile farther north.

▲ A county permit required at both of the parks for tent and trailer camping.

**BELLOWS FIELD BEACH PARK** One of Oahu's ◄ *HIDDEN* prettiest parks, Bellows is a broad white-sand beach bordered by ironwood trees and a marvelous view of the Koolau mountains. It's a great place for swimming and snorkeling and it's also a good surf spot for beginners; fishing usually rewards with *papio*, bonefish and goatfish. Sounds great, huh? The catch is that Bellows Park is situated on a military base and is open to visitors only from Friday noon until 8 a.m. Monday. Facilities include a picnic area, showers, a restroom and a lifeguard. ~ Turn off Kalanianaole Highway (Route 72) toward Bellows Air Force Station.

The park is located near Waimanalo, about 17 miles east of Waikiki.

▲ County permit required.

## Windward Coast

Named for the trade winds that blow with soothing predictability from the northeast, this sand-rimmed shoreline lies on the far side of the *pali* from Honolulu. Between these fluted emerald cliffs and the turquoise ocean are the bedroom communities of Lanikai, Kailua and Kaneohe and the agricultural regions of the Waiahole and Waikane valleys. As suburbs give way to small farms, this florid region provides a relaxing transition between the busy boulevards of Honolulu and the wild surf of the North Shore.

**SIGHTS**

HIDDEN ►

From the southeastern corner of the island, the Kalanianaole Highway flows into **Kailua**, where it intersects with Route 61, or Kailua Road. If you go right for a quarter of a mile along this road you will encounter **Ulupo Heiau** (it's behind the YMCA). According to Hawaiian legend, this temple (which stands 30 feet high and measures 150 feet in length) was built by *Menehunes*, who passed the building stones across a six-mile-long bucket brigade in a one-night construction project.

A slight detour down Route 61 toward the Pacific will bring you to one of Oahu's premier neighborhoods—**Lanikai**—and one of its most beautiful beaches—**Lanikai Beach**. Actually, Lanikai has one of the world's best beaches. The sand is powder-fine; palm trees sway in the wind, providing enough shade to make for ideal sunbathing; and the water, protected by an offshore reef, is the color of Indian turquoise.

Offshore are two small islands, **Moku Iki** and **Moku Nui**, bird sanctuaries known as the **Mokuluas**. Moku Iki is off-limits, but you can kayak (or swim) out to dry, barren Moku Nui from Lanikai Beach; you'll find a fine-sand beach, where hundreds of birds will probably be your only company. The strand where you disembark from your kayak has a unique feature—the waves come from both sides of the island and create an enormous clashing sound. Around the back of the island is a little cove where people often swim, though the currents can be dangerous and the surf quite high, so be cautious.

Heading back to the main highway, you will find that Route 72 immediately merges into Route 61, which then continues for two miles to Route 83, the Kamehameha Highway. Above this thoroughfare, spreading across more than 400 acres at the foot of the *pali* is **Hoomaluhia Botanical Garden**, a relaxing nature conservancy. With sheer cliffs rising on one side and a panoramic ocean view opening in the distance, it is a special place indeed. There is a 32-acre lake (no swimming) as well as a visitors center

# Windward Coast

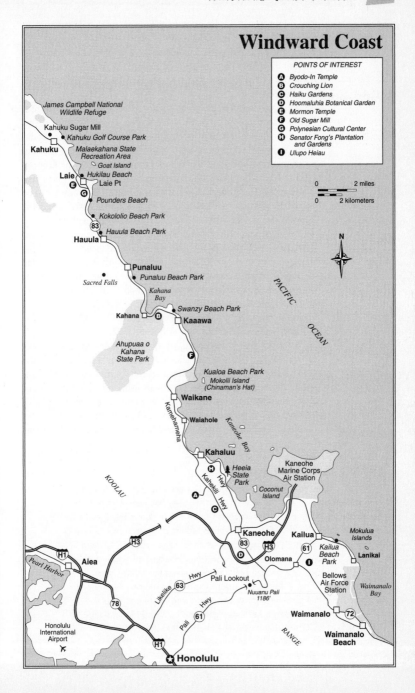

**POINTS OF INTEREST**

- **A** Byodo-In Temple
- **B** Crouching Lion
- **C** Haiku Gardens
- **D** Hoomaluhia Botanical Garden
- **E** Mormon Temple
- **F** Old Sugar Mill
- **G** Polynesian Cultural Center
- **H** Senator Fong's Plantation and Gardens
- **I** Ulupo Heiau

0       2 miles

0       2 kilometers

N

James Campbell National Wildlife Refuge

Kahuku Sugar Mill

**Kahuku**

Kahuku Golf Course Park

Malaekahana State Recreation Area

Goat Island

**Laie**

Hukilau Beach

Laie Pt

Pounders Beach

Kokololio Beach Park

Hauula Beach Park

**Hauula**

**Punaluu**

Punaluu Beach Park

Sacred Falls

Kahana Bay

Swanzy Beach Park

**Kahana**

**Kaaawa**

Ahupuaa o Kahana State Park

Kualoa Beach Park

Mokolii Island (Chinaman's Hat)

**Waikane**

**Waiahole**

Kaneohe Bay

Kamehameha

**Kahaluu**

Heeia State Park

Kaneohe Marine Corps Air Station

Kahekili Hwy

Coconut Island

PACIFIC OCEAN

KOOLAU

H3

**Kaneohe**

**Kailua**

Mokulua Islands

Kailua Beach Park

**Lanikai**

H1

**Aiea**

Pearl Harbor

83

Likelike

Hwy

63

Pali Lookout

Olomana

Bellows Air Force Station

Waimanalo Bay

78

Pali

Hwy

61

Nuuanu Pali 1186'

**Waimanalo**

72

Honolulu International Airport

RANGE

H1

**Honolulu**

**Waimanalo Beach**

and hiking trails. Camping is available on weekends (permit required—get one at the garden office, which is closed Sunday). The fruits, flowers and trees include hundreds of species native to Hawaii as well as tropical regions around the world. ~ Off Route 83 at the end of Luluku Road, Kaneohe; 808-233-7323, fax 808-233-7326.

The Kahekili Highway will also carry you to the graceful **Haiku Gardens**, located just outside Kailua. Formerly a private estate, the gardens rest in a lovely spot with a lofty rockface backdrop. Within this preserve are acres of exotic plant life, including an enchanting lily pond as well as numerous species of flowers. Hawaii specializes in beautiful gardens; the frequent rains and lush terrain make for luxuriant growing conditions. This happens to be one of the prettiest gardens of all. ~ 46-336 Haiku Road, Kaneohe; 808-247-6671, fax 808-247-5886; www.haikugardens.com.

An alternate route through Kailua and Kaneohe will carry you near the water, though the only really pretty views of Kaneohe Bay come near the end. Simply follow North Kalaheo Avenue through Kailua, then pick up Kaneohe Bay Drive, and turn right on Route 836, which curves for miles before linking with Route 83. At Heeia Kea Boat Harbor on Route 836, you can take an hour-long glass-bottom boat ride aboard the **Coral Queen**. Closed Sunday. ~ 808-235-2192, fax 808-236-0722.

**Kaneohe Bay** is renowned for its coral formations and schools of tropical fish that are as brilliantly colored as the coral. This expansive body of water possesses the only barrier reef in Hawaii. Along its shores are **ancient Hawaiian fishponds**, rock-bound enclosures constructed by the early Polynesians to raise fresh seafood. Though they once lined the shores of Oahu, today only a quarter (about 100) remain in usable condition. Several rest along this

**AUTHOR FAVORITE**

*sights*

The **Valley of the Temples** is a verdant chasm folded between the mountains and the sea. Part of the valley has been consecrated as a cemetery honoring the Japanese. Highlighting the region is the **Byodo-In Temple**. Rimmed by 2000-foot cliffs, this Buddhist shrine is a replica of a 900-year-old temple in Kyoto, Japan. It was constructed in 1968 in memory of the first Japanese immigrants to settle in Hawaii. The simple architecture is enhanced by a bronze bell weighing seven tons that visitors are permitted to ring. A statue of Buddha dominates the site. Walk along the placid reflecting pool with its swans, ducks and multihued carp and you will be drawn a million miles away from the bustle of Honolulu. Admission. ~ 47-200 Kahekili Highway, Kaneohe; 808-239-8811.

Windward Coast. One of the largest is located near Heeia State Park. It's an impressive engineering feat that measures 500 feet in length and once contained an 88-acre fish farm. The stone walls in places are 12 feet thick. ~ Located along Kamehameha Highway (Route 836), a few hundred yards before it merges with Route 83.

Continuing along Route 836 you'll come to **Heeia State Park**, a small greensward located on Kealohi Point, anchored by a lighthouse. Kealohi Point was a significant spot for ancient Hawaiians: it was thought to be a jumping-off point of the soul into the spirit world. This park is a perfect spot for a picnic with lovely views of the bay and the ancient fishpond. Offshore you'll see **Coconut Island**, made famous in the opening of TV's "Gilligan's Island." Adjacent to the park is **Heeia Kai Boat Harbor**.

High above Kaneohe, gazing down upon the bay, is **Senator Fong's Plantation and Gardens**. Here you can take a narrated tram tour of 725 acres of gardens and orchards. This luxurious preserve was donated by one of Hawaii's most famous U.S. senators, so be prepared to venture from Eisenhower Valley to Kennedy Valley (sugar cane) to the Johnson Plateau (fruit orchards) to Nixon Valley (gardens) to the Ford Plateau (pine trees). Admission. ~ 47-285 Pulama Road, Kaneohe; 808-239-6775.

Route 83 soon becomes known as the Kamehameha Highway as it courses past lazy fishing boats then enters **Waiahole Valley** and **Waikane Valley**, some of the last places on the island where Hawaiian farmers grow crops in the traditional way. Fruit stands line the highway. The roads off the highway lead to small Hawaiian enclaves, where you'll see taro patches and papaya trees in the backyards.

That cone-shaped island offshore is **Chinaman's Hat**. It was named for its resemblance to a coolie cap, though the Hawaiians had another name for it long before the Chinese arrived in the islands. They called it Mokolii Island, or "little dragon," and claimed it represented the tail of a beast that resided under the water. Watch for frigate birds and delicate white-tailed tropical birds flying overhead.

Just down the road, the **Old Sugar Mill**, Oahu's first, lies in ruin along the side of the road. Built during the 1860s, it fell into disuse soon after completion and has since served only as a local curiosity.

Continuing along you'll pass the community of **Kaaawa** and **Swanzy Beach Park** (see "Beaches & Parks" section below). A few miles later be on the lookout for the Hawaii Visitors Bureau marker noting "**Crouching Lion**" (there's also a restaurant by the same name just below the mountain). To the ancient Hawaiians, who had never experienced the king of the jungle, the stone face was, in fact, that of Kauhi, a demigod from the island of Tahiti who was turned into stone during a struggle between Pele and her sister Hiiaka.

Next is the coral-studded **Kahana Bay**. Once the sight of a burgeoning Hawaiian fishing village, Kahana Bay is now a tranquil spot for a picnic or swim in the sea. Be sure to look out for **Huilua Fishpond**, the oldest of Oahu's many fishponds (it's currently being reconstructed). Across the highway is **Ahupuaa o Kahana State Park.** If you like to hike there's a trail up the valley through lush foliage that weaves past old farmsteads.

Then the highway, still crowding the coastline, traverses the roadside community of **Punaluu**, legendary home of the demigod Kamapuaa, one of Pele's lovers. There's a long, narrow strand of sand and ocean at **Punaluu Beach Park**, which offers pleasant swimming opportunities because of an offshore reef. (However, use caution when the weather is stormy.) The roadway continues up to the small town of **Hauula** with its old **Hauula Door of Faith Church,** a small chapel of clapboard design surrounded by palms. Not far from here is another aging woodframe sanctuary, **Hauula Congregational Christian Church**, built of wood and coral back in 1862.

*50 First Dates* (2004), *The Hulk* (2003), *Blue Crush* (2002) and *Pearl Harbor* (2001) are just a few of the movies that have been filmed on Oahu in recent years.

The nearby town of **Laie**, once thought to have been an ancient place of refuge for Hawaiians, is now a stronghold for Mormons. The Hawaii campus of **Brigham Young University** is located here, as well as the **Mormon Temple**. The Mormons settled here back in 1864; today there are about 55,000 in Hawaii. The courtyards and grounds of the temple are open to the public, but only Mormons are permitted to enter the temple sanctuary.

The Mormons also own Oahu's most popular tourist attraction, the **Polynesian Cultural Center**. Set right on Kamehameha Highway in Laie, it represents one of the foremost theme parks in the entire Pacific, a 42-acre attempt to re-create ancient Polynesia. As you wander about the grounds you'll encounter ersatz villages portraying life in the Marquesas, Tahiti, Fiji, Tonga, New Zealand and old Hawaii. Step over to the Tahitian hamlet and you will experience the rocking *tamure* dance. Or wander onto the islands of Samoa, where the local inhabitants demonstrate how to climb coconut trees. In Tonga a native will be beating tapa cloth from mulberry bark, while the Fijians are pounding rhythms with poles of bamboo. These mock villages are linked by waterways and can be visited in canoes. The boats will carry you past craftsmen preparing poi by mashing taro roots, and others husking coconuts.

The most popular shows are the "Pageant of the Long Canoes," in which the boats head up a lagoon amid a flurry of singing and dancing, and "Horizons." The latter is an evening show similar to Waikiki's Polynesian revues, though generally considered more elaborate. Most of the entertainers and other employees at this

Hawaiian-style Disneyland are Mormon students attending the local university. Closed Sunday. Admission. ~ 55-370 Kamehameha Highway, Laie; 808-293-3000, 888-722-7339; www.polynesia.com.

Be sure to take in the town's natural wonder, **Laie Point**. This headland provides extraordinary ocean views sweeping for miles along the shoreline. Since the breezes and surf are wilder here than elsewhere on the Windward Coast, you'll often encounter waves lashing at the two offshore islets with amazing force. The island with the hole in it is **Kukihoolua** or, as the locals call it, Puka Rock. ~ Head toward the ocean on Anemoku Street, off Kamehameha Highway, then turn right on Naupaka Street.

Along the oceanside, a few miles outside of Laie, hidden behind the vines hugging the road is **Malaekahana State Recreation Area** (see "Beaches & Parks" for added description). This gem of a park offers a long strand of white sand lined with ironwood trees. Offshore is **Goat Island**, or Mokuauia, a bird sanctuary you can actually wade over to when the tide is right (be sure to wear reef slippers or some such foot covering and be careful of the currents).

◄ HIDDEN

Out in the suburban town of Kailua, where trim houses front a beautiful white-sand beach, you'll discover **Pat's Kailua Beach Properties**. Overlooking Kailua Beach Park and about 100 yards from the beach sits a cluster of woodframe cottages. Each is equipped with a full kitchen, cable television and a telephone. Some of the furniture is nicked, but these units (from studios to five-bedroom homes) are clean and cozy. They sit in a yard shaded with monkeypod, coconut and breadfruit trees and provide an excellent value. ~ 204 South Kalaheo Avenue, Kailua; 808-262-4128, 808-261-1653, fax 808-261-0893; www.patskailua.com, e-mail pats.kailua@verizon.net. MODERATE.

**LODGING**

I don't recommend **Hawaii's Hidden Hideaway** just because of its name. It really is a lovely bed and breakfast, with lots of privacy. There are a suite and two studios available; the suite has an outdoor spa with an ocean view. All three have private entrances, parking and decks, and kitchenettes stocked with breakfast goodies. You're quite close to the beaches of Lanikai and Kailua, and a 30-minute or so drive to Waikiki. Three-night minimum stay—not that that will be difficult. ~ 1369 Mokolea Drive, Kailua; 808-262-6560, 877-443-3299, fax 808-262-6561; www.ahawaiibnb.com, e-mail hhhideaway@yahoo.com. MODERATE TO DELUXE.

You can't get much closer to the water than **Schrader's Windward Country Inn**. With about 50 units for rent, this unusual resting place consists of several woodframe buildings right on the edge of Kaneohe Bay. There are picnic tables, barbecue grills and a pool on the two-acre property, as well as a tour boat that can

◄ HIDDEN

take you snorkeling, kayaking or sightseeing on the bay. The guest rooms are cottage style with kitchenettes; many have lanais and bay views. Prices include continental breakfast. ~ 47-039 Lihikai Drive, Kaneohe; 808-239-5711, 800-735-5071, fax 808-239-6658; www.hawaiiscene.com/schrader, e-mail schrader@lava.net. MODERATE.

The **Ali'i Bluffs Bed & Breakfast** offers two rooms with private baths. The Victorian room features antiques and vintage paintings, while the Circus room has large circus posters, many of them originals, from around the world. This contemporary Hawaiian home has a shake roof and is furnished in antiques and Persian rugs. A full breakfast is served poolside every morning. ~ 46-251 Ikiiki Street, Kaneohe; 808-235-1124, 800-235-1151, fax 808-236-4877; www.hawaiiscene.com/aliibluffs, e-mail donm@lava.net. MODERATE.

The **Laie Inn** is a low-slung motel with two floors of rooms surrounding a swimming pool. This is a standard Coke-machine-in-the-courtyard facility located next to the Polynesian Cultural Center. ~ 55-109 Laniloa Street, Laie; 808-293-9282, 800-526-4562, fax 808-293-8115; www.laieinn.com, e-mail laieinn@hawaii.rr.com. MODERATE.

**DINING**    Kailua has a collection of eating establishments spread throughout the town. Among them is **Buzz's Original Steak House**, right across the street from the beach. The place is popular not only with windsurfers, but with Honolulu residents who drive out on the weekends to enjoy the surf and a meal at this upscale beach shack, which has been in business since 1962. Burgers, steaks and seafood are the specialties here, and all entrées include a trip to the salad bar at dinnertime. ~ 413 Kawailoa Road, Kailua; 808-261-4661. DELUXE.

Slide into a booth at **Times Coffee Shop**, where breakfast brings local favorites (Portuguese sausage omelettes, Spam and

---

### BIRDS OF A FEATHER

Featherwork, an ancient island art form, might be of concern to birders and other environmentally conscious visitors. Not to worry, you can appreciate the art form without too much guilt. Conscious of the fragility of their resources, Hawaiians used to trap birds by smearing branches with sticky sap. Once the birds were caught, they would pluck only the choicest feathers, clean the bird's claws and then release them. Passed down through the generations, this art form is practiced today by a handful of skilled artisans. A single feather lei may consist of as many as 2000 feathers.

eggs) and American classics (pancakes, waffles). Fried rice, hamburger steaks, grilled mahimahi and sandwiches make an appearance on the lunch menu. No dinner. ~ 153 Hamakua Street, Kailua; 808-262-0300. BUDGET.

**Saeng's Thai Cuisine** is a freshly decorated ethnic restaurant with a hardwood bar and potted plants all around. Located in a strip mall, it nevertheless conveys a sense of elegance. The menu focuses on vegetarian, seafood and curry dishes. No lunch on weekends. ~ 315 Kailua Road, Kailua; 808-263-9727. BUDGET TO MODERATE.

Known for years as a prime breakfast and lunch place, **Cinnamon's Restaurant** draws a local crowd, which sits beneath the dining room gazebo or out on the patio. The menu is best described as Continental cuisine with local flavors. Try the chicken cashew sandwich or the carrot pancakes—all made from scratch! No dinner Sunday through Wednesday. ~ Kailua Square Shopping Center, 315 Uluniu Street, Kailua; 808-261-8724, fax 808-262-9910; www.cinnamonsrestaurant.com, e-mail cinnamonrest@aol.com. MODERATE TO DELUXE.

◄ HIDDEN

Kailua residents will tell you the pastas at **Baci Bistro** are all homemade and beautifully prepared. You have the option of sitting in the small dining room with greenhouse windows or in the romantic covered lanai. There are veal and fish entrées, risotto dishes and an array of antipasti. No lunch on Saturday and Sunday. ~ 30 Aulike Street, Kailua; 808-262-7555, fax 808-261-2857; www.restauranteur.com. MODERATE TO DELUXE.

In Kaneohe you might like **Koa Omelette House**. It's a tastefully appointed restaurant with a breakfast bill of fare that includes pancakes and crêpes suzette and a lunch menu with salads, sandwiches, teriyaki chicken and seafood. ~ 46-126 Kahuhipa Street, Kaneohe; 808-235-5772. BUDGET.

What sets **Haleiwa Joe's Seafood Grill** apart is its idyllic setting. A terraced dining area overlooks sharp cliffs and peaceful flower beds, making this a choice stop for dinner. The menu consists of steak, seafood and prime rib with a Pan-Asian influence. Dinner only. ~ 46-336 Haiku Road, Kaneohe; 808-247-6671, fax 808-247-5886; www.haleiwajoes.com. MODERATE TO DELUXE.

The setting is the draw at the **Crouching Lion Inn**, a vintage 1927 wood-shingle house at the foot of verdant mountains. The food isn't remarkable—sandwiches and hamburgers, rotisserie chicken, mahimahi and teriyaki steak for lunch and a surf-and-turf menu at dinner. But the beautiful ocean view makes it a worthy stop. One drawback: It's popular with tour buses, so try to arrive at an off-hour. ~ 51-666 Kamehameha Highway, Kaaawa; 808-237-8511, fax 808-237-7061; www.honolulurestaurantguide.com/crouchinglion. DELUXE TO ULTRA-DELUXE.

**GROCERIES**    In Kailua and Kaneohe, you'll encounter large supermarkets. In the Kailua Shopping Center there's **Times Supermarket**. ~ Kailua Road, Kailua; 808-266-4004. **Foodland** is in the Windward City Shopping Center. ~ At Kamehameha Highway and Kaneohe Bay Drive, Kaneohe; 808-247-3357.

Between these major shopping complexes there are smaller facilities such as the **7-11**. ~ 51-484 Kamehameha Highway, Kaaawa; 808-237-8810.

You can get fresh fish at **Masa and Joyce Fish Market** in the Temple Valley Shopping Center. ~ Kahekili Highway (Route 83), just north of Kaneohe; 808-235-6129.

There's a large **Foodland** grocery store in the Laie Village Shopping Center. Closed Sunday. ~ Kamehameha Highway, Laie; 808-293-4443.

**SHOPPING**    Shopping in the Windward Coast is not a major activity. Kailua and Kaneohe both have large shopping centers but the stores are not noteworthy. There are, however, a few places to stop by and browse.

**Island Treasures Art Gallery** offers an exceptional collection of pottery, wooden boxes, jewelry, paintings, handcrafted wooden furniture, shell candles and etched glass with island designs, all created by artists living in Hawaii. ~ 629 Kailua Road, Suite 103, Kailua; 808-261-8131.

The **Livingston Galleries** at the Crouching Lion Inn sells original paintings and prints by local and international artists, as well as estate jewelry, sculpture and handcrafted gift items. ~ 51-666 Kamehameha Highway, Kaaawa; 808-237-7165.

The nearby **Lance Fairly Gallery** has original paintings by local artists, limited-edition prints and enameled tropical fish. ~ 53-839 Kamehameha Highway, Punaluu; 808-293-9009; www.lancefairly.com.

**NIGHTLIFE**    Nights on the Windward Coast are quiet and peaceful, and most people like it that way. For those who prefer a bit of action, however, head to Kailua, where there's always something going on at **Board Riders Bar and Grill**. This sports bar has a pool table and dart boards; on the weekends there are dance tunes from reggae to rock. Occasional cover on Friday and Saturday. ~ 201 Hamakua Drive #A, Kailua; 808-261-4600.

**BEACHES & PARKS**    **KAILUA BEACH** 🏖 🚻 ⚓ Stretching for two miles with white sand all the way and tiny islands offshore, this is one of the prettiest beaches around. It's in the suburban town of Kailua, so you'll trade seclusion for excellent beach facilities. The center of activity is **Kailua Beach Park**, at the end of Kailua Road near the south end of the beach. This 30-acre facility has a grassy expanse shaded by ironwood and coconut trees and perfect for picnicking. There are restrooms and a pavilion with a snack bar. **Kalama Beach County Park**, a small park with restrooms in the middle of Kailua Beach, is less crowded. Swimming, surfing and bodysurfing are good all along the strand and windsurfing is excellent, but exercise caution. ~ You can access Kailua Beach via side streets off Kalaheo Avenue; Kalama Beach County Park is located at 250 North Kalaheo Avenue.

**LANIKAI BEACH** Everyone's dream house is on the beach at Lanikai. This sandy stretch, varying from 20 to 100 feet in width, extends for over a mile. The entire beach in this residential community is lined with those houses everybody wants. The water is the color of cobalt and the protecting reef offshore makes the entire beach safe for swimming. Lanikai has also become a windsurfing favorite. No facilities; the nearest facilities are at Kailua Beach. ~ The strand parallels Mokulua Drive in Lanikai, which in turn is reached by driving south along the beachfront roads in Kailua.

Those beautiful Hawaiian quilts you see are not generally used for snuggling under. Instead, they serve as an expression of historical events and are often gifts of aloha.

**HEEIA STATE PARK** This small pocket park located off of Kamehameha Highway at Kealohi Point is an ideal spot to picnic when traveling around the island. The views of Kaneohe Bay and the ancient Hawaiian fishpond are noteworthy. Numerous indigenous plants thrive here and there are educational programs offered by Friends of Heeia State Park. In addition, there's a pavilion, picnic tables and restrooms. ~ Route 836 (Kamehameha Highway) just outside of Kaneohe.

**KUALOA BEACH PARK** You could search the entire Pacific for a setting as lovely as this one. Just 500 yards offshore lies the islet of Mokolii, better known as Chinaman's Hat. Behind the beach the *pali* creates a startling background of fluted cliffs and tropical forest. The beach is a long and narrow strip of sand paralleled by a wide swath of grass parkland. Little wonder this is one of the Windward Coast's most popular picnic areas. It's also a favorite for swimming, snorkeling and fishing (common catches are *papio*, bonefish, milkfish and goatfish). Facilities include picnic areas, restrooms and showers. ~ 49-479 Kamehameha Highway (Route 83) about ten miles north of Kaneohe.

△ Tent camping permitted. County permit required.

**SWANZY BEACH PARK, PUNALUU BEACH PARK AND HAUULA BEACH PARK** These three county facilities lie along Kamehameha Highway (Route 83) within seven miles of each other. Swimming is generally good at each. Along this coast the most abundant fish is *papio*, followed by bonefish, milkfish and goatfish. Camping is allowed at all except Punaluu, but none compare aesthetically with other beaches to the north and south. Swanzy (open weekends only) is located on the highway but lacks a sandy beach. However, it has the best diving. Its surf break, "Crouching Lion," is for experts only; Punaluu, though possessing a pretty palm-fringed beach, is cramped; and Hauula, a spacious park with a beach and a winter surf break for beginners, is visited periodically by tour buses. So put these beach parks near the bottom of your list, and bring them up only if the other beaches are too crowded. All three beaches have picnic areas and restrooms. ~ These parks are all located along Kamehameha Highway (Route 83). Swanzy lies about 12 miles north of Kaneohe, Punaluu is about four miles north of Swanzy, and Hauula is about three miles beyond that.

Check out the orientation center at Ahupuaa o Kahana State Park. Besides its many natural features, cultural resources within the park include Huilua Fishpond and an ancient fishing shrine and lookout.

▲ Tent and trailer camping allowed at Hauula Beach Park, as well as at Swanzy Beach Park on weekends. A county permit is required.

**AHUPUAA O KAHANA STATE PARK** 🏃 🏊 ↩ This 5228-acre paradise, set on a white-sand beach, offers something for every adventurer. You can pick fruit in a lush forest, picnic in a coconut grove and sightsee an ancient fishpond. You can also fish for *papio*, bonefish, milkfish and goatfish. Swimming is generally good. Surfing is a possibility but is mediocre at best. There are picnic areas and restrooms. ~ 52-222 Kamehameha Highway (Route 83) about 14 miles north of Kaneohe.

▲ There's tent camping on the beach; $5 per night. No camping on Thursday. State permit required; 808-587-0300, fax 808-587-0311; www.hawaii.gov/dlnr/dsp.

**KOKOLOLIO BEACH PARK** 🏊 🏃 ↩ Here's one of the prettiest beaches on the Windward Coast. With trees and a lawn that extends toward the white-sand beach, it's a highly recommended spot for day-tripping. It's also a good beach for swimming and bodysurfing and in winter there are breaks up to six feet, with right and left slide. Common catches include *papio*, bonefish, goatfish and milkfish. There are picnic areas and restrooms. ~ 55-017 Kamehameha Highway (Route 83) in Laie about 20 miles north of Kaneohe.

▲ Camping allowed with county permit.

**POUNDERS BEACH** 🏊 ↩ Named for the crushing shorebreak that makes it a popular bodysurfing beach, this quarter-mile-long strand features a corridor of white sand and a sandy bottom. Swimming is good near the old landing at the western end of the beach. Be careful of currents when swimming anywhere along the beach. Anglers try for *ono*, *moi* and *papio*. There are no facilities here. ~ Located along Kamehameha Highway north of Kakela Beach.

**HUKILAU BEACH**  This privately owned facility fronts a beautiful white-sand beach that winds for more than a mile. Part of the beach is lined with homes, but much of it is undeveloped. Several small islands lie offshore, and the park contains a lovely stand of ironwood trees. All in all this enchanting beach is one of the finest on this side of the island. Swimming is good; bodysurfing is also recommended. Snorkeling is usually fair and there are small surfable waves with left and right slides. The principal catch is *papio*; milkfish, bonefish and goatfish are also caught. There are no facilities here. ~ Located on Kamehameha Highway (Route 83) in Laie about 22 miles north of Kaneohe.

**MALAEKAHANA STATE RECREATION AREA AND GOAT ISLAND** ◄ *HIDDEN*
 This is a rare combination. The Malaekahana facility is one of the island's prettiest parks. It's a tropical wonderland filled with palm, *hala* and ironwood trees, and graced with a curving, white-sand beach. Goat Island lies just offshore. When the tide is right you can wade out to it. Other times, grab a boogie board or surf board and paddle out with a picnic lunch. It's a small, low-lying island covered with scrub growth and scattered ironwood trees. On the windward side is a coral beach; to leeward lies a crescent-shaped white-sand beach. It's a good place to swim because it is shallow and well-protected. There are also good places for snorkeling and, in winter, you can paddle out to a break with a left slide. Feel like fishing? You may well reel in *papio*, the most abundant fish along here; goatfish, milkfish and bonefish are also caught. Goat Island is now a state bird refuge, so you might see wedge-tailed shearwaters nesting. Whatever activity you choose, make sure you don't disturb the birds. Goat Island will return the favor—there'll be nothing here to disturb you either. Facilities include showers, bathrooms and barbecue pits. ~ Located on Kamehameha Highway (Route 83) in Laie about 23 miles north of Kaneohe.

▲ There are two sections to the park. The Laie section includes Goat Island and is administered by the state. The Kahuku section (Puuhonua o Malaekahana, or Place of Refuge) is operated by the Friends of Malaekahana, the first native Hawaiian group to operate a park in the islands.

*Laie Section*: Tent camping allowed. State permit required.

*Kahuku Section*: There are rustic cabins available here. These beachfront units include 40 campsites and 7 beach cabins —6 beach houses with two or three bedrooms, private baths and kitchens ($80 per night on weekends)—and a six-room cabin with a game room and a commercial kitchen ($250 per night). There are seven yurts that sleep two to six people ($40 to $60 per night). Tent sites are $5 to $20 per person, per night. Cabins are equipped with beds, kitchen facilities and bathrooms. Bring your own bedding and cooking gear and be prepared for rustic accommodations. For information or reservations, call 808-293-1736, fax 808-293-2066.

**KAHUKU GOLF COURSE PARK** Other than Goat Island, this is about the closest you'll come to a hidden beach on the Windward Coast. Granted, there's a golf course paralleling the strand, but sand dunes hide you from the duffers. The beach is long, wide and sandy white. Swimming is fair, but exercise caution. In winter, surfers work the "Seventh Hole" breaks, which reach up to eight feet and have a right and left slide. *Papio*, bonefish, goatfish and milkfish are common catches. There are restrooms at the golf course. ~ In Kahuku, about 25 miles north of Kaneohe, turn off Kamehameha Highway (Route 83) toward the ocean. Park at the golf course, then walk the gated road to the beach.

**North Shore**

Wide, wide beaches heaped with white, white sand roll for miles along the North Shore, which curves from Kahuku Point in the east to Kaena Point in the west. Although they can compete with the most beautiful beaches anywhere, it's not the sand or their size that is the main attraction here. Rather it is the winter waves, and these waves have made Oahu's North Shore legendary. Surfers come from around the world to try their skill at one of the world's best spots for the sport.

If you have ever owned a surfboard, or even a Beach Boys album, you know Waimea Bay and Sunset Beach. The names are synonymous with surfing. They number among the most challenging and dangerous surf spots anywhere. During the winter, 15- to 20-foot waves are as common as blond hair and beach buggies. The infamous "Banzai Pipeline," where surfers risk limb and longevity as thunderous waves pass over a shallow reef, is here as well.

Not only is the surf superb, the setting is stunning. Oahu's two mountain ranges form the backdrop, while 4025-foot Mt. Kaala, the island's highest peak, towers above all. Small ranches and farms checkerboard the tableland between the mountains and the sea. The old-time farmers, the surfers and the counterculture types who live in the area all come to Haleiwa for shopping, dining and socializing. Haleiwa, a restored plantation town with old clapboard buildings and wooden sidewalks, preserves the spirit of a rural way of life that is rapidly disappearing.

The plantations that established Oahu's economic base have all closed. In fact, the last sugar mill on the island, located in the North Shore town of Waialua, shut down in 1996, marking the

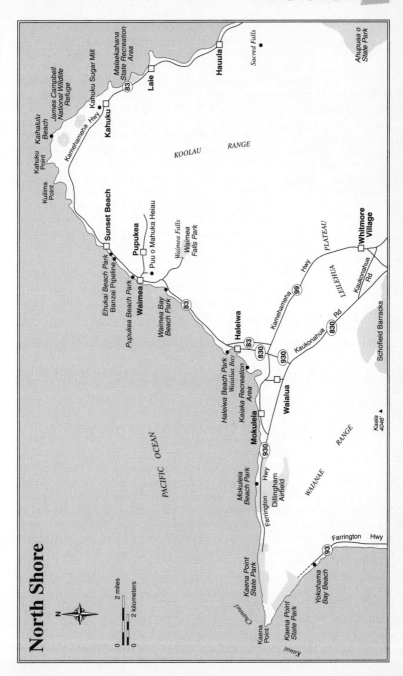

# North Shore

N

0 ___ 2 miles
0 ___ 2 kilometers

KOOLAU RANGE

James Campbell National Wildlife Refuge

Kahuku Sugar Mill

Malaekahana State Recreation Area

Kahalulu Beach

Kahuku Point

Kuilima Point

Kahuku

Kamehameha Hwy

Laie

Hauula

Sacred Falls

Ahupuaa o State Park

Sunset Beach

Pupukea

Puu o Mahuka Heiau

Waimea Falls

Waimea Falls Park

Ehukai Beach Park
Banzai Pipeline

Waimea

Pupukea Beach Park

Waimea Bay Beach Park

Haleiwa

PACIFIC OCEAN

Haleiwa Beach Park
Waialua Bay

Kaiaka Recreation Area

Mokuleia

Mokuleia Beach Park

Farrington Hwy

Dillingham Airfield

Kaena Point State Park

Kawai Channel

Kaena Point

Kaena Point State Park

Kawai

Yokohama Bay Beach

Farrington Hwy

Whitmore Village

LEILEHUA PLATEAU

Kamehameha Hwy

Kaukonahua Rd

Kaukonahua Rd

Schofield Barracks

Waialua

WAIANAE RANGE

Kaala 4046'

end of a major chapter in Oahu's history. Although the Waialua Sugar Company now no longer processes cane, this low-key village west of Haleiwa still has the feel of a sugar town. The mill, which stands at its center, and the Sugar Bar, a bar and pizza place in the old Bank of Hawaii building, serve as reminders of a past that just yesterday was the present.

As the hub of sugar production has shifted to other areas of the world, the farmers of Oahu have filled the vacuum. Coffee experienced a bum crop when it was first planted here in the early 1800s. Locals gave it a more successful try in 1825, however, and it's now experiencing a production boom. The soil and climate of this island lend themselves to excellent crops of the beans, which thrive in moist soil rich in the organic matter of volcanic rock and leaf mold. The land near Waialua, the sleepy little sugar plantation town, is ideal for coffee production: the absorbent soil is loose enough to drain excess water, and the temperature and elevation further the perfect conditions. The sorghum and wiliwili trees of the North Shore currently protect the crop; ultimately, the recently planted Norfolk pines will become the primary guardian against wind damage to the coffee trees.

One of Hawaii's ancient traditions is namegiving. Hawaiians believe the future of a child rests upon the name selected by his or her Hawaiian name giver.

**SIGHTS**

The main road along the North Shore begins with the small town of **Kahuku**. This is where many residents call home. For a taste of the rural Hawaii of old, take a detour into this little village. Kahuku is also the home of the **Kahuku Sugar Mill**, a turn-of-the-20th-century plant. In an effort to refurbish the old mill, the entire complex was turned into a shopping mall. The place has been struggling for years, and the shops never quite made it, but you will find a restaurant there.

**HIDDEN ▶**

Facilitating the recovery of four endangered bird species—the black-necked Hawaiian stilt, Hawaiian moorhen, Hawaiian coot and Hawaiian duck—is the **James Campbell National Wildlife Refuge** in Kahuku. Two units comprise this 142-acre reserve: the Punamaoo Pond is a spring-fed marsh; the Kii Unit is made up of former sugar cane waste–settling basins. Free guided tours of the wetlands are offered October to mid-February. Reservations required. ~ 66-590 Kamehameha Highway, Haleiwa; 808-637-6330 ext. 40.

As you continue along the highway you will skirt **Kaihalulu Beach**, which continues out to **Kahuku Point**, the northernmost point on Oahu. The current here is strong and the rocky bottom makes swimming difficult, but it is a wonderful spot to spend the afternoon beachcombing. The road then makes a bend past **Kuilima Cove**, the windswept white-sand strand fronting the Turtle Bay Resort.

Roadside vendors at locations along the way sell sweet corn, watermelon, papaya, mango and tropical flowers from local farms and gardens, fresh-caught fish and shrimp from the area's aquaculture ponds. You'll get a warm welcome and a chance to "talk story" with the locals as well as the opportunity to enjoy some of Hawaii's natural treasures.

Stretching for two miles and averaging 200 feet in width, Sunset Beach (Kamehameha Highway) is one of Hawaii's largest strands. While Sunset Beach is actually only a single surfing spot, the name has become synonymous with a two-mile-long corridor that includes Banzai Beach and the adjacent Pipeline. When the surf is up you can watch world-class athletes shoot the curl. When it's not, Sunset becomes a great place to swim. The best place to go is Ehukai Beach Park, just off Kamehameha Highway about seven miles northeast of Haleiwa. Just 100 yards to the west sits the Banzai Pipeline (Ke Nui Road), where a shallow coral shelf creates tubular waves so powerful and perfect they resemble pipes. First surfed in 1957, it lays claim to cracked skulls, lacerated legs and some of the sport's greatest feats.

On a plateau between Sunset Beach and Waimea Bay is Puu o Mahuka Heiau, Oahu's oldest temple. A split-level structure built of stone, it once was used for human sacrifices. Today you will encounter nothing more menacing than a spectacular view and perhaps a gentle breeze from the ocean. To get there from Kamehameha Highway, turn left near the Sunset Beach Fire Station onto Pupukea Road, then follow the Hawaii Visitors & Convention Bureau signs.

An altogether different religious site is St. Peter & Paul, a Catholic church. Built on a former rock-crushing plant, this quaint church, with its steeple constructed from the remaining rocks of the plant, seems to stand watch over Waimea Bay.

At Waimea Valley Audubon Center you can wander through a tropical preserve and cultural park stretching across 500 acres. Once a Hawaiian village, it is crisscrossed with hiking trails and archaeological ruins. Weather permitting, you can picnic and swim at Waimea Falls, or browse the arboretum featuring tropical and subtropical trees from around the world, beautiful botanical gardens including one local Hawaiian species. Then there are the birds that populate the complex; since this nature park serves as a bird sanctuary, it attracts a varied assortment. Activities for visitors include self-guided tours any time, or guided tours on Tuesday, Friday, Saturday and Sunday. Admission. ~ Kamehameha Highway, five miles northeast of Haleiwa; 808-638-9199, fax 808-638-9197; e-mail waimea@audubon.org.

Across the road looms Waimea Bay, another fabled place that sports the largest surfable waves in the world. When surf's up in winter, the monster waves that roll in are so big they make the ground tremble when they break. Salt spray reaches as far as the highway. Thirty-foot waves are not uncommon. Fifty-foot giants have been recorded; though unsurfable, these are not tidal waves, just swells rising along the incredible North Shore. In December, the Hawaiian Triple Crown—basically the Super Bowl of surfing— takes place. In summer, Waimea is a pretty blue bay with a white-sand beach. The water is placid and the area perfect for picnicking and sunbathing. So when you visit Waimea, remember: swim in summer, sunbathe in winter.

Next, the Kamehameha Highway crosses Anahula River and a double rainbow–shaped bridge en route to **Haleiwa**, an old plantation town with a new facelift. Fortunately, the designers who performed the surgery on this village had an eye for antiquity. They planned it so the modern shopping centers and other facilities blend comfortably into the rural landscape. The community that has grown up around the new town reflects a rare combination of past and future. The old Japanese, Filipinos and Hawaiians have been joined by blond-mopped surfers and laidback counterculturalists. As a result, this clapboard town with wooden sidewalks has established itself as the "in" spot on the North Shore. Its stylish nonchalance has also proved popular among canny travelers. Despite gentrification, Haleiwa holds on to its relaxed ambience. The surf scene still adds a definite style to Haleiwa.

The little church in town is named for the queen who used to summer on the shores of the nearby Anahulu River, Queen Liliuokalani. **Liliuokalani Protestant Church** dates back to the early 1800s, though the current building was constructed in the mid-1900s. If you have a chance to enter the church, take a look at the clock that was donated by the queen—it shows the phases of the moon as well as the hour, day, month and year.

**AUTHOR FAVORITE**

I'm a surfing enthusiast so I recommend checking out **North Shore Surf and Cultural Museum**. This surfing nook displays related artifacts, boards and old photographs of the local community, and has a mini-theater showing videos of the sport. It also temporarily houses items from an 1824 shipwreck, providing a safe haven for the items while the wreck is being excavated. There's jewelry for sale that was found by underwater metal detection. The museum's other claim to fame is its possession of the last two boards used by famed surfer Mark Foo before he was killed in a surfing accident in 1994. Closed Tuesday. ~ North Shore Marketplace, 66-250 Kamehameha Highway, Haleiwa; 808-637-8888; www.captainrick.com/surf_museum.htm.

A scenic detour takes you to the town of **Waialua**, a former sugar plantation town, via Haleiwa Road. There's not much to see here except the old **Waialua Sugar Mill**, which has been converted into office space. The mill closed its sugar operation in the mid-'90s and the cane fields around this area are being replanted with Waialua coffee. Plantation houses line the streets and it's an interesting area to look around.

If you want to take the faster route toward Kaena Point, pick up Farrington Highway (Route 930). This country road parallels miles of unpopulated beachfront, past wind-battered Mokuleia Beach and arrives at Dillingham Airfield, where you can take **The Original Glider Ride** along the Waianae Mountains. With nearly 30 years of experience, Mr. Bill knows the ins and outs of the countryside. He'll also provide you with a video of your ride. Reservations recommended. ~ 808-677-3404; www.honolulusoaring.com, e-mail mrbill@poi.net.

Beyond this landing strip, the road continues for several miles between a wild ocean and scrub brush–covered mountains before turning into a very rugged dirt track. Along this unpaved portion of roadway you can hike out about ten miles to **Kaena Point** on Oahu's northwest corner (see the "Hiking" section at the end of the chapter). This is the legendary point of departure for Hawaiian souls.

**LODGING**

For a resort experience in a rustic setting, consider the **Turtle Bay Resort**. This rural retreat sprawls across 880 acres on a dramatic peninsula. With a broad beach at the doorstep and mountains out back, it's an overwhelming spot. Add to that riding paths, two golf courses, tennis courts and a pair of swimming pools. Every guest room features an ocean view. ~ 57-091 Kamehameha Highway, Kahuku; 808-293-8811, 800-203-3650, fax 808-293-9147; www.turtlebayresort.com. ULTRA-DELUXE.

Located on the grounds of the Turtle Bay Resort but independently operated, **The Estates at Turtle Bay** offers studio, as well as one-, two- and three-bedroom resort condominiums, each with stove, refrigerator, dishwasher, microwave, washer/dryer and cable television. There are five swimming pools and four tennis courts on the property, and guests can arrange golf and horseback riding through the resort. Rates begin at $95 for a studio and up to $180 for a three-bedroom unit. ~ 56-565 Kamehameha Highway, Kahuku; 808-293-0600, 888-200-4202, fax 808-293-0471; www.turtlebay-rentals.com, e-mail trtlbayest@aol.com. MODERATE TO DELUXE.

**Turtle Bay Condos** has one-, two- and three-bedroom units with kitchen facilities and private lanais that overlook a nine-hole golf course. In high season, studios are $95; one-bedrooms units with a loft sleeping up to four guests are $145; two-bedroom units are $165; and three-bedroom units are $180. ~ 56-565 Kamehameha Highway, Kahuku; 808-293-2800, fax 808-293-2169; www. turtlebaycondos.com.

Surfers, scuba divers and budget-minded travelers will find **Backpacker's Vacation Inn** along Oahu's vaunted North Shore. The central building provides hostel-style rooms and features a TV lounge and kitchen. There's also a back house with private rooms that share a kitchen and bath. Like a hostel, it's budget-priced. Across the street, and directly on the beach, there's a house with private apartments that include their own kitchen and bathroom and are moderately priced. In addition, there are nine re-stored plantation houses with kitchens and baths set on a land-scaped acre. The Vacation Inn has guest laundry facilities and barbecue areas, which provide excellent opportunities for meeting other travelers. ~ 59-788 Kamehameha Highway, Haleiwa; 808-638-7838, fax 808-638-7515; www.backpackers-hawaii. com, e-mail bpacker@maui.net. BUDGET TO DELUXE.

Offering houses right on the beach, **Ke Iki Beach Bungalows** are located between the Banzai Pipeline and Waimea Bay. You'll find moderate- and deluxe-priced duplexes and an ultra-deluxe-priced cottage, all on an acre-and-a-half of palm-shaded property. They are basic woodframe buildings with bamboo and rattan furnishings; all units have full kitchens. The complex includes barbecue facilities, hammocks, a volleyball court and a wide beach. Accommodations are great for families. ~ 59-579 Ke Iki Road, Haleiwa; 808-638-8229, fax 808-637-6100; www.keikibeach. com, e-mail info@keikibeach.com. MODERATE TO ULTRA-DELUXE.

If you need a break from the sterile comforts of commercial hotels, try the **Surfhouse**. There's camping available on the grounds and a "hostel cabin" with bunk beds (linens are provided). The private cabins are clean and comfortable, and as cheap as you'll find. The owners rely mainly on word of mouth for advertising and maintain a commercial kitchen and bathrooms, keeping the prices down and the earthy factor up. ~ 62-203 Lokoea Place, Haleiwa; 808-637-7146; www.surfhouse.com, e-mail info@surf house.com. BUDGET.

**DINING**

Appropriately enough, you'll find the **Kahuku Grill** not far from the old Kahuku Sugar Mill. The menu includes Hawaiian plate lunches as well as shrimp, seafood and steak dishes. Open for breakfast, lunch and dinner daily, it's plain and informal. ~ 55-565 Kamehameha Highway, Kahuku; 808-293-2110. BUDGET TO MODERATE.

HIDDEN ►

Just down the way is **Giovanni's Aloha Shrimp Truck**, serving gourmet plate lunches that the locals claim are the best on Oahu.

There's a choice of scampi, lemon and butter shrimp or hot and spicy shrimp, and, like all plate lunches, they come with two scoops of rice. Eleven picnic tables sit under an awning for this rain-or-shine outdoor eating spot. ~ Beside The Mill, Kamehameha Highway, Kahuku; 808-293-1839. MODERATE.

The **Turtle Bay Resort** features an upscale restaurant, a family restaurant and a poolside snack shop. **21 Degrees North** has sweeping ocean views and features contemporary island cuisine. Expect such delights as seared rack of lamb, pecan duck and charbroiled Hawaiian ahi. At the **Palm Terrace**, overlooking the hotel's lovely grounds, you'll encounter moderate-priced dining in an attractive environment. The restaurant, serving three buffet meals, offers everything from *saimin* and teriyaki to linguine. Children's prices are available. At the **Hang Ten**, munch on a hamburger or taco salad while lounging in the sun. ~ 57-091 Kamehameha Highway, Kahuku; 808-293-8811, fax 808-293-9147; www.turtlebayresort.com. MODERATE TO DELUXE.

◀ HIDDEN

**Sunset Pizza** packs local crowds into its awning-covered picnic tables, with homemade lasagna, pizzas built from scratch, salads and an array of sandwiches made with freshly baked bread. ~ 59-176 Kamehameha Highway, Haleiwa; 808-638-7660. BUDGET.

For relaxed sunset dining overlooking the ocean, try **Jameson's By the Sea**. The inviting dining area features tropical touches like potted plants and rattan furnishing. For lunch there are sandwiches, chowders and fresh fish dishes; at dinner they specialize in seafood. Breakfast on the weekend. ~ 62-540 Kamehameha Highway, Haleiwa; 808-637-4336, fax 808-637-3225. MODERATE TO DELUXE.

The seafood at **Haleiwa Joe's Seafood Grill** is not the best I've ever had, but the salads are large and refreshing, the coconut shrimp pretty good, and the atmosphere a little more chichi than most casual beachside places. Plus, the patio has a beautiful ocean view. ~ 66-011 Kamehameha Highway, Haleiwa; 808-637-8005, fax 808-637-8861. MODERATE TO DELUXE.

**MYTHICAL MAKERS**

The *Menehunes*, in case you haven't been introduced, were tiny Hobbit-like creatures who inhabited Hawaii even before the Polynesians arrived. They were reputed to be superhumanly strong and would work all night to build dams, temples and other structures. Several mysterious manmade objects in the islands that archaeologists have trouble placing chronologically are claimed by mythmakers to be *Menehune* creations.

Mexican restaurants in Hawaii are different from their counter-parts elsewhere in one respect—fish tacos. True to the islands, **Rosie's Cantina** offers them, rounding out a menu filled with the culinary features found in every south-of-the-border eatery. The breakfast menu features American standbys like pancakes and omelettes, while the dinner menu ranges from tacos and enchi-ladas to steaks and seafood. To complement the fare Rosie's stocks the largest selection of premium tequilas in Hawaii. ~ Haleiwa Shopping Plaza, 66-165 Kamehameha Highway, Haleiwa; 808-637-3538, fax 808-637-5086. BUDGET TO MODERATE.

HIDDEN ►   Join the surfers who pour into **Kua Aina Sandwich**, where they order hamburgers, french fries and mahimahi sandwiches at the counter, then kick back at one of the roadside tables. Great for light meals, this place is a scene and a half. ~ 66-160 Kamehameha Highway, Haleiwa; 808-637-6067, fax 808-637-4858. BUDGET.

Steaming fish tacos smothered in spicy salsa. Salty chips that leave oil on your napkin. Cold beer topped with lime (well, you have to provide your own, but you get the idea). Mmmm. But I digress. **Cholos Homestyle Mexican Restaurant** is ideal after-beach fare. You can dine inside or out, and the gorgeous crafts on dis-play are for sale. Open for breakfast (weekends only), lunch and dinner. ~ North Shore Marketplace, 66-250 Kamehameha Highway, Haleiwa; 808-637-3059. BUDGET.

Years ago Haleiwa was home to Da Cuppa Kope, a great café and gathering place. Today it's been supplanted by an even better
HIDDEN ►   coffeehouse, the **Coffee Gallery**, which roasts its coffee on-site. In addition to the best cappuccino on the island, this homespun restaurant, decorated with coffee sacks, serves pastries, bagels, homemade soups and a variety of sandwiches. They also have in-ternet and free wi-fi access. ~ North Shore Marketplace, 66-250 Kamehameha Highway, Haleiwa; 808-637-5355; www.roast master.com, e-mail coffeegalleryhawaii@yahoo.com. BUDGET.

Casual is an understatement at **Paradise Found Café**, where barefoot beachgoers order up fresh-fruit smoothies, soups, salads and vegetarian delights such as tempeh burritos and tofu lemon-grass curry. Vegan substitutions are easily accommodated at this friendly eatery. ~ Inside Celestial Natural Foods, 66-443 Kamehameha Highway, Haleiwa; 808-637-4540. BUDGET.

At **Café Haleiwa** surfers swear by the omelettes, pancakes and "the Barrel"—a blend of eggs, potatoes, green salsa and cheese wrapped in a tortilla. Sandwiches and burgers round out the menu. Located in a century-old building featuring local art-work, surfboards and surfing memorabilia, this local favorite also serves an excellent quesadilla. No dinner. ~ 66-460 Kame-hameha Highway, Haleiwa; 808-637-5516. BUDGET.

# How to Beat the Heat
## with a Sweet Treat

Since the early days of Hawaiian royalty, people have complained about Honolulu's shirt-sticking weather. Come summer, temperatures rise and the trade winds stop blowing. Visitors seeking a golden tan discover they're baking without browning. And residents begin to think that their city, renowned as a cultural melting pot, is actually a pressure cooker.

With the ocean all around, relief is never far away. But a lot of folks, when not heading for the beaches, have found another way to cool off: shave ice. Known as ice frappes among the Japanese originators and snow cones back on the mainland, these frozen treats are Hawaii's answer to the Good Humor man.

They're made with ice that's been shaved from a block into thin slivers, packed into a cone-shaped cup and covered with sweet syrup. Health-minded people eat the ice plain or with a low-calorie or sugar-free syrup, and some folks ask for a scoop of ice cream or sweet black beans (*azuki* beans) underneath the shavings. Most people just order it with their favorite syrup flavors—grape, root beer, cola, cherry, orange, lemon-lime, vanilla, fruit punch, banana, strawberry or whatever.

Whichever you choose, you'll find it only costs about a buck at the many stands sprinkled around town. Watch for stands up on the North Shore, too. No doubt you'll see a long line outside Oahu's most famous shave ice store, **Matsumoto's**. ~ 66-087 Kamehameha Highway, Haleiwa; 808-637-4827.

As a matter of fact, anyplace where the sun blazes overhead you're liable to find someone trying to beat the heat by slurping up a "snow cone" before it melts into mush.

**GROCERIES**  Out by Sunset Beach you'll find a **Foodland Super Market.** ~ 59-720 Kamehameha Highway, Haleiwa; 808-638-8081. There's also **Sunset Beach Store,** which has a small stock but is home to a modest bakery; it's conveniently located near Sunset Beach. ~ 59-024 Kamehameha Highway, Haleiwa; 808-638-8207. **Haleiwa Supermarket,** one of the few large markets on the entire North Shore, is the best place to shop. ~ 66-197 Kamehameha Highway, Haleiwa; 808-637-5004.

Celestial Natural Foods has an ample supply of health foods and fresh produce. ~ 66-443 Kamehameha Highway, Haleiwa; 808-637-6729.

**SHOPPING**  Calling itself **The Only Show In Town** is a slight (very slight) exaggeration, but claiming to be "Kahuku's largest antique and vintage collectible shop" is definitely warranted. Some store specialties include Japanese glass fishing floats, ivory and Coca-Cola memorabilia. Fittingly, this wonderful antique store is located in the old Tanaka Plantation Store, an early-20th-century wood-frame building. ~ 56-931 Kamehameha Highway, Kahuku; 808-293-1295, fax 808-293-8585.

Trendy shoppers head for the little town of Haleiwa. Since Haleiwa is a center for surfers, it's a good place to buy sportswear and aquatic equipment as well as varied artworks and crafts.

**Strong Current** stocks everything imaginable that's related to surfing. They even have a small "surfing museum," consisting of memorabilia from the sport's early days. Then there are the books, videos, posters, boards and other appurtenances, all relating to a single theme. ~ 66-214 Kamehameha Highway,

**ALOHA FROM HAWAII**

Leis mark special occasions in a singular way. In Hawaii, islander graduates are encircled with countless fragrant blossoms to celebrate their accomplishments. When our kids graduated from high school we brought the tradition to the mainland by ordering leis over the internet. **Hawaii Tropical Flowers** went out of their way to ensure our order arrived on time—and they were the friendliest and most helpful people we've ever bought anything from. (Not all internet companies come through with getting you da goods, so stick with Hawaii Tropical Flowers.) Check out their website for both leis and tropical bouquets that whisk away the winter blues. If you call, say aloha to Verna. ~ 888-833-7800; www.hawaiitropicflowers.com.

Haleiwa; 808-637-3406; www.strongcurrenthawaii.com, e-mail info@strongcurrenthawaii.com.

The **North Shore Marketplace** is an eclectic collection of exceptional shops selling everything from surfing gear to handblown glass. **Polynesian Treasures** (808-637-1288) sells handicrafts from Fiji, Tonga, Samoa, Hawaii and lots more. ~ North Shore Marketplace, 66-250 Kamehameha Highway, Haleiwa.

**Iwa Gallery** features a unique collection of artwork by a number of local island artists, including handcrafted candles. ~ 66-119 Kamehameha Highway, Haleiwa; 808-637-4865.

**Oogenesis Boutique** has a creative selection of women's fashions. ~ 66-249 Kamehameha Highway, Haleiwa; 808-637-4580.

Entertainment is a rare commodity on the North Shore, but you will find contemporary Hawaiian music at the Turtle Bay Resort's **Bay View**. Thursday through Sunday has live music outdoors, weather permitted. ~ 57-091 Kamehameha Highway, Kahuku; 808-293-8811.

**NIGHTLIFE**

**SUNSET BEACH** As far as surfing goes, this is the place! I think the best way to do Sunset is by starting from **Ehukai Beach Park**. From here you can go left to the "Banzai Pipeline," where crushing waves build along a shallow coral reef to create tube-like formations. To the right lies "Sunset," with equally spectacular surfing waves. Throughout the area the swimming is fair in summer; however, in winter it is extremely dangerous. From September to April, high waves and strong currents prevail. Be careful! Game fish caught around Sunset include *papio*, *menpachi* and *ulua*. Facilities at Ehukai Beach Park include picnic areas, restrooms and showers. Snorkeling here is poor but it's excellent at **Pupukea Beach Park**, located on Kamehameha Highway six miles northeast of Haleiwa. An 80-acre marine reserve, it has fabulous tidepools and dive sites. ~ Ehukai Beach Park is located off Kamehameha Highway (Route 83) about seven miles northeast of Haleiwa.

**BEACHES & PARKS**

**WAIMEA BAY BEACH PARK** If Sunset is *one* of the most famous surfing spots in the world, Waimea is *the* most famous. The biggest surfable waves in the world (40 feet in winter!) roll into this pretty blue bay. There's a wide white-sand beach and a pleasant park with a tree-studded lawn. It's a marvelous place for picnicking and sunbathing. During the winter crowds often line the beach watching top-notch surfers challenge the curl; in summer the sea is flat and safe for swimming; you can also body-surf in the shorebreak and snorkel when the bay is calm. *Papio*, *menpachi* and *ulua* are common catches. Facilities include a picnic area, restrooms, showers and a lifeguard. ~ On Kamehameha Highway (Route 83) about five miles northeast of Haleiwa.

**HALEIWA BEACH PARK** This is an excellent refuge from the North Shore's pounding surf. Set in Waialua Bay, the beach is safe for swimming almost all year. You can snorkel, although it's only fair. Surfing in not possible here but "Haleiwa" breaks are located across Waialua Bay at Alii Beach Park. Facilities include a picnic area, restrooms, showers, a ball field, a basketball court and a playground. The primary catches at Haleiwa are *papio*, *menpachi* and *ulua*. ~ On Kamehameha Highway (Route 83) in Haleiwa.

**HALEIWA ALII BEACH PARK** Haleiwa Alii Beach Park, across from Haleiwa Beach Park, is where you go to surf. Swells can top 20 feet here, which is why it's the site of several surfing and bodyboarding tournaments—you can watch the pros do things that seem to defy gravity. If you've come on one of the few days that surfing is not ideal, or if you're a beginner, bring your boogieboard and join the kids on the more manageable waves. If you're visiting in winter, you're in luck: lifeguards give free surfing lessons in the morning (it's a good idea to reserve a spot ahead of time; head for the lifeguard tower to sign up). Facilities include a picnic area, restrooms and year-round lifeguards. ~ On Kamehameha Highway (Route 83) in Haleiwa; 808-637-5051, fax 808-637-5052.

**KAIAKA RECREATION AREA** The setting at this peninsular park is beautiful. There's a secluded area with a tree-shaded lawn and a short strip of sandy beach. A rocky shoreline borders most of the park, so it's more for picnics than water sports. You *can* swim and snorkel but there's a rocky bottom. Fishing is good for *papio*, *menpachi* and *ulua*. The facilities here include a picnic area, showers and restrooms. ~ Located on Haleiwa Road just outside Haleiwa.

▲ Permitted; a county permit is required.

### SNORKELER'S PARADISE

Some of the island's best snorkeling is at **Pupukea Beach Park**, a marine reserve on Kamehameha Highway six miles northeast of Haleiwa. This 80-acre park, fringed by rocky shoreline, divides into several sections. Foremost is "Shark's Cove," located on the north side of the fire station, which contains spectacular tidepools. Underwater caves draw divers (experienced only—there have been a number of drownings in these deep and maze-like caverns). ~ Kamehameha Highway at Papukea Road.

**MOKULEIA BEACH PARK AND MOKULEIA BEACH** 🐋 ⟿        ◄ *HIDDEN*

🚶 🛶 ⚓ The 12-acre park contains a sandy beach and large un-
shaded lawn. An exposed coral reef detracts from the swimming,
but on either side of the park lie beaches with sandy ocean bottoms.
If you do swim, exercise caution, especially in the winter months;
there's no lifeguard. There's good snorkeling and in winter the
surf breaks up to ten feet near Dillingham Airfield. Anglers try
for *papio*, *menpachi* and *ulua*. Watch for skydivers, who often
use the shoreline for their beach landings. Whatever your activity of choice, you'll have to contend with the noise of small
planes from nearby Dillingham Airfield. The park is also an excellent starting point for exploring the unpopulated sections of
Mokuleia Beach. Facilities include picnic areas, restrooms and
showers. ~ On Farrington Highway (Route 930) about seven
miles west of Haleiwa. To the west of the park, this beach
stretches for miles along a secluded coast. You can hike down the
beach or reach its hidden realms by driving farther west along
Farrington Highway (Route 930), then turning off onto any of
the numerous dirt side roads.

▲ Tent and trailer camping are allowed with a county permit.
Unofficial camping along the undeveloped beachfront is common.

**MOKULEIA ARMY BEACH** This is the widest stretch of sand along        ◄ *HIDDEN*
the Mokuleia shoreline, and probably the most untamed. Once
maintained by the Army for the exclusive use of their personnel,
it's now open to the public but has no facilities. The high surf in
winter poses no challenge to natives, but surfing really isn't recommended; there have been fatalities here. The treacherous waters mean that you'll pretty much have the spot to yourself. Most
visitors are locals with a strong sense of loyalty to this largely un-
touristed spot. ~ Route 930 near the Dillingham Airfield.

Out along the west coast of Oahu, less than 30 miles ▼▼▼▼▼▼▼▼▼▼▼▼
from the sands of Waikiki, Hawaiian culture is mak-        **Leeward Coast**
ing a last stand. Here on the tableland that separates
the Waianae Range from the ocean, the old ways still prevail.
Unlike the cool rainforests of the Windward Coast or the rain-
spattered area around Honolulu, this is a region of stark beauty,
resembling the American Southwest, with rocky crags and cactus-
studded hills. Farther north, the spartan scenery gives way to wide
vistas of massive mountains sloping gracefully to the sea.

Hawaiian and Samoan farmers tend small fields and raise
chickens. Side roads off the main highway pass dusty houses and
sunblasted churches before turning into dirt tracks that keep
climbing past truck farms and old homesteads. For entertainment,
there are birthday luaus, cockfights and slack-key guitar playing.

The Leeward Coast has become the keeper of the old ways, and residents jealously guard the customs and traditions that they see slipping away in the rest of the state. Although there have been reports of outsiders being hassled by local residents, the reality, in fact, is usually the reverse. Here, far from the madding crowds of tourists and tourist businesses, the true spirit of aloha is alive and well. But who knows for how long?

"Second City," a major development near the town of Ewa, has added thousands of houses to the Central Oahu area. And in the southwest corner of the island the ultra-modern JW Marriott Ihilani Resort & Spa in the Ko Olina area is only the beginning of the inevitable encroachment along this side of the island. So you should consider this one of those places that needs to be seen and seen soon, before the forces of change sweep through.

**SIGHTS**
From Honolulu you can visit the Leeward Coast region by traveling west on Route H-1 or Route 90. If you want to tour what once was a prime sugar-growing area, take Route 90 past Pearl Harbor, then turn left on Fort Weaver Road (Route 760). This country lane leads to the plantation town of **Ewa**. With its old sugar mill and trim houses, Ewa is an enchanting throwback to the days when sugar was king. This town is a slow, simple place, perfect for wandering and exploring.

Near Oahu's southwest corner, Routes H-1 and 90 converge to become the Farrington Highway (Route 93). From here, follow the signs to **Hawaiian Waters Adventure Park**, perfect for those who are afraid of getting a little sand in their pants but love to ride waves or splash in the water. There are inner-tube slides, a 60-foot water slide, artificial waves and much more, spread over 25 acres. Closed Tuesday and Wednesday in winter. A hefty admission. ~ 400 Farrington Highway, Kapolei; 808-674-9283; www.hawaiian waters.com, e-mail questions@hawaiianwaters.com.

**HIDDEN** ►
The first beach you come to along the Leeward Coast is **Barber's Point**. It's not worth a detour, however, so continue along Route 93 to **Ko Olina Resort**. You might want to make a stop here and take a look at the scenery: it can be windy, but it's a beautiful and little-visited spot.

Farrington Highway continues along the coast to Kahe Point. The ugly power plant you see is a good landmark to find **Hawaiian Electric Beach Park** and a top surfing spot by the name of "Tracks." Keep going along Route 93 and you'll pass the towns of Nanikuli, Maili and Waianae.

If you turn up Mailiilii Street in **Waianae**, you will pass placid Hawaiian homesteads and farmlands. This side road also provides sweeping views of the Waianae Range. On the northern side of town is Waianae Harbor, a small port hosting small fishing vessels as well as spiffy yachts.

Farther along is **Makaha Beach,** one of Hawaii's most famous surfing spots, and the site of an annual international surfing championship. It's also a great place for shell hunting. The **Makaha Valley,** extending from the ocean up into the Waianae Mountains, is home to the **Kaneaki Heiau,** a 15th-century temple dedicated to the god Lono. Closed Monday and when raining. ~ Take Manunaolu Street; phone/fax 808-695-8174.

The highway continues along the coastline past several mostly deserted beaches and parks. Across from Kaena Point State Park you'll come upon **Makua Cave,** a lava cavern large enough for exploring and snorkeling. Beyond that, where the paved road turns to dirt, lies **Yokohama Bay,** with its curving sand beach and inviting turquoise waters.

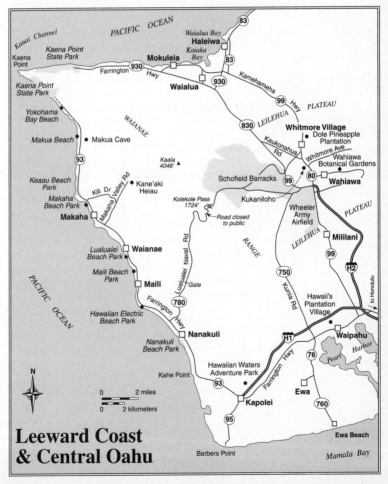

# Leeward Coast & Central Oahu

# Central Oahu

The 1000-foot-high Leilehua Plateau, a bountiful agricultural region once planted with sugar and pineapple, extends from the North Shore to the southern reaches of Oahu. Situated in the middle of the island between the Waianae and Koolau ranges, this tableland has become a vital military headquarters. Wheeler Air Force Base, Schofield Barracks and several other installations occupy large plots of land here. Wahiawa, a small, grimy city, is the region's commercial hub. "Second City," a major development already being built near the town of Ewa, will eventually add thousands of houses to the area. From Haleiwa south to Wahiawa you can take Route 803, Kaukoahuna Road, a pretty thoroughfare with excellent views of the Waianaes, or follow Route 99, the Kamehameha Highway, which passes through verdant pineapple fields.

**DOLE PINEAPPLE PLANTATION**     Located about ten minutes south of Haleiwa along **Route 99**, the Dole Pineapple Plantation, often crowded with tourists, sells (who would have guessed) pineapple products. They offer a self-guided tour and the World's Largest Maze, a 1.7-mile labyrinth made from more than 11,000 Hawaiian plants that covers two acres. Admission for maze. ~ 64-1550 Kamehameha Highway, Wahiawa; 808-621-8408, fax 808-621-1926; www.dole-plantation.com, e-mail sales@dole-plantation.com. The **Pineapple Variety Garden** displays many different types of the fruit in a garden museum. ~ Kamehameha Highway and Kamananui Road, Wahiawa.

**KUKANILOHO**     The east fork of Route 99 becomes **Route 80**, which passes near Kukaniloho, a cluster of sacred stones marking the place where Hawaiian royalty gave birth accompanied by chants, drums and offerings. Studded with eucalyptus trees, this spot has held an important place in Hawaiian mythology and religion for centuries. ~ Follow the dirt road across from Whitmore Avenue just north of Wahiawa.

**HIDDEN ►**     The road past Yokohama is partially passable by auto, but it's very rough. If you want to explore **Kaena Point** from this side of the island, you'll have to hike. It's about two miles to the northwest corner of Oahu, past tidepools teeming with marine life. On a clear day you can see Kauai from this point. (Don't leave valuables in your car in this area.)

**LODGING**     To get away from everything, consider a short stay at the **JW Marriott Ihilani Resort & Spa**. Backed by the Waianaes and facing a curved expanse of ocean, this 387-room hideaway is part

**WAHIAWA BOTANICAL GARDENS**    Farther south along Route 80, Wahiawa Botanical Gardens is a handsome 27-acre retreat studded with tropical vegetation. Plants include orchids, ferns, cacti and bromeliads, as well as heliconias, palms and gingers. ~ 1396 California Avenue, Wahiawa; 808-522-7060; e-mail hbg@co.honolulu.hi.us.

**KOLEKOLE PASS**    For a scenic and historic detour from Route 80, follow Route 80 until it links with Route 99. Take Route 99 west, pull up to the sentry station at **Schofield Barracks** and ask directions to Kolekole Pass. On that "day of infamy," December 7, 1941, Japanese bombers buzzed through this notch in the Waianae Range. You'll be directed through Schofield up into the Waianaes. When you reach Kolekole Pass, there's another sentry gate. Ask the guard to let you continue a short distance farther to the observation point. From here the Waianaes fall away precipitously to a plain that rolls gently to the sea. There's an astonishing view of Oahu's west coast. If you are denied permission to pass the sentry point, then take the footpath that begins just before the gate, leading up the hill. From near the cross at the top, you will have a partial view of both the Waianaes' western face and the central plateau region.

**HAWAII'S PLANTATION VILLAGE**    Back at Wahiawa, Route H-2 provides the fastest means back to Honolulu; the most interesting course is along **Route 750**, Kunia Road, which skirts the Waianaes, passing sugar cane fields and stands of pine. Along the way you can take in Hawaii's Plantation Village, a partially re-created and partially restored village that spreads across three acres of Waipahu Cultural Park in Waipahu. Composed of over two dozen buildings, it includes a Japanese Shinto shrine, a company store and a Chinese Society building. Hawaii's many ethnic groups are represented in the houses, which span several architectural periods of the 19th and 20th centuries. Together they provide visitors with a window into traditional life on a plantation. Closed Sunday. Admission. ~ 94-695 Waipahu Street, Waipahu; 808-677-0110, fax 808-676-6727. From here, Honolulu is about 15 miles east along Route H-1, or you can take Route 750 south to Ewa.

of the 640-acre Ko Olina Resort. There's a golf course, six tennis courts, four restaurants and a spa facility. More important, you'll find a string of four lagoons, each with a crescent beach and a cluster of islets that protects the mouth of the lagoon. ~ 92-1001 Olani Street, Kapolei; 808-679-0079, 800-626-4446, fax 808-679-0295; www.ihilani.com. ULTRA-DELUXE.

**Makaha Shores**, a six-story resort condo complex, overlooks pretty Makaha Beach Park, one of Hawaii's top surfing beaches. There are studios and one- and two-bedroom units, each individually decorated by their owners. The minimum stay is one week, and the units are handled by different agents. ~ 84-265 Farrington Highway, Makaha; 808-696-7121. MODERATE.

**Makaha Valley Towers** is a highrise set along the slopes of Makaha Valley. Units range from studios to two-bedrooms, with nightly, weekly and monthly stays available. Rates vary and accommodations are handled by local realtors. ~ End of Kili Drive, Makaha; 808-695-9568.

**DINING**

By way of resort restaurants, **JW Marriott Ihilani Resort & Spa** at Ko Olina has several deluxe- and ultra-deluxe-priced dining rooms. Foremost is **Azul**, where the fish, lamb and beef are prepared with a Mediterranean flair. **Ushiotei** is the ultimate in Japanese cuisine. And **Naupaka**, a poolside terrace serving cross-cultural dishes, is the Ihilani's answer to informality and easy elegance. Hours for all three vary with the season. Reservations are recommended. ~ 92-1001 Olani Street, Kapolei; 808-679-0079, fax 808-679-3168. MODERATE TO ULTRA-DELUXE.

This sparsely populated strip of shoreline has several other dining spots. All are located on Farrington Highway, the main road, and most are in the town of Waianae. **Cathay Inn Chop Suey** is a good choice for Chinese food. Regulars fill the tables for the crispy *gau gee*, beef broccoli and sweet-and-sour shrimp. ~ 86-088 Farrington Highway, Waianae; 808-696-9477. BUDGET TO MODERATE.

Close by is **Hannara Restaurant**, offering Korean, Hawaiian and American cuisines. This relaxed spot draws locals and tourists alike for sit-down or take-out service. Breakfast, lunch and dinner Monday through Saturday; no dinner Sunday. ~ 86-078 Farrington Highway, Waianae; 808-696-6137. BUDGET.

**GROCERIES**

Sack 'n Save Foods is the prime market in this area. ~ 87-2070 Farrington Highway, Waianae; 808-668-1277.

Another popular place to shop is **The Waianae Store**, a full-service supermarket that includes a bakery and delicatessen. ~ 85-863 Farrington Highway, Waianae; 808-696-3131.

**AUTHOR FAVORITE**

When I'm in Waianae, I have to stop at **L & L Drive-Inn**, which serves breakfast, lunch and dinner. The breakfast combo includes eggs, Portuguese sausage, Spam and rice. Among the hearty plate lunches offered the rest of the day are breaded pork chop with hamburger steak and shrimp curry with chicken *katsu*. ~ 85-080 Waianae Valley Road, Waianae; 808-696-7989, fax 808-696-8803. BUDGET.

**Naupaka Terrace** at the Ihilani Resort features nightly live entertainment. The Ihilani is also home to the **Hokulea**, a cozy lounge perfect for a quiet rendezvous. Hours vary with season. ~ JW Marriott Ihilani Resort & Spa, 92-1001 Olani Street, Kapolei; 808-679-0079.

**NANAKULI BEACH PARK** 🏊 🦀 🎣 ⛵ This park is so large that a housing tract divides it into two parts. The main section features a white-sand beach, *kiawe*-studded camping area and a recreation complex. It's simply a park with everything, unfortunately including weekend crowds. Needless to say, the swimming and snorkeling are good; lifeguard on duty. There are winter breaks with right and left slides. Fishing often rewards with *papio*, *ulua*, *moano* and *menpachi*. Facilities include picnic areas, restrooms, showers, a ball field, a basketball court and a playground. ~ 89-269 Farrington Highway (Route 93) about five miles south of Waianae; 808-668-1137.

▲ Tent and trailer camping are allowed, but a county permit is required.

**HAWAIIAN ELECTRIC BEACH PARK** 🏊 🦀 🎣 ⛵ This once privately owned park, across the highway from a monstrous power plant, is now run by the county. There's a rolling lawn with palm and *kiawe* trees, plus a white-sand beach and coral reef. You can swim, snorkel, surf year-round and fish for *papio*, *ulua*, *moano* and *menpachi*. If you're a proficient surfer, you'll probably head for "Tracks," a top surfing break. The drawbacks are the lack of facilities (there are restrooms and a picnic area) and the park's proximity to the electric company. ~ Located on Farrington Highway (Route 93) about seven miles south of Waianae.

▲ Not allowed here; but tent and trailer camping are okay at nearby Kahe Point Beach Park, with a county permit.

**MAILI BEACH PARK** 🏊 🦀 🎣 ⛵ A long winding stretch of white sand is the high point of this otherwise unimpressive facility. The swimming is good in the summer; reef snorkeling is only fair. Be aware of the reef's steep dropoff. There are winter surf breaks with a right slide. The principal game fish caught here are *papio*, *ulua*, *menpachi* and *moano*. The park contains shade trees and a spotty lawn. There are restrooms and showers. ~ 87-021 Farrington Highway (Route 93) in Maili a few miles south of Waianae.

▲ Not permitted here, but tent camping, with a county permit, is allowed in the summer at nearby Lualualei Beach Park.

**MAKAHA BEACH PARK** 🏊 🦀 🎣 ⛵ Some of the finest surfing in the world takes place right offshore here. In winter, this is the site of international competitions, drawing championship surfers from all across the Pacific. For more relaxed sports, there's a white-sand beach to sunbathe on and some good places to skindive. Swimming and snorkeling are both good when the sea is calm; otherwise, exercise extreme caution. Check with a lifeguard about water conditions. Anglers try for *papio*, *ulua*, *moano* and *menpachi*. The precipitous Waianae Mountains loom behind the park. There are picnic tables, restrooms and showers. ~ 84-369 Farrington Highway (Route 93) in Makaha, two miles north of Waianae.

**KEAAU BEACH PARK** Except for the absence of a sandy beach, this is the prettiest park on the west coast. It's a long, narrow grassy plot spotted with trees and backdropped by the Waianaes. Sunsets are spectacular here, and on a clear day you can see all the way to Kauai. There's a sandy beach just west of the park. Unfortunately, a coral reef rises right to the water's edge, making entry into the water difficult. But once you're in there's great snorkeling, swimming and bodysurfing. In summer there are good surf breaks with a left slide. People fish for *papio*, *ulua*, *moano* and *menpachi*. There are picnic areas, restrooms and showers. ~ Located on Farrington Highway (Route 93) about five miles north of Waianae.

▲ Tent and trailer allowed. County permit required.

*Kaena Point, a great place to spot porpoises, is the legendary home of Nanue the Shark Man.*

HIDDEN ► **KAENA POINT STATE PARK (YOKOHAMA BAY)** This curving stretch of white sand is the last beach along Oahu's northwest coast. With the Waianae Range in the background and coral reefs offshore, it's a particularly lovely spot. Though officially a state park, the area is largely undeveloped. You can walk from Yokohama Bay past miles of tidepools to Oahu's northwest corner at Kaena Point. Keep an eye out for porpoises. Yokohama Bay is a prime region for beach lovers and explorers both. When the sea is calm the swimming is good and the snorkeling is excellent but exercise extreme caution if the surf is up. There are summer breaks up to 15 feet over a shallow reef (left slide). Fish caught in this area include *papio*, *ulua*, *moano* and *menpachi*. Restrooms and showers are the only facilities. ~ Located at the end of the paved section of Farrington Highway (Route 93), about nine miles north of the town of Waianae.

## Outdoor Adventures

**CAMPING**

Along with its traffic and crowds, Oahu has numerous parks. Unfortunately, these disparate elements overlap, and you may sometimes find you've escaped from Honolulu's urban jungle and landed in a swamp of weekend beachgoers. So it's best to plan outdoor adventures far in advance and to schedule them for weekdays if possible.

Currently, camping is allowed at 15 beach parks operated by the City and County of Honolulu. Seven of these parks are on the island's windward side and five on the leeward side. Another two are on the North Shore. Bellows Field Beach Park at Waimanalo on the Windward Coast, only allows camping at its 50 campsites on the weekends. Swanzy Beach Park at Kaaawa, Maili and Kualoa A are also weekend-only campgrounds (Kualoa A is closed in summer). The others permit tent camping every night except Wednesday and Thursday. There are no trailer hookups.

Camping at **county parks** requires a permit. The free permits can be obtained from the Department of Parks and Recreation. ~ Honolulu Municipal Building, 650 South King Street, ground floor, Honolulu, HI 96813; 808-523-4527. They are also available at any of the "satellite city halls" around the island.

**State parks** allow camping for up to five days, depending on the park. It's first-come, first-served on the first day, but after that visitors may reserve spaces. The Division of State Parks issues the free permits. ~ 1151 Punchbowl Street, Room 310, Honolulu, HI 96813; 808-587-0300. You can also write in advance for permits.

There are four state parks on Oahu with camping facilities. **Malaekahana State Recreation Area** on the Windward Coast between Laie and Kahuku offers both tent camping and housekeeping cabins. Also on the Windward Coast, Oahu's largest state park **Kahana Valley State Park**, located between Kaaawa and Punaluu, has campsites. Tent camping is available at **Sand Island State Recreation Area** on Sand Island in Honolulu, as well as at **Keaiwa Heiau State Recreation Area** in the hills above Honolulu.

The **Hoomaluhia Botanical Gardens** allows camping on their grounds Friday through Sunday. There is no fee, but a permit is required and no hookups are available. ~ 808-233-7323.

Remember when planning your trip, rainfall is heaviest on the Windward Coast, a little lighter on the North Shore and lightest of all on the Leeward Coast.

For tent rentals and sales in central Oahu, try **Omar the Tent Man**. Closed Sunday. ~ 94-158 Leoole Street, Waipahu; 808-677-8785.

**FISHING**

From deep-sea fishing to trolling for freshwater bass, Oahu offers challenges to suit any angler. You can try game fishing out in the Pacific, head down to the beach for surf-casting or try one of the island's popular lakes.

Most of the island's fishing fleet dock at **Kewalo Basin** (Fisherman's Wharf) on Ala Moana Drive between Waikiki and downtown Honolulu.

**Hawaii Fishing Adventures and Charters** books deep-sea fishing trips that go out for blue marlin, yellowfin tuna and mahimahi. Charters leave from Kewalo Basin, and reservations are required (all equipment provided). ~ 575 Cooke Street A315; 808-396-2607, 877-388-1376; www.sportfishhawaii.com. Or consider **Sport Fishing**, which runs the *Pacific Blue* and *Ilima* out of Kewalo Basin. Equipment provided. ~ 808-596-2087. **Maggie Joe Sportfishing** does day trips as well as overnight and multiday excursions. An overnight trip to Molokai or a five-day cruise to Kauai and Niihau are among the options. ~ 808-591-8888, 877-806-3474; www.maggiejoe.com.

**DIVING**   One of the great myths about Oahu is that you need to go far off the beaten track to discover its secret treasures. The fact is that within half an hour of Waikiki are excellent snorkeling and diving opportunities. Only an hour away are excellent reefs easily reached by dive boats. From popular Hanauma Bay, just a short ride from the heart of Honolulu, to Kahe Point on the Leeward Coast, there are snorkeling and diving opportunities for beginners and certified pros alike.

Although the most popular snorkeling locale on the island is **Hanauma Bay**, and most people go there, other possible spots are **Shark Cove** on the North Shore and **Electric Beach** on Kahe Point on the northwest Coast. Or you can snorkel at **Makua Beach**, located between Makaha and Yokohama Bay on the Leeward Coast, and swim with the dolphins. Because conditions vary, I strongly recommend seeking instruction and advice from local diving experts before setting out.

**HONOLULU**   **South Seas Aquatics** features dives off a custom 38-foot dive boat. They sell diving equipment. ~ 2155 Kalakaua Avenue, Suite 112, Honolulu, HI 96815; 808-922-0852; www.ssahawaii.com.

**Waikiki Diving Center** takes divers to different sites around Oahu, depending on the time of year and the weather. The company offers two- to three-day PADI and NAUI courses and sells, rents and repairs diving equipment. It will also take nondivers out on an inexpensive introductory scuba charter so they can see what the sport is all about. ~ 424 Nahua Street, Honolulu; 808-922-2121; www.waikikidiving.com.

**SOUTHEAST OAHU**   **Aloha Dive Shop** runs day trips for certified divers and lesson packages for students at Maunalua Bay in the southeast corner of the island. ~ Hawaii Kai Shopping Center, 377 Kehole Street, Hawaii Kai; 808-395-5922.

**LEEWARD COAST**   **Hawaii Sea Adventures** heads to the west side of Oahu and dives the *Mahi* shipwreck. They feature lessons as well as half- and full-day trips and charters. ~ 98-718 Moanalua Road, Pearl City; 808-487-7515.

**WINDWARD COAST**   At **Aaron's Dive Shop** you can choose between beach and boat dives, as well as special night trips. ~ 307 Hahani Street, Kailua; 808-261-1211; www.scubahawaii.com.

**NORTH SHORE**   Depending on the season, the **Haleiwa Surf Center** teaches such sports as snorkeling, surfing, swimming, life-saving and sailing. This county agency is also an excellent source of information on the island's water sports and facilities. ~ Haleiwa Alii Beach Park, Haleiwa; 808-637-5051. **Surf N' Sea** offers half-day beach and boat dives on the North Shore and Leeward Coast including the *Mahi* shipwreck. ~ 62-595 Kamehameha Highway, Haleiwa; 808-637-9887; www.surfnsea.com.

Somewhere between snorkeling and scuba diving is Snuba, created for those who would like to take snorkeling a step further but may not be quite ready for scuba diving. It's a shallow-water dive system that allows underwater breathing. Basically this is how it works. Swimmers wear a breathing device (the same one used in scuba diving) that is connected to a built-in scuba tank that floats on a raft. They also wear a weight belt, mask and fins. The air comes through a 20-foot tube connected to the raft, which follows the swimmer. Groups of six participants are taken out with a guide. They can dive up to 20 feet.

**SNUBA**

    **Breeze Hawaii** offers Snuba tours at Hanauma Bay. Common sightings include an array of fish, eels, dolphins and turtles. ~ 3014 Kaimuki Avenue; 808-735-1857; www.breezehawaii.com.

Surfing, a sport pioneered centuries ago by Hawaiian royalty, is synonymous with Oahu. Stars bring their boards from all over the world to join international competitions that take advantage of ideal surf and wind conditions. From the 30-foot winter rollers on the North Shore to beginner lessons off Waikiki, this is beach boy and girl territory. Windsurfing is equally popular in areas like Kailua Bay and along the North Shore.

**SURFING & WIND-SURFING**

**WAIKIKI**  For everything "on the water, in the water and under the water" see **Prime Time Rentals** near Fort DeRussy Beach. They offer beach accessories, equipment sales and rentals, lessons and

**GLOBAL SURFERS KNOW**

If you plan to surf Oahu (or any of the other Hawaiian islands), check out **www.globalsurfers.com**. This online surf community maintained by surfers offers valuable information on surf spots on Oahu—from beginner breaks like Canoes, Point Panics and Secret, to intermediate breaks like Monster Mush, Pyramid Rock and Hauula Bowls, to expert-only breaks like Off-the-Wall, Pinballs and Pipeline. Not only do they inform you about the break, the type of wave, and the length of the ride, they give you the rap on what to wear (board shorts or wet suits), the crowd level, the best board to use, and the ever-important "localism" of the locale. Remember when surfing in Hawaii, give the locals proper respect.

plenty of friendly advice. Private and group surfing lessons have a "stand and surf" guarantee. ~ Kalia Road; 808-949-8952. The **Aloha Beach Service**, in front of the Sheraton Moana Surfrider Hotel, offers lessons and rents long boards. ~ 808-922-3111.

**DOWNTOWN HONOLULU**  A number of stores located in different parts of the island also rent boards. Near downtown, go to **Local Motion** for surfboard rentals. Check out there selection of beachwear, boards and equipment for sale. ~ 1958 Kalakaua Avenue; 808-979-7873.

**GREATER HONOLULU**  In the Diamond Head area, **Downing Hawaii** rents boards. Closed Sunday. ~ 3021 Waialae Avenue; 808-737-9696.

**WINDWARD COAST**  **Kailua Sailboard and Kayak Company** will teach you the tricks of the trade or help you brush up on your technique. You can also rent sailboards, boogieboards, long boards, kayaks and snorkeling equipment here. ~ 130 Kailua Road, Kailua; 808-262-2555. In the same area, **Naish Hawaii** offers lessons and rentals. This company manufactures its own boards and also operates a shop filled with the latest in sailboarding apparel and accessories, as well as long boards. ~ 155-A Hamakua Drive, Kailua; 808-261-6067.

**NORTH SHORE**  A resource for both the participatory and spectator aspects of surfing and windsurfing is the **Haleiwa Surf Center**. Surf lessons normally run September to early May. ~ Haleiwa Alii Beach Park, Haleiwa; 808-637-5051. In the same area surfing lessons and rentals are also available from **Surf N' Sea**. Lessons last two to three hours; price includes all gear. ~ 62-595 Kamehameha Highway, Haleiwa; 808-637-9887; www.surfnsea.com.

**SAILING**  One of the best ways to enjoy Oahu is aboard a sailboat. From brief cruises off Honolulu to a day-long charter along the North Shore, this is the perfect antidote to the tourist crowds. It's also surprisingly affordable.

### STAYING DRY WHILE EXPLORING THE DEPTHS

If you are not interested in Snuba or scuba diving but do want to see what's down under, try **Atlantis Adventures** (808-973-9811, 800-548-6262; www.goatlantis.com). You'll descend to 100 feet in air-conditioned hi-tech subs and explore an artificial reef complete with sunken ships and airplanes, created to bring back marine life to the area. It's not cheap, though.

If you're eager to charter your own yacht, contact **The Yacht Connection**. The company charters all sizes of vessels ranging from fishing boats to luxury yachts. ~ 1750 Kalakaua Avenue, Suite 3138, Honolulu; 808-523-1383; www.hawaiiyachts.com.

**Above Heaven's Gate** operates charter group cruises to the Diamond Head reef area aboard a teakwood pirate ship. You can also take a guided Hobie-cat tour off the Windward Coast to undiscovered islands most tourists miss (by appointment only). Along the way you'll enjoy Waimanalo, Kaneohe, Lanikai and Kailua Bay. You can also learn how to sail this swift 16-foot craft. ~ 41-1010 Laumilo Street, Waimanalo Bay; 808-259-5429, 800-800-2933, fax 808-259-5633; www.hawaiiweddings.com.

Ever dream of sailing off into the sunset, wind blowing in your hair? Snorkeling trips, swimming in the ocean off Diamond Head, a sunset cruise or a whale-watching venture can all be arranged with **Honolulu Sailing Company**. You can even get married at sea by your licensed and uniformed captain. This personable outfit will sail to meet your needs. ~ 47-335 Lulani Street, Honolulu; 808-239-3900, 800-829-0114; www.honsail.com.

**KAYAKING**

A sport well suited for Oahu, kayaking is an ideal way to explore the island's protected bays, islands and inland rivers. It seems that kayakers are popping up everywhere, particularly around the southeast coast of the island and up the Waimea River. To rent or purchase kayaks and equipment, or to sign up for lessons and tours, consider **Go Bananas** just outside Waikiki. ~ 799 Kapahulu Avenue; 808-737-9514. For kayak rentals and lessons contact **Kailua Sailboard and Kayak Company**. ~ 130 Kailua Road, Kailua; 808-262-2555.

**WAKE-BOARDING & WATER-SKIING**

Snowboarders with the summertime blues gave rise to wakeboarding. If the thrill of waterskiing is a little *too* thrilling, wakeboarding may be the sport to try. A relatively easy-to-control board is pulled slowly (well, 20–35 m.p.h) behind a boat, while the rider skims the wake. The equipment is much easier to maneuver than waterskis, and when your skills are up to par, you can venture into the fancy stuff: jumps, backrolls, zip-zags.

Waterskiing is more physically demanding than wakeboarding, using every muscle in your body, requiring a higher speed and employing narrower, less agile skis.

Near Koko Head, **Wakeboard & Waterski Center** offers instruction every day. A beginning class is 30 minutes, but you can also ski for 15 to 20 minutes. Reservations required. ~ Koko Marina Shopping Center, 7192 Kalanianaole Highway, Hawaii Kai; 808-395-3773; www.hisports.com.

**SKYDIVING & HANG-GLIDING**   You can learn to skydive and participate in a tandem dive with **Skydive Hawaii** at Dillingham Airfield on the North Shore. ~ 68-760 Farrington Highway; 808-637-9700.

Another skydiving operation at Dillingham Field is **Pacific International Skydiving Center**. ~ 68-760 Farrington Highway; 808-637-7472.

**Birdseye View of Oahu** offers daily ultralight airplane and tandem hang-gliding instruction at Kaneohe Marine Base. Call the company, and they'll also give you information on hang gliding in the area. ~ 328 Ilihau Street, Kailua; 808-637-3178.

**JOGGING**   Jogging is very big on Oahu. There are several popular spots, and though they are never quite deserted, the crowds rarely become unmanageable. **Ala Moana Regional Park** is a good area for a run; the paved road fronts the beach, and the cool ocean breezes are welcome. **Kapiolani Park** is another jogger's mecca. **Ala Wai Canal** is a less-recommended road; it's along a main drag and can get chaotic. Oahu also hosts endless races and marathons. For information on participation, pick up a free copy of *Hawaii Race Magazine*, available at most newsstands.

**RIDING STABLES**   It's not the Wild West, but Oahu is *paniolo* country. To explore its beaches, valleys and pasturelands, contact the following listings.

Located on the Windward Coast across from Chinaman's Hat, **Kualoa Ranch & Activity Center** leads one- and two-hour rides that provide startling views of the ocean and surrounding mountains. Guided rides for kids ages three through seven are available. They also offer many other activities including therapeutic horse rides for disabled people, a trip to Secret Island and snorkeling tours. Don't forget your swimsuit. ~ 49-560 Kamehameha Highway, Kaaawa; 808-237-8515; www.kualoa.com, e-mail activityinfo@kualoa.com.

The **Turtle Bay Resort** on the North Shore has riding programs for the general public. They offer 45-minute guided tours. These, and a one-and-one-half-hour evening ride, all take place on the grounds of the hotel, with trails along the beach and through a lovely wooded area. ~ 808-293-8811.

**Happy Trails Ranch** on the North Shore conducts one- to two-hour trail rides through a rainforest valley and pastureland. The ranch has peacocks, chickens, a wild boar and six species of ducks. Children will love this place, and they can ride if they are six years or older. ~ P.O. Box 461, Kahuku, HI 96731; 808-638-7433.

**GOLF**   Even before Tiger Woods, golf has been a very popular sport among visitors in Hawaii, and no other island has more golf courses than Oahu. With more than 30 to choose from, there's one to suit every level of play. And the scenery is spectacular.

**HONOLULU**    For a round of golf in Honolulu, try the **Ala Wai Golf Course**, Hawaii's first municipal course. ~ 404 Kapahulu Avenue; 808-733-7387. **Hawaii Kai Golf Course** is a popular spot with both tourists and *kamaainas* and features two 18-hole courses—one beginner and one championship. ~ 8902 Kalanianaole Highway; 808-395-2358.

**WINDWARD COAST**    The lush **Olomana Golf Links** has an 18-hole course. ~ 41-1801 Kalanianaole Highway, Waimanalo; 808-259-7926. For an inexpensive round of golf visit the **Bay View Golf Park**. ~ 45-285 Kaneohe Bay Drive, Kaneohe; 808-247-0451. Located below the Nuuanu Pali Lookout, the **Pali Golf Course** affords sweeping views of the rugged Koolaus and the windward coastline. ~ 45-050 Kamehameha Highway, Kaneohe; 808-266-7612. If you want to play a casual game, try the nine-hole **Kahuku Golf Course**. ~ Off Kamehameha Highway, Kahuku; 808-293-5842.

The *Guinness Book of World Records* named the Ala Wai Golf Course the busiest in the world.

**NORTH SHORE**    The **Links at Kuilima**, on the grounds of the Turtle Bay Resort, was created around an existing 100-acre wetland preserve, which serves as home to several endangered Hawaiian birds. There are two 18-hole courses designed by golf professional Arnold Palmer. ~ Kahuku; 808-293-8811.

**LEEWARD COAST AND CENTRAL OAHU**    Set amid fields of sugarcane and pineapple along the Leilehua Plateau in the center of Oahu, the **Hawaii Country Club** is a bit rundown, but offers some challenging holes on an 18-hole, par-72 course. ~ 94-1211 Kunia Road, Wahiawa; 808-622-1744. The **Mililani Golf Club**, though not particularly demanding, provides lovely views of the Koolau and Waianae ranges. ~ 95-176 Kuahelani Avenue, Mililani; 808-623-2254. The flat **Ted Makalena Golf Course** is not well-maintained, but is still popular with local golfers. ~ 93-059 Waipio Point Access Road, Waipahu; 808-675-6052.

At the **Ko Olina Golf Club** on the leeward coast, golfers must drive their carts under a waterfall to get to the twelfth hole of this championship course. They will also enjoy the series of lakes, brooks and waterfalls that meanders through the 18-hole course. ~ 92-1220 Aliinui Drive, Kapolei; 808-676-5309.

Especially beautiful is the **Makaha Golf Club** in the Makaha Valley, where sheer volcanic cliffs tower 1500 feet above lush greens, and golfers share the course with birds and peacocks. ~ 84-626 Makaha Valley Road, Makaha; 808-695-9544.

Many Oahu resorts offer complete tennis facilities. But don't despair if your hotel lacks nets. There are dozens of public tennis

**TENNIS**

courts in 47 locations around the island. Following is a partial listing.

**HONOLULU**   In the Waikiki area, try **Kapiolani Park**. ~ Kalakaua Avenue. **Diamond Head Tennis Center** is another option in the area. ~ Paki Avenue. There are courts across from Ala Moana Center at **Ala Moana Tennis Center**. ~ Ala Moana Regional Park, Ala Moana Boulevard.

In Greater Honolulu you can serve and volley at **Keehi Lagoon**. ~ Off the Nimitz Highway. Or opt for a set in the lush Manoa Valley at **Manoa Valley District Park**. ~ 2721 Kaaipu Avenue.

**WINDWARD COAST**   For your tennis needs on the Windward Coast, try Kailua District Park. ~ 21 South Kainalu Drive, Kailua. Or visit Kaneohe District Park. ~ 45-660 Keaahala Road, Kaneohe.

**NORTH SHORE AND LEEWARD COAST**   Sunset Beach Neighborhood Park has two lighted courts. ~ 59-360 Kamehameha Highway, Haleiwa.

Lighted courts are also available at **Waianae District Park**. ~ 85-601 Farrington Highway, Waianae.

Call the County Department of Parks and Recreation for more information on public courts. ~ 808-971-7150.

**BIKING**   Oahu is blessed with excellent roads, well-paved and usually flat, and cursed with heavy traffic. About three-quarters of Hawaii's population lives here, and it sometimes seems like every person owns a car.

Honolulu can be a cyclist's nightmare, but outside the city the traffic is somewhat lighter. And Oahu drivers, accustomed to tourists driving mopeds, are relatively conscious of bicyclists. It's certainly possible to bike through Central Oahu. **Kamehameha Highway** is an option, although it is dotted with steep grades and sections that aren't too bike-friendly.

If you'd really like to get away from it all, try mountain biking. Oahu's most popular mountain bike trail is **Mauna Wili** on

### KITESURFING

Following principles similar to paragliding, windsurfing and even snowboarding, kitesurfers are strapped to a light board and pulled across the water by, well, a big kite. Folks in decent physical condition and nerves of steel pick up the sport quickly, especially if they've had experience with a related activity. After some concentrated study, you'll graduate to bigger kites and speeds of up to 40 m.p.h. Lessons and rentals are provided by **Kailua Sailboards & Kayaks, Inc.**, along with hotel transportation. ~ 130 Kailua Road, Kailua; 808-262-2555; e-mail info@kailuasailboards.com.

the windward side. It starts from the Pali lookout and goes all the way to Waimanalo. In Waimea Bay, the **Ke Ala Pupukea bike path** goes through Sunset Beach Park and Waimea Bay Beach Park. It also conveniently passes a supermarket.

Keep in mind that the Windward Coast and the North Shore are the wet sides, and the south and west coasts are the driest of all. And remember, rip-offs are a frequent fact of life on Oahu. Leaving your bike unlocked is asking for a long walk back.

The Department of Transportation offers a free "Bike Oahu" map that lists detailed routes, road grades and where along the way you can find water and food. The entire brochure is also on their website. ~ 808-527-5044; www.state.hi.us/dot/highways/bike/oahu.

**Bike Rentals**    In Waikiki, **Coconut Cruisers** rents beach cruisers and mountain bikes. ~ 305 Royal Hawaiian Avenue; 808-924-1644. **Blue Sky Rentals** has mountain, road and tandem bikes. ~ 1920 Ala Moana Boulevard; 808-947-0101.

**Bike Repairs**    In addition to doing repair work, **Eki Cyclery** sells accessories and mountain bikes. ~ 1603 Dillingham Boulevard, Honolulu; 808-847-2005. With mountain, road and triathlon bikes for sale, **The Bike Shop** also does repair work. ~ 1149 South King Street, Honolulu; 808-596-0588. **Island Triathlon & Bike** repairs and sells bikes. ~ 569 Kapahulu Avenue; 808-732-7227.

There are numerous hiking trails within easy driving distance of Honolulu. I have listed these as well as trails in the Windward Coast and North Shore areas. Unfortunately, many Oahu treks require special permission from the state, the armed services or private owners. But you should find that the hikes suggested here, none of which require official sanction, will provide you with ample adventure.

**HIKING**

To hike with a group or to obtain further information on hiking Oahu, contact the **Sierra Club**. ~ P.O. Box 2577, Honolulu, HI 96803; 808-538-6616; www.hi.sierraclub.org. Another agency that also has regular weekend hikes is the **Hawaii Trail and Mountain Club**. E-mail ahead; some hikes are for members only. ~ P.O. Box 2238, Honolulu, HI 96804; e-mail htmc@aditl.com. The **Hawaii Nature Center** offers guided hikes one or two times a month. Call ahead to make a reservation. You can also get free maps and general trail information. ~ 2131 Makiki Heights Drive; 808-955-0100, 888-955-0104; www.hawaiinaturecenter.org.

All distances listed for hiking trails are one way unless otherwise noted.

**GREATER HONOLULU**    If you're staying in Waikiki, the most easily accessible hike is the short jaunt up **Diamond Head** crater.

There's a sweeping view of Honolulu from atop this famous landmark. The trail begins inside the crater, so take Diamond Head Road around to the inland side of Diamond Head, then follow the tunnel leading into the crater.

In the Koolau Mountains above Diamond Head there is a trail that climbs almost 2000 feet and affords excellent panoramas of the Windward Coast. To get to the **Lanipo Trail** (3 miles), take Waialae Avenue off of Route H-1. Then turn up Wilhelmina Rise and follow until it reaches Maunalani Circle and the trailhead.

For spectacular vistas overlooking the lush Palolo and Manoa valleys, you can hike **Waahila Ridge Trail** (2 miles). To get there, take St. Louis Heights Drive (near the University of Hawaii campus) and then follow connecting roads up to Waahila Ridge State Recreation Area.

The following trails can be combined for longer hikes. **Manoa Falls Trail** (0.8 mile) goes through Manoa Valley. This is a pleasant jaunt that follows Waihi Stream through a densely vegetated area to a charming waterfall. **Manoa Cliffs Trail** (3.4 miles) a pleasant family hike, follows a precipice along the west side of Manoa Valley. And **Puu Ohia Trail** (.75 mile), which crosses Manoa Cliffs Trail, provides splendid views of the Manoa and Nuuanu valleys. Both trails begin from Tantalus Drive in the hills above Honolulu. **Makiki Loop Trail** (2.5 miles roundtrip) begins near Tantalus Drive. Composed of three interlinking trails, this loop passes stands of eucalyptus and bamboo trees and offers some postcard views of Honolulu. Another loop trail, **Judd Memorial** (.75 mile), crosses Nuuanu Stream and traverses bamboo, eucalyptus and Norfolk pine groves en route to the Jackass Ginger Pool. To get there, take the Pali Highway (Route 61) several miles north from Honolulu. Turn onto Nuuanu Pali Drive and follow it about a mile to Reservoir Number Two spillway.

You can access a two-mile-long portion of the Old Pali Road directly to the right of the Pali Lookout. The narrow paved roadway provides easy hikes that are perfect for family excursions and reward with sweeping panoramas of the Windward Coast. For those with a more strenuous hike in mind, the **Koolaupoko Trail** (9 miles) departs from the Pali Lookout parking lot for magnificent rainforest, valley and ocean views. In places the trail is quite steep and occasionally demanding.

In the mountains above Pearl Harbor, at Keaiwa Heiau State Recreation Area, you will find the **Aiea Loop Trail** (4.8 miles). Set in a heavily forested area, this hike passes the wreckage of a World War II cargo plane. It provides an excellent chance to see some of the native Hawaiian trees—*lehua*, *ohia* and *koa*—used by local woodworkers. (For directions to Keaiwa Heiau State Recreation Area, see the "Greater Honolulu Beaches & Parks" section in this book.)

Another hike is along **Waimano Trail** (7 miles), which climbs 1600 feet to an astonishing vista point above Oahu's Windward Coast. There are swimming holes en route to the vista point. To get there, take Kamehameha Highway (Route 90) west to Waimano Home Road (Route 730). Turn right and go two and a half miles to a point along the road where you'll see a building on the right and an irrigation ditch on the left. The trail follows the ditch.

**SOUTHEAST OAHU** There are several excellent hikes along this shore. The first few are within ten miles of Waikiki, near **Hanauma Bay**. From the beach at Hanauma you can hike two miles along the coast and cliffs to the Halona Blowhole. This trek passes the Toilet Bowl, a unique tidepool with a hole in the bottom that causes it to fill and then flush with the wave action. Waves sometimes wash the rocks along this path, so be prepared to get wet (and be careful!).

At the intersection where the short road leading down toward Hanauma Bay branches from Kalanianaole Highway (Route 72), there are two other trails. **Koko Head Trail** (1 mile), a hike to the top of a volcanic cone, starts on the ocean side of the highway. This trek features some startling views of Hanauma Bay, Diamond Head and the Koolau Range. Another hike, along **Koko Crater Trail** (1 mile), leads from the highway up to a 1208-foot peak. The views from this crow's nest are equally spectacular.

**WINDWARD COAST** There are several other particularly pretty hikes much farther north, near the village of Hauula. In Hauula, if you turn off of Kamehameha Highway and head inland for about a quarter-mile up Hauula Homestead Road, you'll come to Maakua Road. Walk up Maakua Road, which leads into the woods. About 300 yards after entering the woods, the road forks. Maakua Gulch Trail branches to the left. If you continue straight ahead you'll be on Hauula Trail, but if you veer left onto Maa-

**ON WHEELS**

Riders may cruise the Kalanianaole Highway, past Kapiolani Park and around Diamond Head to Hanauma Bay, pedal along the Waianae Coast or zip across the interior from Waialua to Pearl City. Other coastal rides cover the area between Haleiwa and Kahuku and the stretch between Waimanalo Beach and Kaaawa. If you'd like a little two-wheeled company, check out the **Hawaii Bicycling League**, which regularly sponsors weekend bike rides and free annual events. ~ 3442 Waialae Avenue #1, Honolulu, HI 96816; phone/fax 808-735-5756; e-mail bicycle@hbl.com.

kua Gulch Trail, you'll encounter yet another trail branching off to the left in about 150 yards. This is Papali Trail (also known as Maakua Trail).

**Maakua Gulch Trail** (3 miles), en route to a small waterfall, traverses a rugged canyon with extremely steep walls. Part of the trail lies along the stream bed, so be ready to get wet. **Hauula Trail** (2.5 miles) ascends along two ridges and provides fine vistas of the Koolau Range and the Windward Coast. **Papali Trail** (2.5 miles) drops into Papali Gulch, then climbs high along a ridge from which you can view the surrounding countryside.

**NORTH SHORE AND LEEWARD COAST**   You can approach the trail to **Kaena Point** either from the North Shore or the Leeward Coast. It's a dry, rock-strewn path that leads to Oahu's western-most tip. There are tidepools and swimming spots en route, plus spectacular views of a rugged, uninhabited coastline; it's a great place to spot porpoises, and is the legendary home of Nanue the Shark Man. If you're lucky you may sight nesting albatross or rare Hawaiian Monk seals. Keep your distance as both are pro-tected species and a portion of the point is a wildlife preserve. In ancient times, this was sacred land; it was believed the souls of the dead departed from Kaena to the afterworld, called *Po*, the realm of the spirits. To get to the trailhead, just drive to the end of the paved portion of Route 930 on the North Shore or Route 93 on the Leeward Coast. Then follow the trail out to Kaena Point. It's about two miles via the Leeward Coast, and a half-mile via the North Shore.

▼▼▼▼▼▼▼▼▼▼▼▼
## Transportation

### AIR

There's one airport on Oahu and it's a behemoth. **Honolulu International Airport** is a Pacific crossroads, an essential link between North America and Asia. Honolulu International includes all the comforts of a major air-port. You can check your bags; fuel up at a restaurant, coffee shop or cocktail lounge; shop at several stores; or shower.

To cover the eight or so miles into Waikiki, it's possible to hire a cab for $25 to $30. For $8 (roundtrip $14), **Robert's Hawaii** will take you to your Waikiki hotel or condominium. ~ 808-539-9400, 800-831-5541; www.robertshawaii.com.

City buses #19 and #20 travel through Downtown Honolulu and Waikiki. This is the cheapest transportation, but you're only allowed to carry on baggage that fits on your lap. So, unless you're traveling very light, you'll have to use another con-veyance.

### CAR RENTALS

Of all the islands, Oahu offers the most car-rental agencies. At the Honolulu airport, **Avis Rent A Car** (808-834-5536, 800-321-3712), **Budget Rent A Car** (808-836-1700, 800-527-0700), **Dollar Rent A Car** (866-434-2226, 800-800-4000), **National**

Car Rental (808-831-3800, 800-227-7368) and **Hertz** (808-831-3500, 800-654-3011) all have booths. Their convenient location helps to save time while minimizing the problem of picking up your car.

Though not at the airport, **Alamo Rent A Car** provides airport pick-up service. ~ 808-833-4585, 800-327-9633. VIP **Rental** is a cheaper outfit. ~ 234 Beachwalk; 808-922-4605.

There are many other Honolulu-based companies offering very low rates but providing limited pick-up service at the airport. I've never found the inconvenience worth the savings. There you are—newly arrived from the mainland, uncertain about your environment, anxious to check in at the hotel—and you're immediately confronted with the Catch-22 of getting to your car. Do you rent a vehicle in which to pick up your rental car? Take a bus? Hitchhike? What do you do with your bags meanwhile?

If you prefer to go in high style, book a limousine from **Cloud Nine**. ~ 808-524-7999, 800-524-7999.

> TheBus covers 90 percent of the 60-square-mile island. The fleet of 525 buses travel a combined total of 60,000 miles every day, carrying 260,000 passengers—between 30,000 and 35,000 of them are visitors.

**Adventure on 2 Wheels** (808-944-3131) and **Dollar Rent A Car** (808-831-2331) provide jeeps. VIP **Car Rental** (808-922-4605) rents Suzuki Samurais and Geo Trackers.

**JEEP RENTALS**

In Waikiki, **Adventure on 2 Wheels** rents mopeds and bicycles, among other things. ~ 1946 Ala Moana Boulevard; 808-944-3131. You can also try **Blue Sky Rentals**, located on the ground floor of the Inn On The Park Hotel. ~ 1920 Ala Moana Boulevard; 808-947-0101.

**MOPED RENTALS**

Oahu has an excellent bus system that runs regularly to points all over the island and provides convenient service throughout Honolulu. Many of the beaches, hotels, restaurants and points of interest mentioned in this chapter are just a bus ride away. It's even possible to pop your money in the fare box and ride around the entire island.

**PUBLIC TRANSIT**

**TheBus** rumbles along city streets and country roads from 5 a.m. to 10 p.m. (though some lines run past midnight). There are also express buses traveling major highways at commuter times. Most buses are handicapped accessible and many have bike racks.

If you stay in Waikiki you'll inevitably be sardined into a #19 or #20 bus for the ride through Honolulu's tourist mecca. Many bus drivers are Hawaiian; I saw some hysterical scenes on this line when tourists waited anxiously for their stop to be called, only to realize they couldn't understand the driver's pidgin. Hysterical, that is, *after* those early days when *I* was the visitor with the furrowed brow.

But you're surely more interested in meeting local people than tourists, and you can easily do it on any of the buses outside Waikiki. They're less crowded and a lot more fun for peoplewatching.

For information on bus routes call TheBus at 808-848-5555 or visit www.thebus.org. And remember, the only carry-on luggage permitted is baggage small enough to fit on your lap.

**AERIAL TOURS**

The quickest way to see all Oahu has to offer is by taking to the air. In minutes you can experience the island's hidden waterfalls, secluded beaches and volcanic landmarks. Tranquil gliders and hovering whirlybirds all fly low and slow to make sure you see what you missed on the trip over from the mainland. You can also take extended flights that include the outer islands.

**Makani Kai Helicopters** offers helicopter tours of Waikiki and Honolulu, Hanauma Bay, the Koolau Mountains, Chinaman's Hat, Sacred Falls, Kahana Rainforest and the North Shore. They also take trips to the "Jurassic Park Valley," an area where parts of the movie were filmed. Reservations required. ~ 110 Kapalulu Place, Honolulu; 808-834-1111, fax 808-837-7867; www.makanikai.com.

To enjoy a one- or two-passenger glider trip, head out to **The Original Glider Rides** and talk to Mr. Bill. On your 20-minute trip you're likely to see fields of sugar cane, marine mammals, surfers working the North Shore and neighboring Kauai. You'll also enjoy peace and quiet while working your way down from 3000 feet. A videotape of the ride and your reactions makes a memorable souvenir. ~ Dillingham Airfield, Mokuleia; 808-677-3404; www. honolulusoaring.com.

**WALKING TOURS**

**Oahu Nature Tours** offers nine different daily eco-tours that provide an overview of native Hawaiian birds and plants. One focuses on Oahu's volcanic coast, beginning in Diamond Head Crater, continuing through a lagoon wildlife sanctuary, then heading out to the island's southeast corner. Another tour takes you into the Hawaiian rainforest at 2000-feet elevation in the Koolau Mountains. Equipment, transportation and water are provided. Reservations required. Fee. ~ P.O. Box 8059, Honolulu, HI 96815; 808-924-2473; www.oahunaturetours.com.

Ready for goosebumps? Stroll through the past with a company called **Chicken Skin Tours**. Based in Honolulu they offer a number of bus and walking tours. The Ghost Hunter's Bus Tour focuses on the supernatural lore of the island. Reservations highly recommended. Fee. ~ 808-943-0371, fax 808-951-8878; e-mail timewalk@pixi.com.

Chinatown's rich history and culture can be experienced in several inexpensive walking tours that make this exotic place come alive. Explore the markets to find the special ingredients that make up Thai, Vietnamese and Chinese cooking on monthly walks hosted by **Lyon Arboretum**. Fee. ~ 808-988-0456. Learn about the past in a two-hour morning tour offered by the **Hawaii Heritage Center**. Fee. ~ 808-521-2749. Hear tidbits about the economic contributions of the Chinese on a Tuesday-morning tour by the **Chinese Chamber of Commerce of Hawaii**. Fee. ~ 808-533-3181.

# FIVE

# Hawaii

The Big Island, they call it, and even that is an understatement. Hawaii, all 4030 square miles, is almost twice as large as all the other Hawaiian islands combined. Its twin volcanic peaks, Mauna Kea and Mauna Loa, dwarf most mountains. Mauna Loa, the world's largest active volcano, which last erupted in 1984, looms 13,677 feet above sea level. Mauna Kea, rising 13,796 feet, is the largest island-based mountain in the world. It is actually 32,000 feet from the ocean floor, making it, by one system of reckoning, the tallest mountain on earth, grander even than Everest. And in bulk Mauna Loa is the world's largest. The entire Sierra Nevada chain could fit within this single peak.

Kilauea, a third volcano whose seething firepit has been erupting with startling frequency, is one of the world's most active volcanoes. Since its most recent series of eruptions began in 1983, Kilauea has swallowed almost 200 houses. In 1990 it completely destroyed the town of Kalapana, burying a once lively village beneath tons of black lava; then in 1992 it destroyed the ancient Hawaiian village of Kamoamoa and the *heiau* at Wahaula. There is little doubt that the Big Island is a place of geologic superlatives.

But size alone does not convey the Big Island's greatness. Its industry, too, is expansive. Despite the lava wasteland that covers large parts of its surface, and the volcanic gases that create a layer of "vog" during volcanic eruptions, the Big Island is the state's greatest producer of coffee, papayas, vegetables, anthuriums, macadamia nuts and cattle. Its orchid industry, based in rain-drenched Hilo, is the world's largest. Over 22,000 varieties grow in the nurseries here.

Across the island in sun-soaked Kona, one of the nation's only coffee industries operates. Just off this spectacular western coast lie some of the finest deepsea fishing grounds in the world. Between Hilo and Kona, and surrounding Waimea, sits the Parker Ranch. Sprawling across 225,000 acres, it is one of the world's largest independently owned cattle ranches.

Yet many of these measurements are taken against island standards. Compared to the mainland, the Big Island is a tiny speck in the sea. Across its broadest reach it measures a scant 93 miles long and 76 miles wide, smaller than Connecticut. The road around the island totals only 300 miles, and can be driven in a day, though I'd recommend taking at least five. The island's 148,677 population comprises just 8 percent of the state's citizens. Its lone city, Hilo, has a population of only 40,759.

But large or small, numbers cannot fully describe the Big Island, for there is a magic about the place that transcends statistics. Hawaii, also nicknamed the Orchid Island and Volcano Island, is the home of Pele, the goddess of volcanoes. Perhaps her fiery spirit is what infuses the Big Island with an unquantifiable quality. Or maybe the island's comparative youth is what makes the elements seem nearer, more alluring and strangely threatening here. It's still growing in size because of lava flows from Kilauea and Mauna Loa. In fact, recent activity has added more than a square mile to the island. The Big Island is geologically the youngest spot on earth, one million years old. Whatever it might be, the Big Island has always been where I feel closest to the Polynesian spirit. Of all the Hawaiian islands, this one I love the most.

It was here, possibly as early as A.D. 400 or as late as the 9th century, that Polynesian explorers may have first landed when they discovered the island chain. Until the advent of the white man, it was generally the most important island, supporting a large population and occupying a vital place in Hawaii's rich mythology. Little wonder then that Kamehameha the Great, the chief who would become Hawaii's first king, was born here in 1753. He established the archipelago's first capital in Kailua and ruled there until his death in 1819.

Within a year of the great leader's passing, two events occurred in Kailua that jolted the entire chain far more than any earthquake. First the king's heir, Liholiho, uprooted the centuries-old taboo system upon which the native Hawaiian religion rested. Then, in the spring of 1820, the first American missionaries dropped anchor off the coast of Kailua-Kona. It was also near here that Captain James Cook, history's greatest discoverer, was slain in 1779 by the same people who had earlier welcomed him as a god. Across the island another deity, Pele, was defied in 1824 when the high chieftess Kapiolani, a Christian, ate *kapu* (forbidden) fruit on the rim of an active lava lake at Kilauea, and suffered no ill consequence.

As stirring as the Big Island's story might be, much of its drama still awaits the visitor. For the land—the volcanoes, beaches and valleys—is as vital and intriguing today as in the days of demigods and kings. This is a place for the adventurer to spend a lifetime.

On the east coast, buffeted by trade winds, lies Hilo, a lush tropical town that soaks up 140 inches of rain annually. Here anthuriums and orchids are cultivated in a number of spectacular nurseries. Just to the south—smoking, heaving and erupting—sits Hawaii Volcanoes National Park.

The Puna District that straddles the coast between the volcanoes and Hilo has been the site of dramatic eruptions during the past decade. This lush rainforest is also the scene of a major political debate that has pitted environmentalists against developers of a geothermal power plant.

In the north, from the Hamakua Coast to the Kohala Peninsula, heavy erosion has cut through the volcano to form spectacular canyons such as the Waipio

Valley. All along the Hamakua plateau, sugar plantations, fed by waters from Mauna Kea, stretch from the mountains to the surf.

In startling contrast to these verdant mountains is the desert-like Kau district at the southern tip of the island (and, for that matter, the southernmost point in the United States). Along the west coast stretches the Kona district, a vacationer's paradise. Suntan weather, sandy beaches and coral reefs teeming with tropical fish make this an ideal area to just kick back and enjoy. The island's central tourist area is located here in Kailua-Kona, where Hawaiian royalty settled in the 19th century.

Rain or shine, you can get the weather report for the entire island at 808-961-5582, or just for Hilo at 808-935-8555.

And for something unique to the Big Island, there's Waimea with its rolling grasslands, range animals and *paniolos*, or Hawaiian-style cowboys. In fact, one of the biggest Hereford cattle herds is located here in the center of the island.

It's an island I don't think you should miss, an island that offers a string of luxury resorts as well as time-worn tropical retreats hidden along its other shores. To geologists the Big Island is a natural laboratory in which the mysteries of volcanic activity are a fact of everyday life; to many Hawaiians it is the most sacred of all the islands. To everyone who visits it, Hawaii is a place of startling contrasts and unspeakable beauty, an alluring and exotic tropical island.

## Kailua-Kona Area

At the center of the tourist scene on the Kona Coast is the contemporary town of Kailua or Kailua-Kona—a reference to the district in which it's located. Here, extending for eight miles along Alii Drive from the King Kamehameha Hotel to Keauhou Bay, is a string of hotels, restaurants, condominiums and shopping malls. Like a little Waikiki, Kailua-Kona is the commercial focus for this side of the island.

**SIGHTS**

Despite the tinsel and tourist trappings, this old fishing village and former haunt of Hawaiian royalty still retains some of its charm. If you tour **Kailua wharf** around 4 p.m., the fishing boats may be hauling freshly caught marlin onto the docks. Some of the finest marlin grounds in the world lie off this shoreline and the region is renowned for other deep-sea fish. The wharf itself is a departure point not only for fishing charters but for snorkeling tours and glass-bottom boat cruises as well. It's also a favorite place for viewing Kona's fabled sunsets. ~ Alii Drive.

On the grounds of the nearby King Kamehameha's Kona Beach Hotel rests **Ahuena Heiau**, a culturally significant site that has been reconstructed. Ahuena was once part of Kamakahonu ("the eye of the turtle"), Kamehameha's royal compound. It was here that the exalted Kamehameha retired after uniting Hawaii's islands as a single kingdom. Menacing *kii* (sacred wooden figures) stand guard here, while offerings wrapped in *ti* leaves are still left by the faithful. Unfortunately, a hotel luau facility was built immediately next to the site. Tours of the hotel grounds are available by appointment. ~ 75-5660 Palani Road; 808-327-0123.

**Hulihee Palace,** a small but elegant estate built in 1838, sits on Alii Drive in the middle of town. Today it's a museum housing royal Hawaiian relics. This two-story estate was built by the brother-in-law of Kamehameha I and later used by King Kalakaua as a summer palace during the 1880s. Among the fine furnishings are many handcrafted from native *koa.* Admission. ~ 75-5718 Alii Drive; 808-329-1877, fax 808-329-1321; www. huliheepalace.org, e-mail hulihee@ilhawaii.net.

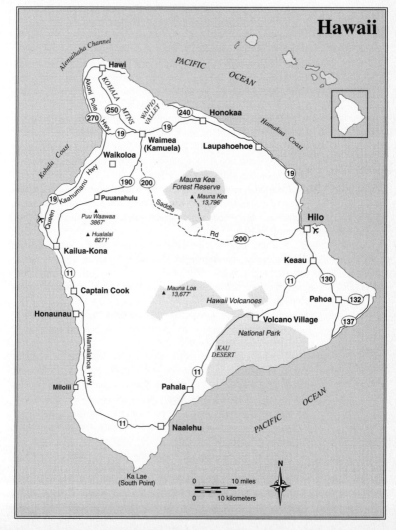

**Mokuaikaua Church,** directly across the street, is the oldest church in the islands. The first missionaries anchored offshore in 1820 after sailing over 18,000 miles around Cape Horn from Boston. By 1836, with most of the Hawaiians converted to Protestant Christianity, the missionaries dedicated this imposing lava-and-coral structure. ~ 808-329-1589.

Contrasting with these venerable sites is **Atlantis Adventures,** an 80-ton made-for-tourists submarine. Diving to depths of 120 feet, this 48-passenger sub explores tropical reefs. During the hour-long voyage, passengers view the underwater world through large viewing ports. Admission. ~ 808-329-6626, 800-548-6262, fax 808-329-1153; www.atlantisadventures.com.

Almost everything in Kailua sits astride Alii Drive, the waterfront street that extends south from town to Keauhou Bay. Several miles from Kailua, this road passes **Disappearing Sands Beach** (or Magic Sands Beach). The lovely white sand here is often washed away by heavy winter surf and then redeposited when the big waves subside as the seasons change.

Farther along, on the rocky shore of Kahaluu Bay, is **St. Peter's Catholic Church.** This stark blue-and-white clapboard chapel, also known as the "Little Blue Church" precariously perched on a lava foundation, is reputedly the world's second-smallest church and was established in 1889.

Located just across the bay are several interesting historical sites: two *heiaus* and the **King's Pool.** You can continue on to Keauhou Bay, where a monument marks the **Birthplace of Kamehameha III.**

You can pay your respects to the crew of the space shuttle *Challenger* at the **Astronaut Ellison S. Onizuka Space Center.** Located eight miles north of Kailua at Kona International Airport, this interactive learning center is a tribute to Onizuka, who lived in Hawaii, and the other astronauts who died in the 1986 tragedy. Videos and interactive displays trace the astronauts' lives and the development of the space program. Admission. ~ 808-329-3441, fax 808-326-9751.

The Big Island is the only place in the United States where cacao beans, the basic ingredient of chocolate, are grown, and the **Original Hawaiian Chocolate Factory** is the only operation on the island that grows, harvests, processes and packages all-Hawaiian chocolate. The Coopers conduct factory tours about five times a week by reservation only. ~ For reservations and directions, call 808-322-2626.

**LODGING**    **Patey's Place in Paradise,** a conveniently priced hostel in the center of Kailua, is small and clean, and boasts a bay view from the huge wraparound deck—remarkable for this area. There are dormitory-style accommodations for 12 people as well as four pri-

*Big Island Getaway*

## Seven-day Itinerary

**Day 1**
- Arrive in **Kailua-Kona** (page 172) and check into a condominium or hotel in town or along the Kohala Coast.
- In the afternoon explore the **Kohala Coast** (page 188) along Route 270, the Akoni Pule Highway, up to the **Pololu Valley Lookout** (page 192).

**Day 2**
- Spend the day snorkeling, swimming, sportfishing, or reading a book.

**Day 3**
- Take Route 190 to the upcountry ranch town of **Waimea** (page 202) and go horseback riding. Or if your rental car company allows, take the Saddle Road up to the road leading to Mauna Kea and the **Onizuka Center for International Astronomy** (page 226). Plan to have dinner in Waimea before heading back.

**Day 4**
- From Kailua-Kona drive around South Point, stopping at **Kealakekua Bay** (page 211) and **Puuhonua o Honaunau National Historical Park** (page 211).
- Continue on Route 11 to Hawaii Volcanoes National Park and spend the night at **Volcano House** (page 228) or a local bed and breakfast. Try to arrive by 4 p.m. so you can see the volcanic activity at dusk, when the glow from the lava is most intense.

**Day 5**
- Explore **Hawaii Volcanoes National Park** (page 221).

**Day 6**
- Head to **Hilo** (page 235) and check in to a hotel or B&B. Explore **downtown** Hilo and the **Liliuokalani Gardens** (page 236). Beach lovers can spend the afternoon at **Richardson Ocean Park** (page 244). Orchid fans should be sure to visit some of the local **flower farms** (page 236).

**Day 7**
- Return to the Kohala Coast via the **Hamakua Coast** (page 245), visiting the **Waipio Valley** (page 247), if time allows, before checking in at the airport.

vate rooms that sleep eight and have ocean views. Kitchen facilities, internet access and television rooms are provided. ~ 75 Ala Ona Ona Street; 808-326-7018, fax 808-326-7640; www.accom modationshawaii.com, e-mail ipatey@gte.net. BUDGET.

**Kona Seaside Hotel**, a sprawling 218-room complex, resides in the heart of Kailua. Located across the street from the ocean, this multi-faceted facility features the Tower Wing; the Garden Wing, where the rooms come with mini-kitchenettes; and the Pool Wing, where the rooms are smaller and less fashionable but are conveniently placed around one of the hotel's two swimming pools. While the more expensive rooms add lanais and wall-to-wall carpeting, all the accommodations are tastefully done. A restaurant is adjacent. ~ 75-5646 Palani Road; 808-329-2455, 800-560-5558, fax 808-329-6157; www.sand-seaside.com. DELUXE.

Part of the **Kona Bay Hotel** is part of the old Kona Inn, the rest of which fell to Kailua developers who have perversely transformed it into yet another shopping mall. What remains is a four-story semicircular structure with a pool, bar, restaurant and lounge in the center. The rooms are large, tastefully furnished and quiet. Some have lava walls that provide a pleasant backdrop plus excellent soundproofing. The staff is friendly, and the atmosphere is very appealing. I once spent a relaxing month here and recommend the place. ~ 75-5739 Alii Drive; 808-329-1393, 800-367-5102, fax 808-935-7903; www.unclebilly.com, e-mail resv@unclebilly.com. MODERATE.

**Kona Tiki Hotel**, a mile down the road, is a quaint hotel neatly situated on the ocean. The rooms are bright and clean. Despite the contrasting decorative themes and the noise from Alii Drive, I recommend this 15-unit establishment for its oceanview lanais, oceanfront pool, barbecue, garden and complimentary continental breakfast. Most of the rooms have kitchenettes. Reservations are recommended. ~ 75-5968 Alii Drive; 808-329-1425, fax 808-327-9402; www.konatiki.com. BUDGET TO MODERATE.

**Kona Islander Inn** occupies several three-story buildings spread across a lush swath of land. Set between Alii Drive and Route 11 on Kailua's outskirts, this hotel has a large lobby, an oval pool, a hot tub and a barbecue flanked by MacArthur palms. All studios have small lanais, cable television, microwaves, refrigerators and air conditioning; two have ocean views. ~ 75-5776 Kuakini Highway; 808-329-3333, 800-622-5348, fax 808-326-4137; www.konahawaii.com, e-mail konahawaii@hot mail.com. BUDGET TO MODERATE.

**Kona White Sands Apartment Hotel**, located just across the street from Disappearing Sands Beach (the nicest beach along Alii Drive), is a ten-unit hotel of one-bedroom apartments. Each comes with a kitchenette and ceiling fans. The cinderblock and plasterboard walls are pretty plain, but who needs fancy interior decoration with that knockout ocean view? Rooms are cross-ventilated, and the cooling breeze will probably bring along noise from cars and sun revelers. That's the extra price for living this close to the Kona Coast. Many people are willing to pay it, so you'll have to reserve a room far in advance. ~ 77-6467 Alii Drive. For reservations here and at Kona Islander Inn, contact the Hawaii Resorts Management, 75-5776 Kuakini Highway, Suite 105-C, Kailua-Kona, HI 96740; 808-329-9393, 800-244-4752, fax 808-326-4137; www.konahawaii.com, e-mail kona hawaii@hotmail.com. MODERATE.

**OHANA Keauhou Beach Resort** is a true sleeper. A large, blocky, seven-story hotel from the outside, it hardly seems like it

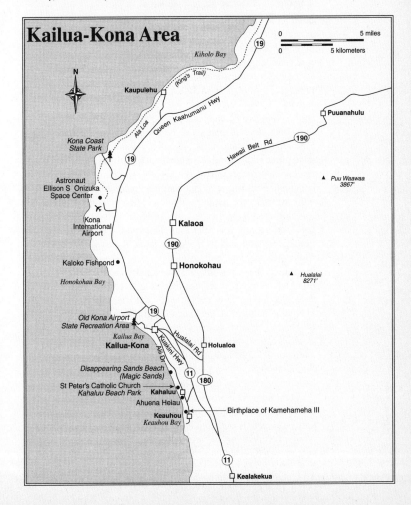

# Kailua-Kona Area

0 — 5 miles
0 — 5 kilometers

N

Kiholo Bay

19

(King's Trail)

Kaupulehu

Queen Kaahumanu Hwy

Ala Loa

Puuanahulu

Kona Coast
State Park

190

Hawaii Belt Rd

19

Astronaut
Ellison S Onizuka
Space Center

▲ Puu Waawaa
3867'

Kona
International
Airport

Kalaoa

190

Kaloko Fishpond ●

Honokohau

Honokohau Bay

▲ Hualalai
8271'

19

Old Kona Airport
State Recreation Area

Kailua Bay
**Kailua-Kona**

Hualalai Rd

Kuakini Hwy

Holualoa

Disappearing Sands Beach
(Magic Sands)

Alii Dr

11

180

St Peter's Catholic Church
Kahaluu Beach Park

Kahaluu

Ahuena Heiau

Keauhou
Keauhou Bay

Birthplace of Kamehameha III

11

Kealakekua

could possess the Hawaiian spirit. But the beautifully landscaped grounds include an ancient *heiau* and other archaeological sites, and the waterfront boasts magnificent tidepools that extend for acres. The airy Hawaiian-style lobby overlooks an oceanfront swimming pool, two restaurants and a lounge. Spacious guest rooms look out over the ocean or gardens. ~ 78-6740 Alii Drive; 808-322-3441, 800-462-6262, fax 808-322-3117; www.ohana hotels.com, e-mail kbr@ohanahotels.com. ULTRA-DELUXE.

Anchoring one end of Kailua Bay is the town's most historic hotel. The **King Kamehameha Kona Beach Hotel** is deserving of note. The lobby alone is worth the price of admission: It's a wood-paneled affair along which you can trace the history of ancient Hawaii. For its guests, the "King Kam" has a pool, tennis courts and jacuzzi, plus a host of other amenities ranging from an activities desk to room service. The rooms themselves are quite spacious, fashionably decorated and well equipped. You'll find plush carpeting, color televisions, air conditioning, refrigerators, coffee makers and lanais with views of the ocean or mountains. ~ 75-5660 Palani Road; 808-329-2911, 800-367-2111, fax 808-329-4602; www.konabeachhotel.com, e-mail roomres ervations@hthcorp.com. DELUXE TO ULTRA-DELUXE.

*Shibui* best describes the **Four Seasons Resort Hualalai at Historic Kaupulehu**. With 243 understated yet elegant bungalow-style guest rooms and 31 suites (each with a private lanai and oceanview), this resort offers a bit of heaven here on earth. Of course, heaven is pricey. But outdoor enthusiasts will be content with the four oceanfront pools—including a seawater pool made for snorkelers—the Sports Club and Spa with its lap pool, eight tennis courts and rock-climbing wall and the PGA championship golf course designed by Jack Nicklaus. Kids will like the game room and parents will appreciate the "Kids for all Seasons Program." (Children under 18 can share their parents' room at no extra charge.) There are three restaurants for dining. What will make it a "Hidden Hawaii" experience is a visit to the Hawaiian cultural center that extends the *Kaupulehu* traditions of Hawaii to the visitor. They offer such diverse classes as ukulele, the Hawaiian language, *lauhala* weaving and Hawaiian navigation. ~ 100 Kaupulehu Drive, Kaupulehu-Kona; 808-325-8000, fax 808-325-8053; www.fourseasons.com/hualalai, e-mail hualalai.reservations@fourseasons.com. ULTRA-DELUXE.

**Hale Kipa 'O Pele** offers three in-house suites and an adjoining bungalow in a plantation-style home with coastal views. A garden jacuzzi is surrounded by lush vegetation. Each suite has a lanai and is decorated with Hawaiian motifs. A *koi* pond provides this B & B with a distinctive feel. ~ P.O. Box 5252, Kailua-Kona, HI 96740; 808-329-8676, 800-528-2456; www.gaystay hawaii.com, e-mail halekipa@gte.net. MODERATE.

Budget accommodations in Kailua-Kona? Well, almost. Centrally located in town, the **Kona Islander Inn Resort** was one of the first condominium complexes built in the area back in the 1960s, and these days it's probably the most affordable. The 145 refurbished, air-conditioned rooms are studio apartments, each with a single large living/sleeping room, a kitchenette and a lanai. The complex consists of three buildings, each three stories tall, linked by pathways that lead among palm trees and gardens. There's a swimming pool and a hot tub, and a white-sand beach directly across the highway. Daily rates run from $79.95 to $99.95. ~ 75-5776 Kuakini Highway; 808-329-3333, 800-244-4752, fax 808-326-4137; www.konahawaii.com, e-mail kona hawaii@hotmail.com.

One-bedroom, two-bath apartments at **Kona Alii** run from $119 double (and from $99 during the off-season, April 1 to December 15). This seven-story building is just across the street from the ocean. ~ 75-5782 Alii Drive; book through Hawaii

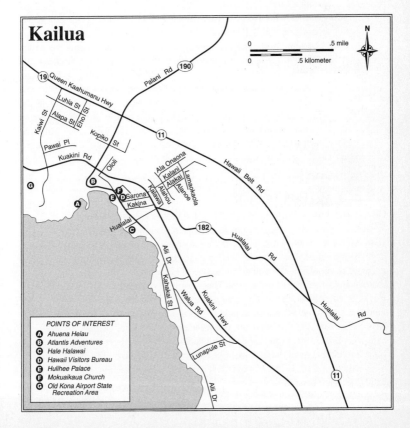

**Kailua**

0      .5 mile
0      .5 kilometer

N

**POINTS OF INTEREST**
- Ⓐ Ahuena Heiau
- Ⓑ Atlantis Adventures
- Ⓒ Hale Halawai
- Ⓓ Hawaii Visitors Bureau
- Ⓔ Hulihee Palace
- Ⓕ Mokuaikaua Church
- Ⓖ Old Kona Airport State Recreation Area

Resorts Management, 75-5776 Kuakini Highway, Suite 105-C, Kailua-Kona; 808-329-9393, 800-244-4752, fax 808-326-4137; www.konahawaii.com, e-mail konahawaii@hotmail.com.

 About one mile south of Kailua is the **Sea Village**, which offers one-bedroom ocean-view units starting at $120 single or double; two bedrooms, two baths are $165 to $180 for one to four people. There's a swimming pool and tennis courts. Oceanfront, but no beach. ~ 75-6002 Alii Drive; book through Sun Quest Vacations, 808-326-7434, 800-367-5168; www.sunquest-hawaii.com, e-mail squest@sunquest-hawaii.com.

**Kona Riviera Villa** is a relatively small condo on a lava-rock beach outside Kailua. It's attractively landscaped, has a pool and rents one-bedroom units for $95 to $115 ($85 to $105 from April 15 to December 14). Three-day minimum. ~ 75-6124 Alii Drive; 808-329-1996. Reserve through Knutson and Associates, 75-6082 Alii Drive, Suite 8, Kailua-Kona; 800-800-6202, fax 808-326-2178; www.konahawaiirentals.com, e-mail knutson@aloha.net.

 Located on Banyans Beach in Kona, **Marc Kona Bali Kai** is one of Kailua-Kona's only oceanfront accommodations. Suites are roomy and nicely appointed, and include studios and one-, two- and three-bedroom suites, all with fully equipped kitchens and ceiling fans. Other amenities include laundry facilities, a convenience store, a snorkeling shop, barbecue areas and limited maid service. There's a courtyard swimming pool and jacuzzi. Rates range from $195 for a mountain studio to $395 for an oceanfront three-bedroom that sleeps eight. ~ 76-6246 Alii Drive; 808-329-9381, fax 808-326-6056; www.marcresorts.com, e-mail kbkai@hawaii.rr.com.

**AUTHOR FAVORITE**

Of course, when money is no object, the place to stay is **Kona Village Resort**, a very plush, private colony located 12 miles north of Kailua. This regal retreat is set along a white-sand cove in an ancient Hawaiian fishing village. The individual guest cottages are thatched-roof structures, variously designed to represent the traditional houses of Hawaiian, Tahitian, Fijian, Samoan and other Polynesian groups. There are no TVs, telephones, radios, clocks or air conditioners in the rooms, but you will find serenity, solitude and a well-heeled version of hidden Hawaii, not to mention a fitness center, tennis courts, sailboats, outrigger canoes and glass-bottom excursion boats. Prices are in the stratosphere and are based on the American plan. Closed the first week of December. ~ P.O. Box 1299, Kaupulehu-Kona, HI 96745; 808-325-5555, 800-367-5290, fax 808-325-0206; www.konavillage.com, e-mail kvr@aloha.net. ULTRA-DELUXE.

**Kona Magic Sands** has a studio apartment renting for $75 without air conditioning, $95 with, year-round, single or double. It's located on the ocean, next to Disappearing Sands Beach. ~ 77-6452 Alii Drive. Book through Hawaii Resorts Management, 75-5776 Kuakini Highway, Suite 105-C, Kailua-Kona; 808-329-9393, 800-244-4752, fax 808-326-4137; www. konahawaii.com, e-mail konahawaii@hotmail.com.

**Aston Kona By The Sea** is a large, trimly landscaped complex on a lava-rock beach. The suites are one- and two-bedroom; all have two baths and a lanai; there's a pool and jacuzzi. Rates start at $235. ~ 75-6106 Alii Drive; 808-327-2300, 800-321-2558, fax 808-327-2333; www.aston-hotels.com.

**DINING**

Kona Coast Shopping Center houses several inexpensive short-order joints. **Don's Chinese Kitchen** (808-329-3770) serves tasty, nutritious, inexpensive meals at its cafeteria-style emporium. **Kamuela Deli** (808-334-0017) is a plate-lunch place next door. You can dine on homemade burgers and lunch plates of teriyaki beef or chicken as well as an array of full meals. Of special interest are the Hawaiian-style roast pork and barbecue. ~ 74-5588 Palani Road. BUDGET.

◄ *HIDDEN*

A local breakfast favorite, **Buns in the Sun** serves bagels, donuts and pastries accompanied by full-flavored Kona coffee. The little blue-and-white bakery-deli also offers a full line of fresh-made bread, cakes and other baked goods. There's a soup, salad and sandwich lunch menu, and they'll pack you a box lunch for your beach picnic or driving excursion. ~ Lanihau Center, 75-5595 Palani Road; 808-326-2774. BUDGET.

If this doesn't intrigue you, head downhill to the North Kona Shopping Center. There you'll find the **Kyotoya Sushi Shop**, a take-out window with a patio and tables. Closed Sunday. ~ Kuakini Highway and Kalani Road; 808-987-8490. BUDGET.

In the King Kamehameha Mall, between the King Kamehameha Hotel and the Kona Industrial Area, is **Ocean Seafood Chinese Restaurant**. The extensive menu has classics including Peking duck, chow mein, chow fun and hot and sour soup. Suffice it to say that it's all there. ~ 75-5626 Kuakini Highway; 808-329-3055. MODERATE.

For Mexican food along Alii Drive, you have two choices. At **Tres Hombres Beach Grill** you'll get a good, filling Mexican meal in a comfortable restaurant. ~ Alii Drive and Walua Road; 808-329-2173, fax 808-331-2850. BUDGET. If you're seeking a tropical drink and a tropical sunset over the water, then **Pancho & Lefty's Cantina & Restaurante** is the place. Similar food, different ambience, higher prices. They also serve Mexican, American and Hawaiian breakfasts. ~ 75-5719 Alii Drive; 808-326-2171. MODERATE.

**Sibu Café** prepares Indonesian and Southeast Asian dishes daily for lunch and dinner. Among the tangy favorites at this outdoor café are beef *saté*, tofu and vegetable stir-fry and Balinese chicken (which is marinated, cooked over an open flame, then served with peanut sauce). ~ Banyan Court, Alii Drive; 808-329-1112. MODERATE.

**HIDDEN ►**

The **Oceanview Inn**, a large, informal dining room opposite Kailua Bay, has a voluminous menu. Chinese, American, Hawaiian, fresh fish and meat dishes, served all day, comprise only part of the selection. There's also a complete breakfast menu. This is the place to go to for local color. Closed Monday. ~ 75-5683 Alii Drive; 808-329-9998. BUDGET.

**Basil's Restaurant**, a hole-in-the-wall bistro punched into a storefront along Alii Drive, has reasonably priced Italian food. The menu is pretty standard as is the red-checkered oilcloth interior, but portions are large and tasty. ~ 75-5707 Alii Drive; 808-326-7836. BUDGET TO MODERATE.

You not only can dine inexpensively at **Aki's Cafe**, you can dine under an umbrella overlooking the water. They may not live up to their motto of "fine Japanese and American food," but the cuisine is passable. They offer hamburgers, fish and chips and spaghetti on the American side of the menu, with sushi, stir-fry and curry dishes on the other. For dinner, there's steak, chicken teriyaki and fish *misoyaki*. ~ 75-5699 Alii Drive; 808-329-0090, fax 808-334-0318. BUDGET.

If you care for Mediterranean, **Cassandra's Greek Tavern** has tables out on the patio as well as in a cozy little dining room. Souvlaki, kebabs, moussaka and dolmas dominate the menu, but they also prepare steak and seafood dishes. ~ 75-5669 Alii Drive; 808-334-1066. MODERATE TO DELUXE.

The commemorative sign at the Kona Inn tells the tale of the old inn—how it was built back in the steamship era when Kona was gaining fame as a marlin fishing ground. The bad news is that the original hotel was converted into a shopping mall—of which this contemporary namesake is a part. The good news is that the restaurant is quite attractive—an open-air, oceanfront affair with two separate dining facilities. The **Kona Inn Restaurant** serves grilled appetizers and sandwiches in its café/grill. The dining room has a separate menu with several fresh fish dishes daily as well as Hawaiian-style chicken. ~ 75-5744 Alii Drive; 808-329-4455, fax 808-327-9358. DELUXE.

Set on a second-story terrace overlooking the ocean, **Lulu's** is one of Kailua's pleasingly windswept addresses. You can lean against the tile bar or sink into a booth, then order from a straightforward sandwiches-salads-and-hamburgers menu. ~ 75-5819 Alii Drive; 808-331-2633, fax 808-329-6766. MODERATE.

**Durty Jake's Café and Bar** serves an "American Continental" menu in an open-air, casual setting, with fresh seafood as well as the usual fare. Open for breakfast, lunch and dinner. ~ 75-5819 Alii Drive; 808-329-7366; www.dirtyjakes.com. MODERATE.

Don't be deceived by the formica tables and cafeteria atmosphere, or the fact that it's located in an industrial park, four miles north of Kailua. **Sam Choy's Restaurant**, established by one of the islands' premier chefs, is a gourmet ghetto. Stop by for breakfast when they serve fried *poke* omelettes, pork chops and eggs, and Spam with Portuguese sausage. No dinner. ~ 73-5576 Kauhola Street, Kaloko Light Industrial Park, located off Kaahumanu Highway; 808-326-1545, fax 808-334-1230. MODERATE TO DELUXE.

**Jameson's By the Sea** is a lovely waterfront restaurant with an emphasis on fresh local seafood dishes. Tucked unpretentiously into the corner of a large condominium, Jameson's conveys a modest sense of elegance: bentwood furniture, potted palms, a seascape from the lanai or through plate-glass windows and good service. Choose from an enticing menu of fresh local catches, steaks, chicken dishes and other gourmet delights. Lunch and dinner weekdays, dinner only on weekends. ~ 77-6452 Alii Drive near Disappearing Sands Beach; 808-329-3195, fax 808-329-0780. ULTRA-DELUXE.

For Continental cuisine in a fashionable setting, consider **La Bourgogne French Restaurant**. This ten-table French country dining room features New York steak with peppercorn sauce, roast saddle of lamb, veal sweetbreads with Madeira sauce, coquilles St. Jacques and fresh fish selections. For appetizers there are escargots, baked brie and lobster cocktail. Round off the meal with cherries jubilee or chocolate mousse and you have a French feast right here in tropical Hawaii. Reservations are highly recommended. Dinner only. Closed Sunday and Monday. ~ Kuakini

**AUTHOR FAVORITE**

Don't let the strip mall setting dissuade you from easing on over to **O's Bistro**. Focus on the fine local art and stellar menu instead. The cuisine varies from Japanese to Thai to Vietnamese to Italian with a single common denominator—everything is prepared with noodles. It's also a showcase for one of Hawaii's finest chefs—Amy Ferguson Ota. If you try the Kona-style tuna casserole, you may be back every day you're on the island. Open for breakfast, lunch and dinner. ~ 75-1027 Henry Street #102; 808-329-9222, fax 808-331-2572; www.osbistro.com, e-mail amy@osbistro.com. DELUXE.

Plaza on Kuakini Highway, four miles south of Kailua; 808-329-6711; e-mail burgundy@gte.net. DELUXE TO ULTRA-DELUXE.

**GROCERIES**    The best place to shop anywhere along the Kona Coast is in the town of Kailua. This commercial center features several supermarkets as well as a number of specialty shops. One of the first choices among supermarkets is **Sack 'n Save** in the center of Kailua. It has everything you could possibly need. Open 5 a.m. to midnight. ~ 75-5595 Palani Road, Lanihau Shopping Center; 808-326-2729.

If you'd prefer another supermarket with a similar selection, try **K.T.A. Super Store**. It's open every day from 5 a.m. to midnight, and is another of the Kailua-Kona area's most convenient and accessible shopping facilities. ~ Kona Coast Shopping Center; 808-329-1677.

**Kona Natural Foods** has an ample stock of vitamins, bathing supplies, grains, fruits and vegetables. By the simple fact that it is the only store of its kind in the area, it wins my recommendation. ~ Crossroads Shopping Center; 808-329-2296.

**SHOPPING**    You might remember that song about how "L.A. is a great big freeway." Well, the Hawaiian version could easily be "Kailua is a great big shopping mall." I have never seen so many shopping arcades squeezed into so small a space. Here are goldsmiths, boutiques, jewelers galore, travel agencies, sandal-makers, knick-knack shops, sundries, T-shirt shops and much, much more, all crowded onto Alii Drive.

Personally, I think most items sold along this strip are tacky or overpriced, and in some cases, both. One place I do recommend, however, is **Middle Earth Bookshoppe**. Here you'll find a good selection of Hawaiian books, as well as paperbacks and current bestsellers. ~ Kona Plaza Shopping Arcade, 75-5719 Alii Drive; 808-329-2123.

The **Kona Inn Shopping Village**, which parallels the waterfront, features dozens of shops. Because of its convenient loca-

---

### A WALK ON THE HISTORIC SIDE

The **Kona Historical Society** will give you a taste of historic Kailua-Kona, including an informative visit to Hulihee Palace. The 75-minute tour starts with the reign of King Umi in the 15th century and leads to the present day with plenty of stops in between. This tour is recipient of the Historic Hawaii Foundation's Preservation Award and is offered weekday at 9 a.m. and 11 a.m. Twenty-four-hour advance reservations are required. Fee. ~ 808-323-3222; www.konahistorical.org.

tion and variety of stores, it is the center of the visitor shopping scene. ~ Alii Drive; 808-329-6573.

The **Coconut Grove Marketplace**, on Alii Drive toward the south end of town, features a selection of restaurants and shops. Drop in at the **Collector Fine Art Gallery**, a gallery that features the works of local and international artists, with a great selection of paintings, ceramics, art glass, woodworks, as well as less pricey art objects. ~ 75-5801 Alii Drive; 808-331-1100.

**Kona Marketplace** is another prime shopping destination. Within this complex is the **Kim Taylor Reece Gallery**, which specializes in artistic photographs of classic hula dancers. ~ 75-5669 C Alii Drive; 808-331-2433.

One of the more tastefully designed malls is **Waterfront Row**, a raw-wood-and-plank-floor shopping complex with perhaps a dozen stores and restaurants. ~ 75-5770 Alii Drive.

The **Hulihee Palace Gift Shop**, a small store located behind the palace, specializes in Hawaiian handicrafts and literature. ~ 75-5718 Alii Drive; 808-329-1877.

Kona's two outdoors "farmers markets" go well beyond fresh produce, macadamia nuts, coffee and flowers to include hand-crafted art, resortwear, and Hawaiian-themed souvenirs. **Kailua Village Farmers Market** (808-329-6573), where local growers gather under plastic tarps to sell their wares, is a good place to pick up home-grown fruits and vegetables. Open Thursday through Sunday, 9 a.m. to 5 p.m. ~ Alii and Hualalai drives. North of town, **Alii Gardens Marketplace** offers a similar range of goods. Open Wednesday, Friday, Saturday and Sunday, 9 a.m. to 5 p.m. ~ Alii Drive. There is also a farmers market in Hilo on Wednesday and Saturday. Tie it in to a visit to the volcano if you're headed that way.

What action there is here is near the shorefront on Alii Drive. **NIGHTLIFE** **Huggo's** has stunning ocean views and is usually packed to the gills. Various live bands perform every evening. ~ Alii Drive and Kakakai Road; 808-329-1493.

The **Billfish Bar**, located poolside at the King Kamehameha Kona Beach Hotel, has live Hawaiian contemporary music on weekends. ~ 75-5660 Palani Road; 808-329-2911.

For an evening of slow rhythms and dancing cheek to cheek, there's the **Windjammer Lounge** at the Royal Kona Resort, which has live music and entertainment on weekends. ~ 75-5852 Alii Drive; 808-329-3111; www.royalkona.com.

To sample Hawaii's own designer beers, check out the **Kona Brewing Company**, a brew pub serving an exotic array of local flavors in addition to specializing in pizzas and salads. ~ North Kona Shopping Center, Kuakini Highway and Palani Road; 808-334-2739.

Another good bet is the **Big Island Comedy Club**, an ever-moving event that's staged at popular nightspots in Kailua and elsewhere along the coast. Call for the current venue. ~ 808-329-4368.

Catering to both a gay and straight clientele, **The Other Side** offers pool tables, dart boards and recorded sounds. ~ 74-5484 Kaiwi Street; 808-329-7226.

Several of the waterfront nightspots in Kailua shine spotlights in the water so you can watch manta rays gliding along the shore.

**BEACHES & PARKS**

**HALE HALAWAI** This small oceanfront park, fringed with coconut trees, has an activities pavilion but no beach. Its central location in Kailua does make the park a perfect place to watch the sunset, though. ~ Located near the intersection of Alii Drive and Hualalai Road in Kailua.

*HIDDEN* ►

**OLD KONA AIRPORT STATE RECREATION AREA** This white-sand beach parallels Kailua's former landing strip, extending for a half-mile along a lava-crusted shore. Very popular with Kailuans, this is a conveniently located spot for catching some rays (sun, that is). The water is shallow, with a rocky bottom. There are a few sand channels for entering the water; and there is a sandy inlet good for kids just north of the lighthouse. This area offers excellent diving. Principal catches are threadfin, big-eyed scad, bonefish, *papio* and especially mullet. Facilities include a picnic area, restrooms and showers. ~ Located about one-half mile northwest of the King Kamehameha Kona Beach Hotel on Kuakini Highway in Kailua. The park gate is closed every evening at 8 p.m.

**KAMAKAHONU** This snippet of sand hugs the south-most corner of Kailua Bay adjacent to the pier. It's a popular spot with local kids and guests at the adjacent King Kamehameha's Kona Beach Resort. Kayakers and distance swimmers also take advantage of the calm beachside to access the waters of Kailua Bay. The restored Ahuena Heiau provides a great backdrop for a swim. Both the beach and temple were part of Kamehameha's royal compound, called Kamakahonu, "the eye of the turtle." ~ Located at the west end of Alii Drive, adjacent to the pier.

*HIDDEN* ►

**HONOKOHAU BEACH** This was once Kailua's nude beach, but prohibitions are in effect. Folks come for miles to soak up the sun on this long narrow strand; it's bordered by a lagoon, backdropped by distant mountains, protected by a shallow reef and highly recommended for the adventurous. Since the water is well-protected, it's good for swimming, although a bit shallow. There are recommended spots for skindiving south of the small-boat harbor but stay away from the harbor itself since sharks are ubiquitous. Surfers enjoy Honokohau's waves.

Rather than fish here try Kaloko Pond about one-half mile north. There are no facilities here. ~ Take Kaahumanu Highway a couple miles north from Kailua. Turn onto the road to Honokohau Small Boat Harbor. From the north side of the harbor, walk about 600 yards farther north to the beach.

### MAHAIULA BEACH—KEKAHA KAI STATE PARK 🏃 🚣 🐟 🏄

A not-very-good road, partly paved, mostly bumpy, leads to beautiful Mahaiula Beach with its white sands and clear blue waters. At the head of a well-protected and deep bay, the swimming is great, as are the snorkeling and diving. In ancient times this coast was (and is) one of the richest in marine resources. There are restrooms, but you must bring your own water. The posted 7 p.m. gate closing should be taken seriously. ~ Located 2.6 miles north of Keahole Airport. Drive down an unpaved ocean road about 1.5 miles to the parking lot. Take the turnoff marked State Park, about five miles north of Kona International Airport.

### MAKALAWENA BEACH 🏃 🚣 🐟 🛶

Makalawena, the next beach to the north of Mahaiula, is another beautiful stretch of North Kona coast. Sand dunes are the backdrop for this beautiful shoreline made up of intricate caves. If you're a shell collector or birder (Opaeula Pond here is a waterbird sanctuary), this is the place to go. Now and then the modern world intrudes, since the beaches are not far from the jets departing Kona International. It can be reached along the coastal foot trail from Mahaiula Beach (about 30 minutes each way; see listing above). This is on private land, so for off-trail activities you need permission from the owner.

### DISAPPEARING SANDS BEACH 🚣 🏄 🛶

A small strand studded with volcanic rocks, this spot is also called Magic Sands. It seems that the white sand periodically washes away, exposing a lava shoreline. When still carpeted with sand, this is a very crowded place. This is a favorite area for swimming and bodysurfing. Kona's best surfing spot is just north of here at "Banyans," with breaks year-round over a shallow reef. For anglers, the major catches include mullet, threadfin, big-eyed scad, bonefish and *papio*. Restrooms and showers are the only facilities. ~ Located on Alii Drive, four miles south of Kailua.

**KAHALUU BEACH PARK** Set along the south shore of Kahaluu Bay, this county park is fringed with palm trees. The salt-and-pepper beach is small and often crowded. Swimming is excellent here since the cove is partially protected by outlying rocks. Tropical fish abound, making this a recommended place for snorkeling, especially beginners. Surfing is good near the reef during periods of high surf. Anglers fish for mullet, threadfin, big-eyed scad, bonefish and *papio*. The bay is also a good spot for throw-netting and surround-netting. Facilities include picnic areas, pavilions, showers and restrooms. ~ Located on Alii Drive, five miles south of Kailua.

## Kohala Coast

Stretching from the northern boundary of Kona to the northwestern tip of the Big Island are the districts of South and North Kohala. One element that comes as a visual shock to many first-time visitors to the Big Island's west coast is the endless stretch of black lava that blankets this dry terrain. Standing in the windshadow of both Mauna Loa and Mauna Kea, this region projects the bald unreality of a moonscape. But the ragged shoreline has been trimmed with stands of palm trees and sections along the roadways are splashed with bougainvillea.

During the last several decades South Kohala, which includes some of the island's prettiest beaches, saw the building of one upscale resort after another and the expansion of residential areas. Farther north, where Kohala Mountain forms a 5000-foot-high spine, the territory remains much as it has for decades. As the Kaahumanu Highway (Route 19) gives way to the northerly Akoni Pule Highway (Route 270), the landscape eventually changes from dry and barren to tropical and luxurious.

Geologically, the Kohala Coast was the section of the island that first rose from the sea. Later, as the volcanoes that formed Kohala Mountain became extinct, the region evolved into a center of historical importance. Kamehameha I was born and raised along this wind-blasted coastline and it was here that he initially consolidated his power base. The region is filled with ancient *heiaus* as well as more recent cemeteries that date to the era when sugar plantations dominated the local economy.

Exploring this region from Kailua-Kona you will find that Kaahumanu Highway cuts across a broad swath of lava-crusted country. There are views of Maui to the north, Mauna Kea to the east and Hualalai to the south.

The site of the Puukohola *heiau* and the main harbor for this stretch of coast, Kawaihae, also offers several shops and restaurants and makes a good stop en route to North Kohala or Waimea.

**SOUTH KOHALA**    Waikoloa's Anaehoomalu Bay provides a dividing line between the districts of North Kona and South Kohala, which runs from Anaehoomalu to a border with North Kohala 20 miles beyond Kawaiahae. Old lava flows, mostly from Hualalai, dominate the landscape, with grasses the primary groundcover.

**SIGHTS**

For evidence of Kohala's historic significance you need look no farther than **Waikoloa**, located between Honokaa and Wai-

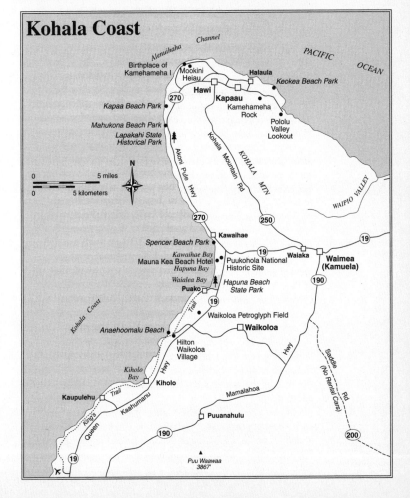

# Kohala Coast

mea. While the area is now heavily developed with tourist resorts, it is also the site of the **Waikoloa Petroglyph Field**. Here you can wander amidst a forbidding lava field etched with ancient symbols. The contrast, with a modern golf course on one side and primitive rock carvings on the other, is ironic to say the least. The path to the petroglyphs is .3-mile in length and begins at the Kings' Shops Mall in Waikoloa. This rough lava course is part of the King's Trail, a mid-19th-century trail built for horseback riders making the 32-mile trip from Kailua to Puako.

Not exactly a hidden destination, the **Hilton Waikaloa Village** is worth a look-see if you are staying on the Kohala Coast. The Hilton Waikoloa, the closest thing to a theme park you'll find on the island, offers a four-acre swimming and snorkeling lagoon, an interactive dolphin guest program, waterfalls, lush gardens and numerous dining spots. You can ride a tram or hop onto a mahagony canal boat (you'll feel like you're on the jungle ride at Disneyland, but without the hippos coming up for air) to tour the facility. Better yet, stroll around and gaze at the stunning artworks that adorn the lobbies and gardens of this massive facility. (Reservations are required for the dolphin encounters.) ~ 425 Waikoloa Beach Drive, Waikoloa; 808-886-1234, fax 808-886-2900; e-mail info@hiltonwaikaloavillage.com.

Next door, the Outrigger Waikoloa fronts one of Hawaii's most beautiful beaches, **Anaehoomalu Beach**. This area, with its sheltered cove and natural ponds, was once a gathering place for Hawaiian royalty. Sea turtles and other marine life call this bay home. (See "Beaches & Parks" below.)

The highway continues north past a desolate desert of black lava to the community of Puako. A short spur off Mauna Lani resort's main road takes you to an easy walk on the Malama Petroglyph Trail that leads to the extensive **Puako Petroglyph Field**. There are hundreds of examples of this Hawaiian art form at Puako, with warriors and outriggers, surfers and sailing ships some of the numerous themes. (It is not permitted to do stencil work on either the old petroglyphs or the contemporary examples that line the trail.)

From Puako, the highway moves north past **Hapuna Beach State Park** (see "Beaches & Parks" below) And the luxurious **Mauna Kea Beach Hotel**. Built by Laurence Rockerfeller, it was the first of the five-star resorts to mushroom along the Kohala coastline.

Continuing north lies the harbor of **Kawaihae**, one of the island's busiest ports and the locale of two major *heiaus*, Mailekini and Puukohola, which have been dedicated as the **Puukohola National Historic Site**. Kamehameha built the impressive triple-tiered Puukohola in 1791 after a prophet related that doing so would ensure his victory over his rivals. At the temple dedication, the ambitious chief aided the prophecy by treacherously slaying his principal enemy. Measuring 224 feet by 100 feet, it was built of lava rocks and boulders that were fitted together using no mortar.

Only one-third of **Pua Mau Place Botanic & Sculpture Garden**'s 45 acres has been planted, but the results are already colorfully spectacular, highlighted by towering hedges of bougainvillaea, and giant plumeria interspersed with giant bronze insect sculptures with a sci-fi appeal. Take the book describing Pua Mau's plants for a self-guided walking tour. ~ 10 Ala Kahua Drive, Kawaiahae; 808-882-0888; www.puamau.org, e-mail irinaprinap@turquoise.net.

**NORTH KOHALA** North Kohala includes much of the mountainous peninsula that provides the Big island with its northernmost lands. The landscape rises from a coastal plain to the lushly forested slopes of the Kohala Mountains.

Just 12 miles to the north along Akoni Pule Highway (Route 270) is **Lapakahi State Historical Park**, where a preserved village provides a unique glimpse into ancient Hawaiian ways. This is definitely worth a leisurely look-see. Dating back 600 years, this one-of-a-kind site includes fishing shrines, canoe sheds, house sites and burial plots. ~ 808-882-6207, fax 808-882-6208.

The old plantation town of **Hawi**, with its trim houses and freshly painted storefronts, harkens back to an earlier era. Back in the 1980s, when the sugar cane industry was in decline, the town looked rather forlorn. But by the beginning of this century it had been completely restored by artists and entrepreneurs. Like neighboring **Kapaau**, it shows its new face in the form of small galleries and local shops. Both are charming enclaves adorned with small churches and relics from the days when sugar was king.

**sights**

**AUTHOR FAVORITE**

Make sure you visit the **Mookini Heiau**, one of the oldest (possibly as old as A.D. 800) and most historically significant archaeological sites from old Hawaii, linked by legend to the arrival of the priest Paao from Tahiti. This holy place measures 250 feet by 130 feet and is reached by taking a left at the Upolu airfield, then following the dirt road for a mile and a half. The **Birthplace of Kamehameha I**, marked with a plaque, lies one-third mile (and two gates) farther west along the same road. The boulders here are reputed to be the original birthstones. The isolated setting is seldom visited, which adds to the spiritual sense of discovery the site offers.

Pride of Kapaau is the original **Kamehameha Statue**, a nine-ton creation cast in bronze. The more famous Honolulu monument is actually only a replica of this gilt figure. Crafted in Florence around 1879 by an American sculptor, the original disappeared at sea on its way to Hawaii but was later recovered and installed here.

The **courthouse** behind the statue is equally historic, providing a glimpse of small-town life enhanced by informational signs. Senior citizens often man an information desk and "talk story" with those with questions or aloha to share.

**HIDDEN** ►  A marked side road off Route 270 just east of Kapaau leads through a macadamia orchard to the **Bond Estate**. One of Hawaii's best preserved missionary estates, it dates back to 1841, when it was built by Reverend Elias Bond and his wife, Ellen. Their Maine background is reflected in the New England–style architecture of the stone house, church, school and plantation buildings. Bond designed the property as a self-sufficient farm to sustain his family, his parishioners and the school where Ellen educated teachers for the 32 one-room schoolhouses the Bonds would eventually establish around the Kohala district. The family eventually converted the farm into a sprawling sugar cane plantation, which became the largest employer in the area and flourished for 100 years. A 1973 earthquake damaged the buildings, and two years later the sugar operation shut down for good. Today Boyd Bond, great-great-grandson of Elias and Ellen, gives tours of the land and the buildings, which are on the National Register of Historic Places (808-889-0657). Call at least a week in advance. ~ Off Route 270, Kapaau.

Along this lush, rainy side of the peninsula are taro patches and pandanus forests. Past the **Kamehameha Rock** (a large boulder that the mighty conqueror reputedly carried from the sea), the road ends at **Pololu Valley Lookout**. The view here overlooking Pololu Valley extends along the monumental cliffs that guard Hawaii's north coast. A half-mile trail leads down to a lovely beach, but watch out for the treacherous riptides.

**HIDDEN** ►  From this cul-de-sac you must backtrack to Hawi, where you can climb the back of **Kohala Mountain** along Route 250 (Kohala Mountain Road), completing a loop tour of North Kohala. Rising to 3564 feet, the road rolls through cactus-studded range country and offers startling views down steep volcanic slopes to the sea. En route are cattle ranches, stands of Norfolk pine and eucalyptus, and curving countryside covered with sweet grasses and wildflowers.

**LODGING**   For years the Kohala district was a placid region strewn with lava and dotted by several pearly beaches. A single resort stood along its virgin coastline. Today, a series of upscale resorts can be found.

**SOUTH KOHALA**  The **Waikoloa Beach Marriott Resort,** a sprawling 545-unit resort, stands along the golden strand of Anaehoomalu Beach, one of Hawaii's most beautiful beaches. An airy lobby decorated with teak furnishings and a stunning century-old *koa* canoe offers a warm island welcome. Guest rooms with rattan furnishings and neutral tones are quite roomy and comfortable, and you can wander the 15 acres of lovely gardens and discover ancient petroglyph fields and a royal fishpond. ~ 69-275 Waikoloa Beach Drive, Waikoloa; 808-886-6789, 800-922-5533, fax 808-886-7852; www.waikoloabeach.com. ULTRA-DELUXE.

The **Mauna Lani Bay Hotel and Bungalows,** a 3200-acre resort, rests on a white-sand beach. Designed in the shape of an arrowhead and boasting 350 rooms, this luxurious facility offers two golf courses, six tennis courts, a spa and fitness center and five restaurants, several of which are award winners. With brilliant green gardens set against black lava, the landscape combines curving lawns and palm-ringed fishponds. Each guest room is spaciously laid out and designed in a pastel motif. ~ 68-1400 Mauna Lani Drive, Kawaihae; 808-885-6622, 800-367-2323, fax 808-885-1484; www.maunalani.com, e-mail reservations@mauna lani.com. ULTRA-DELUXE.

Equally elegant, although a bit bigger and flashier, is the 539-room **The Fairmont Orchid, Hawaii.** With grounds that are spacious, beautifully landscaped and maintained, the Orchid sits on a lovely crescent of white sand that provides swimming. Rooms are spacious, with earth-toned walls. There are a large oceanside swimming pool, ten tennis courts, four restaurants, fitness center, with the resort's two 18-hole golf courses adjacent. ~ 1 North Kaniku Drive, Kohala; 808-885-2000, 800-845-9905, fax 808-885-8886; www.fairmont.com/orchid, e-mail orchid@fair mont.com. ULTRA-DELUXE.

**AUTHOR FAVORITE**

One way to avoid the high cost of the five-star Kohala Coast resorts is to rent a condominium in one of the many complexes. **Mauna Lani Point** is a collection of villa-style condominiums surrounded by a golf course and spread across 19 acres, close to a white-sand beach. Luxuriously appointed, the condos have ocean views, access to Mauna Lani's beaches, jogging trails and a 27-acre historic preserve. Some of the units can fit up to four people; prices range from $340 to $445 a night for one-bedroom units; two-bedroom units run from $450 to $650 a night. Three-night minimum stay required. ~ 68-1050 Mauna Lani Point Drive, Kohala Coast; 800-642-6284, fax 808-885-5015; www.classicresorts.com, e-mail info@classicresorts.com.

The sprawling **Hapuna Beach Prince Hotel at Mauna Kea Resort** is nestled into the bluffs above a wide expanse of sandy beach. The posh Hapuna features beautifully landscaped grounds and offers two golf courses, tennis courts, a spa and children's programs. The 350 rooms are decorated in shades of peach and beige, and all have large lanais and ocean views. ~ 62-100 Kaunaoa Drive, Kohala Coast; 808-880-1111, 800-882-6060, fax 808-880-3142; www.princeresortshawaii.com, e-mail mkrres@maunakearesort.com. ULTRA-DELUXE.

On the Big Island, you can experience 11 of the 13 climatic regions—all in one day.

**NORTH KOHALA**  In the small rustic town of Hawi near Hawaii's northwestern tip, the **Kohala Village Inn** and an adjacent restaurant are the hottest spots around. But there's still privacy and quiet aplenty out back in the sleeping quarters. Rooms in this refurbished establishment feature tin roofs, private baths, ceiling fans, internet access and handsome hardwood floors, and face a small courtyard. The place is tidy. There are also rooms in an adjacent building. ~ 55-514 Hawi Road, Hawi; 808-889-0404; www.kohalavillageinn.com, e-mail info@kohalavillage inn.com. BUDGET TO MODERATE.

**CONDOS**  Located within the Waikoloa Beach Resort, the **Vista Waikoloa** is a three-story, 125-unit condominium complex along Waikoloa Beach that offers air-conditioned two-bedroom luxury suites with large windows and kitchens complete with dishwashers. The dining areas are on private 380-square-foot lanais. There's a heated outdoor pool as well as whirlpools, an exercise room, and washers and dryers. Three-night minimum stay. Prices range from $216 to $252 a night. ~ 69-1010 Keana Place, Waikoloa Village; 808-886-0412, 800-822-4252, fax 808-886-1199.

The only condominium complex in the secluded beachfront community of Puako, **Puako Beach Condominiums** is a long four-story structure located next to the Puako Store, across the street from the beach and one mile from the luxuriant white sands of Hapuna Beach State Park. All 38 units are air-conditioned, mostly three-bedroom, two-bath units designed to sleep up to six, with a king-size bed, a queen-size bed and two twins. Most units have views of the ocean in front and Mauna Kea in back. The grounds are nicely landscaped with flower gardens, and there are a round swimming pool and a children's wading pool. ~ Puako Beach Drive, Puako; 808-882-7711. ULTRA-DELUXE.

**DINING**  **SOUTH KOHALA**  Dining out in this area means resort dining (with prices in the stratosphere) or driving long distances to the north.

The Mauna Lani Bay Hotel hosts some well-known, formal and very expensive restaurants. At the **Bay Terrace** there's an ever-changing menu. The offerings may include black pepper and co-riander–spiced shrimp with watermelon curry or penne pasta with parmesan reggiana sauce and mixed vegetables. Beef dishes might include grilled baby back ribs. Breakfast and dinner are served. ~ Mauna Lani Bay Hotel, 68-1400 Mauna Lani Drive, Kawaihae; 808-885-6622, fax 808-885-1478. ULTRA-DELUXE.

Also located at the Mauna Lani Bay Hotel is the **Canoe House**, one of the Big Island's most highly regarded dining rooms. Spe-cializing in Pacific Rim cuisine and offering spectacular sunsets as an appetizer, it delivers fine food and a fine time. The menu, which changes frequently, is a creative mix of island and Asian dishes. Dinner only. Reservations strongly recommended. ~ 808-885-6622, fax 808-885-1478. ULTRA-DELUXE.

The **Village Steak House** boasts plate-glass views of the Waikoloa Village Golf Course. Selections such as filet mignons, porterhouses, New York strips and T-bone steaks are no surprise, but you can also find fresh fish, shrimp and chicken entrées. Daily specials round out the menu. No dinner Sunday and Monday. ~ Hilton Waikoloa Village; 808-883-9644. DELUXE.

Less expensive eateries can be found at Queen's Court at the King's Shop at Waikaloa. For a little ethnic variety, stop by the **Grand Palace Chinese Restaurant**. Its menu has plenty of choices, with seafood the house specialty. ~ 808-886-6668. MODERATE TO DELUXE.

**NORTH KOHALA** Outside the expensive resorts, you'll find very few restaurants along Hawaii's northwestern shore.

If you cast anchor in the town of Kawaihae, consider **Café Pesto**. Gourmet pizza is the specialty at this simple café. But you'll also find pastas prepared with Asian flair, risottos and fresh fish. ~ Kawaihae Center, Suite 101, Kawaihae; 808-882-1071, fax 808-882-1459; www.cafepesto.com, e-mail cafepesto@excite.com. MODERATE TO DELUXE.

The food is Mexican but the theme is surfing at **Tres Hom-bres Beach Grill**, located in the same complex. There is a great display of surfing memorabilia and some of the bar counters are even fashioned from surfboards. ~ Kawaihae Center, Kawaihae; 808-882-1031. MODERATE TO DELUXE.

Located just across from Kawaihae Harbor, **Kawaihae Har-bor Grill & Seafood Bar**'s menu runs from burgers to catch-of-the-day, pastas to steak. Alfresco seating is a pleasant option at this casual restaurant known for its fresh fish. For dessert, try the *lilikoi* (passion fruit) cheesecake. ~ Route 270, Kawaihae; 808-882-1368, fax 808-882-7005. MODERATE TO DELUXE.

The **Blue Dolphin Restaurant** has a comfortable outdoor din-ing pavilion where you can enjoy Pacific/Mediterranean dishes like nori-wrapped tempura ahi with tropical fruit salsa, and sautéed mahimahi with hot buttered macadamia nuts. Call for dinner hours. Closed on rainy days. ~ Across from Kawaihae Harbor, Kawaihae; 808-882-7771, fax 808-880-1995. DELUXE.

HIDDEN ►   For a taste of funky, traditional Hawaii there's **Kohala Diner**. Set in a tinroof plantation building with bare walls and plastic tablecloths, it serves breakfast, lunch and dinner at super-low prices. ~ Just off Akoni Pule Highway about one mile east of Hawi; 808-889-0208. BUDGET.

In the center of Hawi is the **Kohala Coffee Mill**, a café that serves coffee, smoothies and pastries, but especially Tropical Dreams Ice Cream. Created locally, Tropical Dreams whips up exotic flavors like mango, white chocolate ginger and lychee. ~ Akoni Pule Highway, Hawi; 808-889-5577, 877-301-7683, fax 808-889-5062. BUDGET.

At **Hula La's Mexican Kitchen & Salsa Factory**, nachos, soft tacos and green chicken enchiladas are only part of the full menu. On weekends, you might start your day with breakfast burritos and huevos rancheros. Food is freshly prepared and delicious. ~ Kohala Trade Center, Hawi; 808-889-5668. BUDGET.

**GROCERIES**   **Whaler's General Store** is a convenience store with some groceries. It's located in the King's Shops at Waikoloa. ~ Waikoloa Beach Drive, Waikoloa; 808-886-7057.

Up the mountain several miles above Waikoloa, you'll find **Waikoloa Village Market** in the Waikoloa Highlands Center. ~ 808-883-1088.

On the western side of the island, there are several stores on the Kohala peninsula. Between Kawaihae and Kailua is one store in Puako, **Puako General Store**, with a small collection of groceries and dry goods. ~ 7 Puako Beach Drive, Puako; 808-882-7500.

**K. Takata Store** is an old market with an ample stock of groceries. It's the best place to shop north of Kailua. Closed Sunday afternoon. ~ Route 27, between Hawi and Kapaau; 808-889-5261.

**AUTHOR FAVORITE**

Up near Kohala's northern tip, in the well-preserved historic town of Hawi, is the **Bamboo Restaurant**. Located in the 1920s-era general store turned gallery, this restaurant is decorated with tropical plants and deep wicker chairs. The menu offers a mix of Pacific regional and "local style" cuisine and includes such items as Thai broiled prawns and grilled fresh island fish in a variety of preparations. All meats and produce served are locally grown. There's Hawaiian music Friday and Saturday nights. Reservations required. Closed Sunday night and Monday. ~ Akoni Pule Highway, Hawi; 808-889-5555; www.thebamboorestaurant.com, e-mail bamrest@interpac.net. MODERATE.

**A. Arakaki Store** is conveniently located for campers and pic-nickers headed out to Pololu Valley. ~ Route 270, Halaula; 808-889-5262.

Shopping in Kohala was once a matter of uncovering family-owned crafts shops in tiny towns. Now that it has become a major resort area, you can also browse at designer stores in several top-flight hotels. Simply drive along Akoni Pule Highway between Kailua and the Kohala Peninsula; you'll encounter, from south to north, the **Royal Waikoloan, Hilton Waikoloa Village, Mauna Lani Bay Hotel** and the **Mauna Kea Beach Hotel**. Each of these large resort complexes features an array of boutiques, knickknack shops, jewelers, sundries and other outlets.

**SHOPPING**

Also consider the **Kings' Shops at Waikoloa**. Set on the road leading in to the Waikoloa resort complex, this mall contains clothing stores, a sundries shop and several other promising enterprises.

A beautiful and diverse collection of Hawaii's signature instruments are found at the **Ukulele House**. Choices start at under $25 and price upward into the many hundreds. It's fun browsing even if you have no intention of making a purchase. ~ Kings' Shops at Waikoloa; 808-886-8587.

On the other hand, the diminutive town of Hawi, another of the island's clapboard plantation towns, hosts several artist shops. **The Gallery of Bamboo** has a marvelous collection of island clothes, keepsakes and knickknacks. ~ Akoni Pule Highway, Hawi; 808-889-1441.

Hawaii's largest used book store isn't located in Honolulu, but in small town Kapaau. The **Kohala Book Shop's** selections includes many hard-to-get classics of Hawaiiana as well as a well-stocked contemporary bookshelf. Leave yourself some time to browse. Closed Sunday. ~ 54-3885 Akoni Pule Highway, Kapaau; 808-889-6400; www.kohalabooks.com.

Farther along Akoni Pule Highway, in the falsefront town of Kapaau, you'll find **Ackerman Galleries**. Divided into two different stores on opposite sides of the street, Ackerman's features fine art in one location (closed Sunday) and crafts items in the other. ~ Akoni Pule Highway, Kapaau; 808-889-5971; www.ackerman galleries.com.

Night owls along the Kohala Coast roost at the large resort hotels. The Mauna Kea Beach Hotel has a Hawaiian band at **The Terrace**. ~ Kaahumanu Highway, Kawaihae; 808-882-7222.

**NIGHTLIFE**

The **Honu Bar** at the Mauna Lani Bay Hotel is one of several places in this spacious resort to dance, listen to Hawaiian music, or imbibe. Some guests, however, may prefer a game of chess, pool or backgammon. ~ 68-1400 Mauna Lani Drive, Kawaihae; 808-885-6622.

The **Paniolo Lounge** at the Fairmont Orchid hosts a band that plays Hawaiian and contemporary music. ~ 1 North Kaniku Drive, Kohala; 808-885-2000.

The night scene at the **Royal Waikoloan** centers around a watering hole called the **Clipper Lounge** that offers a diversion of live bands. ~ Kaahumanu Highway, Waikoloa; 808-886-6789.

The **Blue Dolphin Restaurant** features local bands, which draw a lively crowd. The eclectic sounds range from acoustic Hawaiian and jazz to rock and reggae. Closed on rainy days. ~ Across from Kawaihae Harbor, Kawaihae; 808-882-7771.

Also in Kawaihae, there is the **Tres Hombres Beach Grill**, where you can enjoy the original collection of surfing memorabilia that decorates the place. ~ Kawaihae Center, Kawaihae; 808-882-1031.

For Hawaiian music, try the **Bamboo Restaurant** on Friday and Saturday nights. Reservations required. ~ Akoni Pule Highway, Hawi; 808-889-5555.

**BEACHES & PARKS**

**ANAEHOOMALU BEACH** An enchanting area, this is one of the island's most beautiful beaches. There are palm trees, two ancient fishponds filled with barracuda, and a long crescent of white sand. Turn from the sea and take in the gorgeous mountain scenery. Or explore the nearby petroglyph field and archaeological ruins. This beach is very popular and often crowded since it's fronted by a major resort complex. Swimming is excellent along this partially protected shore; there is no lifeguard on duty. Snorkeling is good for beginners but it lacks the scenic diversity elsewhere. Mullet, threadfin, big-eyed scad, bonefish and *papio* are among the usual catches here. Facilities include picnic tables, restrooms and an outdoor shower; there are restaurants in the adjacent Outrigger Waikoloa Beach. ~ Located a half-mile off Kaahumanu Highway, about 25 miles north of Kailua near the 76-mile marker.

**SECRET POND AT MAUNA LANI** Adjacent to the series of fishponds at the Mauna Lani Resort, Secret Pond's cool fresh waters are reached on the trail that leads past the fishponds to the coast. The pool was created in the 19th century when stream waters were enclosed by a lava rock wall. The crystal blue-green waters are inviting, although the pool is too small for much of a swim.

HIDDEN ►    **"69" BEACH OR WAIALEA BAY** No, it's not what you might think. This lovely beach is named for a numbered utility pole at the road turn-off rather than for licentious beach parties. The white-sand shoreline extends several hundred yards along a rocky cove. Despite houses nearby, the spot is fairly secluded; fallen *kiawe* trees along the beachfront provide tiny hideaways. It's a good place to swim but exercise caution. When the water is calm it's also a good spot for snorkeling. Surfers paddle out to the breaks near the southwest end of the bay and off the northwest point. There are no facilities here. ~ Located near the entrance to Hapuna Beach Park, about five miles south of Kawaihae. From Kaahumanu Highway, turn into the park entrance. Then take the paved road that runs southwest from the park (between the beach and the A-frames). Go about six-tenths of a mile on this road and then turn right on a dirt road (the road at the very bottom of the hill). When the road forks, after about one-tenth mile, go left. Follow this road another one-tenth mile around to the beach.

> All along the Kaahumanu Highway, there's a type of graffiti unique to the Big Island. Setting white coral atop black lava, and vice versa, ingenious residents and visitors have spelled out their names and messages.

**HAPUNA BEACH STATE PARK** Here's one of the state's prettiest parks. A well-tended lawn—studded with *hala*, coconut and *kiawe* trees—rolls down to a wide corridor of white sand that extends for one-half mile, with points of lava at either end. Maui's Haleakala crater looms across the water. This is a popular and generally very crowded place. Unfortunately, a major resort hotel was built at one end of the beach. Swimming is excellent at the north end of the beach but beware of dangerous currents when the surf is high. Snorkelers enjoy the coral and fish near the rocks and cliffs at the end of the beach. *Papio*, red bigeye, mullet, threadfin and *menpachi* are often caught here. Facilities include picnic areas, restrooms and showers. ~ Located on Kaahumanu Highway, three miles south of Kawaihae.

▲ No tent or trailer camping is allowed. However, screened A-frame shelters, located on a rise above the beach, can be rented. These cottages, which cost $20 per night, are equipped with a table, sleeping platforms and electricity; they sleep up to four people. Bring your own bedding and cooking utensils. Toilet and kitchen facilities are shared among all six A-frames. For reservations, contact Hawaii State Parks. ~ 808-974-6200.

**SPENCER BEACH PARK** Lacking the uncommon beauty of Anaehoomalu or Hapuna, this spacious park is still lovely. There's a wide swath of white sand, backed by a lawn and edged with *kiawe* and coconut trees. Swimming is excellent here and snorkeling will satisfy beginners and experts alike. Anglers try for *papio*, red bigeye, mullet, threadfin and *menpachi*. There are plenty of facilities: picnic area, restrooms, showers, a large pavilion, volleyball and basketball courts and electricity. This is the only county park with a nighttime security patrol. Also, the gates close you in from 11 p.m. to 6 a.m. ~ Located off Kawaihae Road about one mile south of Kawaihae.

*Text continued on page 202.*

# Snorkeling & Scuba Diving the Gold Coast

**S**imply stated, Hawaii's Kona Coast offers some of the world's most spectacular diving. All along this western shoreline lie magnificent submerged caves, lava flows, cliffs and colorful coral reefs.

Protected from prevailing trade winds by Mauna Kea and Mauna Loa, Kona enjoys the gentlest conditions. Usually the weather is sunny, the surf mild and the water clear (visibility is usually in the 100-foot range). Locals claim they get about 345 ideal diving days a year. It's small wonder, then, that adventurers travel from all over the world to explore Kona's underwater world.

What will you see if you join them? The Kona Coast has over 650 species of reef fish including the brightly colored yellow tang, the aptly named raccoon butterflyfish, the trumpetfish, the coronetfish, the cow-eyed porcupine pufferfish, and the black, yellow and white moorish idol. Large marine animals abound as well, including green sea turtles, hawksbill turtles, manta rays, spotted eagle rays, pilot whales, pygmy killer whales and humpback whales.

When looking for marine life, swim over the coral, looking in, under and around all the corners, caves and crevices. Many spectacular sea creatures await discovery in these hiding spots. Keep in mind that while coral looks like rock, it is a living creature that can be easily killed. Standing on it, touching it, kicking it with your fin or even kicking sand onto it from the ocean floor can damage the coral. So gently drift over the reef and you will be rewarded with new discoveries and close encounters with beautiful tropical fish.

Following are brief descriptions of the best snorkeling and diving spots, as well as shops that provide equipment and tours. For specific information on a particular dive sight, drop by one of these shops. I also recommend you buy waterproof fish identification cards. You can take them into the water and use them to identify these magnificently colored creatures.

**KOHALA COAST SPOTS** Anaehoomalu Beach is good for beginners, but it lacks the scenic diversity of other areas. There's good diving at the end of the road leading to Puako, but it's rocky. "69" Beach (or Waialea Bay) features good underwater opportunities when the surf is mild.

Hapuna Beach State Park has an area that abounds in coral and fish near the rocks and cliffs at the end of the beach. Spencer Beach Park is filled with coral and suits beginners and experts alike.

**Mahukona Beach Park** is an old shipping area littered with underwater refuse that makes for great exploring. **Kapaa Beach Park** offers good diving, but it has a rocky entrance and tricky currents. **Keokea Beach Park**, an excellent spearfishing area, is often plagued by wind and high surf.

**KAILUA-KONA AREA SPOTS**   Kamakahonu Beach, the sand patch next to Kailua's King Kamehameha Kona Beach Hotel, is a crowded but convenient snorkel site. There are corals and many species of fish here, but watch out for heavy boat traffic along the wharf. On the south side of the pier, at the small beach where the Ironman Triathlon swim begins, is good snorkeling.

**Old Kona Airport State Recreation Area**, just a stone's skip north of town, affords excellent diving on either side. The entry is rocky, but once in, you'll find the waters spectacular. Some glass-bottom boats tour this area.

**Honokohau Beach** has some good spots south of the small-boat harbor. **Kaloko-Honokohau National Historic Park**, north of Honokohau Harbor, has a trail that leads to an excellent beach and snorkeling site. Sometimes nudists are on the beach.

**Kahaluu Beach Park**, with its easy entry to the water and complete beach services including restrooms, lifeguard, picnic tables and showers, is the best spot for beginners. The waters here are too shallow for great scuba diving, which means they're all the better for snorkeling.

**SOUTH KONA SPOTS**   Across from Napoopoo Beach Park, at the Captain Cook Monument, is an excellent diving spot—so good, in fact, that it draws diving tours and glass-bottom boats. The best diving is across Kealakekua Bay near the Captain Cook Monument.

**Keei Beach** features a lot of coral and, reportedly, a sea grotto. At **Puuhonua o Honaunau National Historical Park**, also known as the Place of Refuge, there are two natural steps carved into the rocky shoreline that allow for easy entry directly into swarms of reef fish. Because of the abundance of colorful marine life, the accessible location, the easy entry and the variety of depths, this is one of the coast's best spots for snorkelers and scuba divers alike. **Hookena Beach Park** offers good dive spots near the cliffs south of the beach. **Milolii** has excellent diving areas as well as fascinating tidepools.

▲ Both tent and trailer camping are allowed; $3 per night. County permit and reservations are required. This is a very popular place to camp so reserve early—capacity is limited.

**MAHUKONA BEACH PARK** 〜🐟 ⤶ This now-abandoned harbor village and boat landing lies along a rocky, windswept shore. The lawn is shaded with *kiawe* trees; there's no sandy beach here at all. Nicer areas lie to the south, but if you seek a site far from the frenzied crowd, this is a good retreat. The rocks make for poor access for swimming but snorkeling is good. Frequent catches include threadfin, mullet, *menpachi*, *papio* and red bigeye. Facilities include a picnic area, restrooms, showers and electricity. There's no drinking water. ~ Located off Akoni Pule Highway about 13 miles north of Kawaihae.

▲ Tent and trailers are allowed; $3 per night. County permit required.

**KAPAA BEACH PARK** 〜🐟 ⤶ Besides a spectacular view of Maui, this rocky, wind-plagued park has little to offer. It does have a miniature cove bounded by *kiawe* trees, but lacks any sand, which is sometimes nice to have on a beach. Swimming is difficult because of the rocks. Kapaa offers good diving but the entrance is rocky and the currents are tricky. Fishing is probably your best bet here since you can stand on the rocks and try for threadfin, mullet, red bigeye, *papio* and *menpachi*. Picnic areas and restrooms are the only facilities. There's no drinking water. ~ Located off Akoni Pule Highway about 14 miles north of Kawaihae.

▲ Tents and trailers are allowed, but the terrain is very rocky for tent camping; $3 per night.

**KEOKEA BEACH PARK** 🏊 ⤶ Seclusion is the password to this beautiful little park with its cliff-rimmed cove and tiered lawn fringed by *hala* and palm trees. Set way out on the Kohala peninsula, this retreat receives very heavy rainfall. You can swim here but only with extreme caution. It's an excellent area for spearfishing but is often plagued by high wind and high surf. Mullet, *papio*, red bigeye, threadfin and *menpachi* are the main catches here. There are picnic areas, drinking water, restrooms and showers. ~ Take Akoni Pule Highway about six miles past Hawi. Turn at the sign and follow the winding road one mile.

▲ Tent and trailers are allowed; $3 per night. County permit required.

▼▼▼▼▼▼▼▼▼▼

# Waimea

Just 15 miles from the tablelands of Honokaa and ten miles from the Kohala Coast, at an elevation of 2670 feet, sits Waimea. Covered with rolling grasslands and bordered by towering mountains, Waimea (also called Kamuela) is cowboy country. Here, paniolos, Hawaiian cowboys, ride the range on one of the world's largest independently owned cattle ranches. Founded by John Palmer Parker, an adventurous sailor who jumped ship in 1809, Parker Ranch extends from sea level to over 9000 feet. In a typical year the 225,000-acre ranch is home to 55,000 head of cattle.

The cool rustic countryside, seemingly incongruous in a tropical retreat like Hawaii, is dotted with carpenter's Gothic houses and adorned with stables, large grassy lawns and picket fences. Like every place that's discovered, and word is out on Waimea, growth has had its impact with lots of in-migration from the mainland and Honolulu and second-home communities for the wealthy in the vicinity. There area lot more houses, served by several small malls. There are several haute cuisine restaurants worthy of lunch or dinner, and plenty of bed-and-breakfasts to make for a cozy stay.

**SIGHTS**

The museum at **Parker Ranch Visitors Center** presents a history of the Parker family that will carry you back 157 years with its displays of Victorian-era furniture and clothing. In addition to the artifacts and family momentos, there is a movie that tells the story of the Parker family from its earliest days to the present. Admission. ~ 808-885-7655, fax 808-885-7561; www.parker ranch.com, e-mail info@parkerranch.com.

And at the **Historic Parker Ranch Homes** you can view the family's original 1840s-era ranch house and the adjoining 1862 home (which doubles as a museum filled with extraordinary French Impressionist artwork). While the original home was

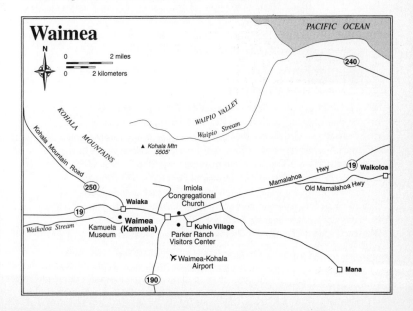

Waimea

built of *koa* and contains a collection of antique calabashes, the latter-day estate boasts lofty ceilings, glass chandeliers and walls decorated with the work of Pissaro and Corot, among others. Closed Sunday. ~ Mamalahoa Highway, one-half mile west of town; 808-885-5433, fax 808-885-6602; www.parkerranch.com, e-mail bfewell@parkerranch.com.

For a splendid example of *koa* woodworking, visit **Imiola Congregational Church** on the east side of town. Built in 1832, this clapboard church has an interior fashioned entirely from the native timber. ~ Mamalahoa Highway; 808-885-4987.

Established in 1985, **Hakalau Forest National Wildlife Refuge** is divided into two sections. Both segments were chosen for their diversity of endemic species of flora and fauna. There are the 5000-acre Kona Forest Unit, upcountry of Kealakekua Bay, which is closed to the public, and the 33,000-acre preserve at Maulua, on the upper slopes of Mauna Kea. The upper portion of Maulua is open to activities such as birdwatching and hiking. Hawaiian owls, hoary bats, hawks and colorful forest songbirds like *apapane* and *akiapolaau* all make their home here. There are no facilities, and no maintained trails. Access is limited to weekends. ~ To reach this isolated acreage means taking the Saddle Road, following the turnoff to Hale Pohaku and the observatories atop Mauna Kea. Turn right where unpaved Mana/Keanakolu Road intersects the summit road. From here it's 12 miles to Hakalau. For entry approval call the refuge between 8 a.m. and 4 p.m.; those approved are given the combination to the locked gate. Information: Fish & Wildlife, 32 Kinoole Street, Hilo; 808-933-6915.

**LODGING**  Set amid the Kohala Mountains in the cowboy town of Waimea are two hotels, both within walking distance of local markets

**AUTHOR FAVORITE**

The cabins at **Mauna Kea State Recreation Area** are convenient for hikers or skiers headed up to Mauna Kea. With its stunning mountain views, sparse vegetation and chilly weather, this rarefied playground hardly seems like Hawaii. A picnic area and restrooms are the only facilities. No tents or trailers are allowed. The cabins can be rented from the Division of State Parks, 75 Aupuni Street, Hilo, Hawaii, HI 96721; 808-974-6200. You must provide your own water. The individual cabins, each accommodating up to six people, have two bedrooms, bath, kitchenette and an electric heater. Cabins have bedding. Rates are $35 for four people and $5 for each additional person. ~ On the Saddle Road about 35 miles west of Hilo.

and restaurants. **Waimea Country Lodge** is a multi-unit motel with exposed-beam ceilings and furniture of knotty pine. Guest rooms are large, carpeted and equipped with telephones, shower-tub combinations and color televisions; some have small kitchenettes. ~ 65-1210 Lindsey Road; 808-885-4100, 800-367-5004, fax 808-885-6711; www.castleresorts.com. MODERATE.

**Kamuela Inn**, a neighbor just down the street, has modest one- and two-room units, as well as suites. These are clean and bright with private baths. All 30 units are equipped with cable TV and some have refrigerators. Guests are served a continental breakfast. ~ Kawaihae Road; 808-885-4243, 800-555-8968, fax 808-885-8857; www.hawaiian-bnb.com/kamuela.html. MODERATE.

Situated at the foot of the Kohala Mountains, **Waimea Gardens Bed and Breakfast** offers another lodging option with its three distinctive studios: one with a fireplace, another with a hot tub and private garden, and a third with a private deck and garden. Benches, which dot the water's edge along the stream out back, are perfect for an afternoon of relaxation. Tropical fruit, breads and pastries start each day. ~ 65-1632 Kawaihae Road; 808-885-8550, fax 808-885-0473; e-mail barbara@waimeagardens.com. DELUXE.

**DINING**

With all the fine-dining possibilities here, Waimea is short on short-order restaurants. There is not much in the way of inexpensive ethnic restaurants. You will find two in Waimea Center (Mamalahoa Highway): **Great Wall Chopsui** has steam-tray Chinese food for lunch and dinner. ~ 808-885-7252. BUDGET. **Yong's Kalbi** serves Korean dishes. Closed Sunday. ~ 808-885-8440. BUDGET.

The pungent scent of garlic soup rolls out the doorway of **Aioli's**, an eat-in or take-out deli, bakery and catering service that doubles as a small gourmet restaurant at dinner hour. Lunch features custom-made sandwiches on homemade bread, from hamburgers to fresh-catch fish. The dinner menu spans the ethnic spectrum, changes constantly and always includes two vegetarian entrées. Typical dinner specials are herb-crusted prime rib, mahimahi and *langostinos en papillote*, walnut-stuffed pasta and herb-marinated grilled shrimp. Closed Sunday and Monday, and the first two weeks of September. ~ Opelo Plaza, Kawaihae Road; 808-885-6325. MODERATE.

If you're hankering for a steak up here in cowboy country, then ride on in to **Paniolo Country Inn**. There are branding irons on the walls and sirloins on the skillet. The booths are made of knotty pine and dishes have names like "Lone Ranger" and "bucking bronco." You can order barbecued chicken, baby back ribs, a "south of the border" special or the veggie quesadillas. ~ 65-1214 Lindsey Road; 808-885-4377. MODERATE.

The **Waimea Ranch House** features dark *koa* panels accented with cowboy gear and photos of *paniolos*. The cuisine is steak and seafood, with a few additional pasta dishes for good measure. ~ 65-1144 Mamalahoa Highway; 808-885-2088. MODERATE TO ULTRA-DELUXE.

**HIDDEN ►** *Paniolos* and other locals hang out at the counter of the **Hawaiian Style Café**, a funky little diner where the portions are huge and the prices ridiculously low. Breakfast might be an omelet bigger than your plate or a stack of buttermilk pancakes 12 inches in diameter. For lunch, you can fill up on cholesterol with a big, fat, juicy hamburger and a heaping pile of fries. The place is justly known for its *luau* plate (served only on alternating Fridays), featuring *laulau*, *kalua* pig, *lomi* salmon, chicken long rice and pickled vegetables. "All-you-can-eat" might be an understatement; it's likely to be all you'll need to eat for your entire stay on the island. Breakfast and lunch only. ~ 64-1290 Kawaihae Road; 808-885-4295. BUDGET.

One of my favorite Waimea dining spots is the **Edelweiss** restaurant, a cozy club with a knockout interior design. The entire place was fashioned by a master carpenter who inlaid *sugi* pine, *koa* and silver oak with the precision of a jeweler. Run by a German chef who gained his knowledge at prestigious addresses like Maui's plush Kapalua Bay Hotel, Edelweiss is a gourmet's delight. The dinner menu includes wienerschnitzel, roast duck and a house specialty—sautéed veal, lamb, beef and bacon with *pfifferling*. For lunch there is bratwurst, sauerkraut and sandwiches. Closed Sunday and Monday, and the month of September. ~ Kawaihae Road; 808-885-6800. DELUXE TO ULTRA-DELUXE.

Chef Daniel Thiebaut blends his French training with local foods and Asian flavors to create exceptional Pacific Rim cuisine at his namesake restaurant, **Daniel Thiebaut**. Artfully presented entrées such as duck breast, mixed seafood in orange chili garlic

**AUTHOR FAVORITE**

Waimea's first contribution to Hawaii regional cuisine is **Merriman's**, a very highly regarded restaurant that has received national attention. The interior follows a neo-tropical theme and the menu is tailored to what is fresh and local. Since the locale is not simply Hawaii, but upcountry Hawaii, the cuisine combines the seashore and the cattle ranch. You might find fresh fish with spicy *lilikoi* sauce or peppercorn-rubbed steak with whiskey butter; gourmet vegetarian dishes round out the fare. I highly recommended it. No lunch Saturday and Sunday. ~ Opelo Plaza, Kawaihae Road; 808-885-6822, fax 808-885-8756; www.merrimanshawaii.com, e-mail goodfood@lava.net. DELUXE TO ULTRA-DELUXE.

sauce on chow fun noodles, and Hunan-style rack of lamb fill the menu. Located in a century-old general store, the interior retains much of its old warmth and feel with polished hardwood floors and period furnishings. No lunch on Saturday and Sunday. ~ 65-1259 Kawaihae Road; 808-887-2200, fax 808-887-0811; www.danielthiebaut.com, e-mail reservations@danielthiebaut.com. ULTRA-DELUXE.

**GROCERIES** The one supermarket located along this route is **K.T.A. Super Store**, open daily from 6 a.m. to 11 p.m. ~ Mamalahoa Highway; 808-885-8866.

**Kona Healthways II** has a large supply of vitamins, baked goods, cosmetics and so on. ~ 67-1185 Mamalahoa Highway; 808-885-6775.

**SHOPPING** In the center of Waimea is the aptly named **Waimea Center**, the shopping complex in Waimea's cattle country. This modern center features boutiques, knickknack shops and more.

**The Quilted Horse** has quilts (without the horse) and decorative items for the home like candles, woodcarvings and wallhangings. ~ Kawaihae Road; 808-887-0020.

**Parker Square** specializes in "distinguished shops." Particularly recommended here is the **Gallery of Great Things**, a store that fulfills the promise of its name. Look for locally made arts and crafts as well as contemporary and tribal art and work representing Polynesia, Indonesia and the Pacific Rim. ~ 808-885-7706.

**Bentley's Home Collection**, in the same complex, offers everything from clothing to greeting cards. ~ Kawaihae Road; 808-885-5565.

Hawaiian and Polynesian art, antiques and artifacts are featured at **Mauna Kea Galleries**. They have a fascinating collection of ceramics, hula dolls, graphics and quilts. ~ 65-1298 Kawaihae Road; 808-969-1184; www.maunakeagalleries.com.

**Dan Deluz's Woods** has beautifully handcrafted bowls, boxes and carvings. The owner, in the business for decades, is a master of his trade. ~ 64-1013 Mamalahoa Highway; 808-885-5856.

Things Hawaiian, which means everything from books to Hawaiian quilt patterns, bric-a-brac to collectible Hawaiiana, and clothing to artworks, even "island edibles," can be discovered at **Cook's Discoveries**. ~ 64-1066 Mamalahoa Highway; 808-885-3633.

**NIGHTLIFE** There's not much to do at night in *paniolo* country except listen to the cows moo. If you're lucky, something will be happening at the 490-seat **Kahilu Theatre**, which offers dance performances, concerts, plays and current movies. ~ Parker Ranch Center; 808-885-6017; www.kahilutheatre.com.

▼▼▼▼▼▼▼▼▼▼▼▼▼
**Kona/Kau District**

South of Kailua lies the Kona/Kau district, a region often overlooked by Big Island visitors. The land at this end of the island was formed from the lava flows of Hualalai and Mauna Loa. Black- and green-sand beaches hug the rugged coastline, while coffee trees and wind-swept grasslands cling to the ragged hillsides. Small towns, unspoiled by tourism, sit along the highway, lost in a time warp of tropical reveries. The southernmost point in the United States is here, as are coffee plantations, historic landmarks and other gems to discover.

**SIGHTS**

*HIDDEN* ►

Along the lower slopes of Hualalai just above Kailua lies **Kona coffee country**. This 20-mile-long belt, located between the 1000- and 2000-foot elevation and reaching south to Honaunau, is an unending succession of plantations glistening with the shiny green leaves and red berries of coffee orchards. If you prefer your vegetation decaffeinated, there are mango trees, banana fronds, macadamia nut orchards and sunbursts of wildflowers. To make sure you remember that even amid all the black lava you *are* still in the tropics, old coffee shacks and tinroof general stores dot the countryside.

So rather than heading directly south from Kailua, make sure you take in the full sweep of Kona's coffee country. Just take Palani Road (Route 190) uphill from Kailua, then turn right onto Route 180. This winding road cuts through old Kona in the heart of the growing region—watch for orchards of the small trees. Before the coast road was built, this was the main route. Today it's somewhat off the beaten track, passing through funky old country towns like Holualoa before joining the Mamalahoa Highway (Route 11) in Honalo.

In the heart of coffee country, **Holualoa** retains its small-town feel, even with its trendy collection of galleries along Mamalahoa Highway, a two-lane road that winds through the three-block-long heart of town.

On Mamalahoa Highway, you'll encounter the old Greenwell Store, a lava stone building that dates to 1875, and a perfect place to combine shopping with museum browsing. The **Kona Historical Society Museum and Gift Shop** has taken over this former general store (now on the National Register for Historic Places). Today it's filled with artifacts from Kona's early days plus notecards, calendars and other items. Of particular interest are the marvelous collections of photos and antique bottles. Closed Saturday and Sunday. ~ Mamalahoa Highway, Kealakekua; 808-323-3222, fax 808-323-2398; www.konahistorical. org, e-mail khs@konahistorical.org.

This main route continues south along the western slopes of **Hualalai**. Located on an ancient Hawaiian agricultural site, the

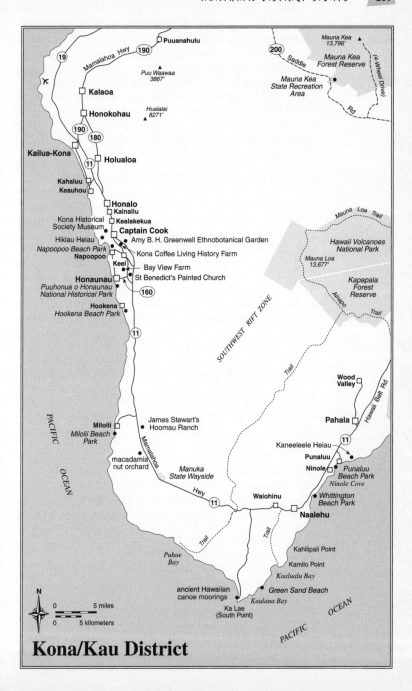

**Kona/Kau District**

HIDDEN ► **Amy B. H. Greenwell Ethnobotanical Garden** spreads across 12 acres of upland countryside. The land is divided into four vegetation zones, varying from seaside plants to mountain forests, and is planted with hundreds of Polynesian and native Hawaiian species. On a self-guided tour, you can wander through fields cleared by Hawaiians in pre-contact days and view the plants that were vital to early island civilizations. Guided tours are offered the second Saturday of every month at 10 a.m. or by appointment. Closed Saturday and Sunday. ~ Off Mamalahoa Highway, Captain Cook; 808-323-3318, fax 808-323-2394; www.bishopmuseum.org/greenwell.

HIDDEN ►    Across the road from the Greenwell Garden is the Kona Historical Society's **Kona Coffee Living History Farm**. Known locally as Uchida Farm, this seven-acre working coffee farm depicts the daily life of immigrant farmers from the 1920s to the 1940s, when small family farms dominated the rural Kona landscape and life in the district revolved around the annual coffee cycle. Access to the grounds is by guided tour only, during which you can view the orchards, a Japanese-style farmhouse, gardens and old processing mills. Closed Saturday and Sunday. Fee. ~ Mamalahoa Highway, Captain Cook; 808-323-2006, fax 808-323-9576; www.konahistorical.org, e-mail coffeefarm@konahistorical.org.

Near the town of Captain Cook, Napoopoo Road leads down to Kealakekua Bay. First it passes the UCC **Hawaii Coffee Factory Outlet**. I don't know about you, but I'm a confirmed "caffiend," happily addicted to java for years. So it was mighty interesting to watch how the potent stuff goes from berry to bean to bag, with a few stops between. For a fee, the Roastmaster tour

**AUTHOR FAVORITE**

*sights*    At **Bay View Farm** you can tour a mill that produces Kona coffee. The trees here, like many you'll see along the roadside, are pruned to six or eight feet. Each will produce about 10 to 12 pounds of berries, which, after being picked by hand, will eventually produce two pounds of beans. Like peas in a pod, there are two beans per berry. A pulping machine squeezes them out of the red berry skin. Next, the beans are dried for up to a week and are turned every hour during daylight. Finally, the outer husks are removed and the beans are graded and bagged for shipping. Small amounts of the premium beans are roasted on the premises (you can watch) and served as free samples (you can also buy more, of course). ~ Painted Church Road, Honaunau; 808-328-9658, 800-662-5880, fax 808-328-8693; www.bayviewfarmcoffees.com, e-mail bayview@aloha.net.

lets you roast your own batch of Kona coffee to take home in personalized bags. If you haven't tried Kona coffee, one of the few
brews grown in the United States, this is the time. ~ 82-5810
Napoopoo Road, Captain Cook; 808-328-5662, fax 808-328-
5663; www.ucc-hawaii.com, e-mail info@ucc-hawaii.com.

**Kealakekua Bay** is a marine reserve and outstanding snorkeling spot with technicolor coral reefs and an array of tropical
fish species. Spinner dolphins swim close to shore in this area. Here
you can also check out the reconstructed temple, **Hikiau Heiau**,
where Captain James Cook once performed a Christian burial
service for one of his crewmen. Captain Cook himself had little
time left to live. Shortly after the ceremony, he was killed and
possibly eaten by natives who had originally welcomed him as a
god. A white obelisk, the **Captain Cook Monument**, rises across
the bay where the famous mariner fell in 1779. The cliffs looming behind the Captain Cook marker in Kealakekua Bay are honeycombed with **Hawaiian burial caves**.

**Puuhonua o Honaunau National Historical Park** sits four
miles south of Kealakekua Bay on Route 160. This ancient cultural site, also known as the Place of Refuge, was one of the
many places established by the *alii* (chiefs) so that *kapu* breakers
and refugees had places to flee for sanctuary. Once inside the
Great Wall, a lava barricade ten feet high and 17 feet wide, they
were safe from pursuers. Free booklets are available for
self-guided tours to the royal grounds, *heiaus* and menacing
wooden images of Native Hawaiian gods that made this beachfront refuge one of Hawaii's most sacred spots. The *heiaus*, dating back to the 16th and 17th centuries, are among the finest examples of ancient architecture on the Big Island. Also explore the
house models, built to traditional specifications, the royal fishpond and the displays of ancient arts and crafts. Picnic tables and
a sandy sunbathing area offer a place to relax—and don't miss
the fascinating tidepools along the lava shoreline. (There's also
great snorkeling here in the area just offshore from the boat
ramp.) If you can, time your visit to Puuhonua o Honaunau for
late afternoon and stay long enough to enjoy the sunset. Facing
west, the setting sun silhouettes the rebuilt Hale o Keawe in vibrant color. You may be the only one there, which adds to a marvelous sense of the past that comes to life with serenity and
power. Admission. ~ 808-328-2288, fax 808-328-8251; www.
nps.org/puho.

An imaginative Belgian priest, hoping to teach his parishioners through color and imagery, transformed St. Benedict's, a
rickety wooden chapel, into a **Painted Church** by covering the interior walls with murals. He depicted several religious scenes and
painted a vaulted nave behind the altar to give this tiny church
the appearance of a great European cathedral. The charming ex-

terior is carpenter's Gothic in style with a dramatic spire. ~ 84-1540 Painted Church Road, Honaunau; 808-328-2227, fax 808-328-8482.

There is little except you, alternating bands of greenery and dark lava, and the black macadam of the Mamalahoa Highway as you proceed toward the southern extremities of the Big Island. Here along the lower slopes of Mauna Loa, lifeless lava fingers cut across lush areas teeming with tropical colors. The contrast is overwhelming: Rounding a bend, the road travels from an overgrown land of poinsettias and blossoming trees to a bleak area torn by upheaval, resembling the moon's surface. Once past the lava flows that have ravaged the countryside, you'll discover a terrain that, though dry and windblown, is planted with macadamia nut orchards and fields of cattle-range grasses.

**HIDDEN ▶** About 30 miles south of Kailua, take the turnoff to the quaint Hawaiian fishing village at **Milolii**. Despite the homes being built, it's quiet and remote, offering a glimpse of life as it once was in Hawaii. (See "Beaches & Parks" section below for more information.)

Continuing south, Mamalahoa Highway passes the late **James Stewart's Hoomau Ranch** (87-mile marker), then a sprawling **macadamia nut orchard**. Eventually, the road arrives at the **South Point** turnoff. South Point Road leads through 11 miles of rolling grassland burned dry by the summer sun to the nation's southernmost point. En route you'll pass a cluster of windmills that draw energy from the trades that blow with ferocity through this region. Fishermen have built **platforms** along the sea cliff here to haul their catches up from the boats that troll these prime fishing grounds.

There are also **ancient Hawaiian canoe moorings** in the rocks below, and the remains of a *heiau* near the light tower. Some ar-chaeologists believe that South Point was one of the places where **HIDDEN ▶** Polynesian discoverers first settled. Another local feature, **Green Sand Beach**, is a two-mile hike along the waterfront from the Kaulana boat ramp. Olivine eroding from an adjacent cinder cone has created a beach with a decidedly greenish hue. It's a hot hike, so if you go, make sure you take water. A rough shorebreak may make swimming risky.

Back on the highway continue on to **Naalehu**, the nation's southernmost town, and then on to **Punaluu Beach Park**. With its palm trees and enchanting lagoon, Punaluu's black-sand beach is simply gorgeous. The tourist complex detracts from the natural beauty, but to escape the madding mobs the explorer need wander only a couple of hundred yards east to the rocky remains of **Kaneeleele Heiau**. Or venture about one-third mile south to **Ninole Cove**. Although there's a condominium complex nearby, this spot is a bit more secluded. Many of the stones along

Ninole's pebbly beach are filled with holes containing "baby" stones that are said to multiply.

From Punaluu to Volcanoes National Park, the highway passes through largely uninhabited grassland and sugar cane areas. **Pahala,** the only town along this stretch, is a plantation colony. For an interesting side trip, go right onto Pikake Street at the first stop sign in Pahala. When it forks after a little more than four miles, go left and proceed along the road as it continues up into luxuriant **Wood Valley,** the scene of a devastating 1868 earthquake and mudslide.

◄ *HIDDEN*

**LODGING**

For a funky country place high in the mountains overlooking the Kona Coast, try the **Kona Hotel.** Catering primarily to workers, this 11-unit hotel remains a real sleeper. It might be difficult to book a room during the week, but on weekends, the lunchpail crowd heads home and you can rent a small place at an unbelievably low rate. Shared bathroom facilities. It's five miles to the beaches and action around Kailua, but if you're after an inexpensive retreat, this is the place. ~ Route 180, Holualoa; 808-324-1155. BUDGET.

One of the more unusual places to stay on the Big Island is the **Dragonfly Ranch.** Spread across two acres, the Dragonfly is billed by owner Barbara Moore as a "healing-arts retreat." The grounds are luxurious and the atmosphere is decidedly New Age. The "honeymoon suite" has an outdoor bed (screened off), complete with mirrored canopy, a sunken bath and shower. Three of the five units have partial kitchen facilities, or, for a small fee, you can participate in the family-style dinner. Don't expect condo-style living, but do prepare yourself for an experience. ~ Route 160, Honaunau; 808-328-2159, 800-487-2159, fax 808-328-9570; www.dragonflyranch.com, e-mail dfly@dragonflyranch.com. DELUXE TO ULTRA-DELUXE.

◄ *HIDDEN*

Upcountry Honaunau has several noteworthy bed and breakfasts that cater to gays. **The Horizon Guest House** has 40 acres

**RIDE TO BRITAIN**

Located on the Kealakekua shoreline, on a stretch of coastline that forms the Bay's northern arm, the Captain Cook Monument (on land given to the British government) is reached by a long, strenuous trail that climbs hillsides before descending to the coast. It's far easier on horseback, with **Kings' Trail Rides O'Kona,** in the upcountry town of Kealakekua, offering daily horseback excursions to the site that include lunch and time for snorkeling and a swim. Snorkels provided by arrangement. ~ P.O. Box 1366, Kealakekua, HI 96750; 808-323-2388; www.konacowboy.com, e-mail sales@konacowboy.com.

of privacy with spectacular views from rooms and the pool and jacuzzi. There are four suites to choose from, all with private lanais. On Route 11 near the 100-mile marker and the Hookena Beach turnoff. ~ P.O. Box 957, Honaunau, HI 96726; 808-328-2540, 888-328-8301, fax 808-328-8707; www.horizonguesthouse. com, e-mail contact@horizonguesthouse.com. ULTRA-DELUXE.

With manicured grounds leading to a tiled-roof villa, **Kealakekua Bay Bed and Breakfast** combines picture-perfect views of Kealakekua Bay with its assortment of accommodations. Three light and airy suites are available. The Alii includes a jacuzzi tub to relax in, but all rooms have private entrances, private baths and refrigerators. Native Hawaiian prints, wicker furniture and ceiling fans adorn each room, including the lounge and dining room. The Ohana Kai cottage has two bedrooms, two-and-a-half baths, a kitchen, laundry, and a private lanai and garden, sleeping up to six. ~ P.O. Box 1412, Kealakekua, HI 96750; 808-328-8150, 800-328-8150, fax 808-328-8866; www.keala.com, e-mail kbaybb@aloha.net. MODERATE TO DELUXE.

At **H. Manago Hotel**, you'll have a varied choice of accommodations. Rooms in the creaky old section have communal baths. The battered furniture, torn linoleum floors and annoying street noise make for rather funky living here. Rooms in the "newer" section rise in price as you ascend the stairs. First-floor accommodations are the least expensive and rooms on the ethereal third floor are the most expensive, but all reside in the budget range. The only advantage for the extra cost is a better view. All these rooms are small and tastelessly furnished—somehow orange carpets don't make it with naugahyde chairs. But you'll find visual relief in the marvelous views of mountain and

### SLEEP UNDER THE BIG TOP

If camping is your idea of vacation fun, check out **Margo's Corner**. Margo's guests are generally bicyclists looking for refuge from highrise hotels and staid inns. Hot showers, breakfast and dinner are provided, and sleeping quarters consist of a number of tent sites situated in a large yard filled with pine trees and organic gardens. Some visitors sleep out in the open under the canopy of trees. For the less adventurous, a guest cottage with a queen-size bed, a private bath and a view of the garden is available, or try the "Adobe Suite" that sleeps six and includes a sauna. Also on the premises are a health food store and a community room. Ask about the art retreats. No smoking. Vegan and vegetarian meals are provided upon request. Closed Thursday and Sunday except with reservations. ~ P.O. Box 447, Naalehu, HI 96772; 808-929-9614; e-mail margos111@ yahoo.com. BUDGET TO MODERATE.

sea from the tiny lanais. There's also a restaurant and television room in the old section. ~ Mamalahoa Highway, Captain Cook; 808-323-2642, fax 808-323-3451. BUDGET.

**Shirakawa Motel**, the country's southernmost hotel, sits on ◄ HIDDEN stunningly beautiful grounds. Once when I stopped by, a rainbow lay arched across the landscape and birds were loudly rioting in the nearby hills. Located 1000 feet above sea level, this corrugated-roof, 12-room hostelry offers quaint rooms with faded furniture, three of which have functional kitchenettes. Without cooking fa-cilities, the bill is even less. A spacious two-room suite with a kitchen is also available. ~ Mamalahoa Highway, Waiohinu; phone/fax 808-929-7462; www.shirakawamotel.com, e-mail shi rak@hialoha.net. You can also write P.O. Box 467, Naalehu, HI 96772 for reservations. BUDGET.

**Wood Valley Temple**, a Buddhist retreat and guesthouse, has ◄ HIDDEN dormitory-style and private rooms. Set on 25 landscaped acres, it provides a serene resting place. The guest rooms are pretty basic but have been pleasantly decorated and are quite comfort-able. Baths are shared and guests have access to the ample kitchen facilities. Call for reservations; two-night minimum. ~ Four miles outside Pahala; 808-928-8539; www.nechung.org, e-mail ne chung@aloha.net. BUDGET.

**Sea Mountain at Punaluu** is a welcome contradiction in terms—a secluded condominium. Situated in the arid Kau Dis-trict south of Hawaii Volcanoes National Park, it rests between volcanic headlands and a spectacular black-sand beach. A green oasis surrounded by lava rock and tropical vegetation, the com-plex contains a golf course, pool, tennis courts and jacuzzi. The several dozen condos are multi-unit cottages (moderate to deluxe). The condos are well-decorated and include a bedroom, sitting room, kitchen and lanai; slightly larger units are available (deluxe to ultra-deluxe). ~ Off Mamalahoa Highway, Punaluu; 808-928-6200, fax 808-928-8075; www.viresorts.com, e-mail seamtn@hialoha.net. MODERATE TO ULTRA-DELUXE.

From Kailua south, the Mamalahoa Highway heads up *mauka*     **DINING** into the mountains above the Kona Coast. There are several restaurants in the little towns that dot the first 15 miles. All sit right on the highway.

At the north end of Holualoa is the **Holuakoa Cafe**, where the sandwiches and baked goods make a great alfresco breakfast or lunch. The changing menu also includes salads, soups and quiche. ~ 76-5900 Mamalahoa Highway, Holualoa; 808-322-2233. BUDGET.

**Teshima's** is a pleasant restaurant modestly decorated with  lanterns and paintings. It's a good place to enjoy a Japanese meal or a drink at the bar. This café is very busy at lunch. Dinner features several Japanese, Hawaiian and American entrées. Breakfast is also served. ~ Mamalahoa Highway, Honalo; 808-322-9140. MODERATE.

There's a different mood entirely at the **Aloha Angel Café**. Here in the lobby of the town's capacious movie house, a young crew serves delicious breakfasts as well as sandwiches, salads and seafood during lunch and dinner. So if for some bizarre reason you've always longed to dine in the lobby of a movie theater . . . . If not, you can eat out on the oceanview lanai. Dinner served Wednesday through Saturday. ~ Mamalahoa Highway, Kainaliu; 808-322-3383; www.alohatheatre.com, e-mail aloha theatre@hawaii.rr.com. MODERATE TO DELUXE.

**Manago Hotel** has a full-size dining room. Primarily intended for the hotel guests, the menu is limited and the hours restricted to "meal times" (7 to 9 a.m., 11 a.m. to 2 p.m., and 5 to 7:30 p.m.). Lunch and dinner platters consist of a set menu. Sandwiches are also available. Closed Monday. ~ Mamalahoa Highway, Captain Cook; 808-323-2642; www.managohotel.com, e-mail manago@lava.net. BUDGET TO MODERATE.

In Kealakekua Ranch Center, a shopping center on Mamalahoa Highway in Captain Cook, there is one low-priced eatery, **Hong Kong Chop Suey**. It is one of those Chinese restaurants that have (literally) over 100 items on the menu. Closed Tuesday. ~ Mamalahoa Highway, Captain Cook; 808-323-3373. BUDGET.

**Canaan Deli** comes recommended by several readers, who like the hoagies and the pastrami sandwiches and their specialty, Philly cheesesteak sandwiches. They also have pizzas and hamburgers at this friendly stopping place, as well as a breakfast menu. Personally, I go for the bagels with cream cheese and lox. ~ Mamalahoa Highway, Kealakekua; 808-322-6607. BUDGET.

On the road down to Puuhonua o Honaunau, there's a great lunch stop—**Wakefield Gardens & Restaurant**. You can wander the tropical preserve, then dine on a papaya boat, sandwiches, a fresh garden salad, or a "healthy burger" (made with natural

**AUTHOR FAVORITE**

Housed in a plantation-style building, the **Keei Café** serves Hawaiian-American and eclectic fusion cuisine, among the best in the area. From Thai curry, Brazilian seafood chowder, pork chops in peppercorn gravy and catch-of-the-day fish specials to peanut-miso salad, vegetarian black beans and tofu fajitas, everything is made from scratch using local ingredients. Leave room for the heavenly coconut flan. Closed Sunday and Monday. ~ Mile marker 113, Mamalahoa Highway, Captain Cook; **808-322-9992**. MODERATE TO DELUXE.

grains), then try a slice of homemade pie. Lunch only. ~ Route 160, Honaunau; 808-328-9930. BUDGET TO MODERATE.

From the outside, the **Coffee Shack** may look something like     ◄ *HIDDEN* a brownish mobile home teetering on the brink of a cliff, but the view from hundreds of feet above the surf is part of what makes this roadside diner south of Captain Cook so special. The breakfast menu features eggs benedict and luau-bread french toast among its offerings. Lunch selections include pizzas and fish sandwiches on homemade bread. ~ 85-5799 Mamalahoa Highway, Honaunau; 808-328-9555. MODERATE.

For something more comfortable, try **Mister Bill's**. The menu includes steak, prawns and chicken. In an area lacking in full-service dining facilities, this restaurant and full bar is a welcome oasis. There is a kid's menu. ~ Mile marker 78, Mamalahoa Highway; 808-929-7447, fax 808-929-8129. MODERATE TO DELUXE.

Down in Naalehu, the nation's southernmost town, you'll find the **Shaka Restaurant**. There are full-course breakfasts; at lunch they serve sandwiches, plate lunches and salads; the dinner menu has beef, seafood and chicken dishes. There's also a full bar. ~ Mamalahoa Highway, Naalehu; 808-929-7404. MODERATE.

Along the lengthy stretch from Naalehu to Hawaii Volcanoes National Park, one of the few dining spots you'll encounter is the **Seamountain Golf Course** in Punaluu. Situated a short distance from the black-sand beach, this restaurant serves a lunch menu consisting of hamburgers, chicken wings and cold sandwiches. Topping the cuisine are the views, which range across the links out to the distant volcanic slopes. ~ Punaluu; 808-928-6222, fax 808-928-6111. BUDGET.

**GROCERIES**     Strung along Mamalahoa Highway south of Kailua is a series of small towns that contain tiny markets.

The only real supermarket en route is **Choice Mart**. ~ Kealakekua Ranch Center (upper level), 82-6066 Mamalahoa Highway, Captain Cook; 808-323-3994.

**Kahuku Country Market**, in the Kau district, has an ample inventory of groceries and drugstore items. ~ Mile marker 78, Mamalahoa Highway; 808-929-9011.

Down at the southern end of the island, the **Naalehu Island Market** is the prime place to stock up. ~ Mamalahoa Highway, Naalehu; 808-929-7527.

**SHOPPING**     After escaping the tourist traps in Kailua, you can start seriously shopping in South Kona. Since numerous shops dot the Mamalahoa Highway as it travels south, I'll list the most interesting ones in the order they appear.

Holualoa offers shoppers some interesting options along downtown's main drag. Check out **Sam Rosen Goldsmith** for artful designs in gold, platinum and silver. Closed Sunday and Monday. ~ Old Holualoa post office, Mamalahoa Highway; 808-324-1688. **Cinderella's Antiques** features antiques and collectibles. ~ Mamalahoa Highway; 808-322-2474. This enclave is also a center for art galleries. Among the most noteworthy is **Studio 7 Gallery**, a beautifully designed multiroom showplace that displays pottery, paintings, sculpture and prints. Closed Sunday and Monday. ~ Mamalahoa Highway; phone/fax 808-324-1335. Artist Matthew Lovein creates *raku*-style wishing jars from a Holualoa workshop; his elegant pottery artwork is for sale at the **Holualoa Gallery**. Closed Sunday and Monday. ~ 76-5921 Mamalahoa Highway; 808-322-8484. A few doors down, housed in an old coffee mill, is the **Kona Arts Center**, where local artists gather to create their wares. ~ Mamalahoa Highway.

For hats and baskets woven from pandanus and bamboo, and sold at phenomenally low prices, turn off the main road onto Hualalai Road, and check out **Kimura Lauhala Shop**. Closed Sunday. ~ Mamalahoa Highway, Holualoa; 808-324-0053.

**Blue Ginger Gallery** displays an impressive array of crafts items produced by local artisans. There are ceramics, custom glass pieces, woodwork and hand-painted silk scarves. ~ 79-7391 Mamalahoa Highway, Kainaliu; 808-322-3898.

Another recommended store is **Paradise Found**, which features contemporary and Hawaiian-style clothes. ~ Mamalahoa Highway, Kainaliu; 808-322-2111. **Knick-Knacks & Paddy-Whacks** is the place for things old and aging. ~ Mamalahoa Highway, Kealakekua; 808-323-2239.

"There's a place in Hawaii that is very dear to me. . . . I want to go back to my little grass shack in Kealakekua, Hawaii." Yes, there really is a little grass shack in Kealakekua and it's been one of my favorite shopping stops. Scaled down from its previous incarnation, **Kealakekua's Grass Shack** still offers a large selection of Hawaiian products, including bowls, jewelry and mirrors made from *koa*, *kou*, *milo*, mango and norfolk pine woods. You

**AUTHOR FAVORITE**

**Big Island Art Farm** specializes in *koa* and other exotic hardwoods. The shop was born when two local woodworkers, alienated by the high prices demanded for their pieces by galleries, decided to go into business for themselves. The result is a shop where the work is not only exquisite but also financially accessible to all. Among the many art pieces and gifts, you'll find bowls and boxes, as well as larger, more elaborate creations. Closed Sunday. ~ 82-6156 Mamalahoa Highway, beside the Manago Hotel, Captain Cook; 808-323-3495.

can also find handmade woven *lauhala* hats, baskets, carved figurines, etched glass, Niihau shell leis and hula accessories. You probably, however, won't see the *humuhumunukunukapuaa* go swimming by. ~ Konwena Junction, Kealakekua; 808-323-2877.

**Kahanahou Hawaiian Foundation,** an apprentice school teaching Hawaiians native arts, sells hand-wrought hula drums and other instruments, as well as masks and other crafts. It also serves as an introduction to Hawaiian music as you view bamboo nose flutes, musical bows, dancing sticks and ceremonial drums. ~ Mamalahoa Highway, Kealakekua; 808-322-3901.

◀ HIDDEN

Given their catchy moniker, it was probably inevitable that the **Bong Brothers Coffee Company,** a long-established Kona coffee growing and roasting operation, would open a retail location. Bong, the Chinese coffee growers' family name, has nothing to do with *pakalolo* paraphernalia, but don't tell that to the folks who have made Bong Brothers (and Bong Sistah) T-shirts a hot Big Island souvenir. You'll find them on sale at **Bong Brothers** on Route 11 in Honaunau, along with local fruits such as cherimoya, star fruit and sugarloaf pineapples. The shop also serves fresh-squeezed juices and smoothies, as well as homemade soups and, of course, coffee straight from their own roasting room. Closed Saturday. ~ 84-5227 Manaloa Highway, Honaunau; 808-328-9289, fax 808-328-8112; www.bongbrothers.com.

The **Kona Association for the Performing Arts** produces an ongoing series of theatrical performances. In addition to plays, it periodically schedules concerts. Call for information. ~ 808-322-9924.

**NIGHTLIFE**

**NAPOOPOO BEACH PARK** 🏖️ 🛶 🎣 ⚓ Small boats occasionally moor off this black-rock beach on Kealakekua Bay. Set amidst cliffs that rim the harbor, it's a charming spot, drawing caravans of tour buses on their way to the nearby Hikiau Heiau. Kealakekua Bay, one mile wide and filled with marine life, is an underwater preserve that attracts snorkelers and glass-bottom boats. In the bay there are good-sized summer breaks. Just north, at "Ins and Outs," the surf breaks year-round. Anglers can try for mullet, *moi*, bonefish, *papio* and big-eyed scad are the common catches. Napoopoo's gray-sand beach was washed away by a storm in 1992, leaving a bouldered beach in its place. The steep incline makes ocean access risky. A picnic area, showers and restrooms are available. There's a soda stand just up from the beach. ~ In the town of Captain Cook, take Napoopoo Road, which leads four miles down to Kealakekua Bay; turn right at the end of the road.

**BEACHES & PARKS**

**KEEI BEACH** 🏖️ 🛶 ⚓ This salt-and-pepper beach extends for a quarter-mile along a lava-studded shoreline. Situated next

◀ HIDDEN

to the creaky village of Keei, this otherwise mediocre beach offers marvelous views of Kealakekua Bay. It is far enough from
the tourist area, however, that you'll probably encounter only
local people along this hidden beach. Darn! The very shallow
water makes swimming safe, but limited. Try the north end. Plenty
of coral makes for good snorkeling. Mullet, threadfin, bonefish,
*papio* and big-eyed scad are common catches here. There are no
facilities. ~ Take the Mamalahoa Highway to Captain Cook,
then follow Napoopoo Road down to Kealakekua Bay. At the
bottom of the hill, go left toward the Puuhonua o Honaunau
National Historical Park. Take this road a half-mile, then turn
right onto a lava-bed road. Now follow this extremely rough
road another half-mile to the beach.

**HOOKENA BEACH PARK** Popular with adventur-
ous travelers, this is a wide, black-sand beach, bordered by sheer
rock walls. Coconut trees abound along this lovely strand, and
there's a great view of the South Kona coast. This is a recommended beach for swimming. Near the cliffs south of the beach
are some good dive spots. Mullet, threadfin, bonefish, *papio* and
big-eyed scad are among the most common catches. A picnic
area and restrooms are the only facilities. There is no drinking
water, but cooking and bathing water is available. ~ Take the
Mamalahoa Highway south from Kailua for about 21 miles to
Hookena. Turn onto the paved road at the marker and follow it
four miles to the park.

▲ Tent camping is allowed; $3 per night. County permit re-
quired.

HIDDEN ▶ **MILOLII BEACH PARK** Even if you don't feel like a character
from Somerset Maugham, you may think you're amid the setting
for one of his tropical stories. This still-thriving fishing village is
vintage South Seas, from tumbledown shacks to fishing nets dry-
ing in the sun. Unfortunately, however, houses have been springing up over the last few years. There are patches of beach near
the village, but the most splendid resources are the tidepools,
some of the most beautiful I've ever seen. This area is fringed with
reefs that create safe but shallow areas for swimming, and wonderful spots for snorkeling. Exercise extreme caution if you go
beyond the reefs. This beach is a prime area for mullet, bonefish,
*papio*, threadfin and big-eyed scad. Facilities include restrooms,
picnic area and a volleyball court. There's no running water. ~
Take the Mamalahoa Highway south from Kailua for about 33
miles. Turn off onto a well-marked, winding, one-lane, macadam
road leading five miles down to the village.

▲ Permitted only in the seaside parking lot. Get there early
and you can park a tent beneath the ironwood trees with the sea
washing in just below; $3 per night. County permit required.

**MANUKA STATE WAYSIDE** This lovely botanic park, almost 2000 feet above sea level, offers a beautiful ocean view. The rolling terrain is planted with both native and imported trees and carpeted with grass. The only facilities are restrooms and a picnic area. ~ On Mamalahoa Highway, 19 miles west of Naalehu.

▲ No tent and trailers are allowed here, but you can park your sleeping bag in the pavilion. No electricity. A state permit is required.

**WHITTINGTON BEACH PARK** 🐟 🏊 🎣 A small patch of lawn dotted with coconut, *hala* and ironwood trees make up this pretty little park. It's set on a lava-rimmed shoreline near the cement skeleton of a former sugar wharf. There are some marvelous tidepools here. Access to the water over the sharp lava rocks is rough on the feet. But once you're in, the snorkeling is very good and there's a surf break in summer with a left slide. Mullet, *menpachi*, red bigeye, *ulua* and *papio* are the most frequent species caught. Facilities consist of picnic area, restrooms and electricity. ~ Across from the abandoned sugar mill on Mamalahoa Highway, three miles north of Naalehu.

> The nene, Hawaii's state bird, can be found nesting on the desolate slopes of Mauna Loa, Mauna Kea and Hualalai.

▲ Tent and trailer camping are allowed; County permit is required.

**PUNALUU BEACH PARK** 🏄 🏊 🎣 A black-sand beach fringed with palms and bordered by a pleasant lagoon, this area, unfortunately, is regularly assaulted by tour buses. Still, it's a place of awesome beauty, one I would not recommend bypassing. One reason for the hubbub is the appearance of the endangered green sea turtles, which should not be disturbed. For more privacy, you can always check out **Ninole Cove**, a short walk from Punaluu. This attractive area has a tiny beach, grassy area and lagoon, which is a good swimming spot, perfect for children, during calm conditions. Exercise caution when swimming outside the lagoon. The snorkeling is only mediocre. Surfers attempt the short ride over a shallow reef (right slide). Principal catches are red bigeye, *menpachi*, *ulua* and *papio*. Facilities include a picnic area, restrooms, showers and electricity. ~ Located about a mile off Mamalahoa Highway, eight miles north of Naalehu.

▲ Tents and trailers are allowed; county permit required.

Covering 344 square miles and extending from the Puna shoreline to the 4090-foot summit of Kilauea to the summit crater of Makuaweoweo atop 13,677-foot Mauna Loa, this incredible park is deservedly the most popular attraction on the Big Island. Its two live volcanoes, still-young Kilauea (the world's most active

# Hawaii Volcanoes National Park

volcano) and towering Mauna Loa (said to be inflating with a possible result of resurgence in 2003) make the region as elemental and unpredictable as the next volcanic eruption.

Currently, the 20-year-long eruption of Kilauea, which resulted in the loss of several hundred homes and the coastal town of Kalapana in 1991, continues unabated. As a result, a visit to the coast when lava is flowing into the sea has been an experience enjoyed by millions under the watchful eye of National Park Service rangers.

*Ohia* trees, with their red pompom flowers, are often the first spots of life in a newly formed lava flow. Maybe that's why Madame Pele deems their flowers sacred.

Unlike Washington's Mt. St. Helens or Mt. Pinatubo in the Philippines, Hawaii's volcanic eruptions are generally less dangerous, their lava released in rivers that flow, largely underground, to the sea, where lava erupts in tall fountains, the release of cinder and ash creates cone-shaped craters called cinder cones. Don't make the park a day trip; it's worth as much time as you can spare.

**SIGHTS**    Contained within this singular park are rainforests, black-sand beaches, rare species of flora and fauna, and jungles of ferns. If you approach the park from the southwest, traveling up the Mamalahoa Highway (Route 11), the points of interest begin within a mile of the park boundary.

Here at the trailhead for **Kau Desert Trail**, you can follow a short (1.5 miles round trip) path that leads to **Footprints**, an area where, according to legend, Halemaumau's hellish eruption overwhelmed a Hawaiian army in 1790. The troops, off to battle Kamehameha for control of the island, left the impressions of their dying steps in molten lava—or so the story goes. According to Park officials, the tracks were left in hot mud by travelers, not warriors. Either way, the tracks can still occasionally be seen in the very fragile hardened ash layers.

Continuing along the highway, turn up Mauna Loa Road to the **Tree Molds**. Lava flowing through a *koa* forest created these amazing fossils. The molten rock ignited the trees and then cooled, leaving deep pits in the shape of the incinerated tree trunks. (Bring mosquito repellent.) It's a little farther to **Kipuka Puaulu** or **Bird Park**, a mile-long nature trail leading through a densely forested bird sanctuary. *Kipuka* means an "island" surrounded by lava and this one is filled with more than 30 species of Hawaiian trees, including *koa*, *kolea* and *ohia*. If the weather's clear, you can continue along this narrow, winding road for about ten miles to a **lookout** perched 6662 feet high on the side of Mauna Loa.

Back on the main road, continue east a few miles to **Kilauea Visitor Center**, which provides a walk-through forest, a film on recent eruptions, a bookstore and an information desk. ~ 808-985-6000, fax 808-985-6004; www.nps.gov/havo.

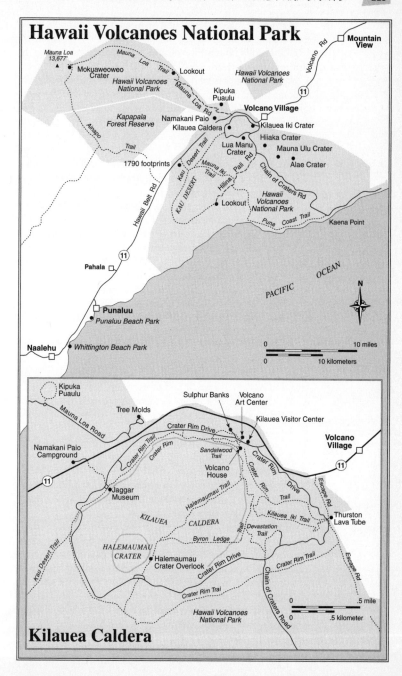

# Hawaii Volcanoes National Park

Mauna Loa
13,677'

Mokuaweoweo
Crater

Mauna Loa Trail

Lookout

Hawaii Volcanoes
National Park

Volcano Rd

Mountain
View

Hawaii Volcanoes
National Park

Mauna Loa Rd

Kipuka
Puaulu

Volcano Village

11

Kapapala
Forest Reserve

Namakani Paio

Kilauea Caldera

Kilauea Iki Crater

Hiiaka Crater

Lua Manu
Crater

Mauna Ulu Crater

Alae Crater

Auwapo

Trail

Kau Desert Trail

Mauna Iki
Trail

Pali Rd

Hilina

Chain of Craters Rd

1790 footprints

KAU DESERT

Lookout

Hawaii
Volcanoes
National Park

Hawaii Belt Rd

Puna Coast Trail

Kaena Point

11

Pahala

PACIFIC

OCEAN

N

Punaluu

Punaluu Beach Park

Naalehu

Whittington Beach Park

0                    10 miles

0              10 kilometers

Kipuka
Puaulu

Sulphur Banks

Volcano
Art Center

Tree Molds

Kilauea Visitor Center

Mauna Loa Road

Crater Rim Drive

Volcano
Village

Crater Rim Trail

Crater Rim

Sandalwood
Trail

Crater Rim Drive

11

Namakani Paio
Campground

Volcano
House

Escape Rd

Jaggar
Museum

Halemaumau Trail

Kilauea Iki Trail

Thurston
Lava Tube

KILAUEA

CALDERA

Kau Desert Trail

Devastation
Trail

HALEMAUMAU
CRATER

Byron Ledge

Halemaumau
Crater Overlook

Crater Rim Drive

Crater Rim Trail

Chain of Craters Road

Escape Rd

0              .5 mile

0           .5 kilometer

Hawaii Volcanoes
National Park

# Kilauea Caldera

Across the road on the rim of Kilauea at **Volcano House**, there's a hotel and restaurant. An earlier Volcano House, built in 1877, currently houses the **Volcano Art Center**, right next to the visitor complex. Here you'll find notable exhibits and gallery works by local artists whose creations relate to the Hawaiian environment and heritage. They also host classes in the Hawaiian language and Hawaiian arts such as hula and lei making, as well as painting, ceramics, glass and photography. ~ P.O. Box 129, Volcano, HI 96715; 808-967-7565, fax 808-967-8512; www. volcanoartcenter.org.

Not far from the Volcano Art Center are the **Sulphur Banks**. You can either walk the ten-minute trail or drive along Crater Rim Drive to get to this odoriferous sightseeing spot. Here, green, red, brown and yellow hues are painted by deposits of crystal that form on the rocks when the gas reaches the surface. Other minerals, including opal, earthy hematite and gypsum, form by the weathering of the rock. These solfataras, or fumaroles, are vents that issue steam, hydrogen sulfide and other gases. Kilauea releases tons of sulphuric gases every day.

*Take note*: People with heart conditions, pregnant women and those with breathing problems should avoid this area, since these gases are unhealthy for them.

The Eruption Update, a 24-hour recorded message, provides information on the latest eruptions. ~ 808-985-6000.

Just beyond the Sulphur Banks are the less smelly **Steam Vents**. Here you can take a steam bath just by approaching the railing of the vent. The steam is caused by groundwater hitting the heated lava. On cooler days you'll find more steam. Steam vents are located on the edge of Kilauea Caldera. A meadow is formed by alterations to the soil that prevent the growth of trees and shrubs. Be careful around the steam vents; they can actually burn you. You'll find larger vents around the crater if you hike around it.

From here you can pick up Crater Rim Drive, one of the islands' most spectacular scenic routes. This 11-mile loop passes lava flows and steam vents in its circuit around and into **Kilauea Caldera**. It also takes in everything from a rainforest to a desert and provides views of several craters.

If Kilauea is active, plan a visit to the eruption zone at dusk. Keep in mind that viewing the volcanic eruption may require a one- or two-mile-long trek from road's-end parking to the eruption zone. Hikers should bring water and wear hiking shoes with a decent tread to navigate the hardened lava rock trail and handle the ground heat generated by cooling lava. Also bring a flashlight. You'll need it if you're heading back from a dusk viewing. The best viewing is from 20 minutes before sunset until 20 minutes after. (Sunset ranges between 5:30 p.m. mid-winter and 7:30 p.m. mid-summer.) This is the stuff of lifetime memories.

# Camping
## near the Caldera

The main campground at Hawaii Volcanoes National Park, **Namakani Paio Campground** is situated in a large, open grassy area dotted with eucalyptus and *ohia* trees at an elevation of 4000 feet. Although there are a handful of designated campsites, it's mostly a matter of simply picking a clear spot, first-come, first-served, and pitching your tent there. The campground has water and restrooms, and there are fire grills and picnic tables in a central pavilion. Bring your own firewood—none is available on-site. There are no reservations, no reservations and no check-in. Open year-round; seven-day maximum stay. ~ Off Route 11, 31.5 miles southwest of Hilo; 808-985-6011.

Located just above the campground of the same name, **Namakani Paio Cabins** are ten extremely basic cabins operated by the Volcano House hotel. Each sleeps up to four people, with one double bed and twin-size bunk beds, all bare-mattress. Amenities include a picnic table and an outdoor barbecue grill. Cabin occupants use the campground restrooms and drinking water supply. Showers are available at the hotel. Rates are $40 a night for two people, $8 per additional person, plus $20 for optional linen rental and a $12 key deposit. Reservations are required; make them through the reception desk at the Volcano House. ~ Off Route 11, 31.5 miles southwest of Hilo; reservations—Volcano House, Hawaii Volcanoes National Park, HI 967128; 808-967-7321.

The national park's **Kulanaokuaiki Campground** has three campsites so far, with more under construction. Located in the middle of the Kau Desert at an elevation of 2700 feet, it offers the remote feel of wilderness camping without the hike. There is a vault toilet but no water; bring plenty. The developed campsites have picnic tables; bring your own firewood. There are no reservations and no check-in. Open year-round. The national park's website (www.nps.gov/havo) is kept up to date and has a lot of helpful information. ~ Five miles southwest from Chain of Craters Road on Hilima Pali Road; 808-985-6011.

## DRIVING TOUR

# Saddle Road

Cutting across the island, Saddle Road climbs from Hilo to an elevation of over 6500 feet (bring a sweater!). The eastern section is heavily wooded with *ohia* trees and ferns and is often fog-shrouded. The central portion includes stark fields of lava only intermittently broken by *kipuka*, "islands" of trees surrounded by lava but left alive—micro-ecosystems that are home to rare native plants and birds. The western portion traverses rolling pastures. The Saddle is a stark landscape, a mosaic of decades-old flows from Mauna Loa's and Mauna Kea's grass-covered cinder cones. You cross lava flows from 1855 and 1935 while gaining elevation that will provide you with the finest view of these mountains anywhere on the island. Before setting out, pack warm clothing and check your gas gauge—there are no service stations or stores en route. And consult your car rental agency: Some do not permit driving on Saddle Road.

**ONIZUKA CENTER FOR INTERNATIONAL ASTRONOMY** Near the 28-mile marker, the road to Mauna Kea leads 13 miles up to the 13,796-foot summit. The first six miles are passable by passenger car and take in a lookout and the Onizuka Center for International Astronomy. There's a free star-gazing program from 6 to 10 p.m. Four-wheel-drive vehicles are recommended for the trip to the summit, although most cars can handle it without problems. ~ 808-961-2180, fax 808-969-4892.

**MAUNA KEA OBSERVATORY** Beyond this point you will need a four-wheel-drive vehicle. Be sure to call ahead since the visitor station at the center sponsors tours of the summit and star-gazing opportunities. At the summit you'll find the Mauna Kea Observatory complex, one of the finest

Proceeding clockwise around the crater, the road leads near **Thurston Lava Tube**, a well-lit cave 450 feet long set amid a lush tree-fern and *ohia* rainforest. The tube itself, created when outer layers of lava cooled while the inner flow drained out, reaches heights inside of ten feet. You can walk through the tunnel and along nearby **Devastation Trail**, a half-mile paved asphalt trail that cuts through a skeletal forest of *ohia* trees regrowing after being devastated in a 1959 eruption.

Another short path leads to **Halemaumau Crater**. This pit, which erupted most recently in 1982, is the traditional home of Pele, the goddess of volcanoes. Even today steam and sulfurous gas blast from this hellhole, filling the air with a pungent odor and adding a sickly yellow-green luster to the cliffs. Halemaumau is actually a crater within a crater, its entire bulk contained

observatories in the world, but be prepared for freezing temperatures. You'll also be treated to some of the most otherworldly views imaginable.

**MAUNA KEA STATE RECREATION AREA**    Mauna Kea State Recreation Area, with cabins and recreation area, lies about midway along the Saddle Road. Situated on the tableland between Mauna Kea and Mauna Loa at 6500-feet elevation, this is an excellent base camp for climbing either mountain. The cabins here are also convenient for skiers headed up to Mauna Kea. With its stunning mountain views, sparse vegetation and chilly weather, this rarefied playground hardly seems like Hawaii. For remoteness and seclusion, you can't choose a better spot. A picnic area and restrooms are the only facilities. No tents or trailers are allowed. The cabins can be rented from the Division of State Parks, 75 Aupuni Street, Hilo, HI 96721; 808-974-6200. The individual cabins, each accommodating up to six people, have two bedrooms, a kitchenette and an electric heater. Bring water for washing and drinking. Rates are $35 for one to four people and $5 for each additional person. Sometimes (depending on water availability) there are also fourplex cabinettes. These aren't nearly as nice as the individual cabins. They are one-bedroom units crowded with eight bunks; cooking is done in a community dining and recreation area next door. ~ On the Saddle Road about 35 miles west of Hilo.

**PANIOLO COUNTRY**    The road continues past a United States military base, then descends through stands of eucalyptus windbreaks into Waimea cattle country. Here you can pick up the Mamalahoa Highway (Route 190) southwest to Kailua, only 87 miles from Hilo. Passing through sparsely populated range country over 2000 feet in elevation, this road has sensational views of the Kona Coast and Maui.

in Kilauea's gaping maw. (People with sulfur sensitivity or heart or breathing problems should probably avoid this site, as should infants, children and pregnant women.)

Around the southern and western edges of the caldera, the road passes part of the **Kau Desert**, a landscape so barren that astronauts bound for the moon were brought here to train for their lunar landing. At the **Jaggar Museum**, adjacent to the U.S.G.S. park observatory, you can catch an eagle's-eye glimpse into Halemaumau Crater and take in a series of state-of-the-art displays on volcanology. Then the road continues on to a succession of steam vents from which hot mists rise continually.

The highway zips into Hilo from the Kilauea Crater area. Until several years ago you could take a more interesting and leisurely route by following **Chain of Craters Road** down to the

Puna district. At present a lava flow several miles wide has closed part of the road. The 20-mile-long section that is still open skirts several pit craters, traverses miles of decades-old lava flows, and descends 4000 feet to the coast. Near the sea, a two-mile trail leads to an excellent collection of **petroglyphs at Puuloa**. The Chain of Craters Road then hugs the cliffs of the shoreline until it abruptly ends, buried for ten miles under lava flows as much as 75 feet deep.

**Volcano Village**, a small rural enclave, lies one mile Hilo-side of the main entrance to Hawaii Volcanoes National Park. The village itself includes a few shops and restaurants on Old Volcano Road, which parallels Route 19 for about one mile. The rest consists of a grid of country roads fronting homes nestled amidst lush vegetation of endemic fern and *koa* forest interspersed with flowering ginger, hydrangea, camellia and other flowering exotics that prosper in the wet, temperate climate.

The village population includes both Native Hawaiians and an assortment of mainland escapists, including many artists and other creative types who revel in Volcano's rural isolation and spiritual energy. Ira Ono, one of Volcano's long-term residents and a key multimedia artist-in-residence, operates **Volcano Garden Arts**, a working gallery, in the vintage 1908 Hopper Estate. The workshop-cum-gallery-cum-sculpture-garden offers special classes in various arts throughout the year. Closed Sunday and Monday. ~ 19-3834 Old Volcano Road; phone/fax 808-967-7261; www.volcanogardenarts.com.

**LODGING**

**Volcano House**, a 42-room hotel, perches 4000 feet above sea level on the rim of Kilauea Crater. Situated in Hawaii Volcanoes National Park, this hotel provides a unique resting place. You can watch the steam rise from Halemaumau Crater or study the rugged contours of slumbering Kilauea. Standard rooms are unfortunately located in a separate building behind the main hotel. For a view of Kilauea, ask for a "crater view," from a superior or deluxe room on the volcano side. The rooms are decorated in an ever tidy and cozy fashion, with wall-to-wall carpeting but no TV or radio. And you certainly won't need an air conditioner at these breathless heights. ~ Near the entrance to Hawaii Volcanoes National Park; 808-967-7321, fax 808-967-8429; e-mail volcanohouse@verizon.com. MODERATE TO ULTRA-DELUXE.

There are quite a number of lovely bed and breakfasts along the Puna/Kau coast in Volcano Village, which plays host to those *akamai* (smart) enough to plan a dusk visit to the eruption site, about 40 to 45 minutes from park headquarters. Since you want to be there at dusk to see the lava at its most awesome, a stay in Volcano is the right choice. (The volcano isn't a good day trip.) It's more than two hours on dark, twisting, country roads to

Kona and Kohala hotels. Besides, the night sky, undimmed by civilization, is a spectacle of brilliant stars and fragrant breezes, which makes an evening walk something memorable.

The wood-shingled buildings at the 1931 **Hale Ohia Cottages** are conveniently located just outside park headquarters on beautifully landscaped grounds. Hale Lehua, Ihilani and #44 cottages are freestanding structures with fireplaces and kitchenettes. There are also five suites (two in the main house and three in another cottage), all with private baths and entrances. The spacious two-story, three-bedroom Hale Ohia suite is well-suited to family travelers, with three bedrooms, a large living space, a full kitchen and a covered lanai with room for barbecuing. ~ P.O. Box 758, Volcano, HI 96785; 808-967-7986, 800-455-3803, fax 808-967-8610; www.haleohia.com, e-mail reservations@haleohia.com. MODERATE TO DELUXE.

**Volcano Accommodations**, a central agency, can help book reservations at a variety of area B&Bs. ~ 808-967-8662, fax 808-985-7028; www.hawaii-volcano.net, e-mail info@hawaii-volcano.net. You can also contact **Volcano Places** for cottage rentals. ~ 808-967-7990, 877-967-7990; www.volcanoplaces.com.

If you're looking for a vista, **Volcano House Restaurant**—perched on the rim of Kilauea Crater—affords expansive views. Located at 4000-foot elevation in Hawaii Volcanoes National Park, this spacious dining room looks out on sheer lava walls and angry steam vents, and on a clear day, the imposing bulk of Mauna Loa. If you can tear yourself away from the stunning scenery,

**DINING**

**AUTHOR FAVORITE**

**Kilauea Lodge** does not rest on the lip of the crater, but that doesn't prevent it from being the finest place in the area to stay. Set on tropically wooded grounds, this hideaway nevertheless conveys a mountain atmosphere. Some guest rooms have fireplaces; all have private baths. This coziness carries over into an inviting common room shared by guests and furnished with rocking chairs and a tile fireplace. The lodge, built in 1938 as a YMCA camp, rests at the 3700-foot elevation and combines the best features of a Hawaiian plantation house and an alpine ski lodge. It also provides a memorable contrast to the ocean-oriented places that you'll probably be staying in during the rest of your visit. One of the two-bedroom cottages has a hot tub. Two-night minimum stay during long holiday weekends. ~ Old Volcano Road, Volcano Village; 808-967-7366, fax 808-967-7367; www.kilauealodge.com, e-mail stay@kilauealodge. com. MODERATE TO DELUXE.

there's buffet-style breakfast and lunch, and an ample dinner menu highlighted by fresh fish, prime rib, linguini marinara and a variety of seafood dishes. ~ 808-967-7321, fax 808-967-8429; www.volcanohousehotel.com. DELUXE.

In L.A. there's the Hard Rock Café; in Volcano Village, it's the **Lava Rock Café**. Breakfast, lunch and dinner feature "magma mini meals," but only at dinner can you get a "full eruption." The lasagna, T-bones and fajitas are, presumably, burning hot. The Lava Rock also serves as an internet café for you e-mail junkies. No dinner on Sunday or Monday. ~ Old Volcano Road, Volcano Village; 808-967-8526, fax 808-967-8090; www.volcanovillage.com. MODERATE.

And for those languorous evenings when time is irrelevant and budgets forgotten, there is **Kilauea Lodge**. You can sit beside a grand fireplace in an atmosphere that mixes tropical artwork with alpine sensibility. The exposed-beam ceiling and elegant hardwood tables comfortably contrast with a menu that features seafood Mauna Kea, duck *a l'orange*, catch of the day and chicken Milanese. Dinner only. ~ Old Volcano Road, Volcano Village; 808-967-7366; www.kilauealodge.com, e-mail stay@kilauealodge.com. DELUXE TO ULTRA-DELUXE.

**GROCERIES**  The **Volcano Store**, located just outside the national park, has a limited stock of groceries and dry goods. ~ Old Volcano Road, Volcano Village; 808-967-7210.

**PARKS**  **NAMAKANI PAIO** Situated in a lovely eucalyptus and *koa* grove in the middle of Volcanoes National Park, this campground offers both outdoor and cabin camping. There is a picnic area and restrooms. ~ On Mamalahoa Highway (Route 11) about three miles west of park headquarters and 31 miles southwest of Hilo.

▲ Tent and trailer camping. No permit required but, as always, campers should note that there is a seven-day limit.

Cabins are rented from the Volcano House (808-967-7321). Each cabin has one double and two single beds, plus an outdoor grill. No firewood or cooking utensils are provided. The units rent for $50 a day for two people, $8 for each additional person up to four. Sheets, blankets and towels are provided, but it's recommended that you bring a sleeping bag. Showers are included with the cabins but campers must pay extra.

▼▼▼▼▼▼▼▼▼▼
**Puna District**

That bulging triangle in the southeast corner of the Big Island is the Puna District, a kind of living geology lab where lush rainforest is cut by frequent lava flows from the East Rift Zone of Kilauea. Here at the state's easternmost point, black-sand beaches, formed when hot lava meets the ocean and explodes into crystals, combine with anthurium farms and papaya orchards to create a region both luxurious and unpredictable. There are lava tubes, arches and caves galore, all formed by the lava that flows inexorably down from the rift zones of Kilauea.

**SIGHTS**

Now that Chain of Craters Road has been covered in a layer of black lava, the only way to visit the area is by following Route 130, which will carry you through the tumbledown plantation town of **Keaau** and near the artistic little community of **Pahoa**, or along Route 137, an enchanting country road that hugs the coast.

In 1990, **lava flows** poured through Kalapana, severing Routes 130 and 137 (which have since been reconnected) and covering many houses. Kalapana, once home to more than 400 people, was largely destroyed. Today, a few isolated houses form oases in a desert of black lava. Just above the town, where the roadway comes to an abrupt halt, you can see how the lava crossed the road.

◀ HIDDEN

The former **Star of the Sea Painted Church** in Kalapana used to be my favorite church in all the Hawaiian Islands. An imaginative Belgian priest, hoping to add color and imagery to the mass, covered the interior walls of this tiny, spired carpenter's Gothic chapel with murals depicting religious scenes and painted a vaulted nave behind the altar to give the little church the appearance of a European cathedral. In 1990, when a slow-moving lava flow destroyed much of Kalapana, villagers lifted the church off its foundation and trucked it to safety just hours before the lava would have engulfed it. The Catholic Church decommissioned it and sold it to the Kalapana Ohana Association for "$1 and love," and it was moved to a three-acre site leased from the state along the Kalapana-Pahoa Highway. The association was awarded a small government grant to convert it into a Native Hawaiian cultural center, but the *hoolaulea*, or celebration, they organized to raise matching funds was scheduled for September 15, 2001— and cancelled at the last minute because of tragic events half a world away. Today, it still stands forlorn by the roadside as vol-

**BLACK HEAT**

Since the latest series of volcanic eruptions began on the Big Island in 1983, the Puna District has been in constant turmoil. During one phase, an average of 650,000 tons of lava a day was spewing from the earth. In all, it has covered 40 square miles of the Big Island, creating 525 acres of new land masses along the ocean, destroying nearly 200 houses and fashioning several new black-sand beaches.

unteers from the 40-member Kalapana Ohana Association work to keep it from deteriorating. As this book goes to press, the association's president says the painted interior is "kind of closed," but check as you pass by and see whether the villagers' dream has come true yet.

After exploring the area of recent volcanic action, you can backtrack along the coast via Route 137, which proceeds northeast through jungly undergrowth and past dazzling seascapes to the tiny villages of **Opihikao** and **Pohoiki** or continue on Route 137 past Kapoho where the paved road ends. Now you're on a red dirt and cinder road, appropriately named **Red Road**. At times the coastline is in sight, at times it is hidden by tall ironwoods and lush vegetation. The road undulates, following the contour of the landscape, giving the drive a roller coaster feel. The rural landscape provides an away-from-it-all feeling, which characterizes Puna's rustic appeal.

**HIDDEN ►**

At the intersection of Route 137 and Route 132, take a right onto the dirt road and follow it seaward toward the site of a truly eerie occurrence. When the 1960 lava flow swept down to destroy this entire region, it spared the **Cape Kumukahi Lighthouse** on the state's easternmost point. Today you can see where the wall of lava parted, flowed around the beacon, then closed again as it continued to the sea. In the process, it added about 500 yards of land to the point—an awesome demonstration of how young this Big Island really is.

**HIDDEN ►**

Now return to Route 132 and head west back toward Pahoa. The road passes more of the **1960 lava flow**, which covered almost 2000 acres and totally leveled the small village of Kapoho.

An eruption, circa 1790, caused the grotesque formations at **Lava Tree State Park**. Here the molten rock swamped a grove of *ohia* trees, then hardened around the skeletons to create a fossil forest. When fissures in the earth drained the molten lava, these petrified trees were left as a lonely legacy. In strange and exotic fashion, these giant skeletons, mixed with fresh growth, loom above huge cracks in the landscape.

**LODGING**

In the beautiful Puna District, a volcanic region fringed with black-sand beaches, there's a marvelous place called the **Kailani Eco-Resort and Adventures**. Situated on Route 137, 13 minutes from Pahoa, it sits just above the ocean on 113 acres. In addition to lodging, this New Age resort provides a lifestyle. There are weekly classes in hula, weaving and lei making; lectures on the history and culture of Hawaii; plus programs in dance, aerobics, yoga and massage. The facilities include a watsu pool, two jacuzzis and a sauna, an Olympic-sized swimming pool and volleyball and tennis courts. Guests stay in multi-unit lodges, sharing a spacious living room, or in private cottages; treehouse units with

**HIDDEN ►**

ocean views are also available. Sleeping accommodations are basic but appealing, with pine walls; the room decorations are crafted at the center. Campsites are available at budget prices. Special events for gays are planned during the year. Meals are $43 a day per person. ~ RR 2, Box 4500, Pahoa, HI 96778; 808-965-7828, 800-800-6886, fax 808-965-0527; www.kalani.com, e-mail kalani@kalani.com. MODERATE TO ULTRA-DELUXE.

**GAY LODGING**    After a long day traversing the dense growth of tropical flowers and macadamia and fruit trees, guests are grateful for a soak in a hot tub, a stint in the steam house or a minute with one of the nearby masseuses. All this and more are obtainable at the **Butterfly Inn**, an all-women lodging, where women bring their own food (and sometimes share in the bounty of the garden), located between Hilo and the village of Volcano. Rooms are cozily decorated, and there's an enclosed deck. ~ P.O. Box 6010, Kurtistown, HI 96760; 808-966-7936, 800-546-2442;

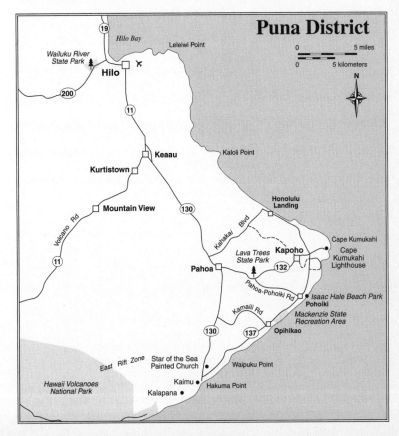

Puna District

www.thebutterflyinn.com, e-mail the.butterfly.inn@prodigy.net.
MODERATE.

**DINING**

In the rustic town of Pahoa, there's **Luquin's Mexican Restaurant**, a friendly Mexican eatery serving a variety of dishes from south of the border. You'll find all the familiar favorites on the menu, from *huevos rancheros* to enchiladas, as well as fish tacos smothered in deliciously *picante* red chili salsa. There's a cantina bar, and the old-time Pahoa-style atmosphere is enhanced by a colorful paint job. ~ Old Government Road, Pahoa; 808-965-9990. MODERATE.

One entry in Pahoa's Italian restaurant scene, **Paolo's Bistro** specializes in Tuscan-style cuisine, highlighting fish dishes and freshly made pasta with pesto or olive oil and garlic. The short menu is supplemented by daily specials. Ingredients are straight from the farm, and the emphasis is on quality rather than quantity. The atmosphere is family-friendly and there's a gazebo in the back for outside dining. ~ 333 Pahoa Road, Pahoa; 808-965-7033. MODERATE.

For more traditional fare consider **Black Rock Cafe**. This booth-lined shrimp-and-steak eatery offers a half-dozen different beef dishes as well as spaghetti, baby back ribs and a catch-of-the-day fish entrée. ~ Old Government Road, Pahoa; 808-965-1177. MODERATE.

**GROCERIES**

A **farmers' market** in the clapboard town of Pahoa convenes every Sunday morning. Otherwise, there are a few small markets. The junction town of Keaau has a **Sure Save**. ~ Old Volcano Road and Keaau–Pahoa Road, Keaau; 808-966-9316.

For health foods in Pahoa, consider **Pahoa Natural Groceries**. ~ 15-1403 Nanawale Homesteads, Pahoa; 808-965-8322.

**SHOPPING**

Out in the volcano region, on the road down to the Puna District, you'll pass through the tiny town of **Pahoa**. Either side of Route 130, the main drag, is lined with falsefront buildings.

## WATCH WHERE YOU WANDER

While in Puna, visitors should not wander off-road. This was, and likely still is, a prime locale for growing *pakalolo*, as marijuana is known in Hawaii. (*Paka* translates as "weed," *lolo* as "crazy.") Ill-conceived State and Federal drug eradication efforts have made for some bad energy concerning marijuana cultivation. The end result has been counterproductive, driving up prices without stopping the flow, pushing more money into an illegal pipeline.

Each one seems to contain yet another ingenious craft shop run
by a local resident.

**ISAAC HALE BEACH PARK** This small park on
the Puna coast is pretty but run-down. There's a patch of black
sand here and some hot springs nearby. A boat landing ramp
makes this a popular park with local folks. Swimming is okay
when the sea is calm. There are both summer and winter breaks
in the center of the bay. The most common catches here are *papio*,
*moi*, mountain bass, *menpachi*, red bigeye, *ulua* and goatfish. A
picnic area and restrooms are the only facilities. ~ Route 137,
about two miles northeast of MacKenzie State Recreation Area.
     ▲ Tent and trailer camping. County permit required. I much
prefer nearby MacKenzie State Recreation Area for overnighting.

**MACKENZIE STATE RECREATION AREA** This beautiful
13-acre park lies in an ironwood grove along a rocky coastline.
King's Highway, an ancient Hawaiian trail, bisects the area. There
is no swimming, snorkeling or surfing because a sea cliff borders
the park. There's good shore fishing from rock ledges but be
careful! Occasional high waves break on these ledges. Picnic area
and pit toilets are the only facilities. There's no drinking water.
~ Route 132, nine miles northeast of Kaimu.
     ▲ Tent camping; state permit required.

**BEACHES & PARKS**

There's one thing you'll rarely miss in this tropical city—
rain. Hilo gets about 130 inches a year. The Chamber of
Commerce will claim it rains mostly at night, but don't
be deceived. It's almost as likely to be dark and wet at midday.
There is a good side to all this bothersome moisture—it transforms Hilo into an exotic city crowded with tropical foliage, the
orchid capital of the United States.
     Hilo is the closest you will approach in all Hawaii to a Som-
erset Maugham–style South Seas port town. With its turn-of-the-
20th-century stores, many badly needing a paint job, and old
Chinese shops, it's a throwback to an era when tourists were few
and Hawaii was a territory. Sections of town, especially around
Waianuenue Avenue, have been refurbished and dabbed with
1990s flash, but much of the downtown still feels like the 1950s,
with a collection of small-town shops and restaurants. The gut-
ters are rusty, the rain awnings have sagged, and an enduring
sense of character overhangs the place with the certainty and fi-
nality of the next downpour.

**Hilo**

Hilo is a tropical wonderland, a rainforest with hotels, shops and
great places to visit. A visit to one of the city's many flower nurseries is an absolute must. These gardens grow orchids, anthuriums and countless other flowers. There are two that I highly rec-

**SIGHTS**

ommend. **Orchids of Hawaii** specializes in *vanda* orchids, birds of paradise and anthuriums. Closed Saturday and Sunday. ~ 2801 Kilauea Avenue; 808-959-3581, 800-323-1449, fax 808-959-4497; www.orchidsofhawaii.com, e-mail hilo@orchidsofhawaii.com. **Nani Mau Gardens** is a 20-acre visual feast that houses a wide variety of tropical flowers and plants. It also has a gift shop. Admission. ~ Several miles south of Hilo near Route 11 at 421 Makalika Street; 808-959-3500, fax 808-959-3501; www.nanimau.com, e-mail nanimau.garden@verizon.net.

A self-guided tour from the Hilo Mainstreet Program Office leads you to 17 sites of historic and architectural significance in this tropical enclave. ~ 329 Kamehameha Avenue; 808-935-8850, fax 808-935-4356.

Banyan Drive is another green thumb's delight. Sweeping past Hilo's nicest hotels, this waterfront road is shaded with rows of giant banyan trees. Plaques proclaim the dignitaries who planted them, including Franklin D. Roosevelt, Babe Ruth and Amelia Earhart. Next to this verdant arcade are the **Liliuokalani Gardens**, 19 acres exploding with color. These Japanese gardens, featuring both Hawaiian and Asian trees, are dotted with pagodas and arched bridges. ~ Banyan Drive and Lihiwai Street.

Be sure to check out the **Suisan Company Limited**. Started in 1907 by a small group of Waiakea fishermen, it is a local institution. Anglers bring their fresh catches—ahi, mahimahi, reef and bottom fish, whatever's jumping—here for sale. Great photo ops! If you'd like to sample some of the fresh fish, buy some tasty *poke ahi* (raw tuna chunks seasoned with chili peppers, seaweed, green onions and soy sauce), a favorite Hawaiian dish. ~ 93 Lihiwai Street; 808-935-9349, fax 808-935-2115; www.suisan.com.

From Banyan Drive, a short footbridge crosses to **Coconut Island,** a palm-studded islet in Hilo Bay. This old Hawaiian sanctuary presents a dramatic view of Hilo Bay and, on a clear day, of Mauna Kea and Mauna Loa as well.

It's not far to **Wailoa River State Park**, where grassy picnic areas surround beautiful **Waiakea Fishpond**. Across one of the pond's arching bridges, at **Wailoa Visitors Center**, there are cultural exhibits and an information desk. ~ Piopio Street, off Kamehameha Avenue; 808-933-0416.

In downtown Hilo, the **Lyman House Memorial Museum** is a fascinating example of a 19th-century missionary home. Built in 1839, the house is furnished with elegant period pieces that create a sense of this bygone era (the house is open to guided tours only). Also on the property is a Hawaiian history museum focusing on Hawaiian culture and the islands' many ethnic groups, and an excellent collection of rocks and minerals. Among the museum's highlights is a 3-D map of the entire Hawaiian chain, from ocean floor to mountain top. Closed Sunday. Admission. ~

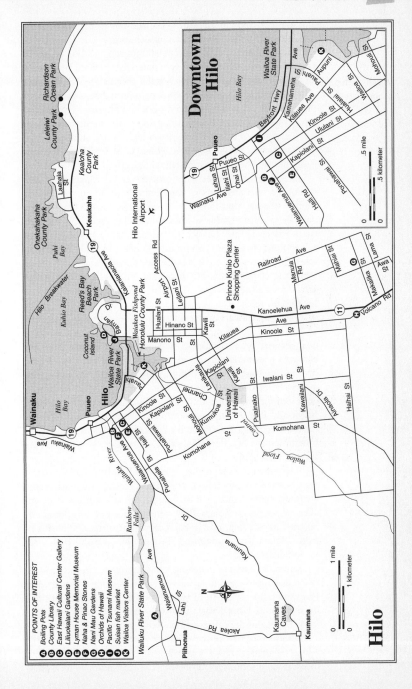

POINTS OF INTEREST
A  Boiling Pots
B  County Library
C  East Hawaii Cultural Center Gallery
D  Liliuokalani Gardens
E  Lyman House Memorial Museum
F  Naha & Pinao Stones
G  Nani Mau Gardens
H  Orchids of Hawaii
I  Pacific Tsunami Museum
J  Suisan fish market
K  Wailoa Visitors Center

**Downtown Hilo**

Hilo Bay

Wailoa River State Park

**Hilo**

Richardson Ocean Park
Leleiwi County Park
Kealoha County Park
Onekahakaha County Park
Keaukaha
Hilo International Airport

Hilo Breakwater
Reed's Bay Beach Park
Coconut Island
Waiakea Fishpond Honolulu County Park
Prince Kuhio Plaza Shopping Center

Wainaku
Pueo
Wailoa River State Park
Wailuku River State Park
Rainbow Falls

Pilihonua
Kaumana
Kaumana Caves

1 mile
1 kilometer
0

276 Haili Street; 808-935-5021, fax 808-969-7685; www.lyman museum.org, e-mail info@lymanmuseum.org.

The **Pacific Tsunami Museum** recaptures in photos, videos and interactive displays the tsunamis that periodically wreak havoc on Hilo. Most notorious was the one in 1946, which swept a half-mile inland and killed 94 people on the Big Island. Computers lead visitors through the history and physics of these infamous phenomena and survivors present first-hand accounts in the museum's videotaped oral histories. Closed Sunday. ~ 130 Kamehameha Avenue; 808-935-0926, fax 808-935-0842; www. tsunami.org, e-mail tsunami@tsunami.org.

Grassroots initiatives have brought about a partial revitalization of what remains of the diminishing number of wood-frame buildings that give Hilo a distinctive look. Luckily there have been some notable successes, including the surprisingly elegant Palace Theater (c. 1925), a restored landmark that's home to top-notch live theater and musicals. The old Police Station (c. 1910) is now an arts complex (the East Hawaii Cultural Center), while the classic Kress Building now houses shops and multi-screen movie theaters and a charter school, each a hopeful sign for the future.

The **East Hawaii Cultural Center Gallery** displays the work of local and international artists in a series of exhibits that change monthly. The building itself, an old police station that has achieved historic landmark status, is a work of art. Closed Sunday and the last week of every month. ~ 141 Kalakaua Street; 808-961-5711, fax 808-935-7536.

Fronting the library on nearby Waianuenue Avenue are the **Naha** and **Pinao Stones**. According to legend, whoever moved the massive Naha Stone would rule all the islands. Kamehameha overturned the boulder while still a youth, then grew to become Hawaii's first king.

Continue up Waianuenue Avenue to **Rainbow Falls**, a foaming cascade in Wailuku River State Park. Here, particularly in the morning, spray from the falls shimmers in spectral hues. It's another two miles to **Boiling Pots**, where a series of falls pours turbulently into circular lava pools. The rushing water, spilling down from Mauna Kea, bubbles up through the lava and boils over into the next pool.

Kaumana Drive, branching off Waianuenue Avenue, leads five miles out of town to **Kaumana Caves**. A stone stairway leads from the roadside down to two fern-choked lava tubes, formed during Mauna Loa's devastating 1881 eruption. Explore the lower tube, but avoid the other—it's dangerous.

HIDDEN ▶    Also be sure to visit the **Panaewa Rainforest Zoo**. Located in a lush region that receives over 125 inches of rain annually, this modest facility houses numerous rainforest animals as well as other species. There are colobus monkeys, pygmy hippos and tigers, plus an array of exotic birds that include crowned cranes, pueos, parrots, Hawaiian coots, laysan ducks and nenes. ~ One mile off the Mamalahoa Highway several miles south of town; 808-959-7224, fax 808-981-2316; www.hilozoo.com, e-mail coh zoo@interpac.net.

**LODGING**

The main hotel district in this rain-plagued city sits astride the bay along Banyan Drive. Most hotels offer moderately priced accommodations, while a few are designed to fit the contours of a more slender purse.

Near the far end of tree-lined Banyan Drive lies the **Hilo Seaside Hotel**. This charming place is actually on a side street fronting Reed's Bay, an arm of Hilo Bay. Owned by the Kimis, a Hawaiian family, it has the same friendly ambience that pervades their other hotels. There's a large lobby decorated with tile, *koa* wood and bamboo. A carp pond complete with footbridges dominates the grounds. The rooms are small and plainly decorated. Most are wallpapered and equipped with telephone, television and a combination shower-tub (perfect for soaking away a rainy day). The lanais overlook lush gardens and the hotel swimming pool. All in all, for friendly ambience and a lovely setting, the Seaside is a prime choice. ~ 126 Banyan Way; 808-935-0821, 800-367-7000, fax 808-969-9195; www.hiloseasidehotel.com, e-mail info@hiloseasidehotel.com. MODERATE TO DELUXE.

The **Hawaii Naniloa Hotel** is a highrise affair located right on the water. Rooms are comfortably furnished and nicely adorned. Restaurants, bars, a lounge and a spa are among the many amenities here, but the most alluring feature is the landscape—the tree-

**AUTHOR FAVORITE**

The former home of the cattle rancher W. H. Shipman and his wife Mary, the historic **Shipman House Bed & Breakfast Inn** has been lovingly restored by the Shipmans' great-granddaughter Barbara Ann and her husband Gary. Much of the furnishings are original and date back to the monarchy, including a Steinway piano Queen Liliuokalani sometimes played while a guest here. Jack London and wife Charmian also spent time at this gracious Victorian. Nowadays, there are five spacious accommodations (two in the detached guest cottage) that are individually decorated with period pieces and fresh flowers. A hula *halau* practices on the premise, and guests are invited to join in on Wednesday-night classes. ~ 131 Kaiulani Street; phone/fax 808-934-8002, 800-627-8447; www.hilo-hawaii.com, e-mail bighouse@bigisland.com. DELUXE.

studded lawn is fringed with tidepools and volcanic rock. Add outdoor swimming pools, a spacious lobby and friendly staff and you have the perfect nesting spot in town. Guests also have access to the Naniloa Country Club's nine-hole golf course across the street. ~ 93 Banyan Drive; 808-969-3333, 800-367-5360, fax 808-969-6622; www.naniloa.com, e-mail hinan@aloha.net. MODERATE TO DELUXE.

**Hilo Bay Hotel** is another economical oceanfront establishment. The theme here is Polynesian, and proprietor "Uncle Billy" carries it off with flair: wicker furniture, thatch and *tapa* in the lobby, a restaurant/cocktail lounge, a bayside swimming pool and several carp ponds dotted about the tropical gardens. Standard rooms have wall-to-wall carpeting, televisions, telephones and air conditioning. The rooms are plainly furnished, located away from the water and rent for a moderate price. Superior rooms (which overlook the gardens, are larger, more attractive and come with ocean views) can be reserved for slightly more. Oceanfront rooms are also available and rent for deluxe prices. ~ 87 Banyan Drive; 808-935-0861, 800-367-5102, fax 808-935-7903; www.unclebilly.com, e-mail reservations@unclebilly.com. MODERATE TO DELUXE.

On a tree-lined residential street just across the Wailuku River sits the **Dolphin Bay Hotel**. This comfortable two-story establishment has 18 units, all equipped with kitchenettes. There are studios, one-bedroom apartments, which can accommodate up to four, and a two-bedroom unit, which houses as many as six. Rooms upstairs have exposed-beam ceilings; all units have cinderblock walls, but personal touches like fresh flowers and fruit, and a garden with a running spring, make this a good choice. ~ 333 Iliahi Street; 808-935-1466, fax 808-935-1523; www.dolphinbayhotel.com, e-mail johnhilo@dolphinbayhotel.com. MODERATE.

Not far away at the **Wild Ginger Inn** you'll find inexpensive guest rooms, which are attractively furnished with wood floors and ceiling fans. There's a laundry room, a large garden and a spacious lobby. This vintage-1940s Hawaiian-style inn is surrounded by flowering trees and trimly manicured grounds. It also features an open-air lobby that's tastefully tiled and equipped with a very inviting hammock. ~ 100 Puueo Street; 808-935-5556, 800-882-1887, fax 808-969-1225. BUDGET.

**Arnott's Lodge** is a clean, bright attractive hostel. Just one block from the waterfront, it is on the outskirts of Hilo in a low-key residential area. There are dormitory rooms available as well as private singles and doubles. Hiking and snorkeling trips are frequently arranged. With low prices, and full kitchen and laundry facilities provided, it's one of the area's best bargains. ~ 98 Apapane Road; 808-969-7097, fax 808-935-6442; www.arnottslodge.com, e-mail mahala@arnottslodge.com. BUDGET.

Scattered throughout Hilo are numerous cafés, lunch counters and chain restaurants serving low-cost meals. This is a great town for ethnic eating on a budget.

**Uncle Billy's Fish and Steakhouse** at the Hilo Bay Hotel sports Hawaiian decor. In addition to its rattan furnishings, this cozy restaurant hosts Polynesian dinner shows nightly. The menu is filled with surf-and-turf dishes priced reasonably. There's no lunch here, but they do offer breakfast and dinner daily. ~ 87 Banyan Drive; 808-935-0861; www.unclebilly.com, e-mail resv@unclebilly.com. MODERATE TO DELUXE.

Right next to Suisan fish market, **Nihon Restaurant & Cultural Center**, a Japanese dining establishment, is a bit light on the culture, but the food is well prepared. Scenic views of Hilo Bay are accented by artwork from local artists. Specialties include noodle dishes, tempura, sukiyaki and sushi. Closed Sunday. ~ 123 Lihiwai Street; 808-969-1133. MODERATE TO DELUXE.

Home-style Japanese meals are made fresh daily at **Miyo's**. A selection of vegetarian specialties, sashimi, tempura and sesame chicken are served in a simple setting of wooden tables and shoji screens. The dining room, which overlooks a fishpond, boasts views of Mauna Kea. Closed Sunday. ~ Waiakea Villas Shops, 400 Hualani Street; 808-935-2273, fax 808-959-6859. BUDGET TO MODERATE.

For breakfast or lunch in downtown Hilo consider **Canoes Café**. This informal dining area serves breakfast wraps in the morning and offers a "sandwich board" and fresh soups at lunch. ~ 14 Furneaux Lane; 808-935-4070; www.canoescafe.com, e-mail info@canoescafe.com. BUDGET.

A local institution, voted Best Breakfast by locals eight years in a row, **Ken's House of Pancakes** has to top the list for all-American fare. If you've ever been to a Denny's or Howard Johnson's, you've been in Ken's. Endless rows of naugahyde booths, a long counter next to the kitchen, uniformed waitresses—the classic roadside America motif. The cuisine is on par with the decor and you'll find 200 items on the menu, but it's a

◀ HIDDEN

### ALL-AMERICAN. . .WITH A HAWAIIAN TWIST

**Don's Grill** is one of those all-American places where dinner comes with soup or salad, hot vegetables, a fresh roll and your choice of mashed potatoes or fries. In this case it's Hawaiian all-American, so the menu switches from pork chops to teriyaki beef, rotisserie chicken to tofu stir-fry, and barbecued ribs to breaded calamari. Very popular with the local folk. Closed Monday. ~ 485 Hinano Street; 808-935-9099, fax 808-961-0162. MODERATE.

great place to join locals for breakfast (yummy banana pancakes) and it's a good late-night option—open 24 hours. ~ 1730 Kamehameha Avenue; 808-935-8711, fax 808-961-5124; e-mail khop@interpac.net. BUDGET.

There are more than three dozen dishes on the menu at **Reuben's Mexican Food**, numbered one to thirty-seven, and they cover the entire territory. Whether you're searching for enchiladas, *camarones empanizado*, beef tostadas, carne asada or huevos rancheros, you'll find it here. ~ 336 Kamehameha Avenue; 808-961-2552. MODERATE.

For creative Italian cuisine in a colorfully romantic atmosphere, the place to go is **Pescatore**, with its yellow exterior, green tablecloths, red chairs, lace curtains and candles in wine bottles. The menu offers such entrées as marinated lamb chops, sautéed chicken breast in lemon caper sauce and pasta puttanesca with anchovy sauce, but as the name suggests, the specialty is fresh seafood, from a traditional cioppino (fisherman's stew) full of lobster, shrimp, scallops and clams to unique sashimi Italian-style. Breakfast served only on weekends. ~ 235 Keawe Street; 808-969-9090. DELUXE TO ULTRA-DELUXE.

**HIDDEN ►** A hole-in-the-wall local favorite well-hidden behind a bowling alley, **Nori's Saimin and Snacks** has nonetheless grown so popular over the years that it even has its own line of souvenir T-shirts, hats, beach towels and packaged snacks. The atmosphere is boisterous, and it's open until 2 a.m. or so. Saimin, noodles similar to ramen, comes prepared in assorted ways—green and flavored with wasabi, fried with Spam, or in seaweed soup, to name a few. There are also other choices. Try the ahi tuna burger. ~ 688 Kinoole Street #124; 808-935-9133. BUDGET.

You can dine or take out at **Café Pesto**, an appealing eatery located in the historic S. Hata Building. This downtown Hilo gathering place serves wood-fired pizza, calzone, risotto, fresh fish and organic salads. ~ 308 Kamehameha Avenue; 808-969-6640, fax 808-969-4858; www.cafepesto.com. MODERATE TO DELUXE.

**HIDDEN ►** **Tsunami Grill and Tempura**, a small café downtown, serves mainly Japanese meals as well as the occasional hamburger and steak. Several *donburi*, *udon* and tempura dishes are on tap as well as special seafood dishes. Closed Sunday. ~ 250 Keawe Street; 808-961-6789. MODERATE.

Thailand is represented by **Royal Siam**, an excellent eatery with a warm ambience, friendly staff, local crowd and exceptional cuisine. You'll find *pad thai* and traditional curries. ~ 70 Mamo Street; 808-961-6100. MODERATE TO ULTRA-DELUXE.

Hilo's foremost steak-and-seafood restaurant is **Harrington's**, a waterfront dining room that is particularly popular with locals. Here you can dine in a congenial atmosphere to the strains of Hawaiian music in the background. Harrington's also has a relaxing bar scene and can be counted on for good food with a view. ~ 135 Kalanianaole Street; 808-961-4966, fax 808-961-4975. DELUXE TO ULTRA-DELUXE.

The island's largest city, Hilo has several supermarkets. Foremost is **Sack-N-Save**. ~ 250 Kinoole Street; 808-935-3113.   **GROCERIES**

Hilo hosts an excellent natural foods outlet—**Abundant Life Wholefoods & Deli**. It contains healthy supplies of vitamins and juices, as well as a deli and fresh organic fruits and vegetables. ~ 292 Kamehameha Avenue; 808-935-7411.

The most convenient way to shop in Hilo is at **Prince Kuhio Plaza**, a full-facility complex with everything from small crafts shops to swank boutiques to a sprawling department store. The Big Island's largest mall, it's a gathering place for local shoppers and a convenient spot for visitors. But bargains and locally crafted products are probably what you're after. So it's a good idea to window-shop through the centers, checking out prices, then do your buying at smaller shops. ~ 111 East Puainako Street; 808-959-3555.   **SHOPPING**

**The Most Irresistible Shop in Hilo** doesn't quite live up to its bold name but does create a strong attraction with jewelry, clothing, ceramics, books and toys. They also feature works by local artists. ~ 256 Kamehameha Avenue; 808-935-9644.

For beach-reading materials, try **The Book Gallery**. This well-stocked shop has many popular titles. ~ 259 Keawe Street; 808-935-4943. If maps, guidebooks, globes, gifts, Hawaiian music and volumes on Hawaiiana sound more inviting, **Basically Books** is an excellent choice. ~ 160 Kamehameha Avenue; 808-961-0144.

Following a similar theme, **Hana Hou** is a shop filled with "vintage and contemporary island treasures." Among those keepsakes are old Hawaiian song sheets, Matson menus and aloha shirts. Closed Sunday. ~ 164 Kamehameha Avenue; 808-935-4555; e-mail hanahou.hilo@verizon.net.

**AUTHOR FAVORITE**

A great spot for original woodwork is south of Hilo about 12 miles on Route 11 at **Dan DeLuz Woods**. The beautiful pieces are fashioned from banyan, sandalwood, *koa* and *milo*, all priced reasonably. The DeLuzes, the craftspeople who own the shop, do all their carving in a separate workshop. If you'd like a description of how the bowls are made, they're happy to provide an informal tour. ~ Mile marker 12, Route 11; 808-968-6607, fax 808-968-6019.

Specializing in "distinct island wearables, bedding and gifts," **Sig Zane Designs** has its own designer line of island dresses and aloha shirts. Closed Sunday. ~ 122 Kamehameha Avenue; 808-935-7077; www.sigzane.com.

**NIGHTLIFE**

The main scene centers around the big hotels along Banyan Drive. By far the best place is the Hawaii Naniloa Hotel. This hotel has a nicely appointed nightclub, **The Crown Room**. The lounge usually books local groups, but every once in a while it imports a mainland band for special events. There's usually a cover charge and two-drink minimum. Then there is **Joji's Lounge**, which sometimes provides piano tunes in the evening. ~ 93 Banyan Drive; 808-969-3333; e-mail hinan@aloha.net.

**Harrington's** hosts a Hawaiian guitarist on Friday and Saturday nights. ~ 135 Kalanianaole Avenue; 808-961-4966.

The **Waioli Lounge** at the Hilo Hawaiian Hotel has live music on weekends. Usually it's a contemporary trio. ~ 71 Banyan Drive; 808-935-9361.

**BEACHES & PARKS**

**KALAKAUA PARK**  Located on the corner of busy Kinoole Street and Waianuenue Avenue, this pretty little park has a grand old banyan tree and a pleasant picnic area. A bronze statue of King Kalakaua adds dignity to the park grounds.

**REED'S BAY BEACH PARK**  Reed's Bay, a banyan-lined cove is a marvelous picnic spot. The bay is actually an arm of Hilo Bay, but unlike the larger body of water, Reed's Bay offers excellent swimming in smooth water (though an underwater spring keeps the water cold). There is also an adjacent body of water popular with the locals. They call it "ice pond" due to its cold waters. Facilities include picnic areas, drinking water, showers and restrooms. ~ Located at the end of Banyan Drive.

**ONEKAHAKAHA, KEALOHA AND LELEIWI COUNTY PARKS**  None of these three parks have sand beaches, but all possess lava pools or other shallow places for swimming. They also have grassy plots and picnic areas, plus restrooms and showers. If you fish along these shores, chances are good you'll net *papio*, threadfin, mountain bass, mullet, big-eyed scad, mackerel scad, milkfish, bonefish or goatfish. Kealoha Park offers good snorkeling, surfing, spear-fishing and throw-netting. ~ All three parks are located within five miles of Hilo, east along Kalanianaole Avenue.

**HIDDEN ►**

**RICHARDSON OCEAN PARK**  This black-sand beach, south of Hilo Bay, is without doubt the finest beach in the area. From there you can see Mauna Kea hulking in the background. Coconut palms and ironwood trees fringe the beach, while a lava outcropping somewhat protects swimmers. The protected areas also make for good snorkeling. This is one of the best spots around Hilo for surfing as well as bodysurfing and bodyboarding. Winter break with right slides. Mornings and evenings are the prime times, but at all times beware of currents, riptides and sharp reefs. Park officials warn beginners to learn the sport at a less treacherous location. Lifeguards are on duty every day. Anglers try for *papio*, mountain bass, mullet, big-eyed scad, mackerel scad, milkfish, bonefish and goatfish. Facilities here include restrooms and outdoor showers. ~ Take Kalanianaole Avenue to within a quarter-mile of where the paved road ends; watch for the sign to Richardson Ocean Park. The beach is behind and to the right of the center; 808-961-8695, fax 808-961-8696.

## Hamakua Coast

Route 19, the Mamalahoa Highway, leads north from Hilo along the rainy, windswept Hamakua Coast. Planted with papaya, macadamia nuts, taro and ginger root, among other crops and teeming with exotic plant life, this elevated coastline is as lushly overgrown as Hilo.

A softly rolling plateau that edges from the slopes of Mauna Kea to the sea, the region is cut by sharp canyons and deep gulches. Waterfalls cascade down emerald walls and tumbling streams lead to lava-rock beaches. Beautiful is too tame a term

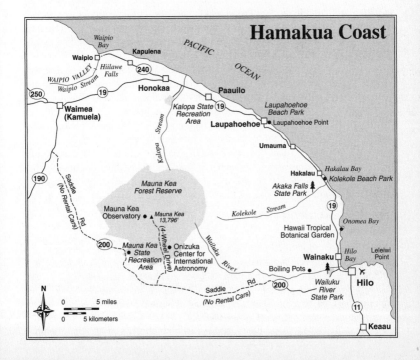

Hamakua Coast

for this enchanting countryside. There are stands of eucalyptus, shadowy forests and misty fields of sugar cane. Plantation towns, built between 1900 and 1910, filled with pastel-painted houses and adorned with flower gardens, lie along the route.

**SIGHTS**

Several miles outside Hilo, follow the signs to the **Scenic Drive**. This old coast road winds past cane fields and shantytowns before rejoining the main highway. Alexander palms line the road. Watch for Onomea Bay: There you'll see a V-shaped rock formation where a sea arch collapsed in 1956.

You might want to stop by **Hawaii Tropical Botanical Garden**, an exotic nature preserve with streams, waterfalls, rugged coastline and over 2000 plant species. This jungle garden, edged by the Pacific and inhabited by shore birds and giant sea turtles, is a place of uncommon beauty. Admission. ~ On the Four Mile Scenic Route, seven miles north of Hilo; 808-964-5233, fax 808-964-1338; www.hawaiigarden.com, e-mail htbg@ilhawaii.net.

Countless gulches ribbon the landscape between Hilo and Honokaa. For a unique tour, take the road from Hakalau that winds down to **Hakalau Gulch**. Literally choked with vegetation, this gorge extends to a small beach. Towering above the gulch is the highway bridge.

*HIDDEN ►*

Another side road several miles north corkscrews down to **Laupahoehoe Point**, a hauntingly beautiful peninsula from which 24 students and teachers were swept away by the 1946 tidal wave. Here gently curving palm trees and spreading lawns contrast with the lash of the surf.

*HIDDEN ►*

Beginning in 1899 and lasting until 1946—when sugar was king—railways were the main source of transportation on the Big Island. Nowadays all that's left of the railroads are relics found in the **Laupahoehoe Train Museum**, housed in a former railroad employee's home. Here you'll find railroad artifacts, photos, memorabilia and a chance to "talk story" with the museum's volunteers, many of whom have spent their lives in the community. Admission. ~ Between mile markers 25 and 26 on Route 19; 808-962-6300, fax 808-962-6957; www.geocities.com/trainmuseum.

**AUTHOR FAVORITE**

On Route 19, traveling north of Hilo, you'll soon come to a turnoff heading inland to **Akaka Falls State Park**. Don't bypass it! A short nature trail leads past bamboo groves, ferns, ti and orchids to Akaka Falls, which slide 442 feet down a sheer cliff face, and Kahuna Falls, 400 feet high. This 66-acre preserve is covered in a canopy of rainforest vegetation. There are birds of paradise, azaleas and giant philodendrons whose leaves measure as much as two feet.

It's a jungle out there. But at **World Botanical Gardens** they're trying to make a tropical paradise out of it. Among the features are a football field–sized children's maze, a 300-acre botanical garden, a pathway through a dense and very beautiful rainforest, and a vista point overlooking a triple-tiered waterfall; many more features are under development. Be sure to try the complimentary fruit and juice. Admission. ~ Located near mile marker 16 on Route 19 in Umauma; phone/fax 808-963-5427; www.wbgi.com, e-mail info@wbgi.com.

The plantation town of **Paauilo** offers a glimpse of vintage Hawaii: decaying storefronts and tinroof cottages. Then it's on to **Honokaa**, a village caught in a lazy-paced time warp and the one-time world center of macadamia nut growing.

◄ HIDDEN

Head out Route 240 to **Waipio Valley**, the island's largest valley. For the hikers and explorers in the group, the lush valley is Eden here on Earth. A riot of tropical colors, swimming holes, 600-foot cascades, taro patches and an occasional wild horse are reasons to spend a day or more in this lush and sacred region. For movie buffs, Kaluahina Falls might bring recognition—but only if you were one of the few to see Kevin Costner's landfall in the monumental flop *Water World*. (See "Hiking" in Outdoor Adventures.) Most people get to see Waipio from this scenic lookout where Route 240 comes to an abrupt end. From the lookout you can see the mile-long black sand beach that marks Waipio's border with the sea. Tall ironwoods mark the site that was once a *heiau*, with the taro patches that remain homage to the Hawaiian past. The steep road that makes its way to the valley floor requires four-wheel drive. It's narrow (in some places only wide enough one vehicle), steep (with up to a 38 degree gradient), with sheer dropoffs that have hosted more than one vehicle.

Taro patches and tumbledown cottages still dot the valley. From the lookout point at road's end, a jeep trail drops sharply into Waipio. Explorers can hike down or take an hour-and-a-half four-wheel-drive tour with the **Waipio Valley Shuttle and Tours**. ~ 808-775-7121. Another agency with tours is **Waipio Valley Wagon Tour**. Its tour is part four-wheel-drive, part mule-drawn, GM shock-equipped wagon. ~ 808-775-9518. Both tours travel several miles up into the valley for eye-boggling views of 1200-foot Hiilawe Falls. Both are closed Sunday.

If you don't have time to explore the valley, be sure to at least take in the vista from the **Waipio Valley Lookout** at the end of Route 240.

**Hotel Honokaa Club**, perched on a hillside above the Hamakua Coast, has a boardinghouse atmosphere. The rooms upstairs are kept thoroughly scrubbed and freshly painted; they're quite adequate. A modest price buys a splendid ocean view, color television

**LODGING**

◄ HIDDEN

plus a tiny private bathroom. Or trade the cable TV away and you can have a small cubicle with community bathroom at even less cost. These rooms are smaller and lack the view, but they're just as clean as the upstairs rooms. Dorm-style hostel accommodations are also available. A continental breakfast is included. ~ Route 240, Honokaa; phone/fax 808-775-0678, 800-808-0678; www. hotelhono.com, e-mail manager@hotelhono.com. BUDGET TO MODERATE.

This is prime bed-and-breakfast country that benefits from a rural setting and hosts with plenty of aloha. The five-room **HIDDEN** ▶ **Waipio Wayside**, on Route 240 between Honokaa and Waipio, offers a convenient base for exploring the valley. The 1930s home has been nicely updated, preserving the feel of the past. An organic tropical continental breakfast is served communally. ~ P.O. Box 840, Honokaa, HI 96727; 808-775-0275, 800-833-8849; www.waipiowayside.com, e-mail info@waipiowayside. com. MODERATE.

At **Mountain Meadow Ranch** in Ahualoa (about five minutes upcountry of Honokaa toward Waimea), you're surrounded by pastureland and tall eucalyptus that scent the air. There are a separate one-bedroom cottage or a two-bedroom suite that can be rented as a two-bedroom booking. Breakfast includes homebrewed coffee, local fruits, breads, pastries and cereal. Rooms are spacious, beds comfortable—fluffy and warm for the cool night air. Owner Gay George is a most pleasant hostess. ~ 46-3895 Kapuna Road, Honokaa, HI 96727; phone/fax 808-775-9376; www.mountainmeadowranch.com, e-mail wgeorge@mountain meadowranch.com. MODERATE.

**DINING**    Jolene's **Kau Kau Korner** has plate lunches, burgers and sandwiches during daylight hours. At dinner, they move on to mahi-**HIDDEN** ▶    mahi, shrimp and vegetable tempura, stir-fry beef and grilled chicken with pineapple. It's a simple café but reasonably priced with good-sized portions and local color. Closed weekends. ~ 45-3625 Mamane Street, Honokaa; 808-775-9498. BUDGET.

Oversize portions, and the fact that on some nights it's the **HIDDEN** ▶    only restaurant in town, makes **Tex Drive-In & Restaurant** a Honokaa landmark and gathering place. Local specialties and standard fare like hamburgers dominate the fast-food menu. ~ Route 19, Honokaa; 808-775-0598. MODERATE.

**GROCERIES**    First you can check out **Jan's Store**. Located in Honomu on the road to Akaka Falls, it has a limited stock, but you may find what you need. ~ Honomu; 808-963-6062. Also try **Ti Kaneshiro Supermarket**, a small-town shop across from the post office in Honokaa. ~ Honokaa; 808-775-0631.

On the road to Akaka Falls in Honomu, you'll happen upon the **Ohana Gallery**. Here is a wide array of work by local artists and craftspeople. Of particular note are photographs of the volcano erupting on the Big Island. The Gallery also serves as an informal area information center. Closed Sunday and Monday. ~ Honomu; 808-963-5467.

The **Waipio Valley Artworks**, located near the Waipio Valley Lookout, is also cluttered with woodcarvings. Made from several different woods, some of these creations are extremely beautiful. This shop also features paintings, ceramics and other locally crafted items. ~ 48-5416 Kukuihaele Road; 808-775-0958.

The **Honokaa People's Theatre**, a 1930 structure with an Old West–style facade and a portico over the sidewalk, is one of the last motion picture houses in Hawaii with a single big screen. Besides showing first-run films and independent and art films, the renovated theater is used for occasional live dance performances and music concerts. Each October or November it is the venue for the Hamakua Music Festival (www.hamakuamusicfestival.com), an extravaganza of jazz, classical and Hawaiian traditional music performances that raises money for music education on the Hamakua Coast. ~ Honokaa; 808-775-0000, fax 808-775-9963.

**KOLEKOLE BEACH PARK** Located at the mouth of a wide gulch lush with tropical vegetation, this comfortable park has a large and pleasant grassy area. A stream and waterfall tumble through the park down to the rocky, surf-torn shore. The sandy beach and natural beauty of the place make it very popular among local residents. You can swim in the stream but the ocean here is forbiddingly rough. Threadfin, *menpachi*, *papio* and *ulua* are the common catches. Facilities consist of a picnic area, restrooms and electricity; there is no drinking water, but spring water is available for cooking and showers. ~ Located just off Mamalahoa Highway (Route 19) about 12 miles northwest of Hilo.

**AUTHOR FAVORITE**
**Kamaaina Woods** in Honokaa has a splendid assortment of handmade bowls and decorations. With items fashioned from *milo*, mango and *koa*, this shop is practically a museum. And if you are interested in learning more about these woods, you can view the factory through the window. Closed Sunday. ~ Lehua Street, Honokaa; 808-775-7722.

▲ Tent and trailer; $3 per night. County permit required.

**LAUPAHOEHOE BEACH PARK** 🏊 🎣 🏃 ⚓ Set on a low-lying peninsula that was inundated by the 1946 tidal wave, this hauntingly beautiful park is still lashed by heavy surf. A precipitous *pali* and lava-strewn shoreline surround the area. Swimming, snorkeling and surfing are good at times, but usually very dangerous. You can fish for *ulua*, *papio*, *menpachi* and *moi*. Facilities include a picnic area, restrooms, showers and electricity. ~ One mile off Route 19 down a well-marked twisting road, about 27 miles northwest of Hilo.

▲ Tent and trailer camping permitted; $3 per night. County permit required.

**KALOPA STATE RECREATION AREA** 🏃 A wooded retreat set in the mountains above the Hamakua Coast, this 100-acre park has both untouched expanses ripe for exploring and several beautifully landscaped acres. Ranging from 2000 to 2500 feet elevation, it's a great place for hiking or just for escaping. There are picnic areas, restrooms, showers and cabins. ~ Take Route 19 southeast from Honokaa for about three miles. A well-marked paved road leads from the highway another two miles to the park.

▲ Tent camping is permitted and cabins are also available. Reservations: 808-974-6200.

**WAIPIO BEACH** 🏃 🏊 Waipio's mile of gray sands are dissected by the waters of Waipio Stream after a journey that begins six miles upstream. With a steep break and often unpredictable currents, swimming requires a careful reading of daily conditions. The setting provides wonderful views of the valley's steep walls. The remains of an ancient *heiau* are situated in an ironwood grove that backs the beach. ~ You can reach the main section of beach by wading the stream, a dangerous task when waters are full. Otherwise it requires a bridge crossing a bit upstream followed by a walk (or drive) to the shore.

▼▼▼▼▼▼▼▼▼▼▼▼▼▼

# Outdoor Adventures

## CAMPING

There are few activities on the Big Island more pleasurable than camping. Beautiful state and county parks dot the island, while enticing hiking trails lead to remote mountain and coastal areas.

No matter what you plan to do on the island, keep in mind that the Kona side is generally dry, while the Hilo side receives considerable rain. Also remember that the mountains can be quite cold and usually call for extra clothing and gear.

Camping at **county parks** requires a permit. These cost $5 per person per day ($2 for ages 13 through 17, $1 for children). Although RV camping is allowed in many county parks, no special parking or electrical hookups are provided. Pick up permits from

the County Department of Parks and Recreation. ~ 101 Pauahi
Street, Suite 6, Hilo, HI 96720; 808-961-8311; www.hawaii-
county.com. Permits are also available at the South Kona Recreation Office. ~ P.O. Box 314, Captain Cook, HI 96740; 808-
323-3060; www.hawaii-county.com. The main county parks and
recreation office for the west side of the island is the Hale
Hawawai office in Kailua-Kona. ~ 808-327-3560; www.hawaii-
county.com. County permits are issued for both tent and trailer
camping, and can be obtained for up to two weeks at each park
(one week during the summer).

Free **state parks** permits can be obtained through the State
Department of Land and Natural Resources, Division of State
Parks. ~ 75 Aupuni Street, Hilo, HI 96720; 808-974-6200. For
information on cabin rentals and camping in Volcanoes National
Park, see the individual listings in the "Beaches & Parks" sec-
tions in this chapter.

**Hilo Surplus** sells sleeping bags, backpacks, tents, stoves and
the like. Closed Sunday. ~ 148 Mamo Street, Hilo; 808-935-6398.

The waters off the Kona Coast are among the Pacific's finest fishing grounds, particularly for marlin. Many charter boats operate
out of Kailua; check the phone book for names or simply walk
along the pier and inquire.

**FISHING**

**Kona Charter Skippers Association** represents one of the
larger outfits. They sponsor daily charters for marlin, yellowfin
tuna, *ono*, mahimahi and other gamefish. Using boats 26 to 54
feet in length, they take out up to six passengers per boat for
half- and full-day trips. Private charters are also available. ~ 74-
857 Iwalani Place, Kailua-Kona; 808-329-3600, 800-762-7546;
www.konabiggamefishing.com.

The **Sea Wife,** with Captain Tim Cox at the helm, sets out
Monday through Saturday from Honokohau Harbor in pursuit

### EELS, CORAL AND A SAIL
Bring your sunscreen, towel and hat for a wonderful half-day of snorkeling
and sailing. Rather than heading out to Molikini with all the other folks,
**Kamanu Charters** takes you to a hidden cove that teems with fish and
otherworldly coral formations. You're bound to see a slinky eel, needle-
nose fish and tons of parrot fish. If you're lucky, spinner dolphins cavort
alongside the boat as you make your way back to the marina. A lively
crew makes the day even more special. ~ P.O. Box 2021, Kailua-Kona,
HI 96745; 808-329-2021, 800-348-3091, fax 808-329-8424; www.ka
manu.com, e-mail kamanu@interpac.net.

of marlin, mahimahi, *ono* and tuna. ~ P.O. Box 2645, Kailua-Kona, HI 96745; 808-329-1806.

Head up to the tuna tower to survey the fishing scene aboard **Pamela**, a 38-foot Bertram that focuses on marlin, short-nosed spearfish, mahimahi, yellowfin and wahoo. ~ Honokohau Harbor, Kailua-Kona; 808-329-3600, 800-762-7546.

Another company offering similar service is the charter desk in the **Kona Fuel and Marine** building. ~ Honokohau Harbor, Kailua-Kona; 808-329-5735.

**DIVING**    The Big Island's coastal waters offer some of the most enticing dive sites in Hawaii. Good visibility, lava and coral formations and, of course, an intriguing variety of marine life assure plenty of fun. Whether you choose a beach or boat dive, you'll find the waters relatively uncrowded. Snorkelers will be attracted to beautiful Kealakekua Bay, where Captain Cook met his maker.

**KAILUA-KONA AREA**    **Sandwich Isle Divers** is a full-service dive shop that offers repairs and instruction, and has two boats for dive trips. Trip destinations include Turtle Pinnacles, Pine Trees, Golden Arches, Kaiwi Point and Kaloko Arches and more locations along the Kona Coast and beyond. They also conduct a night manta ray dive. ~ Kona Marketplace, Kailua-Kona; 808-329-9188, 888-743-3483; www.sandwichisledivers.com.

**Sea Paradise Scuba** leads trips to lava tubes, caverns, caves and other fascinating formations at 40 locations south of Kailua. ~ 78-7128 Kaleopapa Street, Keauhou; 808-322-2500, 800-322-5662; www.seaparadise.com. **Big Island Dives** offers daytime and night dives along the Kona Coast. ~ Kaahumanu Plaza, 75-5467 Kaiwi Street, Kailua-Kona; 808-329-6068.

**KOHALA COAST**    **Kohala Divers** is a full-service diving center providing scuba and snorkeling lessons as well as gear rental. There is a two-tank boat dive available, or go out on their 42-foot custom dive boat. ~ Kawaihae Shopping Center, Kawaihae; 808-882-7774; www.kohaladivers.com.

**HILO**    The only dive shop in Hilo, **Nautilus Dive Center** has been operating one- and two-tank shore dives off the Hilo Coast as well as all over the island since 1982. You'll see a variety of marine life, including sea turtles, as well as coral formations and caves. Closed Sunday. ~ 382 Kamehameha Avenue, Hilo; 808-935-6939.

**SURFING & WIND-SURFING**    For surfing U.S.A., consider the dynamic Kona Coast as well as Hilo Bay. Winter is peak season for surfing popular spots such as Lyman's and Banyan's. Also popular is Pohiki in the Puna area near the Kilauea volcano.

Windsurfing is good year-round. Try Anaehoomalu Beach on the Kona Coast or the South Point area.

**Ocean Sports Hawaii** rents sailboards and offers lessons. ~ Outrigger Waikoloa Resort, Waikoloa; 808-886-6666 ext. 1, 888-724-5234; www.hawaiioceansports.com.

At the Kona Inn Shopping Village, **Honolua Surf Company** sells surfboards and boogieboards and recommends the best locations. ~ 75-5744 Alii Drive, Kailua-Kona; 808-329-1001.

**Pacific Vibrations** will outfit you for a day of surfing and the friendly staff is a great resource for info about local outdoor activities. ~ 75-5702 Likana Lane, Kailua-Kona; 808-329-4140.

One of the authentic pleasures of a Big Island visit is a sail along the Kona or Kohala coast. Choose from a pleasure sail or take an adventure trip that includes a snorkeling excursion.

**SAILING & PARA-SAILING**

Among the popular operators is **Honu Sailing**, which offers half-day, full-day and sunset trips with snorkeling along the Kona coast. ~ Honokohau Harbor, Kailua; 808-896-4668; www.sailkona.com. The **Maile Gulf Star** is a 50-foot sailboat available for a variety of trips around the Big Island. ~ Kawaihae Harbor; 808-326-5174; www.adventuresailing.com.

Another popular sport in Hawaii is parasailing, in which you are strapped to a parachute that is towed aloft by a motorboat. For information, contact UFO **Parasail**. ~ Kailua-Kona; 808-325-5836; www.ufoparasail.net.

**Ocean Eco Tours** has a professional aquatic staff that claims it will take you on a "tour of a lifetime" along the Kona Coast. For paddlers of any skill (beginners to ocean voyagers), they'll find the perfect location for you to view Hawaii's marine world. ~ Honokohau Harbor, 74-425 Kealakehe Parkway, Suite 15, Kailua-

**KAYAKING**

**MAKE A WISH**

You may not associate Hawaii with stargazing, but the vast open spaces and crystal-clear air make it a prime nocturnal viewing spot. A couple of outfitters offer a unique excursion: they'll pick you up and take you to the mountain while providing an informative narrative on the astronomy, geology and geography of Hawaii. After you've experienced a Hawaiian sunset they'll take you mid-mountain, where the highlight of the evening begins: stargazing through portable telescopes with narration provided by knowledgeable experts. The evening concludes with hot chocolate and the peace of the night skies. Contact **Mauna Kea Summit Adventures** (P.O. Box 9027, Kailua-Kona, HI 96745; 808-322-2366, 888-322-2366; www.maunakea.com) or **Hawaii Forest & Trail** (74-5035B Kaahumanu Highway, Kailua-Kona; 808-331-8505, 800-464-1993; www.hawaii-forest.com) to book your excursion.

Kona; 808-324-7873, fax 808-331-1936; www.oceanecotours.com; e-mail ecoinfo@oceanecotours.com.

**Kona Boy** offers guided tours on the island's west side. Rentals of dive, surf, racing or touring kayaks are also available. Kona Boy is a resource for maps, information and advice on sea kayaking. ~ Mamalahoa Highway near Mile marker 113; 808-322-3600.

The Big Island's only Hawaiian-owned and -operated kayak company is **Aloha Kayak Co.** These knowledgeable folks will rent you equipment and take you on exciting tours that include cliff-jumping, snorkeling and even swimming through lava tubes. ~ 79-7428 Kealakekua Highway, Honalo; 808-322-2868; www.alohakayak.com.

**Flumin' Da Ditch** is a unique kayak adventure covering three miles in the century-old flume built to carry water from the Kohala Mountains to hungry sugar plantations. The plantations are gone, but portions of the ditch, as this massive irrigation system was called, remain functional. The ride is tame, accessing the rainforest in a unique and enjoyable way. Reservations are required. ~ 808-889-6922, 877-449-6922, fax 808-889-6944; www.flumindaditch.com, e-mail res@flumindaditch.com.

**WHALE WATCHING & BOAT TOURS**

Between November and May, when about 600 humpback whales inhabit Hawaiian waters, a popular spectator sport is spotting these behemoths in the channels around the islands. The rest of the year, outfitters seek out the lesser-known whales and other marinelife attractions.

**Captain Zodiac** leads four-hour trips twice daily along the Kona Coast. You may see whales, dolphins, sea turtles and other marine life as you journey along the coast and visit sea caves and lava tubes. There's a stop at Kealakekua Bay for snorkeling. ~ Honokohau Harbor; 808-329-3199.

**Captain Dan McSweeney's Whale Watching Adventures** operates three-hour cruises. If you don't see whales, the company will give you another trip at no charge. ~ Honokohau Harbor, Kailua-Kona; 808-322-0028.

**GOLF**

Some of the best golfing in the country is found on the Big Island. From stunning links on the Kohala Coast to community courses in the Hilo area, this island has everything you need for a golf-oriented vacation. Sunny conditions on the Kona side mean you generally don't need to worry about taking a rain check. Throw in views of the lava landscape, verdant shorelines and swaying palm trees, and you've created a duffer's view of paradise.

**KAILUA-KONA AREA**   Located on the slopes of Hualalai, about eight miles north of Kailua-Kona, **Makalei Hawaii Country Club** offers cool Upcountry play between 2000 and 3000 feet above sea level. Play is hilly with narrow fairways that favor accuracy.

# Ski
## Hawaii

During your island tour you'll inevitably pull up behind some joker with a bumper sticker reading "Think Snow." Around you trade winds may be bending the palm trees, sunbronzed crowds will be heading to the beach, and the thermometer will be approaching 80°. Snow will be the furthest thing from your mind.

But up on the 13,796-foot slopes of Mauna Kea, you're liable to see a bikini-clad skier schussing across a mantle of newly fallen snow! Any time from December until April or May, there may be enough dry snow to create ski runs several miles long and fill bowls a half-mile wide and almost a mile long. The slopes range from beginner to expert: Some have a vertical drop of 4500 feet. This is some of the world's highest skiing available.

Situated above the clouds about 80 percent of the time, this snow lover's oasis is baked by a tropical sun many times more powerful than at the beach. So it's easy to tan and easier yet to burn.

Combined with the thin air and winds up to 100 miles per hour, Hawaii's ski slopes are not for the faint-hearted or fair-skinned. But if you're seeking an incredible adventure and want a view of the Hawaiian islands from a 13,000-foot crow's nest, the heights of Mauna Kea await. There are no lifts and no groomed trails; beneath the snow is hard lava rock and cinder. A four-wheel-drive vehicle is required to get you there. It's the same road used to get to the observatories.

**Ski Guides Hawaii** offers all-day downhill skiing and snowboarding tours on Mauna Kea and cross-country skiing on Mauna Loa. The ski season lasts from November through July. This is not an inexpensive trip—but then again, skiing never is. Reservations recommended and deposit required. ~ P.O. Box 1954, Kamuela, HI 96743; 808-885-4188; www.skihawaii.com, e-mail clangan@interpac.net.

The views are rewarding. ~ 72-3890 Hawaii Belt Road (Route 190), Kalaoa; 808-325-6625.

At the **Kona Country Club,** a pair of 18-hole golf courses are ideal for those who want to bunker down. Bring along your camera to capture memorable views of the ocean course. Or head uphill to fully enjoy the challenging Mauka course. If you're looking for over-water holes and hidden hazards, you've come to the right place. ~ 78-7000 Alii Drive, Kailua-Kona; 808-322-2595.

**KOHALA COAST**   The Kohala Coast is where the monied set swings their clubs. So if you're going to play golf at these five-star luxury resorts, bring a fat wallet. Creating a great golf course is easy if you just dip into Laurence Rockefeller's deep pockets, hire Robert Trent Jones, Sr., and buy some lava-strewn oceanfront terrain. What you'll end up with is the 18-hole **Mauna Kea Beach Golf Course.** ~ Kawaihae; 808-882-7222. Quite a challenge, the original links have been complemented by the 18-hole **Hapuna Golf Course** created by Arnold Palmer. ~ 808-880-3000.

**Waikoloa Village Golf Course** is an 18-hole, par-72 layout that also includes a driving range and practice greens. This windy course, designed by Robert Trent Jones, Jr., has great views of Mauna Kea and Mauna Loa. ~ Waikoloa; 808-883-9621. Nearby the **Waikoloa Beach Resort Golf Course** was also designed by Robert Trent Jones, Jr. ~ Waikoloa; 808-886-7888. The adjacent **Waikoloa Kings' Golf Course** has another popular course. ~ Waikoloa; 808-886-7888. Convenient to the Hyatt Regency Waikoloa and the Royal Waikoloan, each course has unique features. The beach course heads through petroglyph fields while the Kings' Golf Course also has beautiful lava hazards.

**Mauna Lani Golf Course** has two 18-hole links built across rugged lava beds. If you miss the fairway, don't expect to find your ball out there in the volcanic landscape. There's also a driving range and practice greens. ~ Kohala Coast; 808-885-6655.

## WHERE THE WILD THINGS ARE

**Hawaii Forest and Trail** is an eco-tourism organization dedicated to the idea that education is fundamental to conservation. Their tours take small groups on explorations through limited-access wildlife refuges and other rarely visited areas. Their eight nature adventure tours (led by experienced naturalist guides) provide an extensive look at the natural history of Hawaii and the threat to endangered plant and wildlife—it's more than just a pretty hike. ~ 74-5035B Queen Kaahumanu Highway, Kailua-Kona; 808-331-8505, 800-464-1993, fax 808-331-8704; www.hawaii-forest.com, e-mail info@hawaii-forest.com.

**KONA/KAU DISTRICT** Sea Mountain Golf Course is a popular 18-hole course located south of Kilauea volcano. It's beautifully landscaped with coconut and banyan trees. ~ Route 11, Puna-luu; 808-928-6222.

**HAWAII VOLCANOES NATIONAL PARK** Volcano Golf and Country Club is the only course I know located in the vicinity of an erupting volcano. The high elevation (4000 feet) will give your ball an extra lift on this 18-hole course. ~ Volcanoes National Park; 808-967-7331.

**HILO** Naniloa Country Club is a nine-hole, par-35 course over-looking Hilo Bay. This narrow course may look easy but don't be deceived: Water hazards and trees along the fairways create plenty of challenges. ~ 120 Banyan Drive, Hilo; 808-935-3000.

Hilo Municipal Golf Course is one of the best bargains on the islands. This 18-hole course has great views of the water and the mountains. Be sure to reserve tee times on the weekends. You can sharpen your skills on the driving range and practice greens. ~ 340 Haihai Street, Hilo; 808-959-7711.

**HAMAKUA COAST** Hamakua Country Club is another inex-pensive choice. Located on the north shore about 40 miles from Hilo, this nine-hole course bans power carts. While it lacks the amenities of the resort links, Hamakua has a nice neighborhood feel. ~ Honokaa; 808-775-7244.

**RIDING STABLES**

Hawaii Forest & Trail offers four types of trips, including mule trips through the Kohala Mountains, where sweeping views of the coastline, Pololu Valley and Haleakala are the attraction. The guides are friendly and informative. ~ 74-5035B Kaahumanu Highway, Kailua-Kona; 808-331-8505, 800-464-1993; www.hawaii-forest.com.

Kings' Trail Rides O' Kona offers a riding/snorkeling combo. Riders descend the Kaawaloa Trail to Kealakekua Bay. Lunch is included, and children over seven with riding experience can par-ticipate. ~ Kealakekua; 808-323-2388; www.konacowboy.com, e-mail sales@konacowboy.com.

In Waipio Valley, **Naalapa Trail Rides** will take you on a two-hour ride through taro patches and waterfalls and (it goes with-out saying) past magnificent views, Monday through Saturday. They also offer excursions in the Kohala Mountains seven days a week. ~ Waipio Valley Artworks, Kukuihaele Village Road, Kukuihaele; 808-775-0419.

**Dahana Ranch** operates a gorgeous spread. Besides offering packages of *paniolo* entertainment and a chance to "brand, rope and pen," they also have rides for the less dedicated. Their one-and-a-half-hour tour takes in views of the working ranch as well as the surrounding valley and mountains. The two-and-a-half-hour option includes participation in an authentic cattle drive. Reservations required. ~ P.O. Box 1293, Kamuela, HI 96743; 808-885-0057, 888-399-0057; www.dahanaranch.com.

**BIKING**  Hawaii offers very good roads and many unpopulated stretches that make it ideal for bikers. Much of the island is mountainous with some fairly steep grades in the interior. Saddle Road, the roads to Waimea, and the road from Hilo up to Volcanoes National Park will all make a heavy breather of you, but the coast roads are generally flat or gently rolling. Most roads have shoulders and light traffic. Keep in mind that the northeast side of the island receives heavy rainfall, while the Kona side is almost always sunny. But wet side or dry, the scenery is spectacular throughout.

**Bike Rentals**  **Dave's Bike and Triathlon Shop** rents mountain and cross-training bikes—with shuttles to and from Kailua hotels—and does repairs. If you want, you can ship your bike and Dave's will have it assembled before you arrive. ~ 75-5669 Alii Drive, Kailua-Kona; 808-329-4522. **B & L Bike & Sports** rents mountain bikes, road bikes and hybrids. Closed Sunday. ~ 75-5699 Kopiko Place, Kailua-Kona; 808-329-3309. **Hawaiian Pedals** offers hybrids and basic mountain bikes as well as gear and accessories. Rental times range from five hours to a couple of weeks. ~ 75-5744 Alii Drive, Kailua-Kona; 808-329-2294; www.hawaiianpedals.com. Hawaiian Pedal's sister company, **HP Bikeworks**, rents front- and full-suspension mountain bikes. ~ 74-5599 Luhia Street, Kailua-Kona; 808-326-2453; www.hpbikeworks.com. There are no bike rentals in Hilo.

**Bike Repairs**  The folks at **Mid-Pacific Wheels** will do repair work or sell you bike accessories. ~ 1133-C Manono Street, Hilo; 808-935-6211. B & L Bike & Sports does repairs. ~ 75-5699 Kopiko Place, Kailua-Kona; 808-329-3309.

**HUMDINGER**

In the mountains of Kohala you'll discover that sports utility vehicles provide more than fashion. The Hummer, originally designed for the military, can pretty much go anywhere, perfect for a tour through the Hawaiian rainforest. **HMV Tours** in Hawi takes groups of two to eight through the Kohala Mountains, which have recently been opened to the public. Waterfalls, local fauna and untouched riverbeds give visitors a glimpse into the beauty of ancient Hawaii before tourism (and Hummers). Closed Sunday and Monday. Reservations required. ~ 808-889-6922, 877-449-6922, fax 808-889-6944; www.flumindaditch.com, e-mail res@flumindaditch.com.

Of all the islands in the chain, Hawaii has the finest hiking trails. The reason? Quite simply, it's the Big Island's size. Larger than all the other islands combined and boasting the highest peaks, Hawaii offers the greatest diversity to explorers.

Mauna Loa and Mauna Kea, each rising over 13,000 feet, provide rugged mountain climbing. To the north, the Kohala Mountains feature trails through dense tropical terrain and along awesome cliffs. In Volcanoes National Park, hikers can experience the challenge of walking through a lava wasteland and into the belly of an active volcano.

Along much of Hawaii's shoreline lies a network of trails that have been under study by the Department of the Interior. Originally a series of access trails for the Hawaiians, they were paid for by local farmers to tax collectors. In 1823, William Ellis, a missionary, tried to follow them to circumnavigate the island. In more recent times, a group of journalists recreated—to the best of their ability—his route.

The plantations in the northeast destroyed any trails in that corner of the island. The sections that remain on the rest of Hawaii contain archaeological sites that should be left unmolested. Some people have proposed National Trail status for the network, but until then you'll need a topographic map, respect for private property and archaeology, and a yen for adventure to tackle the trails that the Hawaiians once tread.

Hawaii's official hiking trails run through three areas: Volcanoes National Park, Kau Desert and the Kohala Mountains. These are popular and well-defined trails, many of which are described below. Permits are required for any overnight backcountry camping within the boundaries of Hawaii Volcanoes National Park, which includes the Kau Desert. Apply the morning of your trip at the Kilauea Visitor Center. Permits are free, but first-come, first-served. All distances listed for hiking trails are one way unless otherwise noted.

**KOHALA COAST**   Stretching along Kohala peninsula's northeast coast is a series of sheer cliffs and wide valleys rivaling Kauai's Na Pali Coast in beauty. At either end of this rainswept *pali* are lush, still valleys that can only be reached by hiking trails. To camp legally in this area can be a challenge, since you need a permit or permission wherever you go, and the land could be State, corporate or owned by one of the dozens of property holders. If you want to camp, start by asking questions at the State Department of Land and Natural Resources; 808-974-4221.

**Pololu Valley Trail** (0.5 mile) descends from the Pololu Valley Lookout at the end of Akoni Pule Highway to the valley floor 400 feet below. There you'll find a secluded beach (beware of the riptides) and a series of trails that lead up through the Kohala Mountains.

**KONA/KAU AREA**    From Volcanoes National Park's southern section several trails lead into the hot, arid Kau Desert. All are long, dusty trails offering solitude to the adventurous hiker.

**Kau Desert Trail** (3.5 miles) branches off Crater Rim Trail and drops 2000 feet en route to the lookout at the end of Hilina Pali Road. The shelter along the way, at Kipuka Pepeiau, provides a welcome resting place on this lengthy trek.

**Mauna Iki Trail** (3.6 miles) leads from Mamalahoa Highway (Route 11) to Hilina Pali Road. The trail passes near Footprints Trail, where a sudden volcanic eruption in 1790 engulfed a Hawaiian army at war with Kamehameha.

**HAWAII VOLCANOES NATIONAL PARK**    The most interesting and easily accessible trails lead through the **Kilauea Caldera** area. The caldera, three miles long and 4000 feet above sea level, can be explored either by hiking along one extended trail or over several shorter connecting trails.

**Crater Rim Trail** (11.6-mile loop) begins near the park headquarters and encircles Kilauea Caldera. An excellent introduction to the volcanoes, this lengthy loop trail passes steam vents, the Kau Desert, the fractured Southwest Rift area and a fascinating fern forest. The views from along the rim are spectacular.

**Sulphur Banks Trail** (0.3 mile) begins at park headquarters and parallels Crater Rim Drive past steam vents and sulphur deposits.

**Halemaumau Trail** (3.5 miles) starts near Volcano House, then descends into Kilauea Caldera. The trail crosses the crater floor and affords astonishing views down into steaming Halemaumau crater, then climbs back up to join Crater Rim Trail. This has got to be one of the park's finest hikes.

**Kilauea Iki Trail** (5 miles) loops from the Thurston Lava Tube parking lot down into Kilauea Iki crater and returns via Crater Rim Trail. Crossing the crater floor, the trail passes over a lava crust beneath which lies a pool of hot rock. Rainwater percolates through the crust, reaches the hot rock, and emerges as steam. The pool was once hot but has cooled significantly (the eruption was in 1959).

**Sandalwood Trail** (1.5-mile loop) loops from near the Volcano House past sandalwood and *ohia* trees and then along the side of Kilauea Caldera.

**Byron Ledge Trail** (4 miles) branches off Halemaumau Trail, crosses the Kilauea caldera floor, and then climbs along Byron Ledge before rejoining Halemaumau. This makes an excellent connecting trail.

Starting within the Kapapala Forest Reserve at 5650 feet, the **Ainapo Trail** (3.5 miles) takes hikers on a moderately challenging trek past mesic *koa* and *ohia* trees. On the way up to the

Ainapo Trail Shelter at Halewai, you'll catch sight of mountain goats and sheep. More experienced hikers can climb the rest of the fog-covered trail (7.5 miles) and will be rewarded with views from the rim of the Mokuaweoweo Caldera in Hawaii Volcanoes National Park. The trailhead begins at the cattleguard between the 40- and 41-mile markers on the Mamalahoa Highway between Volcano and Pahala. This hike requires permits from the Division of Forestry and Wildlife in Hilo (808-974-4221). Reservations for the shelter can be made up to 30 days in advance.

Volcanoes National Park's premier hike is along **Mauna Loa Trail**. This tough 18-mile trek, requiring at least three days, leads to the top of the world's largest shield volcano. Cold-weather equipment and a sturdy constitution are absolute necessities for this challenging adventure. Permits are required for this hike.

Climbers usually hike seven miles the first day from the trailhead at the end of Mauna Loa Strip Road up to Red Hill (Pu'u 'Ula'ula). At this 10,035-foot way station, there is a rudimentary cabin with eight bunks with mattresses, but no provisions. A hearty 11-mile trek the second day leads to the rim of Mauna Loa's summit caldera, and to the Mokuaweoweo cabin (located on the rim). The return trip takes one or two days, depending on how fast you want to come down.

Beware of altitude sickness and hypothermia, and be sure to register for a permit at park headquarters before and after hiking. Purification tablets or filters for the water and white gas for the stoves are also essential; there are no stoves provided in the cabin. Don't treat this as a casual jaunt; it's a real trek. Good planning will ensure your safety and enjoyment.

A single-lane paved road climbs from Saddle Road to an area near Mauna Loa summit. This alternative hiking route lacks the adventure but reduces the time needed to ascend Mauna Loa. This road is not open to rental cars.

**AUTHOR FAVORITE**

Waipio Valley is ripe for exploring, but if you want to leave civilization completely behind, continue instead along the **Waimanu Valley Trail** (9 miles). This track begins at the base of the cliff that marks Waipio's northwest border. It climbs sharply up the 1200-foot rock face in a series of switchbacks, then continues up and down across numerous gulches, and finally descends into Waimanu Valley. This exotic place, half the size of Waipio Valley, is equally as lush. Here, in addition to wild pigs, mountain apple trees and ancient ruins, you'll find naturally running water (requiring purification) and great spots for beachfront picnics. This is a challenging one-day hike, so you may want to camp. You may never want to leave.

**HAMAKUA COAST** Waipio Valley Trail begins from Waipio Valley lookout at the end of Route 24. Waipio is a broad, lush, awesomely beautiful valley ribboned with waterfalls and rich in history. From the trailhead, a jeep trail drops steeply for one mile to the valley floor. Here the trail joins one road leading up into the valley and another heading to the beach. The high road goes toward 1200-foot Hiilawe Falls and to an abandoned Peace Corps training camp.

▼▼▼▼▼▼▼▼▼▼▼▼
## Transportation

**AIR**

Two airports serve commercial flights to the Big Island—Hilo International Airport (General Lyman Field) and Kona International Airport.

The main landing facility is **Kona International Airport** (808-329-2484). Many mainland visitors fly here rather than to Honolulu to avoid Oahu's crowds. Aloha Airlines, American Airlines and United Airlines provide service directly to Kailua-Kona from the mainland and Canada 3000 (seasonally) and Japan Airlines (daily) fly directly from their respective countries.

This facility has snack bars, cocktail lounges, duty-free shops, a restaurant and souvenir shops, but no lockers or bus service. A ten-mile cab ride into town costs about $30.

Passengers flying between the islands use Aloha Airlines or Hawaiian Airlines. They provide frequent jet service from Oahu and the other islands to both Hilo and Kona. Other inter-island carriers include Island Air, Pacific Wings and Paragon Air.

**Hilo International Airport** (General Lyman Field), once the island's main jetport, is now more like a small city airport. Here you'll find a cafeteria-style restaurant, cocktail lounge, gift shop, newsstand and lockers, but no bus service. Covering the two miles into town means renting a car, hailing a cab, hitching or hoofing.

**CAR RENTALS**

When choosing a rental agency, check whether they permit driving on the Saddle Road across the island and on South Point Road, both good paved roads with few potholes and many points of interest. I think it's quite unfair, even irrational, that some rental companies revoke insurance coverage if you drive these thoroughfares. But my protests will be of little benefit in case of an accident. So check first or be prepared to take your chances! It's wise to remember that you will be driving farther on the Big Island than on other islands, sometimes through quite rural areas; it may sound obvious, but remember to watch your gas gauge.

Several companies have franchises at the Hilo and Kailua-Kona airports. Among these are **Avis** (808-935-1290, 808-327-3001, 800-331-1212), **Budget Rent A Car** (808-935-6878, 808-329-8511, 800-527-0700), **Dollar Rent A Car** (800-800-4000),

Hertz Rent A Car (808-935-2896, 808-329-3566, 800-654-3011), National Car Rental (808-935-0891, 808-329-1674, 800-227-7368) and Thrifty Car Rental (800-367-5238).

Alamo Rent A Car is located outside the Hilo International Airport and Kona Airport. ~ 808-961-3343, 808-329-8896, 800-327-9633. Harper Car & Truck Rental is located inside the Kona airport but you must take a shuttle to reach its Hilo location. ~ 808-969-1478, 800-852-9993.

**JEEP RENTALS**

Budget Rent A Car rents four-wheel drives. ~ 808-935-6878, 808-329-8511, 800-527-0700. With offices in Hilo and Kona, Harper Car & Truck Rental offers four-wheel-drive vehicles and allows travel on the Saddle Road and Mauna Kea summit road. ~ 808-969-1478, 800-852-9993.

**MOPED RENTALS**

Harleys and scooters are available through DJ's Rentals, which rents by the half-day, day and overnight. Some three-day and weekly rentals are also available. ~ 75-5663 Palani Road, Kailua-Kona; 808-329-1700, 800-993-4647; www.harleys.com, e-mail info@harleys.com.

**PUBLIC TRANSIT**

The Hele-On Bus provides cross-island service Monday through Saturday between Hilo and Kailua-Kona. There are also limited intra-city buses serving Hilo. The Hele-On runs Monday through Saturday; fares range from 75¢ for short rides to $6 for the Hilo–Kailua cross-island run.

The Hilo bus terminal is on Kamehameha Avenue at Mamo Street. You'll see few bus stops indicated on the island. The official stops are generally unmarked, and you can hail a bus anywhere along its route. Just wave your hand. When it's time to get off, the driver will stop anywhere you wish.

For information and schedules, phone the County Hawaiian Transit. ~ 808-961-8744.

**AERIAL TOURS**

Thanks to the Kilauea eruption, the Big Island offers a wide variety of flightseeing options. In addition to the lava flows, you'll see remote coastlines, the slopes of Mauna Kea and coffee plantations. Bring your camera because the lava flow is one of Hawaii's greatest sightseeing opportunities.

At Blue Hawaiian Helicopter you have a choice of two flights lasting up to two hours. Passengers view the valleys and waterfalls on the island's northern end, as well as volcanic activity at Kilauea. They fly out of two locations. ~ Hilo International Airport; Queen Kaahumanu Highway, Waikoloa; 808-961-5600, 800-786-2583; www.bluehawaiian.com.

**Safari Helicopters'** two tours both emphasize viewings of the Kilauea Volcanic system, with its lava tubes to the ocean, cinder cones and much more. One tour adds a visit to the waterfalls near Hilo to the itinerary. ~ P.O. Box 1941, Lihue, Kauai, HI 96766; Hilo Commuter Air Terminal, Hilo International Airport, Hilo; 808-969-1259, 800-326-3356; www.safariair. com, e-mail info@safarihelicopters.com.

**Big Island Air** takes passengers on a circle island tour featuring Kilauea and the north end valleys and waterfalls. Flights last about 1 hour and 45 minutes. ~ Kona Airport; 808-329-4868.

# SIX

# Maui

Residents of Maui, Hawaii's second-largest island, proudly describe their Valley Isle by explaining that "Maui *no ka oi.*" Maui is the greatest. Few of the island's visitors have disputed the claim. They return each year, lured by the enchantment of a place possessing 33 miles of public beaches, one of the world's largest dormant volcanoes, beautiful people, a breeding ground for rare humpback whales and a climate that varies from subtropic to subarctic.

Named after one of the most important demigods in the Polynesian pantheon, Maui has retained its mythic aura. The island is famous as a chic retreat and jet-set landing ground. To many people, Maui *is* Hawaii.

But to others, who have watched the rapid changes during the past several decades, Maui is no longer the greatest. They point to the 2.4 million tourists (second only to Oahu) who visited during a recent year, to the condominiums and resort hotels now lining the prettiest beaches and to the increasing traffic over once-rural roads. And they have a new slogan. "Maui is *pau.*" Maui is finished. Overtouristed. Overpopulated. Overdeveloped.

Today, among the island's 103,600 population, it seems like every other person is in the real estate business. On a land mass measuring 729 square miles, just half the size of Long Island, their goods are in short supply. During the 1970s and 1980s, land prices shot up faster than practically anywhere else in the country, although the 1990s saw prices decline.

Yet over 75 percent of the island remains unpopulated. Despite pressures from land speculation and a mondo-condo mentality, Maui still offers exotic, untouched expanses for the explorer. Most development is concentrated along the south and west coasts in Kihei, Wailea and Kaanapali. The rest of the island, though more populated than neighboring islands, is an adventurer's oasis. The second-youngest island in the chain, Maui was created between one and two million years ago by two volcanoes. Haleakala, the larger, rises over 10,000 feet, and offers excellent hiking and camping within its summit caldera, the largest such dormant volcanic crater in the world. The earlier of the two firepits created the West Maui Mountains, 5788 feet at their highest elevation. Because of their relative age, and the fact they receive 400 inches of rainfall a year, they are more heavily eroded than the smooth surfaces of Haleakala. Between the two heights lies Central Maui, an isthmus formed when the lava from each volcano flowed together.

The twin cities of Kahului and Wailuku, Maui's commercial and civic centers, respectively, sit in this saddle. Until the 1990s, most of the island was planted in sugar, which became king in Maui after the decline of whaling in the 1860s. Today, a road through what remains of the cane fields leads south to the sun-splashed resorts and beaches of Kihei, Maalaea, Wailea and Makena.

Another road loops around the West Maui Mountains. It passes prime whale-watching areas along the south coast and bisects Lahaina, an old whaling town that is now the island's sightseeing capital. Next to this timeworn harbor is the resort area of Kaanapali, a two-mile stretch of beach backed by hotels, condominiums and a full range of resort facilities. Beyond Kaanapali lies eight miles of coast lined with crescent beaches and lava rock promontories with another collection of hotels, condos and homes at Honokawai, Kahana and Napili. Past Napili the Kapalua Resort adds an upscale alternative, with several hotels and condos and three of Hawaii's best golf courses. Head past Kapalua and the landscape becomes wilder, with the blue-green of pineapple mixing with a series of deep wilderness valleys and grassy headlands that offer magnificently wild coastal views. You'll want to take a break in rustic Kahakuloa, where taro is still grown and the lifestyle is reminiscent of old Hawaii. From Kahakuloa, the road continues around West Maui, returning you to Wailuku and Kahului.

The road girdling Haleakala's lower slopes passes equally beautiful areas. Along the rainswept northeast coast are sheer rock faces ribboned with waterfalls and gorges choked with tropic vegetation. The lush, somnolent town of Hana gives way along the southeast shore to a dry, unpopulated expanse that is always ripe for exploration.

On the middle slopes of Haleakala, in Maui's Upcountry region, small farms dot the landscape. Here, in addition to guavas, avocados and lychee nuts, grow the sweet Kula onions for which the Valley Isle is famous.

Because of its strategic location between Oahu and Hawaii, Maui has played a vital role in Hawaiian history. Kahekili, Maui's last king, gained control of all the islands except Hawaii before being overwhelmed by Kamehameha in 1790. Lahaina, long a vacation spot for island rulers, became a political center under Hawaii's first three kings and an important commercial center soon after Captain Cook sighted the island in 1778. It served as a supply depot for ships, then as a port for sandalwood exports. By the 1840s, Lahaina was the world capital of whaling. Now, together with the other equally beautiful sections of the Valley Isle, it is a mecca for vacationers.

Maui's magic has cast a spell upon travelers all over the world, making the island a vacation paradise. Like most modern paradises, it is being steadily gilded in plastic and concrete. Yet much of the old charm remains. Some people even claim that the sun shines longer on the Valley Isle than any other place on earth. They point to the legend of the demigod Maui who created his own daylight sav-

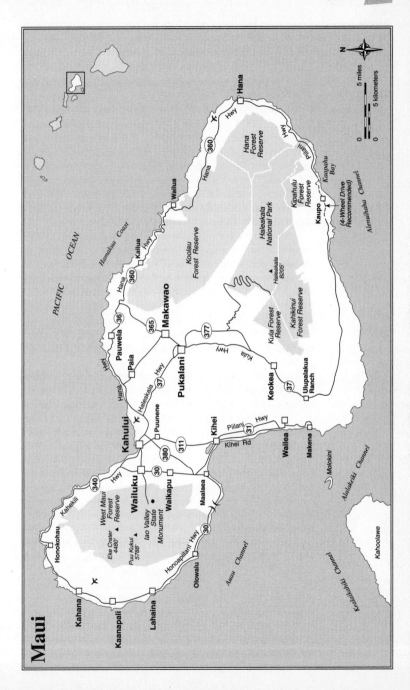

# Maui

N

0 5 miles
0 5 kilometers

PACIFIC OCEAN

**Hana**

Hana Hwy (360)

Hana Forest Reserve

Piilani Hwy

Kaupo

(4-Wheel Drive Recommended)

Kaapahu Bay

Alenuihaha Channel

Kipahulu Forest Reserve

Kahikinui Forest Reserve

Haleakala National Park

Koolau Forest Reserve

▲ Haleakala 8205'

Kula Forest Reserve

**Wailua**

Kailua Hwy

Hana Hwy (360)

Hamakua Coast

(36)

**Pauwela**

(365)

**Makawao**

(377)

**Paia**

Haleakala Hwy (37)

Kula Hwy

**Pukalani**

**Keokea**

(37)

Ulupalakua Ranch

**Kahului**

Puunene

**Kihei**

Piilani Hwy (31)

Kihei Rd

**Wailea**

**Makena**

Molokini

Maalaea Channel

Kahoolawe

Alalakeiki Channel

(311)

(380)

(30)

**Wailuku**

**Waikapu**

**Maalaea**

West Maui Forest Reserve

Iao Valley State Monument

▲ Eke Crater 4480'

▲ Puu Kukui 5788'

(340)

Kahekili Hwy

**Honokohau**

**Kahana**

**Kaanapali**

**Lahaina**

Honoapiilani Hwy (30)

**Olowalu**

Auau Channel

Kealaikahiki Channel

ings by weaving a rope from his sister's pubic hair and lassoing the sun by its genitals. And many hope he has one last trick to perform, one that will slow the course of development just as he slowed the track of the sun.

**Lahaina**

Maui's top tourist destination is a waterfront enclave that stretches for over two miles along a natural harbor, but measures only a couple of blocks deep. Simultaneously chic and funky, Lahaina has gained an international reputation for its art galleries, falsefront stores and waterfront restaurants.

It also happens to be one of Hawaii's most historic towns. A royal seat since the 16th century, Lahaina was long a playground for the *alii*. The royal surfing grounds lay just south of today's town center, and in 1802, Kamehameha I established his headquarters here, taking up residence in the Brick Palace, the first Western-style building in Hawaii.

Although the Hawaiian capital moved to Honolulu in 1850, Lahaina remained a favorite vacation spot for several kings, including Kamehameha III, IV and V, and Queen Liliuokalani. All had second homes in the area and returned often to indulge in those favorite Hawaiian pastimes—rest and relaxation.

It was in Lahaina that the first high school and first printing press west of the Rockies were established in 1831. From Lahaina, Kamehameha III promulgated Hawaii's first constitution in 1840, and established a legislative body that met in town until the capital was eventually moved to Honolulu.

During the 1820s, this quaint port also became a vital watering place for whaling ships. At its peak in the mid-1840s, the whaling trade brought over 400 ships a year into the harbor.

To the raffish sailors who favored it for its superb anchorage, grog shops and uninhibited women, Lahaina was heaven itself. To the stiff-collared missionaries who arrived in 1823, the town was a hellhole—a place of sin, abomination and vile degradation. Some of Lahaina's most colorful history was written when the Congregationalists prevented naked women from swimming out to meet the whalers. Their belligerent brethren anchored in the harbor replied by cannonballing mission homes and rioting along the waterfront.

The town declined with the loss of the whaling trade in the 1860s, and was transformed into a quiet sugar plantation town, serving the Pioneer Sugar Mill that opened during the same decade. Hawaii's first phone line was installed from Lahaina to Haiku in 1877, but not until developers began building resorts in nearby Kaanapali a century later did the town fully revive.

During the 1960s, Lahaina was designated a national historic landmark and restoration of many important sites was begun. By the 1970s, the place was a gathering spot not only for the jet set

*Maui Getaway*

## Five-day Itinerary

**Day 1**
- Fly into Kahului, rent a car and drive to the Lahaina–Kaanapali area.
- Check into your condo or hotel and spend the afternoon relaxing on the beach.

**Day 2**
- Drive up to **Haleakala** (page 347). (For the adventurous, arrive for sunrise, which means you have to leave around 4 a.m.—be sure to check weather conditions before you do this.)
- On the way down from the summit, explore the **Upcountry** (page 340), including the town of Makawao and one of the loop tours, Route 390 or Route 365.
- Plan to spend the afternoon wandering through **Lahaina** (page 268), where you can shop and then have an early-bird dinner.

**Day 3**
- If it's whale-watching season, take an **excursion** from one of the many whale-watching outfits offered in the book. If it's not whale-watching season, you can still view other sea life up close and personal by **kayaking** along Maui's south shore or hopping aboard one of the numerous **snorkeling** adventures to Molokini.

**Day 4**
- Spend the day driving the heavenly **Hana Highway** (page 324).
- Don't miss watching the wind- and kitesurfers at **Hookipa Beach Park** (page 325) and be sure to stop along the way to hike to a waterfall or picnic at **Kaumahina State Wayside** (page 326) or **Puaakaa State Wayside** (page 326).
- Check into a Hana bed and breakfast or hotel. (Be sure to make reservations.) Have dinner at the **Hotel Hana-Maui** (page 332).

**Day 5**
- Return to Kahului via **Ulupalakua** (page 329), the backroad from Hana, if it is open (check weather conditions), stopping at **Oheo Gulch** (page 330) (also known as the "Seven Sacred Pools") and **Charles Lindbergh's grave** (page 330). If the backroad is closed, turn around at Lindbergh's grave and backtrack to Kahului.

but the ultra hip as well. Clubs like the Blue Max made Lahaina a hot nightspot where famous musicians came to vacation and jam.

The jetsetters have moved on, but today, Lahaina retains a semblance of its gentrified charm with shops, galleries, clubs and restaurants lining Front Street, an oceanside "Main Street." Most points of interest lie within a half-mile of the old sea wall that protects this narrow thoroughfare from the ocean, so the best way to explore the town is on foot.

**SIGHTS**   Start at **Lahaina Harbor**, located on Wharf Street, and take a stroll along the docks. In addition to tour boats, pleasure craft from around the world put in here or cast anchor in the Lahaina Roads just offshore. During the heyday of the whaling industry in the 1840s, the Auau Channel between Lahaina and Lanai was a forest of masts.

Across Wharf Street sits the **Pioneer Inn**, a rambling hostelry built in 1901. With its second-story veranda and landscaped garden, this aging woodframe hotel is a great place to bend an elbow and breathe in the salt air. ~ 658 Wharf Street; 808-661-3636, fax 808-667-9366; www.pioneerinnmaui.com, e-mail info@pioneerinnmaui.com.

Just north of here a Hawaii Visitors Bureau sign points out the chair-shaped **Hauola Stone**, a source of healing power for ancient Hawaiians, who sat in the natural formation and let the waves wash over them.

There is nothing left of the **Brick Palace**, the two-story structure commissioned in 1798 by Kamehameha I. Located just inshore from the Hauola Stone and built by an English convict, the palace was used by the king in 1802 and 1803 (although some say he preferred to stay in his grass shack next door). Today the original foundation has been outlined with brick paving.

To the south, a **banyan tree**, the largest in the U.S. and among the oldest in the islands, extends its rooting branches across almost an entire acre. Planted in 1873 to mark the advent of Protestant missionaries in Maui 50 years earlier, this shady canopy is a resting place for tourists and mynah birds alike. ~ Front and Hotel streets.

The sprawling giant presses up against the **Old Courthouse**, constructed in 1859 from coral blocks taken from the home built for King Kamehameha III. The historic building is home to the **Lahaina Visitors Center** (808-667-9193, fax 808-661-4779; www.visitlahaina.com, e-mail info@visitlahaina.com), where you can pick up maps and brochures, including one that provides all the details needed for a self-guided walking tour of Lahaina. The **Lahaina Art Society** (808-661-0111, fax 808-661-9149), a non-profit association of local artists, is also located in the courthouse. Art shows are presented under the banyan tree by the Art

Society every other weekend. On alternate weekends Hawaiian crafts are the theme.

On the third floor of the Old Courthouse is the **Lahaina Heritage Museum** (808-661-1959), which has varying exhibits, such as a selection of traditional canoes.

Those stone ruins on either side of the courthouse are the remains of the **Old Fort**, built during the 1830s to protect Lahaina from the sins and cannonballs of lawless sailors. The original structure was torn down two decades later to build a jail, but during its heyday the fortress guarded the waterfront with numerous cannons.

Across Front Street is the **Baldwin Home**, Lahaina's oldest building. Constructed of coral and stone in the early 1830s, the place sheltered the family of Reverend Dwight Baldwin, a medical missionary. Today the house contains period pieces and family heirlooms, including some of the good doctor's rather fiendish-looking medical implements. Beneath the hand-hewn ceiling beams rests the Baldwin's Steinway piano; the dining room includes the family's china, a fragile cargo that made the voyage around Cape Horn; and in the master bedroom stands a

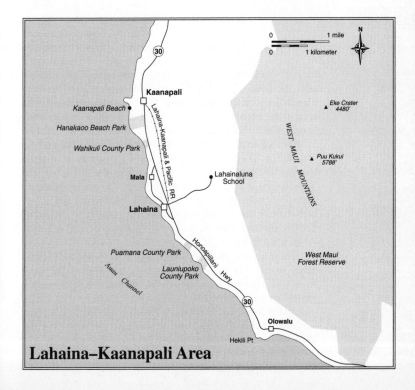

**Lahaina–Kaanapali Area**

four-poster bed fashioned from native *koa*. Admission. ~ 808-661-3262, fax 808-661-9309; www.lahainarestoration.org, e-mail lrf@hawaii.rr.com.

The **Master's Reading Room** next door, an 1834 storehouse and library, is home to the Lahaina Restoration Foundation and not open to the public.

A Chinese gathering place that dates to 1912, the **Wo Hing Museum** has been lovingly restored. While the temple has been converted into a small museum, the old cookhouse adjacent is used to show films of the islands made by Thomas Edison from 1898 through 1906, during the early days of motion pictures. Admission. ~ 858 Front Street; 808-661-5553.

The **Holy Innocents' Episcopal Church** is a small structure dating from 1927. Very simple in design, the sanctuary is filled with beautiful paintings. The Hawaiian madonna on the altar and the tropical themes of the paintings are noteworthy features. Services are Sunday at 7 a.m. and 10 a.m. ~ 561 Front Street; 808-661-4202, fax 808-661-8667; e-mail holyinn@aloha.net.

Lahaina resembles Manhattan when it comes to parking, especially in summer. Lots on Dickerson Street have reasonable rates. If you're parking at a meter, the price of parking can be astronomical if you get a ticket.

Several other historic spots lie along Wainee Street, which parallels Front Street. **Waiola Cemetery**, with its overgrown lawn, dotted with eroded tombstones, contains graves dating to 1829. Queen Keopuolani, the wife of Kamehameha I and the mother of Hawaii's next two kings, is buried here. So is her daughter, Princess Nahienaena, and Governor Hoapali, who ruled Hawaii from 1823 to 1840. Surrounded by blossoming plumeria trees, there are also the graves of early missionaries and Hawaiian commoners. ~ Wainee Street.

Maui's first Christian services were performed in 1823 on the grounds of Wainee Church next door. Today's chapel, renamed the **Waiola Church**, built in 1953, occupies the spot where the Wainee church was constructed in 1832. The earlier structure, Hawaii's first stone church, seated 3000 parishioners and played a vital role in the conversion of the local population to Christianity and Western ways. ~ 535 Wainee Street; 808-661-4349, fax 808-661-1734.

A little farther north on Wainee Street sits the **Lahaina Hongwanji Temple** with its three distinctive turrets. The building dates from 1927, but the Buddhist Hongwanji sect has been meeting at this site since 1910. ~ 808-661-0640.

On the corner of Prison and Wainee streets rise the menacing walls of old **Hale Paahao**, a prison built by convicts in 1854 and used to house rowdy sailors as well as more hardened types. The coral blocks used to build this local hoosegow were taken from the Old Fort on Front Street. ~ 808-667-1985.

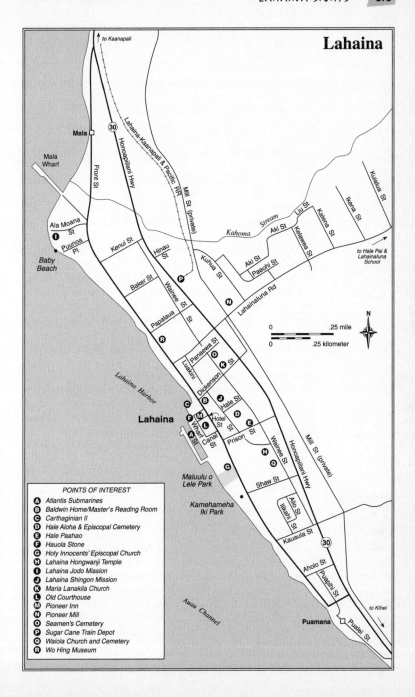

# Lahaina

to Kaanapali

Mala

Mala
Wharf

Lahaina-Kaanapali & Pacific RR

Honoapiilani Hwy

30

Front St

Mill St (private)

Kahoma        Stream

Kulalua St

Ikena St

Liu St

Kalena St

Kelawea St

Aki St

Ala Moana
St

Puunoa
Pl

Baby
Beach

Kenui St

Hinau
St

Kuhua St

Aki St

Paeohi St

to Hale Pai &
Lahainaluna
School

Baker St

Wainee
St

P

Lahainaluna Rd

N

0          .25 mile

0          .25 kilometer

N

Papalaua
St

R

Panaewa St

O

K
St

Luakini
St

Dickenson

J

Hale St

D

C

B

F

Hotel
St

M

E

Lahaina

4
St

L

Prison
St

St

Wharf

Canal
St

H

Wainee St

Honoapiilani Hwy

Mill St (private)

Lahaina Harbor

G

O

Maluulu o
Lele Park

Shaw St

Ailo St

Ilikahi
St

Kamehameha
Iki Park

Kauaula St

30

Auau Channel

Aholo St

Puapihi St

to Kihei

Puamana

Pualei St

## POINTS OF INTEREST

- Ⓐ Atlantis Submarines
- Ⓑ Baldwin Home/Master's Reading Room
- Ⓒ Carthaginian II
- Ⓓ Hale Aloha & Episcopal Cemetery
- Ⓔ Hale Paahao
- Ⓕ Hauola Stone
- Ⓖ Holy Innocents' Episcopal Church
- Ⓗ Lahaina Hongwanji Temple
- Ⓘ Lahaina Jodo Mission
- Ⓙ Lahaina Shingon Mission
- Ⓚ Maria Lanakila Church
- Ⓛ Old Courthouse
- Ⓜ Pioneer Inn
- Ⓝ Pioneer Mill
- Ⓞ Seamen's Cemetery
- Ⓟ Sugar Cane Train Depot
- Ⓠ Waiola Church and Cemetery
- Ⓡ Wo Hing Museum

Just north of the jail along Wainee Street sits the **Episcopal Cemetery** and **Hale Aloha**. Walter Murray Gibson, a controversial figure in 19th-century Hawaiian politics who eventually became an adviser to King David Kalakaua, is buried here. Hale Aloha, completed in 1858 and restored in 1974, served as a church meetinghouse.

Nearby is **Maria Lanakila Church**, a lovely white-washed building with interior pillars that was built in 1928 to replace a 19th-century chapel. Adjacent is the **Seamen's Cemetery**, a poorly maintained ground where early sailors were laid to rest. ~ Wainee and Dickenson streets.

The **Lahaina Shingon Mission**, a simple plantation-era structure with an ornately gilded altar, was built in 1902 by a Japanese monk and his followers. It now represents another gathering place for Maui's Buddhists. ~ 682 Luakini Street between Hale and Dickenson streets; phone/fax 808-661-0466.

The proverbial kids-from-eight-to-eighty set will love the **Sugar Cane Train**, a reconstructed 1890s-era steam train. Operating near the West Maui resort area, the Lahaina–Kaanapali & Pacific Railroad engine and passenger cars chug along a six-mile route midway between the mountains and ocean. Various package tours are available with the train rides, including a sunset dinner train ride, complete with live Hawaiian entertainment. Admission. ~ The main station is off Hinau Street in Lahaina; 808-667-6851, 800-499-2307, fax 808-661-8389; www.sugarcanetrain.com, e-mail mail@sugarcanetrain.com.

Oceanic adventurers might want to take an opportunity to stop in at **Atlantis Submarines** and reserve an underwater tour. The voyage takes you aboard a 48-passenger submersible down more than 100 feet. En route you may see close-up views of technicolor coral reefs and outlandish lava formations. A trip to the depths requires deep pockets; these 90-minute excursions aren't cheap. ~ Wharf Cinema Center, 658 Front Street; 808-667-2224, fax 808-661-1210; www.atlantisadventures.com.

**sights**

**AUTHOR FAVORITE**

For a journey of a spiritual nature, don't miss **Lahaina Jodo Mission**, a Buddhist enclave one-half mile north of Lahaina on Ala Moana Street. There's a temple and a three-tiered pagoda here, as well as the largest ceremonial bell in Hawaii. The giant bronze Buddha, with the West Maui Mountains in the background, is a sight to behold. It rests amid stone walkways and flowering oleander bushes in a park-like setting. The temple grounds are open to the public from dawn to dusk. ~ 12 Ala Moana Street; 808-661-4304, fax 808-661-0939.

And for a splendid view of Lahaina, turn off Route 30 onto Lahainaluna Road, pass the now-closed, century-old Pioneer Mill, and head *mauka* (toward the mountains) to **Lahainaluna School**. Established by missionaries in 1831, it is one of the country's oldest schools west of the Rockies. Today this historic facility serves as a public high school for the Lahaina area. ~ 808-662-4000, fax 808-662-3997.

**Hale Pai**, its printing house dating to 1837, printed Hawaii's first money and many of the first bibles, religious tracts and primers produced in the islands. The first newspaper west of the Rockies was also printed here, written mostly in the Hawaiian language. Hale Pai is open as a museum and research library. It houses a working reproduction of the original printing press. Closed Saturday and Sunday. ~ Phone/fax 808-667-7040; e-mail lrf@hawaii.rr.com.

**LODGING**

To fully capture the spirit of Lahaina, there's only one place to stay—the **Best Western Pioneer Inn**. Located smack on Lahaina's waterfront, this wooden hostelry is the center of the area's action. On one side, sloops, ketches and glass-bottom boats are berthed; on the other side lies bustling Front Street with its false-front shops. The Inn is noisy, vibrant and crowded with tenants and tourists. On the ground floor, you can hunker down over a glass of grog at the saloon, or stroll through the Inn's lushly planted courtyard. Accommodations are located in the section overlooking the courtyard. These are small and plainly decorated, with telephones, overhead fans, air conditioning and lanais. A swimming pool completes the picture. ~ 658 Wharf Street; 808-661-3636, 800-457-5457, fax 808-667-5708; www.pioneer innmaui.com, e-mail info@pioneerinnmaui.com. DELUXE.

My Oscar for most original inn goes to the **Lahaina Inn**. Constructed in the early 20th century, this 12-room beauty was fully restored and appointed in Gay Nineties finery. Each room is wall to ceiling with gorgeous antiques—leaded glass lamps, mirrored armoires, original oil paintings, cast-iron beds and brass locks. Attention to detail is a way of life: the place simply exudes the aura of another era. If you don't stay here, stop by and visit. ~ 127 Lahainaluna Road; 808-661-0577, 800-669-3444, fax 808-667-9480; www.lahainainn.com, e-mail inntown@lahainainn.com. MODERATE TO DELUXE.

While the building is actually quite modern, the **Plantation Inn** possesses the look and ambience of an early-20th-century hostelry. Modeled after the plantation architecture of an earlier era, it features 19 rooms individually decorated in period furniture. Most are adorned with either poster, brass or canopy beds, stained-glass windows and tile bathrooms. Combining the atmosphere of the past with the amenities of the present, guest rooms also feature televisions, refrigerators and air conditioning, as well as VCRs on request. There's a pool with a shaded pavilion and jacuzzi on the premises. Full breakfast included. ~ 174 Lahainaluna Road; 808-667-9225, 800-433-6815, fax 808-667-9293; www.theplantationinn.com, e-mail info@theplantationinn.com. DELUXE TO ULTRA-DELUXE.

The **OHANA Maui Islander** is a warren of woodframe buildings spread across lushly landscaped grounds. The ambience is an odd combination of tropical retreat and motel atmosphere. It features 360 trimly decorated rooms, some of which are small studios (with kitchens) and one-bedroom efficiencies. Amenities include a swimming pool, laundry, tennis court and picnic area. ~ 660 Wainee Street; 808-667-9766, 800-462-6262, fax 808-661-3733; www.ohanahotels.com, e-mail mih@ohanahotels.com. DELUXE TO ULTRA-DELUXE.

**CONDOS**

Though it's more expensive than many others, **Lahaina Shores Hotel** has the advantage of a beachfront location in Lahaina. This sprawling condominium complex offers studio apartments beginning at $180, while one-bedroom units start at $250. With a swimming pool, jacuzzi and the nearby beach, it's quite convenient. ~ 475 Front Street; 808-661-4835, 800-642-6284, fax 808-661-4696, www.classicresorts.com, e-mail info@classicresorts.com.

**DINING**

The **Pioneer Inn Restaurant** brings back the Lahaina of old. The main dining room is a cozy anchorage dotted with nautical fixtures and specializing in regional fare. The emphasis is on the "bounty of Hawaii"; in other words, fresh fish, Upcountry produce and local herbs. Select one of the day's fresh fish specials

**AUTHOR FAVORITE**

Perhaps the nicest complex to stay at on this side of the island is **Puamana**, a 28-acre retreat about a mile southeast of Lahaina. This townhouse complex, a 1920s-era sugar plantation, rests along a rock-strewn beach. The oceanfront clubhouse, open to guests, was once the plantation manager's house, and the landscaped grounds are still given over to mango, plumeria and torch ginger trees. Guests stay in low-slung plantation-style buildings that sport shake-shingle roofs and house from two to six units. To round out the amenities there are three pools and a tennis court. There's a three-night minimum that increases to seven nights during the Christmas season. ~ 34 Pualima Place; 808-667-2551. Reservations through Klahani Resorts: 800-628-6731, fax 808-661-5875; www.klahani.com, e-mail klahani@hotmail.com. DELUXE TO ULTRA-DELUXE.

and you can't go wrong. Breakfast begins at 7 a.m. ~ 658 Wharf Street; 808-661-3636, fax 808-667-5708. MODERATE TO DELUXE.

I'o is the name and creative food is the game. Brainchild of Chef James McDonald, this beachfront restaurant offers both indoor and patio seating in an area that was a favored spot of ancient Hawaiian royalty. The decor is an undersea world of fantasy set against a backdrop of high-tech fixtures. This is the style that matches the chef's cuisine; for example, he creates a New Age salad utilizing an old Hawaii staple, hand-picked pohole fern shoots and sweet papaya from the Hana rainforests, served with a roasted garlic pesto. The local fish preparations are amazing. Dinner only. ~ 505 Front Street, Lahaina; 808-661-8422, fax 808-661-8399; www.iomaui.com. ULTRA-DELUXE.

I can't say much for the nomenclature, but the prices are worth note at **Cheeseburger in Paradise**. This is a rare catch indeed—an inexpensive restaurant smack on the Lahaina waterfront that serves three meals a day and features live rock-and-roll music nightly. Granted, you won't find much on the menu other than hamburgers, salads and sandwiches. But if some couples can live on love, why can't the rest of us live on ocean views? ~ 811 Front Street; 808-661-4855. MODERATE.

**David Paul's Lahaina Grill**, headlining Pacific Rim cuisine, is an intimate dining room with a personalized touch. According to founding chef David Paul Johnson, the menu represents "a gathering of technique, flavors and skills from around the world, utilizing local ingredients to translate each dish into an exceptional dining experience." Tequila shrimp with firecracker rice, steamed Hawaiian lobster with a foie gras–chanterelle sauce, Kona coffee–roasted rack of lamb or macadamia-smoked pork chop were on the regularly changing menu when I was there. Dinner only. ~ 127 Lahainaluna Road; 808-667-5117, 800-360-2606, fax 808-661-5478; www.lahainagrill.com, e-mail reservations@lahainagrill.com. ULTRA-DELUXE.

A defining experience in Lahaina dining is **Gerard's Restaurant**. Here you'll encounter a French restaurant in a Victorian setting with tropical surroundings. Housed in the Plantation Inn, a bed and breakfast reminiscent of early New Orleans, Gerard's provides a chandelier-and-patterned-wallpaper dining room as well as a veranda complete with overhead fans and whitewashed balustrade. The chef prepares fresh fish, rack of lamb, duck *confit* and puff pastry with shiitake mushrooms. Of course, that is after having started off with ahi steak tartar or crab bisque. Dinner only. Highly recommended for a splurge. ~ 174 Lahainaluna Road; 808-667-6077; www.gerardsmaui.com, e-mail gerard@maui.net. ULTRA-DELUXE.

The preferred style of dining in Lahaina is steak and seafood at one of the waterfront restaurants along Front Street. And the common denominator is the ever-popular, usually crowded **Kimo's**, where you can enjoy all the tropical amenities while dining on fresh fish, lobster or prime rib. They have live Hawaiian music Wednesday through Sunday evenings. ~ 845 Front Street; 808-661-4811, fax 808-667-6077; www.kimosmaui.com, e-mail tskimos@aol.com. MODERATE TO DELUXE.

The **Bubba Gump Shrimp Co.** pays homage to the movie *Forrest Gump*. Featuring "shrimp any way you can think of eating it," and other American-style food, it is also filled with *Gump* memorabilia. ~ 889 Front Street; 808-661-3111, fax 808-667-6650; www.bubbagump.com. MODERATE TO DELUXE.

Informality is the password at **Longhi's**, a European-style café that specializes in Mediterranean dishes. The menu changes daily and is never written down; the waiter simply tells you the day's offerings. Usually there'll be several pasta dishes, sautéed vegetables, salads, a shellfish creation, steak, a wine-soaked chicken or veal dish and perhaps eggplant parmigiana. Longhi's prepares all of its own bread and pasta, buys Maui-grown produce and imports many cheeses from New York. The dinners reflect this diligence. Breakfasts and lunches are cooked with the same care. Definitely recommended, especially for vegetarians, who can choose from many of the dishes offered. This is the original location; there's another one in Lahaina and one in Wailea. ~ 888 Front Street; 808-667-2288; www.longhis.com, e-mail longhi@maui.net. DELUXE TO ULTRA-DELUXE.

In the Old Lahaina Shopping Center, the **Thai Chef Restaurant** is a cozy place with an inviting assortment of Southeast Asian dishes. Try the green papaya salad, sautéed chili chicken or seafood with red curry sauce. No lunch on Saturday and Sunday. ~ 880 Front Street; 808-667-2814. MODERATE.

From the aquariums, captain's chairs and marlin trophies, you could never guess what they serve at **Erik's Seafood and Sushi Bar**. What a surprise to discover a menu filled with crabmeat-stuffed prawns, lobster-stuffed chicken breast, salmon and local fish. Early-bird specials. ~ 843 Wainee Street, Lahaina; 808-669-4806, fax 808-662-8784. DELUXE TO ULTRA-DELUXE.

**AUTHOR FAVORITE**

One of my favorite light-food stops is a devil-may-care place called the **Sunrise Café**. Set in a tiny clapboard building with a fresh, airy look, it serves salads, sandwiches and espresso, plus such entrées as smoked kalua pork, grilled chicken breast and mango barbecue chicken. The service is laidback—Maui style. The café serves breakfast and lunch. ~ Located around back at 693A Front Street; 808-661-8558. BUDGET.

Right off the highway in Anchor Square, facing the West Maui Mountains is **Local Food,** a takeout stand that sells local-style breakfasts, plate lunches and juices. No dinner. Closed Saturday and Sunday. ~ 222 Papalaua Street; 808-667-2882. BUDGET.

Light, bright and airy, **Compadres** is a great place to sip a margarita or enjoy a Mexican meal with an island flair. The tropical ambience is as appealing as the steaming dishes served here. Especially popular are the fajitas and pork carnitas, but the menu also offers burgers, salads and vegetarian dishes. Breakfast, lunch and dinner—they open at 8 a.m. ~ Lahaina Cannery Mall, 1221 Honoapiilani Highway; 808-661-7189, fax 808-661-7137. MODERATE.

If you like Greek food, you'll enjoy **Athens Greek Restaurant,** a fast-food stand at the Lahaina Cannery Mall where the gyros are generously stuffed with fresh ingredients and the shish kebabs come in chicken, fish and beef varieties (go for the fish). Take your meal to a nearby table and catch the passing scene. ~ Lahaina Cannery Mall, 1221 Honoapiilani Highway; 808-661-4300. BUDGET.

Slightly (I said *slightly*) off the tourist track is the **Old Lahaina Luau.** Dinner here is based on the traditional luau—from the grass hut buildings to the menu of roast pork, *kalua* pig, sweet potato, mahimahi and poi. Reserve early, show up on time and be prepared to make an evening of Hawaiian feasting. ~ 1251 Front Street, behind the Lahaina Cannery Mall; 808-667-1998, 800-248-5828, fax 808-661-5176; www.oldlahainaluau.com, e-mail info@oldlahainaluau.com. ULTRA-DELUXE.

Voted Best Plate Lunch by locals, **Aloha Mixed Plate,** on the edge of town, is a beach shack by day serving saimin, udon, burgers and plate lunches. The patio is a great place to soak up the beach scene. ~ 1285 Front Street; 808-661-3322, fax 808-661-3087. BUDGET.

◄ HIDDEN

Near the top of the cognoscenti's list of gourmet establishments is an unlikely looking French restaurant in Olowalu called **Chez Paul.** The place is several miles outside Lahaina in a renovated building that also houses Olowalu's funky general store. But for many years this little hideaway has had a reputation far transcending its surroundings. You'll probably drive right past the place at first, but when you do find it, you'll discover a menu featuring such delicacies as homemade duck pâté with mustard seed, grilled rack of lamb with mango chutney, island fish poached in champagne and several other tempting entrées. While the tab is ethereal, the rave reviews this prim dining room receives make it worth every franc. Closed Sunday in summer. ~ Honoapiilani Highway, Olowalu; 808-661-3843, fax 808-667-5692; chezpaul.com, e-mail chezpaul@maui.net. ULTRA-DELUXE.

◄ HIDDEN

**GROCERIES**   Foodland is open daily from 6 a.m. to midnight. ~ Old Lahaina Center, Wainee Street; 808-661-0975.

South of Lahaina, the **Olowalu General Store** has a limited supply of grocery items. ~ Honoapiilani Highway, Olowalu; 808-667-2883.

**SHOPPING**   Lahaina's a great place to combine shopping with sightseeing. Most shops are right on Front Street in the historic wooden buildings facing the water. For a walking tour of the stores and waterfront, start from the Pioneer Inn at the south end of the strip and walk north on the *makai* or ocean side. Then come back along the *mauka*, or mountain, side of the street.

If it's Friday in Lahaina, you can browse the town's art galleries, which sponsor a special **Art Night** every week. This is a great opportunity to meet some of the artists who have made Lahaina an international art scene. The artists, who welcome visitors at galleries where their work is displayed, talk story and add a unique personal touch to a night on the town.

**Lahaina Printsellers**, one of my favorite Maui shops, has an astounding collection of ancient maps and engravings from Polynesia and other parts of the world. ~ 505 Front Street; 808-667-7843.

The **Wharf Cinema Center** is a multilevel complex of shops and restaurants. Most interesting is **Island Coin & Stamps** (808-667-6155), where all sorts of Hawaiiana and other collectibles make tempting souvenirs. The cinema itself is small, but the movies are first-run if you're in the mood for a film while you're on Maui. ~ 658 Front Street.

**The Gecko Store**, the only shop I've seen with a sand floor, stocks inexpensive beachwear as well as T-shirts and toys, many with a gecko theme. ~ 703 Front Street; 808-661-1078.

The **Endangered Species Store**, which features a multitude of conservation-minded items, is a worthy stop. Among other things, you will find chimes, statues and a healthy supply of T-shirts and stuffed animals. ~ 707 Front Street; 808-661-0208.

**Célébrités** is a trendy showcase for the artistic work of several musicians and actors, including John Lennon, Miles Davis, the Rolling Stones' Ronnie Wood, Anthony Quinn and Charles Bronson. They also have album cover art and pieces signed by the Beatles and the Stones. ~ 764 Front Street; 808-667-0727.

**Lahaina Galleries** is of special note not only for the contemporary and classic artworks but also because of the imaginative ways in which they're displayed. Even if you're not just dying to write that five-figure check, stop by for a viewing. ~ 828 Front Street; 808-667-2152, 800-228-2006; www.lahainagalleries.com.

Perhaps the best place in Whalers Village to discover the whaling tradition is **Lahaina Scrimshaw**. During their long journeys, sailors once whiled away the hours by etching and engraving on ivory, creating beautiful articles of scrimshaw. The sale of ivory from animals taken by hunters is banned, but the fossilized remains of ancient mammoths and walruses have kept this art alive. Using ivory that is thousands of years old, artists create a wide array of functional and decorative pieces, many of which are traded by aficionados of this art form. ~ 845 Front Street; 808-661-4034.

If you come across glittering fragments while on the beach, don't buy that million-dollar dream house just yet—these white quartz pieces are merely "Maui diamonds," mistaken by early explorers for the genuine article.

**Sgt. Leisure** has an array of imaginative T-shirts. ~ 855B Front Street; 808-667-0661.

**Contemporary Village Gallery** features paintings by contemporary Hawaiian artists. Amid the tourist schlock is some brilliant artwork. ~ 180 Dickenson Street; 808-661-5559.

Also stop in at the Lahaina Art Society's **Banyan Tree Gallery**. This is a great place if you're in the market for local artwork; on display are pieces by a number of Maui artists. ~ 648 Wharf Street, first floor of the Old Courthouse; 808-661-0111.

The **Lahaina Cannery Mall**, a massive complex of stores housed in an old canning factory, is the area's most ambitious project. **Na Hoku** (808-661-1731) is where you can pick up Hawaiian heirlooms, jewelry, Tahitian and Akoya pearls, or designs by Kabana and Steven Douglas. **Maui Playworks** (808-661-4766; www.mauiplayworks.com) is the place to pick up stunt and sport kites including diamond, box and bird designs. Here you'll also find windsocks, kaleidoscopes, games and a wide array of toys. Complete flying instructions, including tips on where to launch your kite, are provided by the helpful staff. ~ 1221 Honoapiilani Highway.

On the corner of Front and Papalana streets, **Lahaina Center** is another shopping mall, a sprawling complex of theaters, stores and restaurants. Among the shops here is **Hilo Hattie Fashion Center** (808-667-7911), where you and your honey can buy those matching aloha outfits. ~ 900 Front Street.

Front Street's the strip in Lahaina—a dilapidated row of buildings from which stream some of the freshest sounds around.

**NIGHTLIFE**

Tucked into a corner of the Best Western Pioneer Inn, the **Pioneer Inn Grill** features a seagoing motif complete with harpoons, figureheads and other historical nautical decor. Usually packed to the bulkheads with a lively crew, it's a great place to enjoy a tall cold one while listening to live music. ~ 658 Wharf Street; 808-661-3636.

You can enjoy a drink at the **Blue Lagoon Tropical Bar and Grill** in the adjacent courtyard. Occasional live music. ~ Wharf Cinema Center, 658 Front Street; 808-661-8141.

**Moose McGillycuddy's** is a hot club offering a large dance-floor and a variety of live music acts. The house is congenial and the drinks imaginatively mixed; for contemporary sounds with dinner, arrive before 9 p.m. Cover on Tuesday. ~ 844 Front Street; 808-667-7758, fax 808-667-5168; e-mail mooses@maui.net.

**Cheeseburger in Paradise** boasts a variety of performers playing "fun" tunes from 4:30 'til close—around 10 p.m.—every night. There is no dancefloor, however. ~ 811 Front Street; 808-661-4855.

Lahaina's favorite pastime is watching the sun set over the ocean while sipping a tropical concoction at a waterfront watering place. A prime location for this very rewarding activity is **Kimo's**, which features traditional Hawaiian music Wednesday through Sunday, and rock-and-roll on Friday and Saturday. ~ 845 Front Street; 808-661-4811.

Both high-tech and culturally beautiful, **Maui Theatre** is constantly evolving. The mix is one part live theater with two parts Broadway musical and one part Cirque du Soleil. What makes its production 'Ulalena unique is the story—it is a manifestation of the ancient Hawaiian *kumulipo* (creation chant) combined with Hawaii's mythology and history through the ages. The number of performances changes seasonally, so call for the schedule. Admission. ~ Old Lahaina Center, 878 Front Street; 808-661-9913, 877-688-4800; www.ulalena.com.

Another "magical" entertainment experience is **Warren & Annabelle's**. "Warren" is Warren Gibson, a master at sleight-of-hand magic. "Annabelle" is the ghost of a woman who lived in Lahaina during the whaling era and lost her sweetheart to the sea. She can still be seen (or rather, heard) at her piano, playing tunes for the return of her lost love. Elegantly appointed in turn-of-the-20th-century splendor, Annabelle's Parlor is also a restaurant/lounge. The waitstaff sings while helping guests call out song requests to Annabelle. After the preliminaries, doors open to the theater for an entertaining magic show. Unlocking the se-

## MOKUULU, A ROYAL AND SACRED SANCTUARY

Beneath a county park in Lahaina, archaeologists have uncovered one of the islands' most historical sites—**Mokuulu**. It is thought to have once been the political and spiritual center of Maui, with royal residences and a royal mausoleum there, as well as Mokuhinia, a natural wetland and fishpond. Carbon dating shows it to be one of the earliest signs of human existence in the islands. **Friends of Mokuulu** is an organization created to try and restore the site. ~ Friends of Mokuula, 505 Front Street #234, Lahaina; www.mokuula.com, e-mail friends@mokuula.com.

cret passage to enter the parlor is also part of the fun. The show runs Monday through Saturday. Admission. ~ 900 Front Street; 808-667-6244, fax 808-667-6245; www.warrenandannabelles. com, e-mail lisa@warrenandannabelles.com.

**PAPALAUA COUNTY PARK** 🏊 🚣 🎣 *Kiawe* trees and scrub vegetation spread right to the shoreline along Papalaua County Park. There are sandy patches between the trees large enough to spread a towel, but I prefer sunbathing at beaches closer to Lahaina. Bounded on one side by Honoapiilani Highway, this narrow beach extends for a mile to join a nicer, lawn-fringed park; then it stretches on toward Olowalu for several more miles. If you want to be alone, just head down the shore. Swimming is good, snorkeling is okay out past the surf break and surfing is excellent at Thousand Peaks breaks and also very good several miles east in Maalaea Bay. There's an outhouse and picnic area at the county park. ~ Located about ten miles south of Lahaina on Honoapiilani Highway.

🏕 Tent camping. County permit required.

**OLOWALU BEACHES** 🏊 🚣 🎣 ⛵ To the north and south of Olowalu General Store lie narrow corridors of white sand. This is a great spot to hunt for Maui diamonds. Swimming is very good, and south of the general store, where road and water meet, you'll find a coral reef ready for snorkeling. A growing green sea turtle population can be seen by snorkelers at the 14-mile marker. Surfers will find good breaks with right and left slides about a half-mile north of the general store. *Ulua* are often caught from Olowalu landing. There are no facilities, but there is a market nearby. ~ Go south from Lahaina on Honoapiilani Highway for about six miles.

**LAUNIUPOKO COUNTY PARK** 🏊 🚣 ⛵ There is a seaside lawn shaded by palm trees and a sandy beach. A rock seawall slopes gently for entering swimmers, but offers little to sunbathers. It's located near the West Maui Mountains, with views of Kahoolawe and Lanai. When the tide is high, it's a good place to take children to swim safely and comfortably in the tidal pool on the other side of the seawall. Otherwise, swimming and snorkeling are mediocre. There is good surf-casting from the seawall and south for three miles. The park has a picnic area, restrooms and showers. ~ Located three miles south of Lahaina on Honoapiilani Highway.

**PUAMANA COUNTY PARK** 🏊 🚣 🎣 ⛵ A narrow beach and grass-covered strip wedged between Honoapiilani Highway and the ocean, Puamana County Park is dotted with ironwood trees. The excellent views make this a choice spot for an enjoyable picnic. Facilities include portable restrooms and showers. ~

Located about two miles south of Lahaina on Honoapiilani Highway.

**KAMEHAMEHA IKI PARK** 🏊 🤿 🎣 ⛵ The one thing going for this park is its convenient location in Lahaina. Otherwise, it's heavily littered, shadowed by a mall and sometimes crowded. If you do stop by, try to forget all that and concentrate on the sandy beach, lawn and truly startling view of Lanai directly across the Auau Channel. Recent attempts to add more of a native Hawaiian feel to the park include a site where visitors can watch the on-going construction of traditional wooden canoes. Swimming is okay, snorkeling's good past the reef and, for surfing, there are breaks in the summer near the seawall in Lahaina Harbor. This surfing spot is not for beginners! Threadfin and *ulua* are common catches here. Restrooms and tennis courts are across the street at Maluulu o Lele Park near the playing field. ~ Located on Front Street next to the 505 Front Street mall.

**BABY BEACH** 🏊 🤿 🎣 ⛵ This curving stretch of white sand is the best beach in Lahaina. It lacks privacy but certainly not beauty. From here you can look back to Lahaina town and the West Maui Mountains or out over the ocean to Kahoolawe, Lanai and Molokai. Or just close your eyes and soak up the sun. Swimming is good and well protected, if shallow. Snorkeling is only fair. In summer there are breaks nearby at Mala Wharf; left slide. Threadfin is often caught. ~ Take Front Street north from Lahaina for about a half-mile. Turn left on Puunoa Place and follow it to the beach.

**WAHIKULI COUNTY PARK** 🏊 🤿 ⛵ This narrow stretch of beach and lawn, just off the road between Lahaina and Kaanapali, faces Lanai and Molokai. There are facilities aplenty, which might be why this pretty spot is so popular and crowded. Swimming is very good, but snorkeling is only fair. (There's a better spot just north of here near the Lahaina Canoe Club.) The most common catches here are *ulua* and threadfin. Facilities include picnic areas, showers and restrooms; there are tennis courts up the street at the Civic Center. ~ Located between Lahaina and Kaanapali on Honoapiilani Highway.

**HANAKAOO BEACH PARK** 🏊 🤿 ⛵ Conveniently located beside Kaanapali Beach Resort, this long and narrow park features a white-sand beach and grassy picnic ground, and is referred to by locals as Canoe Beach. Practically every Saturday, this is the place to watch Hawaiian canoe racing. The road is nearby, but the views of Lanai are outstanding. Swimming is good, snorkeling fair, but surfing poor. Common catches include *ulua* and threadfin. There are picnic areas, restrooms and showers. ~ Located between Lahaina and Kaanapali on Honoapiilani Highway.

Even in the case of Maui's notorious land developers, there is method to the madness. The stretch of coastline ex-

## Kaanapali–Kapalua Area

tending for six miles along Maui's western shore, crowded to the extreme with hotels and condominiums, is anchored by two planned resorts. Like handsome bookends supporting an uneven array of dog-eared paperbacks, Kaanapali and Kapalua add class to the arrangement.

Supporting the south end, **Kaanapali** is a 500-acre enclave that extends along three miles of sandy beach and includes six hotels, four condominiums, a golf course and an attractive shopping mall. Back in the 19th century it was a dry and barren segment of the sugar plantation that operated from Lahaina. Raw sugar was hauled by train from the mill out to Black Rock, a dramatic outcropping along Kaanapali Beach, where the produce was loaded onto waiting ships.

**SIGHTS**

In 1963, Kaanapali's first resort opened near Black Rock and development soon spread in both directions. Important to devel-

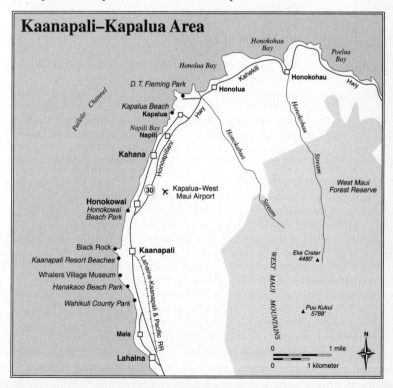

# Kaanapali–Kapalua Area

opers, who built the Sheraton Maui Hotel around it, **Black Rock** (Puu Kekaa) is a volcanic cinder cone from which ancient Hawaiians believed that the dead departed the earth in their journey to the spirit world. According to legend, the great 18th-century Maui chief Kahekili proved his bravery by leaping from the rock to the ocean below.

Kaanapali's modern-day contribution to Pacific culture is the **Whalers Village Museum**. This facility comprises an outdoor pavilion and a museum that details Lahaina's history of whaling. Outdoors, you'll find a 30-foot-long whale skeleton and a whaling longboat on display. The "golden era of whaling" is also portrayed in scrimshaw exhibits, a scale-model whaling ship, harpoons and other artifacts from the days when Lahaina was one of the world's great whaling ports. Self-guided audio tours are available. There's a wonderful shop on site, with a selection of fossilized whale ivory scrimshaw in addition to Victorian-era antiques. ~ Whalers Village, 2435 Kaanapali Parkway, Kaanapali; 808-661-5992, fax 808-661-8584 www.whalersvillage.com.

An earlier chief, Piilani, built a road through the area in the 16th century and gave his name to modern-day Route 30, the Honoapiilani Highway. Translated as "the bays of Piilani," the road passes several inlets located north of Kaanapali that have been developed in haphazard fashion. Honokowai, Kahana and Napili form a continuous wall of condominiums that sprawls north to Kapalua Bay and offers West Maui's best lodging bargains.

**Kapalua**, the bookend holding the north side in place, is a former pineapple plantation that was converted into a luxurious 1500-acre resort. Here two major hotels, three golf courses and

## PUEONE O HONOKAHUA

The Kapalua area includes one of Maui's most important cultural zones, **Pueone o Honokahua**. This 14-acre preserve, near the Ritz-Carlton, Kapalua, was the site of fishing shrines and *heiau* where the ancient Hawaiians worshipped their gods and made astronomical observations. Today you can see a burial ground dating back to A.D. 950 and portions of the King's Highway, a 16th-century stone road around Maui. Also extant are the outlines of terraced taro patches farmed by early inhabitants. Although this land has been claimed in turn by King Kamehameha III, the sugar king H. P. Baldwin, and lastly the Maui Land and Pineapple Company, the state now protects and preserves it as a native Hawaiian sanctuary. The Ritz-Carlton conducts a free tour called "A Sense of Place" at the preserve every Friday from 10 a.m. to noon. ~ 808-669-6200.

several villa-style communities blanket the hillside from the white sands of Kapalua Bay to the deep green foothills of the West Maui Mountains. Like the entire strip along Maui's western flank, Kapalua enjoys otherworldly sunsets and dramatic views of Lanai and Molokai.

In the Kaanapali area the modestly priced hotel is not an endangered species, it's totally extinct! So prepare yourself for steep tariffs.    **LODGING**

Built in 1980, the **Hyatt Regency Maui**, with its its atrium lobby, Asian artwork and freeform swimming pool, set the standard for resorts ever since. Unlike more recent hotels, in which the size of guest rooms is sacrificed for the sake of lavish grounds, the Hyatt Regency maintains an ideal balance between public and private areas. If you're seeking beautiful surroundings, friendly service and beachfront location, this 806-room extravaganza is the ticket. ~ 200 Nohea Kai Drive, Kaanapali; 808-661-1234, 800-233-1234, fax 808-667-4498; www.maui.hyatt. com, e-mail hrmsales@maui.net. ULTRA-DELUXE.

The 430-room **Kaanapali Beach Hotel** sits right on the beach and sports three restaurants and a large lobby. Guest rooms enjoy private lanais and guests lounge around a grassy courtyard, lush gardens and a whale-shaped swimming pool. In addition, there's a giant checkerboard; Hawaiian arts and crafts demonstrations are presented throughout the week. ~ 2525 Kaanapali Parkway, Kaanapali; 808-661-0011, 808-667-5978, fax 808-667-5978; www.kbhmaui.com, e-mail res@kbhmaui.com. ULTRA-DELUXE.

At Black Rock, the sacred lava promontory where cliff divers plunged into the Pacific, the ancient tradition is reenacted as part of a nightly torch-lighting ceremony at the **Sheraton Maui Hotel**. Here 510 rooms and suites are spread across spacious landscaped grounds. The hotel's distinctive architecture (it is partially built atop the rock) places some rooms near the water's edge. Decorated with rattan furniture, tropical prints and seashell-patterned bedspreads, all the rooms are trim and comfortable. You can watch the sunset from several restaurants and lounges, swim in a 140-yard pool or enjoy snorkeling along Black Rock. ~ 2605 Kaanapali Parkway, Kaanapali; 808-661-0031, 888-488-3535, fax 808-661-0458; www.sheraton.com/maui. ULTRA-DELUXE.

The **Royal Lahaina Resort** spreads across 27 acres, encompassing 542 guest rooms, 10 tennis courts, 3 swimming pools, 1 restaurants, a coffee shop and a white-sand beach that extends for a half-mile. Rooms in the highrise hotel price in the ultra-deluxe category, while the rates for the nicest accommodations, the multiplex cottages that dot the landscaped grounds, head for the sky. Note that some readers were neither impressed by the prices nor the accommodations. ~ 2780 Kekaa Drive, Kaanapali;

808-661-3611, 800-447-6925, fax 808-661-6150; www.2maui.
com. ULTRA-DELUXE.

A subtle architectural style gives the **Kapalua Bay Hotel** a low profile. But don't be misled. Part of a 23,000-acre plantation, this relatively small hotel, with 210 rooms and suites, is the hub of one of Maui's most appealing and romantic resorts. A hillside setting overlooking a white-sand crescent beach means that nearly all the rooms have spectacular ocean views. The accommodations are luxurious and tasteful and include rattan- and wicker-furnished sitting areas, baths with sunken tubs and vanity areas; suites also have jacuzzis. Floor-to-ceiling French doors open onto spacious lanais. Rock-lined ponds, tropical gardens, golf courses, restaurants, shops and tennis facilities add to Kapalua's charm. ~ 1 Bay Drive, Kapalua; 808-669-5656, 800-367-8000, fax 808-669-4694; www.kapaluabayhotel.com. ULTRA-DELUXE.

The **Ritz-Carlton, Kapalua**, unique among Ritz-Carltons, sits above the ocean on grounds that overlook not only the formal gardens and manicured lawns associated with this chain, but a sacred resting place for ancient Hawaiian spirits. It was this burial ground that initially put the hotel at odds with Hawaiian culture but then led it to become one of the strongest supporters of the Hawaiian people in the islands, including sponsorship of an annual celebration of Hawaiian culture. It's a luxury accommodation with Hawaiian soul. The 548 guest rooms are spacious and well-appointed with plantation-era furnishings and private lanais; the grounds are as beautiful as they are sacred. The usual five-star hotel amenities include a fitness center, a golf course, two restaurants and 24-hour room service. Kapalua Bay, one of three beaches here, has been designated among the best beaches in America. ~ 1 Ritz-Carlton Drive, Kapalua; 808-669-6200, 800-241-3333, fax 808-669-2028; www.ritzcarlton.com. ULTRA-DELUXE.

**CONDOS**    Most condominiums in this area are on the beach or just across the road from it. They are ideally situated for swimming or sunbathing; the major drawback, ironically, is that there are so many other condos around.

**Kaanapali Alii** ranks as one of Maui's better buys. Here the immense 1500- to 1900-square-foot suites can easily be shared by two couples or a family. All 264 condo units have large living and dining rooms, full kitchens, sitting areas and two baths. Fully carpeted and furnished with rattan, contemporary artwork and potted palms, these units start at $360 and top out at $900. The contemporary highrise facility rests along the beach and has a pool and tennis court. ~ 50 Nohea Kai Drive, Kaanapali; 808-667-1400, 800-642-6284, fax 808-667-1145; www.kaanapali alii.com, e-mail info@classicresorts.com.

Adjacent to the shops of Whalers Village, **The Whaler on Kaanapali Beach** offers spacious units with *koa* parquet floors and some rattan furniture. With its twin 12-story towers, this oceanfront condominium boasts marble baths and has 360 units priced from $245 to $715. ~ 2481 Kaanapali Parkway, Kaanapali; 808-661-4861, 800-922-7866, fax 808-661-8315; www.astonhotels.com, e-mail res.wha@aston-hotels.com.

**Aston Kaanapali Shores** has hotel room–style accommodations for $210 including a refrigerator; studios from $315 double with a balcony and full kitchen; and one-bedroom units with a garden view and full kitchen for $395. ~ 3445 Lower Honoapiilani Road, Kaanapali; 808-667-2211, 800-922-7866, fax 808-661-0836; www.kaanapalishores-maui.com.

The units at **Papakea Resort** provide a pleasant retreat. Ranging from $230 studios to $615 three-bedroom units, all 155 condominiums come with spacious lanais. ~ 3543 Lower Honoapiilani Road, Honokowai; 808-669-4848, 800-922-7866, fax 808-665-0662; www.astonhotels.com, e-mail info@aston-hotels.com.

Two-bedroom apartments at the beachfront **Maui Sands** run from $220 for one to four people. There is a seven-night minimum during the busy season (December 15 through April). ~ 3600 Lower Honoapiilani Road, Honokowai; 808-669-1902, 800-367-5037, fax 808-669-8790; www.mauigetaway.com, e-mail mrmreservations@maui.net.

The one-bedroom apartments at **Honokowai Palms** have a lanai; they run $80 for a double and sleep up to four people. A two-bedroom unit without lanai is $85 for one to six people. The accommodations are located right across the street from the ocean. ~ 3666 Lower Honoapiilani Road, Honokowai; 808-667-2712, 800-669-6284, fax 808-661-5875; www.klahani.com, e-mail jerry@klahani.com.

On the waterfront, **Hale Maui** has one-bedroom condos from $85 double. The drawback to this budget rate is that there is no pool—but you won't miss it with the beach practically in your backyard. ~ 3711 Lower Honoapiilani Road, Honokowai;

### KEIKI RETREATS

Tired of building sandcastles? Want a walk on the beach—adult style? If you're staying in a condo or hotel that doesn't offer a *keiki* (children's) program, you can check your kids into day camps at the Ritz-Carlton, Kapalua's **Ritz Kids** (808-669-6200) or the **Keiki Kamp** (808-667-2525) at the Westin Maui Resort in Kaanapali, even if you're not a guest.

808-669-6312, fax 808-669-1302; www.maui.net/~halemaui, e-mail halemaui@maui.net.

The one-bedroom apartments at the oceanfront **Kaleialoha** start at $125 double; $10 each additional person. ~ 3785 Lower Honoapiilani Road, Honokowai; 808-669-8197, 800-222-8688, fax 808-669-2502; www.mauicondosoceanfront.com, e-mail dford@kal.com.

**Polynesian Shores** has one-bedroom apartments that start at $145 double; two-bedroom units, $185 for four; three-bedroom apartments, $245 for four. All units have ocean views. ~ 3975 Lower Honoapiilani Road, Honokowai; 808-669-6065, 800-433-6284, fax 808-669-0909; mauicondosrentals.com, e-mail info@ mauicondosrentals.com.

**Mahina Surf** features one-bedroom units that start at $140 double ($125 to $175 from April 15 to December 14); two-bedroom accommodations range from $155 to $205. There are oceanfront views with a lava-rock beach. There's a three-night minimum stay. ~ 4057 Lower Honoapiilani Road, Kahana; 808-669-6068, 800-367-6086, fax 808-669-4534; www.mahinasurf.com, e-mail mahinasf@maui.net.

**Kahana Reef All Oceanfront** has studio and one-bedroom apartments for $155 to $170 single or double. As the name suggests, all units are oceanfront; they require a four-night minimum stay. ~ 4471 Lower Honoapiilani Road, Kahana; 808-879-5445, 800-822-4409, fax 808-874-6144; www.resortquestmaui.com, e-mail info@resortquestmaui.com.

One-bedroom condos at **Napili Point Resort** are $239 to $279 for up to four people (reduced rates in low season). Two-bedroom units start at $329. Here sliding doors lead out to oceanview patios. Located on a lava rock coastline, the resort is a short walk from sandy Napili Bay beach. ~ 5295 Lower Honoapiilani Road, Napili; 808-669-9222, 800-669-6252, fax 808-669-7984; www.napili.com.

**Outrigger Napili Shores Resort** is a beautifully landscaped lowrise resort with studios and one-bedrooms running from $182 to $244. The units are individually decorated with tropical themes and the complex is graced by gardens of plumeria and hibiscus. The pool and beach areas are idyllic. ~ 5315 Lower Honoapiilani Road, Napili; 808-669-8061, 800-688-7444, fax 808-669-5407; www.outrigger.com, e-mail reservations@outrigger.com.

Studio apartments at **The Napili Bay** are $143 double for oceanfront views. In addition to private lanais, there's a common barbeque area. ~ 33 Hui Drive, Napili; 808-661-3500, 888-661-7200, fax 808-661-2649; www.mauibeachfront.com, e-mail beachfrt@maui.net.

The **Napili Kai Beach Resort** has 162 units—studios, one-, two- and three-bedroom affairs—that range in price from $200 to $900. Most come with kitchens. All are fully carpeted and have private lanais, rattan furniture, picture windows and direct access to an impressive beach. Closed the first two weeks of December. ~ 5900 Honoapiilani Road, Napili; 808-669-6271, 800-367-5030, fax 808-669-0086; www.napilikai.com, e-mail stay@napilikai.com.

Face it: there are few words in the English language more romantic than "villa." And there are few condominiums on Maui more alluring than **Kapalua Villas**. Situated on a 1650-acre resort and surrounded by three golf courses and an ocean, they offer views that sweep past the mountains and out to the neighbor islands. The units are lowrise structures with sunken tubs, large lanais, and rattan and wicker furniture. Individually owned and decorated, the accommodations provide direct access to swimming, golf and tennis. One-bedroom units range from $199 to $299; two-bedroom units run from $299 to $505. ~ 500 Office Road, Kapalua; 808-669-8088, 800-545-0018, fax 808-669-5234; www.kapaluavillas.com.

**DINING**

Overlooking serene tropical gardens, the open-air **Swan Court** defines the ultimate Maui experience. Guests enter this upscale restaurant in the Hyatt Regency Maui via a grand staircase. With a waterfall and gliding swans in the background, you can choose from a variety of daily-changing entrées such as Hunan marinated lamb chops, grilled lobster satay with coconut and lemongrass, island-style bouillabaisse with macadamia sambal and sautéed *ono* with marinated shrimp won tons. For dessert, there's

**AUTHOR FAVORITE**

**Sansei Restaurant & Sushi Bar** has developed a cult following among both locals and tourists alike for its Pacific Rim sushi. One version incorporates spicy crab, cilantro and various vegetables with sweet Thai chili sauce for dipping instead of the usual soy and wasabi. In another, smoked salmon, Maui onions and cream cheese combine to create the "bagel roll." The tuna sashimi is cut thin and covered with Thai fish sauce and peanuts. It's sushi quite unlike any you've ever tasted. And there's also a selection of entrées, including roasted duck breast with foie-gras glaze. Dinner only. ~ 115 Bay Drive in the Kapalua Bay Shops, Kapalua; 808-669-6286, fax 808-669-0667; www.sanseihawaii.com, e-mail cohen@sanseihawaii.com. DELUXE.

a daily soufflé selection and dessert sampler. Formal dress required. Closed Sunday, Monday, Wednesday and Friday. ~ 200 Nohea Kai Drive, Kaanapali; 808-661-1234. ULTRA-DELUXE.

For an elegant dining experience at a reasonable price, try **Tropica** restaurant in the Westin Maui. Feast on fare prepared on rotisseries, grills and in wood ovens, as well as fresh seafood, while watching the sun set over the bordering beach. Dinner only. ~ 2365 Kaanapali Parkway, Kaanapali; 808-667-2525. DELUXE TO ULTRA-DELUXE.

One way to eat at a reasonable price is by stopping at the takeout stands on the lower level of Whalers Village. There are tables inside or out in the courtyard. **Pizza Paradiso** serves an assortment of pies (including by the slice) plus spaghetti and meatballs and salads. For breakfast you can get bagels or coffee. ~ 808-667-0333. BUDGET.

Honoapiilani, the highway that runs from Lahaina north to Kaanapali, was named after the chieftain who built the original route—Chief Piilani.

The sunsets are otherworldly at **Leilani's On The Beach**, a breezy veranda-style dining room. Trimmed in dark woods and lava rock, the upstairs dining room is dominated by an outrigger canoe that hangs suspended from the ceiling. On the menu you'll find rack of lamb, ginger chicken and teriyaki steak. Downstairs, you can relax and take in the scene from the umbrella shade of the **Beachside Grill**, where cocktails accompany burgers, sandwiches and salads. Frequently there is live rock-and-roll in the afternoon. Touristy but appealing. ~ Whalers Village, 2435 Kaanapali Parkway, Kaanapali; 808-661-4495, fax 808-667-9027; www.leilanis.com. BUDGET TO DELUXE.

Peter Merriman, the chef extraordinaire who earned his reputation with a restaurant on the Big Island, transported his brand of Hawaii regional cuisine across the Alenuihaha Channel to open **Hula Grill** in Kaanapali. Specializing in seafood, this 1930s-era beach house has wok-charred ahi, seafood dim sum dishes and an array of entrées that includes Macadamia nut–crusted mahimahi, grilled herbed ono and pizza baked in the *kiawe* oven. For landlubbers there's Maui-raised steak and goat cheese pizza. ~ Whalers Village, Kaanapali; 808-667-6636, fax 808-661-1148; www.hulagrill.com. DELUXE.

**Giovani's Tomato Pie Ristorante** is located near the entrance to Kaanapali Beach Resort. A patio restaurant overlooking a golf course, it's a pretty place to dine on pizza, pasta and other Italian favorites. The restaurant features a menu that includes veal marsala, chicken parmesan and shrimp scampi. Dinner only. ~ 2291 Kaanapali Parkway; 808-661-3160, fax 808-661-5254. MODERATE.

The **Kaanapali Mixed Plate Restaurant** serves an all-you-can-eat buffet at a price that is surprisingly out of place for this expensive hotel. A complete breakfast is offered; lunch and dinner include a few entrées, a salad bar, soup and dessert buffets. Meat-eaters will revel in the dinner buffets all-you-can-eat prime rib. ~ Kaanapali Beach Hotel, 2525 Kaanapali Parkway, Kaanapali; 808-661-0011, fax 808-667-5616; www.khbmaui.com, e-mail info@kbhmaui.com. MODERATE.

Located on the scenic Kaanapali North Course, **Basil Tomatoes Italian Grille** is a cozy eatery featuring northern Italian versions of veal chop, fresh fish, lasagna and a variety of pastas. Flavorful food and an intimate setting make this a top choice for dinner. Dinner only. ~ At the entrance to the Royal Lahaina Resort, 2780 Kekaa Drive, Kaanapali; 808-662-3210, fax 808-661-5254. DELUXE.

The **Kahana Terrace** is one of those rare finds that you count yourself lucky to have discovered. A wide expanse of the Pacific facing the island of Molokai is the view from the dining room, and in winter and spring, the humpback whales provide an unparalleled show of nature. "Great American food" accurately describes the food—prime rib, meatloaf, steak and lobster are dinner choices, and just plain bacon and eggs, French toast and omelettes are some breakfast items. Try the Sunday beachside barbecue for a good family value. ~ 4299 Lower Honoapiilani Road, Kahana; 808-669-5399, fax 808-669-1027. MODERATE TO DELUXE.

**Dollie's Pub and Café** offers fettuccine alfredo, sandwiches, salads and pizza. Voted Best of Maui by local write-in vote, this is a sports-on-the-TV bar (nine satellite TVs, two 42-inch flat screens) with a small kitchen and adjacent dining room. ~ 4310 Lower Honoapiilani Road, Kahana; 808-669-0266, fax 808-665-0614. MODERATE.

One of Maui's leading restaurants, **Roy's Kahana Bar and Grill** eschews the waterfalls, swans, tinkling pianists and other accoutrements of the island's top dining rooms. Instead, this spacious second-story establishment looks like a gallery with its exposed-beam ceiling, track lighting and paintings. The open kitchen serves up such creations as fresh seared lemongrass *shutome* with Thai basil peanut sauce, *kiawe*-grilled filet mignon with garlic mashed potatoes and Chinese barbecue cabernet, grilled ginger chicken with shoyu glaze and garlic chive rice and blackened ahi with soy-mustard butter. Reservations are a must! ~ Kahana Gateway Shopping Center, 4405 Honoapiilani Highway, Kahana; 808-669-6999; www.roysrestaurant.com, e-mail kahana@roys restaurant.com. DELUXE TO ULTRA-DELUXE.

A good choice for food, libations and conversation is **Fish & Game Brewing Company & Rotisserie**. It's quite a mouthful, but this establishment boasts three dining rooms as well as a microbrewery. The open-hearth rotisserie oven, along with the gleaming copper vats, dominate the first room. The main dining room contains an exhibition kitchen and live lobster tank, while the private dining room showcases a fireplace and leather wingback chairs. Fresh fish and seafood are island-caught; for the carnivorous, there's roasted meats and the tastiest rack of lamb on the island. Sports fans will also enjoy the large-screen TVs in the bar. Breakfast on weekends during football season. ~ Kahana Gateway Shopping Center, 4405 Lower Honoapiilani Road, Kahana; 808-669-3474; www.fishandgamerestaurant.com, e-mail info@fishandgamerestaurant.com. DELUXE TO ULTRA-DELUXE.

For Mongolian beef, kung pao chicken or hot Szechuan bean curd, try **China Boat**. At this family-style restaurant, you can ease into a lacquered seat and take in the Japanese *ukiyoe* prints that adorn the place. Adding to the ambience are lava walls that showcase beautiful Chinese ceramic pieces. Patio dining is also available. No lunch on Sunday. ~ 4474 Lower Honoapiilani Road, Kahana; 808-669-5089, fax 808-669-6132. MODERATE.

In addition to its namesake, **Maui Tacos** has chimichangas, tostadas, burritos, quesadillas and enchiladas. Nothing fancy, just a few formica booths and tables with molded plastic chairs. But the salsa's fresh daily, the beans are prepared without lard and the chips are made with cholesterol-free vegetable oil. Egg burritos and huevos rancheros are served for breakfast. Frozen yogurt and fruit smoothies are also available. ~ Napili Plaza, 5095 Napilihau Street, Napili; 808-665-0222, 888-628-4822; www.mauitacos.com, e-mail eatmaui@maui.net. BUDGET.

Perched on the white sandy beach along one of the most beautiful bays on Maui is **Sea House Restaurant at Napili Kai Beach Resort**. Noted for fresh island fish (offered five different ways), steaks, free-range chicken and seafood pasta, are also available, and the *pupus* menu offers a wonderful selection of island specialties. Open for breakfast, lunch and dinner. ~ 5900 Lower Honoapiilani Road, Napili; 808-669-1500, fax 808-669-5740. DELUXE TO ULTRA-DELUXE.

Maui aficionados agree that **The Plantation House Restaurant** is among the island's best. Capturing their accolades is a spacious establishment with panoramic views of the Kapalua region and a decor that mixes mahogany and wicker with orchids and a roaring fire. Not to be upstaged by the surroundings, the chef prepares fresh island fish seven different ways. The most popular is the "plantation Oscar"—the fish is pan sauteed, then served with butter braised asparagus and sauteed crabmeat with a lemon *buerre blanc*. For lighter appetites there are salads, pastas, honey-guava scallops and, for lunch, a wide range of soups and sandwiches. Breakfast is also served. ~ 2000 Plantation Club Drive, Kapalua; 808-669-6299, fax 808-669-1222; www.theplantationhouse.com, e-mail info@theplantationhouse.com. DELUXE TO ULTRA-DELUXE.

Out in the Kaanapali area, the best place to shop is **Star Market**, **GROCERIES**
a good-sized supermarket that's open from 5 a.m. to 2 a.m. every
day. ~ 3350 Lower Honoapiilani Road, Kaanapali; 808-667-
9590.

Toward Kapalua, try the **Napili Market,** a well-stocked supermarket that's open daily from 6:30 a.m. to 11 p.m. ~ Napili
Plaza, 5095 Napili Hau Street, Napili; 808-669-1600.

Worthy of mention is **Whalers Village** (808-661-4567) in the     **SHOPPING**
Kaanapali Beach Resort. This sprawling complex combines a
shopping mall with a museum. Numbered among the stores
you'll find gift emporia featuring coral and shells, a shirt store
with wild island designs, other stores offering fine men's and
women's fashions.

And then there are the displays. Within this mazework mall
you'll discover blunderbusses, scrimshaw pieces, the skeletal remains of leviathans and whaling boats with iron harpoons
splayed from the bow. Practically everything, in fact, that a whaler
(or a cruising shopper) could desire.

Several shops in this split-level complex should not be missed.
For instance, **Lahaina Printsellers Ltd.** (808-667-7617) purveys
"fine antique maps and prints." **Sgt. Leisure** (808-667-9433) sells
brightly colored resortwear and T-shirts with original designs unlike those seen elsewhere. At **Blue Ginger Designs** (808-667-
5793) original styles in women's and children's clothing are featured. ~ 2435 Kaanapali Parkway.

For serious shoppers, ready to spend money or be damned,
there is nothing to compare with the neighboring hotels. Set like
gems within this tourist cluster are several world-class hotels,
each hosting numerous elegant shops.

Foremost is the **Hyatt Regency Maui,** along whose wood-
paneled lobby are stores that might well be deemed mini-muse-
ums. One, called **Elephant Walk** (808-667-2848), displays *koa*

**STAR LIGHT, STAR BRIGHT**

High atop the Hyatt Regency Maui's Lahaina Tower, a 16-inch reflecting
telescope probes deep space seven nights a week, taking tourists on a trip
through the planets and galaxies. **The Tour of the Stars** is a one-hour
program managed by the hotel's director of astronomy and designed for
the public. It allows ten people at a time to look through stationary
eyepieces while the computer-driven telescope searches the heavens.
Reservations are required, and keep in mind that if a show is cancelled
due to weather, re-scheduling is not automatic. Admission. ~ 200
Nohea Kai Drive, Kaanapali; 808-661-1234.

wood products, baskets and Niihau shell ornaments. There are art galleries, a fabric shop, clothing stores, jewelry stores and more—set in an open-air lobby that is filled with rare statuary and exotic birds. ~ 210 Nohea Kai Drive, Kaanapali; 808-667-7660.

Another favorite Hyatt Regency shop is **Hawaiian Quilt Collection**, where you'll find wallhangings, quilting supplies and an array of quilts. All quilts are Hawaiian related and made by the owner. ~ 210 Nohea Kai Drive, Kaanapali; 808-667-7660.

**La Bareda** is an excellent place to find inexpensive Hawaiian souvenirs such as sarongs, straw hats, jewelry and T-shirts. This shop in the Maui Marriott hotel is also knee-deep in key chains, pennants and ceramic pineapples. ~ 100 Nohea Kai Drive, Kaanapali; 808-667-5082.

The **Kapalua Bay Hotel** sports another upscale shopping annex. If you're traveling with young ones or looking for a souvenir for those you left behind, stop by **Kapalua Kids** (808-669-0033). Here you can buy children's books on Hawaii as well as soft toys and an array of clothing. ~ 1 Bay Drive.

At the **Plantation Course Golf Shop** you'll find an impressive collection of jackets, shirts, sweaters, sweatshirts and shorts, many with a tropical flair. This is also a good place to look for the work of signature designers. ~ 2000 Plantation Club Drive, Kapalua; 808-669-8877.

**NIGHTLIFE** Possibly the prettiest place in these parts to enjoy a drink 'neath the tropic moon is the bar at **Hula Grill**. Located in the Whalers Village mall, this beach house–style gathering place is decorated with original Hawaiian outrigger canoes. It features live Hawaiian music and hula nightly until 9 p.m. The place is located right on the water, so you can listen to a slow set, then stroll the beach. ~ 2435 Kaanapali Parkway; 808-667-6636, fax 808-661-1148; www.hulapie.com.

Hawaiian musicians perform nightly at the Hyatt Regency Maui in the **Weeping Banyan**, an open-air lounge. **Spats Trattoria** (cover) offers deejay dance music on Saturday. ~ 200 Nohea Kai Drive; 808-661-1234, 800-233-1234, fax 808-667-4498.

There's nightly music and Hawaiian entertainment at the Westin Maui in the **'Ono Surf Bar & Grill**. ~ 2365 Kaanapali Parkway; 808-667-2525.

The Sheraton Maui is a prime nightspot both early and later in the evening. Just before sunset you can watch the torch-lighting and cliff-diving ceremony from the **Lagoon Bar**. ~ 2605 Kaanapali Parkway, Kaanapali; 808-661-0031.

There's occasional Hawaiian-style entertainment at the **Royal Ocean Terrace Lounge**, a beachfront watering hole on the grounds of the Royal Lahaina Resort. Arrive early and you can watch the sunset between Lanai and Molokai, followed by the ubiquitous torch-lighting ceremony. ~ 2780 Kekaa Drive; 808-661-3611.

For soft entertainment in a relaxed setting, try **The Lehua,** in the lobby of the Kapalua Bay Hotel, where you can enjoy live music nightly over cocktails and great views of the Pacific. ~ 1 Bay Drive; 808-669-5656.

A Hawaiian duo plays in the evenings at **The Lobby Lounge and Library** at the Ritz-Carlton, Kapalua. ~ 1 Ritz-Carlton Drive, Kapalua; 808-669-6200.

**BEACHES & PARKS**

**KAANAPALI RESORT BEACHES** The sprawling complex of Kaanapali hotels sits astride a beautiful white-sand beach that extends for three miles. Looking out on Lanai and Molokai, this is a classic palm-fringed strand. The entire area is heavily developed and crowded with tourists glistening in coconut oil. But it is an extraordinarily fine beach where the swimming is very good and the skindiving excellent around Black Rock at the Sheraton Maui. The beach has no facilities, but most of the resorts have public restrooms and there are restaurants nearby. ~ Take the public right-of-way to the beach from any of the Kaanapali resort hotels.

**HONOKOWAI BEACH PARK** Compared to the beaches fronting Kaanapali's nearby resorts, this is a bit disappointing. The large lawn is pleasant enough and the beach ample, with a reef that projects right to the shoreline. Still, the view of Molokai is awesome. In the shallow reef waters the swimming and snorkeling are good; surfing is nonexistent. Friendly to kids, the park features a playground, while the reef waters are ideal for youngsters to splash in. *Ulua* and threadfin are among the most frequent catches. Picnic tables, restrooms and showers are available. ~ Located north of Kaanapali in Honokowai on Lower Honoapiilani Road (which is the oceanfront section of Route 30).

It is near the sacred area around Black Rock that divers harvest precious black coral from an underwater shelf.

**NAPILI BAY** You'll find wall-to-wall condominiums along the small cove. There's a crowded but beautiful white-sand beach studded with palm trees and looking out on Molokai. Swimming and snorkeling are delightful and the surfing here is particularly good for beginners. ~ Located several miles north of Kaanapali, with rights-of-way to the beach from Lower Honoapiilani Road via Napili Place or Hui Drive.

**KAPALUA BEACH** This is the next cove over from Napili Bay. It's equally beautiful, but, sadly, has also suffered from the hands of developers. The crescent of white sand that lines Kapalua Bay is bounded on either end by rocky points and backdropped by a line of coconut trees and the Kapalua Bay Hotel. Swimming and snorkeling are excellent; beginners will be especially delighted by the multitude of colorful fish so close to the shore. ~ There's a right-of-way to the beach from Lower Honoapiilani Road near the Napili Kai Beach Club.

**D.T. FLEMING PARK** 🐚 🦞 🏃 ⛱ One of Maui's nicest beach parks, D. T. Fleming has a spacious white-sand beach and a rolling lawn shaded with palm and ironwood trees with a nice view of Molokai's rugged East End. Unfortunately, a major resort resides just uphill from the beach. Sometimes windy, the park is plagued by rough and dangerous surf during the winter. Use caution! You'll find good swimming and bodysurfing and fair snorkeling during the summer. There are also good breaks nearby at Little Makaha, named after the famous Oahu beach. For anglers the prime catches are *ulua* and *papio*. There are restrooms, a picnic area and showers. ~ Located at the Ritz-Carlton, Kapalua, about seven miles north of Kaanapali just off Honoapiilani Highway.

▼▼▼▼▼▼▼▼▼▼▼▼▼
# Northwest Maui

To escape from the crowds and commotion of the Kaanapali–Kapalua area and travel north on the Honoapiilani Highway is to journey from the ridiculous to the sublime. As you curve along the edge of the West Maui Mountains, en route around the side of the island to Kahului and Wailuku, you'll pass several hidden beaches that lie along an exotic and undeveloped shore. This is a region of the Valley Isle not frequented by the tourist crowd.

**SIGHTS**

Near the rocky beach and lush valley at **Honokohau Bay**, the Honoapiilani Highway (Route 30) becomes the Kahekili Highway (Route 340). This macadam track snakes high above the ocean, hugging the coastline. From the highway rises a series of multihued **sandstone cliffs** that seems alien to this volcanic region and creates a picturesque backdrop to the rocky shore.

*HIDDEN* ►

As the road continues, the scenery is some of the most magnificent on Maui. Down a dirt side road sits the rustic village of **Kahakuloa**. Nestled in an overgrown valley beside a deep blue bay, the community is protected by a solitary headland rising directly from the sea. Woodframe houses and churches, which appear ready to fall to the next gusting wind, are spotted throughout this enchanting area. Kahakuloa is cattle country, and you'll find that the villagers live and farm much as their forefathers did back when most of Maui was unclaimed terrain. It was from the shoreline near Kahakuloa that the Polynesian canoe *Hokulea* left on its famous voyage.

The road ascends again outside Kahakuloa. Opening below you, one valley after another falls seaward in a series of spine-backed ridges. Above the road, the mountain range rises toward its 5788-foot summit at Puu Kukui.

There are lush gulches farther along as the road descends into the plantation town of **Waihee**. Here rolling countryside, dotted with small farm houses, slopes from the roadside up to the foothills of the West Maui Mountains.

You're still on the Kahekili Highway, but now once again it really is a highway, a well-traveled road that leads toward Kahului. Located just northwest of town, a side road leads to two sacred spots. The first, **Halekii Heiau**, overlooking Kahului Bay and Iao Stream, dates from the 1700s. Today this temple, once as large as a football field, is little more than a stone heap. **Pihana Kalani Heiau**, a short distance away, was once a sacrificial temple.

Before driving this route, as well as the back road from Hana to Ulupalakua, remember that the car rental agencies probably don't insure you over these winding tracks. Many folks drive the

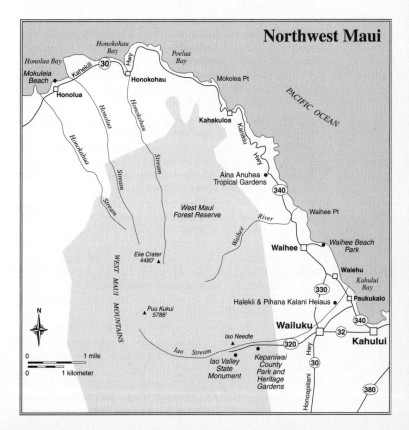

roads anyway, and I highly recommend that you explore them both if weather permits.

**BEACHES & PARKS**

**MOKULEIA BEACH OR SLAUGHTERHOUSE BEACH** 🏊 🏄
🚶 This lovely patch of white sand is bounded by cliffs and looks out on Molokai. Set at the end of a shallow cove, the beach is partially protected. Swimming, snorkeling and surfing are all good. This is part of a marine sanctuary so fishing is not permitted. There are no facilities here. ~ Take Honoapiilani Highway for exactly eight-tenths of a mile past D. T. Fleming Park. Park on the highway and take the steep path down about 100 yards to the beach.

HIDDEN ►

HIDDEN ►

**HONOLUA BAY** 🏊 🏄 🚶 ⚓ A rocky beach makes this cliff-rimmed bay unappealing for sunbathers, but there are rich coral deposits offshore and beautiful trees growing near the water. In winter you're likely to find crowds along the top of the cliff watching surfers work some of the finest breaks in all Hawaii: perfect tubes up to 15 feet. Swimming is good, but the bottom is rocky. Snorkeling is excellent, particularly on the west side of the bay. No fishing is allowed; this is part of a marine sanctuary. There are no facilities (and usually very few people) here. ~ Located about one-and-a-third miles north of D. T. Fleming Park on Honoapiilani Highway. The dirt road to the beach is open only to cars with boats in tow. Park with the other cars along the highway and follow the paths to the beach.

**HONOKOHAU BAY** 🏊 🏄 🚶 ⚓ This rocky beach is surrounded by cliffs. To the interior, a lush valley rises steadily into the folds of the West Maui Mountains. When the water is calm, swimming and snorkeling are good. The surf offers rugged, two- to twelve-foot breaks. Keep in mind the changeable nature of this wave action, since it can vary quickly from the gentle to the dangerous. Milkfish, *papio*, leatherback, *moano* and big-eyed scad are the principal species caught in these waters. ~ Located about six miles north of D. T. Fleming Park on Honoapiilani Highway.

▼ ▼ ▼ ▼ ▼ ▼ ▼ ▼ ▼

# Kihei–Wailea–Makena Area

Stretching from Maalaea Bay to Makena is a near continuous succession of beautiful beaches that make Kihei and Wailea favored resort destinations. Second only to the Lahaina–Kaanapali area in popularity, this seaside enclave rests in the rainshadow of Haleakala, which looms in the background. Maui's southeastern shore receives only ten inches of rain a year, making it the driest, sunniest spot on the island. It also experiences heavy winds, particularly in the afternoon, which sweep across the island's isthmus.

**SIGHTS**

Since the 1970s, this long, lean stretch of coast has become a developer's playground. **Kihei** in particular, lacking a master plan, has grown by accretion from a small local community into a haphazard collection of condominiums and mini-malls. It's an unattractive, six-mile strip lined by a golden beach.

Situated strategically along this beachfront are cement **pillboxes**, reminders of World War II's threatened Japanese invasion. Placed along Kihei Road just north of town, they are not far from **Kealia Pond National Wildlife Refuge**, a reserve of over 700 acres frequented by migratory waterfowl like green wing teals, mallards and pintails, as well as Hawaiian stilts and Hawaiian

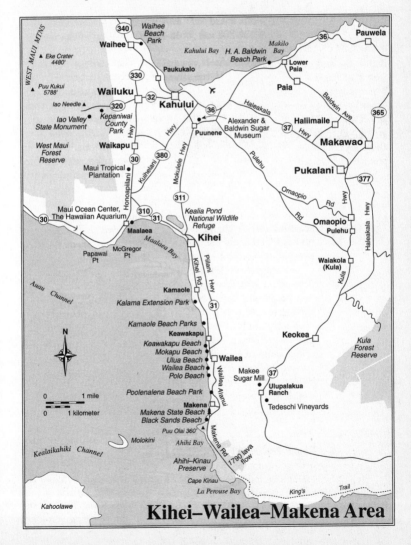

Kihei–Wailea–Makena Area

coots. You can take a nature walk here on dirt paths. Closed weekends. ~ The entrance is on Mokulele Highway near 6-mile marker; 808-875-1582.

To the south lies **Wailea**, an urbane answer to the random growth patterns of its scruffy neighbor. Wailea is a planned resort, all 1450 manicured acres of it. Here scrubland has been transformed into a flowering oasis that is home to top-class hotels and condos, as well as the required retinue of golf courses, tennis courts and overpriced shops. Like Kihei, it is blessed with beautiful beaches.

Home to some of Maui's most luxurious resorts, Wailea is the place to find Picasso originals, 50,000-square-foot spas and villas designed to keep a smile on the face of a high roller. Plantation- and Mediterranean-style architecture, accented by polished limestone tile and granite boulders imported from Mount Fuji, make this swank resort area an international retreat.

> Back in the days of California's gold rush, Maui found its own underground nuggets in potatoes: Countless bushels were grown in this area and shipped to a hungry San Francisco market. Today the crop is used to prepare Maui potato chips.

Connected by a mile-and-a-half-long ocean walk, and lining five crescent beaches, the resort's luxury properties comprise a self-contained retreat. Covering an area three times the size of Waikiki, Wailea has matured from a series of five crescent beaches separated by lava rock promontories into an elegant mix of hotels, condominiums, golf courses (there are three 18-hole championship links and two clubhouses), tennis court and water sports facilities. The Shops of Wailea is the latest addition to the resort's upscale infrastructure.

Adjacent to Wailea, the **Makena** area is a quiet, low-density destination with a single hotel (the Maui Prince) and several small condominiums sharing a full range of resort facilities, including two 18-hole golf courses. The setting, dominated by the upcountry slopes of Haleakala and the dry mix of *kiawe* and cactus that provide ground cover, is highlighted by the wide and luxurious sands of **Makena State Beach**, which I highly recommend visiting. Makena remains one of Maui's finest strands. A hippie hangout in the 1960s and early 1970s, it still retains a free-wheeling atmosphere, especially at nearby **Little Beach** (also known as Baby Beach), Maui's most famous nude beach. ~ Located along Makena Alanui about four miles beyond Wailea.

*HIDDEN ▶*

Past here the road gets rough as it presses south to **Ahihi–Kinau Preserve**. Encompassing over 2000 acres of land and ocean bottom, this preserve harbors an amazing array of marine life and contains the remains of an early Hawaiian fishing village. Almost 100 larval fish species and about two dozen species of stony coral have been found in this ecologically rich reserve. You can hike on a restored portion of the stone-lined Royal Road that in pre-contact times circled the island. The landscape of lava-scarred lowlands is dominated by the green upcountry pastures of Haleakala's mid-level slopes. This was the route of the annual Makahiki procession, when chiefs and their tax collectors made the rounds of the royal dominions, collecting praise and tribute.

The road continues on, bisecting the **1790 lava flow**, which resulted from Haleakala's last eruption. The flow created Cape Kinau, a thumb-shaped peninsula dividing Ahihi Bay and **La** ◄ *HIDDEN* **Perouse Bay**. The bay is named for the ill-starred French navigator, Jean-François de la Pérouse, who anchored here in 1786, the first Westerner to visit Maui. After a brief sojourn in this enchanting spot, he sailed off and was later lost at sea.

Hotels are rare in Kihei. And in Wailea, a hotel in anything less **LODGING** than an ultra-deluxe price range is a contradiction in terms.

The **Nona Lani Cottages**, with eight wooden cottages, provides a little relief. They're situated across busy Kihei Road from a white-sand beach. Each is a one-bedroom unit with lanai, all-electric kitchen and a living room capable of housing one or two extra sleepers. There's wall-to-wall carpeting and a shower-tub combination, plus TV and air conditioners in all bedrooms, but no phone. (Be forewarned: we've had complaints, so you might want to check it out first.) There is a four-night minimum from April 16 to December 15; seven-night minimum from December 16 to April 15. Rooms without kitchens also available; there is a three-night minimum. ~ 455 South Kihei Road, Kihei; 808-879-2497, 800-733-2688, fax 808-891-0273; www.nonalani cottages.com, e-mail nona@nonalanicottages.com. MODERATE.

Spread across 28 acres, the **Aston Maui Lu Resort** is tropically landscaped with palm trees and flowering plants. Within the grounds, which are across the street from a beach, you'll find a Maui-shaped pool and two tennis courts. The guest rooms are furnished in standard fashion and located in a series of interconnecting buildings with some accommodations on the beach. ~ 575 South Kihei Road, Kihei; 808-879-5881, 800-922-7866, fax 808-879-4627; www.astonhotels.com. DELUXE TO ULTRA-DELUXE.

The **Maui Coast Hotel** is a 265-room facility across the street from the beach. It's light, airy, modern and has a pool, outdoor jacuzzis, tennis courts and a cluster of nearby restaurants. There's poolside entertainment nightly. ~ 2259 South Kihei Road, Kihei; 808-874-6284, 800-895-6284, fax 808-875-4731; www.mauicoasthotel.com, e-mail jsoares@mauioceanfrontinn. com. DELUXE TO ULTRA-DELUXE.

Down the road at the **Best Western Maui Oceanfront Inn** you'll find a series of six buildings designed in mock-Hawaiian style and sandwiched between the highway and a white-sand beach. There are 71 rooms and one-bedroom suites, all attractively decorated and featuring air conditioning, television and refrigerator. There's also a workout facility. ~ 2980 South Kihei Road, Kihei; 808-879-7744, fax 808-874-0145; www.maui oceanfrontinn.com, e-mail jsoares@mauioceanfrontinn.com. DELUXE TO ULTRA-DELUXE.

The lushly landscaped **Four Seasons Resort Maui** is the ultimate among ultimate destinations. The only Maui resort we know to feature a trompe l'oeil artwork in the lobby, it's a windswept, Hawaiian palace–style complex set on a luxurious beach. Furnished with wicker and rattan, most of the 380 plantation-style guest rooms offer ocean views. Casablanca fans, tropical plants and marbletop vanities add to the comfort. Louvered doors open onto spacious lanais. Reflecting pools, waterfalls and fountains give the public areas an elegant tropical air. ~ 3900 Wailea Alanui, Wailea; 808-874-8000, 800-334-6284, fax 808-874-2244; www.fourseasons.com. ULTRA-DELUXE.

**PollyMakena** is a pair of oceanfront villas just a hop, skip and a jump from Makena Beach. Ideal for families or small groups, the larger villa has three bedrooms and a loft; the smaller unit has two bedrooms and sleeps up to five people. Beautifully appointed, they're filled with a fascinating assortment of treasures collected by the charming owner, Parks Hay. A hot tub and hammock surrounded by tiki torches adorn the front yard and create a small island of relaxation; a teeming tidepool fronts one of the complexes. PollyMakena is set on "Wedding Cove," so you're bound to witness at least one ceremony during your stay, adding to the romance of this special place. ~ For reservations contact Koolau Vacation Services, P.O. Box 641, Haiku, HI 96708; 808-573-5669, 866-720-7898, fax 708-575-1764; www. koolauvacations.com. ULTRA-DELUXE.

### SNORKELER'S HAVEN

Anywhere along this coastline you can gaze out at **Molokini**, a crescent-shaped islet that is a favorite spot among snorkelers. Resting in the Alalakeihi Channel three miles west of Maui, it measures a scant 19 acres in area and rises 165 feet above sea level. The island is actually a tuff cone created by volcanic eruptions deep underwater that solidified into a hard substance called tuff. Black coral divers harvested the surrounding waters until the 1970s. According to Hawaiian legend, Molokini was created when the volcano goddess Pele cut a rival lover—a lizard—in two, turning the tail into Molokini and the head into the cinder cone near Makena Beach.

Its remote location makes the **Maui Prince Hotel** an unusual find. Built around a courtyard adorned with lush tropical gardens and lily ponds, the 310-room establishment rewards those willing to drive a few extra minutes to Maui's southernmost retreat. Here you're likely to be lulled to sleep by the sound of the surf. Decorated with heliconia and bougainvillea, the rooms and suites open onto lanais. This V-shaped hotel is next door to two of Maui's top golf courses. ~ 5400 Makena Alanui, Makena; 808-874-1111, 800-321-6284, fax 808-879-8763; www.prince resortshawaii.com, e-mail reservationshphw@hiprince.com. ULTRA-DELUXE.

**CONDOS**

**Leilani Kai** is a cozy eight-unit apartment hotel located right on the beach. Studio apartments are $85 double; one-bedroom units are $110 or $115 double; two bedrooms will run you $125 for one to four people. ~ 1226 Uluniu Street, Kihei; 808-879-2606, fax 808-879-0241; www.lkresort.com, e-mail info@lkresort.com.

Oceanside one-bedroom apartments at **Kihei Kai** are $110 to $135 double ($100 to $125 from mid-April to mid-December). Each has television, phone, full kitchen and lanai. Closed Sunday. ~ 61 North Kihei Road, Kihei; 808-891-0780, 888-778-7717, fax 808-891-9403; www.kiheirentals.com, e-mail kihei kai@maui.net.

**Sunseeker Resort** is a small, personalized place where oceanview studios with kitchenettes start at $75 double and one-bedrooms from $99 double. Add $10 for each additional person. ~ 551 South Kihei Road, Kihei; 808-879-1261, 800-532-6284, fax 808-874-3877; www.mauisunseeker.com, e-mail info@mauisun seeker.com.

A highrise condo, **Mana Kai Maui Resort** has "hotel units" that consist of the extra bedroom and bath from a two-bedroom apartment ($280 to $300 in peak season). One-bedroom units with kitchens are $220 to $240. The condo has a beachfront location as well as an adjoining restaurant and bar. ~ 2960 South Kihei Road, Kihei; 808-879-1561, 800-367-5242, fax 808-879-7825; www.crhmaui.com, e-mail res@crhmaui.com.

**Lihi Kai** has nine beach cottages with full kitchens, all renting for $150 single or double. To be sure of getting a cottage, it's best to make reservations far in advance. ~ 2121 Iliili Road, Kihei; 808-879-2335, fax 808-879-0358.

Across the street from a beach park, **Kamaole Beach Royale** is a seven-story condo with one-bedroom apartments for $105 double; two-bedroom units, $130 to $145 double; three-bedroom units, up to $170. Add $10 for each additional person. No credit cards. ~ 2385 South Kihei Road, Kihei; 808-879-3131, 800-421-3661, fax 808-879-9163; www.mauikbr.com, e-mail davi@aloha.com.

**GAY LODGING**  For gay-friendly accommodations, you can stay at the condos or cottage managed by **Maui Suncoast Realty**. Most condos have air conditioning; all have cable TV, ceiling fans and kitchen and laundry facilities. Prices range roughly from $80 to $200. ~ Maui Suncoast Realty, 3134 Hoomua, Kihei, HI 96753; 808-874-1048, 800-800-8608, fax 808-879-6932; www. mauisuncoast.com, e-mail info@mauosuncoast.com.

Another booking agency with both a straight and gay clientele, **Andrea's Maui Oceanfront Condos** has one- two- and three bedroom oceanfront condos surrounded by lush gardens. Amenities include tennis courts, pool, jacuzzi, sauna and putting green. ~ P.O. Box 10799, Truckee, CA 96162; 530-582-8703, 800-289-1522, fax 310-399-0407; www.mauicondos.com, e-mail andrea@mauicondos.com. MODERATE TO ULTRA-DELUXE.

## DINING

HIDDEN ▶

Ever since condominiums mushroomed from its white sands, Kihei has no longer qualified as a poor person's paradise. Yet for inexpensive Korean and local food, there's **Young's Kitchen**. Squeezed into a corner of Kihei Center (next to Longs Drugs) and furnished with plastic seats, it's not much on atmosphere. But it's hard to beat their cheap barbecued ribs, grilled chicken and beef marinated in Korean sauce, *katsu* chicken or Korean soups. A good place for a takeout meal. ~ Kihei Center, 1215 South Kihei Road, Kihei; 808-874-8454. BUDGET.

Parked in the same complex is **Stella Blues Café & Delicatessen**, where you can dine indoors or outside beneath a sidewalk umbrella. The bill of fare includes vegetarian dishes, pastas and sandwiches. Breakfast, lunch and dinner. ~ Azeka Place II, 1279 South Kihei Road, Kihei; 808-874-3779. MODERATE.

If you'd like something from Southeast Asia, drop by **Royal Thai Cuisine**. Here the chairs are wood and the menu includes *dozens* of selections such as crab legs, chili shrimp, cashew chicken or seafood combinations. No lunch on Sunday. ~ Azeka Place Shopping Center, 1280 South Kihei Road, Kihei; 808-874-0813. BUDGET.

**Azeka's Market Snack Shop** runs a take-out window. For atmosphere there's a parking lot, but for food there's a fair choice, with hamburgers and plate lunches priced low. Breakfast and lunch only. ~ Azeka Place Shopping Center, 1280 South Kihei Road, Kihei; 808-879-0611. BUDGET.

What makes **Thailand Cuisine** stand out among the island's Thai restaurants is the ambience. Lush green plants, hand-woven textiles and hand-embroidered silks are everywhere. The dishes are an enticing combination of traditional Thai favorites made with island produce. The chef uses an imaginative blend of spices, herbs, roots and leaves to enhance the natural flavors of the key ingredients, like chicken, beef or shrimp. The Vegetarian

Lovers selections are actually vegan. No lunch on Sunday; dinner is served nightly. ~ 1819 South Kihei Road, Kihei; 808-875-0839, fax 808-874-8961. MODERATE.

Bada-boom, bada-bing, it's a beautiful thing! (Or so Brooklynites say.) Any way you say it, **Bada Bing Restaurant & Rat Pack Lounge** is a great find. Tucked into the colorful ramshackle buildings of Kihei's Kalama Village, this establishment's interior is spacious, with an outdoor lanai under huge shade trees. Anything Italian is hot on Maui these days, and their menu reflects this trend. House specialties like chicken marsala or piccata are good choices, as is the shrimp scampi. Antipasti offerings include spinach, artichoke and roasted garlic dip with croutons. After dinner, swing into the Rat Pack Lounge. No breakfast Monday through Friday. ~ 1945 South Kihei Road, Kihei; 808-875-0188, fax 808-875-4508. MODERATE.

**Surfside Spirits and Deli** has a take-out delicatessen serving sandwiches, salads and slaw, as well as plate lunches. ~ 1993 South Kihei Road, Kihei; 808-879-1385. BUDGET.

**The Sports Page Grill & Bar** offers up salads and sandwiches. The hot dogs—like the Boston Red Sox version topped with baked beans and cheese—pay tribute to baseball teams. The sandwiches immortalize famous sports stars. There's the Bonnie Blair ham, Yogi Berra corned beef and cheese and Fred Couples Par 3 club. ~ 2411 South Kihei Road, Kihei; 808-879-0602, fax 808-874-9078. BUDGET.

For genuine local-style tastes in a clean, inviting diner, stop by **Da Kitchen Express** in the Rainbow Mall. They offer a variety of dishes that represent the different ethnicities that make up the population of Hawaii. Plate lunches, which are composed of a hot entrée, two scoops of white rice and macaroni, potato or green salad, are the way to go. Teriyaki beef and chicken *katsu* are favorites, as are the traditionally Hawaiian dishes *laulau* and *kalua* pork. Breakfast, lunch and dinner. ~ 2439 South Kihei Road, Kihei; 808-875-7782. BUDGET.

◄ HIDDEN

## MAKENA LANDING

Now a peaceful cove, **Makena Landing**, located on Makena Road, was once a port as busy as Lahaina. During the California gold rush, prevailing winds prompted many San Francisco–bound ships coming up from Cape Horn to resupply here. Fresh fruits and vegetables, badly needed by the would-be miners, were traded in abundance. Later local ranchers delivered their cattle to market by tethering them to longboats and swimming the animals out to steamers waiting just offshore from Makena Landing.

At **Canton Chef** the cuisine ranges from roast duck to beef with oyster sauce. This traditional Chinese restaurant offers almost 100 different choices including a selection of spicy Szechuan dishes. ~ Kamaole Shopping Center, 2463 South Kihei Road, Kihei; 808-879-1988. BUDGET TO MODERATE.

Did you say Greek? No problem. Located nearby is the **Greek Bistro** with a full selection of Mediterranean dishes such as moussaka, souvlaki, lamb kebabs and dolmas. Dinner only. ~ Kai Nani Village, 2511 South Kihei Road, Kihei; 808-879-9330. MODERATE TO DELUXE.

The **Five Palms Beach Grill**'s open-air views of the coast combined with a Hawaii Regional–style menu draw a lively crowd that toasts and dines its way through sunset. The casual atmosphere belies the sophisticated cuisine, which includes dishes such as wok-fried *opakapaka* with curry sauce and jasmine rice and Pulehu rack of lamb. Five Palms is also open for breakfast and lunch. ~ Mana Kai Maui Resort, 2960 South Kihei Road, Kihei; 808-879-2607, fax 808-875-4803; www.fivepalmsrestaurant.com, e-mail fivepalmsres@cs.com. ULTRA-DELUXE.

At **Hana Gion** you can choose between tableside *teppanyaki* cooking or a private booth. Built in Japan, broken down and shipped to Maui for reassembly, this beautiful restaurant in the Renaissance Wailea Beach Resort was created with the guidance of one of Kyoto's leading restaurant-owning families. Specialties such as tempura, *shabu-shabu* and sukiyaki are served by kimono-clad waitresses. There's also a popular sushi bar on the premises. It's a good idea to call before going. Dinner only. ~ 3550 Wailea Alanui, Wailea; 808-879-4900, fax 808-874-5370. ULTRA-DELUXE.

**Tommy Bahama's Tropical Café** is like walking into a 1940s movie set on a South Seas island. You'll find soft green wainscoting, bold tropical fabrics and fresh tropical flowers beneath gently rotating ceiling fans—and an oceanview! An open-air lanai invites relaxation, especially with a cocktail from the

**AUTHOR FAVORITE**

A perennial favorite that keeps folks coming back because the food is so *ono* is **Alexander's Fish, Chicken & Chips**, which faces Kihei Road in Kalama Village. It's a casual, open-air café that serves savory, lightly battered island fish. Choose from ahi, *ono* or mahimahi, with cole slaw and french fries or rice. Chicken and ribs are also on the menu. Take-out is a plus for condo vacationers. ~ 1913 South Kihei Road, Kihei; 808-874-0788, fax 808-875-0535. BUDGET TO MODERATE.

Bungalow Bar. The menu is more of a tribute to the restaurant's Florida roots. There are Caribbean-style names for the dishes, such as Rum Runners' Fruit Salad, Mama Bahama's Jerk Chicken Sandwich and Salmon St. Croix. But the quality of the cuisine is excellent, and the desserts are to die for. ~ 3750 Wailea Alanui, Wailea; 808-875-9983, fax 808-875-1398; www.tommy bahama.com. ULTRA-DELUXE.

A fun and casual restaurant at The Shops at Wailea is **Cheeseburger, Mai Tais & Rock-n-Roll**. It's a sister restaurant to Lahaina's Cheeseburgers in Paradise. Along with a familiar decor of tropical prints, bamboo and coconut wood, this Cheeseburger also sports a Hawaiian memorabilia and logo shop. The owners think they provide the best cheeseburger on the island and I have to agree—it's juicy and delectable, and comes with sautéed onions on a sesame-seed bun. The "Beef-Less in Wailea" veggie burgers are worth a try, too. ~ 3750 Wailea Alanui, Wailea; 808-874-8990, fax 808-875-6640; www.cheeseburgerland.com. MODERATE.

**Café Kula** at the Grand Wailea Resort has a terrace dining area that offers light, healthy breakfast, lunch and dinner choices. Start the day with a breakfast burrito, vegetable quiche, muesli or pastries. For lunch try the garden burger or caesar salad served with chicken or ahi. ~ 3850 Wailea Alanui, Wailea; 808-875-1234, fax 808-874-2478. BUDGET TO MODERATE.

**Hakone** is the kind of restaurant you'd expect to find at any self-respecting Japanese-owned resort. The shoji screens, Japanese fans and a sushi bar are authentic; the ocean views are entirely Hawaiian. Start with tempura or miso soup. Entrées include sashimi, sukiyaki and New York steak. Better yet, go on Monday night when they have the Japanese buffet and try a little bit of everything. Outstanding. Reservations are required. Dinner only. Closed Sunday. ~ Maui Prince Hotel, 5400 Makena Alanui, Makena; 808-874-1111, fax 808-879-8763. DELUXE TO ULTRA-DELUXE.

A tranquil oceanfront setting makes the **Prince Court** the place to enjoy Hawaiian regional cuisine. At this signature restaurant in the Maui Prince Hotel, you can choose from a seasonally changing menu that may begin with *panko*-crusted crab cakes, oysters on the half shell or warm lobster and grapefruit salad. The bill of fare continues with such dishes as roasted duckling with Chinese plum sauce or seafood mixed grill (tiger shrimp, catch of the day, lobster and scallops). Tropical foliage add to the elegance. Dinner only except for Sunday brunch. ~ 5400 Makena Alanui, Makena; 808-874-1111. DELUXE TO ULTRA-DELUXE.

**Foodland** is a large supermarket open 24 hours a day. ~ Kihei Town Center, South Kihei Road, Kihei; 808-879-9350. **GROCERIES**

**Star Market,** open all day except between 2 a.m. and 5 a.m., has a large selection of groceries. ~ 1310 South Kihei Road, Kihei; 808-879-5871.

**Azeka's Market** up the road is often price-competitive. Open from 7:30 a.m. to 5 p.m. ~ Azeka Place Shopping Center, 1280 South Kihei Road, Kihei; 808-879-0611.

For healthful items, try **Hawaiian Moons Natural Foods,** which also has a salad bar. Open 8 a.m. to 9 p.m. Monday through Saturday and 8 a.m. to 7 p.m. on Sunday. ~ 2411 South Kihei Road, Kihei; 808-875-4356.

**SHOPPING**    Shopping in Kihei is centered in the malls and doesn't hold a lot of promise. You'll find swimwear shops and an assortment of other clothing outlets, but nothing with style and panache. Foremost among the malls is **Azeka Place Shopping Center,** which stretches along the 1200 South block of Kihei Road.

You're likely to find a bargain or two at the **Maui Clothing Company's Outlet Store** if resortwear and Maui logowear are your thing. There's plenty to choose from. ~ Kihei Gateway Plaza, 362 Huku Li'i Place #106, Kihei; 808-879-0374.

**Kalama Village Shopping Center,** an open-air market with about 20 vendors, is a funky counterpoint to Kihei's other shopping spots. Here you'll find T-shirts, shells, jewelry and souvenirs sold at cut-rate prices by local people. If you're a Kona coffee fan, check out the **Bad Ass Coffee Company** (808-877-5477). There are flavorful blends, pure mild Kona and hearty roasts. ~ 1941 South Kihei Road, Kihei.

If you don't find what you're searching for at any of these addresses, there are countless other strip malls along Kihei Road.

**The Shops at Wailea** is a center of elegance in the already posh Wailea resort. With the look of a Mediterranean seaside village, complete with water fountains, the center is home to several shop-'til-you-drop possibilities. The Shops are comprised of two wings at two levels, and the storefronts lining the East Wing parallel the likes of Rodeo Drive and 5th Avenue. Notable jewelry stores include the Maui-based **Bernard Passman Gallery.** Speaking of art, Wailea boasts galleries galore—**Lahaina Galleries, Dolphin Galleries, Ki'i Gallery, Wyland Galleries, Elan Vital Galleries** and **Celebrités.** Complimentary shuttles run from Wailea hotels to The Shops every 30 minutes. ~ 3750 Wailea Alanui, Wailea; 808-891-6770.

A wonderful place to buy high-quality handicrafts is **Hana Ka Lima,** a market held in the lobby of the Wailea Marriott, an Outrigger Resort every Friday from 9 a.m. to 2 p.m. Artists and craftspeople from around the island sell a variety of crafts including stone carvings, paintings, bead jewelry, and scrimshaw. Some artists even demonstrate their skills. ~ 3700 Wailea Alanui, Wailea; 808-879-1922.

The Grand Wailea Resort Hotel & Spa is home to a $30 million art collection. At the **NaPua Gallery**, you can see original Warhol paintings and some Picasso lithographs. Available for purchase are paintings, mixed-media works and sculpture by leading contemporary artists. ~ 3860 Wailea Alanui, Suite 210, Wailea; 808-874-0510, fax 808-874-2522; www.napua gallery.com, e-mail napuagallery@earthlink.net.

At **Mandalay Imports** you'll find Thai silk, designer dresses, lacquer chests and Chinese opera coats. This shop in the Four Seasons Resort at Wailea also sells innovative necklaces and ceramic vases, and carries fabrics by Anne Namba, a famous Honolulu designer. ~ 3900 Wailea Alanui, Wailea; 808-874-5111.

At night, **Hapa's** hosts an upbeat crowd. There's a deejay nightly **NIGHTLIFE** and live music Monday and Friday. Tuesday is gay night. Cover. ~ Lipoa Center, 41 East Lipoa Street, Kihei; 808-879-9001.

Get your laugh on at the **Rat Pack Lounge** with their Friday-night comedy shows. ~ 1945 South Kihei Road, Kihei; 808-875-0188.

The **Sunset Terrace Lounge** is a pleasant spot to see live Hawaiian entertainment when day turns to night. It's located at the Renaissance Wailea Beach Resort. ~ 3550 Wailea Alanui, Wailea; 808-879-4900.

Live Hawaiian entertainment is a nightly feature at the **Kumu Bar and Grill** in the Wailea Marriott, an Outrigger Resort. Come for dinner or have a drink poolside as you enjoy an appealing island show. ~ 3700 Wailea Alanui, Wailea; 808-879-1922.

> Morning is the best time to go to the beach in Wailea and especially in Kihei. Later in the day, the wind picks up.

Leave it to the Grand Wailea Resort Hotel & Spa—the accent's on Grand—to have Maui's most elaborate high-tech nightclub. **Tsunami** cost $4 million to build and has 20 video monitors and a 14-foot-wide karaoke screen. Open Friday and Saturday only. Cover. ~ 3850 Wailea Alanui, Wailea; 808-875-1234.

A venue at the Four Seasons Resort Maui at Wailea is **Ferraros**, where live Italian music is perfectly timed for enjoying a sunset drink. ~ 3900 Wailea Alanui, Wailea; 808-874-8000.

There is Hawaiian entertainment nightly at the **Molokini Lounge**. ~ Maui Prince Hotel, 5400 Makena Alanui, Makena; 808-874-1111.

**KIHEI BEACH** This narrow, palm-fringed beach that runs from Maalaea Bay to Kihei can be seen from several points along Kihei Road and is accessible from the highway. The entire stretch is dotted with small parks and picnic areas and doesn't actually go by a specific name. There are buildings and numerous condominiums along this strip, but few large crowds on the

**BEACHES & PARKS**

beach. Beach joggers take note: You can run for miles along this unbroken strand, but watch for heavy winds in the afternoon. Shallow weed-ridden waters make for poor swimming and only fair snorkeling (you'll find better at Kamaole beaches). For those anglers in the crowd, bonefish, *papio*, mullet, goatfish, *ulua*, *moano* and mountain bass are all caught here. There are picnic tables and restrooms at Kihei Memorial Park, which is midway along the beach.

**KALAMA EXTENSION PARK** This is a long, broad park (36 acres) that has an ample lawn but very little beach. Rather than lapping along the sand, waves wash up against a stone seawall. Backdropped by Haleakala, Kalama has stunning views of West Maui, Lanai and Kahoolawe. The in-line skating rink features a view so compelling you could easily lose concentration and run into a fellow skater. This park is an excellent place for a picnic but, before you pack your lunch, remember that it, like all Kihei's beaches, is swept by afternoon winds. For surfers there are summer breaks over a coral reef; left and right slides. Snorkeling and fishing are fair; swimming is poor. There are picnic areas, restrooms, a shower and tennis courts. ~ Located on South Kihei Road, across from Kihei Town Center.

**KAMAOLE BEACH PARKS (I, II AND III)** Strung like beads along the Kihei shore are these three beautiful beaches. Their white sands are fringed with grass and studded with trees. With Haleakala in the background, they all offer magnificent views of the West Maui Mountains, Lanai and Kahoolawe—and all are windswept in the afternoon. Each has picnic areas, restrooms, lifeguard and showers. Swimming is very good on all three beaches. The best snorkeling is near the rocks ringing Kamaole III. Goatfish is the main catch for anglers. ~ Located on South Kihei Road near Kihei Town Center.

**KEAWAKAPU BEACH** Ho hum, yet another beautiful white-sand beach . . . . Like other nearby parks, Keawakapu has marvelous views of the West Maui Mountains and Lanai, but is plagued by afternoon winds. The half-mile-long beach is bordered on both ends by lava points. The swimming is good, but Keawakapu is not as well protected as the Kamaole beaches. Snorkelers explore the area around the rocks. The fishing is excellent. There are no facilities except showers. ~ Located on South Kihei Road between Kihei and Wailea.

**MOKAPU AND ULUA** These are two crescent-shaped beaches fringed with palms and looking out toward Lanai and Kahoolawe. Much of their natural beauty has been spoiled by the nearby hotels and condominiums. The beaches have landscaped miniparks and are popular with bodysurfers. Swimming and snorkeling are both good; restrooms and a shower are avail-

*Above: Madame Pele spits fire into the Pacific Ocean on the Big Island.*

*Below: Maui's "House of the Sun," Haleakala, is the world's largest dormant volcano.*

Above: The nene, or Hawaiian goose, is the state bird.

Left: Ancient rock carvings adorn the Puako Petroglyph Field on the Big Island's Kohala Coast.

Below: Colorful anthurium grow in abundance on the Big Island.

*Above: Mahaulepu Beach on Kauai.*

*Left: Niihau, the Forbidden Island.*

*Below: Molokai's historic Kalaupapa Peninsula.*

*Above: Makena State Beach on Maui at sunset.*

*Right: The "Grand Canyon of the Pacific," Kauai's Waimea Canyon.*

One of Lanai's sacred spots: the Garden of the Gods.

*Left: Queen Liliuokalani, Hawaii's last monarch, stands on the grounds of Iolani Palace, where she was imprisoned.*

*Below: Iolani Palace is the only royal residence on United States soil.*

*Above: The dense tropical forest near Hilo on the Big Island of Hawaii.*

*Inset: Hawaiian* keiki.

*Above: Biking down Maui's volcano, Haleakala.*

*Left: Lahaina's celebration of the canoes.*

*Below: Snorkeling in Hanauma Bay, Oahu.*

able. ~ Located in Wailea on Makena Alanui, adjacent to the Renaissance Wailea Beach Resort.

**WAILEA BEACH** 🏊 🤿 Another lovely white-sand strip, once fringed with *kiawe* trees, is now dominated by two very large, very upscale resorts, part of the ultramodern Wailea development here. Swimming is good (the beach is also popular with bodysurfers) and so is snorkeling. Restrooms and showers are available. ~ Located on Makena Alanui in Wailea between the Grand Wailea Resort and the Four Seasons Resort at Wailea.

> Maui's sands run white, gold, salt and pepper, green—even garnet— depending on what Madame Pele decided to spew years ago.

**POLO BEACH** 🏊 🤿 Though not quite as attractive as Wailea Beach, Polo Beach still has a lot to offer. There's a bountiful stretch of white sand and great views of Kahoolawe and Molokini. The beach, popular with bodysurfers, has a landscaped minipark with picnic tables, restrooms and showers. Swimming is good here and the snorkeling is excellent. ~ Located off Makena Alanui on Kaukahi Road in Wailea, adjacent to the Kea Lani Hotel.

**POOLENALENA (OR PAIPU) BEACH PARK** 🏊 🤿 🎣 Once known by locals as Chang's Beach, this is a lovely white-sand strand that has been transformed into an attractive facility frequented by people from throughout the area. The beach has restrooms; unfortunately it also has as its neighbor the Maui Prince Hotel. Swimming is good, snorkeling fair and fishing very good—many species are caught here. ~ Located on Makena Alanui about one-and-one-fifth mile before (north of) the Maui Prince Hotel.

**BLACK SANDS BEACH OR ONEULI BEACH** 🏊 🤿 🎣 Black ◄ *HIDDEN* Sands is a long, narrow, salt-and-pepper beach located just north of Red Hill, a shoreline cinder cone. Fringed with *kiawe* trees, this stretch of beach is less attractive but more secluded than nearby Makena and much rockier. Facilities are nonexistent. Swimming and snorkeling are both fair, but the fishing is very good, many species being caught here. ~ Located on Makena Alanui, four-fifths mile past the Maui Prince Hotel. Turn right on the dirt road at the north end of Red Hill, then bear right and go one-third mile to the beach.

▲ There is unofficial camping but it's illegal and not recommended.

**MAKENA STATE BEACH** 🏊 Much more than a beach, Makena is an institution. Over the years, it's been a countercultural gathering place. There are even stories about rock stars jamming here during Makena's heyday in the early 1970s. Once a hideaway for hippies, the beach today is increasingly popular with mainstream tourists. So far, in my mind, this long, wide corridor of white sand curving south from Red Hill is still the most beautiful beach on Maui. There are toilets. ~ From Wailea Shopping Village, go about four-and-one-half miles south on Makena Alanui. Turn right into the parking lot.

HIDDEN ▶    **LITTLE BEACH (PUU OLAI BEACH OR "BABY BEACH")** 🏖 🦀 This pretty stretch of white sand next to Makena Beach, just across Red Hill, is a nude beach. It's also popular with the island's gay crowd. But if you go nude here or at Makena, watch out for police; they regularly bust nudists. Swimming is good (bodysurfing is especially good here) and you can snorkel near the rocks at the north end of the beach. The fishing is fair, though access is difficult. Beware of strong currents. There are no facilities. ~ Follow Makena Alanui for about four-and-one-half miles south from Wailea Shopping Village. Watch for Red Hill, the large cinder cone on your right. Just past Red Hill, turn right into the parking lot for Makena Beach. From here a path leads over Red Hill to Little Beach.

▲ Camping, though unofficial, is very popular here, but beware of thieves.

▼▼▼▼▼▼▼▼▼▼▼▼▼▼▼
## Kahului–Wailuku Area

The island's commercial, civic and population centers are located in the adjoining towns of Kahului and Wailuku. With no clear dividing place, these two municipalities seem at first glance to be "twin towns." They drift into one another as you climb uphill from Kahului Harbor toward the mountains. Kahului is significantly younger than its neighbor, however, and focuses its daily life around commerce. Maui's main airport is here, together with a skein of shopping malls and a few hotels that line a blue-collar waterfront. Wailuku presents a more rolling terrain and is the seat of government for Maui County.

SIGHTS    **Kahului,** with its bustling harbor and busy shopping complexes, offers little to the sightseer. The piers along the waterfront, lined with container-cargo ships and weekly cruise ships, are the embarkation point for Maui's sugar and pineapple crops. Established as a sugar town more than a century ago, Kahului has a commercial feel about it.

Coming from the airport along Kaahumanu Avenue (Route 32), you can stop and wander through **Kanaha Pond Wildlife Sanctuary.** Once a royal fishpond, this is now an important bird refuge, especially for the rare Hawaiian stilt and Hawaiian coot. There are two one-mile loop roads through the reserve (closed during breeding season, April through August); a permit from the State Division of Forestry is required to hike the trails. The observation area is open year-round.

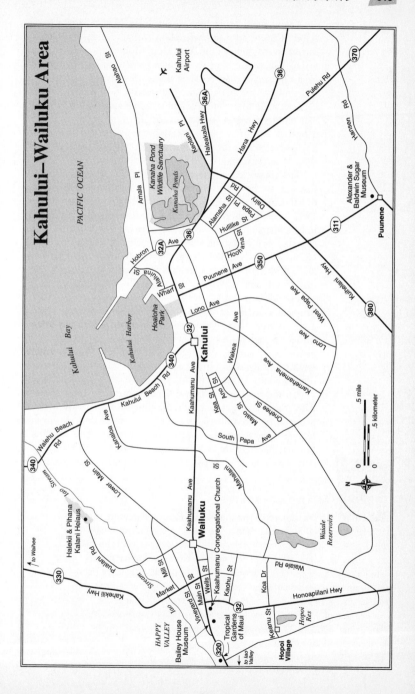

**Kahului–Wailuku Area**

The highway leads uphill to **Wailuku**, Maui's administrative center. Older and more interesting than Kahului, Wailuku sits astride the foothills of the West Maui Mountains at the entrance to Iao Valley. A mix of woodframe plantation houses and suburban homes, it even boasts a multi-story civic building. For a short tour of the aging woodfront quarter, take a right on Market Street and follow it several blocks to **Happy Valley**. This former red-light district still retains the charm, if not the action, of a bygone era. Here you'll discover narrow streets and tinroof houses framed by the sharply rising, deeply creased face of the West Maui Mountains.

The county government buildings reside along High Street. Just across the road rests picturesque **Kaahumanu Congregational Church**. Queen Kaahumanu attended services here in 1832 when the church was a grass shack, and requested that the first permanent church be named after her. Now Maui's oldest church, this grand stone-and-plaster structure was constructed in 1876, and has been kept in excellent condition for its many visitors. With a lofty white spire, it is the area's most dramatic manmade landmark.

Bounded on both sides by the sharp walls of Iao Valley, **Tropical Gardens of Maui** encompasses four densely planted acres of fruit trees, orchids and flowering plants. Iao Stream rushes through the property, which offers garden paths and a lily pond. Closed Sunday. Admission. ~ 200 Iao Road; 808-244-3085; www.tropicalgardensofmaui.com, e-mail info@tropicalgardens ofmaui.com.

Up the road at **Kepaniwai County Park and Heritage Gardens**, there's an outdoor cultural showcase to discover. Backdropped by Iao Valley's adze-like peaks, this adult playground features lovely Japanese and Chinese monuments as well as a taro patch. There are arched bridges, a pool and an Oriental garden. The houses of Hawaii's many cultural groups are repre-

**sights**

**AUTHOR FAVORITE**

In Wailuku, you'll find the **Bailey House Museum**, run by the Maui Historical Society. Lodged in the dwelling of a former missionary, the displays include 19th-century Hawaiian artifacts, remnants from the early sugar cane industry and period pieces from the missionary years. This stone-and-plaster house (started in 1833) has walls 20 inches thick and beams fashioned from hand-hewn sandalwood. Together with an adjoining seminary building, it harkens back to Wailuku's days as an early center of Western culture. Closed Sunday. Admission. ~ 2375-A Main Street; 808-244-3326; www.mauimuseum.org, e-mail baileyh@ aloha.net.

sented by a Hawaiian grass hut, New England saltbox (complete with white picket fence), Filipino bamboo house and a Portuguese villa. On this site in 1790 Kamehameha's forces overwhelmed the army of a Maui chief in a battle so terrible that the corpses blocking Iao Stream gave Kepaniwai ("damming of the waters") and Wailuku ("bloody river") their names.

After exploring Kepaniwai County Park and Heritage Gardens, continue up to the **Hawaii Nature Center**, situated on the edge of Iao Valley, off the gateway to Iao Valley State Monument, features an interactive nature museum designed for adults as well as children. The Nature Center also hosts hikes every day into the Iao Valley, complete with environmental educators. Admission. ~ 875 Iao Valley Road; 808-244-6500, fax 808-244-6525; www.hawaiinaturecenter.org.

◄ HIDDEN

Uphill at the **John F. Kennedy Profile** you'll see Hawaii's answer to Mt. Rushmore, chiseled by nature. Ironically, this geologic formation, which bears an uncanny resemblance to the former president, was never noticed until after his assassination.

◄ HIDDEN

**Iao Valley State Monument** (808-984-8109), surrounded by those same moss-mantled cliffs, provides an excellent view of **Iao Needle**, a single spire that rises to a point 1200 feet above the valley (and 2250 feet above sea level). With the possible exception of Haleakala Crater, this awesome peak is Maui's most famous landmark. A basalt core that has withstood the ravages of erosion, the "Needle" and mist-filled valley have long been a place of pilgrimage for Hawaiians. Be sure to explore the paths from the parking lot that lead across Iao Stream and up to a vista point. Appreciate your visit here: In ancient times the sacred area around the Iao Valley, which translates to "Valley of Dawning Inspiration" or "Supreme Light," was off limits to commoners. When you take a walk through the area you will understand why it is so precious for Hawaiians.

The hotel strip in the harbor town of Kahului lies along the beach on Kahului Bay.

**LODGING**

The **Maui Seaside Hotel** consists of two separate complexes sitting beside each other along Kaahumanu Avenue (Route 32). There is a pool, restaurant and lounge. Rooms in the older poolside wing are a bit less expensive: clean, but lacking in decorative flair, the surroundings are quite adequate. Just a few well-spent dollars more places you in a larger, more attractive room in a newer complex, which has more upscale appointments. Both facilities feature phones, TVs, refrigerators and air conditioning. Some include kitchenettes. Ask about discounts. ~ 100 West Kaahumanu Avenue, Kahului; 808-877-3311, 800-560-5552, fax 808-877-4618; www.mauiseasidehotel.com, e-mail info@maui seasidehotel.com. MODERATE.

The nearby **Maui Beach Hotel**, with 147 air-conditioned guest rooms done in tropical decor, are about as inexpensive as things get on Maui. While conveniently located in Kahului, it is not your made-in-paradise setting, with "oceanfront" meaning the waters of Kahului Harbor. The grounds are appealingly studded with palms, and there is a pleasant pool area with a small adjacent beach, plus two restaurants and a sundries and snack shop. The attitude is island-style friendly. ~ 170 Kaahumanu Avenue, Kahului; 808-986-8095, 888-649-3222, fax 808-242-0865. MODERATE TO DELUXE.

**Aloha North Shore Hostel** is another clean, trim hostel-cum-hotel with shared rooms and private singles or doubles. There are laundry and kitchen facilities, as well as free high-speed wireless internet access; baths are shared. Your seventh night is free. ~ 2080 West Vineyard Street, Wailuku; 808-986-8095, 800-242-0865, fax 808-249-0705; www.northshorehostel.com, e-mail info@northshorehostel.com. BUDGET.

The **Banana Bungalow** is a kind of resort for low-budget travelers. This hotel/hostel caters to windsurfers, surfers and adventurers. It offers a jacuzzi, garden and fruit trees, internet access, cable TV and movies. The folks here conduct their own free tours and have a free airport drop-off. There are laundry facilities and a community kitchen and, of course, hammocks. ~ 310 North Market Street, Wailuku; 808-244-5090, 800-846-7835, fax 808-244-3678; www.mauihostel.com, e-mail info@mauihostel.com. BUDGET.

Built by a wealthy island banker as a wedding gift for his daughter-in-law, this "queen" of historic homes, **The Old Wailuku Inn at Ulupono**, reflects the Hawaii of past generations. The theme of Ulupono and its landscaped grounds are a tribute to Hawaii's poet laureate of the 1920s and '30s, Don Blanding. There are seven individually decorated bedrooms dedicated to an island flower or plant, each with a matching Hawaiian quilt and its own bath. Common areas are the breakfast room, living room, and library, which holds all of Don Blanding's books. The Vagabond's House offers three more lavish rooms. The plantation era at its gentle best. ~ 2199 Kahookele Street, Wailuku; 808-244-5987, 800-305-4899, fax 808-242-9600; www.maui inn.com. DELUXE.

**DINING**

The best place in Kahului for a quick, inexpensive meal is at one of several shopping arcades along Kaahumanu Avenue (Route 32). For common fare, head over to the Maui Mall. Here you can drop in at **Siu's Chinese Kitchen** (808-871-0828), where they serve three meals a day. To round off the calorie count, you can try a cup of *guri guri* sherbet at **Tasaka Guri Guri Shop** (808-871-4513). ~ Maui Mall, Kahului. BUDGET.

The white booths and black-tile tables are an appealing touch
at **Marco's Grill & Deli.** So is the attention to detail at this fam-
ily-operated Italian restaurant. They blend their own coffee and
grind their own meat for sausages and meatballs. The result is a
menu that ranges from chocolate cinnamon French toast at
breakfast to submarine sandwiches and vodka rigatoni later in
the day. In addition to pasta entrées, they serve seafood dishes. ~
444 Hana Highway, Kahului; 808-877-4446, fax 808-873-0011.
MODERATE.

◀ HIDDEN

If you're staying at one of Kahului's bayfront hotels, you
might try **Willy's Restaurant** in the Maui Seaside Hotel. This
open-air Polynesian-style establishment has
steak with fish or shrimp and other assorted dinners. The ambience here is pleasant, and the staff
congenial, but in the past the service has sometimes
been slow. Willy's doesn't serve lunch, but at breakfast (weekdays 7 to 8:30 a.m.; weekends 7 to 9 a.m.)
the specials might include banana hot cakes. Dinner is
from 6 to 8 p.m. Both breakfast and dinner may close
half an hour early on slow days. ~ 100 West Kaahumanu
Avenue, Kahului; 808-871-6494. MODERATE.

Nearly half of Maui's
multicultural population
resides in the Kahalui–
Wailuku area, the seats
of commerce and
government.

The **Rainbow Dining Room** lies along Kaahumanu Avenue
in the Maui Beach Hotel. Overlooking the pool, this spacious
open-air restaurant serves a Japanese buffet; breakfast features
American cuisine. The former includes shrimp tempura, scallops,
mixed vegetables, yakitori chicken, teriyaki steak, many different types of Japanese salad and a host of other dishes. No lunch.
~ 170 Kaahumanu Avenue, Kahului; 808-877-0051, fax 808-
871-5797. DELUXE.

Want something on the healthy side? **Down to Earth Deli &
Cafe** serves veggie burgers, vegetarian subs and other heart-smart
fare in the corner of a full-service natural foods supermarket. ~
305 Dairy Road, Kahului; 808-877-2661, fax 808-877-7548.
BUDGET.

**Bangkok Cuisine** promises "authentic Thai food," though
their menu offers decidedly non-traditional food: Cornish game
hen in a sauce of garlic and black pepper, eggplant beef, and evil
prince shrimp, but their dining room does sport a more authentic vibe. Dinner on Sunday only. ~ 395 Dairy Road, Kahului;
808-893-0026. BUDGET TO MODERATE.

Up the road apiece in Wailuku there are numerous ethnic restaurants guaranteed to please both the palate and the purse. **Sam
Sato's** features local noodle dishes. Open for breakfast and lunch,
it specializes in *manju* (a bean cake pastry), dry *mein* (a noodle
dish) and the ubiquitous *saimin*. Closed Sunday. ~ 1750 Wili Pa
Loop, Wailuku; 808-244-7124. BUDGET.

◀ HIDDEN

In a tropical garden setting, **Saeng's Thai Cuisine** sits in a
beautifully designed building embellished with fine woodwork

and adorned with Asian accoutrements. The menu, which lists three pages of dishes from Thailand, is like an encyclopedia of fine dining. Meals, which are served in the dining room or out on a windswept veranda, begin with *sateh* and spring rolls, venture on to dishes like the "evil prince" and "tofu delight," and end over tea and tapioca pudding. No lunch Saturday and Sunday. ~ 2119 Vineyard Street, Wailuku; 808-244-1567. BUDGET TO MODERATE.

**A Saigon Café** doesn't advertise itself with even a sign on the outside, but business still flourishes. You'll find a small space inside, but a big menu that includes vegetarian, clay pot, seafood and even steak entrées. ~ 1792 Main Street, Wailuku; 808-243-9560, fax 808-243-9566. BUDGET TO MODERATE.

Kahului, then Maui's largest town, was deliberately destroyed by fire in 1890 to kill rats that were spreading an epidemic of bubonic plague.

**Tasty Crust** is famous for its breakfasts, especially pancakes, which it serves in the morning as well as at lunch and dinnertime. If you'd rather not have breakfast in the evening, try the hamburger steak plate. ~ 1770 Mill Street, Wailuku; 808-244-0845, fax 808-242-7170. BUDGET TO MODERATE.

Wailuku's low-rent district lies along Lower Main Street, where ethnic restaurants cater almost exclusively to locals. These are informal, family-owned, formica-and-naugahyde-chair cafés that serve good food at down-to-earth prices. You'll find Japanese food at **Tokyo Tei**. No lunch on Sunday. ~ 1063-E Lower Main Street, Suite C-101, Wailuku; 808-242-9630. BUDGET.

**GROCERIES** Kahului features two sprawling supermarkets. **Foodland** is open daily from 6 a.m. to 11 p.m. ~ Kaahumanu Center, Kaahumanu Avenue, Kahului; 808-877-2808. **Star Super Market** is open daily from 6 a.m. to 10 p.m. ~ Maui Mall, Kaahumanu Avenue, Kahului; 808-877-3341.

**Down to Earth Natural Foods** has a complete line of health food items and fresh produce. Add to that a healthy stock of herbs and you have what amounts to a natural foods supermarket. This gets my dollar for being the best place on Maui to shop for natural foods. ~ 305 Dairy Road, Kahului; 808-877-2661.

There is also **Ah Fook's Super Market** in the Kahului Shopping Center. ~ 55 West Kaahumanu Avenue, Kahului; 808-877-3308.

**Wakamatsu Fish Market** has fresh fish every day but Sunday, when they are closed. ~ 145 Market Street, Wailuku; 808-244-4111.

**Love's Bakery Thrift Shop** sells day-old baked goods at old-fashioned prices. ~ 344 Ano Street, Kahului; 808-877-3160.

**SHOPPING** For everyday shopping needs, you should find the Kahului malls very convenient. Three sprawling centers are strung along Kaahumanu Avenue (Route 32).

Always a favorite with locals, Maui potato chips have by now become a worldwide phenomenon. One of the most popular brands is "Kitch'n Cook'd," made at the family-owned and operated **Maui Potato Chip Factory**. This place has been around since the 1950s, annually increasing in popularity, and it now brings in orders from around the globe. These chips are hard to find in mainland stores, but you can stock up on them here where they're freshly made. No tours. Closed Sunday. ~ 295 Lalo Place, off Route 360, Kahului; 808-877-3652.

**Kaahumanu Center** is Maui's most contemporary shopping mall, with **Macys** (808-877-3361) and **Sears** (808-877-2221), a photo studio, **Waldenbooks** (808-871-6112), boutiques, shoe stores, candy stores, a sundries shop and a jeweler. ~ 275 Kaahumanu Avenue.

Nearby **Maui Mall** has a smaller inventory of shops. Furniture and decorative arts from around the world are showcased at **East to West Trading Company** (808-873-7286). **The Ano Ano Gallery** (808-873-0233) has jade and pearl pieces among its inventory of exotic jewelry. You'll also find Asian antiques and artwork.

If you have children in tow, take a break and head to the **Fun Factory** (808-873-6229). There's enough video games and other electronic attractions to keep them busy for hours. ~ 70 East Kaahumanu Avenue, Kahului; 808-872-4320; www.maui mall.com.

**Summerhouse Boutique** might be called a chic dress shop. But they also sell jewelry and natural fiber garments. ~ 395 Dairy Road, Kahului; 808-871-1320.

Up in Wailuku, a tumbledown town with a friendly face, you'll find the little shops and solicitous merchants that we have come to associate with small-town America. Along North Market Street are several imaginative shops operated by low-key entrepreneurs.

Stop by the **Maui Popcorn Factory** for a new slant on an old-fashioned snack. The Volcano—popcorn mixed with rice crackers, doused with butter and sprinkled with *furikake*—explodes with flavor. After a few tastes of this special treat, you'll be like the Hawaiians, who carry a bag of rice crackers and a jar of *furikake* to the movie theaters to make their own. It's truly addicting. ~ 21 North Market Street, Wailuku; 808-242-9888.

High-end oriental antiques, including a prized collection of Buddhas and estate pieces, are showcased at **Gottling Ltd.** Closed Sunday. ~ 34 North Market Street, Wailuku; 808-244-7779; www.gottlingltd.com.

**Brown & Kobayashi**, another antique store, specializes in rare pieces from the Orient. ~ 38 North Market Street, Wailuku; 808-242-0804.

Central Maui is defined not by what it is but by what lies to the east and west of it. On one side Haleakala lifts into the clouds; on the other hand loom the West Maui mountains, a folded landscape over 5000 feet in elevation. Between them, at the center of the island, sits an isthmus, some areas planted in sugar cane and pineapple. Never rising more than a few hundred feet above sea level, it houses Kahului along its northern edge and serves as the gateway to both the Lahaina–Kaanapali and Kihei–Wailea areas. Three highways cross the isthmus separating West Maui from the slopes of Haleakala. From Kahului, Mokulele Highway (Route 350) tracks south to Kihei through this rich agricultural area. The Kuihelani Highway (Route 380), running diagonally and through open stretches, joins the Honoapiilani Highway (Route 30) in its course from Wailuku along the West Maui Mountains. The low-lying area that supports this network of roadways was formed by lava flows from Haleakala and the West Maui Mountains.

**ALEXANDER & BALDWIN SUGAR MUSEUM**     The Alexander & Baldwin Sugar Museum, an award-winning nonprofit organization, is across from the largest operating sugar plantation in Hawaii. It provides a brief introduction to Hawaii's main crop. Tracing the history of sugar cultivation in the islands, its displays portray everything from early life in the cane fields, the multi-ethnic plantation life, to contemporary methods for producing refined sugar. Closed Sunday except in July and August. Admission. ~ 3957 Hansen Road, Puunene; 808-871-8058.

**MAUI TROPICAL PLANTATION**     The Maui Tropical Plantation is a 60-acre enclave complete with orchards and groves displaying dozens of island fruit plants. Here you'll see avocados, papayas, bananas, pineapples, mangoes, coffee and macadamia nuts growing in lush profusion. There's a tropical nursery and a tram that will carry you through this ersatz plantation. Admission for tram. ~ 1670 Honoapiilani Highway; 808-244-7643.

**MAUI OCEAN CENTER, THE HAWAIIAN AQUARIUM**     Truly both a learning center and a star attraction is Maui Ocean Center, The Hawaiian Aquarium. It's a journey through the living ocean in both open-air and

**Bird of Paradise** carries collectible Hawaiiana including old records, sheet music, bric-a-brac and plantation-style furnishings. Closed Sunday. ~ 56 North Market Street, Wailuku; 808-242-7699.

Some of the island's most reasonably priced souvenirs are found at the **Maui Historical Society Bailey House Museum**, located in the Bailey House Museum. Here you'll find an out-

interior exhibits, each of which are interactive in touch, sight and sound. Showcasing not only Hawaii's unique marine life, from the coral reef to the open ocean, this aquarium also dedicates an exhibit to its host culture, showcasing the language, history and lore of Hawaii. Locally trained marine naturalists are on hand to answer questions and give presentations. In the Shark Dive, certified scuba divers (15 years old and older) can dive in the Open Ocean Exhibit and be surrounded by sharks and rays. Admission. ~ 192 Maalaea Road, Maalaea; 808-270-7000, fax 808-270-7070; www.mauioceancenter.com, e-mail info@mauioceancenter.com.

**LUNCH BREAK**    Overlooking scenic Maalaea Harbor's fishing fleet is the **Blue Marlin Harborfront Grill & Bar**, located on the lower level of the Maalaea Harbor Village complex. The fish is really fresh because it comes straight from the fishing boats, walked over by the fishermen themselves. À la carte favorites make for a good sampling: try the sashimi selection, fresh fish and chips, half-pounds of oysters on the half shell, or a local favorite, ahi *poke*. The ambiance is nautical and casual; diners have a choice of an open-air lanai or wide-view dining room. ~ 300 Maalaea Road, Maalaea; 808-244-8844, fax 808-244-3353. MODERATE TO DELUXE.

**MAALEA BAY**    Past the small boat harbor at Maalaea Bay, the highway hugs the southwest coast. There are excellent lookout points along this elevated roadway, especially near the lighthouse at **McGregor Point**. During whale season you might spy a leviathan from this landlocked crow's nest. Just offshore there are prime whale breeding areas.

**OFFSHORE ISLANDS**    Down the road from McGregor Point, you'll see three islands anchored offshore. As you look seaward, the portside islet is **Molokini**, the crescent-shaped remains of a volcanic crater. **Kahoolawe**, a barren, desiccated island once used for naval target practice, sits in the center. Located seven miles off Maui's south coast, it is a bald, windblasted place, hot and arid. Hawaiian activists long demanded an end to the bombing of this sacred isle by the U.S. Navy. After years of demonstrations, their demands were finally acknowledged in 1994 when the island was turned over to the state of Hawaii. The humpbacked island to starboard is **Lanai**. As you continue toward Kaanapali, **Molokai** sails into view.

standing collection of local history books and art prints. *Koa* bookmarks and Maui-made soaps are also popular. ~ 2375-A Main Street, Wailuku; 808-244-3326.

If you're in the mood for a movie, check out the offerings at the 12-screen **Megaplex**. ~ Maui Mall, 70 East Kaahumanu Avenue, Kahului; 808-249-2222.    **NIGHTLIFE**

The crowd is mostly local at the **Ale House,** which has karaoke on Sunday, a live band on Friday and "Copa Cabana" night on Saturday. ~ 355 East Kamehameha Avenue, Kahului; 808-877-9001.

**BEACHES & PARKS**

**HOALOHA PARK** 🏃 ⛵ Located next to the Kahului hotels, this is one of Kahului's two beaches, but unfortunately the nearby harbor facilities detract from the natural beauty of its white sands. What with heavy boat traffic on one side and several hotels on the other, the park is not recommended. There are much better beaches in other areas of the island. Swimming and snorkeling are poor; surfers will find good breaks (two to six feet, with a left slide) off the jetty mouth near the north shore of Kahului Harbor. It is, however, a good spot to beachcomb, particularly for Maui diamonds. Goatfish, *papio* and triggerfish can be hooked from the pier; *ulua* and *papio* are often caught along the shore. ~ Located on Kaahumanu Avenue (Route 32), Kahului.

**KEPANIWAI COUNTY PARK AND HERITAGE GARDENS** 🏃 This beautiful park is carefully landscaped and surrounded by sheer cliffs. You'll discover paths over arched bridges and through Japanese gardens, plus pagodas, a thatch-roofed hut, a taro patch and banana, papaya and coconut trees. An ideal and romantic spot for picnicking, it has picnic pavilions and restrooms. ~ Located in Wailuku on the road to Iao Valley.

**WAIHEE BEACH PARK** 🏊 🎣 ⛵ This park is used almost exclusively by local residents. Bordered by a golf course and shaded with ironwood trees and *naupaka* bushes, it has a sandy beach and one of Maui's longest and widest reefs. There's a grassy area perfect for picnicking, established picnic areas and restrooms with showers. Beachcombing, *limu* gathering and fishing are all good. Swimming and snorkeling are okay, though the reef is rather shallow. ~ Located outside Wailuku on the rural road that circles the West Maui Mountains. To get there from Route 340 in Waiehu, turn right on Halewaiu Road and then take the beach access road from Waiehu Golf Course.

▼▼▼▼▼▼▼▼▼▼▼▼

# Hana Highway

The Hana Highway (Route 360), a smooth, narrow road running between Kahului and Hana, is one of the most beautiful drives in all Hawaii. Following the path of an ancient Hawaiian trail, it may in fact be one of the prettiest drives in the world. The road courses through a rainforest, a luxurious jungle crowded with ferns and African tulip trees, and leads to black-sand beaches and rain-drenched hamlets. The vegetation is so thick it seems to be spilling out from the mountainside in a cascade of greenery. You'll be traveling the windward side of Haleakala, hugging its lower slopes en route to a small Hawaiian town that receives 70 inches of rain a year.

There are over 600 twists and turns and 56 one-lane bridges along this adequately maintained paved road. It'll take at least three hours to drive the 51 miles to Hana. To make the entire circuit around the south coast, plan to sleep in Hana or to leave very early and drive much of the day. If you can, take your time—there's a lot to see.

**SIGHTS**

About seven miles east of Kahului, you'll pass the quaint, weather-beaten town of **Paia**. This old sugar plantation town, now a burgeoning artist colony and windsurfing mecca, has been painted in nursery colors. Along either of Paia's two main streets, plantation-era buildings have been freshly refurbished.

On the eastern side of town is the **Mantokuji Buddhist Temple**, which celebrates sunset every day by sounding its huge gong.

**Hookipa Beach Park**, one of the world's premier windsurfing spots, lies about three miles east of town. Brilliantly colored sails race along the horizon as windsurfers perform amazing acrobatic stunts, cartwheeling across the waves. The latest craze is kite surfing. You can watch riders "kite the surfzone," jump, jibe or ride upwind.

Within the next ten miles the roadway is transformed, as your slow, winding adventure begins. You'll drive past sugar cane fields, across verdant gorges, through valleys dotted with tumbledown cottages and along fern-cloaked hillsides.

Route 36 becomes Route 360, beginning a new series of mileage markers that are helpful in locating sites along the way. Near the two-mile marker, a short trail leads to an idyllic swimming

**A WORTHY STOP**

For a cultural treat, turn off Route 360 at Ulaino Road following the signs to the **Kahanu Garden**, part of the National Tropical Botanical Gardens. The focus here is on native Hawaiian plants and culture. A highlight of the 90-minute tour is a look at the massive **Hale o Piilani heiau**, which overlooks a moody stretch of coast. The platform, about the size of the three football fields and built of moss- and algae-covered lava rocks, is the largest of the ancient *heiau* sites remaining in Hawaii. The power of the past can be felt here. The sense of authenticity makes this a true encounter with Polynesian Hawaii. The garden is open Monday through Friday for self-guided tours. Closed Saturday and Sunday. Admission. ~ 808-248-8912, fax 808-248-7210; www.ntbg.org, e-mail kahanu@ntbg.org.

hole at **Twin Falls** (the path begins from the west side of the Hoolawa Stream bridge on the right side of the road).

Nearby **Huelo**, a tiny "rooster town" (so named because nothing ever seems to be stirring except the roosters), is known for the **Kaulanapueo Church**. A coral chapel built in 1853, this New England–style sanctuary strikes a dramatic pose with the sea as a backdrop.

Farther along, on **Waikamoi Ridge**, you'll see picnic areas and a nature trail. Here you can visit a bamboo forest, learn about native vegetation and explore the countryside. Remember to bring mosquito repellent, especially if you're planning a rainforest hike.

Another picnic area, at **Puohokamoa Falls** (11-mile marker), nestles beside a waterfall and large pool. If you packed a lunch, this is a perfect place to enjoy it. Trails above and below the main pool lead to other waterfalls.

A few zigzags farther, at **Kaumahina State Wayside** (12-mile marker), a tree-studded park overlooks Honomanu Gulch and Keanae Peninsula. From here the road descends the gulch, where a side road leads left to **Honomanu Bay** (14-mile marker) and its black-sand beach.

Above Keanae Peninsula, you'll pass the **Keanae Arboretum** (16-mile marker). You can stroll freely through paved trails in these splendid tropical gardens, which feature many native Hawaiian plants including several dozen varieties of taro. Another section of the gardens is devoted to exotic tropical plants and there is a mile-long trail that leads into a natural rainforest.

Just past the arboretum, turn left onto the road to the **Keanae Peninsula** (17-mile marker). This rocky, windswept point offers stunning views of Haleakala. You'll pass rustic houses, a patchwork of garden plots and a coral-and-stone church built around 1860. A picture of serenity and rural perfection, Keanae is inhabited by native Hawaiians who still grow taro and pound poi. Their home is a lush rainforest—a quiltwork of taro plots, banana trees, palms—that runs to the rim of a ragged coastline.

Another side road descends to **Wailua** (18-mile marker), a Hawaiian agricultural and fishing village. Here is another luxurious checkerboard where taro gardens alternate with banana patches and the landscape is adorned with clapboard houses. The town is known for **St. Gabriel's Church**, a simple structure made completely of sand and coral, dating from 1870.

Back on the main road, there's yet another picnic area and waterfall at **Puaakaa State Wayside** (22-mile marker). The cascade tumbles into a natural pool in a setting framed by eucalyptus and banana trees. Puaakaa means, by the way, "plenty of pigs."

Past here, another side road bumps three miles through picturesque **Nahiku** (25-mile marker) to a bluff overlooking the sea.

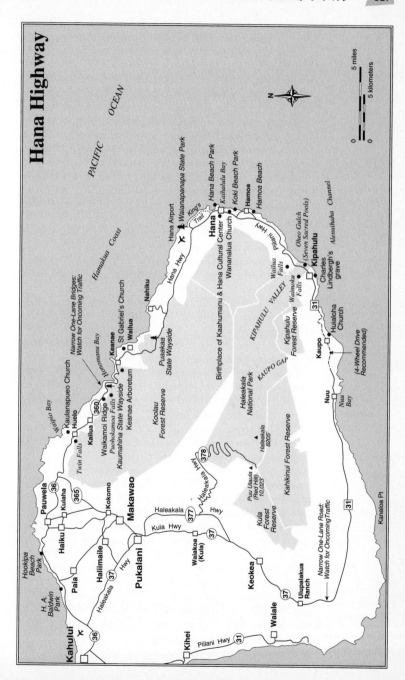

# Hana Highway

PACIFIC OCEAN

PACIFIC

Hamakua Coast

Narrow One-Lane Bridges:
Watch for Oncoming Traffic

Honomanu Bay

Waipio Bay

Kaulanapueo Church

St Gabriel's Church

**Keanae**
**Wailua**

Nahiku

Hana Hwy

King's
Trail

Hana Airport

Waianapanapa State Park

Hana Beach Park
Kaihalulu Bay
Koki Beach Park
**Hamoa**
Hamoa Beach

**Hana**

Birthplace of Kaahumanu & Hana Cultural Center
Wananalua Church

Piilani Hwy

Oheo Gulch
(Seven Sacred Pools)
**Kipahulu**

Charles
Lindbergh's
grave

Puaakaa
State Wayside

Wailua
Falls

Waimoku
Falls

KIPAHULU VALLEY

Kipahulu
Forest Reserve

Huialoha
Church

31

Koolau
Forest Reserve

**Huelo**
**Kailua**

Twin Falls

Waikamoi Ridge
Puohokamoa Falls
Kaumahina State Wayside
Keanae Arboretum

360

KAUPO GAP

Haleakala
National Park

**Kaupo**

(4-Wheel Drive
Recommended)

**Nuu**
Nuu
Bay

Kahikinui Forest Reserve

Alenuihaha Channel

Haleakala
8205

▲ Haleakala Hwy

378

Puu Ulaula
(Red Hill)
10,023'

**Pauwela**
**Kuiaha**

36
365

**Kokomo**

**Makawao**

Haleakala    Hwy

377

Kula Hwy

**Haiku**

**Hallimaile**

37
Hwy

**Paia**

Hookipa
Beach
Park

H. A.
Baldwin
Park

**Kahului**

36

Haleakala    Hwy

**Pukalani**

**Waiakoa (Kula)**

Kula
Forest
Reserve

37

**Keokea**

**Ulupalakua
Ranch**

Narrow One-Lane Road:
Watch for OncomingTraffic

31

Kanaloa Pt

**Waiale**

**Kihei**    Piilani Hwy    31

N

5 miles

5 kilometers

0

0

The view spreads across three bays all the way back to Wailua. Directly below, the ocean pounds against rock outcroppings, spraying salt mist across a stunning vista. Set in one of the wettest spots along the entire coast, Nahiku village is inundated by rainforest and graced by yet another 19th-century church. America's first domestic rubber plantation opened in Nahiku in 1905. You can still see a few remaining rubber plants in the area.

Several miles before you reach Hana, be sure to stop at **Waianapanapa State Park**. Here you will find a black-sand beach and two lava tubes, **Waianapanapa** and **Waiomao caves**. Hawaiian mythology tells of a Hawaiian princess who hid from her cruel husband here, only to be discovered by him and slain. Now every spring the waters hereabouts are said to run red with her blood. Offshore are several sea arches, and nearby is a blowhole that spouts periodically.

Just before the town of Hana, on the right, is **Helani Farm and Gardens**, a sprawling oasis of tropical plant life. Only a section of the gardens is currently open to the public, but it's worth a stop as there's a wealth of flowering plants, trees and vines. You'll also find fruit trees, baobab trees, papyrus, ginger plants and even a carp pond. Visits by appointment only. ~ Hana Highway; phone/fax 808-248-8274, 800-385-5241; e-mail bj4flow ers@aol.com.

As you approach the town of Hana, take the Ulaino Road turnoff going left and follow it to the end. You'll cross a streambed that empties into a pristine freshwater pool, the **Blue Pool**, named for the cobalt color of its icy water. There's limited parking just before the streambed in the grassy meadow (perfect for a quiet picnic); the pool is on the left.

On your way to or from the pool along the same road, watch for the **Ka'eleku Caverns** sign and make a point to visit the island's largest underground lava tube system, created from a flow 1000 years ago. Maui Cave Adventures offers two tours: a one-hour scenic tour or a physically challenging two-and-a-half-hour tour. The latter does not allow anyone under 15 years of age; you have to crawl through a couple of tight spots and climb a ladder on this tour. Tour times vary: please inquire. The visitors center amidst tropical gardens is inviting for a picnic lunch, too. Closed Sunday. Admission. ~ P.O. Box 40, Hana, HI 96713; 808-248-7308; www.mauicave.com, e-mail info@mauicave.com.

To reach the secluded hamlet of **Hana**, you can take the old Hawaiian shoreline trail (see the "Hiking" section at the end of this chapter) or continue on along the highway. This Eden-like town, carpeted with pandanus, taro and banana trees, sits above an inviting bay. Known as "heavenly Hana," it's a ranch town inhabited primarily by folks of Hawaiian ancestry. Because of its remote location it has changed little over the years. The rain that continually buffets Hana makes it a prime agricultural area and adds to the luxuriant, unsettling beauty of the place.

Because of its strategic location directly across from the Big Island, Hana was an early battleground in the wars between the chiefs of Maui and the Big Island, who conquered, lost and regained the region in a succession of bloody struggles. During the 19th century it became a sugar plantation, employing different ethnic groups who were brought in to work the fields. Then, in 1946, Paul Fagan, a San Francisco industrialist, bought 14,000 acres and created the Hana Ranch, turning the area into grazing land for Hereford cattle and opening the exclusive Hotel Hana-Maui.

Hawaiians called Maui's isthmus *Kula o ka Mao Mao*, "the land of mirages."

Head down to **Hana Bay**. Here you can stroll the beach, explore the wharf and take a short path along the water to a plaque that marks the **Birthplace of Kaahumanu**, King Kamehameha I's favorite wife and a key player in the 1819 overthrow of the ancestral Hawaiian religious system. To reach this sacred spot, pick up the trail leading from the boat landing on the right side of the bay. It leads along the base of **Kauiki Hill**, a cinder cone covered with ironwood trees that was the scene of fierce battles between Kahekili, the renowned Maui chief, and the Big Island chief Kalaniopuu.

◀ HIDDEN

Near the Hotel Hana-Maui (where you can request a key to open the gate), you can drive or hike up a short road to **Mount Lyons** (that camel-humped hill with the cross on top). From this aerie, a memorial to Paul Fagan, there's a fine view of Hana Bay and the surrounding coastline.

The **Hana Cultural Center**, an enticing little museum, displays such artifacts from Hana's past as primitive stone tools, rare shells and Hawaiian games. There are antique photographs and elaborately stitched quilts. ~ 4974 Uakea Street; phone/fax 808-248-8622; e-mail hccm@aloha.net.

Also on the grounds, the old **Court House**, built in 1871, is a modest but appealing structure containing five small benches and the original desk for the judge. Be sure to wander through the **Kauhale Complex**, a replica of a Hawaiian village complete with thatched huts to explore.

**Wananalua Church**, a lovely chapel built from coral blocks during the mid-19th century, has been beautifully refurbished. Today, services are conducted in English and Hawaiian. Located atop an ancient *heiau*, stately and imposing in appearance, it is a perfect expression of the days when Christianity was crushing the old Hawaiian beliefs. ~ Hauoli Street and Hana Highway.

**FROM HANA TO ULUPALAKUA** The backroad from Hana around the southeast side of Maui is one of the island's great adventures. It leads along the side of Haleakala past dense rainforest and tumbling waterfalls to an arid expanse covered by lava flows, and then opens onto Maui's vaunted Upcountry region. Since a five-mile stretch is unpaved and other sections are punctuated with potholes, car rental companies generally do not permit driving on parts of this route; so check with them in advance or be prepared to take your chances. Also check on road conditions: The road is sometimes closed during periods of heavy rain.

Past Hana, the road, now designated the Piilani Highway and renumbered as Route 31 (with mileage markers that descend in sequence), worsens as it winds toward an overgrown ravine where **Wailua Falls** (45-mile marker) and another waterfall pour down sharp cliff faces.

At **Oheo Gulch** (known to some as the Seven Sacred Pools) in the Kipahulu District of the Haleakala National Park (42-mile marker), a series of waterfalls tumbles into two dozen pools before reaching the sea. In fact, says Mark Tanaka-Sanders, chief ranger for Haleakala National Park, "there are 24 pools in the area." Who's responsible for the miscount? "Blame it on the tourist industry," he says. "It's also important to know that the Hawaiian people do not consider these pools sacred." They refer to them as the pools at Oheo. The pools are rock-bound, some are bordered by cliffs, and several provide excellent swimming holes. This is an eerie and beautiful place from which you can see up and down the rugged coastline. Used centuries ago by early Hawaiians, they still offer a cool, refreshing experience.

HIDDEN ►   Another special spot, **Charles Lindbergh's grave** (41-mile marker), rests on a promontory overlooking the ocean. The great aviator spent his last days here and lies buried beside **Palapala Hoomau Church** in a grave he designed for himself. This church was built in 1857 of limestone coral, and about one hundred years later was restored by Samuel Pryor, the man who introduced Lindbergh to the area. Pryor had a picture of Jesus dressed in Hawaiian robes painted on a window of the church (and reportedly buried his pet monkeys nearby). The whitewashed chapel and surrounding shade trees create a place of serenity and

## SPRING TRAINING, HANA STYLE

In 1946, Hana hosted the only mainland American baseball team ever to conduct spring training in Hawaii. That was the year that financier Paul Fagan brought the Pacific Coast League's San Francisco Seals to the islands. Arriving with the players was a squadron of sportswriters who sent back glowing dispatches on "Heavenly Hana," helping to promote the destination and the Hotel Hana-Maui, owned of course by Paul Fagan.

remarkable beauty. (To find the grave, continue 1.2 miles past Oheo Gulch. Watch for the church through the trees on the left. Turn left onto an unpaved road and drive several hundred yards, paralleling a stone fence. Turn left into the churchyard.)

Not far from here, in **Kipahulu**, the paved road gives way to dirt. It's five miles to the nearest pavement, so your car should have good shock absorbers; sometimes the weather makes it impassable. The road rises along seaside cliffs, some of which are so steep they jut out to overhang the road. This is wild, uninhabited country, ripe for exploration.

**Huialoha Church**, built in 1859, rests below the road on a wind-wracked peninsula. Once when I visited this aging worship hall, horses were grazing in the churchyard. Nearby you'll encounter the tinroof town of **Kaupo**, with its funky general store. You'll feel like you've entered a time warp . . . and maybe you won't want to return to the present. Located directly above the town is **Kaupo Gap**, through which billowing clouds pour into Haleakala Crater.

◀ HIDDEN

The road bumps inland, then returns seaward to **Nuu Bay's** rocky beach. From here the rustic route climbs into a desolate area scarred by lava and inhabited with scrub vegetation. The sea views are magnificent as the road bisects the **1790 lava flow**. This was the last volcanic eruption on Maui; it left its mark in a torn and terrible landscape that slopes for miles to the sea.

It's several miles farther until you reach **Ulupalakua Ranch**, a lush counterpoint to the lava wasteland behind. With its grassy acres and curving rangeland, the ranch provides a perfect introduction to Maui's Upcountry region.

Owners of North Shore Maui's Mama's Fish House have installed picturesque beachfront cottages next to their restaurant, naming the small complex **The Inn at Mama's Fish House**. Located just east of Paia at Kuau Cove, the inn consists of four two-bedroom units, all facing the ocean, plus two one-bedroom garden-view units. True to form, the owners have named each cottage after a Hawaiian fish. Their beachfront property is known for its lush, tropical gardens and swaying coconut palm grove. Each unit is furnished in bold, Hawaiian print decor, including fresh tropical flowers as well as a complete kitchen and private lanai. ~ 799 Poho Place, Paia; 808-579-9764, 800-860-4852, fax 808-579-8594; www.mamasfishhouse.com, e-mail inn@mamas fishhouse.com. ULTRA-DELUXE.

**LODGING**

◀ HIDDEN

A very convenient accommodation located on the Hana Highway in Keanae is the Maui YMCA's **Camp Keanae**. For just $15 a night, both men and women are welcome to roll out their sleeping bags on bunks in the dormitory or one of five cabins. The camp overlooks the sea, and comes with hot showers, laundry facilities, full-size gym, kitchen and outdoor cooking area. A pair of two-bedroom oceanview cottages sleep up to four people ($100 per night); both have full kitchens. Sorry, the maximum stay here is three nights. Guests must provide their own bedding for the dorms. Reservations required. ~ Hana Highway, Keanae; 808-248-8355, fax 808-244-6713; www.mauiymca.org, e-mail ymcacampkeanae@aol.com. BUDGET.

HIDDEN ►

**Aloha Cottages**, perched on a hillside above Hana Bay, has three two-bedroom cottages, one three-bedroom cottage and one studio that are situated among banana trees; most feature hardwood floors and redwood walls. The decor is simple, the kitchens are all-electric and many of the furnishings are rattan. Representing one of Hana's best bargains, the cottages have been recommended many times over the years by readers and friends. There are only five units at this small complex, so advance reservations are a good idea. ~ 83 Keawa Place; 808-248-8420. MODERATE.

You can also consider heading down toward the water to the **Hana Kai Maui Resort**. Located smack on a rocky beach, this pair of two-story buildings sits amid lush surroundings. The ornamental pool is a freshwater affair fed by toe-dipping spring water. The location and exotic grounds rate a big plus. Both studio apartments and one-bedroom condominiums are available. ~ 1533 Ukea Road; 808-248-8426, 800-346-2772, fax 808-248-7482; www.hanakaimaui.com. DELUXE.

**Hana Accommodations and Plantation Houses** offers cottages and studios. Scattered throughout the Hana area are homes with either mountain or ocean views; each unit is fully equipped

**AUTHOR FAVORITE**

One of the Hawaiian islands' finest resting places is the **Hotel Hana-Maui**, a luxurious retreat on a hillside above the bay. From ocean views to tropical landscape to rolling lawn, this friendly inn is a unique, world-class resort. Spread across the 67-acre grounds are 66 cottage-style accommodations, all elegantly designed to capture the tranquility of Hana. An added bonus is the hotel's health and wellness complex, which sponsors a variety of hiking excursions and nature walks, as well as croquet, tennis, yoga, tai chi and aqua exercise classes. The adjacent pool, landscaped with lava walls and palm trees, enjoys a spectacular setting. The staff has been here for generations, lending a sense of home to an enchanting locale. Rates for this getaway of getaways are stratospheric, but I highly recommend the Hotel Hana-Maui for a splurge. ~ P.O. Box 9, Hana, HI 96713; 808-248-8211, 800-321-4262, fax 808-248-7202; www.hotelhanamaui.com, e-mail info@hotelhanamaui.com. ULTRA-DELUXE.

with (or has access to) a kitchen. Many of the accommodations are decorated with tapa-cloth designs and Hawaiian paintings. Most are cooled with ceiling fans and all have outdoor grills perfect for a private feast. Some facilities are within walking distance of the beach and ancient Hawaiian fishponds. Gay-friendly. ~ Locations throughout Hana; 808-248-7868, 800-228-4262, fax 808-248-8240; www.hana-maui.com. MODERATE TO DELUXE.

**Hana Maui Travel** offers a similar selection of accommodations—including studios and homes—in several price ranges. Here you can settle into a place on Hana Bay or on an idyllic hillside. Some guest units sit atop lava-rock bluffs overlooking the ocean, others are found in secluded five-acre settings. Most accommodations come with lanais, outdoor barbecues and full kitchens. ~ P.O. Box 536, Hana, HI 96713; 808-248-7742, 800-548-0478, fax 808-248-7319; www.hanamauitravel.com, e-mail info@hanamauitravel.com. MODERATE TO DELUXE.

Speaking of scenery, **Heavenly Hana Inn** is blessed indeed.  Located in Hana Town, this hostelry offers three suites and is entered through a Japanese gate. On either side, stone lions guard a luxuriant garden. The interior mirrors this understated elegance. Each suite is decorated in a Japanese style with futon beds, shoji screens and tiled bathrooms with soaking tubs. Breakfast is provided for a fee. ~ Hana Highway; phone/fax 808-248-8442; www.heavenlyhanainn.com, e-mail hanainn@maui.net. ULTRA-DELUXE.

Don't forget the cabins at **Waianapanapa State Park** (for  information, refer to the "Beaches & Parks" section later in this chapter).

**GAY LODGING** The **Huelo Point Lookout** is set on two acres and bounded by pastureland that stretches to the ocean on three sides. There's lodging in three cottages—the Rainbow, Start and Haleakala, each with a full kitchen. Also available is a lookout house, a two-story home complete with a full kitchen, dining room, and space for up to eight people. You can also enjoy your own private hot tub, one of two outdoor showers or the shared pool. ~ P.O. Box 790117, Paia, HI 96779; 808-573-0914, 800-808-871-8645, fax 808-573-0227; www.mauivacationcottages.com, e-mail dreamers@maui.net. ULTRA-DELUXE.

**Napulani O'Hana** offers spacious accommodations within a few miles of Hana, and a mile and a half from the ocean. It's a ranch-style house set on four acres, with decks overlooking the flower-filled gardens; some of the bathroom floors are decorated with handprinted fish. Enjoy the bananas and papaya served in season. ~ P.O. Box 118, Hana, HI 96713; 808-248-8935. BUDGET TO MODERATE.

**DINING**

Paia, once an artsy little town that has since been discovered (there are now nine realtors in town), is located just a few miles out on the Hana Highway. There are several worthwhile restaurants to choose from. If you don't select any of them, however, be forewarned—there are no pit stops between here and Hana.

If you're craving a tasty fish sandwich, the **Paia Fish Market** is the place to go. When you're not in the mood for seafood, this eatery also offers hamburgers, pasta and Mexican dishes such as fajitas. It's is a casual place with plenty of flowers, and prints of water sports on the walls. ~ Corner of Baldwin Avenue and Hana Highway; 808-579-8030. BUDGET TO MODERATE.

For box lunches, drop in at **Cafe Mambo**. Open for breakfast and lunch, this light and airy café serves a variety of items including spinach-nut burgers and mahimahi sandwiches. The menu also offers patrons basic breakfast selections, deli sandwiches, vegetarian options and plain old burgers. ~ 30 Baldwin Avenue, Paia; 808-579-8021. BUDGET TO MODERATE.

**The Vegan Restaurant** is the prime address hereabouts for vegan and vegetarian food. Place your order at the counter—there are salads, sandwiches and hot entrées that include Thai specialties. ~ 115 Baldwin Avenue, Paia; 808-579-9144. BUDGET.

At **Jacques Northshore**, the look is decidedly young and attractive. The Pacific Rim menu of chef Jacques Pauvert hints of French and Italian origins. The fresh fish means a variety of things, depending on the catches of the day. Rich-sauced pastas like smoked chicken breast are hard to resist. The full sushi bar features an excellent selection. Reasonable prices make Jacques a find for value as well as taste. If you're headed back to the coast after a Haleakala sunset, stop here for dinner. You won't regret it. ~ 120 Hana Highway, Paia; 808-579-8844, fax 808-579-8014; e-mail northshorebistro@aol.com. MODERATE TO DELUXE.

You can also try **Mama's Fish House** outside Paia. This oceanfront nook is simply decorated: shell leis, an old Hawaiian photo

**AUTHOR FAVORITE**

Since 1971, **Charley's** has been a favorite spot to drop in for breakfast (and lunch and dinner). Macadamia-nut pancakes, French toast, Cajun ono benedict—you name it, they've got it. At lunch you can try the Woofer burger (Charley is named after a Great Dane); if you prefer the meatless menu, there are veggie burgers, salads or sandwiches. Dinner entrées include "catch of the day," New York steaks, pasta, pizza and calzones. It's a comfortable atmosphere to dine in and practically open all the time. ~ 142 Hana Highway, Paia; 808-579-9453, fax 808-579-8789; www.charleysmaui.com. BUDGET TO MODERATE.

here, a painting there, plus potted plants. During lunch, the varied menu includes Hawaiian seafood sandwiches and salads as well as fresh fish specialties. Other than a few steak and poultry dishes, the dinner menu is entirely seafood. Evening entrées include seafood provençal and fresh Hawaiian lobster. There are always at least four varieties of fresh fish provided by fishermen who bring their catch directly to Mama's, where it is prepared ten different ways. Reservations are highly recommended. ~ 799 Poho Place, off Hana Highway; 808-579-8488, 800-860-4852; www.mamasfishhouse.com, e-mail reservations@mamasfish house.com. ULTRA-DELUXE.

If you plan to stay in Hana for any length of time, pack up some groceries along with your raingear. You'll find only three restaurants along the entire eastern stretch of the island. Luckily, they cover the gamut from budget to ultra-deluxe.

**Tutu's At Hana Bay**, within whistling distance of the water, ◀ HIDDEN
whips up French toast and *loco moco* (rice, hamburger and an egg smothered with gravy) for breakfast and plate lunches, sandwiches and burgers for lunch. ~ Hana Bay; 808-248-8224.

BUDGET.

**Hana Ranch Restaurant** is a small establishment decorated with blond wood and providing marvelous ocean views. A flagstone lanai is perfect for outdoor dining. Open for lunch (either buffet-style or a la carte) and dinner on Wednesday, Friday and Saturday. Wednesday is pizza and pasta night; Friday and Saturday offer steak, fresh fish and baby-back ribs. Reservations are highly recommended. ~ Hana Highway; 808-248-8255. DELUXE TO ULTRA-DELUXE.

Hana's premier restaurant is the main dining room of the **Hotel Hana-Maui**. This extraordinary resort, perched on a hillside overlooking the ocean, provides three gourmet meals a day to its guests and the public alike. The menu blends contemporary cuisine with a regional Hawaiian influence, while ingredients are from Hana-grown produce and the seafood comes from local fishermen: pork tenderloin with rustic potato salad and green apple cole slaw, for instance, or whole opakapaka with stir-fried Asian vegetables and three dipping sauces. ~ Hana Highway; 808-248-8211, fax 808-248-7202; www.hotelhanamaui.com. DELUXE TO ULTRA-DELUXE.

There are few restaurants and even fewer stores in this remote **GROCERIES**
region, so stock up where you can. On the Hana Highway in Paia, **Nagata Store** has a small supply of groceries. It's open Monday through Friday 6 a.m. to 7 p.m., Saturday from 6 a.m. to 6 p.m., and Sunday from 6 a.m. to 12 p.m. ~ 96 Hana Highway, Paia; 808-579-9252. If you can't find what you need here, check the **H&P Market & Seafood**, which keeps the same hours as the

Nagata Store. ~ In the Nagata Store, Hana Highway; 808-579-8362. You can also try the **Paia General Store**. It's open from 6 a.m. to 9 p.m. during the week, and from 7 a.m. to 9 p.m. on weekends. ~ Hana Highway, Paia; 808-579-9514.

**Mana Foods** has a complete range of health foods and organic produce. Open from 8:30 a.m. to 8:30 p.m. every day. Peruse the full-service deli, the plentiful salad bar and hot bar for ultra-fresh dishes. ~ 49 Baldwin Avenue, Paia; 808-579-8078.

With a limited stock of grocery items are **Hana Ranch Store**, open daily from 7:30 a.m. to 7:30 p.m. ~ Mill Street, Hana, 808-248-8261; and **Hasegawa General Store**, open Monday through Saturday from 7 a.m. to 7 p.m., and Sunday from 8 a.m. to 6 p.m. ~ 5165 Hana Highway, Hana, 808-248-8231.

HIDDEN ► Clear across the island, along the back road from Hana, there's a sleeper called **Kaupo General Store** that's open from 10 a.m. to 5 p.m. "most of the time." You'll find it tucked away in the southeast corner of the island. Selling a limited range of food, drinks and wares, this store, founded in 1925, fills the gaps on the shelves with curios from its illustrious history. Closed Sunday. ~ Base of Kaupo Gap; 808-248-8054; e-mail kaupostore@yahoo.com.

**SHOPPING**    Paia, just seven miles outside Kahului, is my favorite place to shop on Maui. Many fine artisans live in the Upcountry area and come down to sell their wares at the small shops lining the Hana Highway. The town itself is a work of art, with old wooden buildings that provide a welcome respite from the crowded shores of Kaanapali and Kihei. I'll mention just the shops I like most. Browse through town to see for yourself. If you discover places I missed, please let me know.

On display at the **Maui Crafts Guild** is a large range of handmade items all by local artists. Here you'll find anything from pressed hibiscus flowers to sculptures. There are also fabrics, ceramics, jewelry, baskets, woodwork and other Maui-made items. ~ 43 Hana Highway, Paia; 808-579-9697.

**Paia Trading Company** has a few interesting antiques and a lot of junk. Among the more noteworthy items: turquoise and silver jewelry, wooden washboards, apothecary jars and antique glassware. Closed Sunday. ~ 106 Hana Highway, Paia; 808-579-9472.

Around the corner on Baldwin Avenue lies another shop worth browsing. **Maui Girl and Co.** features a fine selection of women's beachwear. ~ 12 Baldwin Avenue, Paia; 808-579-9266.

One of my stops in Hana is the **Hana Coast Gallery**, located in the Hotel Hana-Maui. It features native Hawaiian art and artifacts and fine paintings by Hawaiian artists. Also here are beautiful serigraphs, model *koa* racing canoes, ceremonial objects,

# Shell
## Hunting

With over 1500 varieties of shells washing up on its beaches, Hawaii has some of the world's finest shelling. The miles of sandy beach along Maui's south shore are a prime area for handpicking free souvenirs. Along the shores are countless shell specimens with names like horned helmet, Hebrew cone, Hawaiian olive and Episcopal miter. Or you might find glass balls from Japan and sunbleached driftwood.

Beachcombing is the easiest method of shell gathering. Take along a small container and stroll through the backwash of the waves, watching for ripples from shells lying under the sand. You can also dive in shallow water where the ocean's surge will uncover shells.

It's tempting to walk along the top of coral reefs seeking shells and other marine souvenirs, but these living formations maintain a delicate ecological balance. Reefs in Hawaii and all over the planet are dying because of such plunder. In order to protect this underwater world, try to collect only shells and souvenirs that are adrift on the beach and no longer necessary to the marine ecology.

The best shelling spots along Maui's south shore are Makena, Kihei beaches, Maalaea Bay, Olowalu, the sandy stretch from Kaanapali to Napili Bay, D. T. Fleming Park and Honolua Bay. On the north coast, the stretch from Waiehu to Waihee (west of Kahului) and the beaches around Hana are the choicest hunting grounds.

After heavy rainfall, watch near stream mouths for Hawaiian olivines and in stream beds for Maui diamonds. Olivines are small, semiprecious stones of an olive hue. Maui diamonds are quartz stones and make beautiful jewelry. The best places to go diamond hunting are near the Kahului Bay hotel strip and in Olowalu Strea.

feathered art, fiber collages and painted tapa cloth. ~ Hana Highway, Hana; 808-248-8636.

Also on the grounds of the Hotel Hana-Maui is **Noe Noe**, with casual and evening wear for men and women. ~ Hana Highway, Hana; 808-270-5294.

 For everything you could possibly want or need, drop by the **Hasegawa General Store**. This store stocks everything from groceries, clothing, sandals and hardware to placemats, movie rentals, film and cards. The original Hasegawa's burned down years ago, but the name is still famous. ~ 5165 Hana Highway, Hana; 808-248-8231.

**NIGHTLIFE**   If you're looking for something to do in the evening, **Charley's** often offers live music Saturday, Monday and Wednesday nights. Check to see if they have something scheduled. You might even run into Willie Nelson, who favors dining at this local restaurant when he's in town. ~ 142 Hana Highway, Paia; 808-579-9453.

In the early evening, you can enjoy a duo singing Hawaiian music at the Hotel Hana-Maui's **Paniolo Bar**. As relaxed as Hana itself, this low-key establishment is always inviting. ~ Hana Highway, Hana; 808-248-8211.

**BEACHES & PARKS**   **H. A. BALDWIN PARK**   This spacious county park is bordered by a playing field on one side and a crescent-shaped beach on the other. Palm and ironwood trees dot the half-mile-long beach where you can go shell collecting and gaze out to West Maui. The swimming is good, as is the bodysurfing, but beware of currents; the snorkeling cannot be recommended. For surfing there are winter breaks, with a right slide. Fishing for threadfin, mountain bass, goatfish and *ulua* is good. Facilities include a picnic area with large pavilion, showers and restrooms. ~ Located about seven miles east of Kahului on the Hana Highway.

**HOOKIPA BEACH PARK**   For serious surfers, kite-surfers and windsurfers this is the best spot on Maui. It's *not* the place for a novice to try out the sports The beach itself is little more than a narrow rectangle of sand paralleled by a rocky shelf. Offshore, top-ranked windsurfers or kitesurfers may be performing airborne stunts. On any given day you're likely to see a hundred sails with boards attached skimming the whitecaps. The swimming is good only when the surf is low. There are picnic areas, restrooms and showers. ~ Located just off the Hana Highway about three miles east of Paia near Mama's Fish House.

*HIDDEN* ►   **HONOMANU BAY**   A tranquil black-sand-and-rock beach surrounded by pandanus-covered hills and bisected by a stream, Honomanu Bay is a beautiful and secluded area. There are no facilities, and the water is often too rough for swimming, but it's a favorite with surfers. ~ Located off the Hana Highway, about 30 miles east of Kahului. Turn off onto the dirt road located east of Kaumahina State Wayside; follow it to the beach.

**WAIANAPANAPA STATE PARK** 🛶 🦅 ⛵ Set in a heavenly seaside locale, this park is one of Hawaii's prettiest public facilities and is a very popular park. The entire area is lush with tropical foliage and especially palmy pandanus trees. ◆◆◆◆◆◆◆◆◆◆◆◆◆◆◆◆◆◆◆◆◆
There's a black-sand beach, sea arches, a blowhole and two legendary caves. But pack your parkas; wind and rain are frequent. Swimming and snorkeling are good—when the water is calm—as is the fishing. Facilities here include a picnic area, restrooms and showers. ~ Located just off the Hana Highway about four miles north of the town of Hana.

> It takes a good three hours to drive the curvaceous road to Hana. But that's without taking time to stop and smell the ginger. Plan accordingly.

▲ There are sites for up to 60 people on a grass-covered bluff overlooking the sea. There are also plain but attractive accommodations renting for $45 for up to four people. Two additional people are allowed at $5 each. Each cabin contains a small bedroom with two bunk beds, plus a living room that can double as an extra bedroom. All cabins are equipped with bedding and complete kitchen facilities, and some have ocean views. A state permit is required. The cabins are rented through the Division of State Parks. ~ 54 South High Street, Suite 101, Wailuku, HI 96793; 808-984-8109.

**HANA BEACH PARK** 🛶 🦅 ⛵ Tucked in a well-protected corner of Hana Bay, this park has a large pavilion and a curving stretch of sandy beach. It's a great place to meet local folks. Swimming is fine; snorkeling is good near the lighthouse; and beginning surfers will find both summer and winter breaks on the north side of the bay (left slide). Some days are very calm, however. Bonefish, *ulua* and *papio* are routinely taken here and *moilii* run in the months of June and July. As well as the concrete picnic area, there are restrooms and showers and there's a snack bar across the street. ~ Located off the Hana Highway at Hana Bay.

**RED SAND BEACH** 🚶 🛶 🦅 ⛵ Known to the Hawaiians as ◀ *HIDDEN*
Kaihalulu ("roaring sea") Beach, this is one of the most exotic and truly secluded beaches in all the islands. Protected by lofty cliffs, it can be reached by hiking a precarious trail. A volcanic cinder beach, the sand is reddish in hue and coarse underfoot. Most dramatic of all is the lava barrier that crosses the mouth of this natural amphitheater, protecting the beach and creating an inshore pool. Popular with nudists and adventures, it's technically illegal to visit. Swimming, snorkeling and fishing are all good. There are no facilities. ~ This is one place where getting to

the beach becomes an adventure. It is located on the far side of Kauiki Hill in Hana. Follow Uakea Road to its southern terminus. There is a grassy plot on the left between Hana School and the parking lot for the Hotel Hana-Maui's sea ranch cottages. Here you will find a trail leading into the undergrowth. It traverses an overgrown Japanese cemetery and curves around Kauiki Hill, then descends precipitously to the beach. Be careful!

**HAMOA BEACH** Located at the head of Mokae Cove, this stretch of salt-and-pepper sand with rock outcroppings at each end is a pretty place. Unfortunately, the Hotel Hana-Maui uses the beach as a semiprivate preserve. There are restrooms and a dining pavilion that are available only to guests, so a sense of segregation pervades the beach. ~ Follow the Hana Highway south from Hana for a little over a mile. Turn left on Haneoo Road and follow it for a mile to Hamoa.

**KOKI BEACH PARK** A sandy plot paralleled by a grassy park, this beach is more welcoming than Hamoa. Backdropped by lofty red cinder cliffs, Koki can be very windy and the ocean is plagued by currents. With a small island and sea arch offshore, it is also very pretty. Swimmers should exercise caution. ~ Located half a mile back up the Haenoo Road toward the highway.

**OHEO GULCH** The stream that tumbles down Haleakala through the Oheo Gulch forms several large pools (popularly known as the Seven Sacred Pools) and numerous small ones. The main pools descend from above the Hana Highway to the sea. This is a truly enchanting area swept by frequent wind and rain, and shadowed by Haleakala. It overlooks Maui's rugged eastern shore. You can swim in the chilly waters and camp nearby. There are picnic facilities and outhouses; bring your own drinking water. Watch your step and be careful here; frequent accidents have been reported. ~ Located in Haleakala National Park's Kipahulu section (about ten miles south of Hana).

▲ Primitive, meadow-style camping is available on a bluff above the sea. No permit is required and there are no restrictions on the number of occupants, but there is a three-day limit. However, to enter Haleakala National Park a $10 per vehicle fee is required. The permit is good for up to seven days.

## Upcountry

Maui's Upcountry is a belt that encircles Haleakala along its middle slopes and ranges from lush in the north to dry in the south. Situated between coastline and crater rim, it's home to a sparse but growing population, and is ideal for camping, hiking or just wandering. Here the flat agricultural fields that blanket central Maui give way to curving hills of ranch land filled with grazing horses. You may also spot axis deer, Hawaiian owls and pheasants.

Farmers plant tomatoes, cabbages, carrots, giant strawberries and the region's famous sweet Kula onions. Proteas, those delicate flowers native to Australia and South Africa, grow in colorful profusion. Hibiscus, jacarandas, silver oak and other wildflowers sweep along the hillsides like a rainstorm. And on the region's two ranches—35,000-acre Haleakala Ranch and 20,000-acre Ulupalakua Ranch—Angus, Hereford and Brangus cattle complete a picture far removed from Hawaii's tropical beaches.

Home to *paniolo*, Hawaii's version of the Western cowboy, the Upcountry region lies along the highways that lead to the crest of Haleakala. Route 37, Haleakala Highway, becomes the Kula Highway as it ascends to the Kula uplands.

**SIGHTS**

It's impossible to tell from the road the beauty within at the **Enchanting Floral Garden**. This eight-acre floral fantasy, however, is in spectacular bloom much of the year, thanks to dedicated owners Kazuo and Kazuko Taketa, who have spent nearly a decade planting and nurturing an amazing array of flowers. Blossoms drip from vines and trees in great swaths of vibrant color with the Maui lowlands for a backdrop. Admission. ~ Route 37, 10-mile marker, Kula; 808-878-2531, fax 808-878-1805; www.flowersofmaui.com, e-mail info@flowersofmaui.com.

Kula's Surfing Goat Dairy, one of two goat dairies in Hawaii, offers cheese-tasting tours. ~ 3651 Omapio Road; 808-878-2870.

Just outside the village of Waiakoa and still in use, the **Church of the Holy Ghost** (12-mile marker), is a unique octagonal chapel, built along this stretch of road in 1897 for Portuguese immigrants working on Maui's ranches and farms.

Route 37 angles southwest through Ulupalakua Ranch to the ruins of the **Makee Sugar Mill**, a once flourishing enterprise built in 1878.

A currently flourishing business, **Tedeschi Vineyards** sits just across the road. Here at Hawaii's oldest winery you can stop for a taster's tour, sampling a pineapple wine called Maui Blanc, and a sweet dessert wine from pineapple and passionfruit called Maui Splash. The tasting room is located in a building that once served as a retreat for King Kalakaua. This building also houses a gift shop and a history room that includes information about the area—the original families, how the area developed, and the first *paniolos*. A picnic in the lush surroundings that include century-old trees is a bonus. ~ 808-878-6058, fax 808-876-0127; www.mauiwine.com, e-mail info@mauiwine.com.

Just past Keokea Park on Kula Highway (Route 37), you'll see **Grandma's Coffee House**, a local gathering place. Four generations of the Franco family, owners of the coffee shop, have been growing coffee on the slopes of Haleakala and picking the beans by hand. These beans are roasted at the shop in a century-old roaster. Boasting panoramic views, Grandma's Coffee House can also brag about its homemade breakfasts, fresh-baked goodies, and hot lunch specials; the coffee, of course, is very good, too. ~ 9232 Kula Highway; 808-878-2140. BUDGET.

Continuing along Route 37, on the right you'll see a sign for **Sun Yat Sen Park**. What will really draw your attention, though, are the statues that seem to pop up out of the dry grass. They have a distinctly Asian flair because they are monuments to the Chinese immigrants who first settled Upcountry Maui. China's leader from the early 20th century, Sun Yat Sen actually visited Maui and stayed at the Pioneer Hotel in Lahaina, which may be one more reason why the park was named after him.

You can also turn up Route 377 to **Kula Botanical Gardens**. An excellent place for picnicking, the landscaped slopes contain an aviary, a pond, a gift shop and a "Taboo Garden" with poisonous plants and over 60 varieties of protea, the flowering shrub that grows so beautifully in this region. Look for the big black iron gate. Admission. ~ 638 Kekaulike Avenue, Kula; 808-878-1715.

One of the several farms nearby is family-owned **Sunrise Protea Farm**, devoted primarily to proteas. They offer fresh or dried bouquets of these South African native flowers. ~ 378 Haleakala Crater Road; 808-876-0200, fax 808-878-6796; www.sunriseprotea.com.

If you make a right from Route 377 onto the road marked for Polipoli before you get to Kula Botanical Gardens, you'll eventually reach **Polipoli Spring State Recreation Area**. This recreation area is the starting point for uncrowded, easy hikes on Haleakala's upper slopes. Head to Polipoli in the morning and you'll likely catch sight of hang gliders taking off on flights to the lowlands below. Note: The final half of the road to Polipoli is extremely rough; a four-wheel-drive vehicle is recommended. (For more information on trails, see "Hiking" at the end of the chapter.)

Another intriguing place is the tiny town of **Makawao**, where battered buildings and falsefront stores replete with hitching posts create an Old West atmosphere. This is the capital of Maui's cowboy country, similar to Waimea on the Big Island, with a rodeo every Fourth of July. Over the years, Makawao has been transformed from an Old West cow town to a thriving arts center.

HIDDEN ►

From Makawao the possibilities for exploring the Upcountry area are many. There are two **loop tours** I particularly recommend. The first climbs from town along Olinda Road (Route 390) past **Pookela Church**, a coral sanctuary built in 1843.

It continues through a frequently rain-drenched region to the **Tree Growth Research Area**, jointly sponsored by state and fed-

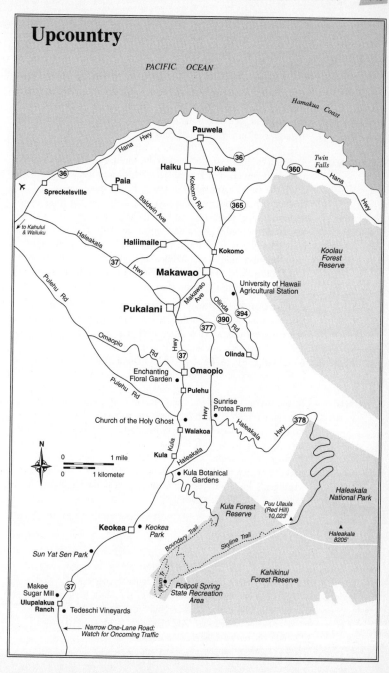

# Upcountry

PACIFIC  OCEAN

Hamakua Coast

Hana  Hwy

**Pauwela**

**Haiku**    Kuiaha    36    360    Twin Falls

36    Hana Hwy

**Paia**    Kokomo Rd    365

**Spreckelsville**

Baldwin Ave

to Kahului & Wailuku

Haleakala    **Haliimaile**    **Kokomo**

37    Hwy    Koolau Forest Reserve

Pulehu  Rd    **Makawao**    University of Hawaii Agricultural Station

**Pukalani**    Makawao Ave    Olinda    394    390    Rd

Omaopio    377

37    Hwy    **Olinda**

Rd    Pulehu Rd

Enchanting Floral Garden    **Omaopio**

**Pulehu**

Sunrise Protea Farm    378

Church of the Holy Ghost    Haleakala Hwy    Hwy

**Waiakoa**

Kula

**Kula**    Haleakala

N    0        1 mile    Kula Botanical Gardens

0        1 kilometer    Kula Forest Reserve    Puu Ulaula (Red Hill) 10,023'    Haleakala National Park

Haleakala 8205'

**Keokea**    Keokea Park    Boundary Trail    Skyline Trail

Sun Yat Sen Park    Plum Tr.    Kahikinui Forest Reserve

Makee Sugar Mill    37    Polipoli Spring State Recreation Area

**Ulupalakua Ranch**    Tedeschi Vineyards

← Narrow One-Lane Road: Watch for Oncoming Traffic

eral forestry services. You can circle back down toward Makawao on Piiholo Road past the **University of Hawaii Agricultural Station**, where you will see more of the area's richly planted acreage.

The second loop leads down Route 365 to the Hana Highway. Turn left on the highway for several miles to Haiku Road, then head left along this country lane, which leads into overgrown areas, across one-lane bridges, past banana patches and through the tinroof town of **Haiku**.

**LODGING**

A mountain lodge on the road to the summit of Haleakala offers a cold-air retreat that is well-situated for anyone who wants to catch the summit sunrise. For years, **Kula Lodge** has rented five chalets, some with fireplaces, sleeping lofts and sweeping ocean and mountain views. The individual chalets are carpeted wall-to-wall and trimmed with stained-wood paneling. The central lodge features a cheery restaurant, bar and stone fireplace. An appealing mountain hideaway. ~ Haleakala Highway, Kula; 808-878-1535, 800-233-1535, fax 808-878-2518; www.kulalodge.com, e-mail info@kulalodge.com. DELUXE.

**GAY LODGING**  **Halfway to Hana House** is a private and secluded studio with a mini-kitchen overlooking the ocean. Guests enjoy a great sunrise view. Stay seven nights or longer and you'll get a 10 percent discount. Three-night minimum. ~ P.O. Box 675, Haiku, HI 96708; 808-572-1176, fax 808-572-3609; www.halfwaytohana.com, e-mail gailp@maui.net. MODERATE.

**DINING**

In the town of Pukalani, there are several good dining spots in Pukalani Terrace Center. Among them is **Nick's Place**, a breakfast-and-lunch-only cafeteria serving Japanese-Chinese-American fare. Choose from such à la carte items as *chow fun*, tempura, Portuguese sausage, stew or corned-beef hash; together they make a hearty meal. At breakfast, try the eggs with Portuguese sausage. ~ Pukalani Terrace Center, Haleakala Highway, Pukalani; 808-572-8258. BUDGET.

**AUTHOR FAVORITE**

**Polli's Restaurant** is a sombreros-on-the-wall-and-oilcloth-on-the-tables eatery offering a full selection of Mexican dishes for lunch and dinner. A local gathering place popular with residents throughout Maui's Upcountry, Polli's has become an institution over the years. It will inevitably be crowded with folks dining on tacos, burritos and tamales, as well as burgers, sandwiches and ribs. ~ 1202 Makawao Avenue, Makawao; 808-572-7808, phone/fax 808-572-0080. MODERATE.

A good local restaurant for breakfast or lunch is the **Ahaaina**.    ◀ *HIDDEN*
The theme here is comfort and family, with Hawaiian print curtains. Breakfast is pretty predictable; lunch includes a wide variety of salads and sandwiches, and fresh fish with home-made tor-
tillas for the fish tacos. Closed Monday. ~ 7-2 Aewa Place at
Haleakala Highway, Pukalani; 808-572-2395. MODERATE.

For something a step more upscale, consider going farther
Upcountry to the **Makawao Steak House**. Redwood plank walls
hold original paintings by some of the best-known local artists.
The popular menu serves a mix of surf-and-turf dishes; unfortunately there is only the salad bar to satisfy vegetarians. Dinner
only. ~ 3612 Baldwin Avenue, Makawao; 808-572-8711, fax
808-572-7103. DELUXE.

Go Mediterranean at **Casanova Italian Restaurant & Deli**, a
stylish bistro that serves Italian-style seafood, pasta dishes and
pizza. For something faster, cheaper and more casual, you can try
the adjacent deli. ~ 1188 Makawao Avenue, Makawao; 808-
572-0220, fax 808-572-4978. DELUXE TO ULTRA-DELUXE.

Upcountry's contribution to Hawaii regional cuisine is **Haliimaile General Store**. A former plantation store that has been
converted into a chic gathering place, it puts a creative spin on
contemporary cuisine and serves roast duckling, fresh island fish
and beef from the Big Island. No lunch on Saturday and Sunday.
~ 900 Haliimaile Road, Haliimaile; 808-572-2666, fax 808-572-
7128; www.haliimailegeneralstore.com. DELUXE TO ULTRA-
DELUXE.

On the lower slope of Haleakala, **Kula Lodge Restaurant** enjoys a panoramic view of the island. Through picture windows
you can gaze out on a landscape that rolls for miles to the sea.
The exposed-beam ceiling and stone fireplace lend a homey feel,
as do the homemade pastries. Specialties include rack of lamb,
pasta dishes and vegetarian entrées. ~ Haleakala Highway, Kula;
808-878-1535, 800-233-1535; e-mail info@kulalodge.com.
DELUXE.

Along the Haleakala Highway there's a **Foodland**, open 24 hours.    **GROCERIES**
~ Pukalani Terrace Center, Pukalani; 808-572-0674.

You can also count on **Down to Earth Natural Foods** for vegetarian health foods and New Age supplies. Open 8 a.m. to 8 p.m.
~ 1169 Makawao Avenue, Makawao; 808-572-1488.

Baldwin Avenue in the Western-style town of Makawao has de-    **SHOPPING**
veloped over the years into a prime arts-and-crafts center.
Housed in the falsefront stores that line the street you'll find galleries galore and a few boutiques besides.

**The Courtyard**, an attractive woodframe mall, contains **Hot
Island Glass** (808-572-4527), with a museum-quality collection

of handblown glass pieces made in the store. Also here is **View-points Gallery** (808-572-5979), which puts many of the higher-priced Lahaina galleries to shame. ~ 3620 Baldwin Avenue, Makawao.

**Gecko Trading Company** is a small boutique that features contemporary fashions at reasonable prices, as well as other gift items. ~ 3621 Baldwin Avenue, Makawao; 808-572-0249.

The kids will love **Maui Child Toys & Books** for its puppets, art supplies, wooden toys and music tapes. ~ 3643 Baldwin Avenue, Makawao; 808-572-2765.

Check out **Goodie's** for gift items: crystal mobiles, locally made jewelry, picture frames. There are also women's fashions, men's shirts and handmade Hawaiian baskets. ~ 3633 Baldwin Avenue, Makawao; 808-572-0288.

Maui's latest "art" destination is not Lahaina's Front Street—surprise, surprise—but rather the small town of Makawao.

What put Makawao on the arts-destination map was the **Hui Noeau Visual Arts Center**. Located on the outskirts of Makawao, the 1917 Mediterranean-style Baldwin mansion offers rotating educational exhibits, and regular workshops on painting, printmaking, ceramics, sculpture and much, much more. For the artistically impaired but pocketbook inclined, works by Maui artists are available for purchase. ~ 2841 Baldwin Avenue, Makawao; 808-572-6560; www.huinoeau.com, e-mail info@huinoeau.com.

In the Kula Lodge complex, the **Curtis Wilson Cost Gallery** sells prints, limited editions and originals by Curtis Wilson Cost. The emphasis is on local landscapes and ocean scenery. ~ Route 377 (Haleakala Highway), Kula; 808-878-6544, 800-810-2678.

**Proteas of Hawaii** specializes in gift boxes, proteas and tropical floral arrangements. They also sell orchids and anthuriums. Closed weekends. ~ 417 Mauna Place, Kula; 808-878-2533.

**NIGHTLIFE**   Upcountry is pretty quiet in the evenings. However, there are live bands on Saturday nights and deejay music on Wednesday and Friday at **Casanova Italian Restaurant**. One of Upcountry's only nightspots, it features a range of live acts—from local Mauian to internationally known. Cover. ~ 1188 Makawao Avenue, Makawao; 808-572-0220.

**BEACHES & PARKS**   **POLIPOLI SPRING STATE RECREATION AREA** 🏃 Located at 6200-foot elevation on the slopes of Haleakala, this densely forested area is an ideal mountain retreat. Monterey and sugi pine, eucalyptus and Monterey cypress grow in stately profusion; not far from the campground there's a grove of redwoods. From Polipoli's ethereal heights you can look out over Central and West Maui, as well as the islands of Lanai, Molokai and Kahoolawe. Miles of trails, some leading up to the volcano summit, crisscross the park. Polipoli has a picnic area, restrooms and running water. ~ From Kahului, take Haleakala Highway (Route 37) through Pukalani and past Waiakoa to Route 377. Turn left on 377 and follow it a short distance to the road marked for Polipoli. About half of this ten-mile road to the park is paved. The second half of the track is extremely rough and often muddy. It is advisable to take a four-wheel-drive vehicle.

▲ There is meadow-style camping (a state permit is required) that holds up to 20 people; the cabin houses up to ten people and rents at $45 per night for the first four guests, and an extra $5 for each additional guest. The spacious cabin (three bedrooms) is sparsely furnished and lacks electricity. It does have a wood heating stove and a gas cooking stove. It can be rented from the Division of State Parks. It's recommended to bring in drinking water. ~ 808-984-8109.

## Haleakala National Park

It seems only fitting that the approach to the summit of Haleakala is along one of the world's fastest-climbing roads. From Kahului to the summit rim—a distance of about 40 miles along Routes 37, 377 and 378—the macadam road rises from sea level to 10,000 feet, and the silence is broken only by the sound of ears popping from the ascent.

At the volcano summit, 10,023 feet in elevation, you look out over an awesome expanse—seven miles long, over two miles wide, 21 miles around. This dormant volcano, which last erupted around 1790, is the central feature of a 30,183-acre national park that extends all the way through the Kipahulu Valley to the sea. The crater floor, 3000 feet below the rim, is a multi-hued wasteland filled with cinder cones, lava flows and mini-craters. It's a legendary place, with a mythic tradition that's as vital as its geologic history. It was from Haleakala ("House of the Sun") that the demigod Maui lassoed the sun and slowed its track across the sky to give his mother more daylight to dry her tapa cloth.

Technically, by the way, this area is an "erosional depression," not a crater. The converging headwaters of eroding valleys met at the top of the mountain and scooped out the seven-mile by two-mile bowl. Later eruptions studded the floor with cinder cones and lava flows. "Erosional depression" is cumbersome compared to "crater," so if you are like me and still say crater, you can at least claim to know the difference.

In the afternoon the volcano's colors are most vivid, but during the morning the crater is more likely to be free of clouds. Before going up Haleakala, call 808-877-5111 for a weather report. Then you can decide what time of day will be best for your explorations. Remember that it takes an hour and a half to two hours to reach the summit from Kahului, longer from the Kaanapali–Kapalua area. Be sure to bring warm clothes since the temperature drop from sea level to 10,000 feet can be 30° or more, which means the temperature may be below freezing. You might even encounter snow. The air is very thin, so pace yourself.

**SIGHTS**

On the way up to the summit you'll pass **Hosmer's Grove** (6800 feet), a picnic area and campground (permit not required) surrounded by eucalyptus, spruce, juniper and cedar, as well as some native trees, like ohia and mamanae.

**National Park Headquarters**, located at the 7030-foot elevation, contains an information desk and maps, and makes a good starting point. You may be lucky enough to see the Hawaiian state bird, the nene, which frequents the area around headquarters. Be sure to keep your distance during nesting season. ~ 808-572-4400; www.nps.gov/hale.

The Brangus cattle that graze along the slopes of Haleakala's ranchland are a Braham-Angus hybrid.

The first crater view comes at **Leleiwi Overlook**, an 8800-foot perch from where, on a clear day, you'll be able to see all the way from Hana across the island to Kihei. Here at sunrise and sunset, under correct meteorological conditions, you can see your shadow projected on the clouds and haloed by a rainbow. To experience this "Specter of the Brocken," stand atop the volcano rim looking toward the cloud-filled crater with the setting sun at your back.

Up the hill, a side road leads to **Kalahaku Overlook**, a 9324-foot aerie that offers a unique view of several cinder cones within the volcano. Just below the parking lot are numerous **silverswords**. Related to sunflowers, these spike-leaved plants grow only on Maui and the Big Island. They remain low bristling plants for five to fifty years or more before blooming into a flowering stalk. Each plant blossoms once, sometime between May and November, and then dies.

The best view of the wilderness area is farther up the road at the **Haleakala Visitors Center**, 9745-feet elevation, where you'll find an information desk, as well as a series of exhibits about the volcano. From this vantage point you can gaze out toward Koolau Gap to the north and Kaupo Gap to the south. Several peaks located along the volcano loom out of the clouds; cinder cones, including 600-foot Puu o Maui, rise up from the crater floor.

From the visitors center a short trail heads up to **White Hill**. Composed of andesite lava and named for its characteristic light color, this mound is dotted with stone windbreaks once used as sleeping places by Hawaiians who periodically visited the summit of Haleakala.

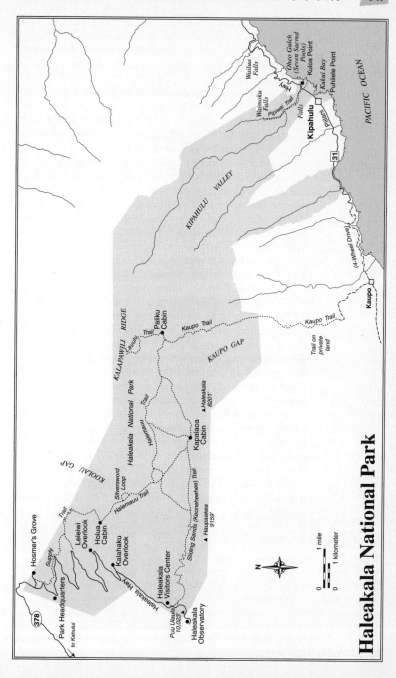

Haleakala National Park

It's a short drive to the summit at **Puu Ulaula Overlook**. From the plate-glass lookout you can view the Big Island, Molokai, Lanai, West Maui and wilderness area itself. On an extremely clear day this 360° panorama may even include a view of Oahu, 130 miles away.

Perched high above atmospheric haze and the lights of civilization, Haleakala is also an excellent spot for stargazing. The white dome-like structure you see is the **Haleakala Observatory**, an important center for satellite tracking and television communications. This area is closed to the public.

While the views along the volcano rim are awesome, the best way to see Haleakala is from the inside looking out. With 36 miles of hiking trails, two campsites and three cabins, the wilderness provides a tremendous opportunity for explorers. Within the belly of this monstrous volcano, you'll see such geologic features as cinder cones and spatter vents. The Hawaiians marked their passing with stone altars, shelters and adze quarries. You may also spy the rare nene (a Hawaiian relative of the Canada goose), as well as chukar partridges and pheasants.

HIDDEN ► The **volcano floor** is a unique environment, one of constant change and unpredictable weather. Rainfall varies from 12 inches annually in the southwestern corner to 200 inches at Paliku. Temperatures, usually hovering between 55° and 75° during daylight, may fall below freezing at night. Campers should come prepared with warm clothing and sleeping gear, a tent, poncho, lantern and stove (no open fires are permitted). Don't forget the sunblock, as the elevation on the bottom averages 6700 feet and the ultraviolet radiation is intense.

Within the wilderness area you can explore three main trails. **Sliding Sands Trail**, a steep cinder and ash path, begins near the Haleakala Visitors Center. It descends from the rim along the south wall to Kapalaoa cabin, then on to Paliku cabin. In the course of this ten-mile trek, the trail drops over 3000 feet. From Paliku, the **Kaupo Trail** leaves the crater through Kaupo Gap and descends to the tiny town of Kaupo, eight miles away on Maui's

**LATE SLEEPERS, TAKE NOTE**

One of Maui's favorite rituals is a predawn trip to the top of Haleakala to watch the sun rise. Unfortunately, the weather can be foggy and cold. Besides that, getting up early is probably the last thing you want to do on vacation. If so, consider the alternative: Sleep late, take your time getting to the top and arrive in time for sunset. But, then again, you'll miss a dazzling, almost religious experience. In any case, call **808-877-5111** to check on the weather before making the trip up!

southeast coast. **Halemauu Trail** (8 miles) begins from the road three-and-a-half miles beyond National Park Headquarters and descends 1400 feet to the crater floor. It passes Holua cabin and eventually joins Sliding Sands Trail at the Kapalaoa cabin.

**LODGING**

There are campgrounds at **Holua** and **Paliku** that require a permit from National Park Headquarters. Permits are given out on a first-come, first-served basis, so plan accordingly. Camping is limited to two days at one site and three days total at both. The campgrounds have pit toilets and nonpotable running water.

There is also a 12-person cabin at each campsite and at **Kapalaoa**. Equipped with wood and gas stoves, pit toilets, cooking utensils, bunks and limited nonpotable water, these primitive facilities are extremely popular. So popular, in fact, that guests are chosen by a monthly lottery two months in advance. ~ For more information, write Haleakala National Park, attention: cabins, P.O. Box 369, Makawao, HI 96768; or call 808-572-4400; www.nps.gov/hale.

▼▼▼▼▼▼▼▼▼▼▼▼▼▼

## Outdoor Adventures

The opportunities for adventuring on the Valley Isle are numerous and the conditions for several activities are outstanding. Whale watching, for example, is top-notch on Maui as humpbacks return each year to the waters off Lahaina to give birth. For cyclists, there are thrilling rides down the slopes of Haleakala and challenging courses on Hana's curving coast. Maui is also home to several of the world's premier windsurfing spots including Hookipa Beach on the island's north shore. In addition, Maui has more miles of swimmable beach than any of the other islands in the chain.

**CAMPING**

Though extremely popular with adventurers, Maui has very few official campsites. The laws restricting camping here are more strictly enforced than on other islands. The emphasis on this boom island favors condominiums and resort hotels rather than outdoor living, but you can still escape the concrete congestion at several parks and unofficial campsites (including one of the most spectacular tenting areas in all Hawaii—Haleakala Wilderness Area).

Camping at **county parks** requires a permit. These are issued for a maximum of three consecutive nights at each campsite, and cost $3 per person per night, children 50¢. Permits can be obtained at War Memorial Gym adjacent to Baldwin High School, Route 32, Wailuku, or by writing the Department of Parks and Recreation Permit Department, 700 Halia Nakoa Street, Unit 2, Wailuku, HI 96793; 808-270-7389.

**State park** permits are free and allow camping for five days. They can be obtained at the Division of State Parks in the State

Building on South High Street, or by writing the Division of State Parks. ~ 54 South High Street, Room 101, Wailuku, HI 96793; 808-984-8109. You can also rent cabins at Waianapanapa and Polipoli state parks through this office.

If you plan on camping in the Haleakala Wilderness Area, you must obtain a permit on the day you are camping from Haleakala National Park headquarters, located on the way to the valley. These permits are allocated on a first-come, first-served basis.

Remember, rainfall is heavy along the northeast shore around Hana, but infrequent on the south coast. Also, Haleakala gets quite cold; you'll need heavy clothing, rain gear and sleeping gear.

It is best to bring along your own camping gear, but in a pinch check **Gaspro Inc.** ~ 365 Hanakai Street, Kahului; 808-877-0056. **Sears** at Kahului's Kaahumanu Center also carries camping gear. ~ 275 Kaahumanu Avenue, Kahului; 808-877-2206.

**ECO-TOURS** More and more adventure tours are becoming eco-tours. Combining the usual tourist activities with a dose of conservation, eco-tours are an edifying way to soak up the beauty and culture of Hawaii while "leaving only footprints."

The flora and fauna of Maui, as well as traces of the ancient Polynesians, are the focus of **Paths in Paradise**. The company's owner/operator is an environmentalist who will lead you on half- and full-day hikes to explore Hawaii's endangered nature. ~ P.O. Box 667, Makawao, HI 96768; 808-264-4827; www.mauibird hikes.com.

An excellent educational opportunity awaits you at the **Ocean Project**, a marine research center studying the coral reefs of Maui. These folks have extensive knowledge and build their events around your interests. At the beach, they'll give you a "class" in the subject of your choice (for example, identification of fish and coral species or the behavior of giant green sea turtles), and then take you snorkeling for an up-close look at what you just learned. The sessions are about two to three hours long and will change the way you view those pretty-colored fish. ~ Lahaina; 808-661-6706; e-mail oceanproject@prodigy.net.

**DIVING** Maui offers a wide variety of snorkeling and diving opportunities ranging from Black Rock off Kaanapali to Honolua Bay, not to mention Olowalu, Ahihi–Kinau Natural Area Reserve and Ulua Beach. While most of the dive operators are located near the island's south coast resorts, there are also good diving and snorkeling opportunities on the north shore at Paia's Baldwin Beach Park, as well as Hana's Waianapanapa State Park. From Maui it's also easy to reach neighboring destinations such as the Molokini Crater Marine Preserve and reefs off Lanai.

Molokini, a crescent-shaped crater off Maui's southern coast, offers one of the island's great snorkeling adventures. Every day dozens of boatloads of people pull up to dive the remarkably clear waters. During winter months, you're also likely to see the humpback whales cavorting nearby.

**LAHAINA** **Extended Horizons** offers half-day excursions to Lanai's west coast. Dive through caverns and lava tubes in search of dolphins, turtles and whales. ~ Mala Wharf, Lahaina; 808-667-0611, 888-348-3628; www.scubadivemaui.com.

*Visibility at Molokini typically ranges between 80 and 150 feet, conditions so clear you can spot fish before even entering the water.*

**Ocean Riders Adventure Rafting** specializes in snorkeling trips; set out from Maui to Lanai or Molokai on full-day snorkel trips accompanied by schools of tropical fish and topped with a continental breakfast and lunch. ~ Mala Wharf, Lahaina; 808-661-3586; www.mauioceanriders.com.

**Lahaina Divers Inc.** is another well-liked dive operator. Their retail store provides equipment and accessories. Scuba classes and trips are available year-round depending on the weather. Equipment repair and service are also available. ~ 143 Dickenson Street, Lahaina; 808-667-7496.

**KIHEI–WAILEA–MAKENA AREA** **Maui Classic Charters** offers half-day dives into the Molokini crater along with catamaran excursions. ~ 179 South Kihei Road, Suite 110, Kihei; 808-879-8188; www.mauicharters.com.

Another recommended tour operator that also rents snorkel and scuba equipment is **Maui Dive Shop**, which has eight locations in Maui. ~ 1455 South Kihei Road, Kihei; 808-879-1175, 800-542-3483; www.mauidiveshop.com.

Well-known by underwater photographers, **Mike Severns Diving** runs trips for certified divers to Molokini and Makena. Dives focus on the southwest rift of Haleakala, a fascinating place to study marine life. Led by informative guides, these trips are an excellent way to see Maui's hidden marine life. ~ Kihei Boat Ramp, Kihei; 808-879-6596; www.mikesevernsdiving.com, e-mail severns@mauigateway.com.

**Scuba Shack** features scuba and snorkeling trips to Molokini Crater. Visibility of 150 feet makes this marine reserve a favorite place to splash down. ~ 2349 South Kihei Road, Kihei; 808-891-0500; www.scubashack.com.

**Maui Sun Divers** provides all gear and offers everything from beginner trips to certification classes to night dives. A true part of "Hidden Hawaii," you won't find them on land. They will take you anywhere around the island, weather permitting. ~ Kihei; 877-879-3337; www.mauisundivers.com.

Experienced divers should sign on with **Ed Robinson's Diving Adventures**. A prominent oceanic photographer, Robinson leads half-day scuba excursions aboard the *Seadiver II* and *Sea Spirit* to the Lanai Cathedrals, Molokini and other favored dive sites. ~ Kihei; 808-879-3584; www.maui-scuba.com.

**Makena Boat Partners** operates the 46-foot *Kai Kanani,* which departs from Makena Beach, and goes closer to the largely submerged volcano than other touring vessels. Prices include all equipment, food and drink. ~ 808-879-7218.

**SURFING WIND-SURFING & KITE-SURFING**

If you must go down to the sea again, why not do it on a board? For surfing, Maalaea, Honolua Bay and Hookipa are consistent world-class venues. La Perouse is an expert's heaven.

Pro windsurfers and kitesurfers will want to head to Hookipa. Pros at other things should confine their windsurfing and kitesurfing to Kanaha, Kihei and Spreckelsville.

**LAHAINA**   **Goofy Fool** gives beginner- to advanced-level lessons and leads surf safaris. ~ 505 French Street, Suite 123, Lahaina; 808-244-9283.

**KAANAPALI–KAPALUA AREA**   **Maui Ocean Activities** offers surfing and windsurfing lessons on the adjacent beach. Ninety-minute windsurfing lessons come with a guarantee of success. Four-person surfing classes are also offered, weather permitting. Rentals are available. ~ Whalers Village, Kaanapali; Maui Ocean Activities reservations 808-667-2001, fax 808-667-4346; www.mauiwatersports.com, e-mail beaches@maui.net.

For weather forecasts on Maui, call **808-877-5111**; marine conditions, **808-877-3477**.

**KAHULUI–WAILUKU AREA**   **Maui Windsurf Company** can help work windsurfing into your visit, either with a car rack and sails or with lessons. Instruction is held in the calmer waters at Kanaha, near the airport. Hookipa's more powerful winds are recommended only for experts. ~ 22 Hana Highway, Kahului; 808-877-4816, 800-872-0999; www.mauiwindsurfcompany.com.

At **Second Wind Sail Surf & Kite**, you can get everything you need for a day (or longer) of surfing, windsurfing or kitesurfing. They offer equipment rental and sales and extensive instruction. ~ 111 Hana Highway, Kahului; 808-877-7467; www.secwindmaui.com.

You can buy surfing gear at **Lightning Bolt,** the oldest surf shop on Maui. ~ 55 Kaahumanu Avenue, Kahului; 808-877-3484.

**HANA AREA**   **Kai Nalu Surf Tours** will take you on two- or four-day excursions to lesser-known Maui surfing spots. ~ 536 Kahua Place, Paia; 808-579-9937.

The deep blue sea around Maui can be nirvana for sportfishing enthusiasts. For deep-sea fishing you'll have to charter a boat, and freshwater angling requires a license, which can be obtained at sportfishing stores.

There is also good fishing from the shore in many places. For information on the best spots, ask at local fishing stores, or try the following beaches: Hoaloha Park, Launiupoko County Park, Honokowai Beach Park, D. T. Fleming Park, Honokohau Beach, Keawakapu Beach, Poolenalena Beach Park, Black Sands Beach, Little Beach and Waianapanapa State Park.

For information on seasons, licenses and official regulations, check with the Aquatic Resources Division of the State Department of Land & Natural Resources. Choose between party boats, diesel cruisers and yachts custom-designed for trolling. All outfits provide equipment and bait. Just bring your own food and drinks and you're in business. Occasionally, your skipper may head for the productive game fishing waters between Maui and the Big Island. It's a treacherous channel, however, so you're more likely to fish the leeward side of the island or off neighboring Lanai.

**LAHAINA**   West Maui Sports & Fishing Supply sails in search of marlin, mahimahi, wahoo and tuna. If a deep-sea excursion is not for you, rent a pole for shore fishing. Based in Lahaina Harbor, West Maui Sports provides shoreline pickup at Kaanapali Beach. ~ 1287 Front Street; 808-661-6252, 888-498-7726; www.westmauisports.com.

Luckey Strike Charters fishes for marlin, mahimahi, wahoo and tuna with light and medium tackle. Light-tackle bottom fishing is also available. ~ Lahaina Harbor; 808-661-4606; www.luckeystrike.com.

Hinatea is a sportfishing boat that offers trips into coastal waters. On half- and full-day trips you'll fish for marlin, mahimahi and *ono*. ~ 27 Lahaina Harbor; 808-667-7548.

**KIHEI–WAILEA–MAKENA AREA**   In the Kihei area, contact Carol Ann Charters for four-, six- and eight-hour fishing trips great for catching marlin, tuna, mahimahi and *ono*. She runs a 33-foot Bertrum. ~ Maalaea Harbor; 808-877-2181.

Rascal Charters fishes for ahi, *ono*, mahimahi and marlin. They also run four-, six- and eight-hour trips aboard a 41-foot Hatteras. ~ Maalaea Harbor; 808-874-8633.

**FISHING**

From mid-December until the middle of May, it is prime whale-watching season on Maui. Humpback whales, measuring about 40 feet and weighing over 40 tons, migrate as many as 4000 miles from their summer home in Alaska. On the journey south, they consume tons of krill and tiny fish, then fast while in Ha-

**SAILING & WHALE WATCHING**

waii. It is in the waters off Maui that they give birth to their young, babies that can weigh as much as three tons and gain up to 100 pounds a day.

These cetaceans are a protected species and power crafts are required by law to keep their distance. But these restrictions are not so severe as to unduly interfere with the many sailing vessels that offer whale-watching opportunities off the Maui coast. You can also enjoy dive trips or pure performance rides on these beautiful vessels.

Between 2000 and 3000 of the world's 10,000 humpbacks make the annual migration to Maui's southwestern coast each year. Today they are an endangered species, protected by federal law from whalers. Several local organizations study these leviathans and serve as excellent information sources.

The **Pacific Whale Foundation** issues daily reports over local radio stations during whale season. This same organization conducts "eco-adventure cruises," the profits from which help fund their whale protection projects. They have snorkeling tours to Molokini and whale-watching cruises, both led by marine naturalists. Most interesting is their dolphin adventure, where you snorkel Lanai's untouched coral reefs and see spinner and bottle-nose dolphins in one of the island's many hidden coves. ~ 300 Maalaea Road, Suite 211, Wailuku; 800-942-5311; www.paci ficwhale.org.

**LAHAINA**  Trilogy Excursions specializes in half- and full-day sailing adventures. They also offer whale-watching trips aboard a 41-foot sloop, as well as snorkeling excursions, scuba trips, instruction and joysailing. Special trips include Molokini crater and Lanai. Trilogy receives high praise from repeat clients who climb aboard the 50-foot catamaran for excursions to Lanai. Once on the nearby island, they can swim and snorkel Hulopoe Bay Marine Reserve, enjoy a Hawaiian barbecue and tour Lanai City. Trips depart from Lahaina and Maalaea harbors and Kaanapali Resort beach. ~ Lahaina Harbor; 808-661-4743.

Scotch Mist Sailing Charters offers half-day snorkeling trips. Whale watching, sailing and champagne-and-chocolate sunset sails are also available. ~ Lahaina Harbor; 808-661-0386.

**BIRD'S-EYE VIEW**

A prime area for whale watching lies along Honoapiilani Highway between Maalaea Bay and Lahaina, particularly at McGregor Point. So while you're visiting Maui, always keep an eye peeled seaward for vaporous spume and a rolling hump. The place you're standing might suddenly become an ideal crow's-nest.

Imagine the thrill of big-time yacht racing when you sail aboard **America II**, a 65-foot America's Cup contender. There are morning whale-watching excursions from December 15 through April and afternoon tradewind and sunset sails year-round. The trips last two hours and include soft drinks and snacks. ~ Lahaina Harbor; 808-667-2133, 888-667-2133.

For an intimate experience, try the six-passenger **Cinderella**, a 50-foot luxury sailboat. ~ Maalaea Harbor; 808-244-0009.

**Island Marine Activities** offers whale-spotting cruises from mid-December to May. They also have fine-dining sunset dinner cruises, Molokini crater snorkel tours, and four package tours to Molokai, from a walking tour to a car rental package. ~ 658 Front Street, Lahaina; 808-661-8397.

**KAANAPALI–KAPALUA AREA** **Kapalua Kai** is a popular cata-maran offering picnic-and-snorkeling and sunset sails. It sails Maui's most scenic waters and features whale-watching excur-sions in winter months. Scuba trips also available. ~ Kaanapali; 808-667-5980; www.sailingmaui.com.

Lahaina and Kaanapali Beach are perfect places to become air-borne. Wonderful views of Maui's west side and neighboring Molokai add to the fun. The typical parasailing trip includes 30 to 45 minutes shuttling out and back to the launch point and eight to ten minutes in the air.

**Parasail Kaanapali** riders rise as high as 900 feet, single or tandem. Closed mid-December to mid-May. ~ Mala Wharf, La-haina; 808-669-6555. UFO **Parasail** lets you ascend up to 800 feet and also fly with a companion. ~ Whalers Village, Kaana-pali; 808-661-7836.

For hang gliding from some of the most beautiful spots on the island, try **Hang Gliding Maui**. They also operate motorized hanggliding in Hana. Reservations required. ~ Hana Airport, Kahului; 808-572-6557; www.hangglidingmaui.com.

**PARA-SAILING & HANG GLIDING**

Cruising Maui's coastline by kayak offers close-up views of sealife as well as neighboring islands and perhaps the largest seasonal population of humpback whales.

**KAYAKING**

**KAANAPALI–KAPALUA AREA** Kayaks are available from **Ka-anapali Windsurfing School**. Trips are offered through the Hyatt Regency. ~ The Hyatt, Kaanapali; Maui Ocean Activities reser-vations 808-661-1234 ext. 3290.

**KIHEI–WAILEA–MAKENA AREA** An easy-going kayaking excursion along the Makena–La Perouse area can be had with **Kelii's Kayak Tours**. Rising early in the morning, you get a quick lesson on ocean kayaking, and then venture off the shoreline in search of Maui's sea life. Those lazy-looking sea turtles bobbing alongside you don't have to work as hard as you do. The trip concludes with a dip in the sea for an up-close-and-personal snorkeling adventure. Kelii's also offers north shore tour excursions in the Honolua Bay/Honokohau area and west shore departures in Lahaina. ~P.O. Box 959, #420, Kihei, HI 96753; 808-874-7652, 888-874-7652; www.keliiskayak.com, e-mail info@keliiskayak.com. Kayak rentals and tours can also be arranged through **South Pacific Kayaks**. Their naturalist-guided trips include snorkeling, and you're likely to see whales, sea turtles and dolphins, depending on the season. ~ 95 Halekuai Street, Kihei; 808-875-4848, 800-776-2326; www.southpacifickayaks.com.

**KAHULUI–WAILUKU AREA**   In Central Maui, **Maui Sea Kayaking** offers day trips to Maui and Lanai and full-moon trips to Molokini. Or they'll lead you on an overnight "romance" retreat, for which a guide will arrange a seaside campsite that is off the beaten track and inaccessible by car. In the morning, the guide will return to prepare your breakfast and lead the way back to civilization. They also lead kayak and wave-ski surfers to beaches good for surfing. Maximum four people. ~ Puunene; 808-572-6299; www.maui.net/~kayaking.

**RAFTING**    Rafting trips are the adventurous way to enjoy the Maui coast. Easily combined with dive and whale-watching trips, these sturdy craft are a great way to reach hidden coves and beaches.

**LAHAINA**   **Action Adventure Tours** operates half- and full-day trips to Lanai and Lanai dive trips. Whale-watching excursions are great fun in the winter months. ~ 1223 Front Street, Lahaina; 808-661-7333; www.actionadventuretravel.com.

**Ocean Riders Adventure Rafting** will take you out to Lanai and, weather permitting, Molokai, for a glorious day of snorkeling, as well as whale watching during whale season. All trips are aboard rigid-hull inflatable boats. ~ Mala Wharf, Lahaina; 808-661-3586; www.mauioceanriders.com.

Another company offering tours is **Captain Steve's Rafting Excursions**, which heads out regularly in search of tropical fish, dolphins and exotic birdlife. One trip not to miss circumnavigates Lanai. ~ Mala Wharf, Lahaina; 808-667-5565; www.captainsteves.com.

Full- and half-day trips are offered aboard **Hawaii Ocean Rafting**'s vessel, a motorized raft that takes you to a variety of different snorkeling spots while spinner dolphins leap picturesquely in your wake. ~ P.O. Box 381, Lahaina, HI 96767; 808-667-2191.

**KIHEI–WAILEA–MAKENA AREA**   **Blue Water Rafting** offers both rafting and snorkeling trips to the very popular Molokini and the Kanaio coast. ~ Kihei Boat Ramp, Kihei; 808-879-7238; www.bluewaterrafting.com.

Maui's volcanic landscape, beaches and sculptured valleys are choice sites for equestrian excursions. A variety of rides are available across the island—from the shoreline of Hana to the slopes of Haleakala, you can count on seeing wildlife, lava fields and those famous Maui sunsets.

**RIDING STABLES**

**KIHEI–WAILEA–MAKENA AREA** **Makena Stables** leads trail rides across the scenic 20,000-acre Ulupalakua Ranch on the south slope of Haleakala. Mountain trails cross a 200-year-old lava flow. Choose among a two-and-a-half-hour morning ride or a three-hour sunset ride. Possibilities include overlooking La Perouse Bay or going through Kalua Olapa, which is an old, inactive volcanic vent, and sunset rides. ~ 8299 South Makena Road, Makena; 808-879-0244; www.makena stables.com.

Brrrr... the lowest recorded temperature in the Hawaiian Islands was 11°F, in 1961, atop Haleakala!

**HANA HIGHWAY** **Lahaina Stables** offers morning, noon and evening rides, presenting history, views of the islands and sunsets along Laniopoko Valley. Lunch provided for midday rides. Eight riders maximum. ~ P.O. Box 10506, Lahaina, HI 96761; 808-667-2222, fax 808-661-5750.

**UPCOUNTRY AND HALEAKALA** At **Thompson Ranch and Riding Stables** ride through pastureland on short day and sunset trips that offer views of the other islands. Excursions are suitable for children. ~ Polipoli Road, Kula; 808-878-1910.

**Charlie's Trail Rides and Pack Trips** provides overnight horseback trips from Kaupo through Haleakala. There is a six-person maximum on overnight trips. Two- and four-hour trips outside the park are also available. Meals can be included in the travel package for groups of four to six. ~ 808-248-8209.

With more than a dozen public and private courses, Maui is golf heaven. Choices on the Valley Isle range from country club links to inexpensive community courses. Also, several resorts offer a choice of championship courses ideal for golfers looking for a change of pace. These are open to the public for a hefty fee. Consider reserving tee-times before your visit, especially during the high season. Some courses allow you to book up to a month in advance.

**GOLF**

**KAANAPALI–KAPALUA AREA** The **Kaanapali Golf Courses** are among the island's finest. The championship par-71 North Course, designed by golf course architect Robert Trent Jones, Sr., has a slight incline. The easier South Course is intersected by Maui's popular sugar cane train. ~ 2290 Kaanapali Parkway, Kaanapali; 808-661-3691; www.kaanapali-golf.com.

With three courses, the **Kapalua Resort** is one of the best places to golf on Maui. For a real challenge, try the par-73 Plantation Course built in the heart of pineapple country. The ocean-front Bay Course and the mountainside Village Course, which ascends into the foothills, were created by Arnold Palmer himself. ~ 2000 Village Road, Kapalua; 877-527-2582.

**KIHEI–WAILEA–MAKENA AREA**   The **Wailea Golf Club**, located in the heart of the Wailea Resort complex, offers three courses, all with ocean views. The 18-hole "blue course" heads uphill along the slopes of Haleakala. The least-challenging "emerald course" is also the shortest. The "gold course" is the longest and most challenging, with 93 bunkers. There are two clubhouses on the premises. ~ 100 Wailea Golf Club Drive; 808-879-2966.

Located next to the Maui Prince Hotel, **Makena Golf Club** has two 18-hole courses. Designed by Robert Trent Jones, Jr., the "North" and "South" courses are intended to blend into the natural Hawaiian landscape while offering high-challenge golf. Rolling terrain and beautiful views of the neighbor islands make these links a treat. ~ 5415 Makena Alanui, Makena; 808-879-3344; www.makenagolf.com.

**KAHULUI–WAILUKU AREA**   **Waiehu Municipal Golf Course** is the island's only publicly owned course. With a front nine on the shoreline and a challenging back nine along the mountains, this course offers plenty of variety. Other amenities include a driving range and practice green. ~ 340 Kahekili Highway, Waiehu; 808-243-7400.

The somewhat hilly, par-72 **Sandalwood** was designed by Nelson and Wright. Three holes have lakes or ponds. There's a restaurant and pro shop on the premises, as well as a practice range, a chipping green and two putting greens. ~ 2500 Honoapiilani Highway, Waikapu; 808-242-7090.

**HANA HIGHWAY**   The **Maui Country Club** is a relatively easy nine-hole course open to the public on Mondays. ~ 48 Nonohe Place, Paia; 808-877-7893.

**UPCOUNTRY AND HALEAKALA**   The upcountry **Pukalani Country Club**, on the slopes of Haleakala, is an 18-hole public course. Boasting the highest elevation of all Maui's courses, this club is a sleeper with great views. Bring a jacket or sweater because these links can get cool. ~ 360 Pukalani Street; 808-572-1314.

**TENNIS**   If you're an avid tennis fan, or just in the mood to whack a few balls, you're in luck. Public tennis courts are easily found throughout the island. Almost all are lighted and convenient to major resort destinations.

**LAHAINA**   In the Lahaina area, you'll enjoy the courts at the **Lahaina Civic Center** ~ 1840 Honoapiilani Highway; or at **Malu-ulu-olele Park** ~ Front and Shaw streets. For more information call the Parks and Recreation Department in Lahaina. ~ 808-661-4685.

**KAANAPALI–KAPALUA AREA**   There are several resorts in the area that open their courts to the public for a fee. One is the **Hyatt Regency Maui.** ~ 200 Nohea Kai Drive, Kaanapali; 808-661-1234. Another is the **Maui Marriott.** ~ 100 Nohea Kai Drive, Kaanapali; 808-667-1200.

The **Kapalua Tennis Garden** offers ten courts. Fee. ~ 100 Kapalua Drive, Kapalua; 808-669-5677.

**KIHEI–WAILEA–MAKENA AREA**   There are public courts at **Kalama Park** on Kihei Road and **Maui Sunset Condominiums** on Waipulani Road. ~ 808-879-4364.

**Makena Resort Tennis Club** is a favorite resort that lets the public use its six courts. Fee. ~ Makena Resort, 5400 Makena Alanui, Makena; 808-879-8777.

**Wailea Tennis Club** has 11 courts. Fee. ~ 131 Wailea Iki Place, Wailea; 808-879-1958.

**KAHULUI–WAILUKU AREA**   In the Kahului area, try the courts at the **Kahului Community Center** on Onehee and Uhu streets. In Wailuku, try **War Memorial** complex at 1580 Kaahumanu Avenue, or the public courts at Wells and Market streets. ~ 808-270-7389.

**HANA HIGHWAY**   In the Hana area try the **Hana Ball Park**.

**UPCOUNTRY AND HALEAKALA**   Popular Upcountry courts are found at the **Eddie Tam Memorial Center** in Makawao and the **Pukalani Community Center** in Pukalani. ~ 808-572-8122.

**BIKING**

If you've ever wanted to zip down a mountainside or go off-road in volcanic highlands, you've come to the right place. While Maui is best known for its downhill cycling trips, there are also many other challenging adventures. For example, you can enjoy the remote route from Hana to Ulupalakua or head from Kapalua to Wailuku via Kahakuloa.

### GIDDY UP

If you'd rather not do the walking, why not mount a steed and ride the trail into the depths of Haleakala? **Pony Express** offers rides down the trail into the crater. On the seven-and-a-half-mile roundtrip (which takes three and a half to four hours) you'll learn about the unique plant and animal life found in the crater, as well as Hawaiian myths and stories. Remember: the altitude is 10,000 feet so dress in layers (you need long pants and closed-toe shoes) because it gets hotter as you go down the trail. (No pregnant women allowed and you must be over 10 and under 65 to ride.) ~ Crater Road, Kula; 808-667-2200, fax 808-878-2821; www.ponyexpresstours.com.

For a friendly cruise down Haleakala on single-gear beach cruisers, contact **Maui Mountain Cruisers.** They serve breakfast or lunch on sunrise or midday rides, stopping for lunch at the Sunrise Market and Protea Farm. ~ 15 South Wakea Street, Kahului; 808-871-6014, 800-232-6284.

**Aloha Bicycle Tours** is a family-run operation that bills itself as a ride-at-your-own-pace tour company with a support van. Sounds like an especially good idea along these gorgeous routes. The volcano tour, for example, swings through Haleakala National Park, stops at a flower farm and Keokea (a.k.a. China Town) and descends to a winery. Minimum age is 14. ~ Kula; 808-249-0911, 800-749-1564.

At **Maui Downhill**, you'll enjoy sunrise daytrips and mid-morning runs on Haleakala. The sunrise run is a beautiful 38-mile trip from the crater to sea level. The longer trips include a meal; helmets, windbreakers, suits and insulated gloves are provided for all rides. ~ 199 Dairy Road, Kahului; 808-871-2155, 800-535-2453, fax 808-871-6875; www.mauidownhill.com.

Family-owned and -operated, **Cruiser Phil's Volcano Rides** also runs Haleakala downhill tours. Phil's has custom-built low-rider, single-gear cruisers and included with the uniform of safety gear are Kevlar motorcycle jackets. ~ 76 Hobron Avenue, Kahului; 808-893-2332.

**HIKING**   Many people complain that Maui is overdeveloped. The wall-to-wall condominiums lining the Kaanapali and Kihei beachfront can be pretty depressing to the outdoors lover. But happily there is a way to escape. Hike right out of it.

The Valley Isle has many fine trails that lead through Hana's rainforest, Haleakala's magnificent valley, up to West Maui's peaks and across the south shore's arid lava flows. Any of them will carry you far from the madding crowd. It's quite simple on Maui to trade the tourist enclaves for virgin mountains, untrammeled beaches and eerie volcanic terrain.

**AUTHOR FAVORITE**

**Hike Maui** has been offering hiking tours longer than anyone else on the island. They emphasize natural history, and their affection for their subject matter shows. One of the hikes wanders through Kipahula Valley, on the track of waterfalls and streams. You can swim through clear pools past ferns and hanging vines, then lunch at the top of a 200-foot waterfall. They also have volcano and coastline hikes. ~ P.O. Box 330969, Kahului, HI 96733; 808-879-5270, fax 808-893-2575; www.hikemaui.com.

Most trails you'll be hiking are composed of volcanic rock. This is a very crumbly substance, so be extremely cautious when climbing rock faces. In fact, you should avoid steep climbs if possible. Stay on the trails: Maui's dense undergrowth makes it very easy to get lost. If you get lost at night, stay where you are. Because of the low latitude, night descends rapidly here; there's practically no twilight. Once darkness falls, it can be very dangerous to move around. You should also be careful to purify all drinking water. And be extremely cautious near streambeds as flash-flooding sometimes occurs, particularly on the windward coast. This is particularly true during the winter months, when heavy storms from the northeast lash the island.

For those ready to take a dip in Iao Stream, be aware that you might be in the water with *leptospirosis*. This bacterium penetrates the body through broken skin or such orifices as the nose, mouth and ears. Flu-like symptoms are the results . . . unless you have a severe case, which can lead to kidney, liver or heart damage. Consult the Hawaii State Department of Health at 808-244-4288 for further information.

It's advisable to wear long pants when hiking in order to protect your legs from rock outcroppings, insects and spiny plants. Also, if you're going to explore Haleakala volcano, be sure to bring rain and cold-weather gear; temperatures are often significantly lower than at sea level and this peak occasionally receives snow.

One note: A number of trails pass preserved cultural or historical sites. Please do not disturb these in any way.

For more information, contact the Division of Forestry and Wildlife, Na Ala Hele Trails and Access Program. ~ 54 South High Street, Room 101, Wailuku, HI 96793; 808-984-8100, 808-873-3509, fax 808-984-8111; www.hawaiitrails.org.

Before arriving in Maui, you might want to obtain hiking maps; they are available on Oahu from **Hawaii Geographic Maps & Books**. They also sell informational guides and books useful for hiking. ~ P.O. Box 1698, Honolulu, HI 96806; 808-538-3952, 800-538-3950.

If you're uncomfortable about exploring solo, you might consider an organized tour. The **National Park Service** provides information to hikers interested in exploring Haleakala National Park. What follows is a basic guide to most of Maui's major trails. ~ Haleakala National Park, P.O. Box 369, Makawao, HI 96768; 808-572-4400, fax 808-572-1304; www.nps.gov/hale.

All distances listed for hiking trails are one way unless otherwise noted.

**KAHULUI–WAILUKU AREA**   The main hiking trails in this region lie in Iao Valley, Wailuku and along Kakekili Highway (Route 340).

Iao Stream Trail (1 mile) leads from the Iao Valley State Monument parking lot for half a mile along the stream. The second half of the trek involves wading through the stream or hopping across the shoreline rocks. But your efforts will be rewarded with some excellent swimming holes en route. You might want to plan your time so you can relax and swim. Watch for falling rocks and flash floods!

Not far from Kahului Airport on Route 360, birders will be delighted to find a trail meandering through the Kanaha Pond Wildlife Sanctuary (2 miles). This jaunt follows two loop roads, each one mile long, and passes the natural habitat of the rare Hawaiian stilt, the Hawaiian duck (a species re-introduced to Maui in 1991) and the Hawaiian coot. The trails in the Kanaha Pond area are closed during bird-breeding season (April–August). The pond-kiosk area, which has a short observation "peninsula," is open year-round, but to hike on the trail, you'll need a permit from the State Division of Forestry. ~ 808-984-8100.

Birders might be interested in knowing that Hawaiian honeycreepers are said to be the most divergently evolved birds on earth.

Northwest of Kahului, along the Kahekili Highway, are two trails well worth exploring, the Waihee Ridge Trail and Kahakuloa Valley Trail.

Waihee Ridge Trail (3 miles) begins just below Maluhia Boy Scout Camp outside the town of Waihee. The trail passes through a guava thicket and scrub forest and climbs 1500 feet en route to a peak overlooking West and Central Maui. The trail summit is equipped with a picnic table rest stop.

KIHEI–WAILEA–MAKENA AREA    King's Highway Coastal Trail (5.5 miles) follows an ancient Hawaiian route over the 1790 lava flow and is considered a desert region. The trail begins near La Perouse Bay at the end of the rugged road that connects La Perouse Bay with Makena Beach and Wailea. It heads inland through groves of *kiawe* trees, then skirts the coast and finally leads to Kanaloa Point. From this point the trail continues across private land. Because segments of the trail pass through the Ahihi–Kinau Natural Area Reserve, which has stricter regulations, call Na Ala Hele Trails and Access Program for more information. ~ 808-873-3508.

HANA HIGHWAY    Hana-Waianapanapa Coastal Trail (3 miles), part of the ancient King's Highway, skirts the coastline between Waianapanapa State Park and Hana Bay. Exercise extreme caution near the rocky shoreline and cliffs. The trail passes a *heiau*, sea arch, blowhole and numerous caves while winding through lush stands of *hala* trees.

Waimoku Falls Trail (2 miles) leads from the visitors center parking lot at Oheo Gulch up to Waimoku Falls. On the way, it goes by several pools and traverses a bamboo forest. (Mosquito repellent advised.) Contact Haleakala National Park Headquarters for information on this trail.

**UPCOUNTRY**   The main trails in Maui's beautiful Upcountry lie on Haleakala's southern slopes. They branch out from Polipoli Spring State Recreation Area through the Kula.

**Redwood Trail** (1.7 miles) descends from Polipoli's 6200-foot elevation through impressive stands of redwoods to the ranger's cabin at 5300 feet. There is a dilapidated public shelter in the old CCC camp at trail's end. A four-wheel drive is required to reach the trailhead.

**Plum Trail** (1.7 miles) begins at the CCC camp and climbs gently south to Haleakala Ridge Trail. The route passes plum trees as well as stands of ash, redwood and sugi pine. There are shelters at both ends of the trail.

**Tie Trail** (0.5 mile) descends 500 feet through cedar, ash and sugi pine groves to link Redwood and Plum Trails. There is a shelter at the Redwood junction.

**Polipoli Trail** (0.6 mile) cuts through cypress, cedars and pines en route from Polipoli Campground to Haleakala Ridge Trail.

**Boundary Trail** (4 miles) begins at the cattle guard marking the Kula Forest Reserve boundary along the road to Polipoli. It crosses numerous gulches planted in cedar, eucalyptus and pine. The trail terminates at the ranger's cabin.

**Waiohuli Trail** (1.4 miles) descends 800 feet from Polipoli Road to join Boundary Trail. Along the way it passes young pine and grasslands, then drops down through groves of cedar, redwood and ash. There is a shelter at the Boundary Trail junction.

**Skyline Road** (6.5 miles) begins at 9750 feet, near the top of Haleakala's southwest rift, and descends more than 3000 feet to the top of Haleakala Ridge Trail. The trail passes a rugged, treeless area resembling the moon's surface. Then it drops below timberline at 8600 feet and eventually into dense scrub. The unobstructed views of Maui and the neighboring islands are awesome. Bring your own water.

**Haleakala Ridge Trail** (1.6 miles) starts from Skyline Trail's terminus at 6550 feet and descends along Haleakala's southwest rift to 5600 feet. There are spectacular views in all directions and a shelter at trail's end.

Three airports serve Maui—Kahului Airport, Kapalua–West Maui Airport and Hana Airport. The latter two are exclusively interisland.

# Transportation

The **Kahului Airport** is the main landing facility and should be your destination if you're staying in the Central Maui region or on the southeast coast in the Kihei–Wailea–Makena area.

**AIR**

Aloha Airlines, American Airlines, Continental Airlines, Delta Air Lines, Hawaiian Airlines, Northwest Airlines, United Airlines and a couple of charter companies offer nonstop service from the mainland.

**Kapalua–West Maui Airport** serves the Lahaina–Kaanapali area. Island Air flies into the facility. ~ 808-669-0255.

**Hana Airport**, really only a short landing strip and a one-room terminal, sits near the ocean in Maui's lush northeastern corner. Island Air lands in this isolated community. And don't expect very much ground transportation waiting for you. There is no bus service, though there is a car rental agency.

**BOAT**

One of the few day-trip services in Hawaii is provided by **Island Marine**. Their 118-foot *Maui Princess* and 100-foot *Molokai Princess* provide trips Monday through Saturday between Maui and Molokai. The price is not cheap. ~ 808-667-6165.

Another ferry, **Expeditions** operates out of Maui and links Lahaina with Manele Bay on Lanai. There are five boats per day in each direction. The 45-minute trip provides a unique way to travel between the islands. ~ 658 Front Street #127, Lahaina; 808-661-3756.

**CAR RENTALS**

If, like most visitors to Maui, you arrive at the airport in Kahului, you certainly won't want for car rental agencies. There are quite a few with booths right at the airport. A number of others are located around town. Most agencies require a credit card and renters to be 25 years old.

In Kahului, the airport car-rental agencies are as follows: **Avis Rent A Car** (808-871-7575, 800-331-1212), **Budget Rent A Car** (808-871-8811, 800-527-0700), **Dollar Rent A Car** (808-877-2732, 800-800-4000), **Hertz Rent A Car** (808-877-5167, 800-654-3131) and **National Car Rental** (808-871-8851, 800-227-7368).

The rental agencies outside the airport include companies that rent older model cars at very competitive rates. One of these is **Word of Mouth Rent A Used Car**, which strongly recommends reservations. ~ 808-877-2436, 800-533-5929; www.mauirentacar.com, e-mail word@maui.net.

If you find yourself in the Lahaina–Kaanapali area wanting to rent a car, try **Avis Rent A Car** (808-661-4588, 800-331-1212), **Budget Rent A Car** (808-661-8721, 800-527-0700), **Dollar Rent A Car** (808-667-2651, 800-800-4000), **Hertz Rent A Car** (808-661-7735, 800-654-3131) or **National Car Rental** (808-667-9737, 800-227-7368). All of these agencies have courtesy phones at the Kapalua–West Maui Airport.

Kihei is served by **Avis Rent A Car**. ~ 808-874-4077, 800-331-1212. For a cheaper alternative, try **Kihei Rent A Car**. ~ 808-879-7257, 800-251-5288.

**Dollar Rent A Car** is the sole company in Hana. ~ 808-248-8237, 800-800-4000.

There are several companies on the island of Maui that rent four-wheel-drive vehicles. If you want to venture on the unpaved roads forbidden by front-wheel drives, check to see if it's okay to take the jeep. Some outfits offering jeeps are **Adventures Rent A Jeep** (190 Papa Place, Kahului; 808-877-6626, 800-701-5337) and **Budget Rent A Car** (808-871-8811, 808-661- 8721, 800-527-0700).

There is almost no public transportation on Maui and the little that is provided lies concentrated in one small sector of the island. The **Maui Public Transit** travels between Wailea, Lahaina, Kaanapali and Kapalua with stops at major resorts. ~ Robert's Hawaii; 808-871-4838 (ask for public transit). **Akina Bus Service** (808-879-2828) operates buses in the Lahaina–Kaanapli area.

**Speedy Shuttle** (808-875-8070) offers transportation from Kahului Airport to resorts on the west to the southside of the island. (It's recommended that you call at least a day in advance, though last-minute pickups are sometimes available.)

Much of Maui's best scenery is reached via serpentine roads or steep mountain drives. While the views are stunning, the best way to get a bird's-eye view is from the air. Helicopters, fixed-wing aircraft and gliders all make it easy to see the volcanic uplands, waterfall splashed cliffs and dreamy back-country beaches.

**AlexAir**, a Maui-based helicopter-tour company, offers a wide range of tours, from 20 to 60 minutes long, as well as private charters. ~ Kahului Heliport; 808-871-0792, 888-418-8458.

If you prefer to see Maui and a bit more, check out **Paragon Air**. Travel aboard a nine-passenger Piper Navajo Chieftain or a six-passenger Partenavia over Maui to the Big Island or Molokai. On Molokai, passengers land and journey by foot or mule to visit Kalaupapa, the leper colony made famous by the work of Father Damien. ~ Kahului Airport; 808-244-3356, 800-428-1231, fax 808-573-8218; www.paragon-air.com.

**Sunshine Helicopters** offers tours that include whale watching when in season, waterfalls, island circumnavigation and private charters. ~ Kahului Heliport; 808-871-0722, 800-469-3000.

Another option is **Blue Hawaiian Helicopters**, a company that has accumulated its share of accolades. The company has also been used in the making of several blockbuster films such as *Jurassic Park* and *Pearl Harbor*. They offer a standard roster of tours using their ultra-quiet ECO-Stars. ~ Kahului Heliport; 808-871-8844, 800-745-2583.

# SEVEN

# Lanai

Eight miles from Maui, across the historic whaling anchorage at Lahaina Roads, lies the pear-shaped island of Lanai. In profile the island, formed by an extinct volcano, resembles the humpback whales that frequent its waters. It rises in a curved ridge from the south, then gradually tapers to the north. The east side is cut by deep gulches, while the west is bounded by spectacular sea cliffs rising 1500 to 2000 feet. Lanaihale, the island's tallest peak, stands 3370 feet above sea level.

First discovered by Captain Cook's men in 1779, Lanai was long avoided by mariners, who feared its reef-shrouded shores and saw little future in the dry, barren landscape. You can still see testaments to their fear in the rotting hulks that lie off Shipwreck Beach.

Ancient Hawaiians believed Lanai was inhabited only by evil spirits until Kaululaau, son of the great Maui chief Kakaalaneo, killed the spirits. Kaululaau, a Hawaiian-style juvenile delinquent who chopped down fruit trees with the gay abandon of young George Washington, had been exiled to Lanai by his father for his destructive behavior. After the wild youth redeemed himself by making the island safe from malevolent spirits, Lanai was settled by Hawaiians and controlled by powerful Maui chiefs.

Most archaeologists doubt that the native population, which lived from taro cultivation and fishing along the eastern shore, ever exceeded 2500. Even periods of peak population were punctuated by long intervals when the island was all but deserted. Lying in Maui's wind shadow, Lanai's rainfall ranges from 40 inches along its northeast face to a meager 12 inches annually in the barren southwest corner.

Like Molokai, its neighbor to the north, Lanai for centuries was a satellite of Maui. (Even today it is part of Maui County.) Then in 1778 it was overwhelmed by the forces of Kalaniopuu, the king of the Big Island. Later in the century, an even more powerful monarch, Kamehameha the Great, set up a summer residence along the south coast in Kaunolu.

During the 19th century, Lanai was a ranchers' island with large sections of flat range land given over to grazing. Missionaries became active saving souls and securing property in 1835 and by the 1860s one of their number had gained control of Lanai's better acreage. This was Walter Murray Gibson, a Mormon maverick whose life story reads like a sleazy novel. Despite being excommunicated by the Mormon church, Gibson went on to become a formidable figure in Hawaiian politics.

Gibson was not the only man with a dream for Lanai. George Munro, a New Zealand naturalist, came to the island in 1911 as manager of a plantation complex that originally tried to grow sugar on the island and then turned to cattle raising. While his herds grazed the island's tablelands, Munro worked in the rugged highlands. He extended the native forest, planting countless trees to capture moisture and protect eroded hillsides. He restored areas ravaged by feral goats and imported the stately Norfolk pines that still lend a mountain ambience to Lanai City. And, most important, Munro introduced an ecological awareness that hopefully will continue to pervade this enchanting island.

The land that Gibson and Munro oversaw changed hands several times until James Dole bought it in 1922 for a mere $1.1 million. Dole, descended from missionaries, was possessed of a more earthly vision than his forebears. Pineapples. He converted the island to pineapple cultivation, built Lanai City, and changed the face of Lanai forever.

Filipinos, now about 50 percent of the island's population, were imported to work the fields. They bent to their labors all over Lanai, wearing goggles and gloves to protect against the sharp spines that bristled from the low-lying plants. Pineapples are cultivated through plastic sheets to conserve precious water and harvesting is done by hand. Up until the early 1990s, you could see hundreds of acres covered in plastic. Downtown Lanai would roll up the streets at 9 p.m., but the lights would burn bright in the pineapple fields as crews worked through the night loading the hefty fruits onto conveyor belts.

That was yesterday, back when Lanai retained something of an ambiguous reputation. Most tourists, hearing that Lanai was nothing but pineapples and possessed only 20 miles of paved roads and a single ten-room hotel, left the place to the antelopes and wild goats.

Now, however, the sleeping midget has awakened. You still rent your car in an old gas station with scuffed floors and deer trophies on the wall. And there are still only three paved roads on the island. But nothing else here is the same.

Stores have been renovated, old plantation homes have received fresh coats of paint, and two small clusters of homes have been constructed on the outskirts of town. Castle & Cooke, the conglomerate that now owns the island, poured millions into the place, building two resorts and transforming little Lanai into luxurious Lanai. The Manele Bay Hotel, a 250-room oceanfront extravaganza, opened in 1991 just one year after the christening of The Lodge at Koele, a rustic but refined 102-room resort situated along Lanai's forested mountain slopes.

Meanwhile the days of pineapple cultivation are over. The output has dropped from a peak of about 16,000 acres to a mere 200 acres, sufficient to supply island needs and give visitors a glimpse at what life was like "back when." Fields are being converted to alfalfa and oats; cattle raising has been reintroduced; and the island's Filipino and Japanese population have quit the plantation and are now working to serve the visitors who make their way to Lanai to enjoy the posh resort hotels and a plethora of outdoor activities like golf, tennis, biking and horseback riding.

The remains of more than 200 shipwrecked vessels dot the coastline of this small island.

In the midst of all the change, this lovely little isle has retained its charm. Even now only a fraction of Lanai's 140 square miles is developed. The rest of the island is covered with a network of jeep and hiking trails guaranteed to keep the heartiest adventurer happy.

Here is an entire island that fits the description "hidden Hawaii." Almost all of Lanai's 3200 citizens live in rustic Lanai City at the island's center and most tourists are concentrated at The Lodge at Koele one mile away or along Hulope Beach at the Manele Bay Resort. Just beyond these clusters lie mountains, rainforests, ranchlands and remote beaches—untouched realms ripe for exploration.

## Lanai City

Situated at 1645 feet, Lanai City is a trim community of corrugated-roof houses and small garden plots. Tourist brochures present the place as a quaint New England village. Most of the houses were constructed around the 1920s in traditional company-town fashion. They are square boxes topped with tin roofs and tend to look alike. Norfolk pines break the monotony, and many homes are freshly painted in a rainbow assortment of hues.

**SIGHTS**

Lanai City is still a company town, but today the company is harvesting tourists instead of planting pineapples. Several housing developments and condominium complexes have been built on the outskirts to house hotel employees. With everything centered around the town square, Lanai City embraces almost the entire population of the island. Situated at the center of the island at an elevation midway between the beach and the mountain peaks, it is cool and breezy with a temperate climate.

The only "sight" in town is the posh mountain resort, **The Lodge at Koele**. It sits amidst a pine forest in a spectacular hillside setting. Pathways lead through manicured fruit and Japanese gardens, sprawling banyan trees and along a koi-filled reflecting pool. It is worth wandering through.

**LODGING**

**HIDDEN ►**

Once the only inn on the entire island, the **Hotel Lanai** is a modest mountain retreat. Set 1600 feet above sea level and surrounded by Norfolk pines, it offers clean, medium-sized rooms equipped with private baths. The lodge was built in the '20s, as was most of Lanai City, but was recently refurbished. It features a restaurant and lounge, and is a local gathering place at dinnertime. A lot of folks hang out in the lobby here, making for a warm, friendly atmosphere, and the staff is congenial. Choose between small- and medium-sized standard accommodations and rooms with lanais. There's a cottage in the back and a U-shaped structure with only ten rooms, so reservations can be troublesome. It's advisable to arrange transportation with the hotel at the time of making reservations. ~ 828 Lanai Avenue; 808-565-7211, 800-795-7211, fax 808-565-6450; www.hotellanai.com, e-mail hotel lanai@wave.hicv.net. MODERATE TO DELUXE.

**The Lodge at Koele**, a fashionable 102-room hideaway, is a study in style and decorum. The most noteworthy feature is the lobby, a vaulted-ceiling affair faced on either end with a stone fireplace that rises to the roofline. Etched-glass skylights extend the length of the room, illuminating the "great hall." The plantation-style guest rooms are done with four-poster beds, hand-stenciled walls, statuettes and decorative plates. To make sure you remember that even here amid the Cook pines you are still in Hawaii, an overhead fan beats the air in languid motions.

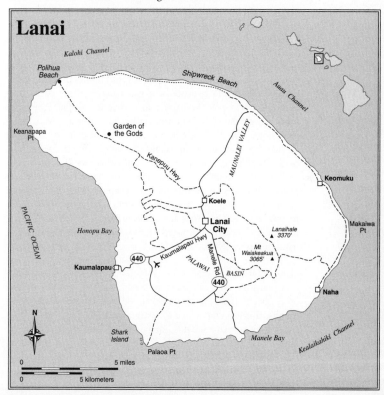

Backdropped by mountains and surrounded by miles of grasslands, the emphasis at The Lodge is on staying put. There are porches lined with wicker chairs, a croquet court, a swimming pool and two jacuzzis that look out on field and forest, and a congenial staff to take care of every request. Five-night minimum at Christmastime. ~ P.O. Box 630310, Lanai City, HI 96763; 808-565-7300, 800-321-4666, fax 808-565-4561; www.lodgeatkoele. com, e-mail reservations@lanai-resorts.com. ULTRA-DELUXE.

You can discover for yourself whether **Dreams Come True on Lanai**. That's what Michael and Susan Hunter, two local jewelry makers, claim can happen when you stay in the six-bedroom house they transformed in 1990 into a bed and breakfast. Set in Lanai City and surrounded by fruit trees and flowering gardens, the house is decorated with hand-carved screens and furniture that the owners transported from Sri Lanka and Bali. There's a large living room for guests as well as a selection of double rooms; some have canopied four-poster beds, and all have private baths with Italian marble and whirlpool tub. Swedish and Shiatsu massage available. Guests are welcome to use the kitchen or laundry. ~ 547 12th Street, Lanai City; 808-565-6961, 800-566-6961, fax 808-565-7056; www.dreamscometruelanai.com, e-mail hunters@aloha.net. MODERATE.

Located on the outskirts of Lanai City, **Bamboo Garden Retreat** offers an ideal vacation haven for families or group gatherings. With seven bedrooms, a sun room and six baths, this plantation home sleeps from two to twenty people. Amenities abound, including a full kitchen, washer and dryer and (too) many televisions. The garden, with its bamboo and palm trees, create an island of solitude on an island of solitude. What does all this cost? The Garden house with 7bed/6bath is $500-$1000/night (will accommodate up to 20); half house with no kitchen and 3bed/3bath is $300-$500/night; half house with kitchen and 3bed/3bath is $350-$550/night. There's also a non-refundable reservation fee. Discounts for weekly rates. ~ P.O. Box 630523, Lanai City, HI 96763; 808-565-9307, fax 808-565-6593; e-mail bambooretreat@yahoo.com.

**DINING**

HIDDEN ►

**Henry Clay's Rotisserie** at the Hotel Lanai offers wholesome dinners featuring an assortment of steak, seafood, pasta, ribs and other selections. Its knotty pine walls decorated with island photographs, this is a cozy place to share a meal. You can strike up a conversation with a local resident, sit back and enjoy the mountain air or bask in the glow of the restaurant's two fireplaces. Dinner only. ~ 828 Lanai Avenue; 808-565-7211, fax 808-565-6450; www.hotellanai.com, e-mail hotellanai@wave.hicv.net. MODERATE TO ULTRA-DELUXE.

If the hotel restaurant is closed, Lanai City has a few other alternatives. First there is **Canoes Lanai**, a luncheonette where locals drop in for breakfast and lunch. They swear Canoes Lanai has the best hamburgers in town. Closed Wednesday. ~ 419 7th Street; 808-565-6537. BUDGET.

A New York style–deli by day, an Italian restaurant at night, **Pele's Other Garden** is another establishment locals frequent. ◀ HIDDEN During the day you can get overstuffed, made-to-order sandwiches, pasta, salads, pizzas, soup and much more. Come nightfall, table-cloths transform the deli into an Italian bistro; you'll find a variety of appetizers, salads and pizzas as well as pasta dishes. The desserts and coffee are tempting. ~ 8th and Houston streets; 808-

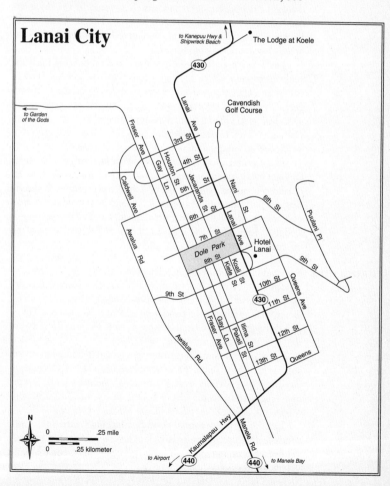

Lanai City

565-9628, fax 808-565-7613; e-mail pogdelibistro@wave.hicv.
net. MODERATE.

HIDDEN ►    The **Blue Ginger Café** rests in an old plantation house and
serves three solid meals a day. Traditional paintings and simple
drawings of tropical fish adorn the place and the red paint on the
cement floor has worn away almost completely. But the white
walls shine and the dinners are served piping hot. ~ 409 7th
Street; 808-565-6363, fax 808-565-6306. BUDGET TO MODERATE.

On Lanai, isolation is the engine of ingenuity. Confronted
with all that land and so few people, The Lodge at Koele transformed sections of the island into an organic garden, hog farm
and cattle ranch. After adding a master chef, they had the ingredients for two gourmet restaurants that would be the pride not
only of tiny Lanai but any island. Meals in The Terrace and The
Formal Dining Room (jackets are required) are as enticing as the
hotel's sumptuous surroundings.

The **Terrace** serves breakfast, lunch and dinner in a fairly casual atmosphere. Here the day begins with Belgian waffles or
bacon and eggs (fresh from the farm). By evening the chef pro-
gresses to shrimp cocktails with jicama slaw and oven-roasted
veal chop with creamy herbed polenta, as well as vegetarian specialties. ~ The Lodge at Koele; 808-565-7300, fax 808-565-
4508; www.islandoflanai.com. DELUXE TO ULTRA-DELUXE.

The **Formal Dining Room** serves dinner only. The menu
changes every four months or so, but imagine lobster with morel
mushroom ragout, and Big Island sweet corn soup with shrimp
beignet. Both restaurants overlook the back of the lodge grounds,
with views of the fishpond, fountain and orchid house. ~ The
Lodge at Koele; 808-565-7300, fax 808-565-4508; www.island
oflanai.com. ULTRA-DELUXE.

**GROCERIES**   For standard food needs, try **Richard's Shopping Center**. This
"shopping center" is really only a small grocery store with a dry
goods department. Richard's is open Monday through Wednesday from 8:30 a.m. to noon and from 1:30 to 6:30 p.m., and Thursday through Saturday from 8:30 a.m. to 6:30 p.m. Closed Sunday. ~ 434 8th Street; 808-565-6047.

If, by some strange circumstance, you can't find what you're
seeking here, head down the street to **Pine Isle Market**. Open Monday through Thursday from 8 a.m. to noon and 1:30 to 7 p.m.,
and Friday and Saturday from 8 a.m. to 7 p.m. Closed Sunday.
~ 356 8th Street; 808-565-6488.

**Lanai City International Food & Clothing Center** sells meat,
produce and canned goods as well as liquor, beer and wine. They
are open 8 a.m. to 6 p.m. Monday through Friday, and 8 a.m. to
4 p.m. on Sunday. Closed Saturday. ~ 833 Ilima Avenue; 808-
565-6433.

# Munro
## Trail

**N**amed for New Zealand naturalist George Munro, this seven-mile jeep trail climbs through rainforest and stands of conifers en route to **Lanaihale**, the highest point on Lanai. From this 3370-foot perch you can see every major Hawaiian island except Kauai.

On the way to Lanaihale, about two miles up the trail, you'll pass **Hookio Gulch**. The ridge beyond is carved with a defense work of protective notches made by warriors who tried futilely to defend Lanai against invaders from Hawaii in 1778.

A footpath leads to an overlook above 2000-foot deep **Hauola Gulch**, Lanai's deepest canyon. Here you may see axis deer clinging to the sharp rockfaces, seeming to defy gravity as they pick their way along the heights.

This knife-edge ridge, little more than 100 feet wide in places, is studded with ironwood and eucalyptus trees, as well as the stately Norfolk pines that New Zealand naturalist George Munro personally planted along the heights. From this aerie the slopes fall away to reveal the twin humps of Maui. The Big Island rests far below you, anchored in open ocean. The sea itself is a flat, shimmering expanse.

From Lanaihale you can either turn around or continue and descend through open fields to Hoike Road, which connects with Route 440. The Munro Trail begins in Koele off Route 430 (Keomuku Road) about a mile north of Lanai City. Be sure to check road conditions and try to go early in the morning before clouds gather along the ridgetop. While it's rough going at times, the trail affords such magnificent views from its windswept heights that it simply must not be ignored by the adventurous sightseer.

You can also pick up deli meat, cheese and other delectables at **Pele's Other Garden**, where they also serve lunch and dinner. Closed Sunday. ~ Corner of 8th and Houston streets; 808-565-9628.

There's also a "Saturday Market" in Dole Park each week.

**SHOPPING**   Don't go home without visiting **Dis 'N Dat**, a shop brimming with lots of dis 'n dat—from exotic wood carvings and boxes to cool jewelry (especially earrings and necklaces). Located in a landmarked building, it's in the hub of laidback Lanai City. ~ 418 8th Street; 808-565-9170; www.disndatlanai.com.

Both a cultural gathering place and gallery, **Lanai Art Center** offers such artworks as *koa*-framed originals, greeting cards, ukuleles, stunning photographs, handcrafted jewelry and ceramics. Traveling artists can stock up on their supplies here as well. Check with the center for ongoing classes and workshops. ~ 339 7th Street, Lanai City; 808-565-7503, fax 808-565-9654.

Once known as the Pineapple Isle, Lanai covers 140 square miles—13 miles wide and 18 miles long.

Granted, it doesn't have much competition, but **Heart of Lanai Art Gallery** would be remarkable regardless of where it was located. Many of the paintings and sculptures are done by local artists and depict the plantation culture that was once Lanai's lifeblood but is now fast becoming its legacy. Open for tea and cookies from 2:30 p.m. to 4:30 p.m., Tuesday through Saturday; call ahead if you want to come at some other time. Closed Sunday. ~ 758 Queens Street (behind Hotel Lanai); 808-565-6678; e-mail den@aloha.net.

In the heart of Dole Park is **The Local Gentry**, a small clothing boutique. If you forgot your swimsuit or sandals, or if you're short on shorts, they have them. They feature clothing from San Francisco City Lights, Putumayo, Tiki, Big Blue, Allen Allen and others. ~ 363-B 7th Street; 808-565-9130; e-mail locgent@aloha.net.

Don't miss **Gifts with Aloha** located next door. This boutique, run by the genial Duprees, features Lanai and Hawaiian artists. Watercolor originals, pottery and wood pieces along with tempting jams, jellies and sauces, hats and casual resort wear round out the offerings at this Lanai-style (i.e., laidback) store. ~ 363 7th Street; 808-565-6589, fax 808-565-9129; www.gifts withaloha.com.

Landscapes and wildlife are celebrated in the oil paintings of local artist Michael Carroll. Stop by the **Mike Carroll Gallery** to see what new works are on the easel. ~ 431 7th Street; 808-565-7122; www.mikecarrollgallery.com.

**Coffee Works Lanai** offers gourmet coffee beans and teas to take home. If you're tired of all of this shopping, stop in for an espresso or ice cream. ~ Corner of Ilima and 6th streets; 808-565-6962.

Otherwise, you will have to seek out the gift shop at **The Lodge at Koele** (808-565-7300) or the **Hotel Lanai** (808-565-7211).

Visitors find this a great spot to get the sleep they missed in Lahaina or Honolulu. If rest isn't a problem, Lanai may be a good place to catch up on your reading or letter writing. One thing is certain—once the sun goes down, there'll be little to distract you. You can have a drink while listening to local gossip at the **Hotel Lanai** (808-565-7211) or while mixing with the gentry at **The Lodge at Koele** (808-565-7300), where the lounge possesses a kind of gentlemen's library atmosphere with an etched-glass-and-hardwood interior. But on an average evening, even these night owl's nests will be closed by midnight (*pupus* are served until 11 p.m.). In addition to its plush lounge, The Lodge at Koele features hula dancers on weekends at lunchtime or other live entertainment in the lobby (the "great hall") at night.

**NIGHTLIFE**

## ▼▼▼▼▼▼▼▼▼▼▼▼▼▼▼▼▼
## Northeast—Shipwreck Beach & Naha

From Lanai City, Route 430 (Keomuku Road) winds north through hot, arid country. The scrub growth and red soil in this barren area resemble a bleak southwestern landscape, but the sweeping views of Maui and Molokai could be found only in Hawaii.

By the way, those stones piled atop one another along the road are neither an expression of ancient Hawaiian culture nor proof of the latest UFO landing. They were placed there by imaginative hikers. Each one is an *ahu*, representative of a local tradition in which columns of three or so stones are built to help ensure good luck.

Near the end of the macadam road you can turn left onto a dirt road. This track leads past colonies of intermittently inhabited squatters' shacks, many built from the hulks of vessels grounded on nearby **Shipwreck Beach**. The coral reef paralleling the beach has been a nemesis to sailors since whaling days. The rusting remains of a barge and a 1950s-era oil tanker still bear witness to the navigational hazards along this coast. Needless to say, this is one of the best areas in Hawaii for beachcombing. Look in particular for the Japanese glass fishing floats that are carried here on currents all the way from Asia.

At the end of the dirt road, a path marked with white paint leads to clusters of ancient **petroglyphs** depicting simple island scenes. Those interested in extensively exploring the coast can

**SIGHTS**

◄ *HIDDEN*

hike all the way from Shipwreck eight miles west to Polihua Beach along jeep trails and shoreline.

Back on the main road (continuing straight ahead as if you had never made that left turn that led to Shipwreck Beach) you will discover that the macadam gives way to a dirt road that leads along the northeast shore for 12 teeth-clicking miles. It was along this now-deserted coast that the ancient Hawaiian population lived. Numbering perhaps 2000 in pre-Western times, they fished the coast and cultivated taro.

The ghost town of **Keomuku**, marked by a ramshackle church that's been partly refurbished, lies six miles down the road. It's another mile and a half to **Kahea Heiau**, a holy place that many claim is the reason Keomuku was deserted. It seems that stones from this temple were used to build the nearby Maunalei Sugar Company plantation despite warnings against disturbing the sacred rocks. So when the plantation failed in 1901 after its sweet water mysteriously turned brackish, the Hawaiians had a heavenly explanation. It was shortly after this incident that most of the rest of Lanai's populace moved up to Lanai City, leaving only spirits along the coast.

Several miles farther, past numerous salt-and-pepper-colored beaches, the road ends at the old Hawaiian village of **Naha**. Today nothing remains of this once prosperous colony.

**BEACHES & PARKS**

**SHIPWRECK BEACH** This strand is actually a string of small sandy patches that stretches for eight miles along the north coast, all the way to Polihua Beach. The glass fishing balls, driftwood and occasional nautilus shells on the beach make this a beachcomber's paradise. The remains of misguided ships that gave the beach its name also add to the allure. It's often windy. You can swim here but the water is shallow and you must beware of sharp coral—a protecting reef is 200 yards offshore. Windsurfers consider Shipwreck one of the prime spots in the islands. Snorkeling is not advised because of sharks. There's good diving for lobsters, but again, be cautious! You'll find good fishing for *ulua*, *papio* and octopus in the area between the squatters' houses and the petroglyphs. There are no established facilities at the beach. ~ Ten miles north of Lanai City. Head north on Route 430 (Keomuku Road) and turn left at the end of the paved road. (See the "Northeast—Shipwreck Beach & Naha" section above for more details.)

**HALEPALAOA BEACH AND NAHA BEACH** A string of salt-and-pepper-colored-sand beaches lies along the 12-mile dirt road to Naha. While most are unattractive and crowded with shoals, they do offer great views of Molokai, Maui and Kahoolawe. The Naha road winds in and out along the seafront, with numerous access roads leading to the shore. The prettiest strand is Halepalaoa Beach, a mile-long white-sand corridor partially bordered by sand dunes. These are swimming beaches; most are well-protected by shoals, but the waters are shallow. Snorkeling is a possibility here but beware of currents. You can also fish here. Several beaches, including Naha, have small picnic areas. ~ Take Route 430 north from Lanai City and continue on after it turns southward and becomes a dirt road. The dirt road extends for about 12 miles, ending at Naha; Halepalaoa Beach is about seven miles out along the dirt road.

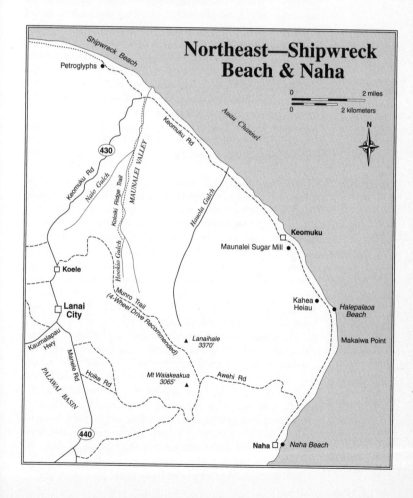

**Northeast—Shipwreck Beach & Naha**

▼▼▼▼▼▼▼▼▼▼▼▼▼▼▼▼
## Southeast—Manele Bay

Heading south from Lanai City on Route 440 (Manele Road), you'll be traveling through the Palawai Basin, the caldera of the extinct volcano that formed the island. This was also the heart of Lanai's once extensive pineapple plantation.

**SIGHTS**

*HIDDEN* ►

The explorer can detour off the main highway to the **Luahiwa petroglyphs**. Finding them requires obtaining explicit directions, then driving through a field, and finally climbing a short distance up a steep bluff. But the Luahiwa petroglyphs—portraying human figures, deer, paddles and turtles—are among the finest rock carvings in Hawaii and are definitely worth the search. As you approach each cluster of boulders, you'll see pictographic stories begin to unfold. One in particular depicts a large outrigger canoe, sails unfurled, being loaded Noah-style with livestock. Preparing, perhaps, for the ancient migration north to the Hawaiian Islands? To locate the petroglyphs, head south from Lanai City on Route 440. Turn left at the first dirt road. Follow the lower road as it curves along the bottom of the hillside. After passing below a watertank and pipeline, the road forks and you follow the left fork. The road goes into a horseshoe curve; when you come out of the curve there will be black boulders on the hillside above you to the left. Spread across a few acres, they contain the petroglyphs.

The main road leads through agricultural fields and winds down to the twin bays at **Manele Small Boat Harbor** and **Hulopoe Bay**, which together comprise a marine life conservation area. Just offshore from the cinder cone that separates these two harbors is a sea stack, **Puu Pehe**, known not only for its beauty but its legends as well. Puu Pehe was a lovely Maui girl kidnapped by a Lanai warrior who kept her hidden in a sea cave. One day when he went off in search of water, a huge sea wave swept the girl to her death. Stricken with grief and remorse, the young warrior buried her on top of the rock island and then jumped to his death from its heights.

The small-boat harbor at Manele, rimmed by lava cliffs along the far shore, contains ruins of ancient Hawaiian houses. You'll also see an old wooden chute protruding from the rocks, a loading platform used years ago to lead cattle onto ships. Today this rock-rimmed anchorage is a mooring place for fishing boats and yachts. Hulopoe offers the island's finest beach, a crescent of white sand with gentle waves, crystalline waters and a fine park facility. You'll find the stone ruins of an ancient Hawaiian home and canoe house at the north end of the beach. Just above the beach, on the grounds in front of the plush Manele Bay Hotel, stands the remains of an *ahu* or traditional Hawaiian shrine.

While The Lodge at Koele is situated at 1600-feet elevation in Lanai City, eight miles from the ocean, Lanai's other fashionable resting spot, the **Manele Bay Hotel**, is a traditional beachfront resort. Set on a bluff overlooking the best beach on the island, it is a 250-room extravaganza designed along both Asian and Mediterranean lines and surrounded by artistically planted gardens. Elegance here is in no way subdued: It speaks from the stone floors and white columns, the dark-paneled library and the recessed ceilings. The two-tiered lobby combines art deco windows with stylized Asian murals; the lower level is a terrace with glass doors that open onto ocean views.

Guest accommodations look out either on the beach or the grounds, which are sculpted into five different theme gardens—Japanese, Bromeliad, Hawaiian, Chinese and Kamaaina. Each

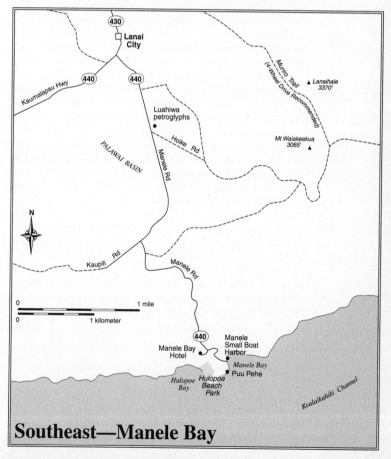

# Southeast—Manele Bay

room is spacious, done in pastel hues and decorated with Asian armoires and color sketches of Hawaiian flora. The four-poster beds are accented with quilts and upholstered throw pillows. Add a pool, three tennis courts, a spa and a workout room and you will realize that once-sleepy little Lanai has joined the 21st century. ~ 1 Manele Bay Drive; 808-565-7700, 800-321-4666, fax 808-565-3868; www.islandoflanai.com, e-mail reservations@lanai-resorts.com. ULTRA-DELUXE.

**DINING**   Outside Lanai City the dining choices—a grand total of three—are concentrated at the Manele Bay Hotel. Here, ladies and gentlemen, lunch is served at the **Pool Grille** on a bougainvillea-covered terrace. Set poolside just above the beach, this patio dining facility features island salads, including a seasonal fruit offering. There is also a standard assortment of sandwiches. Lunch only. ~ 808-565-7700, fax 808-565-2483; www.islandoflanai.com. MODERATE.

This spacious resort offers more formal dining in the **Hulopoe Court Restaurant**, a high-ceiling dining room equipped with glass doors that open onto a veranda overlooking the ocean. Island murals adorn the walls and pineapple-motif chandeliers dominate the room. The decor blends Asian and Polynesian styles while the menu features Hawaiian regional cuisine. Breakfast and dinner only. ~ 808-565-7700, fax 808-565-2483. ULTRA-DELUXE.

Sweeping views of Hulopoe Bay star at the **Ihilani Dining Room**. The menu features Mediterranean cuisine and specializes in lamb, bouillabaisse, and fresh fish dishes. The service is formal, and the wine list and cheese cart extensive. Dinner only. Closed Sunday and Monday. ~ 808-565-7700, 808-565-2996, fax 808-565-2483. ULTRA-DELUXE.

**NIGHTLIFE**   Down along Hulopoe Beach at the Manele Bay Hotel, the **Hale Ahe Ahe Lounge** combines several different settings, each equally inviting. The lounge itself has dark textured walls, a hardwood bar and a clubby ambience. It features piano or contemporary Hawaiian music Tuesday through Saturday. Out on the terrace you can settle into a comfortable armchair or lean against the rail and enjoy the ocean view. The adjacent **Holokai Room** is a game

## HOME, HOME ON THE RANGE

While touring Lanai you're bound to meet more of the island's wildlife than its human citizenry. Asian Axis deer roam everywhere while the mouflon, which look like big horn sheep, tend to be found in the lower elevations of the island. Also keep an eye out for wild turkeys and ring-neck pheasants.

room complete with a pool table, a wide-screen TV and an air of relaxed elegance. The Hale Ahe Ahe lounge is open for hors d'oeuvres only. ~ 808-565-2000, fax 808-565-2483; www.island oflanai.com.

**HULOPOE BEACH PARK** Lanai's finest beach also possesses the island's only fully developed park. Set in a half-moon inlet and fringed with *kiawe* trees, this white-sand beach is an excellent spot for all sorts of recreation. Spinner dolphins are often seen here. It is also the site of the 250-room Manele Bay Hotel, which rests on a bluff about 50 yards above the water-front. Part of a marine life conservation area, Hulopoe has a lava terrace with outstanding tidepools along its eastern point. There is also a wading area for children at this end of the park. If you continue a short distance along this eastern shoreline you'll en-counter **Puu Pehe Cove**, a small beach with abundant marine life that is excellent for swimming and snorkeling. Little wonder that Hulopoe is the island's favorite picnic spot. It's also recom-mended for surfing and fishing. Prime catches are threadfin, *ulua* and bonefish. This is the most accessible surf-casting beach on the island. There are restrooms and showers. ~ Take Route 440 (Manele Road) south from Lanai City for seven miles.

**BEACHES & PARKS**

▲ This is it—the only campground on the island! There are sites at the far end of the beach. Expect to pay a $5 registration fee plus a charge of $5 per camper per day. Permits are issued by the Lanai Company or from the Hulopoe park ranger. Three-night maximum stay. ~ P.O. Box 310, Lanai City, HI 96763; 808-565-2970; www.islandoflanai.com.

**MANELE BAY** Primarily a small-boat harbor, this cliff-fringed inlet is populated by sailboats from across the Pacific. Carouse with the crews, walk along the jetty or scram-ble up the rocks for a knockout view of Haleakala on Maui. It's a very good place for swimming since the harbor is well pro-tected, but you need to be wary of boat traffic. Because Manele Bay is part of a marine preserve the snorkeling is notable and the fishing is limited. Only pole fishing is allowed—no nets. There's a park for picnicking, and just around the corner at Hulopoe Beach are facilities for camping, swimming and other sports. ~ Located Route 440 south of Lanai City.

A southwesterly course along Route 440 (Kaumalapau Highway) will carry you steadily downhill for about six miles to **Kaumalapau Harbor**. This busy lit-tle harbor was built by pineapple interests and used primarily to ship the fruit on barges to Honolulu. During the heyday of Lanai's

## Southwest—Kaumalapau Harbor & Kaunolu

pineapple industry, more than a million pineapples a day were loaded onto waiting ships. On either side of Kaumalapau, you can see the *pali*, which rises straight up as high as 1000 feet, protecting Lanai's southwestern flank. These lofty sea cliffs are an ideal vantage point for watching the sunset.

The most interesting point along this route involves a detour near the airport and a journey down a *very* rugged jeep trail to **HIDDEN ►** **Kaunolu Village**. A summer retreat of Kamehameha the Great and now a national historic landmark, this ancient fishing community still contains the ruins of more than 80 houses as well as stone shelters, petroglyphs and graves. Pick your way through it carefully, lest you step on a ghost. Kamehameha's house, once perched on the eastern ridge, looked across to **Halulu Heiau** on the west side of Kaunolu Bay. Commanding a dominant view of the entire region, these rocky remains are bounded on three sides by cliffs that vault 1000 feet from the ocean.

From nearby **Kahekili's Leap**, warriors proved their courage by plunging more than 60 feet into the water below. If they cleared a 15-foot outcropping and survived the free fall into 12 feet of water, they were deemed noble soldiers worthy of their great king.

Just offshore from this daredevil launching pad lies **Shark Island**, a rock formation that bears an uncanny resemblance to a shark fin. Could it be that warriors skilled enough to survive Kahekili's Leap had then to confront the malevolent spirit of a shark?

## Northwest— Polihua Beach

From Lanai City, a graded pineapple road passes through an eerie stand of iron-wood trees, then disintegrates into an ungraded dirt track that leads about seven miles to the **Garden of the Gods**. This heavily eroded area resembles the Dakota Badlands and features multi-hued boulders that change color dramatically during sunrise and **HIDDEN ►** sunset. A fantasyland of stone, the Garden of the Gods is planted with ancient lava flows tortured by the elements into as many suggestive shapes as the imagination can conjure. The colors here vibrate with psychedelic intensity and the rocks loom up around you as though they were the gods themselves—hard, cold, dark beings possessed of untold power and otherworldly beauty. This is a spot not to be missed.

Past this surreal and sacred spot, Polihua Trail, a rugged jeep road, descends several miles to the ocean. **Polihua Beach**, stretching more than a mile and a half, is the longest and widest white-sand beach on the island.

**POLIHUA BEACH** 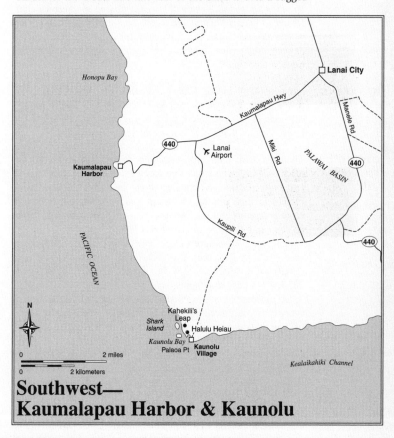 A wide white-sand beach situated along Lanai's northwest shore, this isolated strand, with a stunning view of Molokai, rivals Kauai's trackless beaches. Swimming is allowed here but exercise caution—strong winds and currents prevail throughout this region. The water here is sometimes muddy but when it's clear, and when the Fish and Game Division declares it "in season," you can dive for lobsters. Once a prime nesting beach for green sea turtles, Polihua Beach is an excellent spot to watch whales as they pass close by the shoreline. According to local anglers, this is the best spot on the island for fishing. Common catches include *papio*, *ulua*, bonefish, threadfin and red snapper. There are no facilities here. ~ It's about 11 miles from Lanai City through pineapple fields and the Garden of the Gods. The last half of the drive is over a rugged

**BEACHES & PARKS**

◄ HIDDEN

# Southwest— Kaumalapau Harbor & Kaunolu

jeep trail. For specific directions and road conditions, check with the jeep rental garages.

## Outdoor Adventures

With so much virgin territory, Lanai should be ideal for camping. But here, as on the other islands, landowners restrict outdoors lovers.

### CAMPING

The villain is the outfit that manages the island. It permits island residents to camp where they like, but herds visitors into one area on the south coast. This campsite is located at Hulopoe Beach Park. Reservations are recommended; $5 for camping permit plus $5 per camper per night. ~ Lanai Company, P.O. Box 630310, Lanai City, HI 96763; 808-565-2970.

### FISHING

If you have a hankering to catch marlin, mahi or ono contact **Spinning Dolphin Charters of Lanai**, a private sportfishing charter out of Lanai. Ahi and *aku* (tuna) are found year-round in the waters around Lanai. You can go out for half-day, three-quarter-day or full-day runs. They also offer whale-watching and snorkel tours. ~ 808-565-2970.

### KAYAKING

**Lanai EcoAdventure Centre** features sea kayaking/snorkel combo trips. Explore the reef and the shipwreck on the island's east side or the volcanic history to the west. ~ 328 8th Street, Lanai City; 808-565-7373; www.adventurelanai.com.

### DIVING & SNORKELING

The waters off Lanai are teeming with reef fish and coral formations, enough to make any scuba diver content. One area of Lanai—Cathedrals—is considered the best dive site in Hawaii. Expect to float among Hawaiian green turtles, butterfly fish, black sturgeons and eels. Another favored spot is Kaunalu, with its calm waters and technicolor reef fish.

**Lanai EcoAdventure Centre**, a PADI dive center, offers scuba tours to secluded spots with lava walls and sea caves. Gear rentals are available. ~ 328 8th Street, Lanai City; 808-565-7373; www.adventurelanai.com.

A number of outfitters that operate out of Maui provide everything you'll need (including refreshments) to test the waters off Lanai. Trip departure times can vary by season.

**Trilogy Excursions**, a PADI dive center, conducts snorkel/sail trips with an on-board naturalist from Lahaina Harbor to Hulopoe Beach Park on Lanai. Guests enjoy a light breakfast, a barbecue chicken lunch and an hour-long guided van tour through Lanai's old plantation town. Other options include beach dives at Hulopoe Bay, all-day adventure dives and sunrise dives at Cathedrals. ~ Lahaina Harbor, Maui; 808-661-4743, fax 808-667-7766; www.sailtrilogy.com.

Scotch Mist Sailing Charters offers half-day snorkeling trips from Maui to various locations, at the captain's discretion. ~ Lahaina Harbor, slip 2, Maui; 808-661-0386; www.scotchmistsailingcharters.com.

**GOLF**

Golfers won't be disappointed when they tee off in Lanai. The premier course on the island is one designed by Greg Norman and Ted Robinson, **The Experience at Koele**. Set against the backdrop of forested hills and steep gorges, it lies in the verdant central highlands. Green 17 is completely surrounded by a lake. Reserve tee times up to 90 days in advance. ~ Lanai City; 808-565-7300.

The nine-hole **Cavendish Golf Course**—where the locals play—is open to the public as well. ~ Lanai City.

Or try **Challenge at Manele,** an 18-hole golf course at the Manele Bay Hotel. Designed by Jack Nicklaus, it lies on natural lava outcroppings and follows towering cliffs. The signature hole, number 12, demands a 200-yard tee shot across the ocean. Reserve tee times up to 30 days in advance. ~ 808-565-7700.

**ARCHERY & SPORTING CLAYS**

Ready to test your skills at a medieval sport? **Lanai Pine Archery** has a range for archers of all skills and ages. Instructors provide safety tips and pointers. If bows and arrows are too tame for you, try your luck at shooting clay targets at **Lanai Pine Sporting Clays**. Games include skeet, wobble traps and compact sporting.

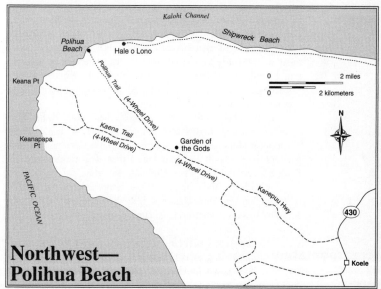

# Northwest— Polihua Beach

Clays are launched to simulate running patterns of various animals and birds. The staff offers instruction. ~ Located one mile north of The Lodge at Koele on Keamoku Highway; 808-559-4600, fax 808-565-4508.

**RIDING STABLES**

The Lodge at Koele offers horseback riding and equestrian tours. Choose between five rides that take you on various trails around the lodge. The Koele Ride is an hour-long leisurely walking ride that follows a wooded trail and gives riders stunning views of Maui, Molokai and Lanai City. ~ 808-565-7300.

**BIKING**

There are a few nice rides from Lanai City, but all are steep in places and pass over pockmarked sections of road. One goes south eight miles to Manele Bay and the beach at Hulopoe, another diverts west to busy little Kaumalapau Harbor, and the last heads north 14 miles to Shipwreck Beach. The **Munro Trail** is perfect for those in good shape and into mountain biking.

Covered in scrub vegetation along much of its surface, Lanai still supports several rare endemic bird species, including the *pueo, uau* and *iiwi*.

Road and mountain bike tours and rentals are available through **Lanai EcoAdventure Centre**. ~ 328 8th Street, Lanai City; 808-565-7373; www.adventure lanai.com. You can also rent them from **The Lodge at Koele**. ~ Lanai City; 808-565-7300.

**Lanai City Service Inc.** is a good place to obtain information concerning Lanai roads. ~ 808-565-7227.

**HIKING**

Hikers on Lanai are granted much greater freedom than campers. Jeep trails and access roads are open to the public; the only restriction is that hikers cannot camp along trails. Since most of the trails lead either to beaches or points of interest, you'll find them described in the regional sightseeing and "Beaches & Parks" sections above. All distances for hiking trails are one way unless otherwise noted.

Beginning behind the Lodge at Koele, the **Koloiki Ridge Trail** (5 miles) leads through forest lands and the Cathedral of Pines (a group of pines resembling a gothic church) to a ridge that runs between Naio Gulch and Maunalei Valley. This moderately difficult hike provides views of Molokai and Maui.

Guided hikes, including overnight camping trips, are offered by **Lanai EcoAdventure Centre**. ~ 328 8th Street, Lanai City; 808-565-7373; www.adventurelanai.com.

**Transportation**

**AIR**

Planes to Lanai land at **Lanai Airport** amid an endless maze of grassland and tilled fields four miles from downtown Lanai City. This tiny landing strip has a small gift shop and a courtesy telephone for car rentals (you'll be picked up in a shuttle). There are no lockers or public trans-

# The Road
## to Adventure

The really interesting places on Lanai lie outside town, and most require driving or hiking over jeep trails. It's advisable to get specific directions wherever you go, since the maze of pineapple roads can confuse even the most intrepid pathfinder. Where possible, I've included directions; otherwise, check with the jeep rental shop in Lanai City or at the hotels.

To be extra safe, ask about road conditions, too. The slightest rain can turn a dusty jeep road into a slick surface, and a downpour can transmogrify it into an impassable quagmire. I once dumped a jeep into a three-foot ditch when the trail to Polihua Beach collapsed. It had been raining steadily for three days and the soft shoulder couldn't support the weight of a vehicle. I was 11 miles from Lanai City with the wheels hopelessly embedded and an hour left until dark.

The way back led past pretty menacing country, heavily eroded and difficult to track through. Rain clouds brought the night on in a rush. I gathered up my poncho and canteen, convinced myself that the worst to come would be a cold and wet night outdoors, and began trekking back to civilization. Fortunately, after five miserable hours I made it. But the entire incident could have been avoided if I had first checked road conditions and had allowed at least several hours of daylight for my return.

This shouldn't discourage you, though. With the proper precautions, exploring Lanai can be a unique experience, challenging but safe. To make things easy, I'll start with a journey to the island's northeastern shore, part of which is over a paved road. Then I'll continue clockwise around the island.

portation. A few rooms house airline offices. Mokulele and Pacific Wings offer service to the islands; IslandAir flies propeller-driven planes and features competitive rates.

If you're staying at any of the island hotels, they will provide transportation into town, as will any of the island's car rental agencies if you're renting a vehicle from them.

**BOAT**

A ferry service called **Expeditions** operates out of Maui and links Lahaina with Manele Bay on Lanai. There are five boats per day in each direction. The 45-minute crossing provides a unique way to arrive on the island and if you're lucky, a chance to spy spinner dolphins and flying fish. ~ P.O. Box 10, Lahaina, HI 96767; 808-661-3756; www.go-lanai.com.

**CAR & JEEP RENTALS**

**Lanai City Service Inc.**, which is affiliated with Dollar Rent A Car, rents automatic compact cars with free mileage. But renting a car on Lanai is like carrying water wings to the desert: there's simply nowhere to go. Rental cars are restricted to pavement, while most of Lanai's roads are jeep trails: four-wheel drive is the only way to fly. ~ 1036 Lanai Avenue; 808-565-7227.

The first time I visited the island of Lanai, I rented a vintage 1942 jeep. The vehicle had bad brakes, no emergency brake, malfunctioning windshield wipers and no seat belts. It was, however, equipped with an efficient shock absorber—me. Today, **Lanai City Service Inc.**, described above, rents new and reliable jeeps. You can also try **Lanai EcoAdventure Centre** for jeep rentals. ~ 328 8th Street, Lanai City; 808-565-7373. (Be aware that the rental car collision insurance provided by most credit cards does not cover jeeps.)

**BOAT TOURS**

There are boat tours of Lanai offered by the Maui-based outfit **Trilogy Excursions**. They'll take you on a full-day excursion, leaving from Lahaina Harbor. Breakfast and lunch is provided, as well as snorkeling equipment and instruction. You'll also go on a one-hour van tour of the island. ~ 808-661-4743.

**GUIDED TOURS**

If you'd rather not do the driving, **Rabaca's Limousine Service** offers tours around the island in limousines or Suburbans ($73.50 an hour) or, if you prefer, 4 x 4s ($50 an hour). There's a two-hour minimum. They also offer 24-hour service. ~ 808-565-6670.

# EIGHT

# Molokai

Between the bustling islands of Oahu and Maui lies an isle that in shape resembles Manhattan, but which in spirit and rhythm is far more than an ocean away from the smog-shrouded shores of the Big Apple. Molokai, Hawaii's fifth-largest island, is 38 miles long and 10 miles wide. The slender isle was created by three volcanoes that mark its present geographic regions: one at West End where the arid Mauna Loa tableland rises to 1381 feet, another at East End where a rugged mountain range along the north coast is topped by 4970-foot Mount Kamakou, and the third, a geologic afterthought, which created the low, flat Kalaupapa Peninsula.

Considering that the island measures a modest 260 square miles, its geographic diversity is amazing. Arriving at Hoolehua Airport near the island's center, travelers feel as though they have touched down somewhere in the American Midwest. Red dust, dry heat and curving prairie surround the small landing strip and extend to the west end of Molokai. This natural pastureland gives way in the south-central region to low-lying, relatively swampy ground and brown-sand beaches with murky water.

The prettiest strands lie along the western shore, where Papohaku Beach forms one of the largest white-sand beaches in the state, and at the east end around Halawa Valley, a region of heavy rainfall and lush tropic vegetation. To the north is the vaunted *pali*, which rises in a vertical wall 3000 feet from the surf, creating the tallest sea cliffs in the world. Here, too, is an awesome succession of sharp, narrow valleys cloaked in velvet green.

Kaunakakai, a sleepy port town on the south shore, is the island's hub. From here a road runs to the eastern and western coasts. Kalaupapa and the northern *pali* are accessible overland only by mule and hiking trails.

Even in a region of islands, Molokai has always been something of a backwater. To the early Hawaiians it appeared desiccated and inhospitable. The rich Halawa Valley was settled in the 7th century and the island developed a haunting reputation for sorcery and mystical occurrences. In ancient times it was also called *pule-oo*, or "powerful prayer," and was revered for the potency of its priests. They were purported to have such power they could pray someone to death.

When Captain James Cook "discovered" the island in November 1778, he found it bleak and inhospitable. Not until 1786 did a Western navigator, Captain George Dixon, bother to land. When Kamehameha the Great took it in 1795, he was actually en route to the much grander prize of Oahu. His war canoes are said to have loomed along four miles of shoreline when he attacked the island at Pakuhiwa Battleground and slaughtered the island's outnumbered defenders.

> Molokai is the only island in the chain, aside from privately owned Niihau, where Hawaiians make up a majority of the population. Along with Lanai, it is really hidden Hawaii.

The next wave of invaders arrived in 1832 when Protestant missionaries introduced the Polynesians to the marvels of Christianity. Around 1850 a German immigrant named Rudolph Meyer arrived in Molokai, married a Hawaiian chieftess, and began a reign as manager of the Molokai Ranch that lasted for almost a half-century.

Leprosy struck the Hawaiian Islands during the 19th century, and wind-plagued Kalaupapa Peninsula became the living hell to which the disease's victims were exiled. Beginning in 1866, lepers were torn from their families and literally cast to their fates along this stark shore. Here Father Damien de Veuster, a Belgian priest, the Martyr of Molokai, came to live, work and eventually die among the afflicted.

For years Molokai was labeled "The Lonely Isle" or "The Forgotten Isle." By 1910 a population that once totaled 10,000 had decreased to one-tenth the size. Then in 1921, Polynesians began settling homesteads under the Hawaiian Homes Act, which granted a 40-acre homestead to anyone with over 50 percent Hawaiian ancestry. Molokai eventually became "The Friendly Isle," with the largest proportion of native Hawaiians anywhere in the world (except for the island of Niihau, which is closed to outsiders). With them they brought a legacy from old Hawaii, the spirit of aloha, which still lives on this marvelous island. Young Hawaiians, sometimes hostile on the more crowded islands, are often outgoing and generous here.

During the 1920s, while Hawaiians were being granted the hardscrabble land that had not already been bought up on the island, Libby (which later sold out to Dole) and Del Monte began producing pineapples across the richer stretches of the island. The company towns of Maunaloa and Kualapuu sprang up and Molokai's rolling prairies became covered with fields of spike-topped fruits. Over the years competition from Asia became increasingly intense, forcing Dole to shut its operation in 1975 and Del Monte to pull out in 1982.

As elsewhere in Hawaii, the economic powers realized that if they couldn't grow crops they had better cultivate tourists. During the 1970s thousands of acres along the island's western end were allocated for resort and residential development and the sprawling Kaluakoi Resort was built. In 1996, vandals opposed to this sort of development destroyed five miles of water pipes on Molokai Ranch, which had earlier closed access to several beaches and evicted a number of former plantation workers from their homes.

Today the island's population numbers under 7000. There isn't a single traffic light here, and the weak economy has saved Molokai from the ravages of devel-

# Molokai

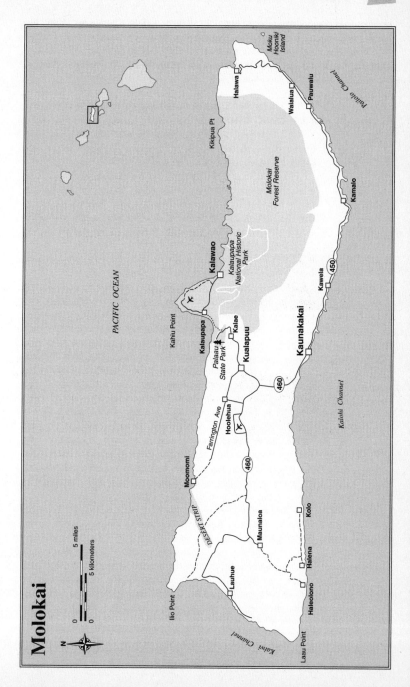

N

0                5 miles

0                5 kilometers

PACIFIC OCEAN

Moku
Hooniki
Island

Halawa

Waialua

Pauwalu

Pailolo Channel

Kamalo

Molokai
Forest Reserve

Kikipua Pt

450

Kawela

Kalawao

Kalaupapa
National Historic
Park

Kahiu Point

Kalaupapa

Kalae

Kualapuu

Kaunakakai

Palaau
State Park

Kalohi Channel

Farrington Ave

Hoolehua

460

Moomomi

460

Maunaloa

Kolo

DESERT STRIP

Halena

Ilio Point

Lauhue

Haleolono

Laau Point

Kalaei Channel

opment that plagued the rest of Hawaii during the 1980s. Change is coming, but like everything on Molokai, it is arriving slowly. Time still remains to see Hawaii as it once was and to experience the trackless beaches, vaulting seacliffs, sweeping ranchlands and forested mountains that led ancient Hawaiians to believe in the mystical powers of Molokai.

## Kaunakakai to East End

You don't need a scorecard, or even a map for that matter, to keep track of the sightseeing possibilities on Molokai. Across its brief expanse, the Friendly Isle offers several rewards to the curious, none of which are difficult to find.

First of course is the falsefront town of Kaunakakai, a commercial hub that more resembles a way station on the road to Dodge City. From here a simple two-lane road, Route 450 (Kamehameha V Highway), threads its way along the southern shore in search of the Halawa Valley at the far east end of the island.

**SIGHTS**

It is only too appropriate that **Kaunakakai** gained its greatest fame from someone who never existed. Known for a song written about "The Cock-eyed Mayor of Kaunakakai," the town has in fact had only one mayor—whether he was cock-eyed, no one will say. This somnolent village, with its falsefront buildings and tiny civic center, is administered from Maui. Poor but proud, it possesses a population of fewer than 3000, and has a main drag (Ala Malama Street) that extends a grand total of three blocks but still represents the hub of Molokai.

According to legend, Molokai was the child of the god Wakea and his mistress Hina, whose cave still lies along the southeastern edge of the island.

Nearby is the **wharf**, extending seaward almost a half-mile and offering a mooring place for a few fishing boats, charter outfits, and private sailboats. A good place to gaze out on the island of Lanai, it is also an ideal vantage from which to take in the green slopes that rise toward the ridgeline of Molokai. Kids love to swim off the Kaunakaki Wharf, where a roped-off area keeps them safe from the boats. It's also a great place to meet local children.

Close to the pier landing rest the rocky remains of **Kamehameha V's Summer Home**, where Hawaii's king luxuriated during the late 19th century.

**HIDDEN ►**

For birdwatching, you'll want to check out the **Wastewater Reclamation Facility**, where the nutrient-rich (read bug-infested) water is a year-round hit with endangered species such as the Hawaiian coot and stilt. In the winter, keep an eye out for the occasional shoveler, green-winged teal, wandering tattler and other migratory waterfowl. Visitors are advised to check in with plant personnel upon arrival. Closed Saturday and Sunday. ~ Located off Maunaloa Highway on the ocean side just before Kaunakakai; 808-553-5341, fax 808-553-4251.

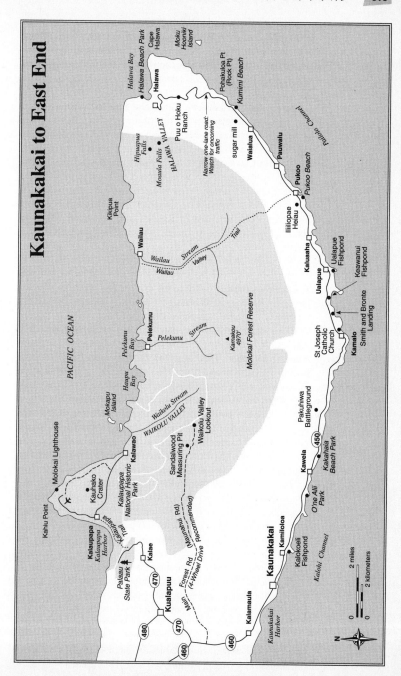

# Kaunakakai to East End

PACIFIC OCEAN

Kahiu Point

Molokai Lighthouse

Kalaupapa
Kalaupapa Harbor

Kalae

Palaau State Park

Kualapuu

Kalawao

Waikolu Valley Lookout

Sandalwood Measuring Pit

WAIKOLU VALLEY

Waikolu Stream

Kauhako Crater

Kalaupapa National Historic Park

Trail
Kalaupapa Trail

Mokapu Island

Haupu Bay

Pelekunu Bay

Pelekunu

Pelekunu Stream

Wailau

Wailau Stream
Wailau Valley

Kikipua Point

HALAWA VALLEY

Hipuapua Falls

Moaula Falls

Halawa Bay
Halawa Beach Park
Cape Halawa
Halawa

Moku Hooniki Island

Puu o Hoku Ranch

Narrow one-lane road: Watch for oncoming traffic

sugar mill

Pohakuloa Pt (Rock Pt)

Kumimi Beach

Waialua

Pauwalu

Pailolo Channel

Pukoo
Pukoo Beach

Trail

Iliiliopae Heiau

Kaluaaha

Ualapue
Ualapue Fishpond

Keawanui Fishpond

Kamalo

Smith and Bronte Landing

St. Joseph Catholic Church

Kamakou 4970'

Molokai Forest Reserve

Pakuhiwa Battleground

Kawela

450

Kakahaia Beach Park

One Alii Park

Kaunakakai

Kamiloloa

Kalokoeli Fishpond

Kalohi Channel

Kaunakakai Harbor

Kalamaula

460

Kualapuu

Forest Rd (Maunahui Rd) (4-Wheel Drive Recommended)

Main Forest Rd

470

480

Kalae

Kualapuu

470

N

0        2 miles

0    2 kilometers

From Kaunakakai to Halawa Valley, a narrow macadam road leads past almost 30 miles of seascapes and historic sites. Route 450 runs straight along the south shore for about 20 miles, presenting views across the Kalohi and Pailolo channels to Lanai and Maui. Then the road snakes upward and curves inland before descending again into Halawa Valley.

Due to the calm, shallow waters along the southeastern shoreline, this area once supported one of the greatest concentrations of fishponds in Hawaii. Numbering as many as five dozen during the pre-Western period, these ancient aquaculture structures were built of lava and coral by commoners to raise fish for Hawaiian royalty. Small fish were trapped within these stone pens, fattened and eventually harvested. You will see the rebuilt remains of several as you drive along the coast, including **Kalokoeli Fishpond**, two miles east of Kaunakakai, **Keawanui Fishpond**, about 12 miles east of town, and **Ualapue Fishpond**, a mile farther east.

About five miles from town lies Kawela, once an ancient city of refuge, now known as the place where two battles were fought at **Pakuhiwa Battleground**. In his drive to become Hawaii's first monarch, Kamehameha the Great launched a canoe flotilla that reportedly extended four miles along this shore.

For a face-to-feather encounter with the endangered nene, Hawaii's state bird, a close relative of the Canadian goose, swing by **Nene O Molokai**. This nonprofit facility raises the birds on a beachfront location and is open for educational visits (by appointment only). ~ P.O. Box 580, Kaunakakai; 808-553-5992, fax 808-553-9029; www.aloha.net/~nene, e-mail nene@aloha.net.

Just past the ten-mile marker (indicating that you are ten miles east of Kaunakakai), a dirt road leads to **Kamalo Wharf**, an old pineapple and cattle shipping point. This natural harbor, once a major commercial center (by Molokai standards!), is now a gathering place for occasional fishermen and boats.

It's a half-mile farther to **St. Joseph Catholic Church**, a tiny chapel built by Father Damien in 1876. A statue of the bespectacled priest, clad in a cape and leaning on a cane, graces the property. A small cemetery completes this placid tableau.

A sign (past the 11-mile marker) designates the **Smith and Bronte Landing**, an inhospitable spot where two aviators crashlanded after completing the first civilian transpacific flight in 1927. The 25-hour flight from California, scheduled to land in Honolulu, ended abruptly when the plane ran out of gas. (An opening in the trees past the 12-mile marker reveals the aforementioned Keawanui Fishpond, one of Molokai's largest.)

Set back from the road in a clearing framed by mountains is **Our Lady of Seven Sorrows Catholic Church**, located 14 miles east of Kaunakakai. Originally built by Father Damien in 1874 and reconstructed almost a century later, it's a pretty chapel surrounded by coconut trees and flanked by a small cemetery.

One of the largest temples in the islands, **Iliiliopae Heiau**, rests   ◄ HIDDEN
hidden in the underbrush on private land just inland from the highway. Measuring about 100 yards in length and 40 yards in width, it was once a center of sorcery and human sacrifice that today consists of a stone platform and adjoining terraces. This is also the trailhead for the Wailau Valley Trail. According to legend, the *heiau*'s stones were all transported from this distant valley and assembled in a single night. Kamani trees were often planted around *heiau*. Considered sacred in many Polynesian cultures, their seeds, gum and bark have been used for medicinal purposes. ~ Located 15 miles east of Kaunakakai; for permission and directions, call Pearl Petro at 808-553-9800.

Nearby is the **Mapulehu Mango Grove**, a stand of over 2000 fruit trees that were planted in 1926 and now represent one of the largest such groves in the world.

The ruins of the island's first **sugar mill** stand near Route 450's 20-mile marker. All that remains of this early factory, which burned down about a century ago, is a solitary stack.

Just beyond the 20-mile marker is Kumimi Beach, which presents your first view of **Moku Hooniki Island**, a popular diving destination, as well as otherworldly vistas of Maui.

The road now begins a sinuous course along a string of pearl-white beaches, then climbs above a rocky coastline. As you curve upward into Molokai's tropical heights, the roadside flora becomes increasingly colorful and dense. First you encounter the

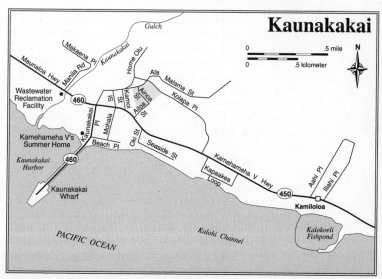

open pastures and rolling ranchland of 14,000-acre **Puu o Hoku Ranch**, then dive into the tropical foliage of Molokai's windblown northeast coast.

As the road winds high above **Halawa Valley** it offers several vista points from which to view this V-shaped canyon bounded by green walls. (*Halawa* means curve.) Directly below, tropical greenery gives way to white surf and then aquamarine ocean. A river bisects this luxuriant region. At the far end, surrounded by sheer walls, two waterfalls—**Hipuapua** and **Moaula**—spill down the mountainside. Obviously East End has withheld its most spectacular scenery until the last.

Archaeologists believe that Molokai's first settlement was established here, possibly as early as the 7th century. The ancient Hawaiians terraced the surrounding slopes, planting taro and living off the largesse of the sea.

In 1946 (and again in 1957) a tidal wave swept through the valley, leveling buildings and leaving salt deposits that destroyed the agricultural industry. Today you can drive down into the valley, where you'll find a park, a lovely curve of sandy beach, freshwater Halawa Stream, an old church and several other structures. A hiking trail leads to 250-foot Moaula Falls and 500-foot Hipuapua Falls, which lie to the interior of this awesomely beautiful vale. Please note, however, that this trail has been closed by the landowner and is not open to the public. You may, however, embark on a guided tour of the area by contacting **Molokai Outdoors** 808-553-4477, 877-553-4477; www.molokai-outdoors.com, e-mail info@molokai-outdoors.com.

**LODGING**

Two miles east of Kaunakakai is the 35-room **Hotel Molokai**, a lowrise hotel with faux-Polynesian architectural details. The accommodations are small but comfortable, and have rattan furnishings, tropical prints; some units also have kitchenettes, refrigerators and ceiling fans. There is an oceanside pool and a pleasant lounge area with an adjacent restaurant and cocktail lounge. The hotel fronts a narrow beach, and shallows offshore are not suitable for ocean swimming, but they're great for fishing, kayaking and windsurfing. The grounds are nicely landscaped with plenty of tall palms that provide a tropical feel. ~ Kamehameha Highway; 808-553-5347, 800-535-0085, fax 808-553-5047; www.hotelmolokai.com, e-mail hotelmolokai@aloha.net. MODERATE TO DELUXE.

If privacy is what you're after, you'll love **Kamalo Plantation Bed & Breakfast**. Set on five acres of orchards and tropical gardens, the secluded cottage lies in the middle of lush grounds. Screen windows let in the tropical smell of the flowering trees, and a private lanai is perfect for the breakfast of homemade bread and fresh fruit from the orchard. The cottage also has a full kitchen. ~ HCO1, Box 300, Kaunakakai, HI 96748; phone/fax 808-558-8236; www.molokai.com/kamalo, e-mail kamaloplan tation@aloha.net. MODERATE.

Ten miles farther east on a sandy beach ideal for whale-watching is the **Moanui Beach House.** Decorated Polynesian style, with vaulted ceilings, the house has two bedrooms with king-size beds, one and a half bathrooms, a living and dining area and a large kitchen. All the home amenities, including TV and VCR, as well as beach gear and grill, are included. Complimentary breakfast breads and fruit are provided with coffee and tea. There's a three-night minimum. ~ HCO1, Box 300, Kaunakakai, HI 96748; phone/fax 808-558-8236; www.molokai.com/kamalo, e-mail ka maloplantation@aloha.net. DELUXE.

In a tropical garden east of Kaunakakai is **A'ahi Place Bed and Breakfast.** Here you'll find a cedar cottage with kitchen and bath, two full-sized beds, and lanais surrounded by fragrant tropical flowers and swaying palms. Best of all—there are no TVs or phones to interrupt your thoughts. ~ P.O. Box 2006, Kaunakakai, HI 96748; 808-553-8033; www.molokai.com/aahi. BUDGET.

On the south shore near the five-mile marker, **Ka Hale Mala** (The Garden House) is a quick walk to the beach. Gourmet breakfasts are included in the moderate host rate, or you can stay there on your own for a lower price. The spacious four-room apartment (that sleeps up to four) is surrounded by a tempting tropical garden—tangelos, pommelos, figs, kau oranges, papayas, limes, breadfruit and more—that you're allowed to pick from. Yum. ~ P.O. Box 1582, Kaunakakai, HI 96748; 808-553-9009; www.molokai-bnb.com, e-mail cpgroup@aloha.net. MODERATE.

**CONDOS**

If you're traveling with several folks or want kitchen facilities, there are also condominiums: **Marc Molokai Shores Suites** offers oceanfront accommodations with full kitchen, lanai and color television. A series of low-slung buildings that forms a U-shaped configuration around a landscaped lawn extending to the beach sits among palm trees, a swimming pool, shuffleboard and barbecue areas. Rates start at $170. ~ Phone/fax 808-553-5954,

**AUTHOR FAVORITE**

*sights*

I love to wander the windswept beach at the edge of **Halawa Valley,** or hike deep into the valley, which has been inhabited by Hawaiians for 1300 years. Ancient *heiau,* two spectacular waterfalls and the remains of a once-rich agricultural industry are some of the highlights of this lush rainforest. See page 398 for more information.

800-535-0085; www.marcresorts.com, e-mail aloha@marcre
sorts.com.

Molokai offers a variety of home and condo rentals, too many
to mention in a guidebook. From one-bedroom facilities to spacious homes, you can probably find something to meet your
budgetary needs. One place to look is www.visitmaui.com—check
the Molokai listings. Property-management and realty companies
are also available in Kaunakakai and Maunaloa. A few include
**Friendly Isle Realty** (800-600-4158) and **Swenson Real Estate**
(800-558-3648).

**DINING**

A gourmet will starve on Molokai, but someone looking for a
square meal at fair prices should depart well-fed. The budget restaurants are clustered along Ala Malama Street in Kaunakakai.

HIDDEN ▶

**Kanemitsu's Bakery** serves tasty meals at appetizing prices. A
local institution, it's a simple café with molded seats, formica tables and an interesting folk-art mural presenting a map of Molokai. The lunch special varies but the price is low whether you are
dining on beef, chopped steak or hamburger steak. Kanemitsu's is
a favorite with the breakfast crowd, which is drawn in by the
bakery as well as by the menu of omelettes, hot
cakes and egg dishes served with Portuguese
sausage or that island favorite, Spam. No dinner.
Closed Tuesday. ~ Ala Malama Street, Kaunakakai;
808-553-5855. BUDGET.

Bet you didn't know this:
Hawaiians consume more
Spam (and that's not the
internet kind) than any-
one else. Don't be shy,
give it a try!

**Outpost Natural Foods** has a takeout counter at
the back of its tiny health food store. Here you can fuel
up with delicious sandwiches, salads and smoothies that
are both nutritious and inexpensive. There are also burritos
and daily specials. No dinner. Closed Saturday. ~ 70 Makaena
Place, Kaunakakai; 808-553-3377, fax 808-553-5857. BUDGET.

If you're into Filipino fare, try **Oviedo's Lunch Counter**. This
mom-and-pop restaurant serves up spicy steaming dishes at low
prices. You'll find plank-board walls surrounding a few plastic
chairs and yellow formica tables. The steam-tray cuisine includes
chicken papaya, pig's feet, turkey tail *adobo* and mango beans.
Open for lunch and early dinner. ~ Puali Street, Kaunakakai; 808-
553-5014. BUDGET.

You're hungry? You want take-out? Why not try **Molokai
Drive Inn**. At breakfast you'll find the usual (eggs and hotcakes)
or the unusual (shrimp omelettes, fried rice, banana pancakes or
eggs and Spam). For lunch or dinner try the ox tail or the Chinese
plate—or stick to burgers if you must. ~ 15 Kamoi Street, Kaunakakai; 808-553-5655, fax 808-553-3693. BUDGET.

**Molokai Pizza Cafe** is an excellent neighborhood pizzeria located just outside of town. Clean and modern, this local hangout is a great place for a tasty lunch or a quick-and-easy dinner.

On Wednesday, Mexican standards are featured, while on Sunday, prime rib is added to the menu. Try one of their burgers on a homemade bun. ~ Kaunakakai Place, Kaunakakai; 808-553-3288, fax 808-553-5400; e-mail molopizza@cs.com. BUDGET TO MODERATE.

The nearest Molokai approaches to a supermarket is **Misaki's**, a **GROCERIES** medium-sized grocery store on Kaunakakai's main drag, Ala Malama Street. The prices are higher and the selection smaller here than at the chain markets, so it's wise to bring a few provisions from the larger islands. Open 8:30 a.m. to 8:30 p.m., Sunday 9 a.m. to noon. ~ 78 Ala Malama Street, Kaunakakai; 808-553-5505, fax 808-553-5575.

**Outpost Natural Foods**, down the street and around the corner from Misaki's, offers a friendly atmosphere as well as juices, herbs, dried fruit, fresh local produce and other health food items. Closed Saturday. ~ 70 Makaena Place, Kaunakakai; 808-553-3377, fax 808-553-5857.

Try **Kanemitsu's Bakery** for delicious raspberry jelly, bread and ◄ HIDDEN pastries. ~ Ala Malama Street, Kaunakakai; 808-553-5855.

On the East End, **Neighborhood Store 'n Counter** has groceries and a stock of liquor. The store is open 8:30 a.m. to 5:30 p.m. daily; the counter is open 10 a.m. to 3 p.m. and is closed on Monday. ~ Kamehameha Highway (near the 16-mile marker); 808-558-8498.

You needn't worry about falling into the shop-'til-you-drop syndrome on Molokai. Long before you have even begun to think about being tired you will have visited every store on the island. Shopping is still an adventure here, since the few stores operating are all owned by local people and provide a window into life on Molokai.

**SHOPPING**

Ala Malama Street, Kaunakakai's main street, offers a modest row of shops. **Molokai Island Creations** specializes in clothing, jewelry, glassware and gift items mostly made by Molokai artists. ~ 63 Ala Malama Street, Kaunakakai; 808-553-5926.

In the same complex, **Molokai Fish & Dive**, "home of the original Molokai T-shirt designs," features its signature clothing and souvenirs as well as beach items and sporting equipment. ~ 61 Ala Malama Street, Kaunakakai; 808-553-5926.

**Imports Gift Shop** features casual wear, cultured pearls, and Hawaiian heirloom jewelry. ~ 828 Ala Malama Street, Kaunakakai; 808-553-5734.

For surfwear you can try **Molokai Surf**. Closed Sunday. ~ 130 Kamehameha Highway, Suite 103, Kaunakakai; 808-553-5093.

Be sure to stop by the **Kamakana Fine Arts Gallery**, above the American Savings Bank in Kaunakakai. Finely turned bowls, blown glass, hula implements, *pahu* drums, *lauhala* hats, painted spirit paintings and marine sculptures are just some of the objects you'll find. Over 75 of Molokai's artists are featured here. Closed Sunday. ~ 40 Ala Malama Street, Kaunakakai; 808-553-8520; www.kamakanagallery.com, e-mail kgallery@aloha.net.

**BEACHES & PARKS**

**O'NE ALII PARK** This spacious park has a large grass-covered field and coconut trees plus a narrow beach with an excellent view of Lanai. A reef far offshore makes this area very shallow and affords ample protection. It's excellent for children. Snorkeling, though, is only mediocre. As for surfing, all the action is far out on the reef and it's rarely any good. Surf-casting isn't bad here but it's even better farther to the east. The most common catches are *manini*, red and white goatfish, parrotfish, *papio*, *ulua*, milkfish and mullet. Facilities here include a picnic area, restrooms, showers and electricity at the pavilion. ~ Located four miles east of Kaunakakai on Route 450; 808-553-3204, fax 808-553-3206.

▲ Mainly tent camping; no hookups, $3 per person per night. Very popular and therefore sometimes crowded and noisy. County permit required.

**KAKAHAIA BEACH PARK** This long, narrow park wedged tightly between the road and the ocean is the site of the Kakahaia National Wildlife Refuge. Since the water is both shallow and murky, swimming and snorkeling are not recommended. Picnicking, surfing and fishing are much the same as at O'ne Alii Park. Day use only. ~ Located six miles east of Kaunakakai on Route 450.

**PUKOO BEACH** This crescent-shaped strand is mirrored by another curving beach just to the west. Maui lies directly across the channel and there are also marvelous views of Lanai. With a shallow, rocky bottom, this beach provides only mediocre swimming. However, it's very popular with anglers. There are no facilities. ~ The old Neighborhood Store 'n' Snack Bar, located on Route 450 near 16-mile marker, is your landmark. Just past here, traveling east, turn into the second driveway on the right. This access road leads a short distance to the beach.

**KUMIMI BEACH, POHAKULOA POINT AND OTHER EAST END BEACHES** Beginning near the 18-mile marker on Route 450, and extending for about four miles, lies this string of small sandy beaches. These are among the island's loveliest, featuring white sands and spectacular views of the islands of Maui and Lanai. The swimming is very good, but beware of heavy currents and high surf. Plentiful coral makes for great snorkeling and good lobster diving. There are numerous surfing breaks throughout this area. Pohakuloa Point (or Rock Point), located eight-tenths of a mile past the 20-mile marker, is one of Molokai's top surfing spots. Barracuda are sometimes caught in the deeper regions. Also bonefish, mountain bass, threadfin, *manini*, red and white goatfish, *ulua*, *papio*, parrotfish, milkfish and mullet. ~ These pocket beaches are located along Route 450 between the 18- and 22-mile markers.

**HALAWA BEACH PARK** Set in lush Halawa Valley, one of Molokai's most splendid areas, the park is tucked neatly between mountains and sea on a grassy plot dotted with coconut palms and ironwood trees. Cliffs, waterfalls, two pocket beaches—altogether a heavenly spot, though sometimes rainy and almost always windy. This is an okay place to swim because it is partially protected by the bay, but exercise caution anyway. Snorkeling is good, though the water is sometimes murky. It's one of the very best spots on the island for surfing. Fishing is also notable; the reefs studding this area make it a prime locale for many of the species caught along East End Beaches. The park is a bit weatherbeaten and overgrown and although there are a picnic area and restrooms, the running water must be boiled or treated chemically. ~ Located 30 miles east of Kaunakakai on Route 450.

▲ Not permitted in the park, but people camp on the other side of Halawa Stream on property owned by Puu o Hoku Ranch (808-558-8109). You will have to park and carry your gear to where you want to camp.

Generally, if you are not pointed east on Molokai, you are headed westerly. The thoroughfare that carries you across the

## Kaunakakai to West End

prairie-like plains of west Molokai is Route 460, also called the Maunaloa Highway, another two-lane track. Along the way you can venture off in search of the plantation town of Kualapuu and the vista point overlooking Kalaupapa, but eventually you will arrive at road's end out in the woodframe town of Maunaloa. From this red-dust municipality it's a short jaunt to Papohaku Beach, Molokai's western shore. If nothing else, Molokai's West End is

### AGED SWIMMERS

Green sea turtles are commonly seen in Hawaiian waters, popping their heads up for a breath of air or sliding along rocky reefs to feed on the seaweed, or *limu*, that gives their flesh its distinctive green tint. The Hawaiians frequently ate *honu*, which was considered a delicacy. These creatures are an amazing 150 million years old, yet in the past century they were hunted so heavily by fishing crews that their population nearly crashed. Since being federally designated as a protected, threatened species, their numbers are rising. But their newest threat is a puzzling disease that causes large tumors to grow on their flesh.

rich in myth and history. As Hawaiian storytellers recount, the region around Maunaloa, the volcano that formed this side of the island, was once a cultural focus of the Polynesians. It was here that the hula originated; from the slopes of Maunaloa the goddess Laka spread knowledge of the sensuous dance to all the other islands.

**SIGHTS**   Just a mile west of the cock-eyed town of Kaunakakai on Route 460 is the **Kapuaiwa Coconut Grove**, planted in the 1860s by Kamehameha V. This magnificent stand of coconut palms, once 1000 in number, consists of particularly tall trees. The grove creates the sensation of being in a tropical dream sequence, with hundreds of palm trees flashing green and yellow fronds and extending to the lip of the ocean. Some appear to stand in columns, but others have bent so far to the wind they have fallen out of formation. Pay a visit toward sunset, when the palms are memorably silhouetted by tropic skies for a wonderful end-of-day setting. Watch out for falling coconuts: these trees are not the trimmed-back kind made safe for the unwary. Adjacent to the coconut grove is the **Kalanianaole Community Hall**, a unique early-20th-century cultural landmark that still serves the community but is considering plans for renovation. ~ Route 460.

Pope John Paul II beatified Father Damien in recognition of his service to leprosy victims banished to Kalaupapa.

Strung like rosary beads opposite the grove are seven tiny churches. This **Church Row** includes Protestant, Mormon, Jehovah's Witness and several other denominations. Like sentinels protecting the island from the devil, they too are gathered in rows. The most intriguing are the oldest, tiny woodframe structures with modest steeples. These one-room chapels lack worldly frills like stained glass and are furnished with creaky wooden pews that seat a few dozen parishioners. Stop by and inquire about services; visitors are always welcome.

**Molokai Plumerias** is a family-run company that will take you on a tour of their 10-acre plumeria farm. Plumeria, with the scent of heaven, are the primary flowers used in lei making. Your guide will teach you about the flower, allow you to pick your own and provide you with the necessary tools to create a lei. There are no regularly scheduled tours, so make reservations in advance. ~ Kalamaula, about two miles west of Kaunakakai; 808-553-3391; e-mail dick@molokaiplumerias.com.

A side trip along Route 470 leads past the tinroof town of **Kualapuu**. Filled with modest plantation houses, it harkens back to an earlier era when Molokai cultivated pineapples rather than tourists. Today its claim to fame is a 1.4-million-gallon reservoir that is reportedly the largest rubber-lined water tank in the world.

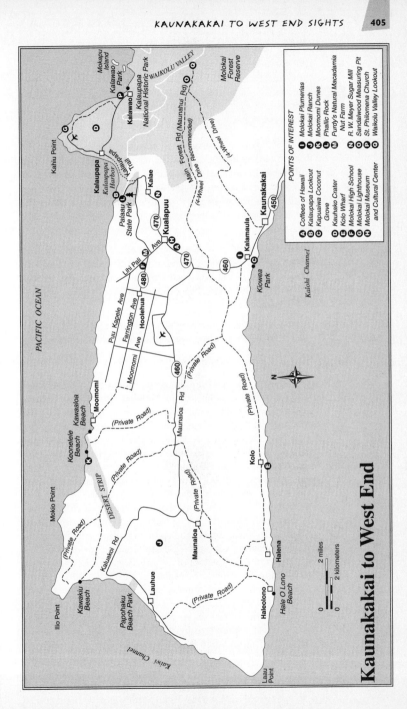

# Kaunakakai to West End

POINTS OF INTEREST

Ⓐ Coffees of Hawaii
Ⓑ Kalaupapa Lookout
Ⓒ Kapuaiwa Coconut Grove
Ⓓ Kauhako Crater
Ⓔ Kolo Wharf
Ⓕ Molokai High School
Ⓖ Molokai Lighthouse
Ⓗ Molokai Museum and Cultural Center
Ⓘ Molokai Plumerias
Ⓙ Molokai Ranch
Ⓚ Moomomi Dunes
Ⓛ Phallic Rock
Ⓜ Purdy's Natural Macadamia Nut Farm
Ⓝ R. W. Meyer Sugar Mill
Ⓞ Sandalwood Measuring Pit
Ⓟ St. Philomena Church
Ⓠ Waikolu Valley Lookout

For a splendid tour of Molokai's mountainous interior, take a drive or hike on the Main Forest Road (Maunahui Road), located four miles west of Kaunakakai. This bumpy dirt road requires four-wheel-drive vehicles along its ten-mile length. To reach the Main Forest Road, take Route 460 west from Kaunakakai. There is a white bridge a little more than three and a half miles from town, just before the four-mile marker. Take a right on the dirt road right before the bridge and you're on the Main Forest Road.

**MOLOKAI FOREST RESERVE**    Deer, quail, pheasant, doves and chukkar partridge populate the route. Numerous secondary roads and trails lead to the very edge of the mammoth Molokai Forest Reserve, through which the main road passes. These side roads offer excellent possibilities for adventurous hikers.

**LUA MOKU ILIAHI**    After nine miles, the main road passes Lua Moku Iliahi, known to the English-speaking world as the **Sandalwood Measuring**

Farther up Route 470, **Kalae** is home to the R. W. Meyer Sugar Mill, which is the highlight of the **Molokai Museum and Cultural Center**. There is an 1878 steam-generated operation that has been restored in sparkling fashion. The mule-driven cane crusher, copper clarifiers and dependable old steam engine are ready and waiting for Molokai to return to its old ways. There are also well-presented displays and heirlooms of the German immigrant family that owned the mill, as well as native Molokai artifacts. Closed Sunday. Admission. ~ Route 470, Kalae; 808-567-6436.

Route 470 ends at the **Kalaupapa Lookout**. Here cliffs as green as Ireland fall away in dizzying fashion to reveal a softly sloping tableland 1600 feet below, the Kalaupapa Peninsula. Fringed by white-sand beaches, this geologic afterthought extends more than two miles out from the foot of the *pali*. A lighthouse and landing strip occupy the point of the peninsula. Nearer the cliffs, a cluster of houses comprises the famous leper colony; while neighboring Kauhako Crater, a nicely rounded circle far below you, represents a vestige of the volcano that created this appendage. Ringed by rock and water, protected by the tallest sea cliffs in the world, Kalaupapa Peninsula is a magnificent sight indeed.

A short hike from the lookout, **Phallic Rock** protrudes obscenely from the ground amid an ironwood stand as thick as pubic hair. This geologic formation, so realistic it almost seems sculpted, was said to represent the Hawaiian fertility god, who was turned

**Pit.** This depression, dug into the earth to match the hull size of an old sailing vessel, was used by 19th-century Hawaiians to gauge the amount of sandalwood needed to fill a ship.

**WAIKOLU VALLEY LOOKOUT**    It's another mile to **Waikolu Picnic Grove**, a heavily wooded retreat ideal for lunching or camping. Here you'll find picnic facilities and an outhouse. (State permit required to camp.) Across the road, Waikolu Valley Lookout perches above Waikolu Valley, which descends precipitously 3000 feet to the sea.

**KAMAKOU PRESERVE**    Here you can also explore Kamakou Preserve, a 2774-acre sanctuary managed by The Nature Conservancy. Home to more than 200 plants that live only in Hawaii, and accessible only by four-wheel drive, the preserve is a lush rainforest and an important watershed for Molokai. There are several forest birds, including the *apapane* and *amakihi*. Closed weekends. For information on visiting the preserve or to check the condition of the Main Forest Road (which may be closed in wet weather), call 808-553-5236, fax 808-553-9870; www.nature.org, e-mail hike_molokai@tnc.org.

to stone when his wife caught him admiring a beautiful young girl. Legend says that a woman offering gifts and spending the night here will return home pregnant.

Route 480 will take you into the town of **Hoolehua**, where you'll find **Purdy's Natural Macadamia Nut Farm**. Located right behind the island's only high school, this small grove of 70-year-old macadamia nut trees is open to the public for free tours and tastings. The owner will explain the growing cycles of the trees and demonstrate harvesting and cooking techniques. Visitors can taste the raw product and also sample the nut after it's been naturally roasted, a process that cuts down greatly on the fat and calories found in nuts sold in stores. Closed Sunday. ~ Lihipali Avenue, Hoolehua; 808-567-6601.

Route 460 continues over dry rolling plains toward Molokai's West End. This arid plateau, windswept and covered by deep red, iron-rich soil, was once planted in pineapple. Today Molokai Ranch, which still owns much of the region, has turned to hay cultivation to feed cattle. Before it was planted with pineapple, Molokai's West End was once a rich adze quarry. The rock, vital to a Stone Age society, was fashioned into tools that were in turn used to create weapons, canoes, bowls and other necessities.

Like the pineapple industry itself, Route 460 ends in **Maunaloa**. With the departure of Dole's operations in 1975, this company town assumed the dusty, falsefront visage of the Wild West after the mines petered out and the saloons shut down. That's all begun to change in the past few years as the Molokai Ranch, which owns just about all of Maunaloa, has started a revitalization program that has seen the more ramshackle plantation houses replaced by contemporary homes, some of the town's more historic buildings upgraded, and several new buildings added, including a lovely 22-room lodge and Molokai's first movie theater. The old post office and general store provide links to Maunaloa's days as a pineapple town, and the overall feeling remains rustically charming, albeit with an increasingly gentrified air.

Any tour of West End should of course finish at the west end. **Papohaku Beach,** a sparkling three-mile long swath of white sand, would be a fitting finale to any tour. Reached by taking Kaluakoi Road from Route 460 and driving through the rolling hills of Kaluakoi Villas, Papohaku is one of the largest beaches in the state. During World War II troops practiced shore landings along this coast. But today you will have the beach and surrounding sand dunes almost entirely to yourself.

**LODGING**   If there is such a thing as luxury camping, a stay at the **Molokai Lodge and Beach Village** would be it. Their idea of "roughing it" includes spacious aluminum-frame "tentalows," canvas-sided bungalows that come with queen-size beds, overhead fans, solar-heated bathrooms and private wooden decks for lounging about. Three hearty meals are served buffet-style in the dining pavilion. There's also a wide range of activities offered to guests: mountain biking, horseback riding, kayaking and cultural hikes. Or you can participate in a cattle roundup at the Paniolo Roundup; and the Cattle Drive, where you'll join *paniolo* as they move cattle from one pasture to another. The staff couldn't be more friendly or helpful. ~ P.O. Box 259, Maunaloa, HI 96770; 808-552-2741, 888-627-8082, fax 808-552-2773; www.molokai ranch.com, e-mail info@molokairanch.com. ULTRA-DELUXE.

**AUTHOR FAVORITE**

The two-story **Molokai Lodge and Beach Village** in Maunaloa was designed and decorated with the town's plantation past in mind—the 22-room lodge exudes a sense of intimacy and charm, with rattan furnishings and '30s-style Hawaiian prints. Rooms are spacious and individually decorated with cheerful upcountry decor. All offer long, unobstructed views of West Molokai's rolling hills, with the ocean in the distance. The eight-acre property includes a day spa, swimming pool, game room and lounge. See above for more information.

Far from the madding crowd on the west end of Molokai, you will find the **Kaluakoi Villas**. These cottage-like accommodations are set near a luxurious three-mile-long beach. This is Molokai's premier resting spot, offering both seclusion and comfort. Here you'll find the essence of plush living: a wasp-waisted pool and a view of Oahu across the channel. Studios (starting at $145 a night) and one-bedroom units (starting at $185 a night) have kitchenettes. The spacious cottage villas are $250 a night and come with a full kitchen. ~ 1131 Kaluakoi Road, Maunaloa; 808-552-2721, 800-367-5004, fax 808-552-2201, www.castleresorts.com.

Nearby **Paniolo Hale Resort** has 15 condos starting at $115 per night. Located just off the shore of Kepuhi Beach, they feature oak floors and beamed ceilings and walls of glass doors that open onto screened lanais. Access to a pool and barbecue area round out the traditional amenities (dishwasher, washer and dryer). Three night minimum. ~ Lio Place; 800-367-2984; www.molokai-vacation-rental.com, e-mail paniolo1@aloha.net.

**CONDOS**

A take-out joint, **Kamuela's Cookhouse** fills the bill when you're hungry. Homemade corned beef hash tops your eggs, if you want, or there's buttermilk pancakes, french toast, breakfast sandwiches and omelettes at breakfast. Lunch brings teriyaki plates, katsu, lemon chicken, mahimahi plates and sandwiches. Friendly folks. ~ Uwao Street, Kualapuu; 808-567-9655. MODERATE.

**DINING**

In Kualapuu, check out **Kualapuu Market**. Open Monday through Saturday 8:30 a.m to 6 p.m. ~ Farrington Highway; 808-567-6243.

Out West End way, **Maunaloa General Store**, in Maunaloa a few miles away from Kaluakoi Villas, has a limited stock of grocery items. Open 8 a.m. to 6 p.m. Closed Sunday. ~ 200 Maunaloa Highway; 808-552-2346.

**GROCERIES**

Over on Molokai's West End in the red-dust town of Maunaloa you'll stumble upon two great shops that share the same building and the same telephone. **Big Wind Kite Factory** has an astonishing assortment of high flyers. There are diamond kites, dancer kites, windsocks and rainbow-tail kites. You can even pick up flags and banners here. At **The Plantation Gallery** there are aloha shirts, batik sarongs, tribal art, shell necklaces and other original pieces by over 30 Molokai craftspeople. They also have the largest collection of books about Hawaii and Hawaiian culture on the island and an extensive selection of Hawaiian music CDs. ~ Maunaloa Highway; 808-552-2364, fax 808-552-2988.

**West Sundries Store** at Kaluakoi Villas carries (what else?) sundries. ~ 808-552-2320.

**SHOPPING**

**BEACHES & PARKS**

**KIOWEA PARK** 🏊 ⛱ Watch for falling coconuts in the beautiful Kapuaiwa Grove, which is the centerpiece of this beach park. Towering palm trees extend almost to the water, leaving little space for a beach. The swimming here is only okay; the water is well-protected by a distant reef, but the bottom is shallow and rocky, and the water is muddy. Beyond the reef, fishing yields mullet, *manini*, parrotfish, milkfish and *papio*, plus red, white and striped goatfish; crabbing is good in the evening. (This park is generally restricted to homesteaders, but if you stop for a picnic you may be allowed by the locals to stay.) A nice place to visit, but I wouldn't want to fall asleep in the shade of a coconut tree. Facilities include a picnic area, restrooms and a pavilion. ~ Located one mile west of Kaunakakai on Route 460; 808-560-6104, fax 808-560-6665.

▲ Camping is usually restricted to homesteaders. If the park is vacant however, the Hawaiian Homelands Department across the street will issue permits for a fee; hours are Monday through Friday from 7:45 a.m. to 4:30 p.m. Reservations are required.

**PALAAU STATE PARK** 🚶 Set in a densely forested area, this 233-acre park is ideal for a mountain sojourn. Several short trails lead to petroglyphs, a startling phallic rock, and the awesome Kalaupapa Lookout. The trail down to Kalaupapa Peninsula is also nearby. There are picnic area, restrooms and a pavilion. ~ Take Route 460 six miles west from Kaunakakai, then follow Route 470 (Kalae Highway) about six more miles to the end of the road; 808-567-6923.

▲ State permit required. Tent camping only.

HIDDEN ►

**MOOMOMI BEACH** 🏊 🎣 🚶 ⛱ A small, remote beach studded with rocks and frequented only by local people—what more could you ask? While Moomomi is a small pocket beach, many people use the name to refer to a three-mile length of coastline that extends west from the pocket beach and includes two

---

## MOLOKAI KA HULA PIKO

If you're in town in mid- to late-May, you'll want to experience **Molokai Ka Hula Piko**, an event that honors the tradition that claims the hula was first danced on Molokai. A mile-long hike to a sunrise ceremony on a hillside leads to where the dances were said to have originated. Cameras are not allowed and decorum is the rule at this spiritual rite. Later in the day beachfront festivities at Papohaku Beach Park include hula and general high spirits. It can be hard to find a room or car during the event, so plan accordingly. Call the Molokai Visitors Association (800-800-6367) for information and updates.

other strands, **Kawaaloa Beach** and **Keonelele Beach**. Moomomi offers good swimming, but use caution because the bottom is rocky and the beach is only partially protected. The snorkeling is very good along reefs and rocks. As for surfing, there are fair breaks at the mouth of the inlet. There's good surf-casting from the rocky headland to the west. Keonelele Beach forms the coastal border of the Moomomi Dunes, a unique series of massive sand dunes that extend as far as four miles inland, covering Molokai's north-western corner; this is also known as the Desert Strip. The preserve protects five endangered plant species and is a habitat for the en-dangered Hawaiian green sea turtle. The only facilities are a pavil-ion and restrooms. ~ Take Route 460 west from Kaunakakai to Hoolehua. Go right on Route 481 (Puupeelua Avenue), then left on Farrington Avenue. Farrington starts as a paved road, then turns to dirt. After 2.2 miles of dirt track, the road forks. Take the right fork and follow it a half-mile to the beach. A four-wheel-drive vehicle may be required.

#### HALENA AND OTHER SOUTH COAST BEACHES 🦆 🛶 🧍     ◀ HIDDEN
🛶 ⚓ Don't tell anyone, but there's a dirt road running several miles along a string of trackless beaches on the south shore. (Note, however, that at last report this road was closed to the public.) The first one, **Halena**, is a very funky ghost camp with a few primitive facilities. To the west lies **Hale O Lono Beach**, with its pleasant bay and lagoon. To the east is **Kolo Wharf** (an abandoned pier col-lapsing into the sea), plus numerous fishponds, coconut groves and small sand beaches. This is an excellent area to explore, camp, hike, fish (bass, threadfin, *enenue*, red goatfish) and commune with hidden Hawaii. The swimming is also good if you don't mind muddy water. It's wise to boil or chemically treat the water if you intend to drink it. *Note:* Only Hale O Lono Beach has a public-access road; the other two are located on Molokai Ranch. ~ Take Route 460 to Maunaloa. As you first enter town (before the road curves into the main section), you'll see houses on the left and a dirt road extending perpendicularly to the right.

Now, to get to Halena, take a right at the fork, then a quick left (there are signs posted), then drive a few hundred yards to the end. The shore is nearby; simply walk west along the beach several hundred yards.

To get to Hale O Lono Beach, walk about a mile west along the beach from Halena.

To get to Kolo Wharf and the other beaches, go straight where the road forks. Kolo is two miles east over an equally rugged road. Sand beaches, coconut groves and fishponds extend for another six miles past Kolo. Then the road turns inland, improving con-siderably, and continues for seven miles more until it meets the main road two miles west of Kaunakakai.

*Text continued on page 414.*

# Molokai Pilgrimage

The ultimate Molokai experience is the pilgrimage to the Kalaupapa leper colony located along the rugged north shore of the island. Isolated on a 12-square-mile lava tongue that protrudes from the north shore, this sacred and historic site can be reached only by foot, mule or plane.

Here about 68 victims of Hansen's Disease, a chronic infectious bacterial disease that causes sores and ulcers and destroys tissue, live in solitude. Doctors have controlled the affliction since 1946 with sulfone drugs, and all the patients are free to leave. But many are 60 to 90 years old, and have lived on this windswept peninsula most of their lives.

The story of the remaining residents goes back to 1866 when the Hawaiian government began exiling lepers to this lonely spot on Molokai's rain-plagued north coast. In those days Kalaupapa was a fishing village, and lepers were segregated in the old settlement at Kalawao on the windy eastern side of the peninsula. The place was treeless and barren—a wasteland haunted by slow death. Lepers were shipped along the coast and pushed overboard. Abandoned with insufficient provisions and no shelter, they struggled against both the elements and disease.

To this lawless realm came Joseph Damien de Veuster—Father Damien. The Belgian Catholic priest, arriving in 1873, brought a spirit and energy that gave the colony new life. He built a church, attended to the afflicted and died of leprosy 16 years later. In 1995, Pope John Paul II made Father Damien "The Blessed Father Damien." Perhaps it is the spirit of this "Martyr of Molokai" that even today marks the indescribable quality of Kalaupapa. There is something unique and inspiring about the place, something you will have to discover yourself.

To visit Kalaupapa, you can fly, hike or ride muleback; there are no roads leading to this remote destination. Once there you must take a guided tour; no independent exploring is permitted. And no children under 16 are allowed. Bus tours are organized by **Molokai Mule Ride** (808-567-6088, 800-567-7550; www.mule ride.com). For flight information, check **Molokai Air Shuttle** (808-567-6847) from Honolulu. **Paragon Air** (808-244-3356, 800-428-1231; www.paragon-air.com) flies from Maui and Honolulu.

As far as I'm concerned, the mule ride is the only way to go. The Molokai Mule Ride conducts tours daily, weather permitting, except Sunday when the park is closed. You saddle up near the Kalaupapa Lookout and descend a 1700-foot precipice, among the tallest sea cliffs in the world. Kalaupapa unfolds below you as you switchback through lush vegetation on a three-mile-long trail. The ride? Exhilarating, frightening, but safe. And the views are awesome.

On the tour you will learn that Kalaupapa has been designated a national historical park. Among the points of interest within this refuge are numerous windblasted structures, a volcanic crater and several monuments. You'll visit **St. Philomena Church**, built by Father Damien in the 1870s, and **Kalawao Park**, an exotically beautiful spot on the lush eastern side of the peninsula. **Father Damien's grave** is also located here.

Definitely visit Kalaupapa. Fly in and you'll undergo an unfor-gettable experience; hike and it will become a pilgrimage.

For current information about road access contact Molokai Ranch. ~ 808-552-2791.

**HIDDEN ►** **KAWAKIU BEACH** 🧍 🏖 🛶 This idyllic spot is my favorite Molokai campground. Here a small inlet, tucked away in Molokai's northwest corner, is edged by a beautiful beach with a sandy bottom. Nearby is a shady grove of *kiawe* trees, fringed by the rocky coastline. On a clear night you can see the lights of Oahu across Kaiwi Channel. This is a very good place to swim because the inlet offers some protection, but exercise caution. Snorkeling is good in summer near the rocks when the surf is low. People fish here for mountain bass, threadfin, *enenue* and red goatfish. There are no facilities. ~ Take Route 460 west from Kaunakakai. At the Kaluakoi Villas, head to the road near the back 9. Drive north until you hit the beach. It's a tricky route, so you may want to check in with the hotel staff for further details; they warn against making the trip without a four-wheel drive.

▲ That shady grove is a perfect site to pitch a tent.

> Molokai has the largest reef system in the United States and the highest bog in the world.

**PAPOHAKU BEACH PARK** 🏊 🧍 🛶 This splendid beach extends for three miles along Molokai's west coast; it's an excellent place to explore, collect puka shells, or just lie back and enjoy the view of Oahu. Backed by *kiawe* trees and low sand dunes, Papohaku is the largest beach on the island, averaging 100 yards in width. Swimming is excellent, but use caution; sit out on the beach and observe the wave action before jumping in. There's not much rock or coral here so the snorkeling is only mediocre. You'll find good breaks for surfing when the wind isn't blowing from the shore. Use caution, especially in the winter months. The beach is also popular with bodysurfers. The fishing is good, usually for mountain bass, threadfin, *enenue* and red goatfish. There are picnic areas, restrooms and showers. ~ Take Route 460 for about 14 miles from Kaunakakai. Turn right onto the road to the Kaluakoi Villas. Continue past the villas (don't turn onto the villas road) and down the hill. Follow this macadam track, Kaluakoi Road, as it parallels the beach. Side roads from Kaluakoi Road and Pohakuloa Road (an adjoining thoroughfare) lead to Papohaku and other beaches.

▲ Tent only. County permit required.

## Outdoor Adventures

With so little development and such an expanse of untouched land, Molokai would seem a haven for campers. Unfortunately, large segments of the island are owned by Molokai Ranch and other private interests; with the exception of a few beaches on Molokai Ranch property, these tracts are closed off behind locked gates.

**CAMPING**

There are a few parks for camping. A county permit is required for Papohaku Beach and O'ne Alii Park. Permits are $3 per person a day (50 cents for children) and are obtained at the County Parks and Recreation office in Kaunakakai. Hours are 8 a.m. to 4 p.m., Monday through Friday, so get your permit in advance. ~ 808-553-3204, fax 808-553-3206.

Camping at Palaau State Park is $5 per person per night and requires a permit from the Department of Land and Natural Resources (808-984-8109) on Maui, or from the park ranger (808-567-6923).

For information on camping at Molokai Ranch, contact the **Molokai Lodge and Beach Village**, Monday through Friday 8 a.m. to 4:30 p.m. ~ P.O. Box 259, Maunaloa, HI 96770; 808-552-2741, fax 808-552-2773; www.molokairanch.com.

**Molokai Fish & Dive** sells camping gear. ~ 61 Ala Malama Street, Kaunakakai; 808-553-5926.

Not the most ideal island for underwater adventures, Molokai does have a few technicolor gems to offer. The best place for snorkeling or diving is at the 20-mile marker on the east side of the island heading out to Halawa Valley. Keep an eye open for **Dragon Tail**, a lava outcropping that zigzags into the Pailolo Channel. There's a large offshore reef here where you're likely to see long skinny trumpet fish, sturgeon and maybe a few green sea turtles.

**DIVING**

If you're not traveling with gear, the following outfitters rent equipment. Several also provide snorkeling and diving trips to prime spots around the island.

Check out **Molokai Fish & Dive** for mask, fin and snorkel rentals. ~ 61 Ala Malama Street, Kaunakakai; 808-553-5926; www.molokaifishanddive.com. **Bill Kapuni's Snorkel and Dive Adventure** rents snorkel equipment. He leads dives to spots where it's not uncommon to see tiger sharks, hammerhead sharks and countless green turtles. He also teaches PADI classes. ~ 808-553-9867. **Molokai Action Adventures** offers three- to four-hour snorkeling expeditions. ~ Kaunakakai; 808-558-8184.

For a scenic paddling adventure, **Lani's Kayak** has full-day North Shore trips that take in breathtaking sea cliffs and lush greenery. Its two-and-a-half-hour Southeast tour features turtles and waterfalls. ~ P.O. Box 826, Kaunakakai, HI 96748; 808-558-8563.

**KAYAKING**

Guided and un-guided ocean kayak tours, including an exploration of the old Kolo wharf are offered by **Molokai Fish & Dive**. Your guides will share their knowledge of the ancient Hawaiian fish ponds. Reservations strongly recommended for non-guests. ~ 808-553-5926.

One- and two-person kayak rentals are available at **Hotel Molokai's Outdoor Activities**. They also have car carriers for rent.

~ Kamehameha V Highway, Kaunakakai; 808-553-4477; www.hotelmolokai.com.

**SAILING**   Providing Molokai's only sailing adventure, **Molokai Charters** operates *Satan's Doll*, a 42-foot sloop that is docked on the wharf in Kaunakakai. Step aboard for sunset cruises, whale-watching tours and snorkeling excursions to Lanai. ~ 808-553-5852.

**FISHING**   Depending on the weather, deep-sea fishing charters will take you to various spots that are within ten to twenty miles of Molokai. Here you're likely to catch mahimahi, tuna, marlin and *ono*.

Alyce C Commercial and Sport Fishing offers half-, three-quarter- and full-day excursions—all equipment included. Bring your own food and drink. They also operate whale-watching tours from late December to early April. ~ Kaunakakai; 808-558-8377. **Molokai Action Adventures** provides all the equipment for half- or full-day charters. ~ Kaunakakai; 808-558-8184.

**BIKING**   Traffic is light and slow-moving, making Molokai an ideal place for two-wheeling adventurers. The roads are generally good, with some potholes out East End near Halawa Valley. The terrain is mostly flat or gently rolling, with a few steep ascents. Winds are strong and sometimes make for tough going.

For those in good shape and who like to climb, contact **Molokai Fish & Dive** for their advanced mountain-bike tour on rugged terrain at Molokai Ranch. Afternoon tours are for beginners and feature a single-track or ranch-road descent to Hale O Lono. All in all, the ranch features 100 miles of trails. ~ 866-282-3483.

### RIDE 'EM COWBOY

For the *paniolo* (cowboy) set, there are a couple of different opportunities on Molokai to check out. **Molokai Fish and Dive** (don't let the name mislead you, you won't be riding a seahorse!) offers a horseback ride along the Kaupoa Beach Trail, with visits to a number of historical sites along the way. For the rodeo set, there's the Paniolo Roundup, an opportunity where you can compete with one another in the Molokai Ranch Rodeo Arena. Here you'll round up and sort cattle and do team penning. The high point of the round-up experience arrives when guests put what they have learned into action during the penning race. Of course, you'll be taught how to do all this by real Hawaiian *paniolo*. Yee haw! ~ P.O. Box 576, Kaunakakai, HI 96748; 808-553-5926, 866-282-3483; e-mail fishand dive@mobettah.net.

**Bike Rentals**   **Molokai Bicycle** sells, repairs and rents mountain and road bikes. Rentals include helmets, locks and maps. Call ahead for hours. ~ 80 Mohala Street, Kaunakakai; 808-553-3931.

Molokai features some splendid country and numerous areas that seem prime for hiking, but few trails have been built or maintained and most private land is off-limits to visitors. Some excellent hiking possibilities, but no official trails, are offered along the beaches described above. Palaau State Park also has several short jaunts to points of interest.

**HIKING**

The only lengthy treks lead to the island's rugged north coast. Four valleys—Halawa, Wailau, Pelekunu and Waikolu—cut through the sheer cliffs guarding this windswept shore.

The **Pelekunu Trail** begins several hundred yards beyond the Waikolu Valley Lookout (see "Molokai's Outback" on page 240). It is unmaintained and extremely difficult. Traversing Nature Conservancy property, the trail leads to a lookout point and then drops into the valley. This is for skilled hikers only.

The **Wailau Trail** is another very difficult trail; it takes about 12 hours and passes through some muddy rainforest regions. The trailhead is off Route 450 about 15 miles east of Kaunakakai. The trail extends across nearly the entire island from south to north. Dangers include deep mud and wild boar. To hike it, you must obtain permission from Pearl Petro. Send a self-addressed stamped envelope with a letter of nonresponsibility. ~ P.O. Box 125, Kaunakakai, HI 96748; 808-558-8113.

The **Kalaupapa Trail** is the easiest and best-maintained trail descending the north *pali*. A trail description is given in the "Kalaupapa" section in this chapter. To hike here you must obtain permission and pay $40 for a mandatory tour of the leper colony. Bring food and water along for this four-hour tour. Call Damien Tours for permission and information. Reservations required. ~ 808-567-6171.

The **Halawa Valley Trail**, one of Molokai's prettiest hikes, extends for two miles from the mouth of the valley to the base of **Moaula Falls**. This 250-foot cascade tumbles down a sheer cliff to a cold mountain pool perfect for swimming. **Hipuapua Falls**, a sister cascade just a third of a mile north, shoots 500 feet down the *pali*. The trail can be accessed only through a guided tour. Call Molokai Fish & Dive to schedule one. ~ 808-553-5926.

**Transportation**

**AIR**

When your plane touches down at **Molokai Airport**, you'll realize what a one-canoe island it is you're visiting. There's a snack bar and adjoining lounge, which seem to open and close all day, plus a few car rental and airline offices. It's seven miles to the main town of Kaunakakai. There's no public transportation available. However, shuttle service can be arranged through some of the hotels, and taxis are available.

IslandAir (800-652-6541) and Molokai Air Shuttle (808-567-6847) fly small prop planes.

You can call Molokai Air Shuttle to arrange various flights. To fly direct from Honolulu to Kalaupapa, try IslandAir, which can always be relied upon for friendly service.

**CAR RENTALS**

The existing companies are **Dollar Rent A Car** (808-567-9012, 800-800-4000 from the mainland, 800-367-7006 in Hawaii), **Budget Rent A Car** (808-567-6877, 800-527-7000 from the mainland, 800-527-0700 in Hawaii) and **Island Kine Auto Rentals** (808-553-5242).

**JEEP RENTALS**

**Budget Rent A Car** rents jeeps, but requires that you drive them only on paved roads! ~ 808-567-6877, 800-527-7000 from the mainland, 800-451-3600 in Hawaii. (Be aware that the rental car collision insurance provided by most credit cards does not cover jeeps.)

**TOURS**

**Molokai Off-Road Tours** (808-553-3369) will take you to see the Coffees of Hawaii plantation, a macadamia nut farm, St. Joseph's Church and the fishponds. They also offer mule tours.

# NINE

# Kauai

Seventy miles northwest of Oahu, across a rough, treacherous channel that long protected against invaders, lies Kauai. If ever an island deserved to be called a jewel of the sea, this "Garden Isle" is the one. Across Kauai's brief 33-mile expanse lies a spectacular and wildly varied landscape.

Along the north shore is the Hanalei Valley, a lush patchwork of tropical agriculture, and the rugged Na Pali Coast, with cliffs almost 3000 feet above the boiling surf. Spanning 14 miles of pristine coastline, the narrow valleys and sheer walls of Na Pali are so impenetrable that a road entirely encircling the island has never been built. Here, among razor-edged spires and flower-choked gorges, the producers of the movie *South Pacific* found their Bali Hai. To the east flows the fabled Wailua River, a sacred area to Hawaiians that today supports a sizable population in the blue-collar towns of Wailua and Kapaa.

Along the south coast stretch the matchless beaches of Poipu, with white sands and an emerald sea that seem drawn from a South Seas vision. It was here in November 1982 that Hurricane Iwa, packing 110-mile-an-hour winds and carrying devastating storm surf, overwhelmed the island. Ironically, it was also this area that sustained some of the most severe damage when Hurricane Iniki struck on September 11, 1992.

The tourist enclave of Poipu gives way to rustic Hanapepe, a former agricultural town now becoming more of an arts community, and Waimea, where in 1778 Captain James Cook became the first Westerner to tread Hawaiian soil. In Kauai's arid southwestern corner, where palm trees surrender to cactus plants, snow-white beaches sweep for miles along Barking Sands and Polihale.

In the island's center, Mount Waialeale rises 5148 feet to trap a continuous stream of dark-bellied clouds that spill more than 480 inches of rain annually, making this gloomy peak the wettest spot on Earth and creating the headwaters for the richest river system in all Hawaii—the Hanapepe, Hanalei, Wailua and Waimea rivers. Also draining Waialeale is the Alakai Swamp, a wilderness bog that covers 30 square miles of the island's interior. Yet to the west, just a thunderstorm away, lies a barren landscape seemingly borrowed from Arizona and featuring the 2857-foot-deep Waimea Canyon, the "Grand Canyon" of the Pacific.

From Lihue, Kauai's county seat and most important city, Route 50 (Kaumualii Highway) travels to the south while Route 56 (Kuhio Highway) heads along the north shore. Another highway climbs past Waimea Canyon into the mountainous interior.

Papayas, taro and bananas flourish in lush profusion along these roads and marijuana is grown deep in the hills and narrow valleys, but coffee is now the most significant crop. Tourism, however, has overtaken agriculture in the Kauai economy and is vital to the island's 55,000 population.

The decline of the sugar industry has intensified demands to replace agricultural income with tourist dollars. But the Garden Isle still offers hidden beaches and remote valleys to any traveler possessing a native's sensibility. And even though sugar is in retreat, some cane fields are still evident across the island. A number of years ago, Kauai provided a window on 19th-century life, when sugar was king. Deep-green stalks covered the landscape in every direction, edging from the lip of the ocean to the foot of the mountains. But foreign competition and a waning industry have led to many cane fields being left fallow or converted to asparagus, papaya and various truck crops and gentlemen's estates.

Nevertheless, one sugar mill is still redolent with the cloyingly sweet smell of cane, and on the westside mammoth cane trucks, sugar stalks protruding like bristles from a wild boar, continue to charge down dusty roads. Depending on the phase of the growing cycle, visitors pass fields crowded with mature cane, tall as Midwest corn, or deep-red earth planted with rows of seedlings. In the evening, when harvested cane is set afire, black smoke billows from deep within the fields.

Historically, Kauai is Hawaii's premier island—the first to be created geologically and the first "discovered" by white men. It was here that Madame Pele, goddess of volcanos, initially tried to make her home. Perhaps because of the island's moist, tropical climate, she failed to find a place dry enough to start her fire and left in frustration for the islands to the southeast.

Formed by a single volcano that became extinct about five million years ago, Kauai is believed by some anthropologists to be the original Hawaiian island populated by Polynesians. After Captain Cook arrived in 1778, explorers continued to visit the island periodically. Ten years later, settlers began to arrive, and in 1820 the first missionaries landed in the company of Prince George, son of Kauai's King Kaumualii. By 1835, the Koloa sugar plantation was founded, becoming the first successful sugar mill on Kauai.

Kauai was the site not only of the original but the anomalous, as well. In 1817, George Scheffer, a Prussian adventurer representing Czar Nicholas of Russia, built a fort in Waimea. He soon lost the support of both the Czar and Kauai's King Kaumualii, but left as his legacy the stone ruins of Russia's imperialist effort.

Kauai was the only island not conquered by Kamehameha the Great when he established the Hawaiian kingdom. Thwarted twice in his attempts to land an attack force—once in 1796 when high seas prevented an invasion from Oahu and again in 1802 when his battle-ready army was suddenly ravaged by disease—he finally won over Kaumualii by diplomacy in 1810.

But Kauai's most fascinating history is told by mythmakers recounting tales of the *Menehune*, the Hobbits of the Pacific. These miniature forest people labored like giants to create awesome structures. Mysterious ruins such as the Menehune Fishpond outside Lihue reputedly date back before the Polynesians and are attributed by the mythically inclined to an earlier, unknown race. Supernaturally strong and very industrious, the *Menehune* worked only at night, completing each project by dawn or else leaving it forever unfinished. Several times they made so much noise in their strenuous laboring that they frightened birds as far away as Oahu.

They were a merry, gentle people with ugly red faces and big eyes set beneath long eyebrows. Two to three feet tall, each practiced a trade in which he was a master. They inhabited caves, hollow logs and banana-leaf huts, and eventually grew to a population of 50,000 adults.

Some say the *Menehune* came from the lost continent of Mu, which stretched across Polynesia to Fiji before it was swallowed by floods. Where they finally

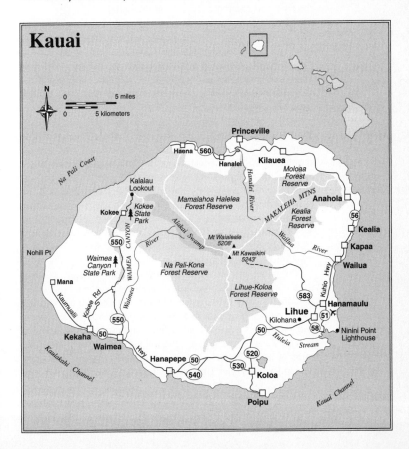

traveled to is less certain. After the Polynesians settled Kauai, the *Menehune* king, concerned that his people were intermarrying with an alien race, ordered the *Menehune* to leave the island. But many, unwilling to depart so luxurious a home, hid in the forests. There, near hiking trails and remote campsites, you may see them even today.

▼ ▼ ▼ ▼ ▼ ▼ ▼ ▼ ▼ ▼

## Lihue Area

Although Lihue is a rather dreary little town of 5700, visitors will likely pass through this tiny city several times because it's so centrally located. This is where the island's two highways converge—Kuhio heading north and Kaumualii going south. Here you'll find Kauai's airport and helicopter facilities, Nawiliwili Harbor and its commodity barges and cruise ships, government offices that issue camping and hiking permits, fast-food joints, industrial parks and big box retailers, and the island's largest shopping mall, Kukui Grove Center. In short, it's the civic and commercial center of the island.

But that doesn't mean the area is devoid of charm. The beautiful Haupu Ridge dominates the landscape to the south while the rambling peaks of Kalepa Ridge loom in the interior, and the Huleia River, which feeds the legendary Menehune (Alekoko) Fishpond, is one of the island's prettiest. And for those seeking convenience, or lacking transportation, Lihue is an excellent choice for home base.

**SIGHTS**

Among the attractions you will find in Lihue is the **Kauai Museum**, a two-building complex rich in Hawaiiana. This is a prime spot to learn about the history, culture and natural history of the island. The main building focuses on Hawaiian heritage with its displays of feather leis, Hawaiian quilts, *koa* furniture and ancient calabashes. In the adjacent exhibition, 19th-century plantation life is revealed in a collection of old photographs, shot by W. J. Senda, a Japanese immigrant. Closed Sunday. Admission. ~ 4428 Rice Street, Lihue; 808-245-6931, fax 808-245-6864; e-mail kauaimuseum@museum.org.

Providing an even wider window on Kauai's sugar-cane heritage, **Grove Farm** is a beautifully preserved 80-acre homestead. Acquired in 1864 by the son of missionaries, the plantation is like a living museum with the main house, farm office, workers' homes and a private cottage still intact. Surrounding these tinroof buildings are banana patches, gardens and pastures. Two-hour guided tours of this fascinating facility are available (Monday, Wednesday and Thursday at 10 a.m. and 1 p.m.) by reservation. ~ 808-245-3202, fax 808-245-7988.

Another interesting side trip from Lihue is down Rice Street to busy **Nawiliwili Harbor**. This deep-water port, with its cruise ships and cargo vessels, is the island's major seaport. Nearby

# Kauai Getaway

## Three-day Itinerary

**Day 1**
- Arrive at the airport in Lihue and drive to the Poipu area. Check in to your condominium or hotel and spend the afternoon relaxing on the beach.

- Have dinner in one of Poipu's many restaurants or venture up to Koloa Town to dine.

**Day 2**
- This is the day to head up to the **North Shore** (assuming it's not raining there). If it's raining on the North Shore, pray for sun and switch to Day 3's activities. First stop in Lihue at **Ma's Family Restaurant** (page 428) for a local-style breakfast.

- Drive on up to **Hanalei** (page 476) for a look around and to stock up on ice-cold water and other provisions. If you're adventurous, hike the first two miles of the **Kalalau Trail** (page 501) at the end of Route 560. If you're in a lazier mood, join the others relaxing at **Kee Beach** (page 477) and snorkeling along the reef.

- Plan to have dinner in Hanalei or Kapaa before returning to Poipu.

**Day 3**
- Drive out Route 50, stopping in **Hanapepe** (page 448) to peruse the local art galleries (page 455).

- Continue on Route 50, turning right on Route 550 out to what is called the Pacific's "Grand Canyon"—**Waimea Canyon** (page 450). Make sure to continue out to the end of the road to visit the **Kalalau Lookout** (page 479), which gives you an extraordinary view of the Kalalau Valley.

- If you want to continue out along Route 50 to the two-mile stretch of white sand at **Polihale State Park** (page 459)—you won't be disappointed.

**Kalapaki Beach** is one of Kauai's most popular strands, both because of its proximity to Lihue and its pretty white sands.

Fronting Kalapaki Beach is the **Kauai Marriott Resort & Beach Club**. Some believe that Mother Nature, in the form of Hurricane Iniki, wreaked havoc on its previous incarnation, the Westin Kauai, because it was so un-Hawaiian in nature—it looked like a Las Vegas version of Rome. Today its lush gardens, massive swimming pool (complete with waterfalls)—the largest in the state—and an extensive art collection spread throughout the public spaces warrant a look and see. If nothing else, a stroll along the granite pathway along the white-sand beach is worth the detour. ~ 3610 Rice Street, Lihue; 808-245-5050, 800-220-2925, fax 808-245-5049; www.marriott.com/lihhi.

From Nawiliwili Harbor, you can continue on to the **Menehune** (or **Alekoko**) **Fishpond**. This 900-foot-long pond, spread across a valley floor and backdropped by the Hoary Head Mountain Range, dates back well before the Polynesians. Or so the mythmakers would like you to believe. Legend has it that a line of leprechaun-like *Menehune* 25 miles long passed rocks from hand to hand and built the pond in a single night. Their only request of the prince and princess for whom they built the structure was ·that these two mortals not watch them while they worked. When the *Menehune* discovered that curiosity had overcome the two, who were watching the midget workers by the light of the moon, the *Menehune* turned them into the pillars of stone you see on the mountainside above the fishpond. ~ Take Rice Street to Nawiliwili, then right on Route 58, a quick left on Niumalu Road and finally right on Hulemalu Road.

A short distance from Lihue, Kuhio Highway (Route 56), the main road to Kauai's north shore, descends into the rustic village of **Kapaia**. Sagging wood structures and a gulch choked with banana plants mark this valley. On the right, **Lihue Hongwanji Temple**, one of the island's oldest, smiles from beneath a modern-day facelift.

Off Kuhio Highway, Maalo Road threads through three miles of fields to **Wailua Falls**. These twin cascades tumble 80 feet into a heavenly pool fringed with *hala* trees. An easily accessible pool lies just a couple hundred yards past the falls.

Follow Kuhio Highway and you'll arrive in **Hanamaulu**, an old plantation town where falsefront stores and tinroof houses line the roadway. If you follow Hanamaulu Road to Hehi Road you'll come to **Hanamaulu Beach Park**. Shaded by coconut palms and ironwood trees, it's a lovely place to picnic. (See "Beaches & Parks" below.)

Or you can head a mile and a half southwest from Lihue on Kaumualii Highway (Route 50) to **Kilohana** for a view of the luxurious side of island life. This 16,000-square-foot Tudor mansion was home to the plantation that once covered these grounds. Today, the 1935 house serves as a center for arts-and-crafts shops and museum displays, and the 35 surrounding acres are devoted to a re-creation of traditional plantation life. Wander down the "coral path" and you'll pass a tropical garden and a succession of corrugated-roof houses. Papaya, banana and avocado trees line the route and roosters crow in the distance. Carriages pulled by Clydesdales tour the grounds and wagon tours lead out into

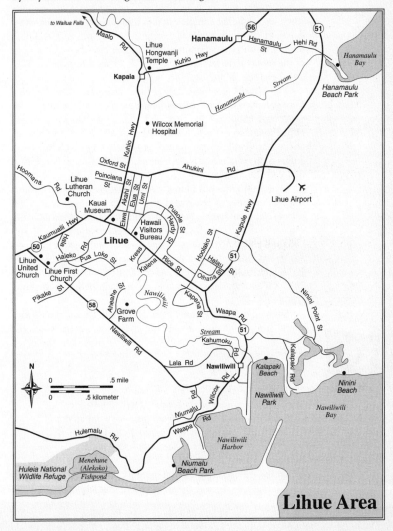

**Lihue Area**

the fields behind the house. There are weekly luaus. ~ Kaumualii Highway; 808-245-5608, fax 808-245-7818; e-mail kilohana@ hawaiian.net.

**LODGING**    If you are in search of budget-priced lodging facilities, there are few places in all Hawaii as inviting as Lihue. And being located near the airport or a block or two from downtown Lihue is convenient for those folks without wheels.

At the **Tip Top Motel** you'll find trim rooms with tile floors, stall showers and air conditioning. The sheer size of this two-story, two-building complex makes it impersonal by Kauai standards, but I found the management to be very warm. You'll have to eat meals in the adjoining restaurant or elsewhere, since none of the rooms have kitchenettes. ~ 3173 Akahi Street, Lihue; 808-245-2333, fax 808-246-8988. BUDGET.

The **Motel Lani**, located three blocks from the Rice Shopping Center, has eight small rooms facing a small patio where guests can lounge about in lawn chairs. The units are clean and comfortable, though sparsely furnished. About half are air-conditioned; all have fans and refrigerators. This place has a noisy lobby (with a television) just off busy Rice Street. ~ 4240 Rice Street, Lihue; 808-245-2965. BUDGET.

Over 100 years old (and the first hotel on the island), **Kauai Inn** was extensively renovated at the end of the millennium, resulting in a comfortable hotel with remnants of old Hawaii. Convenient to the airport, it sits on three acres near the Hapu Mountains and Huleia River, with 48 units, a pool and laundry facilities. All guest rooms have a refrigerator and microwave. ~ 2430 Hulemalu Road, Lihue; 808-245-9000, 800-808-2330, fax 808-245-3004; www.kauai-inn.com, e-mail info@kauai-inn.com. MODERATE.

Situated across the street from Nawiliwili Park is the **Garden Island Inn**. You'll find it near the corner of Waapa Road and

**AUTHOR FAVORITE**

Visible from the vista overlooking the Menehune Fishpond, and accessible only to kayakers, is the **Huleia National Wildlife Refuge** (808-828-1413), a 238-acre preserve that rises from the river basin up the wooded slopes of Huleia Valley. This estuary is home to 31 bird species including four different endangered species of waterbirds—the Hawaiian stilt, Hawaiian duck, Hawaiian gallinule and Hawaiian coot. If a trip up-river begins to look familiar, it's because it was the setting for scenes in *Raiders of the Lost Ark*. Hawaiian medicinal plants and wild fruit line the banks of the river.

Wilcox Road, a short walk from Kalapaki Beach. Each room is light and airy with comfortable furnishings, fresh flowers, attractive appointments and overhead fans. You'll hear occasional noise from passing trucks and planes. Children are welcome, and several of the large rooms are sufficiently spacious for families. All of the fully equipped units have refrigerators, wet bars and microwave ovens. Second- and third-story rooms have air conditioning. Beach gear, including boogieboards, is loaned free to guests. The grounds are trimly landscaped and highlighted by a koi pond in which several dozen carp flash their colors. ~ 3445 Wilcox Road, Lihue; 808-245-7227, 800-648-0154, fax 808-245-7603; www. gardenislandinn.com, e-mail info@gardenislandinn.com. MODERATE TO DELUXE.

Fronting a quarter-mile of white sandy beach, one of the island's loveliest, the **Kauai Marriott Resort & Beach Club** is the Lihue area's premier resting spot. The 356-room hostelry is a stone's throw from the airport and Lihue. Most rooms, appointed in island-style decor featuring Hawaiian tropical floral designs, offer views of the ocean and come with a lanai. A beach promenade of granite tile leads from one end of the beach to the other. For those not interested in swimming in the ocean, the resort sports the largest swimming pool in the islands, replete with waterfalls. A myriad of water sports is available to guests. Restaurants and a fitness center round out the amenities. ~ 3610 Rice Street, Lihue; 808-245-5050, 800-872-6626, fax 808-245-5049; www.marriott.com/lihhi, e-mail kauai@marriott.com. ULTRA-DELUXE.

**CONDOS**

**Banyan Harbor Resort**, a collection of woodframe buildings across a busy street from Nawiliwili Harbor, has condos with ocean and garden views; one-bedroom units are $110 per night while two-bedroom units are $140 per night. Each unit has a full kitchen and laundry facilities. Most of the 148 units here are leased by the month, but a handful rent by the night. ~ 3411 Wilcox Road, Lihue; 808-245-7333, 800-422-6926, fax 808-246-3687; www. vacation-kauai.com, e-mail reservations@banyanharbor.net.

**DINING**

For good food at modest prices, Lihue is a prime spot. This is the center of most island business so it contains numerous restaurants that cater largely to local folks.

◄ *HIDDEN*

You're liable to see lots of local faces lining **Hamura Saimin**'s curving counter. When I ate there the place was packed. I had the *"saimin* special," a combination of noodles, wontons, eggs, meat, onion, vegetables and fish cake in a delicious broth. ~ 2956 Kress Street, Lihue; 808-245-3271. BUDGET.

◄ *HIDDEN*

**Oki Diner** is open 19 hours a day. A small and spare eatery, this is a favorite place for locals to dine on ramen, wonton soup and various other Asian dishes. ~ 3125 Kuhio Highway, Lihue; 808-245-5899. BUDGET.

Want to go Japanese? Try **Restaurant Kiibo,** a contemporary-style restaurant with a tatami room. You'll find the menu filled with yakitori, tempura and tofu dishes, as well as sushi and sashimi. Closed Sunday. ~ 2991 Umi Street, Lihue; 808-245-2650. MODERATE.

HIDDEN ►

A local institution since 1939, the **Lihue Barbecue Inn** offers Asian dishes in addition to all-American meals. Breakfasts at this comfortable establishment are pretty standard: the lunch menu includes salads, soups, sandwiches, hamburgers and a daily special that often features teriyaki and Pacific Rim–influenced dishes; at dinner, there's steak, shrimp tempura and scampi. Closed Sunday. ~ 2982 Kress Street, Lihue; 808-245-2921. MODERATE TO DELUXE.

A favorite among tourists is the **Tip Top Café and Bakery.** Visitors can take their pick from any in a succession of booths in this large and impersonal eatery. Breakfasts are inexpensive—the macadamia-nut pancakes are delicious. Lunch entrées, however, are not very imaginative and have received negative reviews from readers. The well-known bakery serves macadamia-nut cookies, the house specialty. No dinner. Closed Monday. ~ 3173 Akahi Street, Lihue; 808-245-2333, fax 808-246-8988. BUDGET.

HIDDEN ►

For the money, the best breakfast spot on the island is **Ma's Family Restaurant.** This nondescript café makes up in clientele what it lacks in physical beauty. Early in the morning the place is crowded with locals on their way to work. In the world of breakfasts, this is the bargain basement. Or if you want to go Hawaiian, order a *laulau,* poi and *lomi* salmon dish. No dinner. ~ 4277 Halenani Street, Lihue; 808-245-3142. BUDGET.

The **Café Portofino** at the Kauai Marriott serves up several pasta dishes as well as house specialties like calamari, scampi, eggplant parmigiana and sautéed rabbit. Dinner only. ~ 3610 Rice Street, Lihue; 808-245-2121. DELUXE TO ULTRA-DELUXE.

HIDDEN ►

Visit **Kalena Fish Market** for the best plate lunch in Lihue. Fish and meat specials, like breaded mahi, Korean-style barbecue spare ribs and local foods like *laulau* and *kalua* pig with cabbage, change daily. You can choose from a wide array of side dishes: macaroni salad, marinated bean sprouts and *kim chee.* It's clean and modern with a few tables. ~ 2985 Kalena Street (off Rice Street), Lihue; 808-246-6629, fax 808-246-2174. BUDGET.

Whatever the time of day or night, **Garden Island BBQ** is generally packed with customers, nearly all of them locals. The reason? Great food, ample portions, three pages of menu choices that are the same for lunch and dinner, super casual setting and low prices. The menu is predominantly Chinese and the barbecue is more local or Korean-style than Texas, but you can also get burgers, sandwiches and plate lunches. Closed Sunday. ~ 4252 Rice Street, Lihue; 808-245-8868. BUDGET.

Just a coconut's throw from a sandy beach, **Duke's Canoe Club** is on Kalapaki Bay at the Kauai Marriott Resort & Beach Club. Besides the fresh fish, grill items and celebrated salad bar, this open-air restaurant has surfboards, photos and memorabilia commemorating the granddaddy of surfing, Duke Kahanamoku. Roaming musicians entertain nightly. ~ Kalapaki Beach, Lihue; 808-246-9599, fax 808-246-1047. MODERATE TO ULTRA-DELUXE.

**JJ's Broiler** is a family-style eatery with standard steak dishes, seafood platters and a salad bar. The waterfront location overlooks Kalapaki Beach and has a sunny Southern California ambience. ~ 3416 Rice Street, Nawiliwili; 808-246-4422, fax 808-245-7019; www.jjsbroiler.com, e-mail jjsbroiler@hotmail.com. DELUXE TO ULTRA-DELUXE.

Also located in Nawiliwili is **The Beach Hut**. They offer a full breakfast menu; for lunch and dinner, there are hamburgers, sandwiches and salads. Order at the window and dine upstairs on a deck overlooking the water. ~ 3474 Rice Street, Nawiliwili; 808-246-6330. BUDGET.

Good news for those who want to get away from city life—only 3 percent of Kauai is "urbanized."

At **Ara's Sakana-ya Fish House** you can kill two birds with one stone. Their deli has good plate lunches, sushi and fresh fish, but the best part is you can take your food to the laundromat next door and eat while you wash. Lunch and take-out only. ~ Hanamaulu Plaza at Kuhio Highway and Hanamaulu Road, Hanamaulu; 808-245-1707. BUDGET.

If it's atmosphere and a taste of the Orient you're after, reserve a tea room at the **Hanamaulu Café**. My favorite is the garden room overlooking a rock-bound pond filled with carp. Lunch and dinner are the same here, with an excellent selection of Japanese and Chinese dishes. There's also a sushi bar at night. Children's portions are available. Closed Monday. ~ Kuhio Highway, Hanamaulu; 808-245-2511, fax 808-245-2497. MODERATE.

Take a plantation manor, add a flowering garden, and you have the setting for **Gaylord's**. Elevating patio dining to a high art, this alfresco restaurant looks out on the spacious lawns and spreading trees of Kilohana plantation. The menu features fresh island fish, pasta, farm-raised venison, baby back ribs, slow-roasted prime rib and chicken Kauai in addition to exotic specials on Monday and a well-rounded wine list. Or consider attending their luau on Tuesday or Thursday. A rare combination of Old World elegance and tropical ambience; lunch, dinner and Sunday brunch served. Reservations required. ~ At Kilohana on Kaumualii Highway, one and one half miles southwest of Lihue;

808-245-9593, fax 808-246-1087; www.gaylordskauai.com, e-mail gaylords@hawaiian.net. DELUXE TO ULTRA-DELUXE.

**GROCERIES**    Lihue has by far the greatest number of grocery, health food and fresh fish stores on the island. This commercial center is an ideal place to stock up for a camping trip, a hike or a lengthy sojourn in an efficiency apartment.

The **Big Save Market** is one of Lihue's main grocery stores. Its doors are open daily from 7 a.m. to 11 p.m. ~ Lihue Shopping Center, 4444 Rice Street, Lihue; 808-245-6571.

**Star Market**, located in the Kukui Grove Center, is another local grocery staple. They're open from 6 a.m. to 11 p.m. every day. ~ 3-2600 Kaumualii Highway, Lihue; 808-245-7777.

**Vim 'N Vigor** has an excellent line of vitamins, juices and bath supplies, plus natural foods and sandwiches. Closed Sunday. ~ Rice Shopping Center, 3122 Kuhio Highway, A-9, Lihue; 808-245-9053; www.vimnvigor.com.

HIDDEN ►    Don't miss the **Sunshine Market** every Friday afternoon in the parking lot of the town stadium. Local folks turn out to sell homegrown produce, "talk story," and generally have a good time. It's a great place to buy island fruits and vegetables at bargain prices, and an even better spot to meet Kauai's farmers. Early morning is the best time to arrive—before the best produce has disappeared. ~ Kapule Highway.

If you hanker for fresh fish, be sure to check out **The Fish Express**. ~ 3343 Kuhio Highway, Lihue; 808-245-9918.

**Love's Bakery** sells day-old products including delicious breads at a discount. ~ 4100 Rice Street, Nawiliwili; 808-245-6113.

**SHOPPING**    **Kukui Grove Center** is the island's largest shopping mall, an ultramodern complex. Here are department stores, bookshops, specialty stores and other establishments. Though lacking the intimacy of Kauai's independent handicraft outlets, the center provides such a concentration of goods that it's hard to bypass. ~ 3-2600 Kaumualii Highway, Lihue; 808-245-7784.

**AUTHOR FAVORITE**

At the **Kapaia Stitchery** half the items are designed and stitched by local women. There's an array of T-shirts, aloha shirts, Hawaiian quilting pillow kits and patterns, plus stunning patchwork quilts. This is an excellent place to buy Hawaiian fabrics and hand-dyed batiks from Bali. Closed Sunday. ~ Kuhio Highway, just north of the hamlet of Kapaia; 808-245-2281, fax 808-245-1772.

Why not stop in at the **Kauai Museum Shop** if you're interested in taking home some Niihau shell leis, local crafts or books? They have a nice selection. Closed Sunday. ~ 4428 Rice Street, Lihue; 808-246-2470.

The **Kauai Fruit & Flower Company** can put together custommade baskets of coffee, macadamia nuts, papaya salsa, coconut syrup, fresh bread, dried fruit, etc. They make a great gift for anyone you left at home. The store also sells traditional Hawaiian musical instruments. Closed Sunday. ~ 3-4684 Kuhio Highway, Lihue; 808-245-1814, 800-943-3108; www.kauaifruit.com.

**Kilohana** (808-245-5608) is one of Hawaii's most beautiful complexes to shop. Set in a grand sugar plantation house, it rests amid acres of manicured grounds. Many rooms in this museum-cum-mall are furnished in period style to recapture 1930s-era plantation life. The galleries, boutiques and crafts shops are equally enchanting. Here you'll find pillows, hand-blown glassware, Niihau shell leis, pottery and much, much more. ~ Kaumualii Highway, one and one half miles southwest of Lihue.

**Two Frogs Hugging** got its campy name from a statue the owners saw that began their foray into imports. Their merchandise consists mainly of intricate, imported wood furniture and stone carvings. Closed Sunday. ~ 3215 Kuhio Highway, Lihue; 808-246-8777; www.twofrogshugging.com, e-mail kauaimp@aloha.net.

You'll find a lot of local color at the **Lihue Café**. The drinks are cheap, the tourists are few. ~ 2978 Umi Street, Lihue; 808-245-6471.

**Duke's Canoe Club**, an attractive watering hole overlooking the beach at the Kauai Marriott Resort & Beach Club, has strolling musicians nightly and live shows on Thursday and Friday evenings. ~ Kalapaki Beach, Lihue; 808-245-5050.

Every small town needs its quirky band of players, and Lihue is no exception. The island's only theater troupe is located here, in the **Kauai Community Players**. The non-profit has been around since 1971, producing old standbys like *Joseph and the Amazing Technicolor Dreamcoat*, *The Miracle Worker* and *Sweeney Todd*, as well as lesser-known productions. ~ Lihue; 808-245-7700; www.kauaicommunityplayers.org, e-mail kcp@hawaiian.net.

Or you can always head to the **Lihue Bowling Center** and knock down a few pins. ~ 4303 Rice Street; 808-245-5263.

**NIGHTLIFE**

**KALAPAKI BEACH** 🏄 🎣 ♨ This wide strand stretches for a quarter-mile in front of the Kauai Marriott hotel. Popular with surfers since ancient Hawaiian times, Kalapaki is situated right on Nawiliwili Bay, an appealing but busy harbor. It is also one of the best swimming beaches on the island since the harbor protects it from heavy shorebreak. Out past the harbor, the Hoary Head

**BEACHES & PARKS**

mountains rise in the background. Beginner's surfing is best in the center of Nawiliwili Bay, where there is a right slide. More experienced surfers will find good breaks next to the rock wall near the lighthouse, where there's a left slide. There's also good surfing on the right side of the bay. Nicknamed "Hang Ten," these left slide breaks are a good place for nose-riding. Snorkeling is so-so at Kalapaki, but anglers should have better luck. Both off the pier and near the lighthouse are good spots for mullet, big-eyed scad, *papio*, bonefish and threadfin; sometimes *ulua*, *oama* and red bigeye can be caught here, too. Nawiliwili Park, next to the beach, has a picnic area and restrooms. ~ Take Rice Street from Lihue to Nawiliwili Park. Enter from the park.

**NIUMALU BEACH PARK** 🏊 🚣 This tree-lined park is tucked into a corner of Nawiliwili Harbor near a small-boat harbor. With neighbors like this and no swimming facilities, the park's key feature is its proximity to Lihue. It is popular nonetheless with picnickers, and the adjacent Huleia River attracts kayakers, fishermen and crabbers. Facilities include a picnic area, restrooms and showers. ~ Take Rice Street to Nawiliwili, turn right on Route 58, then left on Niumalu Road.

▲ Camping allowed with county permit.

HIDDEN ►   **NININI BEACH** Hidden along a rocky coastline between Nawiliwili Bay and the lighthouse on Ninini Point are two small sand beaches. Lying at the base of a sea cliff, these pocket beaches are separated by a lava rock formation. The smaller beach is about a quarter-mile from Ninini Point and the larger is known as **Running Waters Beach**, named for the numerous springs that bubble out of the lava and percolate up into the sand. Both are excellent for sunbathing but generally not safe for other water activities due to strong currents and undertow; bodysurfers, however, fre-

---

### FROM THE MENEHUNE TO INDIANA JONES

Board your kayak and head down the Huleia River, home to the legendary Menehune Fishpond. **Island Adventures**, an eco-friendly kayaking company, escorts you to the heart of the Huleia National Wildlife Refuge. Spottings of Koloa ducks, egrets, Hawaiian stilts and jumping fish are all part of the adventure. You can even play Indiana Jones at the rope swing used in *Raiders of the Lost Ark*. To complete the trip, you'll take a short hike through the wildlife refuge, where your local guide will point out Hawaiian medicinal plants and fruits as you squish along a muddy trail. A very enjoyable, laidback Hawaiian adventure. ~ Nawiliwili Small Boat Harbor, Lihue; 808-245-9662, fax 808-246-9661; www.kauaifun.com, e-mail funkauai@hawaiian.net.

quent Running Waters Beach. Since both beaches are pretty close to civilization, I don't recommend camping at either beach. There are no facilities here. ~ Take the road leading through the Kauai Marriott property in Nawiliwili. Follow this road to the golf course clubhouse. Park and walk across the golf course in a direction several degrees to the right of the lighthouse. The smaller beach can be reached by walking from Running Water Beach toward the lighthouse for about three-tenths of a mile.

**HANAMAULU BEACH PARK** Here's an idyllic park nestled in Hanamaulu Bay and crowded with ironwood and coconut trees. The beach is a narrow corridor of sand at the head of Hanamaulu Bay. The bay is well-protected, affording excellent swimming, but the water is usually murky so there is not much snorkeling. I found this a great place for picnicking and shell collecting. Anglers can expect to hook bonefish, mullet and bigeyed scad. A picnic area, restrooms, showers and a playground are some of the facilities here. ~ Take Kuhio Highway to Hanamaulu, then turn down the road leading to the bay.

▲ Needles from the ironwood trees make a natural bed at this lovely site. Tent and trailer camping (closed Wednesday); county permit required.

**NAWILIWILI PARK** Not the most beautiful setting on the island, this park nevertheless offers a swath of grass and picnic tables as well as access to good surf and fishing grounds. There's also playground equipment for the little ones. Picnic tables, a pavilion and restrooms round out the facilities. ~ Located north of Nawiliwili Harbor. Take Waapa Road north until it connects with Rice Street (Route 51). The park is east of the junction.

## Poipu Area

The Poipu area, crown jewel of the southside of Kauai, specializes in beaches—along with a steady stream of sunshine. What you'll find in this warm, dry, white-sand corner of the island is a prime example of everyone's favorite combination—the old and the new. The traditional comes in the form of Koloa Town, site of Hawaii's first successful sugar mill, a 19th-century plantation town that has been splashed with tropical colors. For the modern, you need look only a couple miles down the road to Poipu, a series of scalloped beaches that has become action central for real-estate developers.

Anchoring these enclaves to the east is Puuhi Mount, scene of the last volcanic eruption on Kauai. To the north rises the Hoary Head Range, a wall of wooded mountains that divides the district from the Huleia Valley and Lihue. Everywhere else you'll find fields lying fallow or acres that are still planted with sugar. The tiny, old communities of Lawai and Omao comprise the rest of what is known locally as the southside.

**SIGHTS**    Without doubt, you'll want to drive out from Lihue along Kaumualii Highway (Route 50) to explore the south coast. Along the
way, if you possess a Rorschach-test imagination, you'll see **Queen
Victoria's Profile** etched in the Hoary Head Range. (Need a helping eye? Watch for the Hawaii Visitors Bureau sign on the side
of the highway.)

When you turn south toward Poipu on Maluhia Road (Route
520), you won't need a road sign to find what locals refer to as
**Tree Tunnel,** an arcade of towering swamp mahogany trees that
forms a shadowy tunnel en route to the timeworn town of **Koloa.**
The remains of the original sugar plantation stand in an unassuming pile on the right side of the road as you enter town; a plaque
and sculpture near this old chimney commemorates the birth of
Hawaii's sugar industry, a business that dominated life in the islands throughout most of the 19th and 20th centuries. A sugar
mill continued to operate until 1996 just outside town and Koloa
still consists primarily of company-town houses and humble
churches surrounded by former sugar cane fields. But the main
street was gentrified during the 1980s as tropical-colored paints
were added to the old woodframe and falsefront town center.

The tiny **Koloa History Center,** located in the Old Koloa Town
mall, provides a brief introduction to the history of the area in the
form of artifacts from the old plantation days. ~ Koloa Road, Koloa.

A dirt road at the end of Weliweli Road near the sugar mill leads
to the largest manmade reservoir in Kauai and on the islands.
Covering over 420 acres **Waita Reservoir** is built on former marsh-
lands on the eastside of Koloa and is now used by local anglers.

From Koloa, Poipu Road takes you through fields two miles
to the coast and the vacation community of **Poipu.** If a one-word
association test were applied to Poipu, the word would be "beach."
There really is no town here, just a skein of hotels, condominiums
and stores built along a series of white-sand beaches. Nevertheless, this is Kauai's premier playground, a sun-soaked realm that
promises good weather and good times.

Near the center of Poipu, tucked into the grounds of Kiahuna
Plantation, are the **Moir Gardens.** What was once a labor of love
for the Koloa Sugar Plantation manager's wife has grown over
the years from a small cactus garden into its present-day incarnation, filled with a variety of tropical plants as well as a broad
collection of succulents. If you're staying in Poipu, it's worth
strolling through. ~ Kiahuna Plantation, 2253 Poipu Road,
Poipu; 808-742-6411, fax 808-742-1698.

While civilization has encroached to the very side of the sea,
nature continues to display some of its gentle wonders along the
colorful reefs and pearly sands. Most remarkable of all is **Spouting
Horn,** an underwater lava tube with an opening along the shore.
Surf crashing through the tube dramatically transforms this blow-

hole into a miniature Old Faithful. The mournful sounds issuing from Spouting Horn are said to be the plaintive cries of a legendary lizard or *mo'o*. It seems that he was returning from another island where he had been told of the death of his two sisters. Blinded by tears he missed his landing and was swept into the blowhole. Try to time your visit with the high tide when the spumes from Spouting Horn reach their greatest heights. You should look around at this intriguing coastline, which is covered by coral outcroppings and tidepools. ~ End of Lawai Road.

During the 1800s, **Koloa Landing** was a major port for whalers in the islands and was, until the 20th century, the main port of Kauai. Now it's a major spot for scuba divers.

On Lawai Road, a small park commemorates the life of Prince Kuhio, who died in 1922 and was the last designated heir to the Hawaiian throne. A statue of the prince graces **Prince Kuhio Park**, as well as the well-preserved **Hoai Heiau**, the foundation of the prince's home and the remains of an ancient fishpond. This is a pretty palm-framed greensward steeped in history. ~ Lawai Road, Poipu.

Beyond the park is **Kukuiula Bay**, a popular spot for fishing and scuba diving. There's an offshore reef and boaters and kayakers often launch their vessels here.

The **National Tropical Botanical Garden** encompasses 300 acres in the Lawai Valley, and within its lush grounds are offered two distinct tours: the Allerton Garden Tour and the McBryde

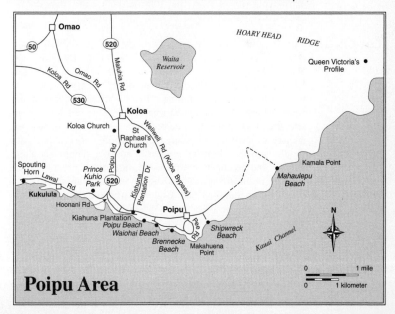

Poipu Area

Garden Tour...

Garden Tour. The Allerton tour is guided and includes the summer cottage of the late Queen Emma and the former home of Chicago millionaire Robert Allerton. The McBryde tour is self-guided and explores the scientific garden as well as some historic buildings that were part of the old McBryde sugar plantation tours. Both tours offer a wealth of information about the 10,000 species of plants cultivated in the valley, as well as NTBG's mission to save rare tropical plants from around the world. Each tour costs $30 per person. The NTBG Visitor Center is located across from Spouting Horn. ~ Lawai Road, Poipu; 808-742-2623 (reservations); www.ntbg.org.

For a real "Hidden Hawaii" adventure, follow Poipu Road east past the Hyatt Regency Kauai. The pavement will end and you'll find yourself on an old cane road. Follow it for about two miles. Minor cane roads will intersect the main one—ignore them. When you come to a major cane road (you'll know it by the telephone poles), turn right and follow this road. After about a mile you'll see roads leading to the beach. There's a guard shack at the turnoff (you're venturing into private property) and **HIDDEN ▶** you may have to sign a waiver to continue on to **Mahaulepu Beach**—the south shore's hidden strands. In addition to being incredibly beautiful and ripe with potential for outdoor sports, Mahaulepu Beach is important scientifically. Look around for petroglyphs or play in the 100-foot-high sand dunes. (See "Beaches & Parks" below for more information.)

**LODGING**

One place for people wanting to rough it or to establish a base camp is **Kahili Mountain Park**, run by the Seventh Day Adventist Church. Facing the Hoary Head Range and backdropped by Kahili Mountain, this 197-acre domain offers an easy compromise between hoteling and camping. The two-bedroom cabin comes equipped with lanai and private bathroom, plus a funky kitchenette; the other cabins are one-bedroom units. The facilities also include cabinettes with shared baths. Both types of facilities should be reserved several months in advance. Though cooking utensils and bed linens are provided, furnishings are a bit spartan: The floors are uncarpeted and the sole decoration is the surrounding mountains. Thank God for nature. At this rustic resort you can enjoy the swimming pond or hike the nearby trails. ~ Write to Kahili Mountain Park, P.O. Box 298, Koloa, HI 96756. The park is five miles from Koloa town and about one mile off Kaumualii Highway; 808-742-9921, fax 808-742-6628; www.kahilipark.org, e-mail reservations@kahilipark.org. BUDGET TO MODERATE.

**HIDDEN ▶**

Located on a small bluff overlooking the ocean is **Garden Isle Cottages Oceanfront**. These pretty one-bedroom hideaways are decorated with artistic flair: Oil paintings and woven pieces adorn the walls, the furnishings are rattan and the kitchens are modern. The rooms, which are decorated with Asian, Polynesian and Indonesian themes, overlook Koloa Landing, site of the best snorkeling on the island. There is usually a two-night minimum stay. Closed Saturday and Sunday. ~ 2660 Puuholo Road, Koloa; 808-742-6717, 800-742-6711, fax 808-742-1933; www.oceancottages.com, e-mail vacation@oceancottages.com. DELUXE.

In a renovated plantation house near Poipu Beach you'll find the **Old Koloa House**. The rooms are pleasant, and decorated à la old Hawaii, complete with flowered drapes and ceiling fans; they all have private entrances. One room has a private bath (with clawfoot tub and shower); the other two share a bathroom. A continental breakfast is served in your room on the first morning. After that, you have to fend for yourself, but you'll be armed with a refrigerator and a microwave. ~ 3327 Waikomo Road, Koloa; 808-742-2099; www.oldkoloahouse.com, e-mail information@oldkoloahouse.com. MODERATE.

**Koloa Landing Cottages** in Poipu offers five cottages, a studio, a one-bedroom unit, and three two-bedroom units, one of which sleeps up to six; all are walking distance to the ocean. These are attractive facilities with kitchens. With a garden setting and family atmosphere, they evoke a comfortable sense of old Hawaii. Four-night minimum. ~ 2704-B Hoonani Road, Poipu; 808-742-1470, 800-779-8773; www.koloalanding.com, e-mail infokoloalanding@aol.com. MODERATE.

**Poipu Bed & Breakfast Inn** is a lovely woodframe house with four guest rooms. The decor is dominated by white wicker furniture and merry-go-round horses (there's one in the living room and in three of the bedrooms). You can also expect wall-to-wall carpeting and overhead fans. There are large covered lanais in front and back plus a yard complete with garden and fruit trees. ~ 2720 Hoonani Road, Poipu; 808-743-0100, 800-808-2330, fax 808-245-3004; www.kauai-inn.com, e-mail info@kauai-inn.com. DELUXE.

It would be an elastic stretch of the imagination to call the **Hyatt Regency Kauai Resort & Spa** a hidden destination. This *is*, after all, a Hyatt Regency—with over 600 guest rooms, several pools, six restaurants, six lounges and several acres of manmade lagoons. But before this luxury resort was built, the beach on which it sits was one of the great hidden locales on Kauai. Shipwreck Beach is still a magnificent crescent of white sand, and the Hyatt Regency Kauai Resort & Spa, backdropped by cane fields and deep-green mountains, enjoys some of the seclusion for which Keoneloa Bay was renowned. With its wood-paneled lobby, atrium garden and plush guest rooms, it is one of Kauai's prettier hotels. ~ 1571 Poipu Road, Poipu; 808-742-1234, 800-554-9288, fax 808-742-1557; www.kauai-hyatt.com. ULTRA-DELUXE.

With one of the southside's few truly oceanfront locations, as well as a pool that takes full advantage of the enviable view, the **Sheraton Kauai Resort** is a pleasant, subdued hotel. The 413 rooms, like the resort itself, are totally comfortable and standard Sheraton, but with an understated elegance. The grounds are lushly landscaped, giving the resort a private feel. ~ 2440 Hoonani Road, Poipu; 808-742-1661, 800-782-9488, fax 808-742-9777; www.sheratonkauai.com. ULTRA-DELUXE.

**Marjorie's Kauai Inn** overlooks grazing horses in the Lawai Valley, and you can enjoy the view from your private deck. All three spacious guest rooms have a refrigerator, a microwave, a coffee maker and a toaster; you'll receive bread, fruit, juice and coffee on your arrival. Guests have access to a swimming pool, and you can ask your hostess for use of a barbecue grill, a blender and beach chairs. Marjorie's a good resource for information about local attractions. Adults only. ~ Lawai; 808-332-8838, 800-717-8838; www.marjorieskauaiinn.com, e-mail marjorie@marjorieskauai inn.com. MODERATE.

**CONDOS**   The best way to shop for value and location among Poipu condos is to contact one of the local rental agencies. They include **Poipu Beach Resort Association** at 2440 Hoonani Road in Koloa (808-742-7444, 888-744-0888, fax 808-742-7887; www.poipubeach. org, e-mail info@poipubeach.org.), **Grantham Resorts** at 3176 Poipu Road in Poipu (808-742-2000, 800-325-5701, fax 808-742-9093; www.grantham-resorts.com, e-mail info@grantham-resorts.com) and **R & R Realty & Rentals, Inc.** at 1763 Pee Road in Poipu (808-742-7555, 800-367-8022, fax 808-742-7434; www. r7r.com, e-mail randr@r7r.com). Talk to these agencies at length. Ask them about the best deals they have to offer in the season you're going. If interested, you can also ask about packages that include rental cars.

**AUTHOR FAVORITE**

For a place located right on the water, there's **Gloria's Spouting Horn Bed & Breakfast**. This custom-designed beachhouse features three ocean-front guest rooms outfitted with canopy beds, handmade Hawaiian quilts and *koa* furniture. Open and airy, Gloria's is a place where you can relax on the lanai that sits just above the waves, lie in a hammock, swim in the pool, or go surfing outside your front door. Full breakfast served. ~ 4464 Lawai Beach Road, Poipu; phone/fax 808-742-6995; www.glorias bedandbreakfast.com, e-mail glorbb@gte.net. ULTRA-DELUXE.

A particularly well-known destination, **Kiahuna Plantation** is a 35-acre beachfront spread and an ideal family resting spot. This complex of resort condominiums is landscaped with lily ponds, lagoon and a spectacular cactus garden. The beach here provides lots of fun for bodysurfers. The units are housed in attractive plantation-style structures, which dot the resort's rolling lawns. In peak season, one-bedroom condos are $225 to $460; two-bedroom units are $365 to $505. Ask for a condo away from the street and parking lot. ~ 2253 Poipu Road, Poipu; 808-742-6411, 800-688-7444, fax 808-742-1698; www.outrigger.com.

Neatly situated near the oceanfront just a short jaunt to the beach, **Poipu Kapili** offers you a great place to unpack your bags. It's a 60-unit complex with a pool and tennis courts amid lush vegetation. Each condo, uniquely decorated by its owner, offers views (and sounds) of the blue Pacific. One-bedroom condos start at $220. ~ 2221 Kapili Road, Koloa; 808-742-6449, 800-443-7714, fax 808-742-9162; www.poipukapili.com, e-mail aloha@poipukapili.com.

**Whaler's Cove** is a secluded condominium resort that serves up an idyllic shoreline setting. Its roomy, two-bedroom units (which sleep up to six and range from $479 to $619) feature oceanfront lanais that face onto the bright blue Pacific; one-bedroom units run from $349 to $469. Koloa Landing, an excellent snorkeling and shoreline dive spot, is right next door. Each condo has cheery, modern decor. The resort has a pool, a hot tub and the ubiquitous barbecue. ~ 2640 Puuholo Road, Koloa; 808-742-7571, 800-225-2683, fax 808-742-1185; www.whalers-cove.com, e-mail stay@whalers-cove.com.

One of the most unique condos around is **Poipu Crater Resort**. ◄ HIDDEN
Located just 600 yards from the beach, it's also one of the best deals. This entire 30-unit facility rests in the crater of an extinct volcano. The accommodations are contained in attractive wood-frame houses; all are two-bedroom condos and rent for $130 to $210 in peak season, depending on length of stay. There's a pool, tennis courts, a sauna and a barbecue area. ~ Hoohu Road, Poipu; 808-724-7400, 800-367-8020, fax 808-742-9121; www.suite-paradise.com, e-mail mail@suite-paradise.com.

**Poipu Kai Resort** consists of a succession of separate buildings spread around a spacious lawn. There are seven pools and nine tennis courts plus a restaurant, jacuzzi and barbecues. The entire complex fronts Shipwreck and Brennecke's beaches. Studio units start at $95 and one-bedroom condos start at $124, depending on the length of your stay. ~ 1941 Poipu Road, Poipu; 808-742-7400, 800-367-8020, fax 808-742-9121; www.suite-paradise.com, e-mail mail@suite-paradise.com.

**Poipu Shores** is a small (39-unit) complex right on the ocean with a swimming pool so close to the water the waves seem poised to break across it. One-bedroom units start at $290 ($230 off-season). ~ 1775 Pee Road, Poipu; 808-742-7700, 800-367-5004, fax 808-742-9720; www.castleresorts.com.

At **Sunset Kahili Condominiums**, one-bedroom apartments start at $225 and sleep up to four, and two bedrooms house up to six and begin at $325. All units have ocean views. Four-night minimum stay gets a discount; two-week stay required during holiday season. ~ 1763 Pee Road, Poipu; 808-742-7434, phone/fax 800-827-6478; www.r7r.com, e-mail info@r7r.com.

At **Kuhio Shores**, one-bedroom apartments are $220 for one to four people; two bedrooms, two baths, cost $325 for one to six people. On the shore, but lacking a beach. Lower rates for stays longer than four days. ~ 5050 Lawai Road, Poipu; 808-742-7555, 800-367-8022, fax 808-742-1559; www.r7r.com, e-mail randr@r7r.com

**DINING**

South-of-the-border cuisine comes in the form of tamales, chile verde, enchiladas and tacos at **Mi Casita Mexican Restaurant**. With oilcloth on the tables and a desert-and-cactus mural covering an entire wall, this home-style eatery is a good bet for a filling meal. No lunch on Sunday. ~ 5470 Koloa Road, Koloa; 808-742-2323. BUDGET TO MODERATE.

For patio dining stroll down the street to **Tom Kats Grill**. Situated in a small interior courtyard, this easy-going restaurant has prime rib, lobster and fresh seafood, as well as sandwiches and chicken fingers for the kids. ~ 5400 Koloa Road, Koloa; 808-742-8887. MODERATE.

This area is not known for an abundance of restaurants, so you're lucky to find **Pizzetta**. Tastefully decorated with Italian scenes and tiles, the full bar will mix you up a drink while you wait for your order. The menu is basic Italian: calzones, mozzarella sticks, etc. But the pizza is particularly good, with its homemade crust and sauce, and reasonably priced. You can eat in, dine on the deck, or take it to go. Delivery is also an option. ~ 5408 Koloa Road, Koloa; 808-742-8881, fax 808-742-2715. MODERATE TO DELUXE.

HIDDEN ►

For super fresh sashimi, a variety of fish *poke* and hearty plate lunches, stop in at the **Koloa Fish Market**. These plate lunches are several steps above the competitors in quality, and the raw fish items are fresh. Lunch only. ~ 5482 Koloa Road, Koloa; 808-742-6199, fax 808-742-1018. BUDGET.

The stars, the ocean and the **Beach House Restaurant** is a showcase for Maui-born chef Scott Lutey's island cuisine and for painter Jan Kasprzycki's land- and seascapes. Signature items include the "Ahi Taster," Kauai asparagus salad, lemongrass-and kaffir lime–crusted scallops, wasabi-crusted snapper and a kahlua taro cheesecake. Not only is the food worth the splurge, the oceanfront location, on the road to Spouting Horn, is a perfect setting for watching the waves under the stars. Dinner only. ~ 5022 Lawai Road, Koloa; 808-742-1424, fax 808-742-1369; www.the-beach-house.com. DELUXE TO ULTRA-DELUXE.

At **Pattaya Asian Cafe**, you can settle back at a teak dining table. This small patio eatery serves broccoli noodles, lemon chicken, fresh sweet basil beef, and numerous other Southeast Asian dishes. The food has never disappointed me the several times I've dined here. Worth a stop. ~ Poipu Shopping Village, 2360 Kiahuna Plantation Drive, Poipu; 808-742-8818. MODERATE.

It seems like everywhere you go in Hawaii these days, Roy Yamaguchi has a restaurant. On Kauai it is **Roy's Poipu Bar & Grill**, an informal dining room with the kitchen behind a glass partition. The menu is a sample of what the staff calls Hawaiian fusion cuisine. You can order steamed fresh fish, hibachi-style salmon or *kiawe*-grilled ribeye steak. Or at least that's what was on the ever-changing menu last time I was in. In any case, it's hard to go wrong. Reservations are strongly recommended. Dinner only. ~ Poipu Shopping Village, 2360 Kiahuna Plantation Drive, Poipu; 808-742-5000, fax 808-742-5050. MODERATE TO ULTRA-DELUXE.

Families will love **Poipu Tropical Burgers**, with its *keiki* meals, casual, open-air setting, low prices and wide range of items. Gourmet burgers, sandwiches, meal-sized salads, fresh fish, steak and pasta make up the menu. Portions are hearty, and it's open for three meals a day. ~ Poipu Shopping Village, 2360 Kiahuna Plantation Drive; 808-742-1808. MODERATE.

Overlooking Poipu Beach is **Brennecke's Beach Broiler**. Downstairs at this two-level dining spot you'll find a budget-priced deli serving sandwiches and shave ice. The upper deck is occupied by an open-air restaurant that serves appetizers, lunch and dinner daily, then stokes the *kiawe* broiler for dinner selections that include fresh fish dishes, steak, chicken and seafood kebab. There is also pasta. ~ 2100 Hoone Road, Poipu; 808-742-7588, 888-384-8810, fax 808-742-1321; www.brenneckes.com, e-mail bob@brenneckes.com. MODERATE TO ULTRA-DELUXE.

**AUTHOR FAVORITE**

**Keoki's Paradise**, a beautiful patio-style restaurant centered around a tropical garden and pond, is located in Poipu Shopping Village. They feature a steak-and-seafood menu. Some say the seafood is the best you'll get for the price. The setting alone makes it worth a visit. ~ Poipu Shopping Village, 2360 Kiahuna Plantation Drive, Poipu; 808-742-7534, fax 808-742-7847. MODERATE TO ULTRA-DELUXE.

Huge (and tasty) portions that will last you two meals, or can be shared, are served up at **Taqueria Nortenos** in the Poipu Plaza. The decor isn't much to write home about, but you can take your Mexican food to go, and with prices like this it's hard to complain. You might want to try the *chalupas* or burritos. For dessert order the *bunuelos*. Closed Wednesday. ~ 2827 Poipu Road, Poipu; 808-742-7222. BUDGET.

The setting at **The Plantation Gardens Restaurant** is a restored Polynesian-style home tucked away in the densely landscaped grounds of Kiahuna Plantation Resort. Meals, served inside and on the open-air veranda, have a Pacific Rim influence. The menu emphasizes organic, locally grown herbs and vegetables as well as a grill using *kiawe*—the native Hawaiian mesquite. Filet mignon, double-cut lamb chops and a variety of fresh options will make your mouth water. Vegetarians will be pleased with a choice of creative entrées. Dinner only. ~ 2253 Poipu Road, Koloa; 808-742-2216, fax 808-742-1570. DELUXE TO ULTRA-DELUXE.

The Hyatt Regency Kauai Resort & Spa's most imaginative restaurant is without doubt **Tidepools**. The theme is grass-shack Polynesia, with each of the several dining rooms resembling a classic *hale pili*. Set in a quiet lagoon and graced with classic Hawaiian sunsets and ocean breezes, it's a great place to dine. The offerings include charred ahi sashimi and a mixed seafood grill with lobster, scallops, shrimp and fish. Dinner only. ~ 1571 Poipu Road, Poipu; 808-742-1234, fax 808-742-1557; www.kauai-hyatt.com. ULTRA-DELUXE.

**GROCERIES** The **Big Save Market** includes a dry goods section and is definitely the place to shop on the way to Poipu Beach. ~ Koloa Road, Koloa; 808-742-1614.

Also popular with local shoppers is **Sueoka Store**, a classic old grocery store with a takeout stand located right in the center of town. ~ Koloa Road, Koloa; 808-742-1611.

If you're stuck, you might want to check out the **Whaler's General Store**, which is open 7:30 a.m. to 10 p.m. The prices are higher and the grocery selection is limited, but the hours are handy. ~ Poipu Shopping Village, 2360 Kiahuna Plantation Drive, Poipu; 808-742-9431.

If you're already soaking up the sun at Poipu, you have a few grocery options. **Brennecke's Mini-Deli** is conveniently situated across the street from Poipu Beach Park. This mom-and-pop business has liquor, cold drinks and a limited selection of groceries. ~ 2100 Hoone Road, Poipu; 808-742-7583.

To increase your choices and decrease your food bill, head up Poipu Road to **Kukuiula Store**. This market has prices that are nearly competitive with the Big Save Market on Koloa Road. ~ 2827 Poipu Road, Poipu; 808-742-1601.

# The Forbidden
## Island

There's little doubt that the most hidden place in "hidden Hawaii" is **Niihau**, Hawaii's westernmost inhabited island. About 250 native Hawaiians live on this privately owned island under conditions similar to those prevailing during the 19th century. Used as a cattle and sheep ranch and closed to the public, it is Hawaii's last unspoiled frontier.

The Robinsons, a Scottish family that came to Hawaii from New Zealand, purchased the island in the 1860s and have protected (some critics say segregated) its inhabitants from the rest of the world ever since. Residents of Niihau are free to leave the island but must ask permission to return, and while the situation does have a company-town aura about it, the Robinsons have historically shown an abiding concern for the people and ecology of Hawaii.

While Niihau measures a mere 73 square miles and rises only 1281 feet above sea level at its highest point, the island lays claim to rich fishing grounds and is famous for its Niihau shell necklaces, fashioned from rare and tiny shells that wash up on the windward shore only a few times a year.

Until the 1980s, Niihau fully deserved its nickname, "The Forbidden Island." But today outsiders with a sense of adventure (and some extra cash) can climb aboard a **Niihau Helicopter** flight and tour a part of the island. You'll fly over most of the island, avoiding the village where the population is concentrated, and land on a remote beach for beachcombing, snorkeling and a picnic lunch. You won't meet any Niihau residents, but you will have an experience that could prove to be your ultimate encounter with "hidden Hawaii." ~ Kaumualii Highway; 808-335-3500.

If you'd rather explore the island by ground, **HoloHolo Charters** offers an interesting option. Leaving from Port Allen and including a continental breakfast, their "Supertour" first stops at the Na Pali Coast to view the natural wonders of the area. They then head to Niihau for a snorkeling visit, during which you'll receive instruction by the crew. A buffet-style lunch follows. During the meal, the crew discusses the people and history of Niihau. ~ Elele; 808-335-0815, 800-848-6130.

**SHOPPING**  On the way to Poipu, the former plantation town of Koloa supports a cluster of shops as well as a miniature mall. Several clothing stores line Koloa Road. The minimall, called **Old Koloa Town** (even though it was totally overhauled in the 1980s), houses a string of small jewelry stores, a T-shirt shop and a photo studio. ~ Koloa Road, Koloa.

**Atlantis Gallery & Frames** has contemporary Hawaiian paintings and prints. ~ 5400 Koloa Road, Koloa; 808-742-2555.

Walk into **Island Soap & Candle Works** and get an education in how to make both. This amazing little shop has soaps made from coconut, guava, plumeria and every other island product imaginable. There are bath gels, botanical hand lotions and, oh yes, candles—dozens of different kinds. ~ 5428 Koloa Road, Koloa; 808-742-1945.

> The island of Kauai boasts one of the wettest spots on earth, but its southern flank resembles the Arizona desert.

**Poipu Shopping Village** is a resort-style shopping complex with several businesses, including restaurants, a store that sells only designer jewelry, two art galleries, a surf shop and a sundries shop. It's a good spot to stop at before a day at the beach. ~ 2360 Kiahuna Plantation Drive, Koloa; 808-742-2831.

**Hale Mana** offers a wonderful selection of designer island clothing, art prints, Chinese antiques, and "gifts for the spirited." Its sister store **Hale Mana Fine Arts** specializes in fine art and museum pieces. ~ 2360 Kiahuna Plantation Drive, Poipu; 808-742-1027.

At **Spouting Horn,** next to the parking lot that serves visitors to the blowhole, local merchants set up tables to sell their wares. You're liable to find coral and *puka* shell necklaces, trident shell trumpets, rare Niihau shell necklaces and some marvelous mother-of-pearl pieces. You are free to barter, of course, though the prices are pretty good to begin with. If you're interested in jewelry and want to meet local artisans, this is the spot. ~ End of Lawai Road, Poipu.

**NIGHTLIFE**  To catch a local crowd, head down to **Brennecke's Beach Broiler**. There's no music, but the crowds are young and the views otherworldly. ~ 2100 Hoone Road, Poipu; 808-742-7588.

**Keoki's Paradise** (808-742-7534) in Poipu Shopping Village features contemporary Hawaiian music every Tuesday, Thursday, Friday and Saturday nights and Sunday during the day. You can sit outdoors in a garden setting and enjoy the sounds. Also in the mall, check out the Polynesian dance show Tuesday and Thursday evenings on the mall's center stage. ~ 2360 Kiahuna Plantation Drive, Poipu.

**Joe's On The Green** has live Hawaiian music during their Wednesday and Thursday evening dinner. Locals love the place, so make reservations ahead of time or prepare to squeeze in at the bar. ~ 2545 Kiahuna Plantation Drive, Poipu; 808-742-9696.

There's live Hawaiian and light contemporary music at **The Point** Tuesday through Thursday from 8 to 11 p.m., and dancing on Friday and Saturday. The 225-degree view and wavefront location are an even stronger draw. Great at sunset. ~ Sheraton Kauai Beach Resort, 2440 Hoonani Road, Poipu; 808-742-1661 ext. 52.

The Hyatt Regency Kauai, with its spectacular location on Shipwreck Beach, hosts the area's upscale nightspots. **Stevenson's Library** is a stately wood-paneled lounge that evokes a sense of colonial-era Polynesia. For a drink with a view of the beach, try the **Tidepools Restaurant**. Hawaiian sunsets and music go hand in hand at **Seaview Terrace**, located in the hotel's lobby. ~ Hyatt Regency Kauai Resort & Spa, 1571 Poipu Road, Poipu; 808-742-1234, 800-633-7313.

**POIPU BEACH AND WAIOHAI BEACH** Extending along the main hotel area in Poipu are two adjacent white-sand beaches crowded with visitors. Popular with sunbathers, swimmers and water-sport aficionados, both are protected by a series of offshore reefs. At Poipu Beach there is good surfing for beginners near the beach, for intermediate surfers about 100 yards offshore and for expert surfers about a half-mile out at "First Break." This beach is also popular with windsurfers. Waiohai Beach has an offshore break near the reef known as "Waiohai." There's fishing from the nearby rocks (the beach area is usually crowded). There are lifeguards. ~ Located along Poipu Road near the closed Waiohai hotel.

**BEACHES & PARKS**

**POIPU BEACH PARK** This has got to be one of the loveliest little parks around. There's a well-kept lawn for picnickers and finicky sunbathers, a crescent-shaped beach with a protecting reef and the sunny skies of Poipu. Since the water here is relatively flat, most days it's not good for surfing. However, swimming is excellent, and the entire area has some of the best diving on the island. An offshore sandbar makes for good bodysurfing. Bonefish, rockfish and *papio* are common catches; there's also good spearfishing on the nearby reefs. You'll find a picnic area, restrooms, showers and lifeguards. ~ Located on Hoone Road in Poipu.

**SHIPWRECK BEACH** Back in the 1980s, this was one of the greatest of Kauai's hidden beaches. Then condominiums began crawling along the coast and eventually the Hyatt Regency Kauai was built right on the strand. Today, it's a sandy but rock-studded beach, quite beautiful but bordered by the resort. Swimming is good when the surf is low. This is also an outstanding bodysurfing and windsurfing area (the best spot is at the east end of the beach). Fishing is good from nearby Makawehi Point. ~ From the Poipu Beach area, follow Poipu Road east and simply look for the Hyatt Regency Kauai, which borders the beach.

HIDDEN ► **MAHAULEPU BEACH** 🏊 🏄 🏊 ⚓ If you've come to Kauai seeking that South Seas dream, head out to these lovely strands. Mahaulepu is a tropical corridor of white sand winding for two miles along a reef-protected shoreline and including several strands and pocket beaches. Flocks of seabirds inhabit the area, and if that's not enough, the area boasts 100-foot-high sand dunes. There are well-protected sections of beach where you can swim, as well as rocky areas where you can fish. Snorkeling and surfing are also good here. The beach has no facilities. ~ From the Poipu Beach area, follow Poipu Road east past the Hyatt Regency Kauai at Shipwreck Beach. Beyond Shipwreck, the pavement ends and the thoroughfare becomes a cane road. Continue on the main cane road (which is like a dirt road continuation of Poipu Road). Follow this road for about two miles (even when it curves toward the mountains and away from the ocean). Numerous minor cane roads will intersect from the right and left: ignore them. Finally, you will come to a crossroads with a major cane road (along which a line of telephone poles runs). Turn right and follow this road for about a mile (you'll pass a quarry off in the distance to the right), then watch on the right for roads leading to the beach. You will encounter a guard shack at the turnoff where you are required to sign a waiver to continue onto the property. The beach entrance is closed from 7 p.m. to 7:30 a.m.

## Waimea Area

The Western world's relationship with Hawaii, a tumultuous affair dating back more than two centuries, began in southwest Kauai when Captain James Cook set anchor at Waimea Bay. Cook landed on the leeward side of the island, a hot, dry expanse rimmed by white-sand beaches and dominated to the interior by Waimea Canyon, the "Grand Canyon of the Pacific."

The climate at the southwestern end of the island is conducive to sugar cane, which is partly why Gay & Robinson is the only plantation to still survive on Kauai. Its fields line the roads, along with Kauai Coffee groves.

The towns here have retained an old-Hawaii feel, even though vacation rentals are now creeping up along the handsome stretch of coastline. Beyond the towns, it's either west to the Pacific Missile Range Facility and enough long, broad, thick, sandy beaches to satisfy the most dedicated beach bum, or north to the cool, often misty, forested elevations of Kokee.

Although the westside is a place of many topographic contrasts, when it comes to population and lifestyle, it's still local to da max. The old ways of hunting, fishing and farming prevail here, supported by the expanses of open space running from the mountains to the sea.

**THE COAST**    One of the first plantation towns you'll encounter driving west on Kaumualii Highway (Route 50) is **Kalaheo**. A detour up the hillside in Kalaheo, up **Puiilima Road**, will give you a broad overview of the area, as well as a taste of residential life on this part of the island. Or take a left on Papalina Road, which will lead a mile up to **Kukuiolono Park**, a lightly visited Japanese garden complete with stone bridge, ornamental pool and florid landscaping. Take a stroll through this peaceful retreat and you'll also enjoy a stunning view that sweeps across a patchwork of fields to the sea.

Route 50 continues along to the small town of **Eleele,** another residential neighborhood. From here you can take Route 541 to the

**SIGHTS**

◄ *HIDDEN*

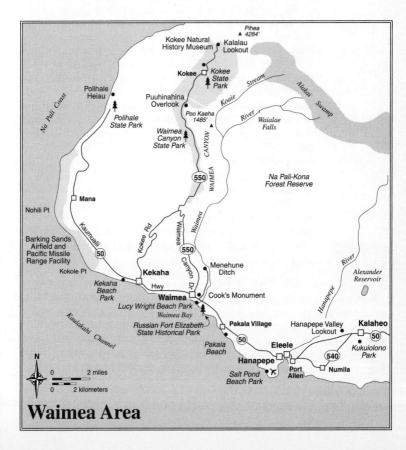

# Waimea Area

community of **Port Allen** and its small boat harbor and shopping center. If you're interested in fishing charters or tour boats, a few operate out of this area.

Back on Route 50, en route from one tinroof town to the next, you'll pass the **Hanapepe Valley Lookout**, which offers a view of native plant life dramatically set in a gorge ringed by eroded cliffs. Taro patches grow in abundance in this wet and lush valley.

HIDDEN ►

Be sure to take the nearby fork into **Hanapepe**, a vintage village complete with wooden sidewalks and weather-beaten storefronts. During the 1924 sugar strike, 16 workers were killed here by police. Even today, the independent spirit of those martyrs pervades this proud little town. It has become a haven for artists, and galleries seem to outnumber residents.

For a sense of Hanapepe during the plantation days, drive out **Awawa Road**. Precipitous red lava cliffs rim the roadside, while rickety cottages and intricately tilled fields carpet the valley below.

On the outskirts of Hanapepe, turn right on Route 543 toward the ocean. Here you'll see ancient **salt ponds**, which are still used today. Continue to the end of the road to get to **Salt Pond Beach Park**, a spot frequented by windsurfers and locals.

A short detour off Route 50 from either Kalaheo or Hanapepe leads to the **Kauai Coffee Visitor Center**. Housed in a former plantation-worker's home, the center has pictures from the area's sugar-plantation days, as well as information about contemporary coffee production. Best of all, they have a small café and free tastings. ~ Route 540, between Kalaheo and Hanapepe; 808-335-0813, fax 808-335-3149; www.kauaicoffee.com, e-mail greensales@kauaicoffee.com.

As Kaumualii Highway winds its way past small communities, you'll see that this is still sugar country. A side trip to one of Hawaii's few remaining sugar plantations leads to the mill and to **Gay & Robinson Tours**. The road is lined with monkeypod trees and passes by former plantation-managers' homes, with their manicured gardens. Even if you don't go on a tour, it's worth seeing this

**AUTHOR FAVORITE**

sights  It's a short drive onward and upward from Kokee Natural History Museum to the **Kalalau Lookout**, where Kauai's other face is reflected in knife-edged cliffs and overgrown gorges that drop to the sea 4000 feet below. Another nearby overlook gazes out across the **Alakai Swamp** to **Mount Waialeale**. (Because of cloud cover in the valley, it's best to arrive at the overlook before 10 a.m. or after 4 p.m.) One more spectacular scene along the way, one more reason to bring you back to this magnificent island.

street. The tour office features a mini-museum, and the tour itself takes in the cane fields and factories of a classic Hawaiian plantation. (If you take the tour, you'll need to wear closed-toe shoes and clothes you don't mind being stained red by the soil.) Reservations required. Admission. ~ Near the 19-mile marker on Kaumualii Highway, Waimea; 808-335-2824; www.gandrtours-kauai.com, e-mail info@gandrtours-kauai.com.

Just past the 22-mile marker is a road that takes you to **Russian Fort Elizabeth State Historical Park**. Now just a rubble heap, historically it represents a fruitless attempt by a maverick adventurer working for a Russian trading company to gain a foothold in the islands in 1817. Designed in the shape of a six-pointed star, the original fort bristled with guns and had walls 30 feet thick. Two other forts were built on the island—one in Princeville and another in Hanalei. Nothing is left of them.

An earlier event, Captain James Cook's 1778 "discovery" of Hawaii, is commemorated with a lava monolith near his landing place in Waimea. Watch for roadside markers to **Cook's Monument**. ~ Just after you cross the Waimea River, on the road to Lucy Wright Park.

Cook was not the only outsider to assume a role in Waimea's history. It seems that those industrious leprechauns who built the fishpond outside Lihue were also at work here constructing the **Menehune Ditch**. This waterway, built with hand-hewn stones in a fashion unfamiliar to the Polynesians, has long puzzled archaeologists. ~ Outside town on Menehune Road.

◀ HIDDEN

In the early 20th century, **Waimea** was a thriving sugar community. Drive around town and you'll see several structures that have withstood the test of time, like the restored **Waimea Theater** and the **Yamese** and **Masuda** buildings. Those interested in getting up close and personal with the past might take the "mill camp walking tour." Plantation life and homes and gardens are highlighted. Tours are held Tuesday, Thursday and Saturday at 9 a.m. Reservations are required. Admission. ~ 808-335-2824, fax 808-335-6852.

Back on Kaumualii Highway, you'll pass the town of **Kekaha**, home of a now-defunct sugar mill and a colony of plantation houses, before arriving at the next stop on this scenic itinerary—**Barking Sands Airfield**. Actually, it's not the airfield but the sands that belong on your itinerary. These lofty sand dunes, among the largest on the island, make a woofing sound when ground underfoot. This, according to scientists, is due to tiny cavities in each grain of sand that cause them to resonate when rubbed together. If you have trouble making the sound, remember what one local wag told me: The hills actually got their name from tourists becoming "dog-tired" after futilely trying to elicit a growl from the mute sand. (Since the beach here at Major's Bay is on a military reservation, call 808-335-4229 to make sure the facility is open to the public.) Nearby is the **Pacific Missile Range Facility** (808-335-4229), an important launch area for military and meteorological rockets and the site of periodic war games.

Having made a fool of yourself trying to get sand to bark, continue on past the deserted town of **Mana** (along a graded dirt road for the last five miles) to the endless sands of **Polihale State Park**. This very hot, very dry, very beautiful retreat represents the last stretch of a 15-mile-long sand beach, one of the longest in the state, that begins way back in Kekaha. The sand marathon ends at the foot of the Na Pali cliffs, in an area sacred to the Hawaiians. Here the ancients built **Polihale Heiau**, a temple whose ruins remain. This sacred place is where the spirits of the dead made their leap into the spiritual world. And here the road ends, further passage made impossible by the sea cliffs that wrap around Kauai's northwest corner.

The sand at Barking Sands Airfield is similar to that found in Egypt's Sinai Desert, the Gobi Desert of Mongolia and in Saudi Arabia.

**THE MOUNTAINS** Another candidate in the contest for ultimate adventure—one that is free, doesn't require a helicopter and always lies open to exploration—is **Waimea Canyon** (808-274-3433). Touring the "Grand Canyon of the Pacific" involves a side trip from either the town of Waimea or Kekaha. Waimea Canyon Drive leads from the former and Kokee Road climbs from the latter; they join about halfway up the mountain. For an overview of the entire region, go up along Waimea Canyon Drive, since it hugs the canyon rim and provides the best views, then follow Kokee Road down.

As the paved road snakes along the side of this 2857-foot-deep canyon, a staggering panorama opens. The red and orange hues of a barren southwestern landscape are splashed with tropic greens and yellows. Far below, the **Waimea River**, which carved this ten-mile-long chasm, cuts a sinuous course. Several vista points provide crow's-nest views of the territory, including **Puuhinahina Overlook** at 3500-feet elevation, which offers views of the canyon to the east and Niihau to the west.

The road continues deep into Kauai's cool interior before arriving at **Kokee State Park**, a preserve of *koa* trees, with their crescent-shape leaves, and *ohia* trees, with their gray bark and red pompon flowers. You're apt to see a variety of birds here, including the red *apapane*, the yellow-green *amakihi*, the white-tailed tropic bird and maybe the state bird, the nene. Wild boar roam the area and trout fishing is a favorite sport in the park. Hiking trails meander through the park. (See "Hiking" at the end of the chapter for more information.) Within this 4345-acre park you'll find a restaurant and cabins.

At the **Kokee Natural History Museum** is a small display space devoted to the flora, fauna and natural history of the area,

as well as an exhibit about Hurricane Iniki. Collections of shells
and Hawaiian artifacts are also featured. ~ 808-335-9975, fax
808-335-6131; www.kokee.org, e-mail information@kokee.org.

Accommodations on Kauai's southwest side include beachside
cottages in Waimea and ethereal facilities in Kokee State Park.

**LODGING**

Nightly, weekly or monthly, the **Kalaheo Plantation** is a good
bargain. The 1926 plantation-style home, located a couple of
miles from the beach, once belonged to a district judge. The man-

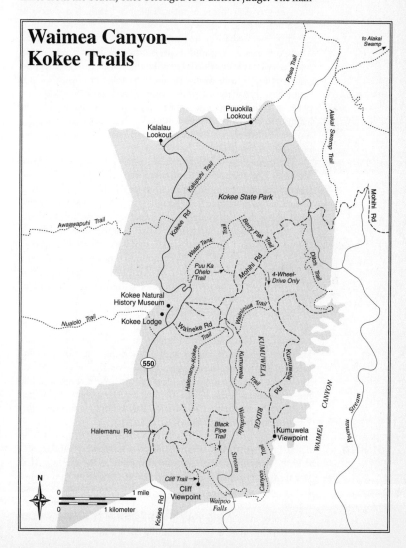

# Waimea Canyon—
# Kokee Trails

agement polished up the floors, added some new windows and, they won't hesitate to tell you, 500 plants, and opened for business. There are six modern suites with either a kitchenette or full kitchen; some have private lanais. You can rent the whole house but you can't wear your shoes inside. ~ 4579 Puuwai Road, Kalaheo; phone/fax 808-332-7812; www.kalaheo-plantation.com, e-mail kalaheo1@gte.net. BUDGET TO MODERATE.

**Waimea Plantation Cottages** is one of the most alluring and secluded facilities on the entire island. Here in a spectacular coconut grove, fronting a salt-and-pepper beach, is a cluster of charmingly rustic 1920s-era plantation cottages. Each has been carefully restored and many are furnished with rattan furniture. These one-, two- and multibedroom houses have full kitchens. Maid service is every third day. Like the rest of the complex, the swimming pool follows the style of an earlier era (most visitors swim here since the offshore waters are usually murky). The place is a little gem out on Kauai's remote westside. ~ 9400 Kaumualii Highway, Waimea; 808-338-1625, fax 808-338-2338; www.waimea-plantation.com, e-mail paul.schow@aston-hotels.com. ULTRA-DELUXE.

**HIDDEN ►**

Those seeking a neighborhood setting may prefer **Classic Vacation Cottages**, seven stand-alone vacation rentals of varying sizes at the end of a residential cul-de-sac in the quiet, hilly town of Kalaheo. They range from a modest studio to an attractive full-sized home that sleeps eight. The larger units have full kitchens, too, making them a bargain for two couples or a family. Of course, the beach isn't nearby, although Kukuiolono hilltop park and golf course aren't far. The communal hot tub is another plus. ~ P.O. Box 901, Kalaheo, HI 96741; 808-332-9201, fax 808-332-7645; www.classiccottages.com, e-mail clascot@hawaiian.net. BUDGET TO MODERATE.

Nestled in secluded woods between Waimea Canyon and the Kalalau Lookout are the **Kokee Lodge Cabins**. Each of the 12 mountain cabins, varying in size from one large room to two-bedroom complexes, comes with a wood-burning stove, a basic kitchen and rustic furnishings. These wood cabins, 3600 feet above sea level, are a mountaineer's dream. With forest and hiking trails all around, Kokee is ideal for the adventurer. It gets chilly, so bring a jacket or sweater. Reservations are essential. ~ Kokee State Park; 808-335-6061. BUDGET.

**DINING**

Traveling west toward Waimea Canyon and Barking Sands, you'll find the watering places decrease as rapidly as the rainfall. Most restaurants en route are cafés and takeout stands. If you're on a budget, you're in luck; if you're looking for an exclusive, elegant establishment, you'll find slim pickings out Waimea way.

Family-owned and -operated **Brick Oven Pizza** is commonly touted as having the best pies on the island. But don't expect the

Americanized version of the dish. Brick Oven specializes in authentic Italian: thin crust brushed with garlic butter and minimal sauce. Red-and-white-checked tablecloths and an amiable staff complete the image. The place is often jammed, so plan ahead if you have hungry kids in tow. Closed Monday and for one week in September. ~ 2-2555 Kaumualii Highway, Kalaheo; 808-332-8561, fax 808-332-3800. BUDGET TO MODERATE.

At the **Kalaheo Steak House** you'll step into a comfortable wood-paneled dining room. Pull up a chair, rest your elbows on the table (it's permitted) and choose among sirloin, filet mignon, scampi, Cornish hens and several other appealing entrées. No reservations accepted. Dinner only. ~ 4444 Papalina Road, Kalaheo; 808-332-9780. MODERATE TO DELUXE.

**Kalaheo Coffee Co. and Cafe** is always bustling. Locals arrive ◄ HIDDEN in droves for the omelettes, hearty deli sandwiches and burgers, yummy homemade cinnamon rolls and coffee drinks. With small wooden tables and a few stools at a counter, it's a tiny, clean place, with friendly service. Breakfast and lunch only. ~ 2-2436 Kaumualii Highway, Kalaheo; 808-332-5858, fax 808-332-5868; www.kalaheo.com. MODERATE.

**Camp House Grill** is a trim little café with an island-style ◄ HIDDEN menu. Favored by nearby residents, they serve *huli huli* chicken and pork ribs, and big, satisfying breakfasts. The homemade pies are a big draw. ~ 2-2431 Kaumualii Highway, Kalaheo; 808-332-9755, fax 808-332-7052. BUDGET TO MODERATE.

A family-run eatery, **Toi's Thai Kitchen** serves a lunch and ◄ HIDDEN dinner menu consisting primarily of Thai food such as yellow curry chicken and stir-fried eggplant with tofu. Fried chicken and mahimahi are also served. The decor is simple but the food is good. Closed Sunday. ~ Eleele Shopping Center, 178 Hanapepe Bay, Eleele; 808-335-3111. MODERATE.

**Da Imu Hut Café** has Hawaiian dishes, *saimin*, fried chicken, ◄ HIDDEN teriyaki chicken, fried noodles and hamburgers at 1950s prices.

**AUTHOR FAVORITE**
You don't get to eat outside at Hanapepe's **Green Garden Restaurant**, but the tropical plants convey a genuine garden feeling. The deliciously varied dinner menu ranges from pork chow mein to rock lobster tail and includes homemade old-fashioned vegetable soup and a salad bar. I particularly enjoyed the seafood special, a platter of mahimahi, shrimp, oysters and scallops. Children's and senior portions are available. Dinner only. Closed Tuesday. ~ Kaumualii Highway, Hanapepe; 808-335-5422, fax 808-335-5528. MODERATE.

It's not much on looks, but it fills the belly. With unusual hours, always call ahead. ~ 3771 Hanapepe Road, Hanapepe; 808-335-0200. BUDGET.

Gourmet vegetarian with an Italian flair is the way they describe the food at **Hanapepe Cafe and Espresso**. Every Friday night you'll find them preparing such entrées as marinated eggplant lasagna, pasta primavera with portobello mushrooms or marinara dishes made with locally grown produce. They're also open for lunch Tuesday through Saturday. That's when you can stop by for a caesar salad, a "healthnut sandwich," pasta specials, garden burgers or baked frittata. Reservations recommended. Closed Saturday and Sunday. ~ 3830 Hanapepe Road, Hanapepe; 808-335-5011. DELUXE.

HIDDEN ► Breakfast burritos, melts and deli sandwiches, fish plates and other specials are found at **Waimea Bakery & Deli**, a roadside eatery that also prepares an especially good taro-teriyaki burger. Their smoothies, milk shakes, tropical fruit turnovers, Hawaiian sweetbread and other baked goodies add to the appeal. Closed Tuesday. ~ 9875 Waimea Road; 808-338-1950. BUDGET.

**Waimea Brewing Company**, at Waimea Plantation Cottages, is one of those places you go to for the novelty value as much as the refreshment. Alongside the beer are served sandwiches and burgers, pasta dishes, grilled meats, chicken and fresh fish. There's relaxed, plantation-style decor inside, with a delightful, broad lanai for outdoor dining. ~ 9400 Kaumualii Highway, Waimea; 808-338-9733, fax 808-338-2338; www.waimea-plantation.com/brew, e-mail info@kikiaola.com. MODERATE TO DELUXE.

Because Kauai has been around longer than the other Hawaiian islands, its lusher and filled with more exotic wildlife and vegetation.

At **Pacific Pizza and Deli** you can certainly order a typical cheese pie, but they also offer more exotic versions such as Thai or Mexican pizza. Deli sandwiches, wraps and coffee drinks are available, too. Closed Sunday. ~ Wrangler Restaurant Building, 9852 Kaumualii Road, Waimea; 808-338-1020. BUDGET TO MODERATE.

Steaks, naturally, are the order of the day at **Wranglers Steakhouse**. Here guests can choose to take their meals outside or indoors in a rustic dining room. Hardwood floors and galvanized awnings contribute to the Western feel, as do the old wagon and wooden horse. The menu features classic surf and turf dishes. You might want to take a peek at the *paniolo* artifacts in their small museum. No lunch on Saturday. Closed Sunday. ~ 9852 Kaumualii Highway, Waimea; 808-338-1218, fax 808-338-1266. MODERATE TO DELUXE.

When you're up in the heights above Waimea Canyon you'll be mighty glad to discover **Kokee Lodge** in remote Kokee State Park. From the dining room of this homey hideaway, you can gaze out at the surrounding forest. The restaurant offers a light break-fast and lunch menu. The emphasis is on fresh, healthy dishes and local specialties like *lilikoi* pie. For breakfast try the corn-bread, and for lunch choose from soups, sandwiches and salads. ~ 808-335-6061, fax 808-335-5431. BUDGET.

There are two **Big Save Markets** along Kaumualii Highway. Tra-veling west from Lihue, the first is in the Eleele Shopping Center. ~ Eleele; 808-335-3127. The second is in the center of Waimea. ~ Waimea; 808-338-1621. Both are open from 6:30 a.m. to 10 p.m., Monday to Saturday, and 6:30 a.m. to 9 p.m. on Sunday.

**GROCERIES**

Also along the highway is the **Menehune Food Mart**, a con-venience store. ~ Kalaheo; 808-332-7349. For groceries past Wai-mea, try the **Menehune Food Mart** on Kekaha Road. ~ Kekaha; 808-337-1335.

Head up to Eleele off of Route 50 near Kalaheo and you'll dis-cover **Red Dirt Hawaii**, home of the "original Red Dirt shirt." Made with stains from the iron-rich soil of Kauai, these T-shirts are a cottage industry with workers all over the island coloring them. If your shirt starts fading, don't worry—just roll it in the dirt or wash it with mud and it will look like new again! ~ 4352 Waialo Road, Eleele; 808-335-5670, fax 808-335-3478; www.dirtshirt.com, e-mail onlinesales@dirtshirt.com.

**SHOPPING**

Hanapepe, a turn-of-the-20th-century town with a falsefront main street, has developed into an arts center.

**8 Bells Gallery** displays a range of mediums by local artists. They feature oil, sculpture, watercolor and limited-edition prints, and are known for their excellent framing with Hawaiian wood. Closed Sunday. ~ 4510 Hana Road, Hanapepe; 808-335-0550.

Well-known local watercolorist Arius Hopman is spot-lighted at the eponymous **Arius Hopman Gallery**. Closed Sun-day and Monday. ~ 3840-C Hanapepe Road, Hanapepe; 808-335-0227.

The **Dawn M. Traina Gallery** has paintings, drawings and prints of native Hawaiian people created by the store's namesake. Closed Sunday and Monday. ~ 3840-B Hanapepe Road, Hana-pepe; 808-335-3993.

Hanapepe is also the home of **Kauai Fine Arts**, a singular gal-lery housing an outstanding collection of antique maps and prints. Open Sunday by appointment only. ~ 3905 Hanapepe Road, Hanapepe; 808-335-3778; www.brunias.com.

Consider a tropical oil painting or one of the sculptures at **Giorgio's Gallery**. Closed Sunday. ~ 3871 Hanapepe Road, Hana-pepe; 808-335-3949.

**Collectibles & Fine Junque** has an amazing collection of glass-ware, aloha shirts, dolls and old bottles. It's a good place to pick

up antiques or knickknacks. Closed Sunday. ~ 9821 Kaumualii
Highway, Waimea; 808-338-9855.

**NIGHTLIFE**   Every week Hanapepe hosts **"Friday Art Night,"** showcasing
local artists in the numerous galleries in town. From 6 to 9 p.m.
most galleries in this artist enclave keep their doors open, offering refreshments, a chance to talk story with the artists, and frequent musical performances. Art demonstrations, poetry readings and other performances can be found along the street.

**Hanapepe Cafe and Espresso** is a bit of an anomaly, with
gourmet vegetarian food that would seem more at home in
California than in this tiny town. On Friday night the place is
packed, with local entertainers performing Hawaiian slack-key
guitar. There's no bar, but you can sit and have an espresso and
dessert. Closed Sunday and Monday. ~ 3830 Hanapepe Road,
Hanapepe; 808-335-5011.

**BEACHES**    **SALT POND BEACH PARK** 🐾 🛶 ⛷ 🎣 ♨ A pretty, crescent-
**& PARKS**    shaped beach with a protecting reef and numerous coconut trees,
this park is very popular with locals and may be crowded and
noisy on weekends. It's a good place to collect shells, though. The
road leading to the park passes salt ponds that date back hundreds of years and are still used today to evaporate sea water and
produce salt. Swimming is good in this well-protected area. Snorkeling is fair and there is diving near rocks and along the offshore
reef. For surfing, there's a shore break by the mouth of the Hanapepe River nearby in Port Allen. Sandy and shallow with small
waves, this area is safe for beginners. There are left and right
slides. Along the outer harbor edge near Port Allen Airport runway there are summer breaks, for experienced surfers only, which
involve climbing down a rocky shoreline. At Salt Pond there are
occasional summer breaks (left and right slides) requiring a long
paddle out. This is also a very popular windsurfing area. Rockfish and mullet are the most common catches here. Facilities include a picnic area, restrooms, showers and lifeguards. ~ Take

**FLYING HIGH**

An unmanned, solar-powered aircraft named *Helio* has been built by NASA
and AeroVironment and launched from Barking Sands, Kauai. A long, thin
flying wing that researchers hope will reach 100,000 feet in altitude, more
than three times higher than commercial jets fly, it is to be used as a
surrogate satellite or low-cost telecommunications platform. On its
first test flight from Barking Sands it soared to 76,000 feet.

Kaumualii Highway to Hanapepe. Turn onto Route 543 and follow it to the end.

▲ There's a grassy area near the beach for tent camping; a county permit is required.

**PAKALA BEACH** ⚓ 🏄 ⚓ 📷 This long narrow ribbon of    ◄ HIDDEN
sand is bounded by trees and set in perfectly lush surroundings.
Surfers will probably be the only other people around. They may
come out of the water long enough to watch the spectacular sunsets with you and to tell you of the fabled summer waves that
reach heights of 10 to 12 feet. If this book were rating beaches
by the star system, Pakala Beach would deserve a constellation.
When the surf is low it's a good place to swim. You can also
snorkel along the reef. This is one of Hawaii's top summer surfing spots. The incredibly long walls that form along a wide shallow reef allow you to hang ten seemingly forever. Hence the nickname for these breaks—"Infinity." The one drawback: It's a long
paddle out. Fishing is good from the rock outcropping off to the
left. There are no facilities here. ~ Located along Kaumualii
Highway near the 21-mile marker (two miles east of Waimea)
you'll see a concrete bridge crossing Aakukui stream with the
name "Aakukui" chiseled in the cement. Go through the gate
just below the bridge and follow the well-worn path a few hundred yards to the beach.

**LUCY WRIGHT BEACH PARK** ⚓ 🏄 📷 This five-acre park at
the Waimea River mouth is popular with locals and therefore
sometimes a little crowded. Despite a sandy beach, the park is
not as appealing as others nearby: The water is often murky from
cane field spillage. If you're in need of a campground you might
stop here, otherwise, I don't recommend the park. Swimming is
fair, unless the water is muddy. Surfing varies from small breaks
for beginners to extremely long walls that build four different
breaks and is best near the river mouth. There's a left slide. In
Waimea Bay, there are parrotfish, red goatfish, squirrelfish, *papio*,
bonefish, bigeyed scad and threadfin. You can also fish from the
pier a few hundred feet west of the park. Facilities include a picnic area, restrooms and showers. ~ Located in Waimea.

▲ Tent camping only. County permit required.

**KEKAHA BEACH** 🏄 This narrow beach parallels Kaumualii
Highway for several miles along the eastern edge of Kekaha. Although close to the highway, the lovely white strand offers some
marvelous picnic spots, but the rough surf and powerful currents
make swimming dangerous. There are many surfing spots along
here; the foremost, called "Davidson's," lies off Oomano Point.

**KEKAHA BEACH PARK** ⚓ 🏄 📷 Set on a beautiful ribbon of
sand, this 20-acre park is a great place to kick back, picnic and

catch the sun setting over the island of Niihau. Swimming is good when surf is down; otherwise it can be dangerous. For surfers, immediately west of the park are several breaks, including "Inters" (near Kaumualii Highway and Akialoa Street) and "First Ditch" and "Second Ditch," located in front of two drainage ditches. Anglers try for threadfin. There are picnic facilities and restrooms. ~ Located on Kaumualii Highway in Kekaha.

HIDDEN ▶   **KOKOLE POINT** 🏃 ⤵ Out by an old landing strip/drag strip, a local dump and a rifle range, there is a wide sandy beach that stretches forever and offers unofficial camping and outrageous sunsets. Fishermen, joggers and beachcombers love the place, but those who hold it nearest their hearts are surfers. The breaks here go by such names as "Rifle Range," "Targets" and "Whispering Sands." Currents and high surf usually make swimming unadvisable. However, fishing is good. There are no facilities. ~ Take the road that leads off Kaumualii Highway one mile west of Kekaha (there's a sign directing traffic to the dump). Follow any of the dirt roads in as far as possible. These will lead either to the dump or to a nearby landing strip. Walk the last three-tenths of a mile to the beach.

**BARKING SANDS** 🏊 🛶 🏃 🎣 ⤵ The military installation at Major's Bay is bounded by very wide beaches that extend for miles. You'll see the Barking Sands dunes and magnificent sunsets and get some of the best views of Niihau anywhere on Kauai. The weather is hot and dry here: a great place to get thoroughly baked, but beware of sunburns. The Pacific Missile Range Facility is located here, and the area is sometimes used for war games, so these beaches are sometimes closed. Swimming is good, but exercise caution. The coral reefs make for good snorkeling. **Major's Bay** is an excellent surfing spot with both summer and winter breaks. Other breaks include "Rockets" near the rocket launch pad, "Kinkini" at the south end of the airfield runway, and "Family Housing" just offshore from the base housing facility. Windsurfers also frequent Major's Bay and "Kinkini." A particularly good fishing spot is around Nohili Point; the most common catches are bonefish, threadfin and *ulua*. There are no facilities. ~ Take Kaumualii Highway several miles past Kekaha, then watch for signs to the Pacific Missile Range Facility. Due to heightened security measures, obtaining access to the beach can be complicated. Upon arrival in Hawaii, those wishing to visit must contact the local naval center, where they will be asked to complete a clearance form. The completed form must be taken to the Lihui Police Department for a criminal background check. A photo I.D. pass will be issued, though the entire process takes a week. Call ahead for public hours; 808-335-4221.

**POLIHALE STATE PARK** 🏊 🚻 💧 This 300-foot-wide beach blankets the coast for over two miles along Kauai's west end. It borders the sea cliffs of the Na Pali Coast, covering 138 acres. The hot, dry weather is excellent for sunbathing and prime for burning, so load up on sunscreen. You might even want to bring an umbrella or other form of shade. The afternoons bring great sunsets. This park has magnificent mountain surroundings: Niihau looms in the distance. Swimming is for experts only. The safest swimming is at **Queen's Pond**, an area that, depending on the year's weather conditions, floods and creates a protected lagoon along the beachfront near the middle of the park. Surfing is okay; there's a shore break with left and right slides. There's good windsurfing off Queen's Pond. This beach is also especially great for shell collecting. Bonefish, threadfin and *ulua* are the most common game fish. Facilities include a picnic area, restrooms and showers. ~ Take Kaumualii Highway until it ends, then follow the signs along dirt roads for about five miles.

> Polihale State Park, the United States' westernmost state park, is worth visiting—just to see the endless white-sand expanse.

▲ You can pitch a tent on the beach under a star-crowded sky, or find a shady tree (though they are rare in these parts) for protection against the blazing sun. This is a wonderful place to camp for a day or two. After that, the barren landscape becomes tiresome and monotonous. Tent camping allowed. A state permit is required.

**KOKEE STATE PARK** 🚶 💧 This spectacular park, high in the mountains above Waimea Canyon, is a mecca for hikers, campers and other outdoor enthusiasts. Sprawling across 4345 heavily wooded acres, this rugged country offers a unique perspective on the Garden Isle. In the rivers there's excellent freshwater angling for rainbow trout during August and September; a state license is required, though. Kokee has everything but a grocery store, so come well-stocked or plan to eat at the lodge restaurant (breakfast and lunch only; 808-335-6061). There is seasonal plum picking, and pig, goat and deer hunting is allowed in the public hunting and fishing areas. The lodge (808-335-6061) also has a museum and gift shop. Nearby are cabins, restrooms, showers, a picnic area and hiking trails. ~ Take Kaumualii Highway to Waimea, then pick up Waimea Canyon Drive from Waimea or Kokee Road from Kekaha. They eventually join and lead about 15 miles up to the park. Contact the park at 808-335-9975, fax 808-335-6131; www.aloha.net/~kokee, e-mail kokee@aloha.net.

▲ An area at the north end of the park has been allocated for tent camping. There are also several wilderness camps along the hiking trails. A state permit is required for nonwilderness camping.

▼▼▼▼▼▼▼▼▼▼▼▼▼▼

**Wailua–Kapaa Area**     If Lihue is the commercial center of Kauai, Wailua is the cultural heart of the island. Here along the Wailua River, the only navigable river in Hawaii, the *alii* built *heiau* and perpetuated their princely lines. There are broad surfing beaches here as well as cascades and grottos up along the Wailua River. What attracted Hawaiian royalty to Kauai's east coast was the weather along this windward shore, cooler in the summer than the baking sands of Poipu but not as moist as the tropical rainforests to the north. The Hawaiian nobility added fishponds and coconut groves to these natural features and forbade commoners from entering their domain. The oral tradition they handed down tells of a Tahitian holy man named Puna, one of the first Polynesians to arrive in Hawaii, who chose this sacred spot to live. Other legends recount the lost tribe of Mu, a pre-Polynesian people, dwarfish and cruel, who inhabited caves far up the Wailua River.

Developed as a resort destination before Poipu and Princeville, this area has nevertheless avoided the overdevelopment that plagues other parts of the island. Wailua and Kapaa, while hosting a string of oceanfront condominiums, remain working-class towns, maintaining a contemporary version of the cultural pride of the ancient *alii*.

**SIGHTS**     **Lydgate Park**, at the confluence of the Wailua River and the ocean, is the center of sacred Kauai. The *alii* established the rocky remains of the **Hauola Place of Refuge** on this site. Here *kapu* breakers under sentence of death could flee; once inside its perimeter, their crimes were absolved. A stone retaining wall also marks the ancient **Hikina a ka la Heiau**. The **petroglyphs** etched in the rocks at the mouth of the river can be seen at low tide. Near the entrance to the marina you'll find the **Malae Heiau**. It is easy to see why this area was sacred to ancient Hawaiians—the serenity is palpable, the beauty extraordinary. ~ Kuhio Highway, Wailua.

On the other side of Route 56 you can step from the sacred to the profane. Billing itself as "Kauai's best-kept secret," **Smith's Tropical Paradise** has elements of the classic tourist trap. Covering 30 riverside acres is a series of gardens and mock Pacific villages in the form of a tropical theme park. There are hibiscus, bamboo and Japanese gardens as well as re-creations of life in Polynesia, the Philippines and elsewhere. Budding botanists will enjoy the labeled plants and trees. On Monday, Wednesday and Friday, they have a luau and show. Admission. ~ Wailua Marina State Park, Wailua; 808-821-6895, fax 808-822-4520; www.smiths kauai.com, e-mail smiths@aloha.net.

Fittingly, the adjacent marina is the departure point for boat trips up the Wailua River to **Fern Grotto**. The scenery along the way is magnificent as you pass along a tropical riverfront that is luxuriously overgrown. The grotto itself is a 40-foot cavern draped with feathery ferns, a place so beautiful and romantic that many people choose to marry here. But the boat ride is one of the most cloyingly commercial experiences in Hawaii, a 20-minute voyage during which you are crowded together with legions of tourists and led in chants by a narrator with an amplifier. Admission. ~ 808-821-6892, fax 808-822-4520; www.smithskauai.com, e-mail smiths@aloha.net.

For those not interested in joining in on this tourist institution, you can rent a kayak and paddle yourself upriver to the grotto.

Movie buffs should take note when passing along Route 56. The large abandoned complex surrounded by a beautiful stand of palm trees is the **Coco Palms**. This resort, the first constructed on Kauai, was built around a coconut grove planted in the 1800s by a German immigrant; the area around the resort was home to Kauai's Queen Kapule in the mid-1800s. The final 20 minutes of *Blue Hawaii*, Elvis' last movie, were filmed here. Some scenes

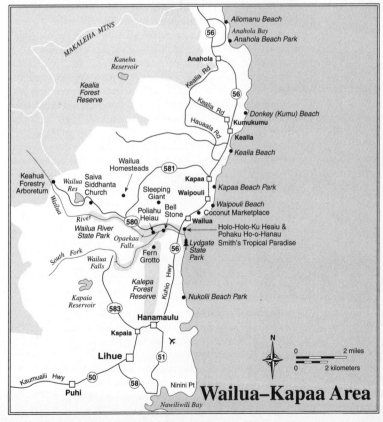

**Wailua–Kapaa Area**

from *South Pacific* and *Miss Sadie Thompson* were also filmed here, and for "Fantasy Island" viewers, this is where Tatoo goes zipping by in his jeep. In fact, Hollywood was drawn to this location numerous times. However, it has stood empty since September 1992, when Hurricane Iniki ravaged the resort. Renovation plans are in the works.

Take a detour onto Kuamoo Road (Route 580). This road courses through Kauai's most historic region, the domain of ancient Hawaiian royalty. Watch for Hawaii Visitors Bureau signs pointing out the **Holo-Holo-Ku Heiau**, one of the oldest temples on the island, a place where human sacrifices were performed. A short distance uphill, you'll find a small but interesting **Japanese cemetery**. Ironically, this is also the site of **Pohaku-Ho-o-Hanau**, a sacred spot where royal women came to give birth.

As you continue up Route 580, the lush Wailua Valley opens to view. On the left along the hilltop rest the rocky remains of **Poliahu Heiau**, purportedly used by Kauai's King Kaumualii. A short path leads down to the **Bell Stone**, which resounded when struck with a rock, loudly signaling the birth of royal infants. All these places, vital to Hawaii's past, were located along the old King's Highway, a sacred thoroughfare used only by island rulers.

*HIDDEN ►*

For vivid mountain scenery, continue on Route 580 past the 40-foot, multi-cascade **Opaekaa Falls** (a path along the highway brings you to a great viewpoint). The road then proceeds past **Wailua Homesteads**, what used to be a ranch and farm region filled with fruit orchards, pastures and vegetable fields but is now rapidly becoming residential.

*HIDDEN ►*

A detour off of Kuamoo Road takes you to a cultural experience unique in Kauai—the **Saiva Siddhanta Church**, the Hindu monastery in Wailua. The Kadavul Hindu Temple is open mornings between 9 and 11:30 a.m., and tours are offered weekly. Currently, the Iraivan Temple—the first all-stone, hand-carved, granite Agamic temple ever built in the West—is under construction there. ~ Located about four miles up Kuamoo Road (Route 580) at 107 Kaholalele Road; 808-822-3012 (tour information); www.gurudeva.org, e-mail iraivan@hindu.org.

*sights*

**AUTHOR FAVORITE**

The original town of Anahola was along the coast. Here a beautiful white strand curves along Anahola Bay, a prime beachcombing area. (See "Beaches & Parks" below.) On the far side of the bay is **Aliomanu Beach**, a beach shaded by ironwood trees and fringed by one of Kauai's longest reefs. (See "Beaches & Parks" below.) These are favorite local haunts.

Route 580 ends at **Keahua Forestry Arboretum**, where hiking trails wind through groves of painted gum trees. The adjoining state forest climbs all the way to one of Kauai's tallest peaks **Mount Waialeale** (5208 feet), although no trails lead there. The mountain has an annual rainfall of more than 400 inches.

Back on Route 56, as the road dips down into **Kapaa,** you'll be passing from one Hawaiian era to another. At one time Kapaa was a center for rice cultivation. Later came sugar. Now this 19th-century town, with its falsefront stores and second-story balconies, is home to everyday folks. This is where the local plumber, carpenter and fisherman live. The population is Japanese, Hawaiian, Caucasian, Filipino and Chinese. They reside in small plantation houses and attend the local churches that dot the surrounding countryside.

The **Hawaiian Museum** is administered by Serge Kahili King, a local teacher of *huna*, the ancient Polynesian tenet reminiscent of today's New Age principles. After gaining shaman status at age 14, King traveled extensively through Africa, Asia and the Americas, bringing back to Kauai not only his techniques for spiritual growth but an enviable collection of artifacts and art. You'll find statues of Hawaiian gods, tools such as poi pounders, African dance masks and a Maori war club. The museum is open by appointment only, but they insist this can be "anytime." *Huna* workshops and discussions are also held here, at the heart of the *huna* movement. ~ 4504 Kukui Street, Suite 11, Kapaa; 808-823-8381; www.huna.org, e-mail huna@huna.org.

◀ *HIDDEN*

In its northerly course between Wailua and Kapaa, Kuhio Highway (Route 56) passes the **Coconut Marketplace** with its sprawling shopping mall and grove of royal palm trees.

From Kapaa, there's an excellent view of the **Sleeping Giant,** a recumbent figure naturally hewn out of the nearby mountain range. Follow the highway and you'll arrive at a curving ribbon of sand known as **Kealia Beach.** Across the road are a store and post office. These clapboard buildings represent in its entirety the tiny town of **Kealia.** From Kealia, the Kuhio Highway climbs and turns inland through sugar cane fields and continues through the town of **Anahola,** a small Hawaiian homestead settlement.

◀ *HIDDEN*

**LODGING**

**Rosewood** exudes cheerfulness, charm and high standards, making this Wailua Homesteads bed and breakfast a reliable choice. Units include a Victorian cottage, rooms in the main house and a secluded thatched cottage. A bunkhouse, which has private sleeping lofts and shared toilets and showers, is a super budget option. Hardwood floors, color-washed walls, quality linens, nice landscaping with old shade trees and a lily pond, along with delightful outdoor showers, are just a few of the highlights. All room options come with kitchens or kitchenettes. There's also a common room with internet access. A breakfast basket comes with the more expensive units, or daily breakfast is served in the main house for an extra charge. Rosewood is set in a rural area, with mountain views and sheep grazing across the road, but there is some traffic noise. Not totally secluded, it's located three miles from the east side, beaches and restaurants. ~ 872 Kamalu Road, Wailua; 808-822-5216, fax 808-822-5478; www.rosewoodkauai. com, e-mail rosewood@aloha.net. BUDGET TO DELUXE.

The **Kauai Sands Hotel** costs a little more, but it's still a bargain. This beachfront accommodation is part of the only hotel chain in the world owned by a Hawaiian family, the Kimis. You'll find a relaxed and spacious lobby, restaurant, two pools, a well-tended lawn, carpeting, a lanai, imaginative decor and a touch of Hawaiiana. Ask about discounts. ~ 420 Papaloa Road near the Coconut Marketplace, Wailua; 808-822-4951, 800-560-5553, fax 808-822-0978; www.kauaisandshotel.com. MODERATE TO DELUXE.

**HIDDEN ►**    **Rainbows End**, a classic restored plantation cottage, has romance written all over it. Set in a secluded rural area near the hosts' home, it has special features like floors with inlaid mahogany, cozy country-decor furnishings, extra thick towels, a clawfoot whirlpool tub and an enclosed outdoor shower. It's a one-bedroom place with a kitchenette, as well as a futon in the living room for extra guests. Amenities include cable TV, VCR, videos, books, beach equipment and good information about nearby trails and activities. Breakfasts include fruit grown on-site. Gay-friendly. ~ 6470 Kipapa Road, Kapaa; 808-823-0066, fax 808-823-0071; www.rainbowsendkauai.com, e-mail info@ rainbowsendkauai.com. MODERATE.

To get any closer to the water than the **Hotel Coral Reef**, you'd have to pitch a tent in the sand. Located on Kuhio Highway in Kapaa, it's within strolling distance of markets and restaurants and is an excellent choice for the wanderer without

### THE VILLAGE THAT TIME FORGOT

The **Kamokila Hawaiian Village** is so isolated, it appears to have been carved out of the surrounding tropical labyrinth. The re-created village evokes authentic early Hawaii with food- and craft-making demonstrations. Self-guided tours will take you through the paces of ancient Hawaiian life, including an assembly hall, birthing house, chief's quarters, cooking pit and athletic ground. It's also the site of a decidedly contemporary obsession: movie making. *Outbreak*, starring Dustin Hoffman and Morgan Freeman, for example, was filmed here. Closed Sunday. Admission. ~ 6060 Kuamoo Road, off Route 580, just past the Wailua Bridge across from Opaekaa Falls; 808-823-0559.

wheels. A floral garden leads out to a comfortable strip of sand next to Kapaa Beach Park. In this beachfront building you can enjoy a touch of wood paneling, soft beds, refrigerator and a delightful seascape just beyond those sliding glass doors. A second building offers rooms with fans and ocean views. ~ 1516 Kuhio Highway, Kapaa; 808-822-4481, 800-843-4659, fax 808-822-7705; www.hotelcoralreef.com, e-mail hotel.coralreef@gte.net. MODERATE TO DELUXE.

The **Kauai International Hostel** has both dormitory and private rooms at low prices. Facilities, as you might expect, are spartan. There's a scruffy yard with two buildings; guests share a television room, a kitchen, a washer/dryer and a pool table. Like hostels everywhere, it's a good deal for the dollar. ~ 4532 Lehua Street, Kapaa; 808-823-6142. BUDGET.

**GAY LODGING**    There are four comfortable, airy guest rooms at the gay-friendly bed and breakfast **Mohala Ke Ola**. It's situated near the river from Opaekaa Falls and offers grand views of Mount Waialeale and Secret Falls. Amenities include a pool and jacuzzi; continental breakfast served on the deck. ~ 5663 Ohelo Road, Kapaa; 808-823-6398, 888-465-2824; www.waterfallbnb.com, e-mail kauaibb@aloha.net. MODERATE TO DELUXE.

Looking like it has been lifted straight out of the Japanese countryside, **Mahina Kai Ocean Villa** has a Japanese garden and teahouse to match. Three suites and one single guest room are fitted with kimono quilts and shoji screen doors and share a kitchen; a cottage includes a kitchenette. There's an indoor pond and a pool as well as an ocean view from this two-acre property. ~ 4933 Aliomanu Road, Anahola; 808-822-9451, 800-337-1134; www.mahinakai.com, e-mail reservations@mahinakai.com. ULTRA-DELUXE.

**Kaha Lani** isn't a place you'd find unless you were looking for it, making these isolated condominiums, perfect for a quiet retreat. Families will also enjoy the property's proximity to Lydgate State Park, with its child-designed Kamalani playground and protected *keiki* pools along the water. The comfy condos have well-equipped kitchens, and most are demurely decorated in a muted tropical theme. (They are individually owned, so the decor varies.) One-bedroom units start at $225; two bedrooms start at $325. ~ 4460 Nehe Road, Wailua; 808-822-9331, 800-922-7866, fax 808-822-2828.

**CONDOS**

**Wailua Bay View** offers one-bedroom apartments, $125 for up to four people; three-night minimum stay. Ocean view. ~ 320 Papaloa Road, Kapaa; 808-245-4711, 800-767-4707, fax 808-245-8115; www.prosserrealty.net, e-mail holiday@prosserrealty.net.

Studio apartments at **Kapaa Sands Resort** are $110 single or double, $128 for an oceanfront unit. Two-bedroom apartments,

$147 (one to four people); $168 for an oceanfront location. ~ 380 Papaloa Road, Kapaa; 808-822-4901, 800-222-4901, fax 808-822-1556; www.kapaasands.com.

The **Kauai Coast Resort** is another appealing place. Located behind the Coconut Marketplace, it's popular with swimmers and shoppers alike. You'll find a pool, a spa, a fitness center and tennis courts amid the central grounds, plus a windswept lobby with adjoining restaurant. For pleasant surroundings near the center of the action, it's definitely among the area's top choices. All the condominiums are air-conditioned and include TVs, full kitchens, washer/dryers and lanais. Studios start at $195; one-bedroom units start at $255 per night; and two-bedroom units start at $330. The decor is quite tasteful, and the rates, considering the amenities, are reasonable. ~ 520 Aleka Loop, Kapaa; 808-822-3441, 877-977-4355, fax 808-822-0843; www.kauaicoastresort.com.

> To ease the congestion through Kapaa, the Kapaa Bypass Road was built. Pick it up just before the Coconut Plantation in Wailua. It takes you to the north side of Kapaa, cutting through fields behind town.

**Mokihana of Kauai** has studio apartments that run $65 single or double. These units are supplied with a hotplate and small refrigerator. ~ 796 Kuhio Highway, Kapaa; 808-822-3971, fax 808-822-7387.

**Kauai Kailani** features two-bedroom apartments, $75 for up to four people; $7.50 for each extra person. This offers a lot of square footage for the money, but there's one catch—reservations are difficult to obtain and should be made a year in advance. Three-night minimum. ~ 856 Kuhio Highway, Kapaa; 808-822-3391, fax 808-822-7387.

**DINING**

**HIDDEN** ►

Never mind the stark setting of fluorescent lighting and booths with formica-topped tables, the food at **Korean BBQ** is good, plentiful and cheap. Of course, they offer a variety of Korean dishes such as fish *jun*, barbecue chicken or beef, cold noodles with mixed veggies and soups. You can substitute tofu for many of the meat dishes. Eat in or take-out. ~ 4-356 Kuhio Highway (Kinipopo Shopping Village), Wailua; 808-823-6744. BUDGET.

Antique Japanese screens set the theme at **Restaurant Kintaro**, where you can dine at the sushi bar or enjoy *teppanyaki*-style cooking. If you decide on the latter, choose between filet mignon, shrimp, scallops, steak teriyaki or oysters sautéed with olive oil. They also prepare traditional tempura and yakitori dinners as well as *yosenabe* (Japanese bouillabaisse). Closed Sunday. ~ 4-370 Kuhio Highway, Wailua; 808-822-3341, fax 808-822-2153. DELUXE.

There are short-order stands galore at the Coconut Marketplace. **Harley's Ribs-'n-Chicken** delivers what its name promises.

~ 808-822-2505. The **Fish Hut** lives up to its name. ~ 808-821-0033. You'll never guess what they serve at **Aloha Kauai Pizza**. ~ 808-822-4511. Any time from early morning until 8 or 9 p.m., several of these stands will be open. An interesting way to dine here is by going from one to the next, nibbling small portions along the way. ~ 4-484 Kuhio Highway, Wailua. BUDGET.

A favorite breakfast institution, **Eggbert's** is a perfect place for people watching. Try the hotcakes with coconut syrup, or the sour-cream-and-chives omelette. Lunch offerings are mainly sandwiches and salads, while dinner choices include steak, meatloaf, pork and chicken; the stir-fry is a good vegetarian option. No dinner on Sunday. ~ Coconut Marketplace, 4-484 Kuhio Highway, Wailua; 808-822-3787, fax 808-822-2012. MODERATE.

If cost is a consideration, stop by **Waipouli Deli & Restaurant**, located next to Blockbuster and behind McDonald's, for supercheap and decent local-style food. The stark decor is a bit gritty and uninspired, but you can fill up on *saimin*, various fried meats, eggs and rice without running up a large tab. Closed Monday. ~ Waipouli Town Center, 4-771 Kuhio Highway, Kapaa; 808-822-9311. BUDGET.

◀ HIDDEN

For a light, healthful meal, you can cross the street to **Papaya's Natural Foods**. This takeout counter with outdoor tables has pasta, pizza, sandwiches, vegetable stir-fry, grilled fish and salads. Papaya's also caters to vegetarians and vegans. Closed Sunday. ~ Kauai Village Shopping Center, 4-831 Kuhio Highway, Kapaa; 808-823-0191, fax 808-823-0756. BUDGET.

Thai restaurants have mushroomed in Kapaa, but old-timer **King and I** is still the best bet. The small, pink dining room is decorated with ornate Thai art and cascading orchids. The food is reliably good, with lots of vegetarian choices. Try the garlic eggplant, pungent green papaya salad, *pad thai* noodles and curries. Black rice pudding is a must for dessert. ~ 4-901 Kuhio Highway (Waipouli Plaza), Kapaa; 808-822-1642. MODERATE.

It's beef, beef and beef at **The Bull Shed**. We're talking about prime rib, beef kebab, top sirloin, garlic tenderloin and teriyaki steak. All this in a casual restaurant that's so close to the surf your feet feel wet. Speaking of surf, they also serve lobster, broiled shrimp, Alaskan king crab and fresh fish. Dinner only. ~ 796 Kuhio Highway, Kapaa; 808-822-3791, fax 808-822-4041. MODERATE TO DELUXE.

When nothing will do but a hearty, old-fashioned breakfast, **Kountry Kitchen** also delivers the goods. Booths line the place, which strives for an old-fashioned coffee shop look, and it's been around long enough to carry it off. Lunch is sandwiches, burgers, salads and other simple fare. Breakfast and lunch only. ~ 1485 Kuhio Highway, Kapaa; 808-822-3511. BUDGET.

In the center of Kapaa, there's a restaurant known to Mexican food aficionados for miles around. **Norberto's El Café** draws a hungry crowd of young locals for dinner. The owners raise a lot of their own vegetables, and they serve monstrous portions. If you're not hungry, order à la carte or one of the smaller dinners. If you are, choose from a solid menu ranging from enchiladas (including Hawaiian taro-leaf enchiladas) to burritos to chiles rellenos. Children's portions are available and all meals can be converted to cater to vegetarians. Definitely worth checking out. Dinner only. Closed Sunday. ~ 4-1373 Kuhio Highway, Kapaa; 808-822-3362. MODERATE.

*HIDDEN* ►  A breakfast jewel is **Ono Family Restaurant,** which offers a more exotic take on the day's main meal. Fried rice with *kim chee* omelettes are balanced by simpler selections. Lunch centers around sandwiches (cod, egg salad) and burgers (bacon, chili). Plate lunches and stir-fry are also on the menu. Their coconut syrup and pineapple/papaya jam can be bought here, too. ~ 1292 Kuhio Highway, Kapaa; 808-822-1710, fax 808-823-8784. BUDGET.

**Mema Thai Cuisine** is slightly overpriced, but the food, a mix of Thai and Chinese, is pretty good. The ambience here is casual, although the silk-clad waitstaff glide around elegantly. No lunch on Saturday and Sunday. ~ 4-369 Kuhio Highway, Kapaa; 808-823-0899. MODERATE.

In north Kapaa, **The Shack** serves up burgers, sandwiches and salads, but the sports bar atmosphere, live music, big-screen TV and games seem to be a bigger draw than the rather uninspired menu. Still, it's cheap and open until midnight, making it a good choice for a simple or late meal. ~ 1394 Kuhio Highway, Kapaa; 808-823-0200. MODERATE.

The local crowds attest to the quality and value at **Mermaid's Café.** Serving lunch and dinner, this tiny place offers vegan and vegetarian choices as well as wraps, burritos, and chicken satay and curry plates. The menu favorite, an ahi nori wrap, contains

**AUTHOR FAVORITE** 🍽

Some of the best hamburgers on the island are found at **Duane's Ono Char-Burger**, a wood-planked burger stand next to the Anahola Post Office. Cheddar, mushrooms, bleu cheese and pineapple are some of the toppings heaped onto the thick patties. The juicy teriyaki burger is an island favorite. Don't feel like ground beef? You can also opt for a veggie burger, broiled chicken or fried fish. To round off your meal, order a fruit shake and a side of crispy fries. ~ 4-4350 Kuhio Highway, Anahola; 808-822-9181. BUDGET.

local tuna. ~ 4-1384 Kuhio Highway, Kapaa; 808-821-2026.
BUDGET TO MODERATE.

Portions are hearty at the **Olympic Café**, which looks out    ◄ *HIDDEN*
right on the main Kapaa drag, making it a great place to people
watch. The food is high-quality and well-prepared: tasty egg dishes,
omelettes and pancakes for breakfast; a choice of big salads, sandwiches and burgers for lunch. Or try one of the Mexican entrées,
like burritos. Juices, coffee drinks and drinks from the full bar
soothe parched throats. The open-front dining room is casual and
has views of the ocean and mountains. ~ 4-1354 Kuhio Highway,
Kapaa; 808-822-5825. BUDGET.

There are two major grocery stores in the Wailua–Kapaa area.    **GROCERIES**
Try **Foodland** in the Waipouli Town Center. ~ Kapaa; 808-822-
7271. Or shop at **Safeway**. ~ Kauai Village Shopping Center, Kapaa; 808-822-2464. There's a **Big Save Market** at the Kapaa Shopping Center. ~ 1105-F Kuhio Highway; 808-822-4971.

To the north is the **Whaler's General Store**. This well-stocked
market is the largest store between Kapaa and Princeville. ~ 4-
4350 Kuhio Highway, Anahola; 808-822-5818.

In the Kinipopo Shopping Village, **Tin Can Mailman** (808-822-    **SHOPPING**
3009) specializes in new, used and rare books, particularly Pacific Island titles. It is also rich in stamps, maps, tapa cloth and
botanical prints. Closed Sunday. ~ 4-356 Kuhio Highway, Wailua.

For campy antiques, "tropical wear" plus new and vintage
clothing, try **Bambulei,** hidden behind the Wailua Shopping Plaza.
If Hawaiiana from the 1950s appeals to you, this is the place for
a little treasure hunting. Be careful: Two cottages filled to the rim
with funky knickknacks may make you forget the beach. ~ 4-
369D Kuhio Highway, Wailua; 808-823-8641.

The **Coconut Marketplace** is a theme mall that consists of
wooden stores designed to resemble little plantation houses. For
decor you'll find the pipes, valves, gears and waterwheels characteristic of every tropical plantation. This is a good place for
clothing, curios, jewelry, toys, Asian imports and T-shirts. If you
don't want to buy, you can always browse or have a snack at the
many short-order stands here. ~ 4-484 Kuhio Highway, Wailua;
808-822-3641.

Two galleries within the Marketplace are worthy of note.
**Kahn Galleries** (808-822-3636) features locally and internationally known artists. Focusing on Hawaiian seascapes and landscapes, the gallery offers work by Roy Tabora. Also consider
**Ship Store Galleries** (808-822-7758) and its antiques, weapons
and maritime themed paintings by an eclectic group of artists.
**Overboard** (808-822-1777), also in the Coconut Marketplace,

has aloha shirts and other Hawaiian wear. ~ 4-484 Kuhio Highway, Wailua.

**Kauai Village Shopping Center,** a multi-store complex in the center of Kapaa, is another of Kauai's shopping destinations. Anchored by a grocery store, it features a string of small shops.

> The largest of Kauai's towns—population wise—Kapaa has a real local feel to it.

**Hula Girl** sells clothing and gifts for the entire family. Their focus is Hawaiiana, with a great selection of bowls, books and prints. ~ 4-1340 Kuhio Highway, Kapaa; 808-822-1950.

Talk about unusual. **Island Hemp & Cotton** specializes in things made from the "evil" weed. There's an attractive line of women's clothing here, not to mention soap, paper, and body lotion, all fabricated from hemp. ~ 4-1373 Kuhio Highway, Kapaa; 808-821-0225.

**NIGHTLIFE**    If your image of the perfect paradise vacation includes tropical drinks, you're in for a treat at the **Lizard Lounge.** The place is on the funky side but the drinks are delicious and the mood festive. You can play darts, watch the game and gnaw on buffalo wings while you sip one of thirty beers. ~ Waipouli Town Center, 4-771 Kuhio Highway, Kapaa; 808-821-2205.

**BEACHES & PARKS**    **NUKOLII BEACH PARK** Located adjacent to the Outrigger Kauai Hilton Hotel, this is a long narrow strand with a shallow bottom. From the park, the beach extends for several miles all the way to Lydgate Park in Wailua. One of the island's prettiest beaches, it provides an opportunity to use the park facilities or to escape to more secluded sections (adjacent to Wailua Golf Course). A dirt road parallels the beach north of the park for about a half-mile, but if you seek seclusion, just start hiking farther north along the shore. You'll find places galore for water sports. Swimming is good in well-protected and shallow waters. Snorkelers will be content swimming among reefs and there are good surf breaks on the shallow reef at "Graveyards." Fishing is best near the reefs. ~ Located at the end of Kauai Beach Drive. To reach the more secluded sections, go north from Lihue on Kuhio Highway and take a right onto the road that runs along the southern end of the Wailua Golf Course. This paved road rapidly becomes a dirt strip studded with potholes. Driving slowly, proceed a quarter-mile, then take the first left turn. It's another quarter-mile to the beach; when the road forks, take either branch.

**LYDGATE BEACH AND LYDGATE PARK** The awesome ironwood grove and long stretches of rugged coastline make this one of Kauai's loveliest parks. Near the Wailua River, it is also one of the most popular. The Hauola Place of Refuge and other sacred sites are located within the state park. (See "Sights" above for more information.) Two large lava pools, one perfect for kids and the other protecting swimmers and snorkelers, make it a great place to spend the day. Surfers must take a long paddle out to breaks off the mouth of Wailua River. There's a right slide. This park is also favored by windsurfers. *Ulua* is the most common catch. You'll find a picnic area, showers, restrooms, a playground and lifeguards. With kids in tow, Kamalani Playground in Lydgate Park offers a distracting alternative to making sandcastles. ~ From Kuhio Highway, turn toward the beach at Leho Drive, the road just south of the Wailua River.

**WAILUA RIVER STATE PARK** Home to the famous Fern Grotto, this small park features sacred historic sites and breathtaking views of river and mountains. It also has a marina and is the launching point for motorized and kayaking tours up the famous river, which is billed as the only truly navigable waterway on the island. In addition, waterskiing is allowed and canoe clubs practice here. There are lots of shady areas and picnic tables. Although the park is public, boat companies pay to maintain the landing at Fern Grotto upriver, which is technically off-limits to kayakers. Restrooms are available here. ~ Take Route 56 to Kuamoo Road (Route 580).

**WAILUA BEACH** One of east Kauai's nicest and most accessible stretches of broad sand, Wailua Beach is perfect for sunbathing and beachwalking. Conditions can be treacherous for swimming, however, because the frequently blowing trade winds often create rough waters and the Wailua River empties into the ocean here. In rainy weather, the river often creates a strong current at the south end of the beach. Boogieboarders challenge the waves here, and a hot surf break known as "Horner's" is found at the northern end of the beach. Children gravitate toward the river area. A lifeguard is on limited duty but there are minimal facilities. The best parking is near the Wailua Bridge. ~ This beach, near the Coco Palms Resort, is easily accessed only when traveling north on Kuhio Highway.

**WAIPOULI BEACH** The longest, narrowest strip of sand on the eastside begins behind the Coconut Marketplace shopping center and ends about two miles down the road at Waikaea Canal in Kapaa. Even though many condos and resorts border this beach, it isn't that crowded and it's easy to find lots of hidden coves. The ocean in this area is usually rough, and most of the coastline is either beachrock or reef. Swimming is not recommended. Fishermen are common here, pole fishing or hunting octopus in the sand. About midway along this stretch is a protected shallow section in the reef known as "Baby Beach," because many families come here with small children. No facilities except at the boat-launching area near the canal, where you'll find restrooms and pavilions, and often some hard-drinking locals just hanging out. There's a nice trail for getting your exercise biking or walking along Waipouli Beach. ~ The beach can be accessed at a number of points behind Coconut Marketplace and along the shoreline road that runs parallel to Kuhio Highway, a few blocks *makai* (toward the ocean).

Monk seals, one of two species of tropical seals left, sometimes snooze in the sand at Waipouli Beach; don't disturb their naps!

**KAPAA BEACH PARK** 🏊 While it sports an attractive little beach, this 15-acre facility doesn't measure up to its neighbors. Located a block from the highway as the road passes through central Kapaa, the park is flanked by ramshackle houses and a local playing field. The area has a picnic area with barbecue pits and restrooms. Swimming and fishing are only fair, but there is good squidding and torchfishing. ~ Located a block from Kuhio Highway, Kapaa.

**KEALIA BEACH** 🏊 This strand is one of those neighbors that makes Kapaa Beach the pimply kid next door: It's a wide, magnificent beach curving for about a half-mile along Kuhio Highway. The swimming is good, but requires caution. Surfing and bodysurfing can be found at the north end of the beach. Fish here for *papio*, threadfin and *ulua*. There are no facilities. ~ Located on Kuhio Highway, Kealia.

HIDDEN ▶ **DONKEY BEACH OR KUMU BEACH** 🏊 This broad, curving beach is flanked by a grassy meadow and towering ironwoods. Favored as a hideaway and nude beach by locals, it's a gem that should not be overlooked. Also note that the two-mile stretch from here north to Anahola is lined by low sea cliffs that open onto at least four pocket beaches. This entire area is popular with beachcombers, who sometimes find hand-blown Japanese glass fishing balls. Swimmers, take care: currents here can be treacherous and the nearest lifeguard is a world away. Surfers get their kicks at Donkey Beach, or try "14 Crack" just north of the beach. Anglers frequent this beach for pole-fishing and throw-netting. There are no facilities here. ~ Follow Kuhio Highway north from Kealia. At the 11-mile marker the road begins to climb slowly, then descends. At the end of the descent, just before 12-mile marker, there is a parking area and a path to the beach.

▲ Unofficial camping is common.

HIDDEN ▶ **ANAHOLA BEACH PARK** 🏊 A slender ribbon of sand curves along windswept Anahola Bay. At the south end, guarded by ironwood trees, lies this pretty little park. Very popular with neighborhood residents, this is a prime beachcombing spot where you may find Japanese glass fishing balls. There is a protecting reef here; but as elsewhere, use caution swimming because of the strong currents. Snorkeling is good behind the reef. Surfers have a long paddle out to summer and winter breaks along the reef (left and right slides). There is a break called "Unreals" offshore from the old landing. This is also a popular bodysurfing beach. There's good torchfishing for lobsters, and anglers often catch *papio*, rudderfish, *ulua*, threadfin, bonefish and big-eyed scad. Facilities include a picnic area, restrooms, showers and limited lifeguard duty. ~ Turn onto Anahola Road from Kuhio Highway in Anahola; follow it three-quarters of a mile, then turn onto a dirt road that forks left to the beach.

▲ You can pitch a tent on the grassy area near the beach; county permit required.

**ALIOMANU BEACH** 🏊 ⚓ On the far side of Anahola Bay, separated from the park by a lagoon, sits another sandy beach. Shady ironwood trees, several roadside houses and a picnic table dot this area, which is a favorite among locals. What makes Aliomanu particularly popular is the offshore reef, one of Kauai's longest and widest fringing reefs. This is an excellent area for gathering edible seaweed. Swimming is fairly safe in the lagoon but use caution seaside. Local residents spear octopus and go torchfishing here. ~ Turn off Kuhio Highway onto Aliomanu Road just past Anahola.

◄ HIDDEN

## North Shore

It is no accident that when it came time to choose a location for Bali Hai, the producers of *South Pacific* ended their search on the North Shore of Kauai. The most beautiful place in Hawaii, indeed one of the prettiest places on earth, this 30-mile stretch of lace-white surf and emerald-green mountains became Hollywood's version of paradise.

Backdropping this thin line of civilization is the Na Pali Coast. Here, sharp sea cliffs vault thousands of feet from the ocean, silver waterfalls streaming along their fluted surfaces. There are pocket beaches ringed by menacing rock formations and long, wide strands as inviting as a warm tub.

The North Shore is wet and tropical, drawing enough precipitation to dampen the enthusiasm of many tourists. It is suited for travelers who don't mind a little rain on their parade if it carries with it rainbows and seabirds and a touch of magic in the air.

**SIGHTS**

You might want to begin your introduction to the North Shore at the **Guava Kai Plantation**, which offers 480 acres that produce more than half of Hawaii's guava crop, making them the largest producer in the country. The guava was introduced to Hawaii in the late 1700s and now grows wild throughout the islands. The fruit at Guava Kai Plantation is hand-picked. The visitors center, which also sports a snack shop, will give you taste of guava products. There's a self-guided tour of the guava-juicing process. Bring a picnic and follow the short path leading past tropical plants and a pond to a pretty picnic area. ~ 4900 Kuawa Road, Kilauea; 808-828-6121, fax 808-828-1880; e-mail info@guavakai.com.

Kilauea itself is a former sugar town with a cluster of stores and a couple of noteworthy churches. The cottages that once housed plantation workers are freshly painted and decorated with flowering gardens and the place possesses an air of humble well-being.

The Christ Memorial Episcopal Church is an ideal spot for reflection. The beautiful building was consecrated in 1941. It's built out of lava stone and has stained-glass windows imported from England. ~ Kilauea Road, Kilauea; 808-826-4510.

Another chance for history cum meditation is St. Sylvester's Roman Catholic Church, an octagonal building containing works by Jean Charlot, a local artist. The church was constructed, in part, to illustrate the importance of art to the Catholic religion. ~ Kilauea Road, Kilauea; 808-822-7900, fax 808-822-3014.

HIDDEN ▶

Along the North Shore, humankind is a bit player in the natural drama being presented here. To take in that scene, you need venture no farther than Kilauea Point National Wildlife Refuge. Here on Kilauea Point, a lofty peninsula that falls away into precipitous rockfaces, you'll have the same bird's-eye view of the spectacular coastline as the boobies, tropicbirds, albatross and frigate birds. As you stand along this lonely point, gazing upon the ocean and along the cliffs, birds—graceful, sleek, exotic ones—swarm like bees. A vital rookery, the refuge is also frequented by Hawaiian monk seals and green turtles, as well as occasional whales and dolphins. Offshore is Mokuaeae Island, a state bird preserve. Admission. ~ End of Kilauea Road, Kilauea; 808-828-1413, fax 808-828-6634.

Counterpoint to this natural pageant is the Kilauea Lighthouse, a 52-foot-high beacon built in 1913 that bears the world's largest clamshell-shaped lens. Capable of casting its light almost 100 miles, it is the first sign of land seen by mariners venturing east from Asia. This old lighthouse, now replaced by a more modern beacon, sits on the northernmost point of Kauai. People gather at the point for interpretive talks of the bird life and natural history of the region.

Along Route 56 you'll see Kalihiwai Bay. There's another (ho-hum) beautiful beach here, surrounded by ironwood trees. A sweeping but shallow lagoon has been formed by the Kalihiwai River. (See "Beaches & Parks" below for directions to Kalihiwai Beach.)

Civilization stakes its claim once again at Princeville, a one-time plantation named by R. C. Wyllie in honor of the son of Kamehameha IV and Queen Emma. This 11,000-acre planned resort community combines private homes, condominiums and the elegant Princeville Resort. Set along a luxurious plateau with

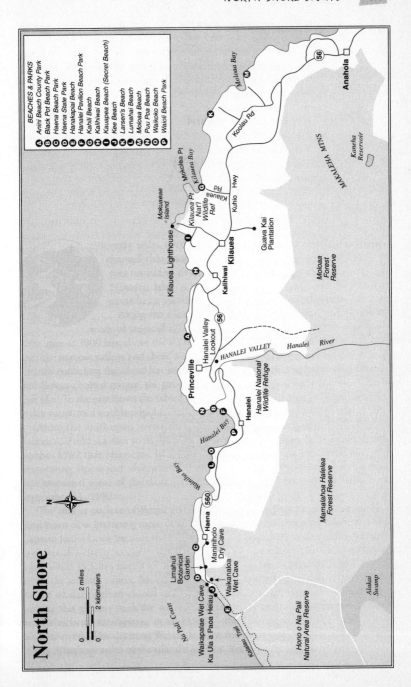

# North Shore

N

0       2 miles
0       2 kilometers

Na Pali Coast

Limahuli Botanical Garden

Maniniholo Dry Cave

Waikapalae Wet Cave

Ka Ula a Paoa Heiau

Waikanaloa Wet Cave

Kalalau Trail

Haena

560

Hono o Na Pali Natural Area Reserve

Makua Bay

Hanalei Bay

Princeville

Hanalei Valley Lookout

56

HANALEI VALLEY

Hanalei

Hanalei Bay

Hanalei National Wildlife Refuge

Hanalei River

Mamalahoa Halelea Forest Reserve

Alakai Swamp

Kilauea Lighthouse

Mokuaeae Island

Kilauea Pt Nat'l Wildlife Ref

Mokolea Pt

Kilauea Bay

Kilauea Rd

Kilauea

Kalihiwai

Kuhio Hwy

Guava Kai Plantation

Moloaa Forest Reserve

Koolau Rd

Moloaa Bay

MAKALEHA MTNS

Kameha Reservoir

56

Anahola

scintillating views of the Na Pali Coast, it is a tastefully designed complex complete with golf courses and acres of open space.

The adventurous might want to make the trek down to **Queen's Bath**, a large lava tidepool at the end of a slippery trail. ~ In Princeville, near the Pali Ke Kua condominium parking lot. There is a sign pointing to the trail.

These taro patches and surrounding wetlands comprise the 917-acre **Hanalei National Wildlife Refuge,** home to the Hawaiian duck, Hawaiian stilt, the Hawaiian coot and the Hawaiian moorhen, all of which are endangered. For a close-up version of this panorama, turn left onto Ohiki Road near the old bridge at the bottom of the hill. It will lead you back several eras to a region of terraced fields and simple homesteads. There is no parking or facilities.

**HIDDEN ▶**

In town, a combination of plantation-style buildings, dramatic mountain views and curving beaches creates a mystique that can only be described in a single word—**Hanalei**. It makes you wonder if heaven, in fact, is built of clapboard. The town is little more than a string of woodframe bungalows and falsefront stores lining the main road. On one side a half-moon bay, rimmed with white sand, curves out in two directions. Behind the town the *pali*, those awesome cliffs that fluctuate between dream and reality in the focus of the mind, form a frontier between Hanalei and the rest of the world.

The **Hanalei Pier**, on the National Register of Historic Places, was constructed in 1892. Although the pier has since been reinforced with concrete, it still adds a touch more romance to the already unreal seascape.

That little green-and-white church along the highway is the **Waioli Hulia Church,** part of the Waioli Mission, built in 1912. If you get a chance to go in, take a look at the beautiful stained-glass windows. ~ Kuhio Highway, Hanalei; 808-826-6253, fax 808-826-9625.

It's almost superfluous that the **Waioli Mission House,** built in 1836, provides glimpses of a bygone era: The entire town seems a reflection of its former self. But this one-time home of Abner and Lucy Wilcox, missionaries from New England, extends a special invitation to step back into the 19th century. A small but stately house, shiplap in design with a second-story lanai, it sits amid palm and *hala* trees on a broad lawn. The rooms look undisturbed since the days when the Wilcoxes prayed and proselytized. The china rests in the cupboard and an old rocker sits in one room while the canopied bed and cradle still occupy a bedroom. The walls are decorated with photos of Abner and Lucy Wilcox and knickknacks from their era are scattered about the entire house. Guided tours are led Tuesday, Thursday and Saturday between 9 a.m. and 3 p.m. ~ 808-245-3202, fax 808-245-7988.

The road winds on from Hanalei past single-lane bridges and overgrown villages. The air seems moister and the real world more distant as you pass **Lumahai Beach**, a sandy scimitar where Mitzi Gaynor vowed to "wash that man right out of my hair" in the 1957 movie *South Pacific*. ~ Off Kuhio Highway about five miles west of Hanalei.

Several caves along this route were created eons ago when this entire area was underwater. The first is **Maniniholo Dry Cave**, which geologists claim is a lava tube but which legend insists was created by *Menehune*. The **Waikapalae** and **Waikanaloa Wet Caves** nearby are said to be the work of Pele, the Hawaiian goddess of volcanos, who sought fire in the earth but discovered only water.

A loop trail three-quarters of a mile long winds through the **Limahuli Botanical Garden**. Devoted to conservation of native and Polynesian-introduced plants, the valley is rich in history and contains several archeological sites. A path winds through ancient terraces with Hawaiian taro, into a forest being restored with many endangered Hawaiian plants, and out to ocean and mountain views. Self-guided and guided tours are available; reservations required for guided tours. Closed Monday and Saturday. Admission. ~ 808-826-1053; www.ntbg.org.

The cinematic appears once more at **Kee Beach**, a lovely strand with protecting reef that was used to film some of the torrid love scenes in "The Thorn Birds." It was at Kee Beach that the 1960s encampment, dubbed Taylor Camp after actress Elizabeth Taylor's brother, who owned a piece of the land, was located. Now it's "occupied" by daytrippers. This is the end of the road, beyond which the fabled Kalalau Trail winds along the Na Pali Coast.

Just above Kee Beach at the far west end of the strand rises **Ka Ulu a Paoa Heiau**. This grass-covered terrace was also the site of a hula platform and ceremonial hall; Hawaii's greatest hula masters once taught here. According to legend, the volcano god-

◄ HIDDEN

**AUTHOR FAVORITE**

Past Princeville, the road opens onto the **Hanalei Valley Look-out**, a vista point that transcends prose with its beauty. Below you spreads a patchwork of tropical vegetation, fields of broad-leafed taro that have been cultivated for over 1200 years. This green carpet, swaying and shimmering along the valley floor, is cut by the thin silver band of the Hanalei River. Framing this scene, as though a higher power had painted the entire tableau, are deep-green cliffs, fluted and sharp, that rise 3500 feet from the tilled fields.

dess Pele departed Kauai from here, settling on the Big Island, where she still lives. ~ Follow the path on the top of the stone wall just above Kee Beach. About ten yards past the end of the beach, take the left fork in the path. Another 20 yards and you will be on the platform.

Kee Beach is the end of the road. But what awaits the adventurer lies beyond—the **Na Pali Coast**. With sea cliffs sculpted by wind and rain that seem to reach to the stars, towering over lush mountain valleys—this is hidden Kauai. There are various ways to explore this misty and mystical region. Numerous outfitters offer catamaran, sailboat or zodiac rafting trips along the coast. Kayakers can cruise the coastline in a group tour or on their own. Helicopters fly deep into the valleys, swooping like birds, brushing up against waterfalls and adze-like cliffs. Or you can hike along an ancient Hawaiian trail 12 miles to Kalalau Valley. (See "Hiking Kalalau" later in this chapter) Anyway you can, do it. This is truly one of the most magnificent spots on earth.

For those wanting just a taste of the coastline, there's a two-mile hike to **Hanakapiai Beach**. It's an arduous trek climbing up some 800 feet, hugging cliffs along a narrow trail, crossing streams, and walking in mud. But the reward at the end is a spectacular valley with a picture-perfect white-sand beach. (The current can be tricky here; use caution when swimming.) Two more miles inland are **Hanakapiai Falls**, which feed a large swimming pond.

Tucked into this verdant area is the **Hono o Na Pali Natural Area Reserve**. This was once a major crop-growing region, with remnants of terraced hills still clearly visible. Wild fruit and coffee plants thrive in the rain-soaked valleys and on surrounding cliffs.

If you're on foot, it's another five and a half miles to **Kalalau Beach** and the once-thriving **Kalalau Valley**. Two miles wide and

## BEEN HERE BEFORE?

Does this place seem familiar? Are you on the set of *Jurassic Park*? Isn't that Bali Hai from *South Pacific*? Kauai's beauty and tropical ambience have provided numerous backdrops for blockbuster movies and television shows. The Huleia River still sports the rope swing used in *Raiders of the Lost Ark*, and the Coco Palms Resort, abandoned after Hurricane Iniki in 1992, awaits Elvis' return to *Blue Hawaii*. **Hawaii Movie Tours** will take you to some of these sites while you watch the featured scenes in your "theater on wheels." If you want to take home the scenes, purchase *The Kauai Movie Book* by Chris Cook. ~ Kapaa; 808-822-1192, 800-628-8432, fax 808-822-1608; www.hawaiimovietour.com, e-mail tourguy@hawaiian.net.

three miles deep, studded with guava and mango trees, it was not so very long ago, in the early 1900s, that a community populated this area. Now, hikers and kayakers, who need permits to visit, seek out the freshwater pools and pristine beach. For the less adventurous, the valley can be viewed from the **Kalalau Lookout** at Waimea Canyon.

A note of caution: If you do venture along the coast in a kayak or on foot, remember that this coastline is wild and unpredictable. Even experienced adventurers have needed to be rescued here.

Farm life, North Shore Kauai–style, is the experience at **North Country Farms**, a small organic family farm with two separate cottages (one of which can accommodate up to six people) that are run like a bed and breakfast. The setting is pleasant and quiet, amid fields and orchards, with mountain views, and owner Lee Roversi strives to use and serve natural products. The cottages are clean, simple and comfortable, with an instant homey feel that families, couples or those planning a longer stay would appreciate. Each sleeps at least four comfortably, with no cleaning fee, making this a real bargain for the $120 per night price. Both have a TV/VCR (one with cable), but plenty of books, puzzles, games and toys will keep you occupied, if that's what you prefer. ~ Kahili Makai Street, Kilauea; 808-828-1513, fax 808-828-0805; www.northcountryfarms.com, e-mail ncfarms@aloha.net. BUDGET TO MODERATE.

**LODGING**

◄ *HIDDEN*

The North Shore's premier resting place is a clifftop roost called the **Princeville Resort**. Situated on a point and sporting one of the best views this side of paradise, it's a 252-room complex decorated in European style with a large touch of Hawaiiana. The hotel rises above a white-sand beach and features several restaurants as well as a pool and jacuzzi. Trimmed in gold plating and marble, this is a concierge-and-doorman resort long on service. ~ Princeville; 808-826-9644, 800-325-3589, fax 808-826-1166; www.luxurycollection.com. ULTRA-DELUXE.

**Hanalei Bay Resort**, spectacularly perched on a hillside overlooking the coastline, provides full vacation facilities. The 22-acre property, which descends to a beach, contains a restaurant, lounge, tennis courts and two spacious swimming pools. The guest rooms are located in three-story buildings dotted around the grounds; some include kitchens. Be forewarned: We have had complaints that the facilities do not warrant the price tag. ~ 5380 Honoiki Road, Princeville; 808-826-6522, 800-827-4427, fax 808-826-6680; www.hanaleibaykauai.com. ULTRA-DELUXE.

**Mana Yoga** is a great little vacation hideaway in a rural North Shore area that has stunning mountain views. It's on a five-acre farm, and is the downstairs portion of the Edwards' family home. But not to worry—there's plenty of privacy, with your own lanai,

◄ *HIDDEN*

entrance, kitchen and bath. It has two bedrooms and easily sleeps four people. Yoga classes, private and public, are provided by the owner, who is also a masseuse. Three-night minimum stay. ~ Ahonui Place, Princeville; 808-826-9230; www.manayoga.com, e-mail michaelle@manayoga.com. MODERATE.

At the YMCA's beachfront **Camp Naue**, there are dormitory accommodations in bunkhouses. Bring your own bedding. There is also an adjacent area for camping. Reservations can only be made for large groups; otherwise, it is on a first-come, first-served basis. Calls will only be returned if they're local or if the campsite can call collect. ~ The camp is located off Kuhio Highway, Haena; 808-246-9090. BUDGET.

**CONDOS**   In the Princeville Resort complex, a few miles east of Hanalei, are several condos: The **Pali Ke Kua** offers one- and two-bedroom apartments for $131 and up. ~ 808-826-9066, fax 808-826-4159. **Pahio at Kaeo Kai** has studios from $115. These are modern units with wet bars, but no kitchens. There is a swimming pool on each property. ~ 808-826-6549, fax 808-826-6715.

Although the Princeville Resort area is awash with condos, they're generally pretty bland. **Sealodge**, tucked away on a quiet side street, is the exception. The privacy and setting make these condos distinct. One-bedroom units are $120 per night, with a $75 one-time cleaning fee. Two-bedroom apartments run $145, with a $85 one-time cleaning fee. A pool, barbecue area, and plenty of parking round out the special features. ~ Princeville; 808-826-6751.

For information on other condominiums, as well as cottages and houses, and to learn where the best deals are available during any particular time, check with **Hanalei Vacations**. You can also browse (virtually) through every one of their properties at their

**AUTHOR FAVORITE**

The **Hanalei Colony Resort** is the only beachfront condominium complex on the North Shore. It's a five-acre lowrise complex with the ocean as your only distraction (no TVs or phones). You can choose one of 48 two-bedroom condos, most with two bathrooms, all with fully equipped kitchens and private lanais. Each unit is stylishly furnished with Hawaiian-style decor. In summer they run a special program for families. The Hanalei Day Spa (treatments, yoga classes), Tunnels Bar and Grill (lunch and dinner) and Napili Art Gallery and Coffee House are recent additions. Check their website for more information. Two-bedroom apartments run $195 to $385. ~ Kuhio Highway, Hanalei; 808-826-6235, 800-628-3004, fax 808-826-9893; www.hcr.com, e-mail aloha@hcr.com.

website. ~ P.O. Box 223206, Princeville, HI 96722; 808-826-
7288, 800-487-9833, fax 808-826-7280; www.800hawaii.com,
e-mail rentals@aloha.net.

If you'd simply like a pizza, the little town of Kilauea offers up **Pau Hana Pizza**, a combination kitchen and bakery that cooks up some delicious pies. ~ Kong Lung Center, Lighthouse Road, Kilauea; 808-828-2020. MODERATE TO DELUXE.

**DINING**

In the Princeville market you'll find the informal **Paradise Bar & Grill**. It serves sandwiches at lunch and steak and seafood every evening. ~ Princeville Market, Princeville; 808-826-1775. MODERATE.

The prize for prettiest dining room on the North Shore goes to **La Cascata**, the Princeville Resort's signature restaurant. That is not even taking into account the edenic views of the Na Pali Coast or the soft breezes wafting in from the ocean. All we're counting is the tilework, the murals and the Mediterranean pastel colors. The bill of fare is mostly Italian-influenced Mediterranean. Dinner only. ~ Princeville; 808-826-9644, fax 808-826-1166. ULTRA-DELUXE.

Any restaurant critic in the world would immediately award five stars to the view at **Bali Hai Restaurant**. Perched on a deck high above Hanalei Bay, it overlooks a broad sweep of mountains and sea. The menu features classic island fare, ranging from fresh catches to steak to pasta. Reservations are recommended. ~ Hanalei Bay Resort, 5380 Honoiki Road, Princeville; 808-826-6522, fax 808-826-6680. MODERATE TO ULTRA-DELUXE.

As beautiful and popular as Hanalei happens to be, the area possesses only a few low-priced facilities. If you've ever tried to find a place to stay here, you know how tight things can be. And the budget restaurant situation is not a whole lot better.

The **Hanalei Wake-Up Café** is a low-key eatery with omelettes and other egg dishes in the morning. There's a small dining room with a deck. Breakfast only. ~ Aku Road, Hanalei; 808-826-5551. BUDGET.

**Postcards** is a fun, gourmet semi-vegetarian restaurant tucked into an old plantation cottage on the outskirts of town. The dinner menu features lots of organic produce and is short and simple: fresh fish specials, pasta with veggies or seafood, Cajun crusted ahi with chipotle sauce, phyllo wraps with veggies and taro fritters. Smoothies, juices and salads, too. Service can be sketchy, but then, it *is* Hanalei. Dinner only. ~ 5075-A Kuhio Highway, Hanalei; 808-826-1191. MODERATE TO DELUXE.

**Hanalei Taro & Juice Co.**, owned by a couple who farm taro just down the road, lays to rest the notion that taro equals sour poi. The roadside cart, with a couple of covered picnic tables out front, sells fruit smoothies, sandwiches, awesome *laulau* and des-

◄ *HIDDEN*

sert treats, all made from the wholesome, starchy vegetable that was a mainstay of Hawaiian diets. They bake their own sandwich rolls and the taro *mochi*. Lunch only. Closed Sunday. ~ 5-5070 Kuhio Highway, Hanalei; 808-826-1059. BUDGET.

The atmosphere of **Hanalei Gourmet** is laidback and local. To fit this feeling, the menu is solid but unpretentious. There are numerous salads, including a chicken salad boat and an ahi pasta salad. The sandwich selection features a shrimp sandwich and a special concoction with eggplant and red peppers. Following this seafood and vegetable theme are the dinner entrées, which change nightly. The bar scene is lively, there's live entertainment at least three nights a week and the kitchen prepares good food at favorable prices. ~ 5-5161 Kuhio Highway, Hanalei; 808-826-2524, fax 808-826-6007; www.hanaleigourmet.com. MODERATE TO DELUXE.

**Hanalei Mixed Plate**, a takeout stand, serves everything from buffalo burgers to veggie burgers as well as stir-fry, tofu, ginger chicken and *kalua* pig. ~ Located next to Ching Young Village, Kuhio Highway, Hanalei; 808-826-7888. BUDGET.

There are several luncheonettes, including **Village Snack and Bakery**, which serves standard lunch fare. ~ Ching Young Village, Kuhio Highway, Hanalei; 808-826-6841. BUDGET.

**Sushi Blues Grill**, a Hanalei hotspot, combines industrial decor with live entertainment every night. The menu at this second-floor restaurant/club includes sizzling seafood stir-fry, coconut shrimp, linguine and scallops, and of course a host of sushi selections. Dinner only. ~ Ching Young Village, Kuhio Highway, Hanalei; 808-826-9701; www.sushiandblues.com. DELUXE.

HIDDEN ►
Hearty, Mexican meals like fajitas and enchiladas, as well as quiche, veggie burgers, salads, wraps and more, are prepared well at the **Polynesian Café**. Coffee drinks, ice cream smoothies and yummy baked goods baked on-site add to the appeal, along with a cheerful staff. ~ Ching Young Village, Kuhio Highway, Hanalei; 808-826-1999. BUDGET TO MODERATE.

Forget all this nonsense about good health and low cholesterol, step up to the window at **Bubba's** and order a hot dog or a "Big Bubba" (a half-pound hamburger with three patties). ~ 5-5161 Kuhio Highway, Hanalei; 808-826-7839. BUDGET.

On the road since 1978 was the **Tropical Taco**, a van cum taco stand that is now dispensing its mouth-watering fish tacos from a permanent location. Dine inside or on the deck, where you can do some serious people watching. Closed Sunday. ~ 5088 Kuhio Highway, Hanalei; 808-635-8226. BUDGET.

HIDDEN ►

The **Tahiti Nui Restaurant** is a refreshing alternative to the commercialized luaus of big hotels—this is a family affair. If you miss it, try offerings from the menu, which features steak, fresh fish, calamari, scampi, pasta and chicken dishes. And check out the bamboo-fringed lanai, or the lounge decorated with Pacific Island carvings and overhung with a thatch canopy. ~ 5-5134 Kuhio Highway, in the center of Hanalei; 808-826-6277. MODERATE.

With woven *lauhala* walls, bamboo bar and outrigger canoe, **Zelo's Beach House** certainly looks the part. It's airy and informal—a great spot to relax. When you're ready to order, you'll find an eclectic menu. The central focus is pasta: linguine and clams with toasted pine nuts, Cajun chicken pasta and an all-you-can-eat spaghetti dish. But they also have steak, baby back ribs and fresh seafood. ~ 5-5256 Kuhio Highway, Hanalei; 808-826-9700; www.sushiandblues.com, e-mail sushi.blues@verizon. net. DELUXE.

From the porthole windows to the Japanese fishing balls, the **Hanalei Dolphin Restaurant and Fish Market** presents an interesting aquatic decor. Built smack on the bank of the Hanalei River, this eatery offers a turf-and-surf menu that includes fresh fish, shrimp dishes and New York steak. The restaurant, which is highly recommended, does not take reservations. The fish market at the back of the restaurant offers many of the same fish found on the menu to take home and cook yourself. ~ 5-5016 Kuhio Highway, Hanalei; 808-826-6113, fax 808-826-6699. ULTRA-DELUXE.

**GROCERIES**

The best place on the North Shore is **Foodland**. It's very well stocked and open from 6 a.m. to 11 p.m. ~ Princeville Shopping Center, off Kuhio Highway; 808-826-9880.

Hanalei supports one large grocery store on Kuhio Highway, **Big Save Market**. ~ Ching Young Village, Hanalei; 808-826-6652.

**Hanalei Health Foods** carries organic and health-related items. Open 9 a.m. to 6 p.m. ~ Ching Young Village, Kuhio Highway, Hanalei; 808-826-6990.

**Banana Joe's Tropical Fruit Farm** has ripe, delicious fruits as well as smoothies and dried fruit. ~ 5-2719 Kuhio Highway, Kilauea; 808-828-1092.

**AUTHOR FAVORITE**

The romantic **Lighthouse Bistro**, in the historic Kong Lung Center in Kilauea, offers bistro-style fare with European and Asian influences in an open-air setting. This translates into shrimp parmesan; blackened, broiled or sautéed fresh fish with various sauces, like Thai mango sesame; chicken and steak. Lunch is sandwiches, pasta and salads. Full bar and good wine list. ~ Kong Lung Center, Lighthouse Road, Kilauea; 808-828-0480, fax 808-828-0481; www.lighthousebistro.com, e-mail finedining@ lighthousebistro.com. MODERATE TO DELUXE.

**SHOPPING**   Kong Lung Co. has a marvelous assortment of Pacific and Asian treasures as well as a selection of Hawaiian books. Don't miss this one. ~ Kilauea Lighthouse Road, Kilauea; 808-828-1822.

Princeville is the closest you will come to a shopping center on the North Shore. The **Princeville Shopping Center** features a cluster of shops that represents the area's prime spot for window browsers. Kids define heaven as **Magic Dragon Toyland and Supply,** (808-826-9144), which specializes in unique toys and games and a variety of fine art supplies—fun for the whole family. ~ Off Kuhio Highway, Princeville; 808-826-3040.

Hanalei's **Ching Young Village** is a small shopping mall that contains a variety store, clothing shops and several other outlets. There's a **Hot Rocket** here for beachwear (808-826-7776) and **On the Road to Hanalei** (808-826-7360) for tapa cloth, woodcarvings, jewelry, quilts and other locally and globally fashioned craft items. **Pedal 'N Paddle** (808-826-9069) provides any equipment you may need for a variety of outdoor activities, from kayaking to camping. The shopping center also has **Blue Kauai Tattoos** (808-826-0114), for obvious reasons. ~ Kuhio Highway, Hanalei; www.chingyoungvillage.com.

Across the street you'll find the **Hanalei Center,** made up of seven buildings, six of which are restored historical structures including the Old Hanalei School Building. There are shops, restaurants, a health clinic, a yoga studio, and more. ~ Kuhio Highway, Hanalei; 808-826-7677; www.hanaleicenter.com.

**Ola's** showcases the work of over 100 craftspeople from Hawaii and the mainland. ~ Off Kuhio Highway, next to Hanalei Dolphin Restaurant, Hanalei; 808-826-6937.

**Kai Kane** is an attractively decorated shop featuring fashions of their own design. It's a great place to shop for alohawear. ~ 5-5088 Kuhio Highway, Hanalei; 808-826-5594.

**Yellowfish Trading Company** has a marvelous collection of antiques and Hawaiian collectibles. ~ Hanalei Center, Kuhio Highway, Hanalei; 808-826-1227.

**NIGHTLIFE**   In all the world there are few entertainment spots with a view as grand as the Princeville Resort's **Living Room Bar.** Overlooking Hanalei Bay, it also features a singer and pianist playing standards and contemporary music nightly. ~ Princeville Resort, Princeville; 808-826-9644.

At nearby Hanalei Bay Resort's **Happy Talk Lounge,** you can enjoy the views of Hanalei Bay and relax with contemporary Hawaiian music daily and jazz on Sunday. ~ 5380 Honoiki Road, Princeville; 808-826-6522.

**Amelia's,** located out at the Princeville Airport, has live music Friday and Saturday nights. ~ 5-3541 Kuhio Highway, Princeville; 808-826-9561.

For a tropical drink amid a tropical setting, place your order at **Tahiti Nui Restaurant**, which has live entertainment nightly as well as a satellite feed. ~ 5-5134 Kuhio Highway, Hanalei; 808-826-6277. Or try the **Hanalei Dolphin Restaurant**. ~ Kuhio Highway, Hanalei; 808-826-6113.

The **Hanalei Gourmet** has live performances by local artists Wednesday and Friday evenings and Sunday afternoons. Call to see if any extra shows have been scheduled. ~ 5-5161 Kuhio Highway, Hanalei; 808-826-2524.

There's music seven nights a week at the **Sushi Blues Grill**. One night there's karaoke, another night there's dancing, and the rest of the time they have jazz and blues. Occasional cover on Friday and Saturday. ~ Ching Young Village, Hanalei; 808-826-9701.

**MOLOAA BEACH** 🏊 🌊 ⚓ Nestled in Moloaa Bay, a small inlet surrounded by rolling hills, Moloaa Beach is relatively secluded, though there are homes nearby. A meandering stream divides the beach into two strands. You'll see a coral reef shadowing the shore. There is good beachcombing at the west end of the strand. Swim with caution. Snorkeling and fishing are good, as is lobster diving. There are no facilities. ~ Take Koolau Road where it branches off Kuhio Highway near the 16-mile marker. Go one and three tenths miles, then turn onto Moloaa Road. Follow this to the end. All roads are paved.

**BEACHES & PARKS**

**LARSEN'S BEACH** 🏊 🌊 ⚓ This narrow, sandy beach extends seemingly forever through a very secluded area. Rolling hills, covered with small trees and scrub, rim the strand. Glass fishing balls and other collectibles wash ashore regularly, making this a prime beachcombing spot. A protecting reef provides excellent

◄ HIDDEN

---

**AIRBORNE ATHLETES**

Seabirds are amazing creatures, flying thousands of miles to their seasonal feeding and nesting grounds and even spending years at sea. Boobies, Laysan albatrosses, wedgetail and Newell's shearwaters, tropic birds and frigate birds are commonly seen on Kauai's north and east shores, soaring on the currents and dipping into the sea to pluck out fish or squid. Albatrosses often nest on the golf courses and expansive lawns at Princeville and elsewhere from February through June, and their elaborate courtship rituals are an entertaining sight. With wing spans reaching five feet or more, these big, beautiful birds are awkward on land, giving rise to their nickname "goonie birds," but very graceful in flight. The Kilauea National Wildlife Refuge is the best place to see all these seabirds, as well as Hawaii's state bird, the endangered nene goose.

swimming and snorkeling. It is also very popular for seaweed gathering and throw-netting. There are also good fishing spots. Surf is sometimes dangerous here, so exercise caution. There are no facilities. ~ It's hard to get to, but more than worth it when you arrive. Take Koolau Road as it branches off Kuhio Highway near the 16-mile marker. Go two and a half miles to a cane road on the right, which switches back in the opposite direction. Get on this road, then take an immediate left onto another dirt road (lined on either side with barbed wire). Don't let the fences scare you—this is a public right of way. Follow it a mile to the end. Hike through the gate and down the road. This leads a half-mile down to the beach, which is on your left. (There is also an access road from Koolau Road that is located one and a fifth miles from the intersection of Koolau Road and Kuhio Highway.)

> The Hanalei River, one of the largest rivers in the state, is said to be the most pristine in Hawaii. Together with its estuarine bay it's considered "outstanding for the abundance and quality of natural, cultural and scenic resources."

HIDDEN ►  **KAHILI BEACH** 🏊 🚶 🎣 Tucked away in Kilauea Bay, this beach is bordered by tree-covered hills and a rock quarry. It's a lovely, semi-secluded spot with a lagoon that represents one of Hawaii's most pristine estuaries. Kahili is also a prime beachcombing spot. For a spectacular view of windswept cliffs, follow the short quarry road that climbs steeply from the parking area. Swimming is good when the sea is calm. The favorite surf break is "Rock Quarry," located offshore from the stream. Fishing is rewarding, and the reef at the east end of the beach is also a favored net-throwing spot. There are no facilities. ~ From Kuhio Highway, about two miles south of Kilauea town, head east on Wailapa Road for about three-quarters of a mile. Look to your left for the white post that marks the dirt beach access road. Take this road about one mile to the beach; it's rough, but passable, although it can be very muddy during wet weather.

▲ Unofficial camping.

HIDDEN ►  **KAUAPEA BEACH OR SECRET BEACH** 🏊 Inaccessibility means seclusion along this hidden strand. Ideal for birdwatching, swimming and unofficial camping, this half-mile-long beach lies just below Kilauea Lighthouse. Very wide and extremely beautiful, it is popular with nudists and adventurers alike. No facilities spoil this hideaway. Note that this place is notorious for car break-ins so leave nothing in your vehicle. ~ The beach can be seen from Kilauea Lighthouse, but getting there is another matter. From Kuhio Highway just west of Kilauea turn onto Kalihiwai Road (be sure to get on the eastern section of Kalihiwai Road, near Banana Joe's Tropical Fruit Farm). The road immediately curves to the left; go right onto the first dirt road; proceed three-tenths mile to a parking lot; from here follow the fenceline down into a ravine to Kauapea Beach.

▲ Unofficial camping.

**KALIHIWAI BEACH** 🏃 🛶 Bounded by sheer rock wall on one  ◀ HIDDEN
side and a rolling green hill on the other, this semi-secluded beach is crowded with ironwood trees. Behind the ironwoods, the Kalihiwai River has created a large, shallow lagoon across which stretches the skeleton of a bridge, a last grim relic of the devastating 1946 tidal wave. "Kalihiwai" is one of the top expert winter surfing breaks on the North Shore. It's also popular for bodysurfing. Swimmers should exercise caution. Bonefish and threadfin are the most common catches. This is also a great spot for surround-netting of akule. No facilities. ~ Take heed—there are two Kalihiwai Roads branching off Kuhio Highway between Kilauea and Kalihiwai. (The washed-out bridge once connected them.) Take the one closest to Lihue. This bumpy macadam road leads a short distance directly to the beach.

**ANINI BEACH COUNTY PARK** 🏖 🎣 🏃 🚿 ⚓ 🚤 🛶 Here a grass-covered park fronts a narrow ribbon of sand, while a protecting reef parallels the beach 200 yards offshore. I thought this an ideal place for kids: The ocean is glass smooth and the beachcombing is excellent. As a result, it's very popular and sometimes crowded. Swimming is excellent and very safe. Snorkeling is also topnotch. Surfers' note: There are winter breaks on very shallow reef (left and right slides). This is also a very popular windsurfing site. The beach has the only boat launch on this side of the island, and anglers take advantage of it to catch bonefish, *papio* and *ulua*. People also torchfish, throw-net, spear octopus and harvest seaweed at Anini. Facilities include a picnic area, restrooms and a shower. ~ Between Kilauea and Hanalei, turn off Kuhio Highway onto the second Kalihiwai Road (the one farthest from Lihue, on the Hanalei side of the Kalihiwai River). Then take Anini Road to the beach.

▲ Pleasant, but lacks privacy. A county permit is required. Tent camping only.

**PRINCEVILLE BEACHES** 🏖 🎣 🏃 There are three beaches directly below the plateau on which the Princeville Resort complex rests. The most popular is **Puu Poa Beach**, a long and wide strand located next to the Princeville Resort and reached through the hotel. It offers good swimming and easy access to the hotel's (expensive) facilities but is often crowded. The other two are pocket beaches. **Sealodge Beach**, reached via a right of way behind Unit A of the Sealodge condominium, is a white-sand beach backdropped by cliffs. Offshore is a surfing break called "Little Grass Shacks." **Hideaways** consists of two mirror-image beaches, one below Pali Ke Kua condos and the other below Puu Poa condos. They are both good spots for swimming and snorkeling and feature a well-known surf break. ~ To reach Sealodge Beach, turn right from Kuhio Highway onto Kahaku Road and into the Princeville complex. Turn right on Kamehameha Road and follow it to the Sealodge condos. Access to Hideaways is located between Puu Poa condos and the Princeville Resort near the end of Kahaku Road.

**HANALEI BAY BEACHES** A sandy, horseshoe-shaped strip of sand curves the full length of Hanalei Bay. Along this two-mile strand there are four beach parks. **Black Pot Beach Park**, a local gathering place, lies at the eastern end of the bay and is bounded on one side by the Hanalei River and on the other by a 300-foot-long pier (Hanalei Landing). With showers and lifeguard facilities available to beachgoers, it is very popular with watersport enthusiasts of all stripes—swimmers, surfers, bodysurfers, windsurfers, kayakers and anglers. It is located at the eastern end of Weke Road. **Hanalei Pavilion Beach Park**, located along Weke Road between Pilikoa and Aku roads, is a favorite picnic spot. **Waioli Beach Park**, a small facility set in an ironwood grove, is situated near the center of the half-moon-shaped bay. It can be reached from the end of either Hee Road or Amaama Road. Black Pot Beach Park, Hanalei Pavilion Beach Park and Waioli Beach Park all have lifeguards on duty. **Waikoko Beach** is a slender strand paralleled by a shallow reef. Popular with families who come here to swim and snorkel, it lies along Kuhio Highway on the western side of the bay.

There are three major surf breaks here. "Impossible" breaks require a long paddle out from the pier; right slide. "Pine Tree" breaks, off Waioli Beach Park, are in the center of the bay. "Waikoko" breaks are on the shallow reef along the western side of the bay. All are winter breaks. Surfing in Hanalei is serious business, so be careful. Early morning and late afternoon are the best surfing times. The bay is also a popular bodysurfing area. Fish for squirrelfish, rockfish, red bigeye, *oama*, big-eyed scad, *ulua* and *papio*. There is crabbing off Hanalei Landing pier. All beaches have picnic areas, restrooms and marvelous ocean and mountain views. ~ Located in Hanalei just off Kuhio Highway.

▲ Tent camping permitted on weekends and holidays at Black Pot Beach Park only. A county permit is required.

**LUMAHAI BEACH** Many people know this strand as the Nurse's Beach in the movie *South Pacific*. Snuggled in a cove and surrounded by lush green hills, Lumahai extends for three-fourths of a mile. With white sand against black lava, it's a particularly pretty spot. Swim only when the sea is very calm and exercise ex-

> Mount Kawaikini, at 5243 feet, is Kauai's tallest peak.

treme caution. During the winter months, it's one of the most treacherous spots on the island. You can try for *papio* and *ulua*. There are no facilities. ~ Watch for a vista point near the 5-mile marker on Kuhio Highway. From here, a crooked footpath leads to the beach. The beach can more easily be accessed about a mile down the road, at the Lumahai River bridge. Do not swim at the river mouth because of strong currents.

## TUNNELS (MAKUA) BEACH AND OTHER HAENA BEACHES

There are beach access roads all along Kuhio Highway near Haena. Taking any of these dirt roads will shortly lead you to secluded strands. Most popular of all is "Tunnels," a sandy beach with a great offshore reef. According to divers, the name "Tunnels" derives from the underwater arches and tunnels in the reef; but surfers claim it's from the perfect tunnel-shaped waves. Windsurfers consider this one of the best sites on Kauai. You'll also find swimmers, snorkelers, sunbathers and beach-combers here. Kepuhi Point is one of the best fishing spots on the North Shore; Tunnels attracts fishermen with nets and poles. There are no facilities here. ~ These beaches are located along Kuhio Highway near Wainiha Bay and Kepuhi Point. Tunnels is two-fifths mile east of Maniniholo Dry Cave.

## HAENA BEACH PARK

This grassy park, bounded by the sea on one side and a sheer lava cliff on the other, is right across the street from Maniniholo Dry Cave. It's very popular with young folks and provides good opportunities for beachcombing. There are very strong ocean currents here, which make swimming impossible in winter but fine in summer. Surfing "Cannon's" breaks on a shallow reef in front of Maniniholo Dry Cave is for experts only (right slide). There is excellent surfcasting and torch-fishing for red bigeye, squirrelfish, *papio* and *ulua*. Cardinal fish are sometimes caught on the reef at low tide during the full moon. A picnic area, restrooms and a shower are the facilities here. ~ Located on Kuhio Highway five miles west of Hanalei.

▲ It's an attractive campground, sometimes crowded, open to both tents and trailers, and requiring a county permit. There is also camping nearby at the YMCA's **Camp Naue** (808-246-9090).

## HAENA STATE PARK AND KEE BEACH

At the end of Kuhio Highway, where the Kalalau trail begins, 65.7-acre Haena State Park encompasses a long stretch of white sand, with Kee Beach at its western end. This reef-shrouded beach is one of the most popular on the North Shore. When the surf is gentle, swimming is superb. At such times, this is one of the best snorkeling beaches for beginners, with its protective coral reef brilliantly colored and crowded with tropical fish. In addition, there are 4000-year-old sea caves to explore. The Haena shoreline is also one of the island's best shelling beaches. Surfing is good at "Cannons" and "Bobo's" breaks. This is also a prime windsurfing area. There is good fishing along the reef. There are restrooms and showers. ~ Located at the end of Kuhio Highway.

## Outdoor Adventures

To visit Kauai without enjoying at least one camping trip is to miss a splendid opportunity. This lovely isle is dotted with county and state parks that feature ideal locations and complete facilities. There are also many hidden beaches where unofficial camping is common.

### CAMPING

Camping at **county parks** requires a permit. These are issued for seven days. You are allowed to camp a total of 60 days per year at all county parks. Permits cost $3 per person per night; children under 18 are free. Permits can be obtained weekdays at the Division of Parks and Recreation. ~ 4444 Rice Street, Suite 330, Lihue; 808-241-6660, fax 808-241-4497.

**State park** permit fees vary by location. They allow camping five consecutive days at each park, and should be requested at least one month in advance for winter, at least a year in advance for summer reservations. These permits are issued by the Department of Land and Natural Resources. ~ 3060 Eiwa Street, Lihue, HI 96766; 808-274-3445.

The State Division of Forestry also maintains camping areas in the **forest reserves.** Currently, these are free (but call the Division of Forestry to see about new fees); permits are available at the State Division of Forestry. ~ 3060 Eiwa Street, Room 306, Lihue, HI 96766; 808-274-3433. Camping is limited at each site, and there's a four-night maximum at the Kukui Trail campsites near Waimea Canyon and a three-night limit at the Sugi Grove and Kawaikoi sites in the rainforest area at the top of Waimea Canyon.

Camping elsewhere on the island is officially prohibited. While local people and visitors do sometimes camp on hidden beaches anyway, the authorities crack down on this regularly. By the way,

### FLY LIKE AN EAGLE (OR A GOONIE BIRD)

What better way to see Kauai than to soar on high with the birds? Okay, so you don't have wings. How about trying a motorized hang glider, accompanied by a fully certified flight instructor from **Birds in Paradise**? Be assured, you'll get a briefing on the basics of flying in a "weight-shift aircraft," and you will always be in communication with the pilot through an intercom on your helmet. ~ 808-822-5309; www.birdsinparadise. com, e-mail birds@birdsinparadise.com.

an extra effort should be made to keep these areas clean. One of the best suggestions I've ever heard is to leave your campsite cleaner than when you arrived.

Rainfall is much heavier along the North Shore than along the south coast, but be prepared for showers anywhere. The Kokee area gets chilly, so pack accordingly. And remember, boil or chemically treat all water from Kauai's streams. Water from some of these streams can cause dysentery and leptospirosis, a serious illness with flu-like symptoms, and none of the waterways are certified safe by the Health Department.

Fishing in Kauai is superb year-round, and the offshore waters are crowded with many varieties of edible fish. For deep-sea fishing you'll have to charter a boat, and freshwater angling requires a license, which can be obtained at sportfishing stores. For information on seasons, licenses and official regulations, check with the **Division of Aquatic Resources**, which is part of of the State Department of Land and Natural Resources. ~ 3060 Eiwa Street, Room 306, Lihue, HI 96766; 808-274-3344, fax 808-274-3448.

**FISHING**

Both saltwater and freshwater fishing opportunities make Kauai popular with anglers. Intriguing possibilities include overnight adventures off the Niihau coast, fishing for giant tuna and marlin. Keep a sharp eye out on your trip and you may spot spinner dolphins or breaching whales along the way.

**Wild Bill Sport Fishing** provides everything you need to fish for marlin, ahi, *ono* and *aku* on Kauai's south and east coasts. The four-hour charter accommodates up to six people; six- and eight-hour charters are also available. ~ Nawiliwili Harbor, Lihue; 808-822-5963.

The Garden Isle offers snorkeling and scuba opportunities at such spots as Haena Beach, Tunnels Beach, Moloaa and Koloa Landing. In the Poipu area, Koloa Landing has a number of green sea turtles in its midst and is mainly for experienced snorkelers. The beach in front of Lawai Beach Resort is another popular spot for snorkelers. Even if you have your own equipment, it's a good idea to stop by one of the local dive shops to pick up a map, as well as advice on local conditions.

**DIVING**

Snuba was created for those who would like to take snorkeling a step further but may not be quite ready for scuba diving. It's a shallow-water dive system that allows underwater breathing. The air comes through a 20-foot tube connected to the raft, which follows the swimmer. Groups of six participants are taken out with a guide. They can dive up to 20 feet. **Snuba Tours of Kauai** leaves from Lawai Beach in Poipu. The personalized instruction extends to the underwater tour; all equipment (and fish food) is provided. Closed Sunday. ~ 808-823-8912; www.snuba kauai.com, e-mail snuba@snubakauai.com.

**POIPU AREA**   To familiarize yourself with the area's treasures you may want to begin with a group tour. **Fathom Five Divers** rents diving and snorkeling equipment and takes groups, limited to a maximum of six people to ensure personal attention, to hot spots such as Sheraton Caverns and Brennecke's Ledge. Divers often spot fish unique to Kauai such as bandit angel fish, long-nosed hawkfish and boarfish. Half-day dives leave every morning and afternoon. ~ Poipu Road, Koloa; 808-742-6991; www.fathom five.com. **Seasport Divers** rents snorkeling and scuba equipment and offers lessons, tours, and day and night dives. ~ 2827 Poipu Road, Poipu; 808-742-9303; www.kauaiscubadiving.com.

**WAILUA–KAPAA AREA**   **Snorkel Bob's Kauai** rents snorkeling equipment returnable at branches on all the other islands. The shop puts together a tip sheet of the best current snorkel spots (factoring in the weather, tides and so forth). ~ 4-734 Kuhio Highway, Kapaa, 808-823-9433; and also at 3236 Poipu Road, Koloa, 808-742-2206; www.snorkelbob.com.

**NORTH SHORE**   **Hanalei Water Sports Inc.** offers certification classes. Beginners start right at Princeville Beach; more advanced divers may join small groups in exploring the lava tubes and caverns of Tunnels Beach. ~ Princeville Resort, Princeville; 808-826-7509. Another good possibility for snorkeling rentals is **Hanalei Surf Company**. Check out their supply of boogieboards, wet suits and surfboards. ~ 5-5161 Kuhio Highway, Hanalei; 808-826-9000; www.hanaleisurf.com. **Pedal 'N Paddle** has snorkels, masks and fins as well as single and double kayaks for rent. ~ Ching Young Village, Hanalei; 808-826-9069.

## GO FLY A KITE, LITERALLY

For a kitesurfing spot on Kauai, look for an uncrowded beach free of trees and powerlines. Then take to the wind. But if a 30-foot leap seems like a little too much excitement for you, enjoy watching others jump, jibe and "kite the surfzone." Because the sport is relatively new, and Kauai remains off the beaten path, it's a bit difficult to find an instructor here. But call **Anini Beach Windsurfing** on the North Shore and speak with Foster. He'll conduct private kitesurfing lessons with folks of all levels, and fix you up with the gear. His office address is "the beach," but you can make reservations and get information by phone. ~ 808-826-9463; www.windsurfingandkitesurfingonkauai.com.

Kauai surfers can lead you to such breaks as Tunnels, Donkey
Beach, Pakalos, P.K.s, Centers or Acid Drops. You might want
to consult with a local surf shop or the internet about what the
swells look like that day and which locales are appropriate for
your skill level (some are mellow, some are awesome). Surfing on
Kauai means summer breaks in the south and winter breaks in
the north.

**SURFING
& WIND-
SURFING**

**POIPU AREA**    Surfers head for the Poipu coastline. **Progressive
Expressions** not only sells and rents surfboards, they make their
own. Bodyboards and swim fins are also available. ~ 5420 Koloa
Road, Koloa; 808-742-6041. Surfing champion Margo Oberg's
**Nukaumoi Beach and Surf Center** offers beginner's surfing lessons
on Poipu Beach. Boogieboards, snorkel gear and accessories are for
rent. ~ Next to Brennecke's Beach Broiler, Poipu; 808-742-8019.

If you're new to surfing, or just want a refresher course, sign
up for a lesson with the **Kauai Surf School**. They give two-hour
private and group lessons, mainly aimed at beginners, although
intermediate and advanced classes are also available. Groups are
limited to four per instructor so that everyone receives personalized instruction. ~ Poipu; 808-332-7411; www.kauaisurfschool.
com.

**WAILUA–KAPAA AREA**    The **Kauai Water Ski and Surf Company**
rents surfboards and offers all levels of lessons, usually conducted
on Wailua Beach. They also have a boat on Wailua River for knee
boarding or wake boarding. Boards and accessories are also for
sale. ~ 4-356 Kuhio Highway, Wailua; 808-822-3574.

**NORTH SHORE**    Both fiberglass and soft surfboards, boogieboards and swim fins can be rented at **Hanalei Surf Company**. ~
5-5161 Kuhio Highway, Hanalei; 808-826-9000; www.hanalei
surf.com. Rentals and beginner-to-expert windsurfing lessons are
offered at **Windsurf Kauai**. The North Shore's Anini Beach, with
its reef-protected lagoon, is often the setting for the lessons. ~
Near Anini Park, Hanalei; 808-828-6838. Windsurfing lessons
of all levels are conducted right on Anini Beach at **Anini Beach
Windsurfing**. ~ 808-826-9463; www.windsurfingandkitesurfing
onkauai.com.

The trade winds ensure excellent sailing in Kauai waters. From
a catamaran trip along the southern shore to a thrilling trip along
the rugged Na Pali Coast, these waters are ideal for cruising.
Many of the cruises stop at isolated beaches and also offer excellent snorkeling opportunities.

**BOAT
TOURS**

**LIHUE AREA**    **True Blue Charters** offers sailboat rentals. With
exclusive boating rights to Kalapaki Bay, they conduct one-hour
rides of the area; personalized tours will take you to remote des-

tinations of your choice. All levels of sailing lessons are offered, as well as kayak tours of Huleia River. Boogieboards and snorkel gear are also rented. ~ Kalapaki Beach, Lihue; 808-245-9662, 888-245-1707, fax 808-246-9661; www.truebluecharters.com.

**WAIMEA AREA**   For south coast sailing tours on the 55-foot-long *Spirit of Kauai* or the *Akialoa* catamaran, weigh anchor with **Captain Andy's Sailing Adventures**. Along the way, you may spot humpback whales or giant green sea turtles. Sunset sails are among the intriguing possibilities. ~ Port Allen; 808-335-6833. **Holoholo Charters** runs 5.5-hour snorkel sails to the Na Pali Coast. 3.5-hour sunset sails are also available. ~ Port Allen Boat Harbor; 808-335-0815, 800-848-6130; www.sail-kauai.com. **Na Pali Riders** has a rafting trip that explores the entire Na Pali Coast including the sea caves, and offers snorkeling at the Nualolo Kai reef. Lunch and equipment included. ~ P.O. Box 1082, Kalaheo, HI 96741; 808-742-6331; www.napalirid ers.com.

**Captain Zodiac** offers rafting expeditions along the Na Pali Coast. Six-hour trips include visits to sea caves, beautiful reefs and an ancient fishing village. All trips include some snorkeling, and equipment is provided. Sunrise and sunset cruises are offered in the summertime, while whale watching along the north shore in the winter months is also featured. ~ Port Allen; 808-335-2719, 800-535-0830; www.napili.com, e-mail fun@capt-andys.com.

Zodiac and catamaran tours of the Na Pali Coast are also offered by **Kauai Sea Tours**. Half-day snorkeling tours take you to a landing on a secluded beach for first-rate snorkeling during the summer, while winter and spring whale-watching tours are led by naturalists. Or choose the sunset dinner cruise (with or without snorkeling). ~ Port Allen; 808-826-7254, 800-733-7997; www.seatours.net, e-mail seatour@aloha.net.

**WAILUA–KAPAA AREA**   **Paradise Kayaks** leads kayaking and hiking tours and rents kayaks, ideal for exploring rivers and wildlife refuges. Snorkel gear and boogie boards are also for rent. They also provide sea kayaking lessons. ~ 4-1596 Kuhio Highway, Kapaa; 808-822-1112.

**KAYAKING**   Kayaking is one of Kauai's fastest growing water sports. And why not? Choose from verdant river valleys or, if you like, go down to the sea again.

**LIHUE AREA**   **Aloha Canoes & Kayaks** conducts tours up the Huleia River through the midst of the Huleia National Wildlife Refuge. Among the sights you'll pass are ancient taro fields and the Menehune Fishpond. The tour continues with a hike through the *Jurassic Park* rainforest and a gourmet lunch beside a waterfall. The way back is the easy part: gliding on a motorized canoe, you'll be entertained with stories of the history and legends of Kauai. Closed Sunday. ~ Lihue; 808-246-6804, 877-473-5446; www.hawaiikayaks.com, e-mail info@hawaiikayaks.com.

**POIPU AREA**  **Outfitters Kauai** offers paddling around Poipu during the winter months, and North Shore trips in the summer. Bring your snorkel gear along, as there will be time to explore. ~ 2827-A Poipu Road, Poipu Beach; 808-742-9667, 888-742-9887; www.outfitterskauai.com, e-mail info@outfitterskauai.com.

**WAILUA-KAPAA AREA**  **Kayak Kauai** rents kayaks and runs snorkel trips. They also sponsor river tours of waterfalls on the Wailua River, as well as all-day tours of the Na Pali Coast from May to September. This trip includes a lunch break at the ruins of an ancient Hawaiian fishing village. ~ Kapaa and Hanalei; 808-826-9844, 800-437-3507; www.kayakkauai.com, e-mail info@kayakkauai.com.

If you want to go out on your own, you can rent a kayak from **Kauai Waterski and Surf Company**. Kayakers are provided with a map leading them to such Wailua River highlights as the Secret Falls, a waterfall and a remote Hawaiian village. ~ 4-356 Kuhio Highway, Wailua; 808-822-3574; e-mail surfski@aloha.net.

**Kayak Wailua** provides guided adventures: they'll supply equipment and a laminated map and guide you two and a half miles up Wailua River. At a Hawaiian village along the way, you can secure your boats and continue on foot. Here you'll discover canyons, waterfalls, a swimming hole where ancient Hawaiian kings and high chiefs once bathed, as well as other natural treasures. ~

**AUTHOR FAVORITE**

Expect more than a cruise along the extraordinary Kauai coastline when you board the **Na Pali Explorer**. In addition to providing descriptions of flora, fauna and Hawaiian culture that make the experience educational, the crew is always on the lookout for dolphins and sea turtles. They are attentive to your needs, ecologically oriented, and will lead you along one of the most beautiful coastlines in the world, past craggy cliffs and into remote sea caves. Then they'll take you snorkeling amid the region's colorful coral reefs. You can't miss with one of their trips. These five-hour expeditions run from May through September; snorkeling gear, light snacks and deli-style lunch are provided. ~ 9935 Kaumualii Highway, Waimea; 808-338-9999, 877-335-9909, fax 808-338-0742; www.napali-explorer.com.

808-822-3388; www.kayakwailua.com, e-mail info@kayak wailua.com.

**NORTH SHORE**   Kayak Hanalei will take you on a relaxing tour of the river, stopping to snorkel, eat and laze. Or, if you prefer, they'll introduce you to the rich history of Kauai on a narrated tour. All equipment is provided. ~ In the Ching Yong Shopping Center, Kuhio Highway, Hanalei; 808-826-1881; www.kayak hanalei.com, email a1kayak@aloha.net.

**WATER SKIING**   If you've ever wondered what it feels like to waterski through paradise, why not head for the town of Wailua. The serene Wailua River is the perfect place to glide through verdant canyons graced by waterfalls. You can practice your slalom technique, try out a pair of trick skis or enjoy yourself on the hydroslide.

**Kauai Waterski and Surf Company** offers trips for intermediate to advanced waterskiers. Hot doggers will want to try out the competition slalom course; 15-minute, half-hour or hourlong runs can be arranged. ~ 4-356 Kuhio Highway, Wailua; 808-822-3574; e-mail surfski@aloha.net.

**RIDING STABLES**   From scenic coastal trail rides to journeys up North Shore valleys, Kauai is an equestrian's delight.

In the Poipu area, try CJM **Country Stables**. Possibilities include two-hour rides along the south shore to Mahaulepu and Haupu beaches. They also offer a three-hour "breakfast ride" departing at 8:30 a.m. and covering some of the best beaches in the Poipu area. You may be tempted to return later on foot to explore these hidden spots. (No rides on Sunday.) ~ At the end of Poipu Road; 808-742-6096, fax 808-742-6015.

## ADVENTURE AFOOT AND AFLOAT

Combine an education about the history, flora and fauna of Kauai's interior with a hiking/kayaking adventure. **Princeville Ranch Hike & Kayak Adventures** offers a number of options. Tours include the "waterfall excursion" (which takes you first to a spectacular 360° view of ocean and mountain and then on to a five tiered waterfall), the "Jungle Waterfall Kayak Adventure" (a combination kayaking/hiking/inner-tubing experience), and the "Zip 'n' Dip Expedition" (which includes jumping with a zipline from a suspension bridge into a very deep swimming hole). There is also a range of private excursions available, with length and destinations tailored to your interests. Children over five are welcome (over 12 for the "Zip 'n' Dip"). ~ Princeville; 808-826-7669, 888-955-7669; www.kauai-hiking.com.

In the Hanalei area, contact **Princeville Ranch Stables** for three- or four-hour picnic rides to waterfalls (includes a moderately strenuous hike), as well as 90-minute country rides to the bluff overlooking Anini Reef. Closed Sunday. ~ Kuhio Highway, Princeville; 808-826-6777; www.princevilleranch.com.

**GOLF**

Some of the best golfing in Hawaii is found on the Garden Isle. In addition to outstanding resort courses at Princeville, the Kauai Marriott and the Hyatt Regency Kauai, you can enjoy several excellent public courses. Beautifully situated with dramatic ocean and mountain backdrops, all of these links will make your game a pleasure.

**LIHUE AREA** **Kiele Course** and the **Mokihana Course**, both created by Jack Nicklaus, are two of the island's best-known golfing spots. Both courses have 18 holes, full equipment rental, spectacular ocean views and guava and mango forests. ~ Both are adjacent to the Kauai Marriott, Nawiliwili; 808-241-6000, 800-634-6400.

**POIPU AREA** Next door to the Hyatt Regency Kauai is the Robert Trent Jones, Jr.–designed 18-hole **Poipu Bay Resort Golf Course**. Full equipment rental is available at this course that was specifically designed to provide an ocean view from each hole. ~ 2250 Ainako Street, Koloa; 808-742-8711.

**WAIMEA AREA** On the south side of the island, the semiprivate **Kukuiolono Golf Course** in Kalaheo is also popular. This ninehole course offers views of ocean and Kalaheo mountains. ~ 854 Puu Road, Kalaheo; 808-332-9151.

**WAILUA–KAPAA AREA** The golfing public is well served at the 18-hole, oceanfront **Wailua Golf Course**, and the low green fees make this course a best buy. ~ Wailua; 808-241-6666.

**NORTH SHORE** The 27-hole **Princeville Makai Golf Course** was designed by Robert Trent Jones. Full equipment rental is available and the scenery is beautiful. ~ Princeville; 808-826-3580. It is complemented by the demanding 18-hole **Prince Country Club** course next door. There's also a driving range to help sharpen your skills. ~ 428 Kuhio Highway, Princeville; 808-826-5000.

**BIKING**

There are no bikeways on Kauai and most roads have very narrow shoulders, but the Garden Isle is still the most popular island for bicycling. Roads are good and, except for the steep 20-mile climb along Waimea Canyon, the terrain is either flat or gently rolling. The spectacular scenery and network of public parks make this a cyclist's dream.

One local spot for biking is along **Route 56**. This is a narrow road with one-lane bridges that keep tour buses and large trucks out of the area, though car traffic can be quite heavy.

For hearty mountain bikers, the **Powerline Trail** (15 miles) is an arduous but rewarding challenge. It follows a powerline that connects the North Shore with the east side of Kauai. The trail takes you into the interior of the island, offering views of Mt. Waialeale, one of the wettest spots on earth. Be sure to bring a U.S. Survey map (available at local camping stores), water and food with you. This journey is for experienced mountain bikers who are in the best of shape. ~ To get to the trailhead, turn inland at the corner of Princeville stables and continue beyond the row of houses.

**Bike Rentals**   **Outfitters Kauai** rents hybrid, full-suspension and road bikes as well as children's mountain bikes and baby seats. ~ 2827-A Poipu Road, Poipu; 808-742-9667; www.outfitters kauai.com. In Hanalei, **Pedal 'N Paddle** rents beach cruisers. Popular destinations from here include Princeville and the lagoon at Kee Beach. ~ Ching Young Village; 808-826-9069.

**Bike Repairs**   **Bicycle John's** in Lihue offers a full-service sales and repair shop. Closed Sunday and Monday. ~ 3215 Kuhio Highway, Lihue; 808-245-7579.

**Bike Tours**   **Outfitters Kauai** has an afternoon bike tour. The tour stops along the way for photo ops and interesting lectures on the history and folklore of the area. The best part is: they'll bring you up the hill in a van. ~ Poipu Plaza, 2827A Poipu Road, Poipu; 808-742-9667, 888-742-9887; www.outfitterskauai.com, e-mail info@outfitterskauai.com.

**HIKING**   Hiking is among the finest, and certainly least expensive, ways of touring the Garden Isle. Kauai's trails are concentrated in the Na Pali Coast and Waimea Canyon–Kokee regions, with a few others near the Wailua River. Most are well maintained and carefully charted. For further information, contact the State Depart-

**AUTHOR FAVORITE**

**Kauai Nature Tours** is a company that encourages "effective co-existence of earth's environment and its human inhabitants." To this end, all tours are led by local scientists and provide a detailed look into the natural wonders of Hawaii. The "Waimea Canyon Explorer" tour explores Kauai's geologic past. The "Mahaulepu Coast" hike shows you Kauai's limestone ledges and discusses the history of the coastline. This is a perfect way to learn to "take only pictures, leave only footprints." ~ Koloa; 808-742-8305, 888-233-8365; www.teok.com, e-mail teok@aloha.net.

ment of Land and Natural Resources. ~ 808-984-8100; www.
hawaiitrails.org.

All distances listed for hiking trails are one way unless otherwise noted.

**WAILUA RIVER**    While none of these hikes actually follow the
Wailua, all begin near Route 580, which parallels the river.

**Nounou Mountain Trail—East Side** (1.75 miles) begins off
Haleilio Road at the parking lot in the Wailua Houselots and
climbs 1250 feet to the Sleeping Giant's head at Mount Nounou
summit. This trail is strenuous.

**Nounou Mountain Trail—West Side** (1.5 miles) begins off
Route 581 and ascends with moderate difficulty 1000 feet to join
the East Side trail.

**Keahua Arboretum Trail** (0.5 mile) begins two miles past the
University of Hawaii Wailua Experiment Station on Route 580.
This easy nature trail is lined with foreign plants.

**Kuilau Ridge Trail** (1.2 miles) begins on Route 580 near the
Keahua Arboretum. This moderate, scenic hike goes past several
vista points and picnic areas.

**WAIMEA CANYON–KOKEE**    Kokee State Park has about 45 miles
of hiking trails through rugged, beautiful country. Along the mountain paths listed here, you'll discover some of the finest hiking in
all Hawaii.

**Alakai Swamp Trail** (3.5 miles) passes through bogs and
scrub rainforests to the Kilohana Lookout. This moderate once-
muddy trail is now partially covered with boardwalks. It begins
off Mohihi (Camp 10) Road, but is also accessible by the Pihea
Trail.

**Awaawapuhi Trail** (3.1 miles) starts on Route 550 midway
between Kokee Museum and Kalalau Lookout. This physically
challenging trail leads through a forest to a vista at 2500-feet elevation that overlooks sheer cliffs and the ocean. The trail then
connects with Nualolo Trail for a 13-mile loop.

**Berry Flat Trail** (0.6 mile) and **Puu Ka Ohelo Trail** (0.5 mile)
combine off Mohihi (Camp 10) Road to form an easy loop that
passes an interesting assortment of trees, including California redwood, *ohia*, *sugi* pine and *koa*.

**Black Pipe Trail** (0.5 mile) links Canyon Trail with Halemanu Road. It follows a cliff past stands of the rare *iliau* plant,
a relative of Maui's famous silversword.

**Canyon Trail** (1.8 miles) forks off Cliff Trail and follows a
relatively easy path around Waimea Canyon's northern rim to a
vista sweeping down the canyon to the sea.

**Cliff Trail** (0.1 mile) begins at the end of the right fork of
Halemanu Road and offers a pleasant walk to a viewpoint above
Waimea Canyon. Feral goats are often spotted.

**Ditch Trail** (1.7 miles) runs from Mohihi Road at one end to Waininiua Road at the other. It's a moderate trail with spectacular views of forest areas and the Poomau River.

**Halemanu-Kokee Trail** (1.2 miles) sets out from the old ranger station. Birdwatchers should especially enjoy this easy jaunt.

**Iliau Nature Loop** (0.3 mile roundtrip) starts along Route 550 on a short course past 20 local plant species, including the *iliau*, endemic only to the Garden Isle. This easy trail offers good views of both Waimea Canyon and Waialae Falls.

**Kalupuhi Trail** (1.6 miles) begins at Route 550 en route to a plum grove. The plums are in season every other year. In a good year, you can enjoy both plums and a pleasant hike.

**Kawaikoi Stream Trail** (1.8 miles roundtrip), an easy loop trail, starts on Mohihi (Camp 10) Road across from Sugi Grove and follows near the stream through a manmade forest.

**Koaie Canyon Trail** (3 miles) branches off the Waimea Canyon trail near Poo Kaeha. It's a moderate hike that crosses the Waimea River and passes ancient terraces and rock walls en route to Lonomea camp, a wilderness campsite. Here you'll find a shelter and a stream chock-full of swimming holes.

**Kumuwela Trail** (1 mile) begins off Mohihi (Camp 10) Road and passes through a fern-choked gulch. Good for birdwatchers.

**Nature Trail** (0.1 mile) begins behind the Kokee Museum and passes through a *koa* forest.

**Nualolo Trail** (3.75 miles) starts near Park Headquarters. Along the strenuous path you'll be able to see Nualolo Valley on the Na Pali Coast.

**Pihea Trail** (3.7 miles) offers excellent views of Kalalau Valley and the Alakai Swamp. This moderate trail also features a variety of birds and plant life. It begins at Puuokila Lookout.

**Poomau Canyon Lookout Trail** (0.3 mile) heads through a stand of Japanese *sugi* trees and a native rainforest. It begins from Mohihi (Camp 10) Road and ends at a vista overlooking Poomau and Waimea Canyons.

**Waimea Canyon Trail** (11.5 miles) can be reached from the Kukui Trail. Its very challenging path follows the Waimea River through the center of the canyon.

**Waininiua Trail** (0.6 mile) leads from the unpaved Kumuwela Road through a forest where ginger grows.

**NORTH SHORE**   The **Powerline Trial** (11.2 miles) is a strenuous hike through Kauai's interior. Beginning in Princeville, it follows the Hanalei River, offering views of countless waterfalls and Mt. Waialeale, ending on the east side of the island near Kapaa. If you're feeling less adventurous, hike in a few miles and enjoy the waterfalls and lush vegetation before turning back the way you came. ~ To get to the trailhead, turn inland at the corner of Princeville stables and continue beyond the row of houses.

# Hiking
## Kalalau

**K**auai's premier hike, one of the finest treks in all the islands, follows an 11-mile trail along the rugged Na Pali Coast. This ancient Hawaiian trail to Kalalau Valley descends into dense rainforests and climbs along windswept cliffs. Streams and mountain pools along the path provide refreshing swimming holes. Wild orchids, guavas, *kukui* nuts, mangos and mountain apples grow in abundance.

The trail begins near Kee Beach at the end of Kuhio Highway. After a strenuous two-mile course the trail drops into Hanakapiai Valley. From here, it climbs through the valley and up to Hanakapiai Falls. Fringed by cliffs and possessing a marvelous sand beach, Hanakapiai makes an excellent rest point or final destination.

If you bypass the side trails and continue along the Kalalau Trail, you'll find that as it climbs out of Hanakapiai Valley, it becomes slightly rougher. Sharp grass presses close to the path as it leads through thick foliage, then along precipitous cliff faces. Four miles from Hanakapiai Valley, the trail arrives at Hanakoa Valley. There is an open-air shelter for public use here, as well as a steep one-third-mile trail that goes up to Hanakoa Falls.

The final trek to Kalalau, the most difficult section of the trail, passes scenery so spectacular it seems unreal. Knife-point peaks, illuminated by shafts of sunlight, rise thousands of feet. Frigate birds hang poised against the trade winds. Wisps of cloud fringe the cliffs. The silence is ominous, almost tangible. A foot from the trail, the ledge falls away into another sheer wall, which plummets a thousand feet and more to the surf below.

The narrow, serpentine trail then winds down to Kalalau Valley. A well-fed stream rumbles through this two-mile-wide vale. If you must use the water here, be sure to boil or otherwise purify it. Farther along, a white-sand beach sweeps past a series of caves to the far end of the valley. You may want to stop awhile and explore the caves, but if you swim here or at Hanakapiai, exercise extreme caution. The undertow and riptides are wicked.

Kalalau has many fine campsites near the beach, but firewood is scarce and cutting trees is *kapu*, so you'd best bring a campstove. Camping at Hanakapiai, Hanakoa or Kalalau will necessitate a state permit. Anyone hiking beyond Hanakapiai also needs a permit. These are available from the State Parks office. ~ 3060 Eiwa Street, Lihue; 808-274-3445.

▼▼▼▼▼▼▼▼▼▼
**Transportation**

**AIR**

Visiting Kauai means flying to the centrally located Lihue Airport. ~ 808-246-1400. Aloha Airlines, Hawaiian Air, American Airlines, North American, Air Trans Air and United Airlines operate here.

The Lihue Airport has a restaurant, a cocktail lounge, lockers, a newsstand, a gift shop and a flower shop. What you won't find are buses, far more useful to most travelers than cocktails and flowers. Transportation (it's two miles into town) requires reserving a seat on a shuttle, renting a car, hailing a cab, hitching or hoofing. Cabs generally charge about $6 to Lihue.

**CAR RENTALS**

Across the street from the terminal at Lihue Airport you'll find a series of booths containing car-rental firms. These include **Alamo Rent A Car** (808-246-0645, 800-327-9633), **Avis Rent A Car** (808-245-3512, 800-331-1212), **Budget Rent A Car** (808-245-9031), **Dollar Rent A Car** (800-800-4000) and **National Car Rental** (808-245-5636, 800-227-7368).

**JEEP RENTALS**

**Budget Rent A Car** has four-wheel drives. However, most Kauai roads, including cane roads, are accessible by car so you probably won't need a jeep. ~ Lihue Airport; 800-527-0700.

**PUBLIC TRANSIT**

**Kauai Bus** is a shuttle that travels between Lihue and Hanalei seven times a day from 6:45 a.m. to 6 p.m. It stops at about a dozen places, including two major shopping centers. ~ 808-241-6410.

**JEEP TOURS**

**Aloha Kauai Tours** has half- and full-day, off-road four-wheel-drive tours into the mountains of Kokee State Park and other areas of the island. Bring comfortable walking shoes and binoculars, as the tours often include a hike. Lunch is included in the full-day tours. ~ 800-452-1113; www.alohakauaitours.com.

**AERIAL TOURS**

Whether you choose a whirlybird's-eye view from a helicopter or prefer the serenity of a glider, aerial sightseeing is one of Kauai's great thrills. From simple flyovers to thrilling acrobatic flights, you'll gain a unique perspective on the island's canyons and rainforests, hidden beaches and tropical retreats.

**Island Helicopters** offers a one-hour tour of all the major scenic areas of the island, from the Na Pali Coast to the Mount Waialeale Crater. ~ Lihue Airport; 808-245-8588, 800-829-5999.

**Ohana Helicopter Tours** provides a 50-minute Makihana tour that hits all the major sights of Kauai—Waimea Canyon, Sleeping Giant, and the Na Pali Coast. The 65-minute Maile Tour offers a more extensive view of the Na Pali Coast, Alakai Swamp and Olokele Canyon. Shuttle service is available from southern resorts. ~ Lihue Airport; 808-245-3996, 800-222-6989.

Heli USA, based in Princeville Airport, features unique glimpses of scenic treasures like Waialeale, the Na Pali Coast and Waimea Canyon. ~ 808-826-6591, 866-936-1234; www.heliusa.com.

If you want an airplane tour, Tropical Biplanes will take you up in a bi-plane for a thrilling tour of the island. ~ Lihue Airport; 808-246-9123.

Niihau Helicopters specializes in trips to the Forbidden Isle. Bring your own snorkeling equipment because the twin-engine helicopter will land on one of the island's remote beaches, ideal for exploring its pristine underwater environment. Book tours at least a week in advance. Closed Sunday. ~ Kaumualii Highway; 808-335-3500, 877-441-3500.

# Recommended Reading

*The Beaches of Oahu*, by John R.K. Clark. University of Hawaii Press, 1977. This book, and companion volumes that cover the other islands, provides excellent background information on all the beaches.

*Hawaii,* by James Michener. Bantam Books, 1978. This lengthy historic novel skillfully blends fact and fiction, dramatically tracing the entire course of Hawaiian history.

*Hawaii Pono*, by Lawrence H. Fuchs. Bess Press, 1993. A brilliant sociological study of 20th-century Hawaii that vividly portrays the islands' ethnic groups.

*Hawaii: The Sugar-Coated Fortress*, by Francine Du Plessix Gray. Random House, 1972. A hard-hitting analysis of modern-day Hawaii that details the tragic effect Western civilization has had on the Hawaiian people.

*Hawaiian Antiquities*, by David Malo. Bishop Museum Press, 1995. Written by a Hawaiian scholar in the 19th century, this study contains a wealth of information on pre-European Hawaiian culture.

*Hawaiian Hiking Trails*, by Craig Chisholm. Fernglen Press, 1994. The best single-volume hiking guide available, this handbook provides excellent descriptions of Hawaii's most popular treks.

*The Legends and Myths of Hawaii*, by David Kalakaua. Charles E. Tuttle Company, 1972. Written by Hawaii's last king, this fascinating collection includes fables of the great chiefs and priests who once ruled the islands.

*Polynesian Researches: Hawaii*, by William Ellis. Charles E. Tuttle Company, 1969. This missionary's journal originally appeared in the 1820s. Despite some tedious sermonizing, it poignantly portrays Hawaii at a historic crossroads and graphically describes volcanoes and other natural phenomena on the big island.

*Shoal of Time*, by Gavan Daws. University Press of Hawaii, 1994. The finest history written on Hawaii, this volume is not only informative but entertaining as well.

*Shore Fishing in Hawaii*, by Edward Y. Hosaka. Petroglyph Press, 1995. This how-to guide is filled with handy tips on surf-casting, fabricating your own equipment and identifying Hawaii's fish species.

# Index

# Lodging Index

# Dining Index

## HIDDEN GUIDES

Adventure travel or a relaxing vacation?—"Hidden" guidebooks are the only travel books in the business to provide detailed information on both. Aimed at environmentally aware travelers, our motto is "Where Vacations Meet Adventures." These books combine details on unique hotels, restaurants and sightseeing with information on camping, sports and hiking for the outdoor enthusiast.

## PARADISE FAMILY GUIDES

Ideal for families traveling with kids of any age—toddlers to teenagers—Paradise Family Guides offer a blend of travel information unlike any other guides to the Hawaiian islands. With vacation ideas and tropical adventures that are sure to satisfy both action-hungry youngsters and relaxation-seeking parents, these guides meet the specific needs of each and every family member.

Ulysses Press books are available at bookstores everywhere. If any of the following titles are unavailable at your local bookstore, ask the bookseller to order them.

You can also order books directly from Ulysses Press
P.O. Box 3440, Berkeley, CA 94703
800-377-2542 or 510-601-8301
fax: 510-601-8307
www.ulyssespress.com
e-mail: ulysses@ulyssespress.com

## HIDDEN GUIDEBOOKS

____ Hidden Arizona, $16.95
____ Hidden Bahamas, $14.95
____ Hidden Baja, $14.95
____ Hidden Belize, $15.95
____ Hidden Big Island of Hawaii, $13.95
____ Hidden Boston & Cape Cod, $14.95
____ Hidden British Columbia, $18.95
____ Hidden Cancún & the Yucatán, $16.95
____ Hidden Carolinas, $17.95
____ Hidden Coast of California, $18.95
____ Hidden Colorado, $15.95
____ Hidden Disneyland, $13.95
____ Hidden Florida, $18.95
____ Hidden Florida Keys & Everglades,
      $13.95
____ Hidden Georgia, $16.95
____ Hidden Guatemala, $16.95
____ Hidden Hawaii, $18.95
____ Hidden Idaho, $14.95
____ Hidden Kauai, $13.95
____ Hidden Los Angeles, $14.95
____ Hidden Maui, $13.95

____ Hidden Miami, $14.95
____ Hidden Montana, $15.95
____ Hidden New England, $18.95
____ Hidden New Mexico, $15.95
____ Hidden New Orleans, $14.95
____ Hidden Oahu, $13.95
____ Hidden Oregon, $15.95
____ Hidden Pacific Northwest, $18.95
____ Hidden San Diego, $14.95
____ Hidden Salt Lake City, $14.95
____ Hidden San Francisco & Northern
      California, $18.95
____ Hidden Seattle, $13.95
____ Hidden Southern California, $18.95
____ Hidden Southwest, $19.95
____ Hidden Tahiti, $17.95
____ Hidden Tennessee, $16.95
____ Hidden Utah, $16.95
____ Hidden Walt Disney World, $13.95
____ Hidden Washington, $15.95
____ Hidden Wine Country, $13.95
____ Hidden Wyoming, $15.95

## PARADISE FAMILY GUIDES

____ Paradise Family Guides: Kaua'i, $16.95
____ Paradise Family Guides: Maui, $16.95

____ Paradise Family Guides: Big Island of
      Hawai'i, $16.95

Mark the book(s) you're ordering and enter the total cost here ➭ [         ]

California residents add 8.25% sales tax here ➭ [         ]

**Shipping,** check box for your preferred method and enter cost here ➭ [         ]

☐ BOOK RATE                          FREE! FREE! FREE!

☐ PRIORITY MAIL/UPS GROUND      cost of postage

☐ UPS OVERNIGHT OR 2-DAY AIR    cost of postage                          [         ]

**Billing,** enter total amount due here and check method of payment ➭

☐ CHECK              ☐ MONEY ORDER

☐ VISA/MASTERCARD _____ EXP. DATE _____

NAME _____ PHONE _____

ADDRESS _____

CITY _____ STATE _____ ZIP _____

MONEY-BACK GUARANTEE ON DIRECT ORDERS PLACED THROUGH ULYSSES PRESS.

## ABOUT THE AUTHOR

**RAY RIEGERT** is the author of eight travel books, including *Hidden San Francisco & Northern California*. His most popular work, *Hidden Hawaii*, won the coveted Lowell Thomas Travel Journalism Award for Best Guidebook as well a similar award from the Hawaii Visitors Bureau. In addition to his role as publisher of Ulysses Press, he has written for the *Chicago Tribune*, *Saturday Evening Post*, *San Francisco Chronicle* and *Travel & Leisure*. A member of the Society of American Travel Writers, he lives in the San Francisco Bay area with his wife, co-publisher Leslie Henriques, and their son Keith and daughter Alice.

## ABOUT THE PHOTOGRAPHER

**ROBERT HOLMES,** born in England, first visited the U.S. in 1976 at the invitation of Ansel Adams. Since moving to the United States to live in 1979, his photographs have appeared in virtually every major travel magazine including *National Geographic*, *GEO, Islands* and *Travel & Leisure*. In addition to his magazine credits, he has illustrated 37 books and authored 4. He is the first photographer to have twice received the Travel Photographer of the Year award. He lives in Mill Valley, California, with his two daughters.